THE PRACTICAL WOODWORKER

A COMPLETE GUIDE TO THE ART
AND PRACTICE OF WOODWORKING

Written and Illustrated by Experts

and Edited by

BERNARD E. JONES

Editor of "Work," "The Amateur Mechanic," etc.

VOLUME II

Copyright © 2013 Read Books Ltd.
This book is copyright and may not be
reproduced or copied in any way without
the express permission of the publisher in writing

British Library Cataloguing-in-Publication Data
A catalogue record for this book is available from the
British Library

Woodworking

Woodworking is the process of making items from wood. Along with stone, mud and animal parts, wood was one of the first materials worked by early humans. There are incredibly early examples of woodwork, evidenced in Mousterian stone tools used by Neanderthal man, which demonstrate our affinity with the wooden medium. In fact, the very development of civilisation is linked to the advancement of increasingly greater degrees of skill in working with these materials.

Examples of Bronze Age wood-carving include tree trunks worked into coffins from northern Germany and Denmark and wooden folding-chairs. The site of Fellbach-Schmieden in Germany has provided fine examples of wooden animal statues from the Iron Age. Woodworking is depicted in many ancient Egyptian drawings, and a considerable amount of ancient Egyptian furniture (such as stools, chairs, tables, beds, chests) has been preserved in tombs. The inner coffins found in the tombs were also made of wood. The metal used by the Egyptians for woodworking tools was originally copper and eventually, after 2000 BC, bronze - as ironworking was unknown until much later. Historically, woodworkers relied upon the woods native to their region, until transportation and trade innovations made more exotic woods available to the craftsman.

Today, often as a contemporary artistic and 'craft' medium, wood is used both in traditional and modern styles; an excellent material for delicate as well as forceful artworks. Wood is used in forms of sculpture, trade, and decoration including chip carving, wood burning, and marquetry, offering a fascination, beauty, and complexity in the grain that often shows even when the medium is painted. It is in some ways easier to shape than harder substances, but an artist or craftsman must develop specific skills to carve it properly. 'Wood carving' is really an entire genre itself, and involves cutting wood generally with a knife in one hand, or a chisel by two hands - or, with one hand on a chisel and one hand on a mallet. The phrase may also refer to the finished product, from individual sculptures to hand-worked mouldings composing part of a tracery.

The making of sculpture in wood has been extremely widely practiced but survives much less well than the other main materials such as stone and bronze, as it is vulnerable to decay, insect damage, and fire. It therefore forms an important hidden element in the arts and crafts history of many cultures. Outdoor wood sculptures do not last long in most parts of the world, so we have little idea how the totem pole tradition developed. Many of the most important sculptures of China and Japan in particular are in wood, and the great majority of African sculptures and that of Oceania also use this medium. There are various forms of carving which can be utilised; 'chip carving' (a style of carving in which knives or chisels are used to remove small chips of the material), 'relief carving' (where figures are carved in a flat panel of wood), 'Scandinavian flat-plane' (where figures are carved in large flat planes, created primarily using a carving knife - and rarely rounded or sanded afterwards) and 'whittling' (simply carving shapes using just a knife). Each of these techniques will need slightly varying tools, but broadly speaking, a specialised 'carving knife' is essential, alongside a 'gouge' (a tool with a curved cutting edge used in a variety of forms and sizes for carving hollows, rounds and sweeping curves), a 'chisel' and a 'coping saw' (a small saw, used to cut off chunks of wood at once).

Wood turning is another common form of woodworking, used to create wooden objects on a lathe. Woodturning differs from most other forms of woodworking in that the wood is moving while a stationary tool is used to cut and shape it. There are two distinct methods of turning wood: 'spindle turning' and 'bowl' or 'faceplate turning'. Their key difference is in the orientation of the wood grain, relative to the axis of the lathe. This variation in orientation changes the tools and techniques used. In spindle turning, the grain runs lengthways along the lathe bed, as if a log was mounted in the lathe. Grain is thus always perpendicular to the direction of rotation under the tool. In bowl turning, the grain runs at right angles to the axis, as if a plank were mounted across the chuck. When a bowl blank rotates, the angle that the grain makes with the cutting tool continually changes between the easy cuts of lengthways and downwards across the grain to two places per rotation where the tool is cutting across the grain and even upwards across it. This varying grain angle limits some of the tools that may be used and requires additional skill in order to cope with it.

The origin of woodturning dates to around 1300 BC when the Egyptians first developed a two-person lathe. One person would turn the wood with a rope while the other used a sharp tool to cut shapes in the wood. The Romans improved the Egyptian design with the addition of a turning bow. Early bow lathes were also developed and used in Germany, France and Britain. In the Middle Ages a pedal replaced hand-operated turning, freeing both the craftsman's hands to hold the woodturning tools. The pedal was usually connected to a pole, often a straight-grained sapling. The system today is called the 'spring pole' lathe. Alternatively, a two-person lathe, called a 'great lathe', allowed a piece to turn continuously (like today's power lathes). A master would cut the wood while an apprentice turned the crank.

As an interesting aside, the term 'bodger' stems from pole lathe turners who used to make chair legs and spindles. A bodger would typically purchase all the trees on a plot of land, set up camp on the plot, and then fell the trees and turn the wood. The spindles and legs that were produced were sold in bulk, for pence per dozen. The bodger's job was considered unfinished because he only made component parts. The term now describes a person who leaves a job unfinished, or does it badly. This could not be more different from perceptions of modern carpentry; a highly skilled trade in which work involves the construction of buildings, ships, timber bridges and concrete framework. The word 'carpenter' is the English rendering of the Old French word *carpentier* (later, *charpentier*) which is derived from the Latin *carpentrius;* '(maker) of a carriage.' Carpenters traditionally worked with natural wood and did the rougher work such as framing, but today many other materials are also used and sometimes the finer trades of cabinet-making and furniture building are considered carpentry.

As is evident from this brief historical and practical overview of woodwork, it is an incredibly varied and exciting genre of arts and crafts; an ancient tradition still relevant in the modern day. Woodworkers range from hobbyists, individuals operating from the home environment, to artisan professionals with specialist workshops, and eventually large-scale factory operations. We hope the reader is inspired by this book to create some woodwork of their own.

CONTENTS

	PAGE
LIST OF THE CHIEF CONTRIBUTORS	vii
SHEDS AND OUTDOOR ERECTIONS (94 *Illustrations*)	417
WHEELBARROWS (48 *Illustrations*)	440
BOXES FOR SPECIAL PURPOSES (49 *Illustrations*)	454
TOOL CHESTS (27 *Illustrations*)	468
WORK BENCHES (105 *Illustrations*)	478
GARDEN CARPENTRY (132 *Illustrations*)	507
GARDEN BASKETS (33 *Illustrations*)	540
TRELLISES, PORCHES AND ARCHES (95 *Illustrations*)	546
SUMMERHOUSES (57 *Illustrations*)	577
GARDEN ROOMS OR BUNGALOWS (22 *Illustrations*)	596
GARDEN LIGHTS (41 *Illustrations*)	603
GREENHOUSES (56 *Illustrations*)	613
TENTS (28 *Illustrations*)	625
POULTRY HOUSES (35 *Illustrations*)	634
INCUBATORS AND CHICKEN REARERS (34 *Illustrations*)	648
TUBS AND CHURNS (30 *Illustrations*)	663
DOORS AND WINDOWS (48 *Illustrations*)	670
FIXING WOODWORK TO WALLS (27 *Illustrations*)	689
BEVELLED WORK AND CURVED WORK (36 *Illustrations*)	698

CONTENTS

	PAGE
CRAMPS AND CRAMPING (39 *Illustrations*)	708
SIMPLE BOOK-RACKS AND BOOK-SHELVES (48 *Illustrations*)	717
DWARF BOOKCASES (54 *Illustrations*)	729
REVOLVING BOOKCASES (20 *Illustrations*)	741
TALL BOOKCASES (49 *Illustrations*)	748
HALL FURNITURE (96 *Illustrations*)	764
DRESSERS AND SIDEBOARDS (98 *Illustrations*)	788
COAL-BOXES (29 *Illustrations*)	817

List of the Chief Contributors

H. Alexander	Machine Woodworking
I. Atkinson	Toys, etc.
A.M.	Upholstery
W. A. C. Ball	Examples
J. D. Bates	Metal Fittings
R. V. Boughton	Drawing
G. S. Boulger	Woods and Timber
John Bovingdon	Veneering and Examples
R. S. Bowers	Examples
C. W. D. Boxall	Equipment, Examples, etc.
Sydney Camm	Aeroplane Woodworking
A. Claydon	Examples, etc.
T. W. Corkhill	Joint Making, Construction, etc.
J. L. Devonshire	Examples
G. Eldridge	Examples
H. E. V. Gillham	Examples
P. R. Green	Examples
R. Greenhalgh	Tools, Processes, etc.
T. Holt	Joint Making
W. J. Horner	Turning, Pattern Making, etc.
H. Jarvis	Joint Making, etc.
F. W. Loasby	Billiard-table Making
R. H. Lomas	Barrow Making
W. J. Moseley	Wood Finishing
G. F. Rhead	Inlaying, etc.
W. S. Rogers	Picture Framing, etc.
C. F. Shackleton	Examples
G. Strethill-Smith	Examples
C. S. Taylor	Upholstery, etc.
H. Turner	Wood Carving
C. E. A. Wyatt	Examples

Sheds and Outdoor Erections

SMALL PORTABLE CYCLE SHED

THE portable cycle shed here illustrated is designed to accommodate one, although it can be easily arranged to extend the size, so that it would allow of another being placed alongside.

In Figs. 1 and 2 are shown elevations of the framing at the front and back, whilst Fig. 3 is a plan of the floor and framing, also showing in the broken section a view of the framed joists carrying same and forming the groundwork on which the floor and sides are supported clear of the ground. The framing shown is intended to be covered with stout rot-proof canvas or thin "Ruberoid" or "Congo" roofing felt, otherwise with stout plain canvas which must be well painted. The framing also allows of using, instead of these materials, the ordinary fireproof board or thin planed matchboarding, say $\frac{3}{8}$ in. or $\frac{1}{2}$ in. thick.

The sides are framed up for the purpose of securing together, and forming complete parts in themselves. This is sometimes a great consideration when moving about the country. The base is dovetailed at the corners (see Fig. 5), and the intermediate bearers are stub-tenoned into the front and back pieces. It should be framed and pinned together truly square, and then the floorboards can be neatly nailed down, keeping back from the edges just the thickness of the framing and boring at the ends to prevent the nails from splitting and spoiling the job.

Tongued-and-grooved red deal boards are the best, in fact, all the stuff, excepting the top, should be red deal sound and dry. The framing stuff is prepared from 1-in. material. It should be mortised and tenoned together, keeping the thickness of the tenon one-third of the whole thickness, or way $\frac{5}{16}$ in. thick tenons all round (see Figs. 6, 7, 8, and 9). The braces are cut into the middle rail (see Fig. 8), and well screwed. The other end stub-tenons into top and bottom rails and stiles as shown. The intermediate or middle rails of the side and back framing, besides stiffening the frame, serve the purpose of keeping the wheels and handles off the canvas, which will then only be liable to injury from the outside.

The isometric details at the top and bottom (Figs. 4 and 5) show how the side framing forms the hanging part for the doors in front (see Fig. 11), using T or cross-garnet hinges on the top and bottom rails. The sides at the top are mortised to receive the sub-tenons of the cross-rail (see Fig. 10) which runs through. It could be preferably got out of $1\frac{1}{2}$-in. stuff and then rebated to receive the doors, although shown as 1 in. thick with a nailed or screwed fillet to form the stop. The roof board, being all in one piece of sequoia, whitewood, or a well-seasoned ash or elm board, lays on the sides and rests on intermediate bearers carried at the back and front, to which it is screwed from the inside. It should hang well over all round to keep off the rain, and either be well-painted, creosoted, or covered with a roofing material. The cross bearers are half-boxed into the front and back framing, and have angle irons well screwed on to tie them across the top (*see* Fig. 12).

If canvas is used the edges should fold all round the framing edges and be tacked inside, care being taken to plane off the sharp edges so as not to cut the canvas. If any other flexible material is used, the edges should be protected with fillets. Fillets or stops are nailed up the sides, along the top and on the door edges to form a tight joint. The usual fastening can be a couple of bolts and a padlock. The sides and back are neatly screwed at the corners when erecting same on the baseboard framing. The joint at the bottom is covered with a plinth or skirting well bevelled on the top edge and snugly fitting to the framing to exclude the wet. To make a satisfactory job the writer would recommend 2-in. copper nails for the floor and brass screws for the other parts.

The base should be thoroughly creosoted and lightly fixed to creosoted sleepers buried in the ground, keeping the bottom just clear for through-ventilation purposes. Inside the shed there will be found ample room for a neat shelf or two to carry the accessories or cleaning appliances. The whole should be kept well painted with pleasing colours, and placed in a convenient position. The drawings are to scale, the internal dimensions being 6 ft. long by 4 ft. high and 2 ft. deep back to front.

CHEAP CYCLE SHED

The illustrations (Figs. 13 to 16) give a plan, two sections, and an elevation of a small shed that will hold four cycles, using the junction made by two walls. Cycles require to be stored in as dry a

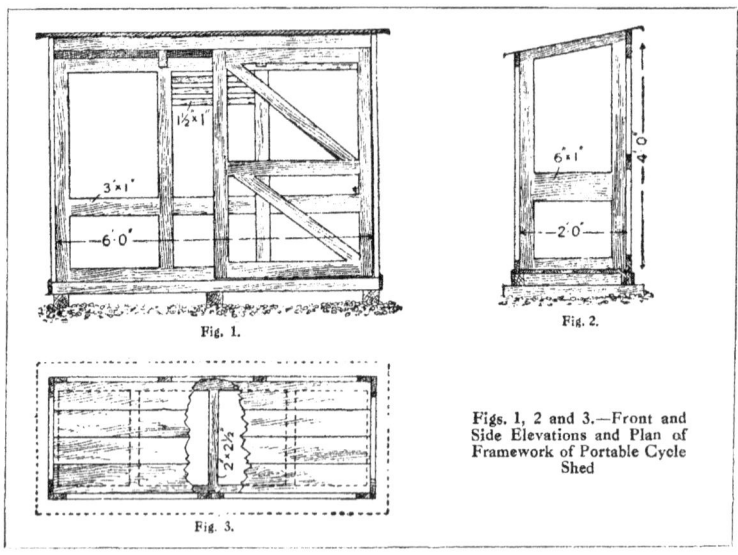

Figs. 1, 2 and 3.—Front and Side Elevations and Plan of Framework of Portable Cycle Shed

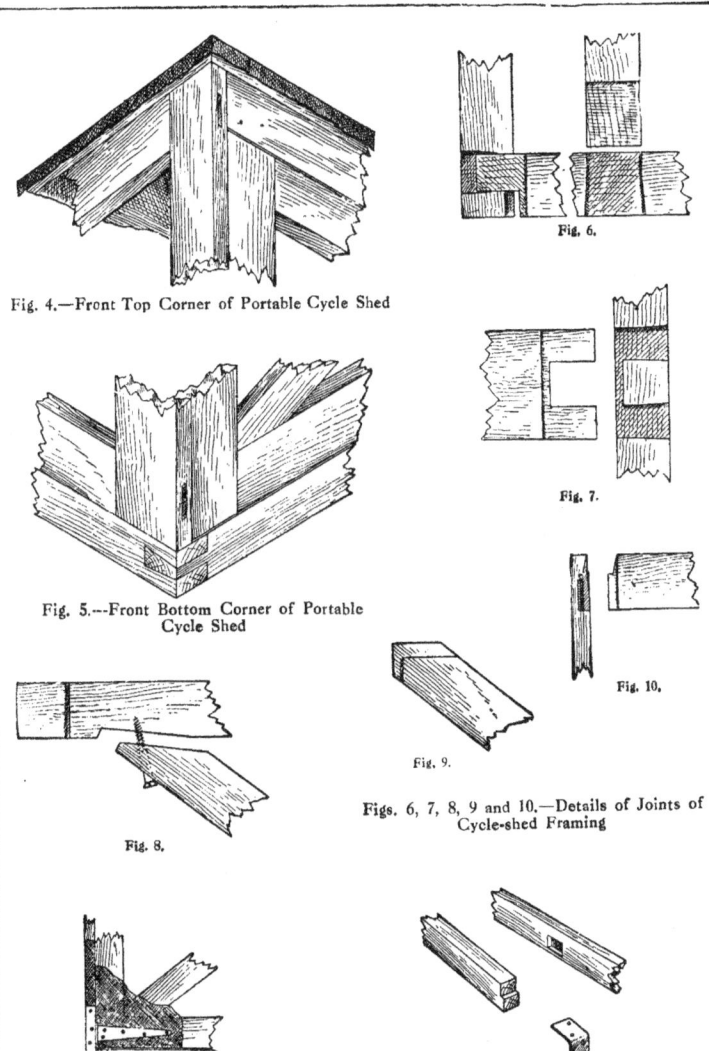

Fig. 4.—Front Top Corner of Portable Cycle Shed

Fig. 5.—Front Bottom Corner of Portable Cycle Shed

Fig. 6.

Fig. 7.

Fig. 8.

Fig. 9.

Fig. 10.

Figs. 6, 7, 8, 9 and 10.—Details of Joints of Cycle-shed Framing

Fig. 11.—Corner showing T-Hinge Joint

Fig. 12.—Detail of Cross Bearer and Joint with Angle-iron

place as possible, to avoid trouble and expense by rusting and frequent cleaning. This essentially means special precautions for keeping out wet and the prevention of dampness rising from the earth. Each cycle requires a width of 1 ft. 3 in. to 1 ft. 6 in., according to the the shed should be formed wheel racks of small scantling timber, placed in pairs diagonally, and at a distance apart sufficient to allow for the front wheel of the cycle to enter.

The following particulars should give a clear indication as to construction. A

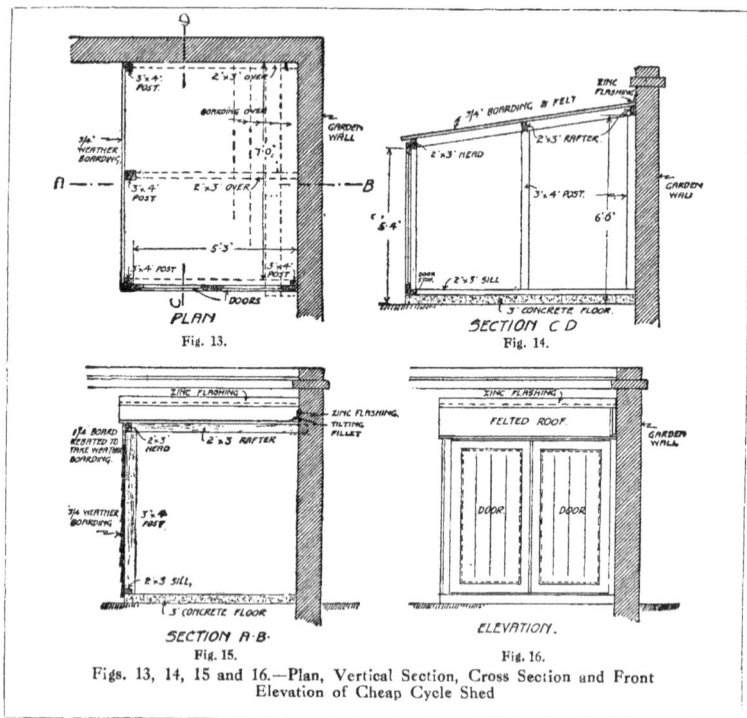

Figs. 13, 14, 15 and 16.—Plan, Vertical Section, Cross Section and Front Elevation of Cheap Cycle Shed

width of the handle bars, if each is stored on a flat floor. If every alternative cycle is raised about 9 in. above its neighbour, then a much lesser width is required. Each cycle is about 6 ft. 6 in. long, and a length of 7 ft. should be allowed. The sizes shown on the illustrations will be sufficient to accommodate four cycles if raising blocks are used. At the rear of boarded floor, laid on wood joists, is not good unless a layer of concrete is laid over the site to prevent dampness. A cheap method of construction is to lay a 3-in. thickness of good concrete over the site, and to render the top of same. The concrete to be composed of one part of portland cement to four parts of fine aggregate, such as broken brick and sand.

SHEDS AND OUTDOOR ERECTIONS

The rendering to the top of the concrete to form the floor should be $\frac{1}{2}$ in. thick, and composed of one part of cement to three parts of sand. The sizes of sills, posts, heads and rafters are shown, and a careful adherence to the methods of framing will result in a very economical form of construction with dead bearings for nearly all members.

The side may be weather-boarded as shown, or by adding a rail between the head and the sill, it may be vertically matchboarded with $\frac{5}{8}$-in. or $\frac{3}{4}$-in. matching, which will require painting; this will be unnecessary in the case of weather-

The doors should be formed of stiles not less than $1\frac{1}{2}$-in. by 4-in. (nominal thickness), and top and bottom rails, with $\frac{3}{4}$-in. matching rebated into the framing as shown. The hanging stiles fit into the rebated posts; the top rails abut against the 2-in. by 3-in. head; and the bottom rails against small stops at the floor level. The quantities of timber required will be: 26 ft. run of 2-in. by 3-in.; 23 ft. run of 3-in. by 4-in. fir for the framing; 32 ft. run of $1\frac{1}{2}$-in. by 4-in. (cut of 3-in. by 4-in.) for the doors; 8 ft. run of 2-in. by 3-in. triangular tilting fillet (out of 2-in. by 3-in.) $\frac{1}{4}$ square of $\frac{3}{4}$-in. average thickness weather-

Fig. 17.—Motor-cycle and Side-car Shed

boarding. The roof may also be weather-boarded; but the slope will have to be steeper than shown. A better method is to use $\frac{3}{4}$-in. boarding, covered with bituminous felt. The water-tighting of the joint between the roof and wall requires careful attention to avoid constant trouble. A zinc flashing is the only practical method, and will be cheapest in the end. A cement fillet is not good. A small tilting fillet is necessary, as shown, to prevent water gravitating under the flashing.

boarding; $\frac{1}{4}$ square of $\frac{3}{4}$-in. grooved-and-tongued matching; $\frac{1}{4}$ square of bituminous felt; $4\frac{1}{2}$ yd. super of 3-in. concrete floor with rendering; $4\frac{1}{2}$ yd. levelling ground.

SHED FOR MOTOR-CYCLE AND SIDE-CAR

The motor-cycle and side-car shed shown above has folding-doors at one end, (Fig. 17), although a single door would suit in the case of a narrower erection, and it has a small window in the centre of

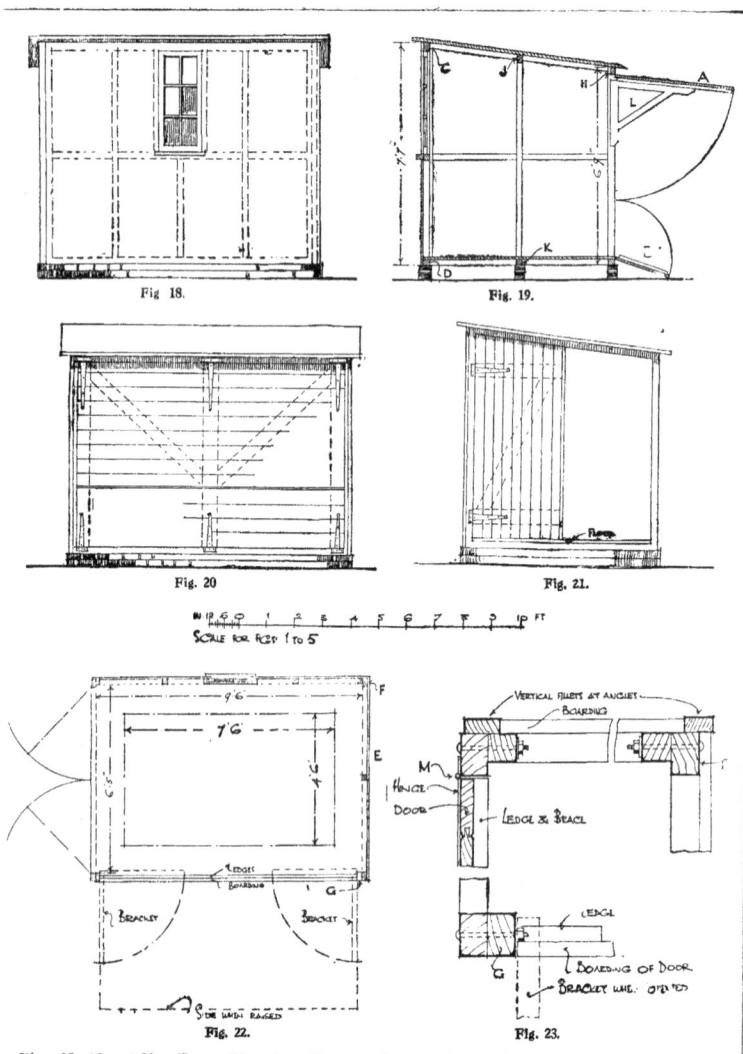

Figs. 18, 19 and 20.—Front Elevation, Cross-section and Back Elevation of Motor-cycle and Side-car Shed

Figs. 21, 22 and 23.—End Elevation, Plan and Detailed Plan of Framing of Motor-cycle and Side-car Shed

the back which could be omitted if not thought necessary. The front is in two portions, one hinged to lift upwards and form a shelter, as at A in Fig. 19, and the other falling as at B to form a convenient slope from the floor to the ground. A somewhat smaller shed would suffice for motor-cycles without side-cars, and other purposes; but working to the sizes given would result in a shed large enough to allow at least 12-in. margin round any cycle and side-car.

Each side is constructed as a separate section, thus simplifying the work and permitting an easy taking to pieces for removal, the whole being fixed together with $\frac{3}{8}$-in. bolts. The back is framed as dotted in Fig. 18, with 2-in. by 2-in. uprights and middle rail, a 3-in. by 2-in. head C (Fig. 19) fixed upright and splayed to suit the slope of the roof, and a 3-in. by 2-in. sill D (Fig. 19) laid flat. The fixed light shown can easily be inserted if desired. The end at E (Fig. 22) has a 2-in. by 2-in. centre upright a middle rail and head (raking to suit roof), a 3-in. by 2-in. sill as before, and 3-in. by 2-in. angle-posts, as at F in Figs. 22 and 23. The front has a 3-in. by 2-in. sill and uprights G (Figs. 22 and 23) and a 5-in. by 2-in. splayed head H (Fig. 19).

When the framework has been bolted together and set on a base of bricks or sleepers clear of the ground, a longitudinal bearer, as at J (Fig. 19), about 3 in. by 2 in., can easily be fixed to take the roof boarding, which should be felted, tarred and sanded. A similar central bearer, as at K (Fig. 19) serves to take the floor; but as it can be supported at close intervals it need only be 2 in. deep. The ends of the boards will rest on the sill as shown, and if desired they could be put together in sections by means of ledges on the underside.

The back and fixed end can be covered with vertical tongued-and-grooved boards, or horizontal feather-edged boarding, either of which will stiffen the work considerably. Horizontal boarding will look best if stopped against vertical fillets at the angles, as shown at the top corners of Fig. 23. The entrance end is filled in with doors of boarding ledged and braced, as dotted in Fig. 21. The front is filled in with boarding, as in Fig. 20, with ledges at the extreme ends and centre, and braces in addition on the upper portion. This latter is hinged, as in Fig 19, with crossgarnets and supported when open by means of two framed brackets as at L. The pins of the hinges for these should be arranged at the point marked M in Fig. 23, so that when closed the brackets are clear of the closed front, and when open, as dotted in the same figure, they come under the end ledges previously mentioned. Shorter hinges will suffice for the lower flap of the front.

TOOL SHED OR GARDEN SHELTER

A tool shed and shelter, the making of which will neither be very costly nor tax the skill of the average handyman, is shown in Fig. 24. The shed is constructed in sections consisting of a front, two sides, a back, and a roof, which are made separately and screwed together. A seat is fitted to the interior of the shed. The framework could be of deal, covered with grooved-and-tongued matchboarding The sizes to which the shed should be made are shown in the illustrations. It will not be advisable to interfere with the height of the shed, but, if desired, it could be made either larger or smaller on plan. The dimensions 3 ft. wide by 3 ft. 6 in. deep will give a shed of very useful size; but for those who require a smaller shed these dimensions could be reduced to 2 ft. 6 in. by 3 ft., and this will, of course, result in a saving of material.

The front framework of the shed, which is shown by Fig. 26, consists of two side rails 6 ft. 6 in. long by 3 in. wide by 1 in. thick, top rail 3 ft. long by 3 in. deep by 1 in. thick, and a bottom rail 2 ft. 8½ in. long by 2 in. deep by 1 in. thick. The top and side rails are half-lapped and screwed together, as shown by Fig. 31, and the bottom rail is screwed to the inside of the side rails, as shown by Fig. 32, a space of 1¾ in. being allowed between the ends of the bottom rail and the outer edges of the side rails for the thickness of the sides of the shed.

The framework of the sides, which is shown by Fig. 27, consists of a front rail 6 ft. 6 in. long, back rail 5 ft. 9 in. long, and top, middle, and bottom rails, which are 3 ft. 6 in. long by 2 in. wide by 1 in. thick. The framework is half-lapped and screwed together, as shown by Fig. 31. Struts, which should be of a similar section to the framework, are fitted from the front bottom corner to the back of the middle

Fig. 24.—Tool Shed or Garden Shelter

rail, and from this point to the front top corner. The sides are covered on the outside with $\tfrac{3}{4}$-in. matchboarding. The back is made to the dimensions shown in Fig. 28, being formed with $\tfrac{3}{4}$-in. matchboarding, which is held together at the top with a batten 2 ft. $8\tfrac{1}{2}$ in. long by 3 in. deep by 1 in. thick; and at the bottom with a batten 2 ft. $8\tfrac{1}{2}$ in. long by 2 in. deep by 1 in. thick. Struts which are 2 in. wide by 1 in. thick should be fixed across diagonally between the battens, as shown in Fig. 28.

The front, sides, and back are fixed together, as shown by Figs. 30 and 33. The sides fit between the front and back, and screws are driven through the front and back into the sides. A floor could be provided, being formed of 1-in. boards, which rest on the top edges of the bottom members of the framework, and are supported in the middle with a bearer, as shown by the dotted lines in Fig. 30. A seat should be fitted across the back of the house, as shown in Fig. 25, and should be about 1 ft. 6 in. wide, formed with 1-in. boards resting on cleats fixed to the sides of the shed. The seat should be about 1 ft. 6 in. high, and should be slightly higher at the front than at the back. The roof could be formed with $\tfrac{3}{4}$-in. or 1-in. grooved-and-tongued boards, which run from the front to the back of the shed and are held together with two cross battens, as shown by Fig. 34. It should overhang about 3 in. at the sides and back, and about 8 in. at the front, while it is either screwed or nailed to the top edges of the front, sides, and back. The roof should be covered with roofing felt or a piece of canvas, the wood being well painted before the material is fixed.

The door of the shed is made up of $\tfrac{3}{4}$-in. matchboarding, as shown by Fig. 29, being held together by two cross battens about 6 in. by 1 in. in section, and a diagonal batten about 3 in. by 1 in. in section. The door is hung on the righthand side with a pair of long-flap T-hinges, as shown in Fig. 24, and it should also be provided with a lock and key. A small fillet should be fitted to the shutting edge of the door, as shown in Fig. 35. Ordinary boards of almost any width could be used for covering the shed, if desired, instead of the matchboards; but it will be well in that case to cover the joints with fillets, as shown in Fig. 36. The shed when complete should rest on a row of bricks to protect the base from wet rot.

Needless to say, the work should be finished with two or three coats of good oil paint; a coat of varnish over the paint will help to repel the weather.

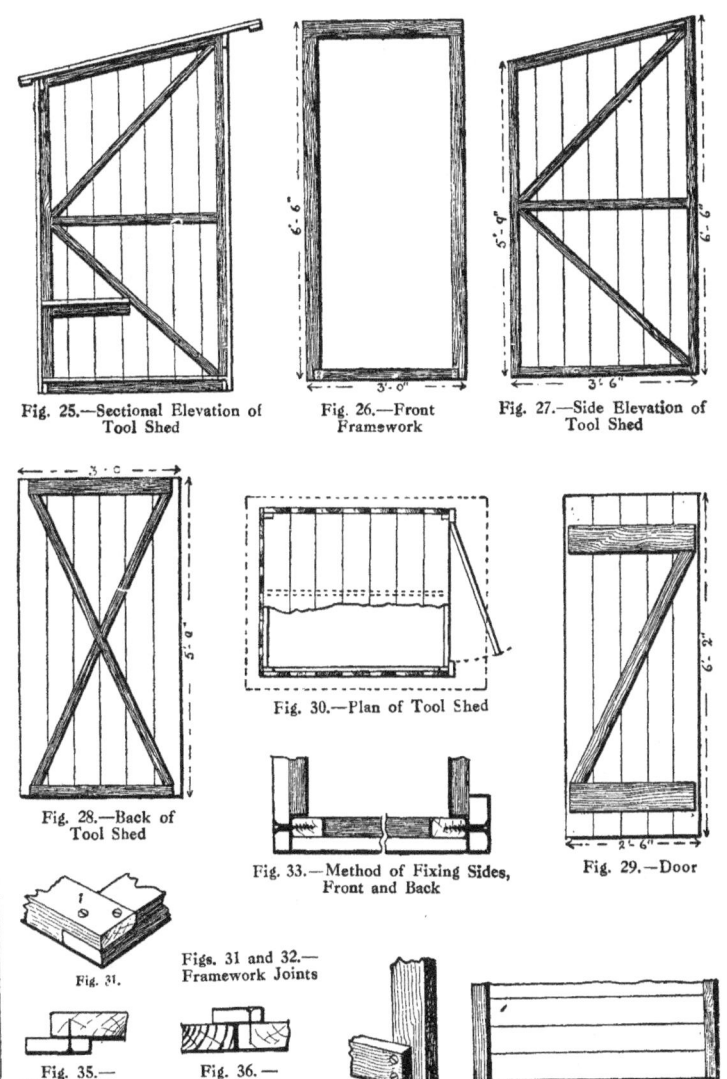

SANATORIUM FOR OPEN-AIR TREATMENT

A sanatorium for open-air treatment is here described and illustrated in such a manner as to render the construction of a similar one a matter of plain straightforward carpentry.

In size the structure measures 6 ft. long by 4 ft. deep on the inside, the height

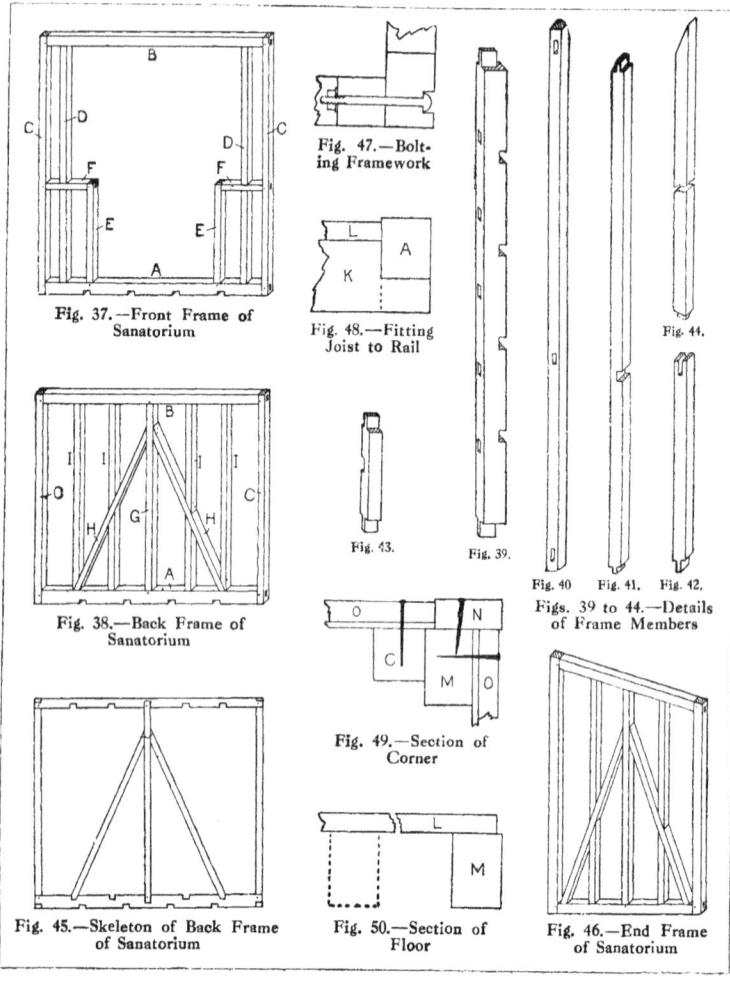

Fig. 37.—Front Frame of Sanatorium

Fig. 47.—Bolting Framework

Fig. 48.—Fitting Joist to Rail

Fig. 43.

Fig. 39.

Fig. 40. Fig. 41. Fig. 42.

Fig. 44.

Figs. 39 to 44.—Details of Frame Members

Fig. 38.—Back Frame of Sanatorium

Fig. 49.—Section of Corner

Fig. 45.—Skeleton of Back Frame of Sanatorium

Fig. 50.—Section of Floor

Fig. 46.—End Frame of Sanatorium

SHEDS AND OUTDOOR ERECTIONS

being 6 ft. 10 in. at the front and 5 ft. 4 in. at the back, also on the inside. It may be stated that it will be better to make the structure larger than this rather than

Fig. 51.—Framing of Building without Joists

smaller, the appearance when finished being quite different than when the various parts are being put together. A width of five feet would perhaps be better than four feet.

As shown by the photographs, the front is practically entirely open, the ends and sides being closed in and made as nearly draught-proof as possible. The whole structure revolves on a platform so that the patient can have the sun or not, as he pleases, and can turn his back to the cold winds at will. The outside is weather-boarded with feather-edged boards, and the inside is lined with three-ply wood, thus making it practically airtight. The roof is formed with tongued-and-grooved boards, also lined with three-ply and covered outside with Ruberoid felt. The floor is of tongued-and-grooved boards and should be covered with linoleum.

The actual construction of the building will now be dealt with. For convenience of removal at any time it is made in sections, and can be unshipped in two or three hours. As being the most complicated, begin with the front section, as shown by Fig. 37. This consists of the bottom rail A (4 in. by 2 in.), the top rail B (3 in. by 2 in.), the outside uprights C, the long and short intermediate uprights D and E, and the intermediate rails F, all of these latter being 2 in. square. The back section is as shown by Fig. 38, and consists of the bottom rail A, similar to that on the front section, the top rail B, to which the same applies, and also to the outside uprights C. After this, however, the similarity ends, the middle upright G, the braces H, and the filling-in studs I, are all 2 in. square, as in the front section. The framing of these two sections can be dealt with at the same time, there being to a certain extent a likeness between them.

The whole construction is, of course, based on mortise-and-tenon joints, and in Fig. 39 is shown the bottom rail of the back section (Fig. 38) tenoned to fit the outside uprights, and mortised to take the braces and the upright studs; also slotted on the underside to fit the floor joists, of which more later on. In fact,

Fig. 52.—Building Turned Up to Cut Slots for Joists, Two Slots Cut, One Joist in Position

it will be as well to leave this out at present and cut them after the sections are fixed together. The bottom rail of the front section must be done in exactly the same way as Fig. 39, except as regards the mortises for the studs, which must, of course, be made to suit the positions of the long and short intermediate uprights.

In describing the back section the two rails and the two outside uprights are the ones that have, so far, been mentioned. The middle upright, which is the only one

Fig. 53.—Building Framed with Joists in Position

Fig. 54.—Stops for Weather-board Fixed and Floor Laid

The outside upright is shown by Fig. 40, mortised to take the top and bottom rails, and also the intermediate rail. The four uprights (for the front and back sections) will be exactly alike, except that those for the back section will not require the middle mortise, there being no intermediate rail.

Fig. 41 shows the intermediate upright D, tenoned to fit into the top and bottom rails, and halved to fit the short intermediate rail. Fig. 42 shows the short intermediate upright E tenoned to fit into the bottom rail and slot-mortised to take the short rail, while Fig. 43 shows the latter tenoned to fit the outside upright and the short upright E, and halved to fit to the intermediate upright D. As regards the front section, the various parts will be fixed together with wood pins, the joints either pulled up tightly with cramps, or, what is better, each tenon can be drawbored so that the driving in of the pin will pull the joint up tightly. The halving joint connecting D and F is best fastened together with a screw inserted from what will be the inside of the building.

needed the full length, must be tenoned at each end to fit into the top and bottom

Fig. 55.—Building Weather-boarded, but without Roof

rails, the length from shoulder to shoulder being the same as the distance between the mortises in the uprights. This section

SHEDS AND OUTDOOR ERECTIONS

can now be put together with the five parts which are ready, after which the two braces can be tenoned to fit in the two mortises nearest the outside uprights, cutting the Fig. 45, the fact of bringing the upper ends on the same level against the middle upright will ensure the frame being square. The remaining four uprights in the back

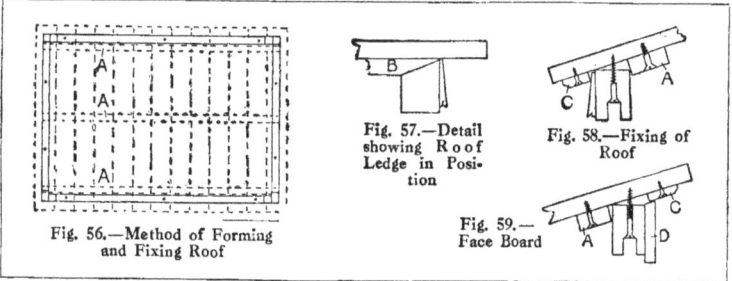

Fig. 56.—Method of Forming and Fixing Roof

Fig. 57.—Detail showing Roof Ledge in Position

Fig. 58.—Fixing of Roof

Fig. 59.—Face Board

shoulders to the angle required, which, as well as the correct length and angle of the upper end, can be obtained by laying one of them in position and marking by section will simply require tenoning at one end and cutting to the length and angle to fit the braces, to which they will be fixed by nailing. The bottom

Fig. 60.—Front View of Building with Roof

Fig. 61.—Back View of Building with Roof

the parts to which they have to fit. The brace, tenoned and cut to the required angle, is shown by Fig. 44, and the other one should be cut to the same length and angles, but the opposite way so that they form a pair.

On fixing the two braces, as shown in end will require no further fixing beyond insertion into the mortises in the rails.

The back and front sections are now finished for the time being, and attention can next be given to the ends, one of which is shown by Fig. 46. These are framed and fixed together in precisely the same way as the back, the angle and lengths of the top rail, uprights and braces, being found by laying the various pieces in position and marking. Remember that the outside uprights at the back and front must be the same length as the corresponding parts on the back and front sections, to which they have to finish level at both the top and the bottom. It will also be noticed that there will be no tenon on the bottom ends of the braces, these simply resting against the bottom rail, to which they are fixed with nails as at the upper end. The uprights at the outside of the end frames are 3 in. wide, and the top and bottom rails are the same width ; the remaining parts are 2 in. only, and the whole of the parts are 2 in. thick.

The four sections can now be bolted together, using three bolts at each corner. The end sections will fit against the sides, the 3-in. wide upright on the former projecting beyond the narrower side upright, as in Fig. 47, the purpose of this projection being seen later on. The heads of the bolts must be sunk in as shown, and the two parts must be kept level while the holes for the bolts are made. If the slots for the floor joists have been left as mentioned before, the whole erection can now be turned on its side and these slots made. The joists should be cut to fit so that they will be as in Fig. 48, where K is the joist, cut so as to come level with the front (and back) bottom rail on the underside, and leaving a space for the floorboard L to fit against the rail as shown.

The joists will not require fixing to the rails in any way ; in fact, they must not be fixed, but the rails must be simply allowed to rest on them. To make the structure firm for the time being, blocks should be so placed under the joists that these will all take equal weight, and no other part rest on anything but the joists, and while in this position the backs, two ends and the front can be weatherboarded. In order to give a finished appearance to the building, upright strips must be fixed at each corner and the boards fitted between. These strips must be fixed to the edge of the upright on the

ends of the building, as in Fig. 49, where M is a part of the end frame with the upright " stop " N fixed to it, and C is the part of the front frame to which the " stop " must not be fixed ; O is the weather-boarding. In like manner, in fixing the weatherboards they must be fixed only to the parts as shown, otherwise the sections will not come apart when required. Similar stops must be fixed at the openings in the front of the building, as shown in the photographs.

After finishing the weather-boarding the floor can be laid, but the boards must be fixed to the joists only. They will run over and rest on the bottom rails of the end framing. Fig. 50 shows a section of the floor at the end framing, the boards resting on the bottom rail, the dotted line being one of the joists. Photographs, showing the various stages of the construction so far described, are reproduced in Figs. 51 to 55 inclusive.

The next part to give attention to is the roof. This consists of 1-in. tongued-and-grooved boards held together by three ledges formed of strips of the same board. Fig. 56 shows in detail the method of forming and fixing the roof to the building. The solid lines represent the top rails of the front, back, and the two end frames ; the dotted lines A represent the three ledges for holding the roof boards together ; and the dotted lines at right angles to these are the boards forming the actual roof.

The ends of the ledges are cut off at a slope, as at B (Fig. 57), and the top rails of the end frames are cut away to suit, so that when the ledges are laid in position the upper surface will be level with the top rails. The roof boards are then laid on the ledges, and one by one screwed to them from the inside, one screw through each ledge into each board, allowing the first and the last boards to project over the ends of the building some $1\frac{1}{2}$ in., as shown in Figs. 56 and 57. This will fix the roof boards together ; but at present they are not fixed to the building itself. To do this, screws are inserted from the inside through the top rails of the frames into the roof boards, as in Figs. 58 and

SHEDS AND OUTDOOR ERECTIONS

59, which show sections at the back and front respectively. Three screws should be used at the front and back, and two at each end, as shown in Fig. 56.

Fig. 63.—Platform on Stumps with Floor in Position

It will be found in fixing the roof boards together that the two outside boards are not very firmly fixed owing to the ledges not reaching the outside. To obviate this, strips as at C should be screwed to the underside of the boards at both top and bottom, as in Figs. 58 and 59. At the front also it is as well for the sake of appearance to fix the face piece D along the top rail, as in Fig. 59.

It can now be seen that to remove the roof intact, all that is needed is to withdraw the ten screws from the inside, and the whole is free. Front and back views of the complete building are shown in the photographs, Figs. 60 and 61. The frame for the platform on which the building will revolve is shown by Figs. 62 and 63. It is 3 ft. 10 in. square, and is built up from 3-in. by 2-in. deal, placed edgewise as shown; and as the construction is simple no description is necessary.

The platform frame must be covered with 1-in. tongued-and-grooved boards (Fig. 64), allowing them to project over it about 2 in. all round, and cutting off the corners, as in Fig. 64. This illustration also shows the metal rack as fixed, and as this is important that it be fixed to an exact circle, the method adopted to attain this must be described in detail. The section of the track is as E (Fig. 65), the ball-bearing runner working on it as at F; but at intervals of about 8 in. the base of the track is flattened out to the section G, and the flange thus formed is drilled for screws, this forming the means of fixing in position. It thus follows that the track must be bent to the circular form.

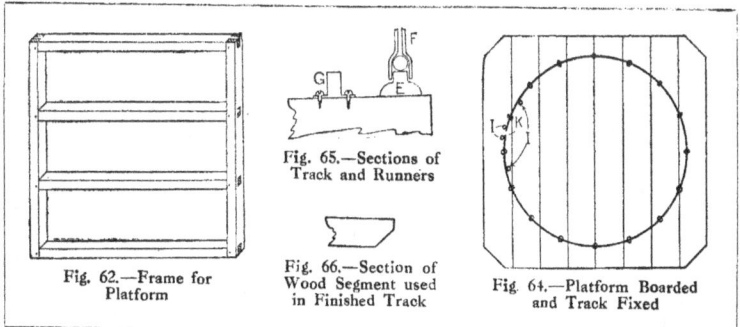

Fig. 62.—Frame for Platform

Fig. 65.—Sections of Track and Runners

Fig. 66.—Section of Wood Segment used in Finished Track

Fig. 64.—Platform Boarded and Track Fixed

The method adopted by the writer, and which was a perfect success, is as follows: A circle of the size of the inside of the track proper (not the base) is described on the platform, and a piece of board about 15 in. long is cut to the same radius, the under edge being bevelled off, as in Fig. 66. This segment is screwed to the platform with the circular edge coinciding with the circular mark, as at H

(Fig. 67), and the track placed in contact with the wood at one end and fixed. The track is then gradually bent round into contact with the wood and the other screws inserted, moving the wood to a fresh position as required until the circle is complete. It is obvious that only the track in and out as wanted until the true circle is complete. These extra screws are shown at I (Fig. 64), the joint in the track being at K.

The platform with the track complete is fixed to four oak stumps planted firmly in the ground, projecting above the ground

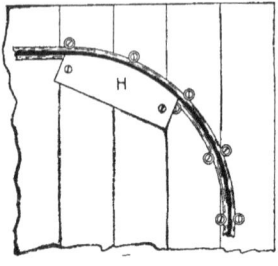

Fig. 67.—Detail showing Fixing of Track

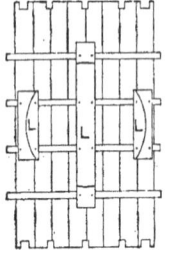

Fig. 68.—Detail showing Boards Fixed under Floor to which Runners are Fixed

the outer screws can be inserted to fix the track until the wood is removed to a fresh position. After this is done, however, the inner screws should be inserted at once in case the track is strong enough to have a tendency to draw out the outer screws.

to the height required, and finished perfectly level at the top, this being absolutely necessary if the building is to revolve easily when finished.

To prepare the underneath part of the floor for the ball-bearing runners, and to do this conveniently, the building should

Fig. 69.—Platform showing Track being Fixed

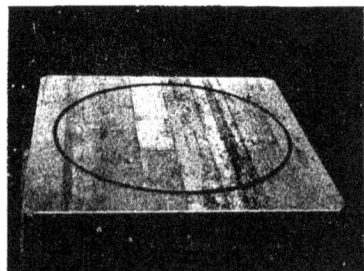

Fig. 70.—Platform, with Track Complete

The only difficulty encountered in the fixing of the track is where the ends of the track meet. Here the stiffness of the metal has the tendency to resist the bending to the circle; but this is overcome by inserting extra screws inside and outside the track as required. These screws, acting on the bevelled base, force

be taken to pieces so that the floor can be turned up. This being done, the three pieces of board (not less than 1 in. in thickness) must be screwed to the joists as at L (Fig. 68). On these boards the circle must be struck as before, as shown, and this is the guide for the insertion of the runners, which will simply be let in

SHEDS AND OUTDOOR ERECTIONS

so that the flanges can be screwed to the boards. If the circle, as marked on the boards L, is made to the same radius as that on the platform to which the track of the runners pressing against the inside or outside of the track; but if care is taken to get it right, the building will revolve quite easily. Fig. 69 is a photo-

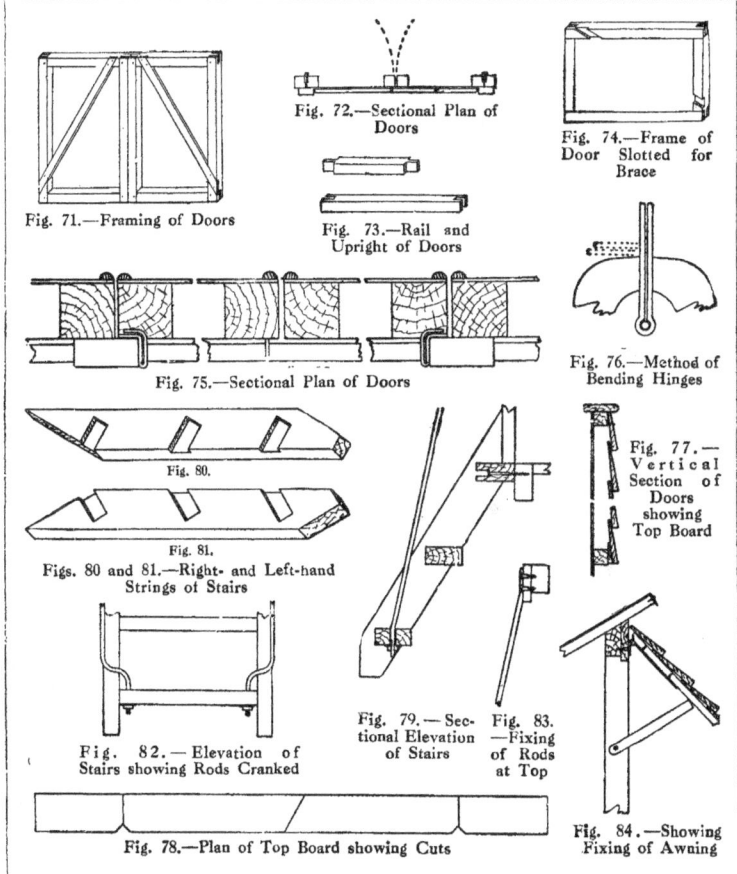

Fig. 71.—Framing of Doors

Fig. 72.—Sectional Plan of Doors

Fig. 73.—Rail and Upright of Doors

Fig. 74.—Frame of Door Slotted for Brace

Fig. 75.—Sectional Plan of Doors

Fig. 76.—Method of Bending Hinges

Fig. 77.—Vertical Section of Doors showing Top Board

Fig. 80.

Fig. 81.

Figs. 80 and 81.—Right- and Left-hand Strings of Stairs

Fig. 82.—Elevation of Stairs showing Rods Cranked

Fig. 79.—Sectional Elevation of Stairs

Fig. 83.—Fixing of Rods at Top

Fig. 78.—Plan of Top Board showing Cuts

Fig. 84.—Showing Fixing of Awning

is fixed, the inside face of the balls must be at the same distance when the pulleys are fixed. Some care is necessary here, or there may be friction through the flanges graph showing the actual fixing of the track, and Fig. 70 a photograph of the platform and track complete.

The lower part of the opening at the

front of the building is closed in with folding doors, the frames for which are shown by Fig. 71. They are covered with weather-boarding, that on one door overlapping that on the other, as in Fig. 72, thus forming the necessary rebate. The frames of the doors are put together with slot mortise-and-tenon joints. One of the rails with tenons cut, and one of the uprights with mortises made, are shown by Fig. 73.

In order to be certain that the doors will keep their shape it is best to fix a small brace as shown. This is simply a plain strip of wood, the door framing being cut away to take it, as in Fig. 74. To revert back to Fig. 72, it will be noticed that the door fits behind the stop on the framing of the building; but the boards fit between these stops, thus preserving the same line in the boarding throughout, and causing the boarding of the doors to form a part with, and to agree with, the rest of the building.

In the illustration the doors are shown as opening inwards, but as this takes up a certain amount of room, an alternative method of arranging them to open outwards is described.

This is shown in Fig. 75. The framing of the doors fits up to the framing of the building, and as the stops project forward beyond this, it follows that the knuckle of the hinge must come to the face of the stops, and fit between these and the ends of the weather-boards on the doors. Outside hinges would solve the difficulty easily, of course, but in a very clumsy manner, and back flaps adapted by bending them as shown, are preferable.

In order that the doors should open properly, it is necessary that all the hinges shall be bent alike, and also that the two parts of each hinge shall be bent at the same time, otherwise they would not fit easily and closely together. The hinges are bent as shown in Fig. 76; screwing each one tightly in the vice with the jaws at the line where the bend is to be, the upper part can be forced to the position shown by dotted lines by means of a heavy hammer. If this is done carefully, there is no risk of breakage, or of the hinges not being practically all alike when finished. In hingeing the doors, the hinges must be let into the wood as required, the best way being to let the full thickness into the doors, not cutting away the wood of the stop at all. Good hold for the screws will be found in both the edge and back of the stop, and in the framing of the doors and the ends of the weather-boards.

The boards of the right-hand door should overhang the frame about $\frac{1}{2}$ in., thus forming the necessary rebate where the doors meet, and obviating the need for any stop being fixed on. Bolts on the inside, shooting into the floor, will be all that is wanted in the way of fastenings, as it is easy to reach over from the outside to either open or fasten them up. Along the top of the doors is fixed a plain board with the nosing worked on each edge, as shown in the section (Fig. 77). This board should be fixed to the doors and to the side openings in one piece, cutting it afterwards as required; that is, immediately over each hinge (where it will have to be notched, as shown in Fig. 78) and in the middle where the doors open. This latter cut must be on the slope as shown, to allow the right-hand door to open freely; if the cut is square the door will bind.

The building being on a fairly high platform requires a step or two to get to it comfortably. In the present case a flight of three steps is needed and provided, the upper step being on a level with, and forming a continuation of, the floor. These steps are made entirely of 4-in. by 2-in. deal, the treads being trenched into the strings, and fixed together with nails from the outside. The strings continue upwards, and are fixed to the stops at each side of the door opening; but as this would not be sufficient fixing, even with the assistance of the screws through the upper tread into the sill, make them perfectly safe by the use of two iron rods which pass through the lower tread, fixing with bolt and nut, and screwed firmly to the facia board at the top ends. These rods are cranked just above the stair tread, to allow the doors to open to the

SHEDS AND OUTDOOR ERECTIONS

full width of the opening. They also serve as very efficient handrails to the stairs, a necessary item in the case of an invalid.

The construction of the stairs is very simple, and should be perfectly plain to

Fig. 85.—Section of Window at Side

Fig. 86.—Section of Window at Bottom

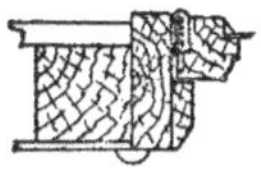

Fig. 85.    Fig. 86

anyone who will study the illustrations for a few minutes. Fig. 79 is a sectional elevation after the stairs are fixed, and Figs. 80 and 81 are the pair of strings with

The front awning is necessary to keep the wet from driving into the front, if for any reason it is not convenient to turn the building back to the weather for the time being; but it is more necessary to keep off the direct rays of the sun, when for any reason it has to be kept facing that way. The awning is made up of weatherboards (feather-edged) held together with three ledges, and is hinged at the top just under the roof, as in Fig. 84. It can thus be raised to a nearly horizontal position; or, if required, it can be allowed to fall to a vertical position; or it may be fixed at any point between by varying the adjusting rods, one of which is fixed on the inside of each lining at the extreme width of the opening. Two small windows in the back are a great improvement, and the building would be better framed to take the windows.

Stops must be fixed round the openings to form rebates to take the sashes, those at the sides and top being simply a chamfered moulding of the necessary width,

Fig. 87.—Back of Finished Sanatorium

Fig. 88.—Front of Sanatorium, with Doors Closed

the trenches made to take the treads. The latter are not illustrated, as they are simply cut off square at the ends to the correct length, when they are ready for fixing. Fig. 82 is a front elevation of the stairs (bottom part only), and will make the cranking of the rods plain, while Fig. 83 shows the fixing of the rods at the upper end to the facia board.

as shown in Fig. 85; but that at the bottom should be as in Fig. 86, to form a stop to prevent the water driving in and over. The sashes are simply a square frame to fit each opening, made of ordinary sash moulding to take the glass. They are hinged on opposite sides, one opening to the right and the other to the left, and are fixed and adjusted by means of ordinary casement stays.

The inside of the sanatorium is lined throughout with three-ply birch $\frac{1}{8}$ in. in thickness, the joints and also the angles being covered with a half-round moulding. This method of lining makes it practically draught-proof, while it is easy to do, and is not costly. It can be finished in any style, paint or stain, the former preferably, unless the stain is varnished. If this is done, outside varnish should be used, the inside being really in a great measure exposed to the weather sufficiently to call it outside. To prevent damage to the three-ply lining at the floor level, it will be as well to fix a narrow skirting entirely round the inside, on the face of the thinner wood. Two photographs of the completed building are shown in Figs. 87 and 88.

PORTABLE WORKSHOP

The method of construction of a workshop or storeroom building measuring 24 ft. long by 18 ft. wide, of a portable nature, would be first to prepare to a rectangular shape the concrete foundation, spacing the $\frac{3}{4}$-in. holding-down bolts, with their 6-in. by 6-in. by $\frac{1}{2}$-in. anchor plates, as shown in the longitudinal and transverse sections, Figs. 90 and 91, and also in Fig. 92. Protection must be provided for the screw thread and the nut at the top in the form of sacking, tied tightly on, and temporary boarding, bored with $\frac{3}{4}$-in. holes the correct distances apart to keep the bolts upright and in proper position, should be fitted and maintained while the concrete and brickwork is being put in. The concrete should be of about 4 to 1 proportions. A dampcourse composed of either asphalte, slate, or heavily tarred felt is an essential provision if the lasting qualities of the timber superstructure are to be considered, and this should be laid both horizontally and vertically. The brick base is then built and should be well grouted in with the mortar as the work rises. All these matters are shown in the detail drawing, Fig. 92.

The upper part of the building should be of good quality deal or fir, and all the sections should be strongly mortised and tenoned together, spiking being only resorted to where absolutely unavoidable. The main erection, as will be seen from the plan of the floor in Fig. 89 at A, is of 4-in. by 3-in. angle-posts, and 6-in. by 2-in. to carry the roof trusses, with 4-in. by 3-in. forming the door posts. The sections are of 4-in. by 2-in., being placed into position, and bolted with $\frac{1}{2}$-in. bolts to the 6-in. by 2-in. constructional uprights, etc. The bolting at the angles is arranged by allowing one bolt to be at a trifle lower level than the other to permit it to pass (see Fig. 91, sectional elevation E). Reference to Fig. 89 at A will clear up any point on this matter.

The sectional panels, which measure about 8 ft. by 9 ft. 6 in., are framed complete with the casement windows fitted in them, and these, by carefully arranging the galvanised-iron sheeting in width as well as height, can be taken out and replaced at will upon the simple removal of the $\frac{1}{2}$-in. bolts. It is obvious that the two end panels would have to be fixed first, and the centre one with the laps in width of the corrugated iron provided on each side of it afterwards.

Galvanised corrugated iron should not be cut if possible to avoid doing so, and certainly not extensively, but the correct size and shape of the sheets required should be ordered from the works to ensure the galvanising covering entirely the surfaces, together with the edges. A shearing machine is the correct method of cutting this material, specially designed for the purpose, but these are not readily available. Small holes such as those for the projection of a window sill can be managed by the careful working of a hack saw. The other method, and the one usually resorted to, is by means of a cold chisel and heavy hammer. This, as can be well imagined, makes a very rough job, and the edges should be trimmed and filed up to a true line for exposed positions. These facts only accentuate the desirability of ordering carefully and accurately, and should it be a case of cutting as against giving an extra lap in the iron, to select

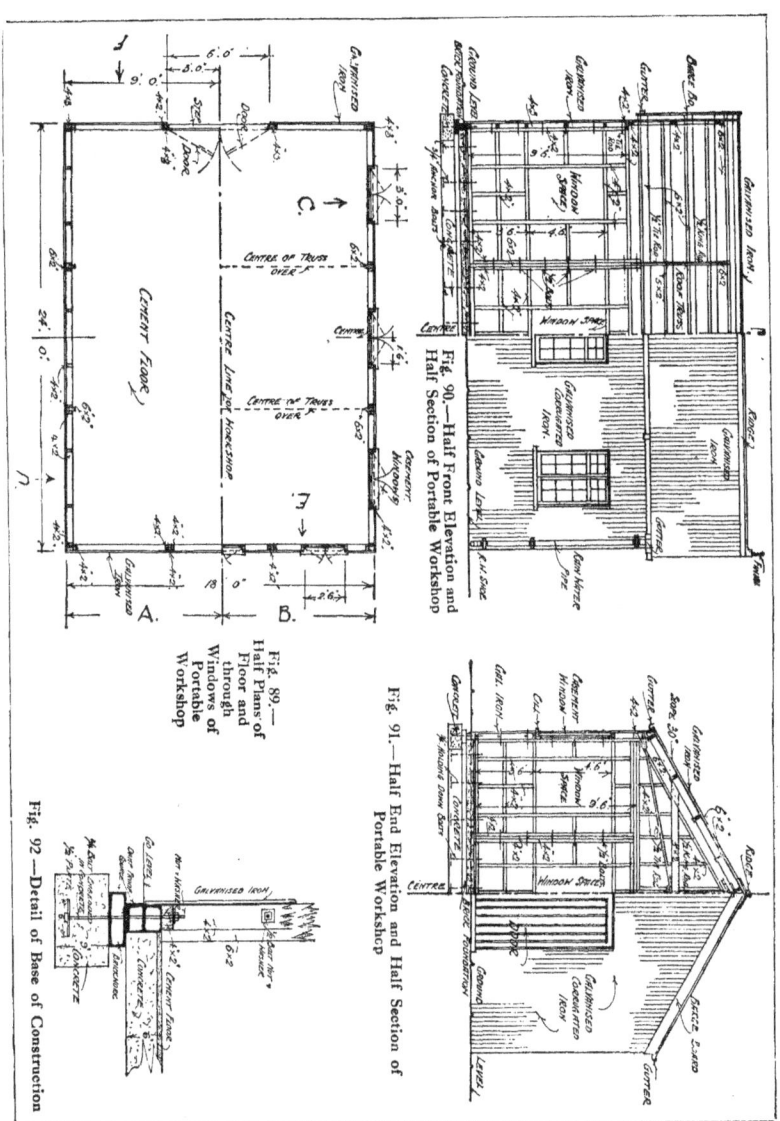

Fig. 89.—Half Plans of Floor and through Windows of Portable Workshop

Fig. 90.—Half Front Elevation and Half Section of Portable Workshop

Fig. 91.—Half End Elevation and Half Section of Portable Workshop

Fig. 92.—Detail of Base of Construction

THE PRACTICAL WOODWORKER

the latter as the proper course, for weather acts on the ungalvanised edges, and the ends of the sheets rust away very rapidly. It is well to arrange the building to enable stock size sheets to be used, and 24-gauge corrugated iron will be found

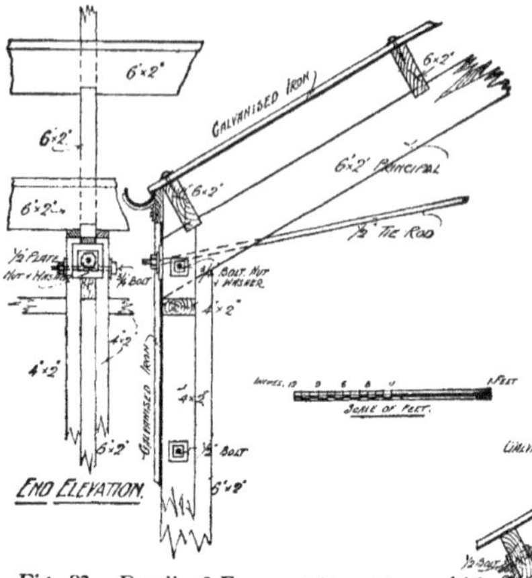

across the front of the building inside, over the door, would be a wise precaution so as to tie this end securely together.

A light form of roof is shown, but an ordinary king-post truss would suffice if it is desired to keep the constructional part of the erection particularly in timber. The span is not enough to introduce the bow-string kind of truss. It is a cheap, strong type of truss, consisting, as is seen in Fig. 91, transverse section, of 6-in. by 2-in. principal rafters, 5-in. by 2-in. collar halved into same with the ½-in. king and tie rods. Each is made as one section and slipped in between the extended 4-in. by 2-in. sides of the side panels, and on to the 6-in. by 2-in. upright, and then

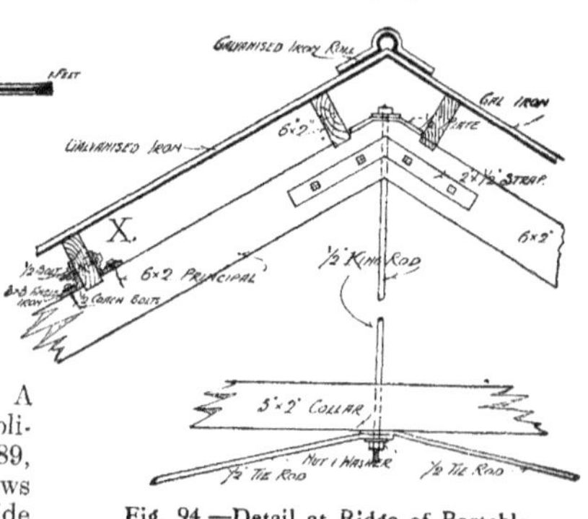

Fig. 93.—Detail of Eaves of Portable Workshop

Fig. 94.—Detail at Ridge of Portable Workshop

sufficient for all ordinary purposes. A list of sizes can be easily obtained on application to the manufacturers. Fig. 89, at B, gives a half plan through the windows and doorway, which is arranged 6 ft. wide in two widths. Three windows are provided each side and at the back, which should prove sufficient lighting for ordinary purposes. However, one extra each side of the doorway could be inserted if, for instance, working benches are situate there.

Before proceeding to put on the roof, the assembling of the made sections (of which there are eleven) and fastening them together should be complete. They are simply passed over the holding-down bolts through the holes corresponding in position with the same in the 4-in. by 2-in. sill, washered, and the nuts tightened up, which is followed by the bolting up of the sides. The introduction of a ½-in. tie rod

securely bolted through the three thicknesses. The end elevation (Fig. 93) shows this point very clearly. Further explanatory details of the roof trusses are illustrated in Figs. 93 and 94, and will be easily followed and understood from them. On these trusses 6-in. by 2-in. purlin rafters are notched down parallel to the length of the workshop on to them at 2-ft. 6-in. intervals, and then in turn the galvanised corrugated iron is secured to same by galvanised pins each provided with a washer on top.

Fig. 94 at the point x shows a way by

SHEDS AND OUTDOOR ERECTIONS

which the roof can be placed on in sections. Each principal rafter of the trusses is provided with two 3-in. by 3-in. angle irons as shown, drilled to receive the $\frac{1}{2}$-in. bolts through the same to secure the purlins rafters and similarly drilled to enable the coach bolts to be screwed into the principal rafters. The rafters and the sheets of iron fastened to them are removed by lifting as soon as the bolts through the angle cleats are taken out. The two end sections would have to be fitted first, and then the centre one. The roof in this case is portable and in six pieces. The $2\frac{1}{2}$-in. rain-water pipes, 4-in. half-round gutters, ridge pieces, and barge boards are separate portions, and must be treated as such.

In Figs. 90 and 91 half front elevation and side elevation are given, and, as will be seen, the appearance complete would not be at all objectionable. The floor is shown to be in concrete with cement floating, but this, together with the provision for ventilation, etc., is dependent entirely upon the class of user. Other minor points will be easily cleared up by reference to the drawings, which to a large extent are self-explanatory. The letters on the plans (Fig. 89) apply to the other illustrations for reference and to facilitate the reading of them.

Wheelbarrows

EASILY-MADE BARROW

THE useful barrow shown by Figs. 1 to 4 can be made with few tools. All the work is quite straightforward, and has been greatly simplified by the introduction of a solid-wood wheel in place of the usual spoked wheel. A plan of the barrow is shown by Fig. 6.

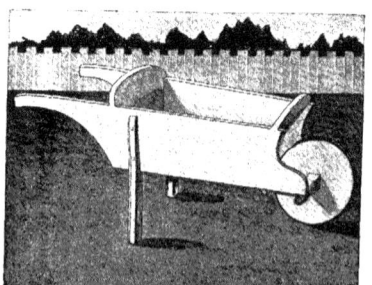

Fig. 1.—Sketch of Easily-made Barrow

In making, it is best to employ English elm, but a barrow made of good red deal is very serviceable and will last quite a number of years. The sides, back, front, and bottom should all be 1 in. thick. The sides are cut as shown in Fig. 5, and the top and bottom edges are bevelled to the side bevel of the barrow. The back is cut as shown in Fig. 7, and the front as shown in Fig. 8. Both the back and front are housed $\frac{1}{4}$ in. into the sides, and are fixed by driving screws through the sides. The bottom fits between the sides, and against the bottom edges of the back and front. It is fitted in from the back, and when in position screws are driven through the sides into the edges of the bottom, and others inserted through the bottom into the edges of the back and front.

The legs should, if possible, be of ash $1\frac{1}{2}$ in. square, shaped as shown by Fig. 9. They are bolted to the sides of the barrow, and may either be fixed square with the bottom, as shown in Fig. 2, or square with the ground. Neat chamfers about $\frac{1}{4}$ in. wide worked on the edges of the legs will improve the appearance.

The wheel is 1 ft. 2 in. in diameter by 1 in. or, if possible, $1\frac{1}{4}$ in. thick, having an iron tyre of either flat or half-round section $\frac{3}{8}$ in. thick. The tyre is welded slightly smaller in circumference than the wheel. It is heated for driving on, and when in place is cooled down. Three nails or screws are driven through the tyre. The hub is shown by Fig. 10; it is 10 in. long by $2\frac{1}{4}$ in. square, shouldered down to 2 in., and mortised through the wheel. The ends of the hub are rounded down to $1\frac{1}{2}$ in., and iron ferrules, as shown by Fig. 11, are driven on the ends. The wheel revolves on iron pegs $\frac{1}{2}$ in. in diameter, and similar to that shown by Fig. 12, driven into the ends of the hub. The wheel is held in

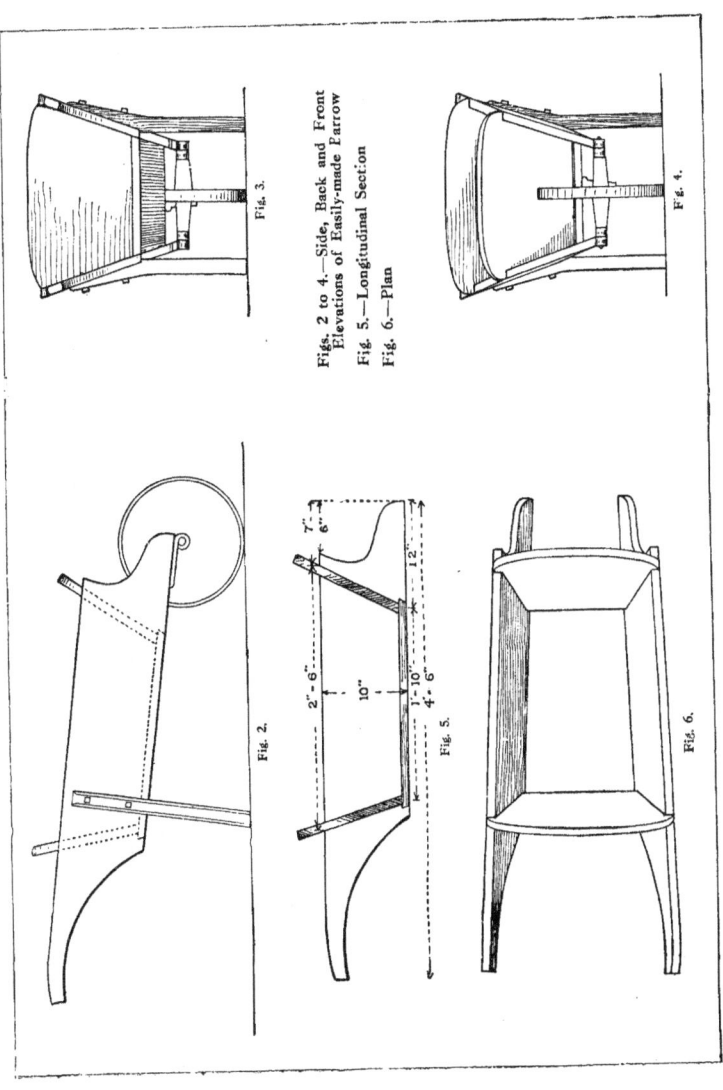

Figs. 2 to 4.—Side, Back and Front Elevations of Easily-made Parrow
Fig. 5.—Longitudinal Section
Fig. 6.—Plan

position on the hub with a key, as shown by Fig. 13, which is mortised through the hub. The wheel is attached to the barrow and works in two iron eyes, as shown by Fig. 14, which are turned up from iron 1 in. wide by ⅜ in. thick, each eye being provided with two screw holes.

The painting of the barrow must not be overlooked, quite three good coats being necessary, green for the outside and red inside being usual colours.

of the barrow, and Fig. 17 a plan as seen from underneath.

For the framework, English oak and ash are most suitable, the former being more durable than the latter when exposed to alternate wet and dry weather; but it has the disadvantage of being heavier than ash and less elastic. The panels or linings may be of either elm or red deal, the latter

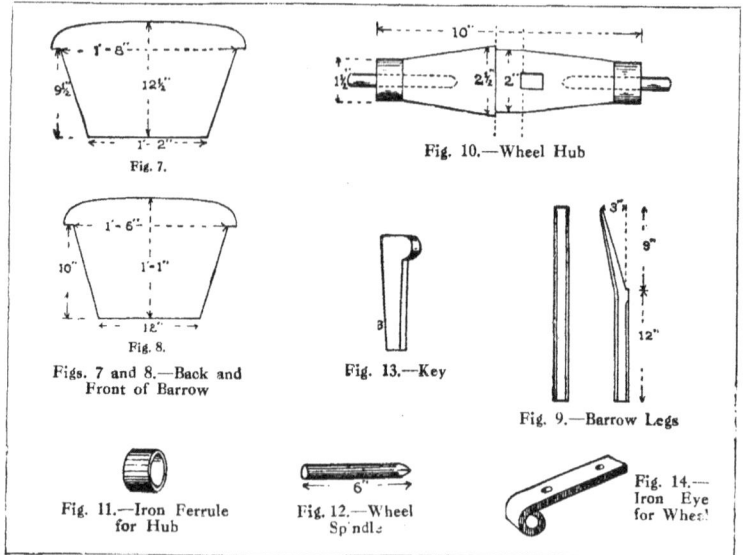

Fig. 7.

Fig. 10.—Wheel Hub

Fig. 8.

Figs. 7 and 8.—Back and Front of Barrow

Fig. 13.—Key

Fig. 9.—Barrow Legs

Fig. 11.—Iron Ferrule for Hub

Fig. 12.—Wheel Spindle

Fig. 14.—Iron Eye for Wheel

GARDEN OR STABLE WHEELBARROWS

Garden barrows and farm or stable barrows are alike, except that the former have removable top boards for carrying leaves, etc., large bodies fairly wide at the front being required for both purposes. Two standard patterns will be dealt with, the first one a full-size barrow of substantial build being shown in side elevation by Fig. 15. Fig. 16 is a front elevation

being most suitable for the bottom boards as regards durability. When getting out the stuff, which should be well seasoned and free from large knots and checks, allowance must be made for waste in cutting to length and planing up, as the finished sizes will be given. The large timber merchants keep special barrow timber in stock. The following pieces will be required for the framework: Two crooked strines A, 5 ft. long by 3 in. deep by 2 in. thick; three sloats B, 1 ft. 11 in., 1 ft. 8¾ in., and 1 ft. 6¼ in. long respectively by 2½ in. by 1¼ in.; two legs C, 2 ft. 4 in. long by 2¼ in. by 2¼ in.; two front

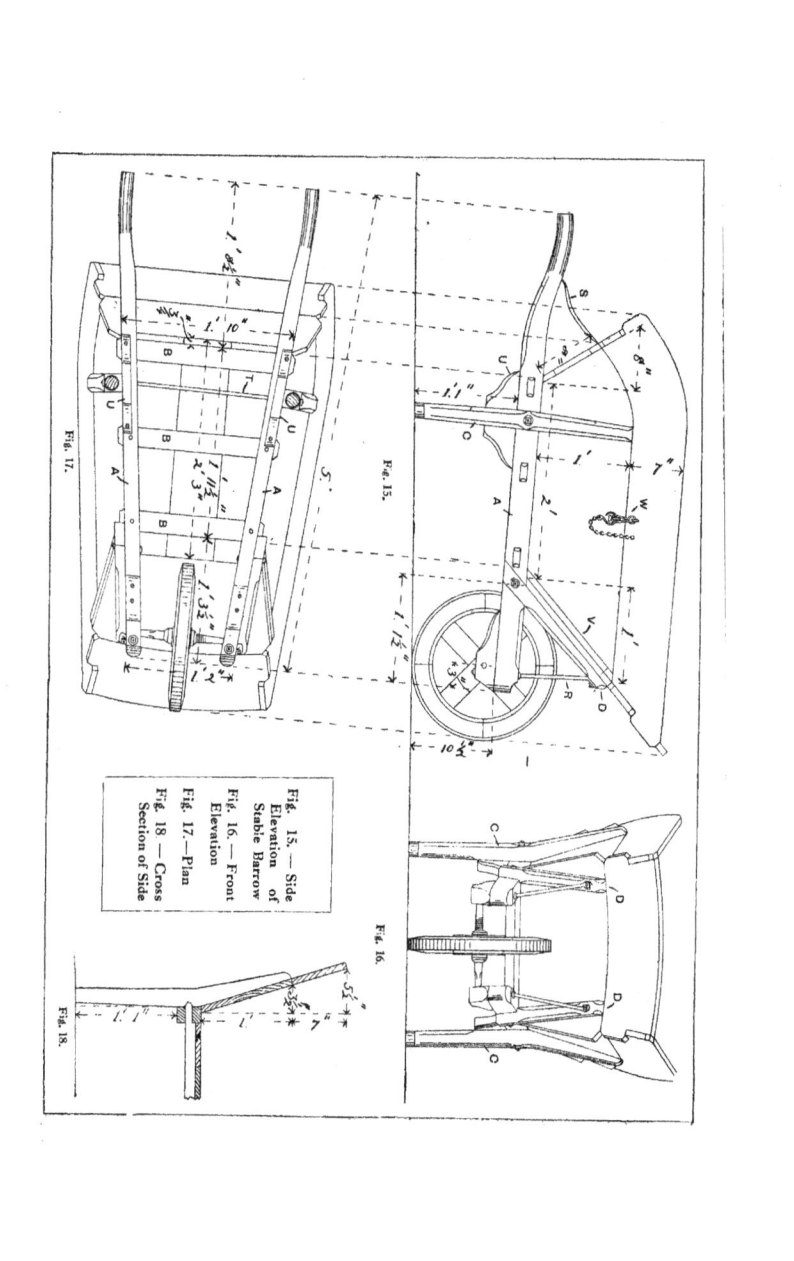

Fig. 15.—Side Elevation of Stable Barrow
Fig. 16.—Front Elevation
Fig. 17.—Plan
Fig. 18.—Cross Section of Side

standards D, 1 ft. 8¾ in. long by 2 in. wide by 1⅞ in. thick ; and 16-ft. run of 2½-in. by 1-in. ash for the top board battens ; also 2 ft. of 2½-in. by 2-in. oak for the trunnion blocks.

The principal dimensions of the barrow are as follow : Length inside at bottom, 2 ft. ; ditto at top, 3 ft. 5 in. ; width at bottom inside, 1 ft. 8¼ in. at back and 1 ft. 3⅛ in. at the front ; vertical depth of sides, 1 ft. ; ditto of top boards, 7 in. ; splay of sides, 3½ in. ; splay of front panel or head, 1 ft. or 45° ; splay of back panel, 8 in. in 1 ft. ; capacity of body without top boards, 5 cub. ft. The width of the bottom frame over the strines is 1 ft. 2 in. at the front, and 1 ft. 10 in. at the back of the hind sloat. The length on the centre line of the plan from the front end of the strines to the front sloat is 1 ft. 3⅛ in. ; over the front and back sloats, 1 ft. 11½ in. ; and from hind sloat to end of handles, 1 ft. 8½ in.

Having planed up the stuff true to size and out of wind, place the strines on the floor the required distance apart and the sloats across them in their respective positions, using small cramps to keep them in position, testing for truth with a waxed line diagonally across opposite corners until found correct. Then scribe the position of the mortises on the strines and the shoulder on the sloats. The sloats are made with bare-faced tenons ¾ in. thick, the shoulder being on the upper side, so that the ⅝-in. bottom boards will come flush at the top with the strines as shown in the cross-sectional view (Fig. 18). Square lines on both sides of the strines from the marks previously made, and gauge the width of the mortises from the upper edge.

Having cut the mortises and tenons, bore a ¼-in. pinhole through each mortise, and knock the frame together temporarily to see whether it is true, testing again with the waxed line. When true, scribe the position of the pinholes on the tenons, take the frame apart, and bore the holes a trifle nearer the shoulder to give the joints a little draw and ensure the shoulders coming up tight. After dressing the handles to shape, and rounding the ends of the tenons on the sloats, which project ½ in. from the face of the strines, give all the joints a good coat of white-lead mixed with linseed oil, and fix together permanently with lancewood or hickory pins.

The bottom boards, 2 ft. 3 in. long, run longitudinally between the strines, and are nailed to the sloats, the ends of the boards being rounded. To set out the front and back panels, first mark the inside length of the body on the frame as at E and F (Fig. 19), then the amount of splay, namely, 1 ft. at the front and 8 in. at the back, fixing two straightedges G and H at the two latter marks by means of cramps or wire nails. Then place another straightedge J across the others at a distance of 3½ in. from one of the strines and parallel with it, marking the inner edge where they cross at K and L, repeating the operation for the other side.

Next obtain the width of board required for the front and back by setting them out on a board to the given splay, as shown in Fig. 15, which is 1 ft. 6¼ in. for the front panel and 1 ft. 2¼ in. (8½ in. + 5¾ in.) for the back panel. Having planed the stuff and shot the edges true, gauge a line 1⅛ in. from the upper edge of the front panel, this being the amount of camber, and, with square and scriber, strike a centre line M (Fig. 20) across the board. Then take the outside width across the bottom at F F and the width across the top at L L (Fig. 19), divide by 2, and set off the measurements obtained on each side of the centre line at F F and L L (Fig. 20), afterwards drawing lines from F to L for the required bevels. For the back panel, take the widths E E and K K (Fig. 19), setting off half their respective lengths on each side of the centre line in Fig. 21, and drawing the bevels through the points obtained. Then gauge the true width 8½ in. up from the bottom as shown by line N. As the front and back panels project 1¼ in. over the sides, scribe parallel lines O that distance from F L (Fig. 20) and E K (Fig. 21).

The top swept line P (Fig. 20) is struck by first inserting a bradawl at each side L, and another in the centre at Q, then nailing two crossed laths together, their edges touching the three awls, as shown by Fig. 22. Then by withdrawing the centre awl, but holding it in the same place given splay, then setting the bevel to the taper of the bottom frame and applying it to the inner or acute bottom edge of the

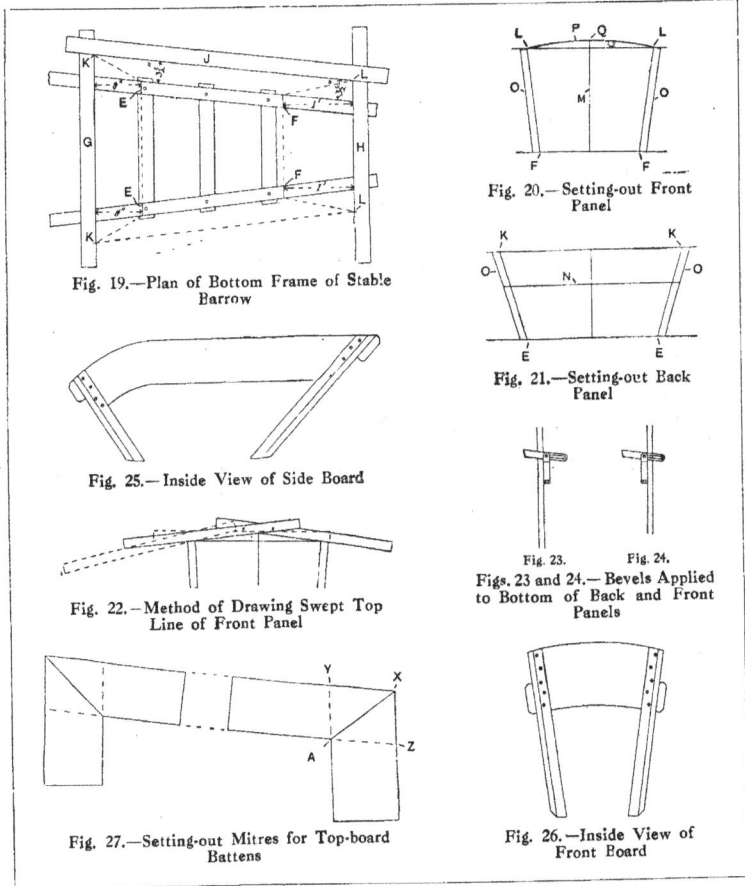

Fig. 19.—Plan of Bottom Frame of Stable Barrow

Fig. 25.—Inside View of Side Board

Fig. 22.—Method of Drawing Swept Top Line of Front Panel

Fig. 27.—Setting-out Mitres for Top-board Battens

Fig. 20.—Setting-out Front Panel

Fig. 21.—Setting-out Back Panel

Figs. 23 and 24.—Bevels Applied to Bottom of Back and Front Panels

Fig. 26.—Inside View of Front Board

as a scriber, move the laths round from one side to the other, as indicated by dotted lines, the scriber bearing lightly on the panel. The end bevels are obtained by first bevelling the bottom edge to the panels, as shown by Figs. 23 and 24, from which points lines are scribed on the face to the same bevel as those on the back. The front standards taper at the top to $1\frac{3}{4}$ in. wide by $\frac{7}{8}$ in. thick, and are shouldered down $\frac{3}{8}$ in. at the bottom, where they are lapped to the face of the strines and secured with $\frac{5}{16}$-in. bolts.

The head is supported by braces R (Fig. 15) of $\frac{7}{16}$-in. round bar iron with a flap at the top and a $\frac{7}{16}$-in. bolt through it and the standard, the $\frac{3}{8}$-in. bolt-end at the bottom taking the strine and trunnion block, the latter being further secured with screws. The holes for the axle are only bored $1\frac{1}{2}$ in. deep, and should be lined with pieces of iron tubing an easy fit on the ends of the axle. The back panel is supported by brackets s (Fig. 15) $1\frac{1}{2}$ in. thick, fixed to the strines with dowels and screws. Having nailed the front and back panels in position, the side panels can be marked from them after bevelling the bottom edge. Place the side panels on the side of the barrow with the lower edge level with the top of the frame, and scribe on the inner side along the ends of the front and back panels to get the correct length and shape. Then mark the end bevels on the lower edge, continuing the lines on the face to the same bevel as those scribed on the back, so that there will be no mistake when cutting to shape and dressing the ends.

Dress the legs to the side splay as shown in Fig. 18, and taper them to 2 in. by 2 in. at the bottom and 2 in. by $\frac{7}{8}$ in. at the top, chamfering the edges where they do not bear against anything. The legs are fixed to the face of the strines with a $\frac{3}{8}$-in. long-bolt T (Fig. 17) and $1\frac{1}{4}$-in. brackets U. The lower ends of the legs are shod with hoops of 1-in. by $\frac{1}{8}$-in. iron. Fillets V (Fig. 15) $1\frac{1}{4}$ in. by $\frac{3}{4}$ in. are fixed across the front panel close to the ends to strengthen the side panels and form a better fixing for them.

The removable top boards are held in position by a long batten at each end, fixed to the back with screws, as shown by the inside views of a side and front board (Figs. 25 and 26 respectively), the battens extending to the bottom of the body, and mitre-jointed to those of the adjacent boards, which prevents their falling outwards. The top boards are halved together edgewise at the corners, the end boards being inserted first, then the side boards, which are fitted with a hasp and staple W (Fig. 15) secured with a pig-tail or hook cotter attached to a chain, thus locking the whole securely.

The easiest way of obtaining the correct bevels for the mitres will be to place the battens in the inside corners of the body, and mark and cut the bevels at the foot to fit perfectly level on the bottom boards. Then mark the thickness at the foot of the ends battens on the foot of the side battens from X to Y (Fig. 27), and the thickness at the foot of the side battens on the foot of the end battens from X to Z. With the bevel as previously set (Figs. 23 and 24), draw lines across to A (Fig. 27), taking care to place the blade the right way. Join A to X, and gauge the width on the inner side of the batten. The bevel is held the opposite way for the other end of the barrow, as on the left of Fig. 27.

The wheel is 1 ft. 6 in. high in the wood main spoke, $2\frac{1}{2}$ in. by $1\frac{7}{8}$ in.; the other one, $2\frac{1}{2}$ in. by $\frac{3}{4}$ in.; felloes, $2\frac{1}{4}$ in. deep by 2 in. thick; tyre, $1\frac{1}{2}$ in. by $\frac{5}{16}$ in. The light spoke is mortised through the heavy one, the latter being dressed to $\frac{3}{4}$ in. thick at the ends. The axle, of 1-in. square bar iron, has a solid collar $1\frac{3}{4}$ in. square by $\frac{1}{2}$ in. thick on one side of the wheel, and a nut the same size on the other side, a $2\frac{1}{2}$-in. by $\frac{1}{8}$-in. washer being interposed between the nut and the spoke. The ends of the axle are rounded to $\frac{3}{4}$-in. diameter.

ALTERNATIVE DESIGN FOR BARROW

Another design of wheelbarrow, of medium size, is given in side elevation by Fig. 28, and in front elevation by Fig. 29. Fig. 30 is a plan of the bottom frame, and Fig. 31 a sectional elevation of the body, Fig. 32 being a cross section through one leg.

The framework of this barrow consists of two strines B, 4 ft. 5 in. long by $2\frac{3}{4}$ in. deep by 2 in. thick; a front sloat C, 1 ft. $6\frac{1}{2}$ in. long by $3\frac{3}{4}$ in. wide by $1\frac{1}{4}$ in. thick; a hind sloat D, 1 ft. 9 in. long by $2\frac{1}{2}$ in. wide by $1\frac{1}{4}$ in. thick; two legs E, 2 ft. $\frac{3}{4}$ in. long by 2 in. by 2 in.; two front pillars F, 1 ft. $7\frac{1}{2}$ in. long by $1\frac{1}{2}$ in. wide by $1\frac{1}{4}$ in.

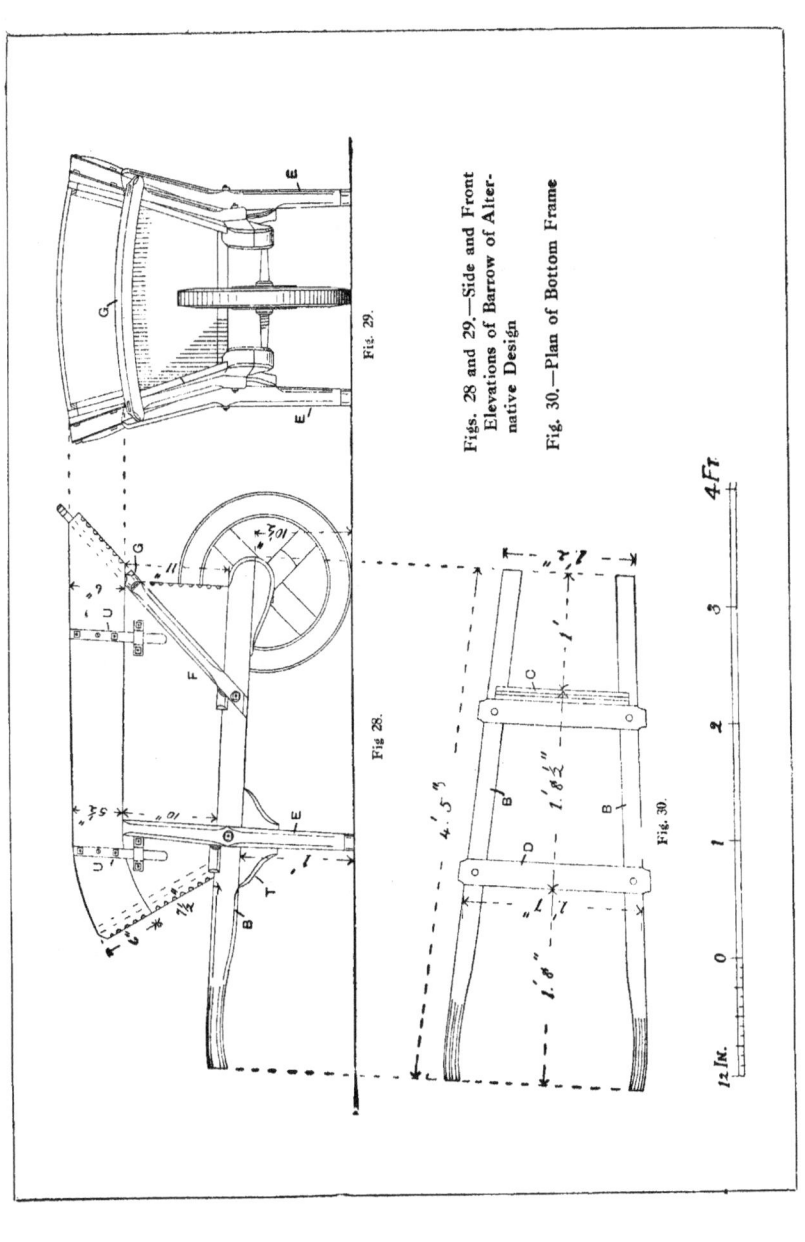

Figs. 28 and 29.—Side and Front Elevations of Barrow of Alternative Design

Fig. 30.—Plan of Bottom Frame

thick; and a front cross-rail G, 2 ft. 2 in. long by $1\frac{1}{2}$ in. wide by $1\frac{5}{8}$ in. deep, compassed to $1\frac{1}{4}$ in. at the centre; also 2 ft. of $2\frac{1}{4}$-in. by 2-in. oak for the trunnion blocks.

The principal dimensions are as follow: Length inside at bottom, 1 ft. 6 in.; splay of front, $9\frac{3}{4}$ in.; splay of back, $4\frac{1}{4}$ in. in its own depth; vertical depth of side, 11 in. at the front, 10 in. at the leg, and $6\frac{1}{2}$ in. at the back; width of board for back panel $7\frac{3}{4}$ in.; width of bottom inside, 1 ft. $5\frac{1}{8}$ in. at back and 1 ft. $2\frac{3}{8}$ in. at front; splay of sides, $3\frac{1}{2}$ in. at the leg; vertical depth of top boards, 6 in. at the ends and $5\frac{1}{4}$ in. at the leg; capacity of body without top boards, 3 cub. ft. The width of the bottom frame over the strines is 1 ft. 2 in. at the front and 1 ft. 7 in. at the back of the hind sloat. The length on the centre line of the plan from the front end of the strines to the front sloat is 1 ft.; over the sloats, 1 ft. $8\frac{1}{2}$ in.; and from the hind sloat to the end of the handles, 1 ft. 8 in.

The bottom frame is marked out as previously described. The sloats and strines are let into each other $\frac{5}{16}$ in., as shown by Fig. 33, the sloats standing $\frac{3}{8}$ in. above the strines to come flush with the top of the bottom boards, which run crosswise between the sloats. The front sloat is grooved $\frac{1}{2}$ in. from the front edge for the $\frac{5}{8}$-in. front boards H (Fig. 31), the ends of the sloat being cut, as shown by the enlarged view (Fig. 34), to the angle of the front pillars, the back of which falls in line with the back of the front boards. The ends of the sloats project 1 in. over the strines, and after being rounded in and shaved out, the joints are given a coat of white-lead before they are finally fixed together with $\frac{5}{16}$-in. bolts.

To make the front pillar pattern, first take the length at the front from the top of the strine to the shoulder at the upper end from Fig. 28, and set it off on the edge of a board as at J K (Fig. 35), also the total length of the foot at L. Then take the vertical height at the shoulder from Fig. 28, set it off on the vertical dotted line M (Fig. 32), and square a line across to the splayed side line. The distance between the vertical and splayed lines at this point is the amount of splay required for the pillar, which must be set off on a line squared from K (Fig. 35), as at N. Join J and N, and mark in the thickness $1\frac{1}{4}$ in.

After the pillars have been cut to pattern a horizontal square (Fig. 36) will be required in dressing the inner side to the required bevel. The steel blade O is securely fixed to the end of a bolt, which turns in a gunmetal stock P, the blade being fixed to any angle by means of a knurled nut Q. To use the square, first draw a number of horizontal lines across the front edge of the pillars as shown, hold the stock of the square parallel to one of the lines, and swing the blade round to a horizontal position when the pillar is inclined to the front splay, as shown by the lower shoulder line R (Fig. 35) on the inner side of the pillar, securing it by tightening up the nut. Then dress the inner side of the pillars to the square from point to point, holding the stock to the horizontal lines on the front.

Dress the legs to the side splay obtained from Fig. 32, making them $1\frac{3}{4}$ in. by $\frac{7}{8}$ in. at the top and $1\frac{3}{4}$ in. by $1\frac{3}{4}$ in. at the bottom. Having prepared the panels, which are $\frac{3}{4}$ in. thick, bevel the bottom edge of the side ones to suit the side splay, and mark on them the forward splay of the front pillars, also the position of the sloats. Notch out the lower edge of the panels to fit over the sloats, place the front pillars to the splayed lines, and fix them temporarily with a couple of screws at the back. Fix the legs temporarily in position on the frame with $\frac{3}{8}$-in. bolts, and also the side panels, and pillars, securing the latter with cramps, or, if preferred, with the $\frac{5}{16}$-in. bolts by which they will be afterwards fixed permanently. Then by placing a straightedge across the front of the pillars at the top, the amount to be dressed off to make them level with the top cross-rail can be measured, which will be barely $\frac{1}{16}$ in., as the pillars are slightly on the twist.

Having taken off the pillars and dressed the front edge to line at the top, mark the tenons from the inner side and gauge them from the front across the top, when they will have the requisite amount of twist to

WHEELBARROWS

line with the cross-rail. As the front cross-rail is compassed 1½ in., the shoulders on the pillars should be marked to correspond, although they will be almost square. Also mark the inclination of the tenons on the rail. After mortising, place the project 1¼ in. Give the joints a coat of white-lead and fix together, either screwing or nailing the panels to the pillars and legs.

The front ends of the side panels are fixed to the strines with half-round strap-

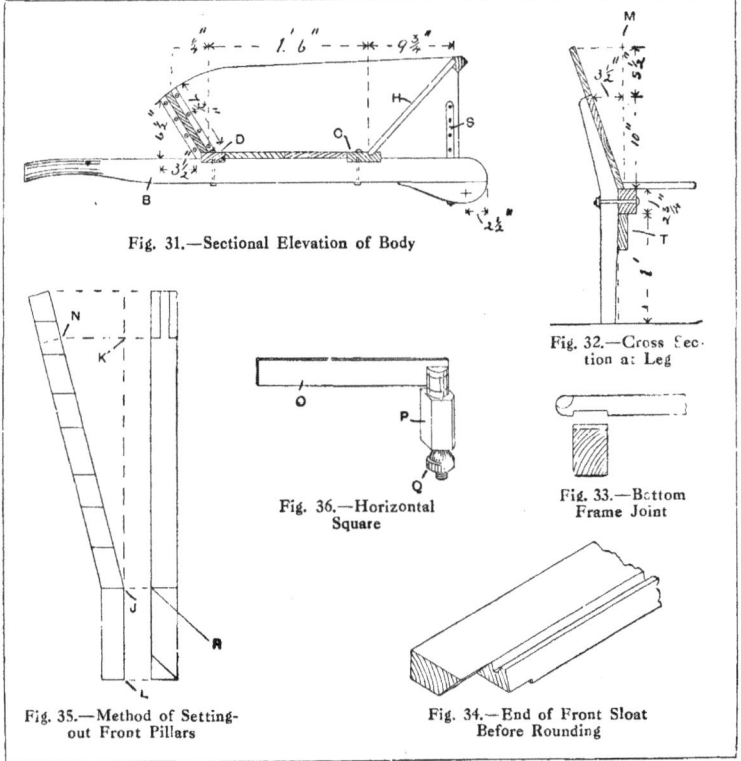

Fig. 31.—Sectional Elevation of Body

Fig. 32.—Cross Section at Leg

Fig. 36.—Horizontal Square

Fig. 33.—Bottom Frame Joint

Fig. 35.—Method of Setting-out Front Pillars

Fig. 34.—End of Front Sloat Before Rounding

sides, pillars, and rail in position, marking all bearings, also the pinholes on the tenons, then take apart, box out the inside bottom edge of the rail ⅝ in. deep by ¾ in. on, for the front boards, and chamfer the edges as desired, rounding in and shaving out the ends of the rail, which bolts s (Fig. 31), which also take the trunnion blocks, the latter being further secured with screws. The front boards are ⅝ in. thick, and run the same way as the pillars, the bottom ends fitting into the groove in the front sloat, and the top ends into the boxing in the cross-rail to

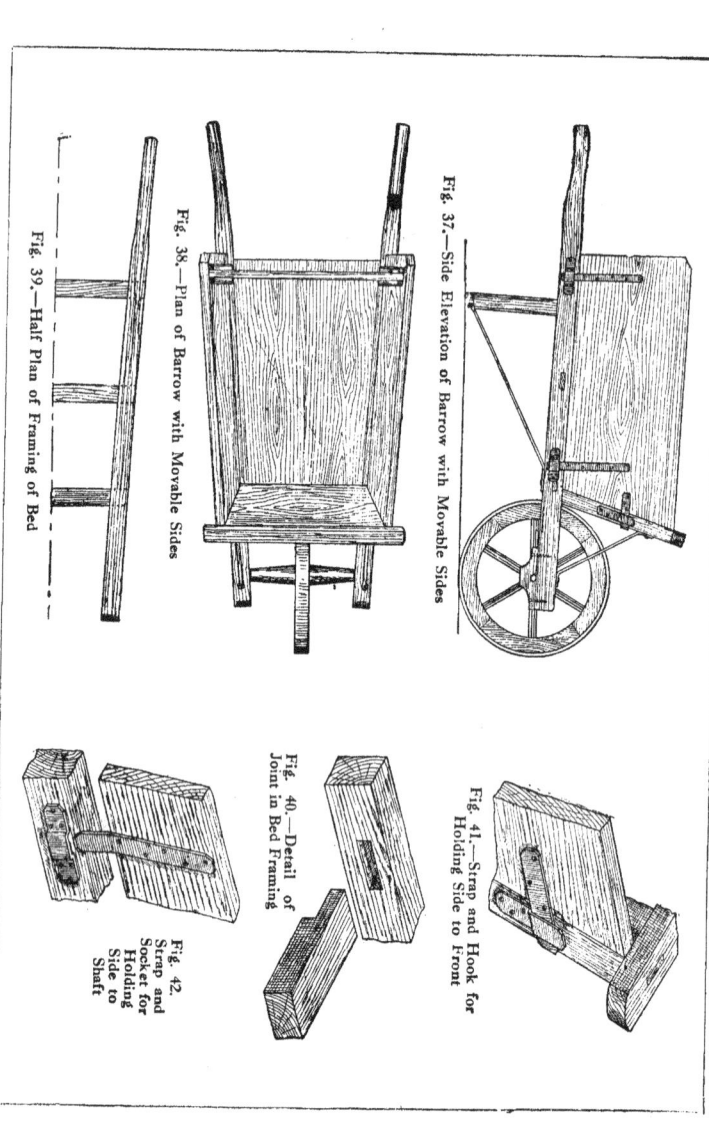

Fig. 37.—Side Elevation of Barrow with Movable Sides

Fig. 38.—Plan of Barrow with Movable Sides

Fig. 39.—Half Plan of Framing of Bed

Fig. 40.—Detail of Joint in Bed Framing

Fig. 41.—Strap and Hook for Holding Side to Front

Fig. 42.—Strap and Socket for Holding Side to Shaft

WHEELBARROWS

which they are nailed. The projecting upper corner of the top rail is dressed off level with the top of the side panels. The bottom boards, $\frac{5}{8}$ in. thick, are next fitted and nailed to the strines.

The back panel can either be made to slide in and out between $\frac{3}{4}$-in. by $\frac{5}{8}$-in. fillets screwed to the side panels, as shown in Fig. 31, or it can be a fixture; but there is not much advantage in making a low back removable. When the back is removable, the legs require staying to prevent the sides of the body spreading. The legs are strengthened by means of wood brackets T (Fig. 28) firmly screwed in position.

The portable side boards, $\frac{3}{4}$ in. thick, are attached with 1-in. by $\frac{3}{16}$-in. iron plates U, which drop into staples made from the same bar and fixed to the side panels with $\frac{1}{4}$-in. bolts. When fixing the upright irons to the side boards, care should be taken to place them parallel with each other, otherwise they will not drop into position. The loose front and back boards are battened at the back, and slide down between $\frac{3}{4}$-in. by $\frac{5}{8}$-in. fillets screwed to the side boards.

The wheel is the same as described for the other barrow.

A WHEELBARROW WITH MOVABLE SIDES

An easily constructed barrow with movable sides is shown by Figs. 37 and 38. The sizes can be easily obtained from the illustrations, which are reproduced to a scale of $\frac{3}{4}$ in. to a foot, except the details (Figs. 40, 41, and 42), which are twice that size; but these can be modified to meet requirements. Suitable woods are, ash for the framework, and oak, poplar, or best red deal for the boarding.

The framing is mortised and tenoned together, Fig. 39 being half plan of framing of bed, and Fig. 40 an enlarged detail of one of the joints. From the latter figure it will be noticed that the rails have barefaced tenons. The legs and uprights of the front are tenoned into the under and upper sides of the shafts respectively, and are kept in position more rigidly with iron stays, which are about $\frac{3}{8}$ in. in diameter and forged at the ends for screw holes.

Figs. 37, 41, and 42 show the ironwork for holding the sides in position. The iron straps, $1\frac{1}{4}$ in. by $\frac{1}{4}$ in., are screwed to the sides, the vertical ones fitting into iron sockets screwed to the side of the shafts, and the horizontal straps fitting into hooks on the uprights of the front framing. To hold the backboard in position, fillets are screwed to the barrow sides. The construction of the wheel should present no difficulties, the felloes being dowelled together, the spokes are tenoned into them, and the hub and the latter are bored for the axle, which runs in hardwood bearing blocks screwed to the shafts.

WHEELBARROW OF MODIFIED DESIGN

Wheelbarrows are usually very heavy things to use, for much of the weight is borne directly by the arms of the user A barrow which has been designed with a view to obviate this is shown in side elevation in Fig. 43. It is so built that the greater part of the load is carried over the wheel, thus taking much of the weight off the arms. The barrow is also shorter than an ordinary one, and narrow enough to pass through a 2 ft. 6 in. doorway, this, together with the deep sides, being desirable features for stable use. Figs. 44 and 45 are back and front views respectively. Fig. 46 is a plan as seen from underneath, and Fig. 47 is a sectional elevation of the body.

Either oak or ash should be used for the framework, and the panels and bottom boards of elm or good red deal. The two strines A are 4 ft. 1 in. long by $2\frac{3}{4}$ in. deep by 2 in. thick; the two sloats B, 1 ft. $10\frac{1}{2}$ in. and 1 ft. $7\frac{3}{4}$ in. respectively by $2\frac{5}{8}$ in. wide by $1\frac{1}{8}$ in. thick; two legs C, 2 ft. $2\frac{1}{4}$ in. long by 2 in. by 2 in.; and two standards D, 1 ft. $8\frac{1}{2}$ in. long by $1\frac{1}{2}$ in. by $1\frac{3}{8}$ in. The width of the bottom frame over the strines is 1 ft. 3 in. at the front and 1 ft. 9 in. at the back of the hind sloat. The length on the centre line of the plan, from the front end of the strines to the front sloat, is 1 ft. $\frac{3}{4}$ in.; over the sloats, 1 ft. $3\frac{1}{4}$ in.;

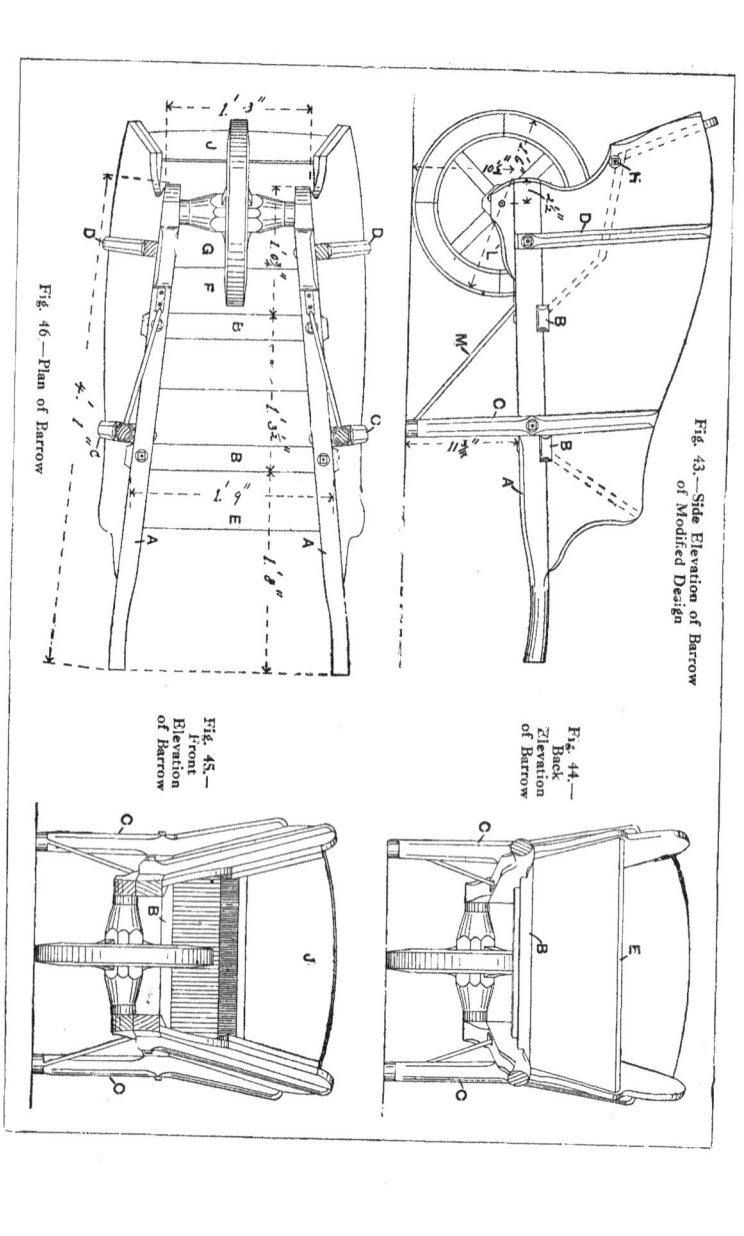

Fig. 43.—Side Elevation of Barrow of Modified Design

Fig. 44.—Back Elevation of Barrow

Fig. 45.—Front Elevation of Barrow

Fig. 46.—Plan of Barrow

from the hind sloat to the end of the handles, 1 ft. 8 in.

The strines and sloats are let into each other ¼ in. so that the latter stand ⅝ in. above the former to come level with the top of the bottom boards, which run extends across the front of the body, underneath the board G, embracing the side panels, to resist inside pressure. The front panel J, 10½ in. wide, slides between fillets, and can be taken out to facilitate tipping the load. This panel should be

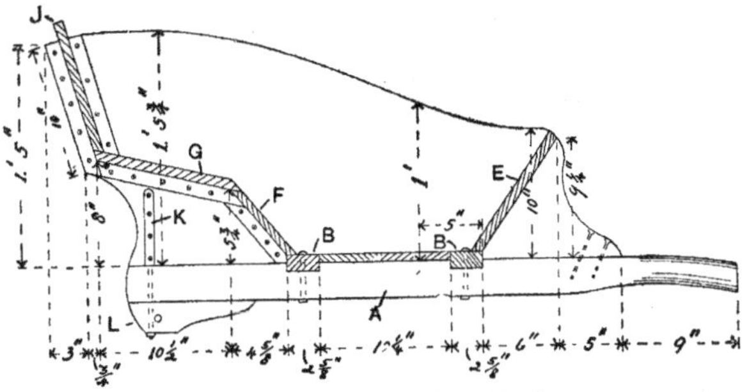

Fig. 47.—Sectional Elevation of Body

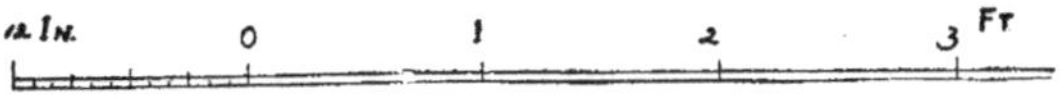

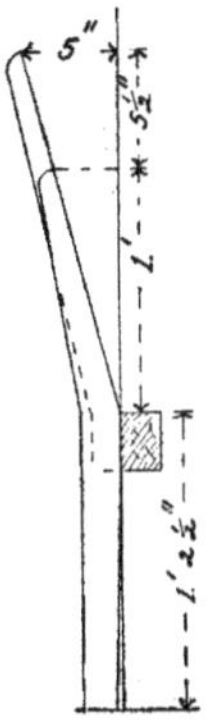

Fig. 48.—Side Splay of Leg and Standard

crosswise between the sloats, the frame being fixed together with $\frac{5}{16}$-in. bolts. The legs and standards are got out to the side splay obtained from Fig. 48, and is 5 in. in 1 ft. 5½ in. The legs are tapered to 1¾ in. by 1¾ in. at the bottom, and 1¾ in. by ⅞ in. at the top, the standards also tapering to ⅞ in. thick at the top. The legs are fixed to the face of the strines with ⅜-in. bolts, and the standards with $\frac{5}{16}$-in. bolts.

The length of the various sections should be taken from the side line on the plan, and the height or width of the board from the side splay line (Fig. 48), when setting out the side panels. The panels are all ¾ in. thick, the back panel E, 11 in. wide, being housed $\frac{3}{16}$ in. into the side panels and nailed in position, being strengthened with corner plates at the top. The raised front is fixed to 1⅛-in. by ⅝-in. fillets screwed to the side panels, the board F being ⅝-in. thick, and the other one G ¾ in. thick. A $\frac{5}{16}$-in. long-bolt H battened at the back to prevent its splitting. At the front, a half-round strap-bolt K is fixed to the inner side of the side panels, with screws, the bolt taking the front end of the strines and trunnion blocks.

The trunnion blocks L are 10 in. by 2¼ in. by 2 in., their back ends being fixed with screws, and the trunnion holes lined with iron tubing. The legs are strengthened with stays M of $\frac{7}{16}$-in. round iron, the lower end being welded to the hoop on the leg.

The wheel is 1 ft. 6 in. high "in the wood"—that is, without the tyre; nave, 1 ft. long by 3½ in. by 3½ in.; one spoke, 3¼ in. by 1¼ in.; and the other one 1¼ in. by 1¼ in.; felloes, 2¼ in. by 2¼ in.; tyre, 1¾ in. by $\frac{5}{16}$ in.; trunnions of ⅝-in. iron. The wide spoke is mortised through the centre of the nave and the square spoke at right angles, the wide spoke being then dressed to 1¼ in. in width at the ends. The tangs at the ends of the spokes should be ⅞ in. in diameter.

Boxes for Special Purposes

STRONG WOODEN BOX

Fig. 1 is a general view of a strong wooden box of general utility. The box may be of oak, walnut, teak, mahogany, or other hardwood, and if made as here shown and polished, will have a good appearance. Fig. 2 is a longitudinal section. The dimensions are, of course, only suggestive, and can be varied to meet requirements. The thickness of the wood may be $\frac{1}{2}$ in. to $\frac{3}{4}$ in., according to the size and strength required.

Assuming that the material has been sawn to the various sizes and planed up true, the angles of the sides and ends should be set out for dovetailing. One of the best forms for this class of work is secret lap-dovetailing, as shown at Fig. 3. On the right hand piece about $\frac{1}{8}$ in. is allowed to project beyond the ends of the pins, and thus after the joints are glued together, the small amount of end grain can be rounded (as indicated at Fig. 4), which will show so little when polished as to be no detriment. The top edges of the sides and ends are tongued, as shown in Figs. 3 and 5, the top being grooved to receive these tongues, as shown in Fig. 6. Fig. 7 is a conventional view of a corner of the bottom, showing how its edges are tongued so as to slide in the grooves of the sides and ends in Figs. 3 and 8.

The fitting being satisfactory, the sides, ends, and bottom should be glued together, and the joints held close by cramps until the glue is dry. The top can next be glued on and cramped. The outside should then be smoothed off, and the angles (except the bottom) slightly, but neatly, rounded off. A neat finish to the bottom can be made by rounding the edge of a piece of stuff, mitreing, and gluing and screwing it on as shown. Before putting on the fillet, additional strength would be given to the box by inserting a few screws obliquely through the bottom into the sides and ends, as shown in section at Fig. 8.

A gauge should be set to the depth of the portion forming the lid, and a line marked round and then sawn. If this sawing is carefully done, an even shaving taken off each of the surfaces should be sufficient to leave the edges at once smooth and truly fitting. If desired, a small bead may be worked round the outside of the edge of the lid, as shown at Figs. 1 and 9. The lid should now be hinged, and as it is necessary for them to be of a strong character in such a box, chest hinges which screw on the inside, or ornamental flap hinges which screw on the outside are the most suitable. A handle and plate, in which the handle drops down flush when not in use as shown, should be neatly let into the lid as shown and fixed with screws. A suitable lock and staple should also be fixed on, as shown in Fig. 1. The box can then be polished.

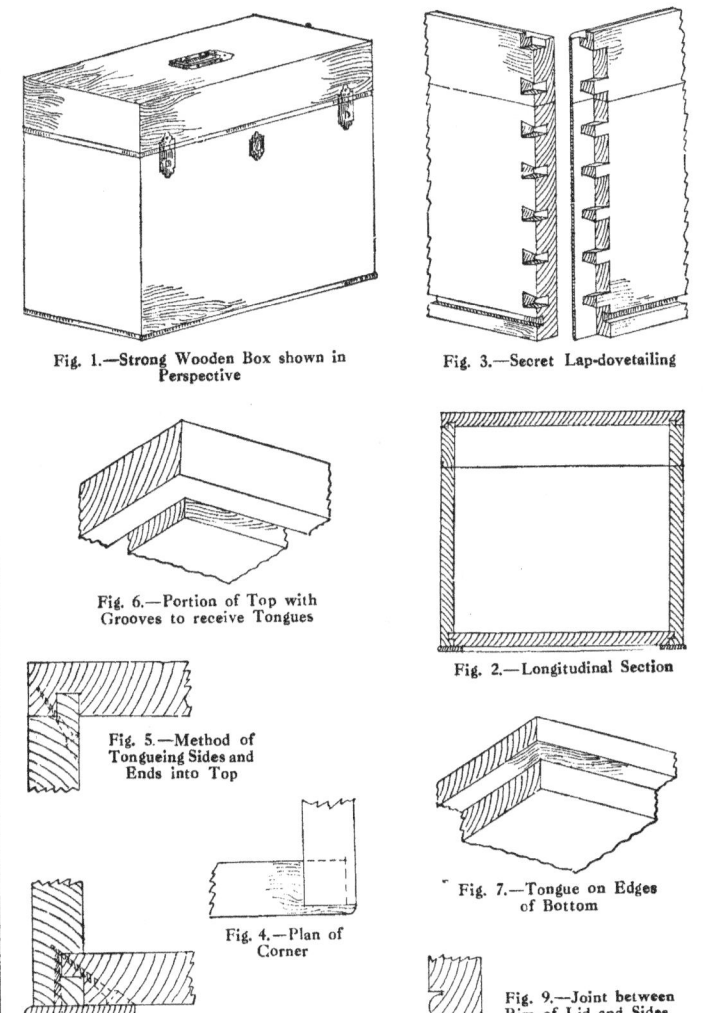

Fig. 1.—Strong Wooden Box shown in Perspective
Fig. 3.—Secret Lap-dovetailing
Fig. 6.—Portion of Top with Grooves to receive Tongues
Fig. 2.—Longitudinal Section
Fig. 5.—Method of Tongueing Sides and Ends into Top
Fig. 4.—Plan of Corner
Fig. 7.—Tongue on Edges of Bottom
Fig. 8.—Joint between Bottom, Sides and Fillet
Fig. 9.—Joint between Rim of Lid and Sides

CLOTHES BOX FITTED WITH TRAYS

The clothes-box shown in front elevation in Fig. 10 is 3 ft. 6 in. long, 2 ft. 3 in. high, and 2 ft. from the back to the front. The material to be used may be good pine, red deal, or white deal, according to choice; red deal would, of course, stand the most wear. The boards for the sides, ends, bottom, and top should be about $\frac{7}{8}$ in. thick after being planed, and should be carefully jointed and ploughed and cross-tongued and glued. It is important when jointing up for a box not to have the glued joints of the front and back in the same plane as those of the ends. Fig. 10 shows the front formed of two pieces jointed, and Fig. 11 shows the end formed of three pieces. In a box of this description it is a good plan to make the rim of the lid and the sides and the ends all in one; then, when the top and bottom are fixed on, the part to form the rim is separated from the sides and ends by sawing along

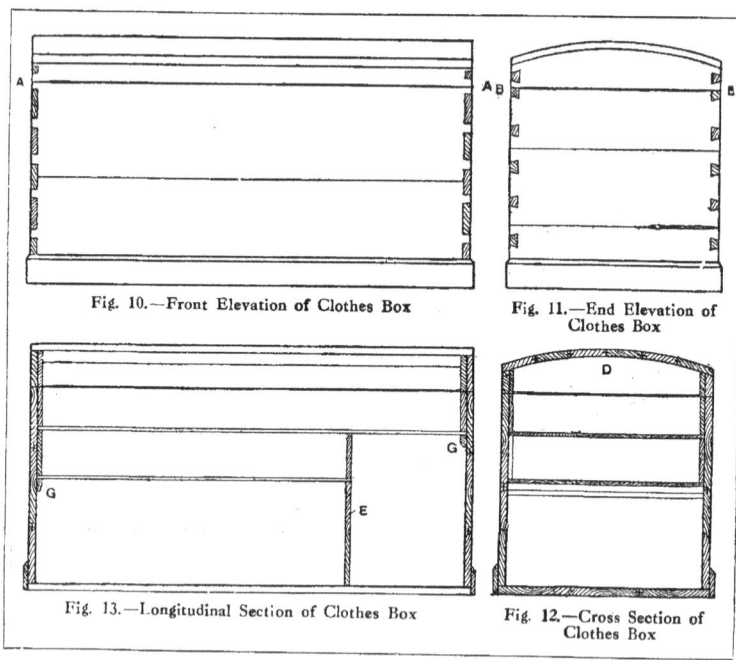

Fig. 10.—Front Elevation of Clothes Box

Fig. 11.—End Elevation of Clothes Box

Fig. 13.—Longitudinal Section of Clothes Box

Fig. 12.—Cross Section of Clothes Box

the lines as shown at A A (Fig. 10) and B B (Fig. 11). The sides and ends should be dovetailed together as shown. The lid being curved on the top, it will be necessary to form it of strips about 4 in. wide, which should be carefully jointed and ploughed and tongued together, as shown at D (Fig. 12).

The bottom can be formed of three boards jointed and tongued together. By referring to the illustrations it will be seen that the bottom is nailed direct to the lower edges of the sides and the ends;

BOXES FOR SPECIAL PURPOSES

it will be much stronger if glued to them before nailing. The plinth round the chamfered as shown; it should be fixed with glue and a few small nails. The division E (Figs. 13 and 14) should be about $\frac{1}{2}$ in. or $\frac{5}{8}$ in. thick, and may be slightly housed into the sides. The trays should be made of wood about $\frac{5}{8}$ in. thick, the corners being dovetailed together, as shown in Figs. 14, 15 and 16; the bottoms of the trays may be thin boarding about $\frac{3}{8}$ in. thick, jointed together. For most purposes it will be better for the top tray to have a bottom formed of webbing interlaced, as shown in Fig. 16. Two fillets of wood about $1\frac{1}{4}$ in. by $\frac{3}{4}$ in. (G, Figs. 13 and 14) should be fixed to

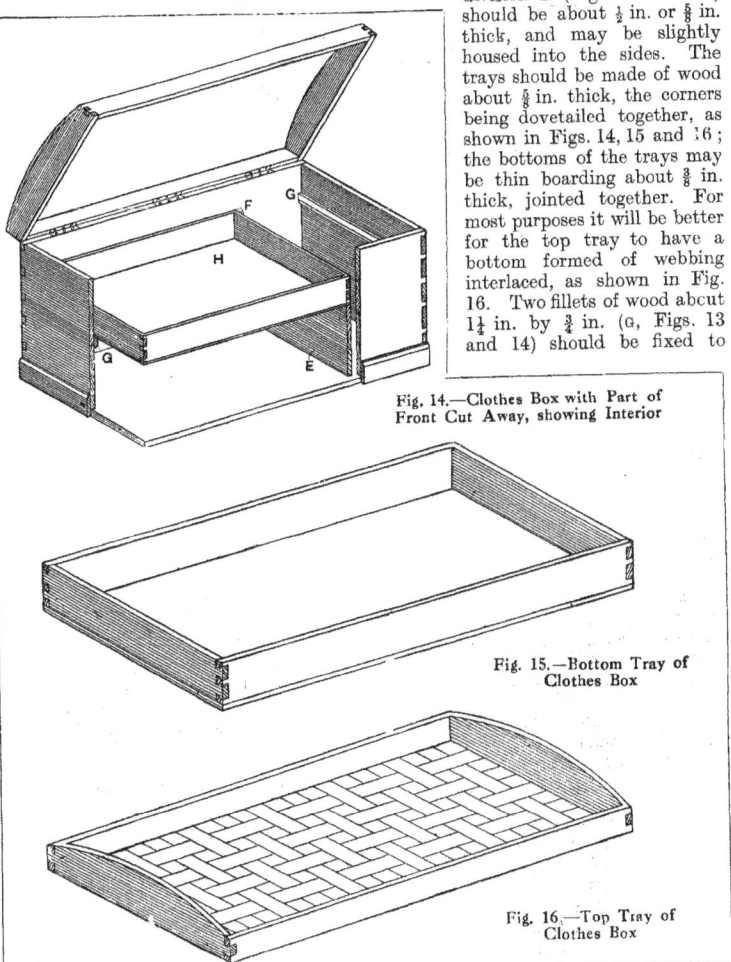

Fig. 14.—Clothes Box with Part of Front Cut Away, showing Interior

Fig. 15.—Bottom Tray of Clothes Box

Fig. 16.—Top Tray of Clothes Box

lower part of the box should be about $3\frac{1}{2}$ in. wide and $\frac{5}{8}$ in. thick, and the ends to support the trays. Two small fillets will also be required to keep the lower tray H (Fig. 14) in position as shown at F (Fig. 14). The box should be fitted with three hinges and a lock.

BOX FOR TRANSPORT OF EGGS

A box for the special purpose of packing eggs for transit is shown in Figs. 17 and 18. It will be necessary to construct it strongly in order to withstand the rough usage it is likely to receive.

Fig. 17.—Egg Box, Closed, shown in Perspective

The chief sizes for the box shown are, length 1 ft. 4 in., breadth 1 ft., and height 1 ft. The thickness of the wood for the bottom, sides, ends, and lid should be about ¾ in. finished, for the sides and ends of trays ⅜ in. finished, and for the divisions and bottom ¼ in. finished. A plan of the box, showing an egg-tray in position, is shown by Fig. 19.

The ends and back are dovetailed together, as shown in Fig. 22, and the bottom should be strongly screwed to the under edges of these. It will be seen that the lid and front are clamped (Fig. 20), which will be found to greatly strengthen these parts. Of course, if desired, the front could be dovetailed to the ends ; but it will give more ready access to the trays and facilitate their removal if the front is made to drop as in Fig. 18, the particular kind of strap hinges required being clearly shown. Fig. 21 shows the method of fixing the hinges for the front and lid so as to allow of their tight fitting when closed. For fastening the box, a good method is shown in Fig. 17, two hinged staples with eyes and flange plates being screwed to the front. The eyes have holes sufficiently large to allow of an iron rod passing through. The rod has a head or ring at one end and an eye at the other, the latter for fastening by a padlock as shown. The sides and ends of the trays should be notched or cogged together, as indicated in Fig. 23. The sides and ends can be grooved to receive the ends of the divisions ; but this is hardly necessary. Where the divisions cross each other they should be halved together, as shown in Fig. 24. The joints can be glued together, and further secured with a few sprigs. The bottom can then be nailed on to the edges of the sides and ends.

Each division can be lined with felt or straw, and a layer of felt between each tray would be an advantage. For lightness, the bottoms and divisions of the trays could be of three-ply wood. If exceptionally hard wear is anticipated, the angles might be protected with metal corners screwed on, and a strong metal

Fig. 18.—Egg Box, Open

handle would be useful. The box should be clearly marked " EGGS " in order to ensure careful handling.

DONATION BOX

A suitable form of donation box is shown by the photograph (Fig. 25) on page 460. The door forms a convenient shelf with sides when open, so that the coins cannot roll out, and can be counted whilst being

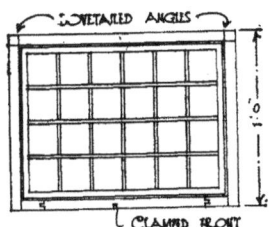

Fig. 19.—Plan of Egg Box, showing Tray

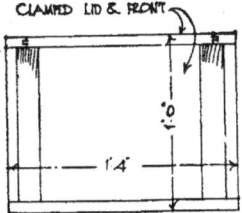

Fig 20.—Front Elevation

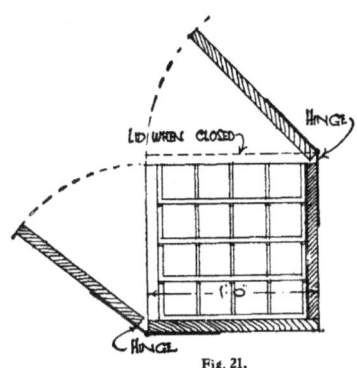

Fig. 21.

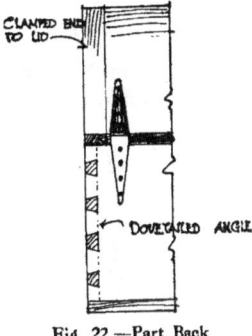

Fig. 22.—Part Back Elevation

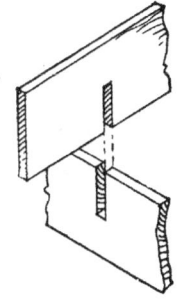

Fig. 21.—Section showing Trays and Method of Hinging Front and Lid

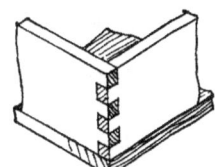

Fig. 23.—Angle of Tray

Fig. 24.—Halved Joint for Divisions of Tray

removed (*see* Fig. 26). The box is to be fixed to wood panelling with four screws through the back. The construction will be understood from Fig. 27.

The top, bottom and sides are of $\frac{1}{2}$ in. thick wood, strongly dovetailed together,

Fig. 25.—Photograph of Donation Box, Closed

Fig. 26.—Photograph of Donation Box, Open

and they are rebated at the back edge to receive the back panel of $\frac{3}{8}$-in. stuff in flush, which is glued and secured with screws. The door also is of $\frac{1}{2}$-in. stuff, with the shaped sides of $\frac{1}{4}$ in. thickness fixed on with glue and screws. The square end of these latter is bevelled (about $\frac{3}{4}$ in. on the inner side) to $\frac{1}{4}$ in. For hinging the door, two 2-in. brass butt hinges are used, put on flat and let level, with the outside uppermost, ther fore it is necessary to countersink t. screw holes on that side. This is do to keep the inside quite level. It shou be neatly fitted so as to have no visib space at the hinged joint, and ensure against any slight shrinka which might occur to make a spa through which a very thin coin mig escape. The bottom and inside door is covered with leather glued o This also serves to cover the hinge A stop-slip is screwed under the to for the door to shut against, and

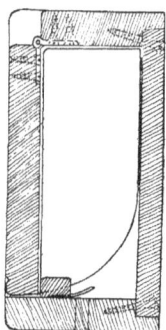

Fig. 27.—Cross Section of Box showing Construction

piece of leather is put between an just under the slot to send the coin to the back of the box. The size the slot is to take easily a 5s. piece.

In cleaning up the box for polish ing, all the outside corners should b slightly rounded, and the wood the oiled over and french polished in th usual way.

LETTER BOX FOR DOOR

Most entrance doors are furnished wit slots through which letters can be slippe but it is not invariably that a receptac is placed to receive them, and even whe this is the case it is not always particular easy to extract the contents from the bo

BOXES FOR SPECIAL PURPOSES

This objection, however, will not apply to the letter box here shown, the whole front of which slides up, leaving the interior fully exposed. A general view of the box is shown in Fig. 28. Front and side elevations are shown in Figs. 29 and 30. It can be of any desired size, although as drawn and figured it is likely to meet the average requirements. The material of which it is constructed is quite optional.

The chief point is that, as on most ordinary doors the letter box would unavoidably come partially over some of the panels, either these must have pieces planted on them in order to bring them out to a surface flush with that of the framing, or alternatively the two sides and bottom must be cut to the requisite outline at the back in order to come close up to the surfaces of the framing, mouldings and panels, as at A A (Fig. 30). The whole work can suitably be made out of stuff ¼ in. thick, and a beginning had better be made with two side pieces cut to the contour in Fig. 30, measuring about 2⅞ in. in width at the top, and increasing as necessary in order to meet the panels (if any), as at A A (Fig. 30). The sides are kept apart by a top piece B (Fig. 30) 2½ in. wide, and a bottom piece C 2⅞ in. wide, plus whatever is found necessary to fit close up to the sunk panel face. These pieces would be 6 in. or a little more in length according to the slot in the door, and when their positions have been set out on the sides a small groove should be worked along each of the latter, ¹⁄₁₆ in. wide, ⅛ in. deep, and ¹⁄₁₆ in. back from the front edges of the sides. These grooves are required to begin at the upper face of the bottom piece C (Fig. 30), and continue right up.

The door may next be fitted in these grooves (see Fig. 31), and is intended to consist of ¼-in. stuff 11¾ in. long and 6¼ in. wide, having a flat bevel about ¾ in. wide taken off it on all edges, thus reducing their thickness to ⅛ in. A diamond-shaped opening can then be cut, and its edges slightly bevelled and filled in with a piece of glass or celluloid. Immediately below the diamond a wood stop should be planted on the back in order to strike against the top, and so prevent the door coming completely out of the grooves. A small knob or handle will complete the box, which can be stained or painted to match the door for which it is intended.

Fig. 32 shows a method of forming the

Fig. 28.—Letter Box shown in Perspective

grooves with two neat little fillets planted on the sides, thus obviating the need for ploughing the latter; while should any trouble be found in attaching the box to the door it may be useful to employ pieces, as at D (Fig. 33), measuring ¾ in. across. Another sample of a letter box was given in the section dealing with elementary examples.

TRAVELLING TRUNK

Fig. 34 is a general view of a strong travelling trunk made of wood. Fig. 35 is a front elevation. The following are the main particulars of its construction.

THE PRACTICAL WOODWORKER

Useful sizes are given on the drawings, but, of course, these may be varied to meet requirements.

The necessary boarding, ¾ in. to 1 in. thick (according to strength required), having been obtained and cut to length for the sides, ends, bottom and top, it should arrange the boards to the top and bottom transversely, as shown at Figs. 36 and 37. The sides and ends should next be set out for lengths, and then the ends set out for dovetail pins. These should be arranged in the portion to form the rim of the lid, as shown at x x (Figs. 36 and 37).

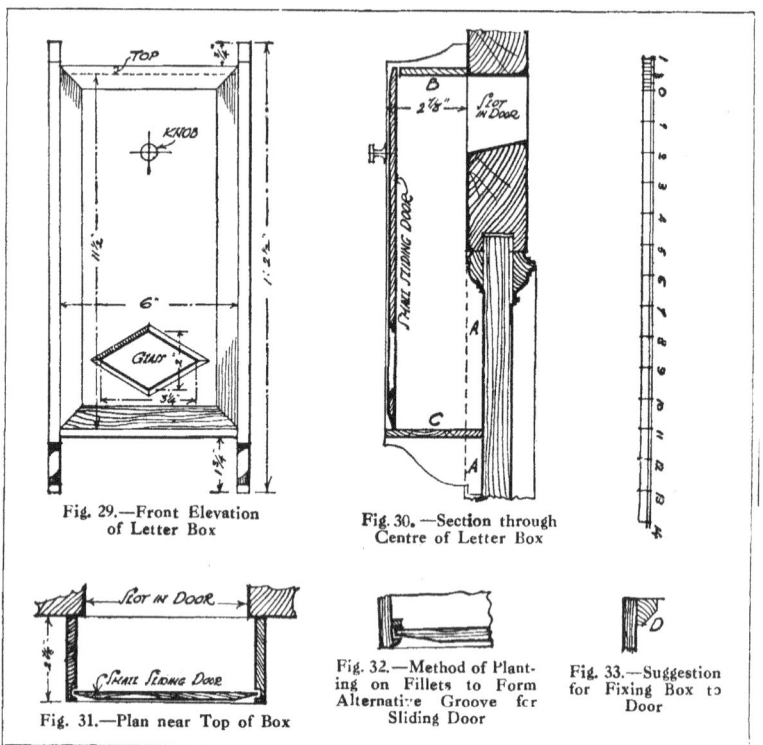

Fig. 29.—Front Elevation of Letter Box

Fig. 30.—Section through Centre of Letter Box

Fig. 31.—Plan near Top of Box

Fig. 32.—Method of Planting on Fillets to Form Alternative Groove for Sliding Door

Fig. 33.—Suggestion for Fixing Box to Door

be jointed and ploughed for tongues. Instead of this, machine-prepared grooved-and-tongued floor boarding of good quality and well seasoned will answer the purpose admirably. The joints should be glued and cramped close together until the glue is dry. Care should be taken not to have the joints in the sides and ends in the same plane. It is a stronger method to After these are sawn and the waste cut out, the pins should be placed on the sides, and the sockets marked out from them. A strong form of dovetail is shown at Fig. 38. Fig. 39 shows the box pin joint, which is rather easier to make, but is not so strong as dovetailing. When ready, the joints should be glued and further secured with a few nails. The

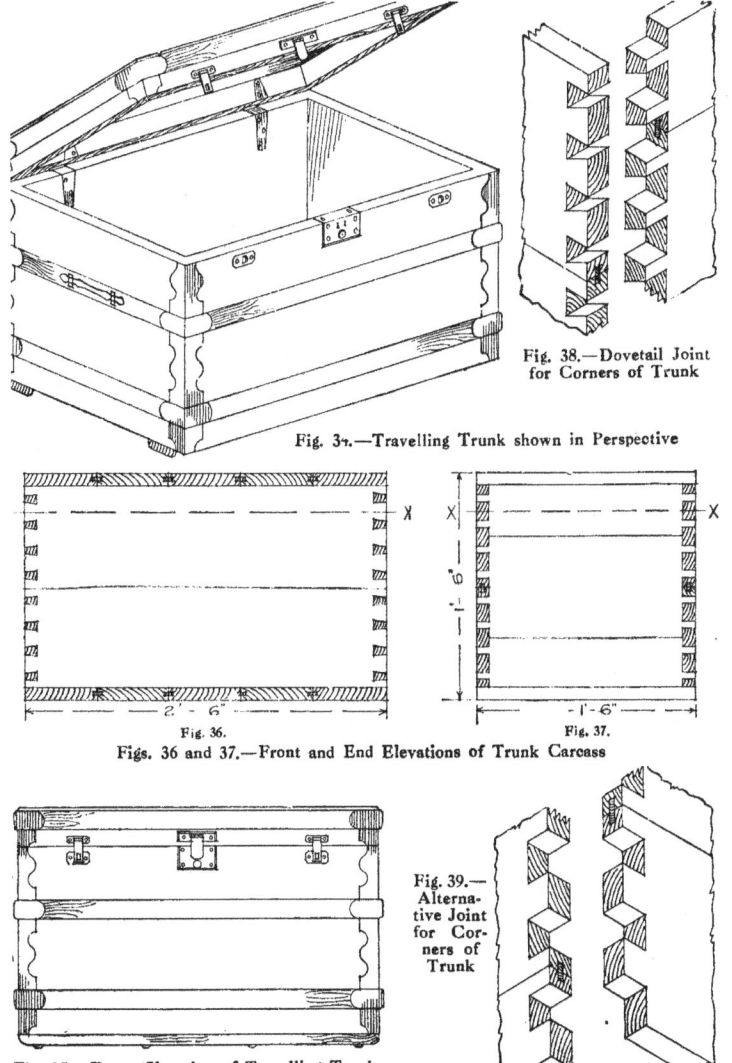

Fig. 38.—Dovetail Joint for Corners of Trunk

Fig. 34.—Travelling Trunk shown in Perspective

Figs. 36 and 37.—Front and End Elevations of Trunk Carcass

Fig. 39.—Alternative Joint for Corners of Trunk

Fig. 35.—Front Elevation of Travelling Trunk

the top and bottom can be glued and nailed to the sides and ends, and planed flush where necessary. The part forming the lid should next be separated by cutting along the lines x x (Figs. 36 and 37).

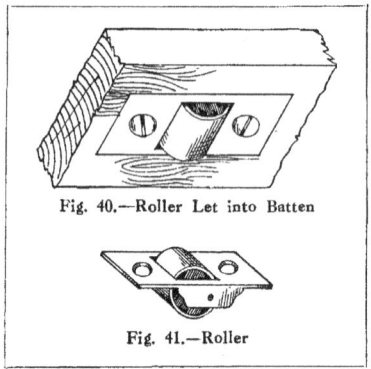

Fig. 40.—Roller Let into Batten

Fig. 41.—Roller

The whole of the outside can be covered with american cloth or a stout close-woven canvas; in each case the material must be stuck down firmly and evenly to the wood with strong glue.

Two or three battens about ¾ in. by 2½ in. should be fixed on to the bottom of the box, preferably with screws, and an iron roller should be let in near each end, so that its plate is flush with the surface of the batten, as shown at Fig. 40. Fig. 41 shows the form of roller used. Some strips of ash or oak about ⅝ in. by 1¾ in. should be fixed to the sides and ends as shown. These may be secured with screws inserted from the inside, if desired. Some sheet-iron plate or mild steel plate, about 1/16 in. thick, should be cut into strips, 3 in. to 4 in. wide, and bent down the centre at right angles. The outer edge may be straight or shaped, as shown at A

(Fig. 35). Holes should next be punch and countersunk, so that the plates c be fixed to the angles of the box w screws. Care should be taken to file all the outer arrises of these iron an bindings. The bindings of the fillets ne only be slightly narrower than the fille The lid should be fixed with a pair of b hinges, as shown in Fig. 34. A suita lock, and a staple fastening at each er should also be fixed.

If the box is covered with strong canv this may be painted brown, or any otl colour desired, and a coat of varnish v improve the appearance of the batte The ironwork should be japanned coated with an enamel. The interior the trunk can be fitted with a mova tray, etc., as necessary. To make t box dust-proof, a fillet should be nai round the inside, so as to project into 1 rim of the lid.

CLOTHES BOX WITH SECRET DRAWER

Fig. 42 shows a clothes chest which divided into three parts by means of t trays, so as to keep the various clotl separate. The bottom space is intenc

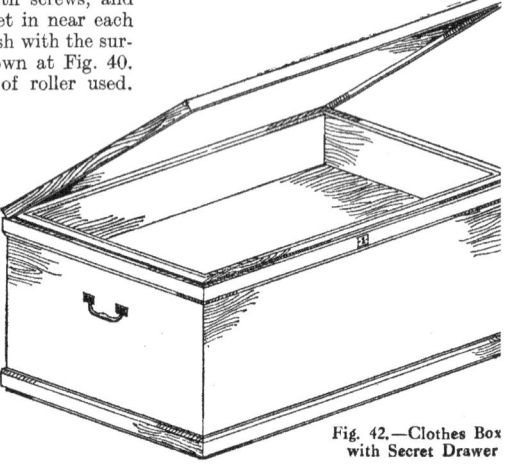

Fig. 42.—Clothes Box with Secret Drawer

BOXES FOR SPECIAL PURPOSES

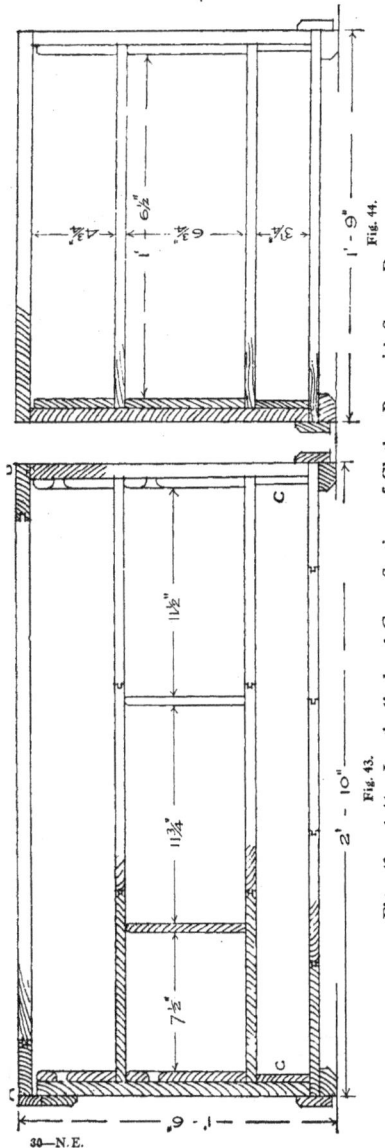

Figs. 43 and 44.—Longitudinal and Cross Sections of Clothes Box with Secret Drawer

for trousers; the middle one (which is divided into three) is for shirts and collars; and the top one for coats. Longitudinal and cross sections are shown in Figs. 43 and 44.

The chest is made from ¾-in. yellow pine, dovetailed together, with a ½-in. bottom nailed on, and 1½-in. by 1-in. pieces screwed to the bottom to keep it off the floor. The end and side wood at the bottom is covered by a base, which is mitred at the corners and nailed on. The lid is made of ¾-in. wood, with 3-in. cross-ends mortised and tenoned to it. There are two arrangements shown for the lid: A (Fig. 43) shows an arrangement with one facing nailed to the lid and resting on the other, which is nailed to the box, and kept down ⅛ in. from the top edge; B shows a throating cut out of the top edge of the chest, and a small bead fastened to the lid.

The trays are dovetailed together, and a grip hole is cut out at each end, and nicely rounded. The tray bottoms, which are feathered and grooved together, having the grain running the short way are screwed to the under side of the trays. Small pieces are put in at the bottom of the box to carry the bottom tray, the top tray resting on the bottom one. The top edges of the trays are rounded, and should be mitred at the corners, the divisions being mitred to the middle of the round. The base is only shown on one part of Fig. 43, but it should be carried all round.

If desired, a secret drawer can be fixed to the chest as described below. Fig. 45 is a vertical section, and Fig. 46 a horizontal section taken just below the underside level of the bottom C (Fig. 43).

The divisions A and B (Fig. 45) should be prepared with small flush beads as shown; this will hide the joint between the front of the drawer and the division. The divisions A and B and the sides of the till should

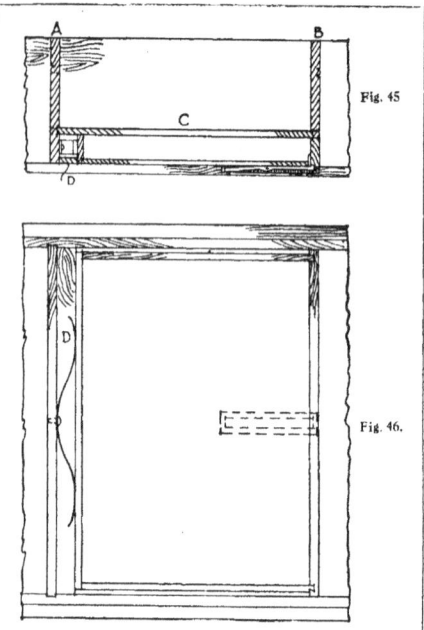

Figs. 45 and 46.—Vertical and Horizontal Sections of Secret Drawer

be grooved to receive the bottom c as indicated. The front of the drawer should be a good fit at each end up to the sides of the till. The sides of the drawer should be dovetail-grooved into the front, as shown in Figs. 45 and 47, the joints with the back being ordinary dovetails. It will be seen that the sides of the drawer are about ¼ in. away from the sides of the till; this will allow of the drawer coming out more easily, as the front can be placed a little obliquely while withdrawing it, and thus it will not bite against the sides of the till. The bottom of the drawer should be accurately fitted in rebates made in the front, sides and back. A piece D (Figs. 45 and 46) should be fixed to the bottom of the till and fit just to the back of the drawer, so that the front of the latter is flush with the face of the division E. A piece of steel spring should be bent to shape and fixed with a screw (see Fig. 46); of course the spring should be sufficiently

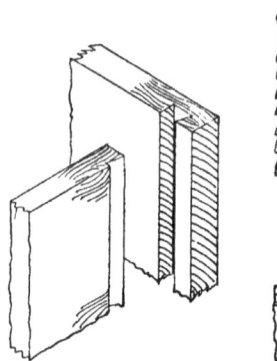

Fig. 47.—Dovetail Housing for Drawers

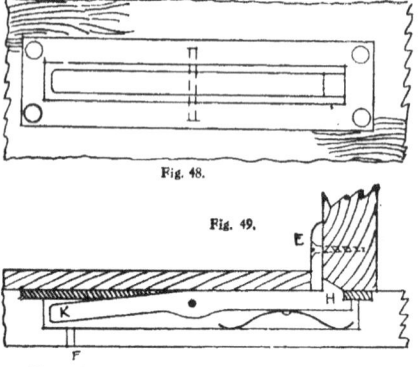

Figs. 48 and 49.—Plan and Section of Drawer Fasteners

BOXES FOR SPECIAL PURPOSES

strong to push the drawer forward 1 in. or more on the fastening being released.

The fastening is shown in plan by Fig. 48 and in section by Fig. 49. A small hole is made in the bottom of the till as indicated at F. This hole only need be large enough to admit the point of a penknife or anything similar, but, if desired, it may be sufficiently large to admit the tip of the finger. On pushing up the end of the lever at K, the end H is lowered and detached from the brass plate E (screwed to the inside of the front of the drawer), and immediately the spring at the back pushes the drawer forwards. To close the drawer, it is simply pushed so that the brass plate E, coming in contact with the catch H, pushes it down; then H, of course, rises and clips E as shown. It will be seen that the catch and lever are kept in position by a spring, and the end H is prevented from being pushed too high by the spring, as the brass plate catches it.

Tool Chests

PORTABLE TOOL BOXES

TOOL CHESTS are an obvious convenience, and are usually made by the workmen in all trades for convenience in storing their tools.

The box (Fig. 1) should be large enough to hold the hand-saw and the panel-saw in the lid. A useful size is 2 ft. 7 in. long,

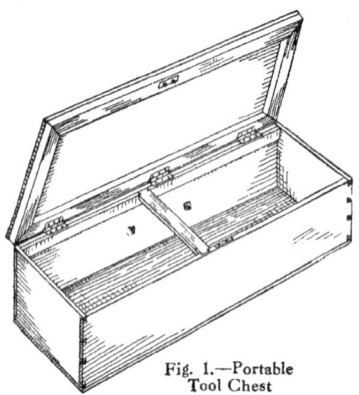

Fig. 1.—Portable Tool Chest

11 in. wide, and 7 in. deep, outside measurements. This is just large enough to take a 26-in. hand-saw and a 22-in. panel-saw. The box may be made a little narrower if the panel-saw is put with the rest of the tools in the body of the box. The sides, top, and bottom are made of ½-in. stuff, preferably pine. The sides are dovetailed together, and the bottom then screwed on. Pieces 1¼ in. by 1 in. are screwed to the top to strengthen it, form a deep panel to hold the saws, and to afford good fastening for the hinges. The latter are three 3-in. brass butts. A strip 1½ in. by ⅜ in. is screwed to the inside top edge of the back to receive the hinges and to strengthen the back.

A handle is bolted to the back of the box for carrying purposes. To strengthen the back and front whilst carrying, a 1½-in. by ½-in. strip is dovetailed to the top edge of the front side and to the strip at the top of the back. This strip is removable, and is only placed in position when the box is to be carried. The box is fitted with a reliable box lock. The saws are held in the lid panel by cleats for the blade ends, and by wooden turn-buttons (about 2 in. by ¾ in.) through the holes in the handles. The box should be given two coats of black paint, with the initials of the owner lettered in white on the top of the lid.

Alternative Design.—Fig. 2 is a photograph of an alternative design of box.

The framework of this may be ⅝-in. cypress dovetailed at the corners, a suitable size being 34½ in. by 16 in., one half being 3 in. deep, the other 2 in. A rebate joint as shown enlarged in Fig. 5 joins the two parts, and prevents strain on the hinges when the case is closed. The tongue on the wider half measures ¼ in. by ¼ in., and a ³⁄₁₆-in. bead is also wrought on this edge to improve the appearance of the job.

TOOL CHESTS

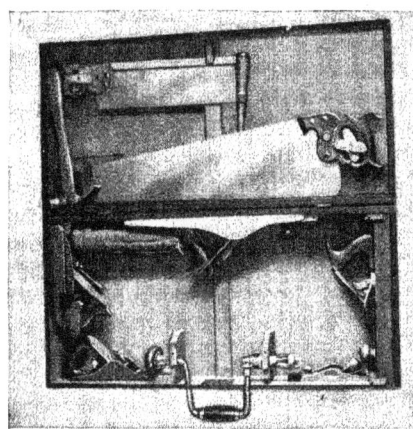

Fig. 2.—Alternative Form of Portable Tool-box

The sides of the framework are covered in with $\tfrac{3}{16}$-in. plywood. The bar across the middle of each side is a strengthening member, which should only be omitted if the sides are of thicker stuff, say $\tfrac{1}{4}$ in. The sides are secured by gluing and screwing, $\tfrac{3}{4}$-in. brass button-head screws at 3-in. spacing being used.

As the photograph shows (Fig. 2), the brace is utilised as a carrying handle, two slots being cut in the deeper side of the chest to accommodate it, while the two brackets shown transmit the weight of the chest solidly to the chuck-neck and handle-neck respectively. The methods of accommodating the planes and saws will be obvious from the illustrations, Figs. 2

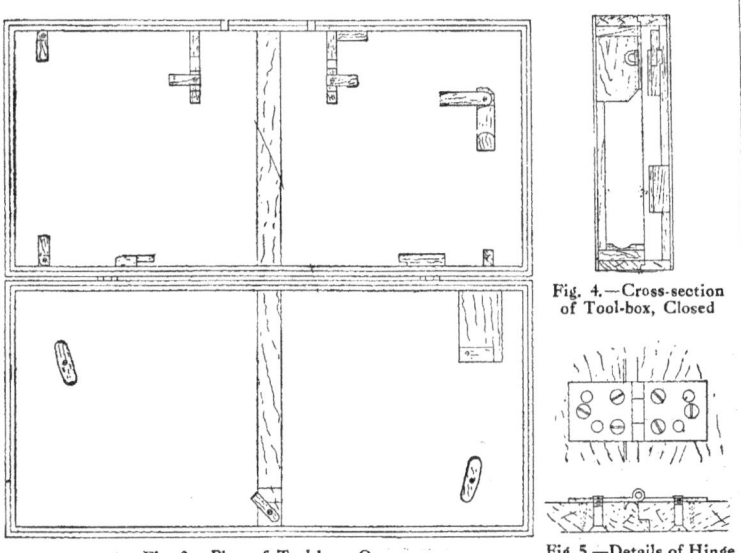

Fig. 3.—Plan of Tool-box, Open

Fig. 4.—Cross-section of Tool-box, Closed

Fig. 5.—Details of Hinge Fastening

THE PRACTICAL WOODWORKER

and 3. Attention may be drawn to the position of the square in the corner behind the rip-saw, the blade fitting into a saw-cut in the block shown. The handle of the smoothing plane fits into a shaped block lined with baize, wherein it is held by the turnbutton. All the planes, in fact, are secured by blocks appropriately shaped to hold one end, suitable turn-buttons fastening the other. All blocks attached to the three-ply sides are secured by screwing through from the outside plus gluing. Fig. 4 shows a cross-section of the box.

No special provision is made in building the chest for the smaller odd tools, as the actual selection of these carried naturally varies very much with the nature of the work to be done, and therefore the construction of fitments likely to suit every possible grouping is impossible. The case is fitted with a lock and key; but for ordinary securing, a couple of strong hooks and eyes are fitted. The hinges for strength's sake are backflaps, and are secured as shown in Fig. 5. In addition to the ordinary wood-screws attaching the hinges, two $\frac{3}{16}$-in. Whitworth countersunk screws are tapped through each fla] from the inside, and the projecting point riveted over, thus rendering it impossibl for the contents of the chest to be go at by tampering with the hinges. Fo greater protection against hard usage iron corner-plates should be screwed t the eight corners of the chest.

No dimensions other than the externa sizes have been given, as these will natur ally differ according to the actual tool carrying requirements of the individua maker.

PATTERNMAKERS' TOOL-CHEST

A tool-chest to hold patternmakers tools is shown in Fig. 6.

The largest tool likely to require accom modation is the jack plane, for which a box 18 in. long would be sufficient. Bu if a hand-saw is included it would requir to be not less than 31 in. inside measure ment. A trying plane is large and coul not be dispensed with. A tenon saw i continually wanted, and if kept in th box must be easy to get at. The bo should be long enough to take the longes tool, and should be less in depth than it i in width. A depth of 10 in. and a widtl of 12 in. should be ample; in fact, the depth might be cut down to 8 in. and stil leave room for all the tools a pattern maker requires, provided they are suitably arranged in the box. This, of course means that the tools must be packed ir on top of one another, and the lowe ones be inaccessible until those above are removed.

A plain interior with no fittings of any kind is scarcely desirable even when it is important to cut down the size. A simple arrangement is to fit two sliding tills, as shown in the illustration, for small tools. including the paring tools, and reserve the body of the box for large ones. These tills can be lifted out or slid to the back or the front of the box as required, their width being half that of the box. The ledges on which they slide are nailed or screwed to the ends, the lower ones being an additional thickness on the upper, so that the lower till is about $\frac{1}{2}$ in. shorter

Fig. 6.—Patternmakers' Tool chest

TOOL CHESTS

than the upper to allow of lifting out. The tills should not be very deep, or they will occupy too much of the interior space. A depth of 1½ in. for the top one and 2¼ in. for the other is sufficient. They can be dovetailed or simply nailed.

The body of the box itself should be dovetailed. Either hard or soft wood can be used as preferred. A suitable thickness for the box is about ⅝ in. Tills need not be more than ¼ in. to ⅜ in. thick. The sides and ends are prepared first, and are planed to thickness, width, and length. The length, both of sides and ends, will be the overall measurement if the corners are to be dovetailed ; the width will be the inside measurement. Sometimes the sides are screwed or nailed temporarily face to face, while the edges and ends are planed and the dovetails marked and cut, as this is a little quicker than dealing with each piece separately. The ends are treated similarly except that the dovetail lines on them are usually transferred direct from the sides which they have to fit, each end in this case having its dovetails marked and cut separately. The dovetails may be measured and their angles marked with a bevel, or they may be simply divided and marked by freehand, the lengths, of course, which correspond with the thickness of the wood, being gauged on both sides of the pieces in all cases. If this method is adopted each joint, at the time the transference of the dovetail lines to the end pieces is made, must have a number or other mark pencilled on each piece to show the position for fitting together.

When the sides and ends are fitted they are glued and nailed, and then the bottom is nailed on. It is important at this stage to see that the dovetailed frame is square, for the nailing on of the bottom fixes it unalterably. A piece for the cover is prepared similar in length and width to the bottom. There is the choice, however, of making the cover longer and putting its border strip across the under surface instead of on the end grain as illustrated.

Plinths are nailed round the bottom and top edges as shown, those at the top being ⅛ in. or so below the top edge, and the border round the cover coming down to meet them when the cover is closed. Those at the bottom may be protected and strengthened by corner pieces of sheet-iron screwed on. The bottom, and the cover also, may be stiffened with battens across the grain. The grain of the bottom need not necessarily run lengthwise, as that of the cover and sides does. It may be composed of a number of short pieces with grain the other way.

Sometimes the under surface of the cover does not bear directly on the top edge of the box, but has a depth of 1 in. or more, so that saws and other suitable tools can be attached to the inside of the cover, and allow the latter to be closed with the box filled level with its top edge with other articles. The same effect can be produced by keeping the top till 1 in. below the top edge of the box and not packing tools above that mark. A plain flat cover, with the usual border, can then be used and still have fittings for the attachment of tools ; but attachment in this way is scarcely convenient for tools in constant use, and is a matter of taste rather than convenience for tools seldom used.

When the box has to be packed for travelling, plenty of cotton waste or paper or other suitable material should be used to keep the tools immovable, as it must not be assumed that the box will always be handled carefully and kept the right side up. The cover also should be screwed down instead of merely locked.

WOODWORKERS' TOOL CHEST

In constructing the tool chest shown in perspective by Fig. 7, and cross-section by Fig. 8, the length must be sufficient to accommodate a rip-saw. This will make the chest 2 ft. 9 in. long internally, and if it is made 1 ft. 8 in. wide by 1 ft. 9 in. deep, it will be found convenient for all purposes.

The material for the outside case should be good white deal or yellow pine, and as the chest may have to stand some rough usage, it should not be less than 1 in. thick. In gluing up the front, back, and ends to obtain the necessary width the joints should be tongued or dowelled, the former being the better method. In dovetailing the chest together, the number of tails should not be stinted, and they should not be more than 1½ in. apart, as in Fig. 9, as the closer they are the stronger will the chest be. Care should be taken that the joints (see Fig. 10) do not come immediately opposite those in the ends.

The plinths run all round the chest, and should be 6 in. and 2½ in. wide and 1 in. thick, respectively, with one edge finished with a plain bevel. The plinths, or skirting, can be mitred at the corners, but it will be stronger to dovetail them. The top plinth, or rib under the lid, must be kept down about ¾ in. from the top of the chest, so as to form a rebate for the lid to shut on. The bottom should be 1 in. thick, tongued and grooved, and nailed on crosswise; that is, the grain to run from the front to the back of the chest.

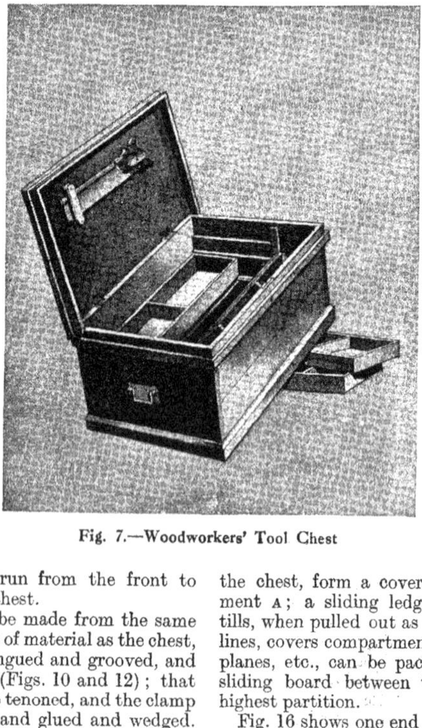

The lid should be made from the same kind and thickness of material as the chest, with the joints tongued and grooved, and the ends clamped (Figs. 10 and 12); that is, the lid should be tenoned, and the clamp mortised through and glued and wedged. The lid should be fitted so as to overhang the chest all round about $\frac{1}{16}$ in., and be hung with a pair of strong brass butts, and the lock (which should be a spring one, self-acting) put on, after which the rim of the lid can be mitred together at the corners, and grooved in the front and the ends (see Figs. 13 and 14).

For the inside of the chest good yellow deal or pine is recommended, which can be finished by staining. If desired, a more fancy wood can be used. As shown in Figs. 15, 16, and 17, the chest is divided in width into three parts; A, for bead planes, plough, etc., this is 7 in. wide, and is covered by the sliding tills; B, for miscellaneous tools, best planes, or anything which is not in every day use; and C (which is 3½ in. wide inside) is the saw till. These compartments are divided by the two partitions shown, that between A and B being 9 in. high, and that between B and C 1 ft. 2 in. The three tills G, H, and J slide to and fro to give access to the compartments beneath, and when in place at the back of the chest, form a covering for compartment A; a sliding ledge D beneath the tills, when pulled out as shown by dotted lines, covers compartment B. The bench planes, etc., can be packed away on the sliding board between the tills and the highest partition.

Fig. 16 shows one end of the chest with the cleats fixed, between which the partitions fit, and which are about 1 in. wide by ½ in. thick. Those which hold the partition between B and C should be fixed

Fig. 7.—Woodworkers' Tool Chest

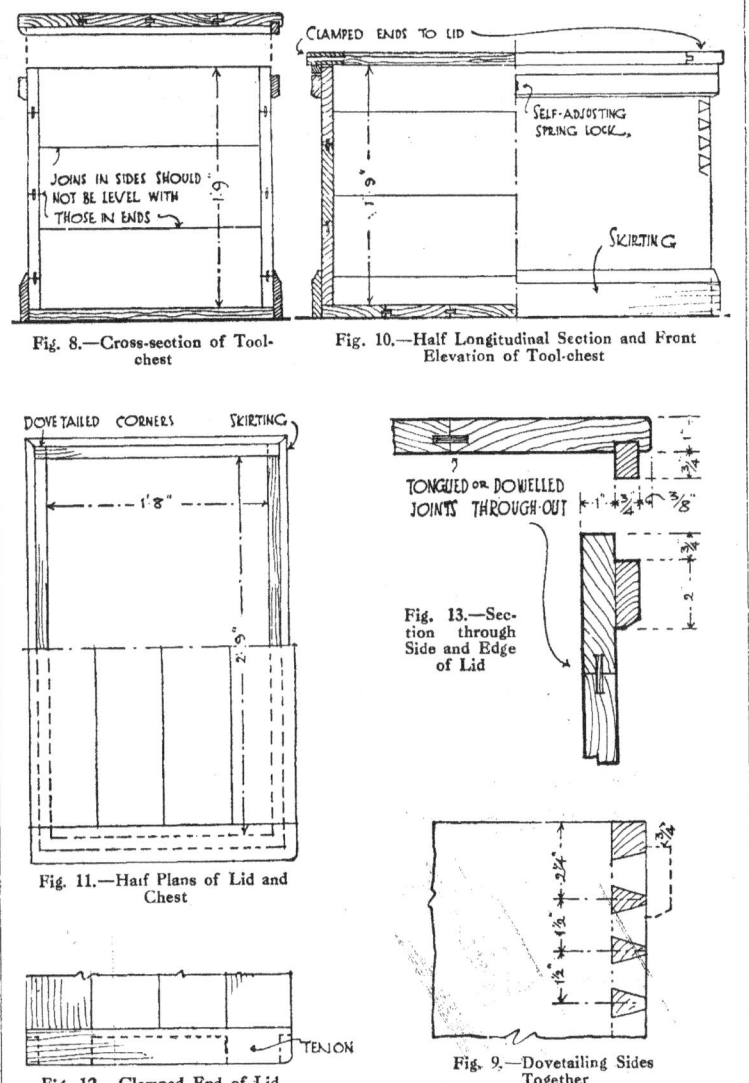

Fig. 8.—Cross-section of Tool-chest

Fig. 10.—Half Longitudinal Section and Front Elevation of Tool-chest

Fig. 11.—Half Plans of Lid and Chest

Fig. 12.—Clamped End of Lid

Fig. 13.—Section through Side and Edge of Lid

Fig. 9.—Dovetailing Sides Together

first, ½ in. apart, the one nearest the back of the chest reaching nearly to the top, the other, nearest the front, stopping at the same height as the partition The back partitions having been placed in position, the horizontal cleats can be fixed, the top edges of which must be 9½ in. from the bottom of the chest, and they must run from the back of the chest to the long upright cleat, as shown in Figs. 16 and 19. On these the sliding ledge D works, which is 9 in. by ¾ in., clamped at the ends,

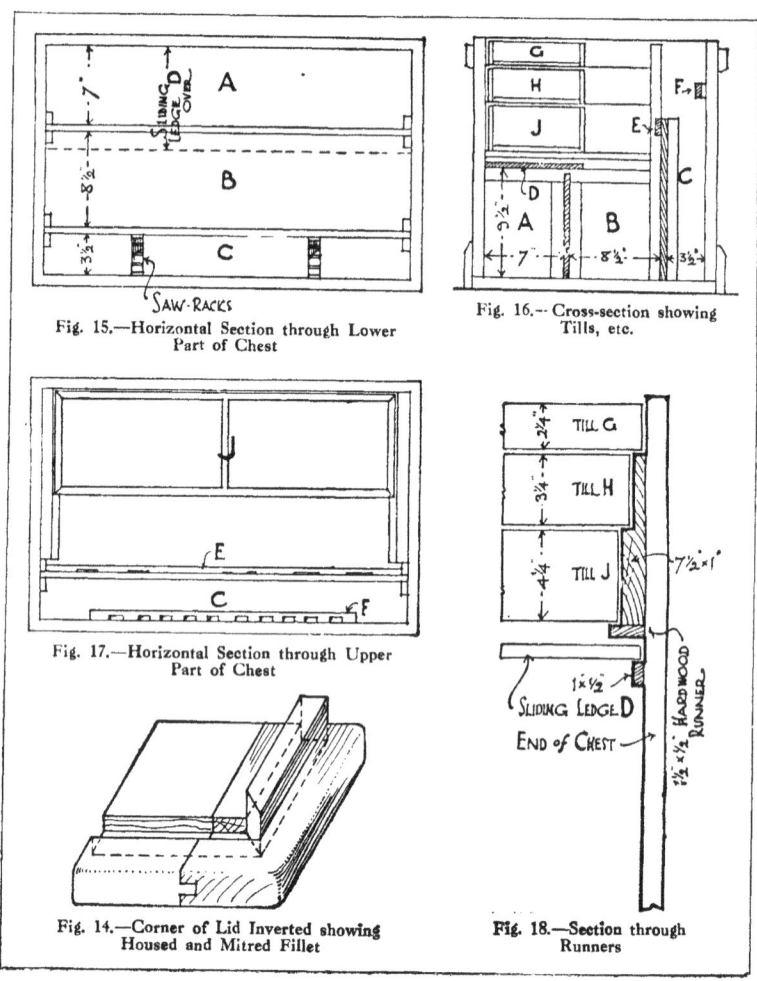

Fig. 15.—Horizontal Section through Lower Part of Chest

Fig. 16.—Cross-section showing Tills, etc.

Fig. 17.—Horizontal Section through Upper Part of Chest

Fig. 14.—Corner of Lid Inverted showing Housed and Mitred Fillet

Fig. 18.—Section through Runners

TOOL CHESTS

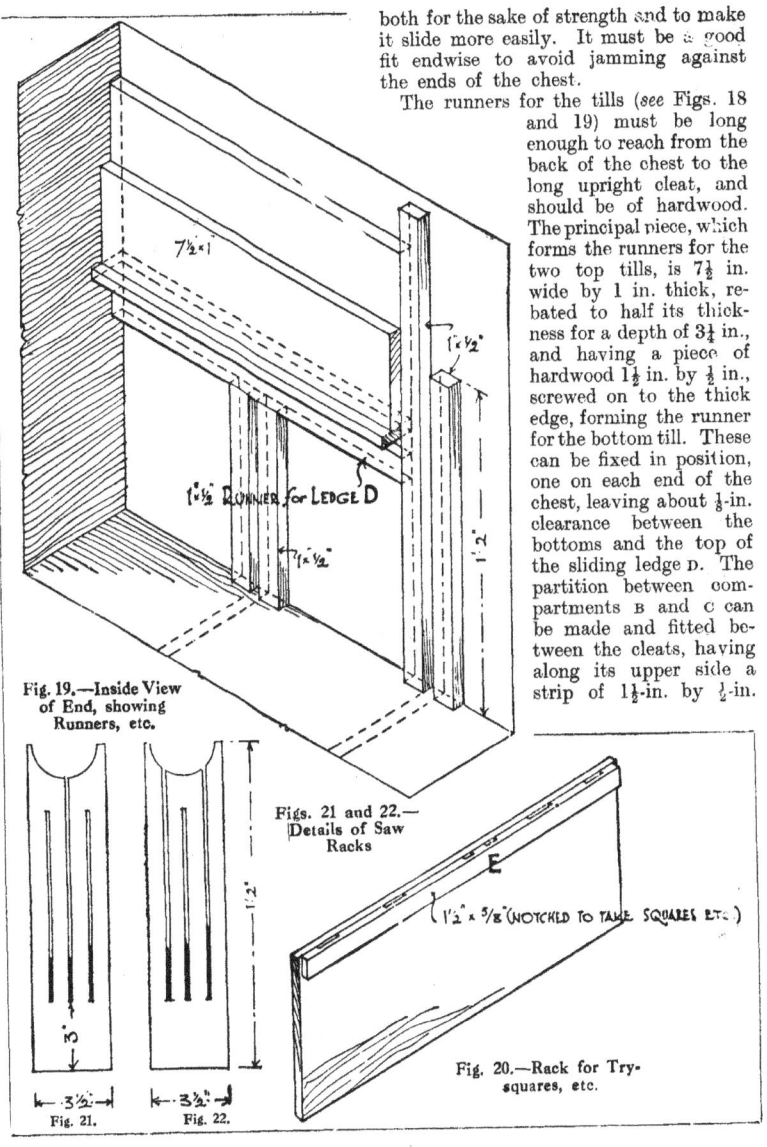

Fig. 19.—Inside View of End, showing Runners, etc.

Figs. 21 and 22.—Details of Saw Racks

Fig. 20.—Rack for Try-squares, etc.

both for the sake of strength and to make it slide more easily. It must be a good fit endwise to avoid jamming against the ends of the chest.

The runners for the tills (see Figs. 18 and 19) must be long enough to reach from the back of the chest to the long upright cleat, and should be of hardwood. The principal piece, which forms the runners for the two top tills, is $7\frac{1}{2}$ in. wide by 1 in. thick, rebated to half its thickness for a depth of $3\frac{1}{4}$ in., and having a piece of hardwood $1\frac{1}{2}$ in. by $\frac{1}{2}$ in., screwed on to the thick edge, forming the runner for the bottom till. These can be fixed in position, one on each end of the chest, leaving about $\frac{1}{8}$-in. clearance between the bottoms and the top of the sliding ledge D. The partition between compartments B and C can be made and fitted between the cleats, having along its upper side a strip of $1\frac{1}{2}$-in. by $\frac{1}{2}$-in.

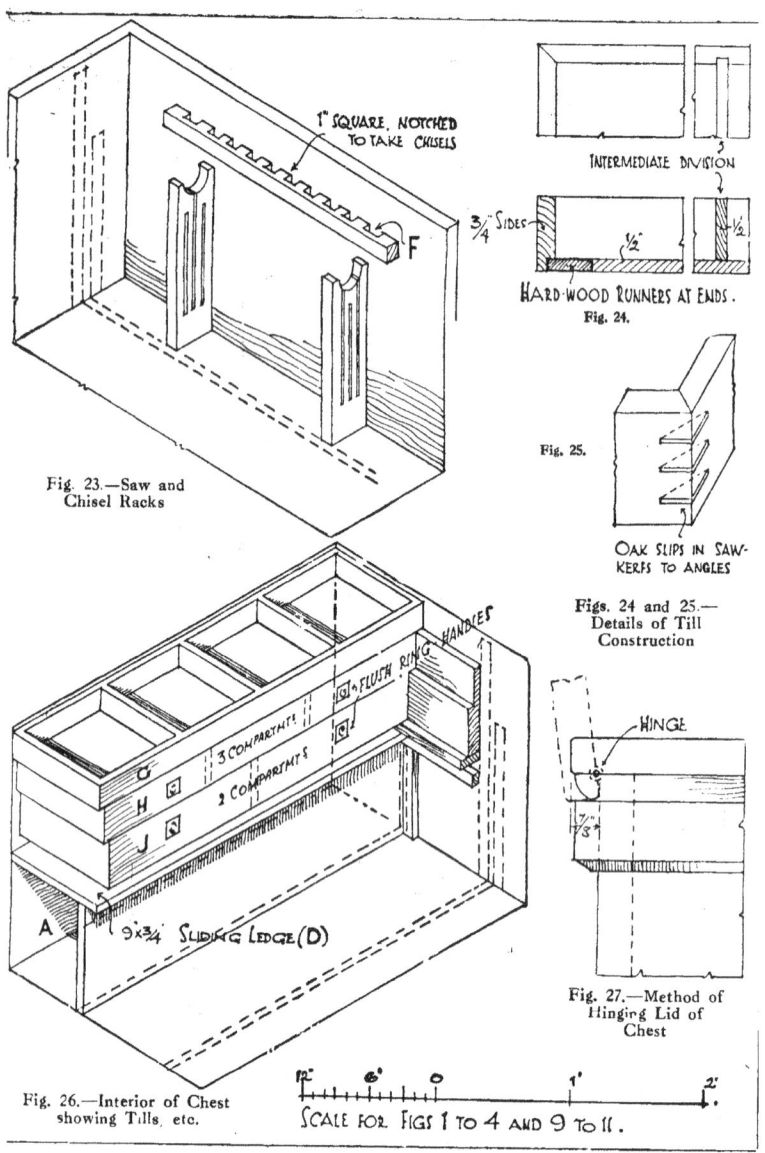

Fig. 23.—Saw and Chisel Racks

Figs. 24 and 25.—Details of Till Construction

Fig. 26.—Interior of Chest showing Tills, etc.

Fig. 27.—Method of Hinging Lid of Chest

SCALE FOR FIGS 1 TO 4 AND 9 TO 11.

TOOL CHESTS

deal, cut to fit between the cleats on each end of the chest, fixed level with the top edge, on the side nearest the front of the chest, and notched about $\frac{1}{8}$ in. at intervals. The slots thus formed can be used for squares, etc., the stocks resting on top of the partition and the blades hanging down inside the saw till (see Fig. 20).

The saw-racks (Figs. 21, 22, and 23) are 1 ft. 2 in. long, $3\frac{1}{2}$ in. wide, and 1 in. thick, shaped at the top ends, and with three slots made in each. The middle slot, in Fig. 21, runs from the top to within 3 in. of the bottom, the remainder stopping the same distance from the bottom, and about $1\frac{1}{2}$ in. from the top. In the other (Fig. 22) the middle slot is stopped at both the top and the bottom, and the other cuts through at the top end. These two racks are fixed at about 8 in. from each end, by screwing through the horn at the top to the front of the chest, as shown in Fig. 23. The partition being then put into its place, screws can be put through it into each saw-rack, which will hold all in place. In placing the saws in the racks, the points are inserted in the closed slots, and the handle ends dropped into the open slots, one saw pointing one way and two the opposite.

A piece of hardwood, 2 ft. long and 1 in. square, with a series of notches cut into it wide enough to take the various chisels, etc., and with about $\frac{1}{2}$ in. of solid wood left between each, can be screwed to the front of the chest just above the top of the partition (leaving an equal space at each end to allow room for the hand to be inserted to remove the saws) to furnish a resting-place for the larger chisels, the handles being just inside the front of the chest, the blades hanging in the saw till (see F Fig. 23).

The three sliding tills are of the same width, namely, 9 in. outside, but vary in depth. They should be of $\frac{3}{4}$-in. stuff, with $\frac{1}{2}$-in. bottoms and divisions, the rims dovetailed together, or mitred, as in Figs. 24 and 25. The fronts and back should be rebated to receive the bottoms, the grain of which should run across the width of the tills. At each end the bottom should be of hardwood. The divisions should be trenched into the sides, forming in G, H, and J respectively two, three, and four compartments (see Fig. 26). One of the bottom divisions should be fitted up for the brace and bits, with racks for the bits fitted round the brace, by which means one division can be made to accommodate the former and a whole set of the latter. Other divisions can be fitted with racks for small chisels, gouges, gimlets, bradawls, and various other tools.

Turn-buttons to take the tenon and dovetail saws can be screwed to the underside of the lid, so that when it is closed they will be in position between the top till and the front of the chest. The sliding ledge D can be grasped underneath with the fingers when it is desired to draw it forward, and it should have a couple of thumb-holes cut in its top by which to push it back. Each till should have a pair of flush-rings inserted in the front, so that it can be pulled forward without touching the others.

Owing to the rib under the lid running round the box the method of hinging will be as shown in Fig. 27. A strong iron handle on each end of the chest will make it complete.

Work Benches

BENCH ATTACHMENTS FOR TABLES

A SIMPLE contrivance which can be attached to a kitchen table so as to form a bench suitable for light work is shown by Figs. 1 and 2. Fig. 3 is a plan of the together at right angles. Next obtain a wooden screw and box, or nut; a wooden screw cheek must also be prepared, and a runner. Prepare a box of wood about 1 in. thick, to fit the runner. The bench cheek must next be mortised for the runner

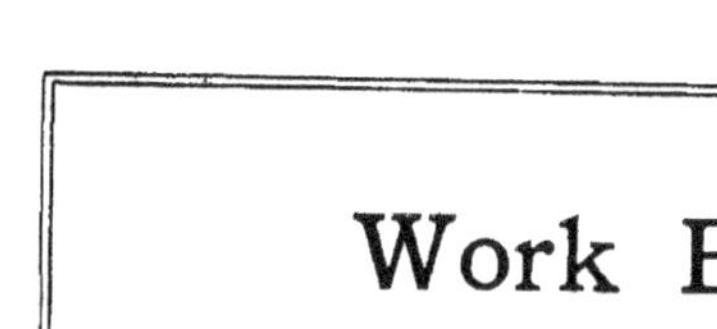

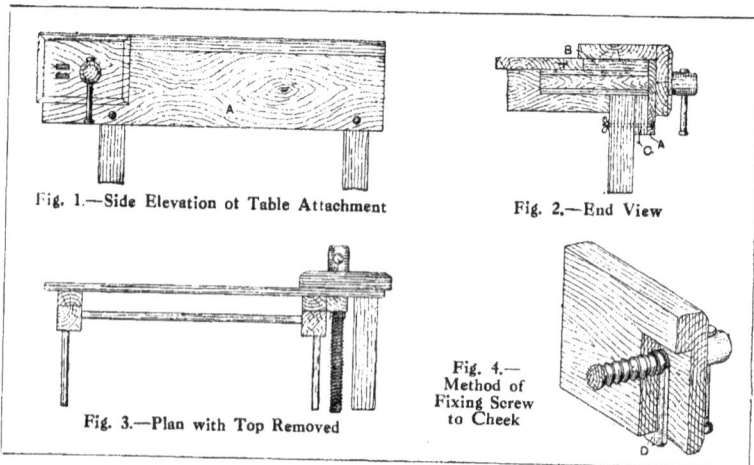

Fig. 1.—Side Elevation of Table Attachment

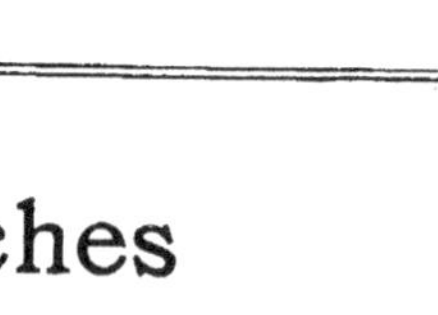

Fig. 2.—End View

Fig. 3.—Plan with Top Removed

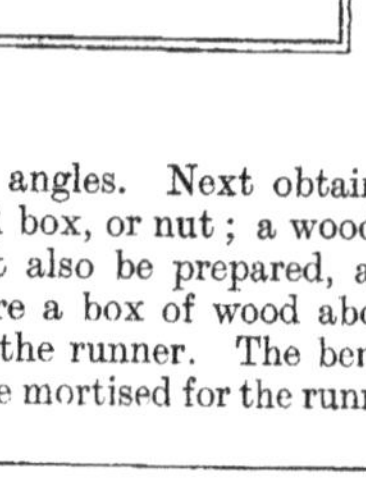

Fig. 4.—Method of Fixing Screw to Cheek

attachment with the top removed. The only damage to the table will be the boring of one hole through two legs for two bolts that hold the attachment.

The cheek of the bench is formed by the board A. The plank forming the top and this cheek should be firmly screwed and the box fixed to it, and also the plank forming the top. It will be necessary to insert a block B (Fig. 2) between the box and the top. The screw cheek can be bored to receive the screw, and to hold these two together properly it will be necessary to mortise through from the bottom edge of the cheek into the hole to receive the screw, as indicated in Fig. 4. Then a piece of hardwood D, shaped to fit into the groove made in the plain part of the screw, will hold the screw and cheek Finally bore through the cheek, the blocks, and through the two legs for a bolt, which can be tightened up at the back by an ordinary nut, or by a fly-nut, as shown in Figs. 2 and 6. It will be best to sink

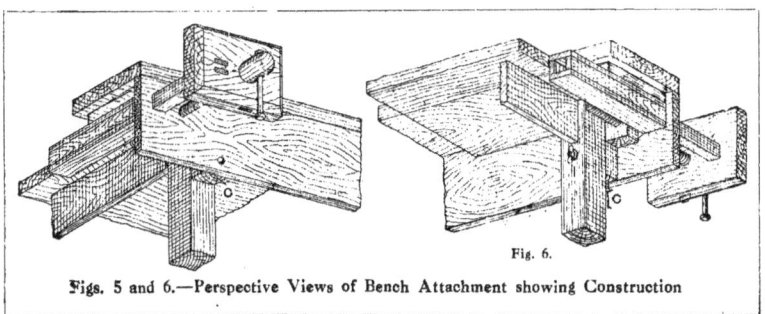

Figs. 5 and 6.—Perspective Views of Bench Attachment showing Construction

properly together. Now the hole for the screw in the cheek of the bench can be cut out and the nut screwed into position behind it. When this part is complete, place it in position on the table. Then prepare two blocks C (Figs. 2, 5, and 6), which fit between the legs and the bench cheek, and secure these blocks to the cheek with a couple of screws in each.

the head of the bolt so that it does not project and damage the work.

Alternative Arrangement.—An even simpler arrangement is shown in Fig. 7. A plan of the working top is shown in Fig. 10.

It consists of a piece of white pine 8 in. longer than the table, so that it projects 5 in. at one end and

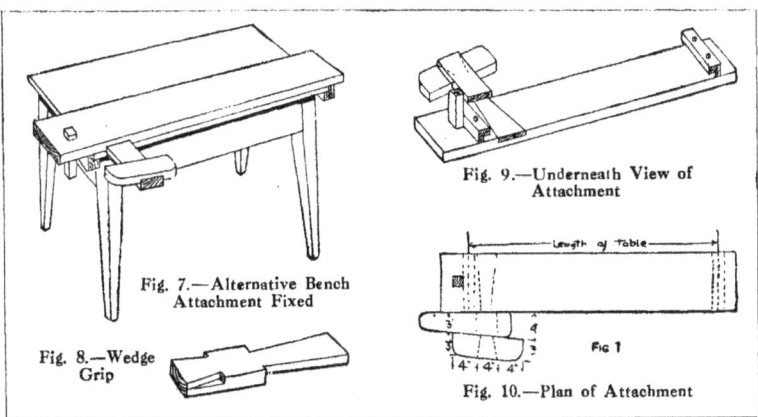

Fig. 7.—Alternative Bench Attachment Fixed

Fig. 8.—Wedge Grip

Fig. 9.—Underneath View of Attachment

Fig. 10.—Plan of Attachment

3 in. at the other. The reason that a greater projection is required at one end is to give room for the bench pin. The width of the working top may be 9 in. and the thickness 1½ in. The top is secured to the table by means of two checked fillets, which allow the top to slide off and on easily. These are shown clearly in an inverted position in Fig. 9. The wedge grip is secured to the top by a piece of 4-in. by 1½-in. framing which is dovetailed across the top, and is also dovetailed on the opposite end to receive the lug. A sketch of this piece ready for jointing to the other pieces is shown by Fig. 8. The long dovetail, which is also half-checked, is fitted to the top, while the small one is for the lug. By half-checking the long dovetail a check is formed and keeps the working top from being forced out of position while the work is going on. The thickness of the wedge should be ¾ in., and is fitted well forward to allow an average thickness to be held in position.

The bench pin is 1½ in. by 1½ in. square, and is fitted into a hole which is cut through the working top. The best position for it is against the front checked fillet, and as this part depends only on the tightness of the fit, it should be made of well-seasoned timber.

BENCH TOP WITH VICES

A design fitted with light side and end vices is shown in Fig. 11.

The timber used should be thoroughly seasoned. Four window-sash screws, 5 in. by ⅜ in., will be required. If the bench is wanted for heavy work, it will be advisable to use $\frac{7}{16}$-in. screws. Two 3-in. hand cramps, such as fretworkers use, and two bars of wrought-iron, 1 in. by ⅜ in. and 9 in. long, with five countersunk holes drilled in each will be required for fastening the bench in position.

The bench-top A (Figs. 11, 12, and 13) is a 1¾-in. deal board, 4 ft. long by 9 in. or 10 in. wide. Choose the best side for the face, and plane it up quite true, squaring up all the other sides from it. The mortises for the movable stop B (Fig. 11) are 1 in. by 2 in., and 2 in. from the front edge of the bench, a convenient distance apart being 5 in. (*see* Fig. 12). A piece of oak quartering, 2 in. square when planed up by fully 3 ft. 9 in. long, will be wanted for the two vices. Saw off a 6-in. length for the tail vice C (Fig. 11) and mortise a 1-in. by 2-in. hole through the centre for the stop D. Next mark the position of the thumbscrews E, centrally in the thickness of the bench-top, and 1 in. from each end of the block. Bore with brace and bit, and let in the washer plates F (*see also* Fig. 14) across the way of the grain. Mark the centres for the screws on the end of the bench, to coincide with the holes in the block, taking care that the mortise in the block falls in line with those in the bench-top; then with a centre-bit bore the recess for the boss on the nut plate G (Fig. 14), and the smaller ones for the thumbscrews, afterwards letting the plates in flush on the outside and firmly fixing them with screws. The oak stops B and D (Fig. 11) should be a moderately tight fit in the mortises, and, as the movable stops C cannot be knocked up from underneath, a recess ¼ in. deep is made in the back, ⅜ in. from the top. Opposite this an inclined sinking is made in the top of the bench, so that a ¼-in. chisel can be inserted to force up the block as required.

The remaining 3-ft. 3-in. length of quartering is for the side vice H, which is fitted in the same manner as the tail vice, except that the top face stands ⅛ in. higher than the top of the bench, so that when a number of narrow strips of stuff have to be planed, they can be placed side by side on the bench, between the vice, and a slip of wood nailed or screwed to the bench. The same purpose is served by using two or more stops knocked into the mortises, the strips to be planed being forced against these by pressure from the vice. This vice is fixed 1 in. from the end of the bench, so as to leave room for one of the small cramps, the thickness of which is cut out of the top and front edge of the bench as at J, so as to be level on the outside. The other cramp fits into the recess K at the opposite end of the bench.

WORK BENCHES

The two iron bars are fixed underneath the bench across the grain, and firmly screwed to keep it from warping. The bar next to the tail vice should be fixed close to the end of the board, to act as a stop against the end of the table, whilst the bar near the other end of the bench is let in level on the under side. Before these plates are drilled it should be ascertained that the holes for the screws will be out of the way of the screws securing the vice.

ledges screwed on. These must also be 1½ in. thick, and cut out at the front so as to fit all three boards; and leave them plain at the top. Make two frames, as c, of about 3-in. by 1¼-in. stuff, 6 in. less in length than the bench, and the same height as the latter has to be, and hinge them to the outside ledges so that they will fold inwards. Then hinge the bench to the back piece B, using wrought-iron

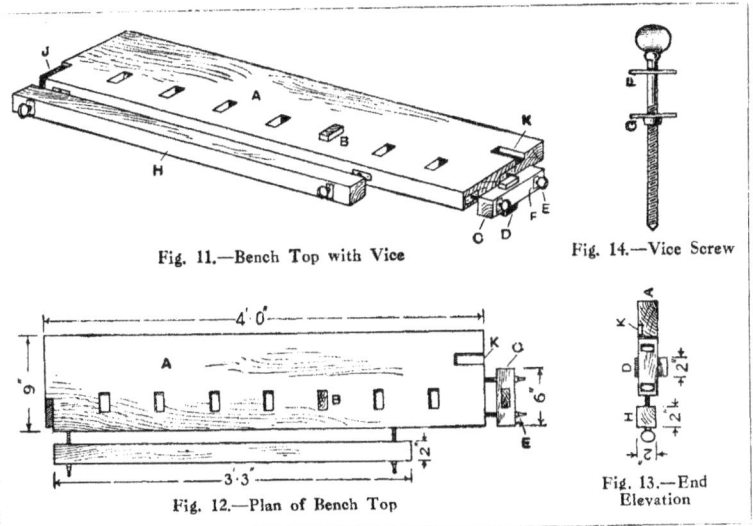

Fig. 11.—Bench Top with Vice

Fig. 14.—Vice Screw

Fig. 12.—Plan of Bench Top

Fig. 13.—End Elevation

FOLDING BENCH

Figs. 15 and 16 show a bench for fixing against a wall, so that it will hang down the side of the wall when not in use. Plug a piece of 4-in. by 1½-in. deal firmly to the wall, the same length as the proposed bench and 1 in. lower than the top will be (see A, Fig. 16), and on this screw a piece of 3-in. by 1-in. stuff of the same length, as at B. Make the bench of three boards in width, the front one 1½ in. thick, the others 1 in., fixed together with three

flap hinges, and scribe the bottoms of the frames c to the floor, so that the whole weight of the bench will rest on them, not on the hinges; and the result will be a good firm bench. If a bench more than about 5 ft. long is required, three hinges should be used at the back; and the bench will be considerably firmer if a stretcher is made with notches to fit over the bottom rails of the two frames which form the legs, to keep them from spreading, and a pair of braces hinged to it at the ends, the latter cut the right length to squeeze tightly in at each side of the middle ledge, as shown by dotted lines in Fig. 15. If a vice is required, use one of the self-fixing ones, which clip the boards of the bench by means of a screw underneath. The proper height of a bench is from 2 ft. 9 in. to 2 ft. 11 in., according to the height of the user.

more readily handled than a bench of the folding type.

The top is mortised to drop over tenons formed on the posts (Fig. 20), and is secured to the posts with wedges. It i

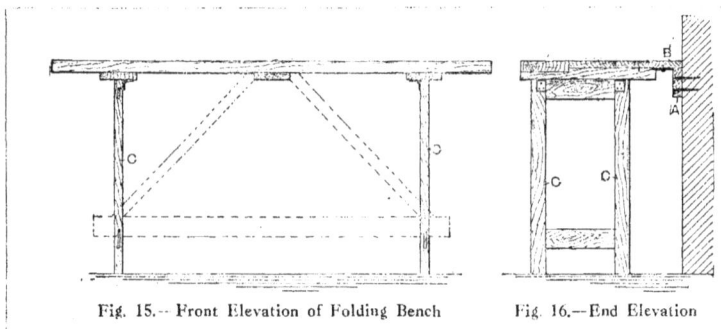

Fig. 15.—Front Elevation of Folding Bench   Fig. 16.—End Elevation

To dismantle the bench, it is only necessary to fold the legs towards one another, and it will fold down to the wall, with the legs out of sight.

made of three planks, the two outer ones being 11 in. by 1⅞ in., and the centre one being 12 in. by 1 in., rebated to fit grooves on the outer planks. Stout battens are

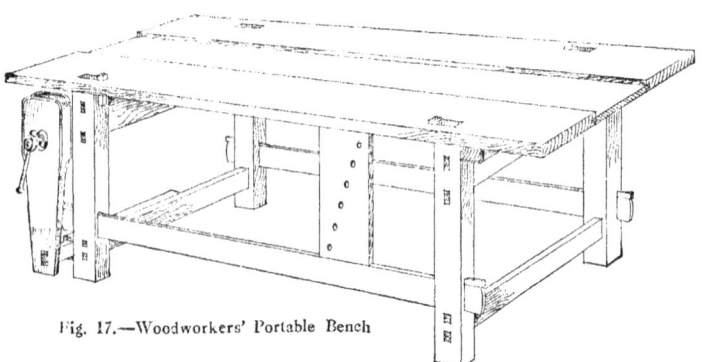

Fig. 17.—Woodworkers' Portable Bench

WOODWORKERS' PORTABLE BENCH

The bench shown by Figs. 17 to 19 can be quickly taken apart or erected, and being in three primary portions, it is

screwed to the underside, the end batten abutting against the outsides of the posts (see Fig. 19). The posts are a fixture in pairs; but are joined longitudinally by two rails, with half dovetailed bare-faced tenons secured with wedges. The rail

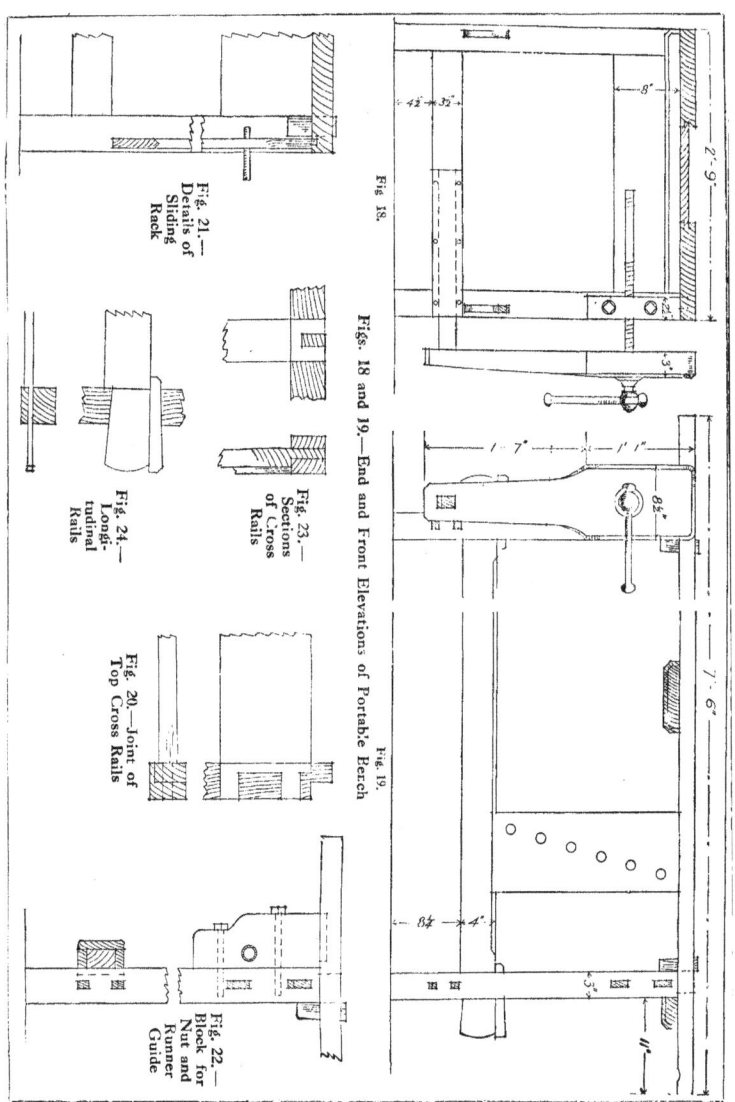

Figs. 18 and 19.—End and Front Elevations of Portable Bench. Fig. 20.—Joint of Top Cross Rails. Fig. 21.—Details of Sliding Rack. Fig. 22.—Block for Nut and Runner Guide. Fig. 23.—Sections of Cross Rails. Fig. 24.—Longitudinal Rails.

and wedges (Fig. 8) should be numbered to their respective places, and a hole bored in each wedge, so that, if necessary, they may be corded together to prevent loss during transit. The front rail has a double chamfer worked on its top edge to retain the sliding rack, The top edge of the rack fits in a groove under the top of the bench, as shown in section by Fig. 21.

Two forms of vices are shown. Each constitutes a part of the particular section to which it is attached, and in no way interferes with the dismantling of the bench. Fig. 22 shows the back check of

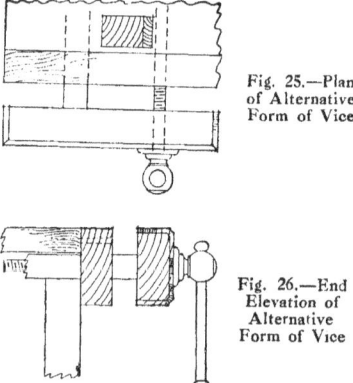

Fig. 25.—Plan of Alternative Form of Vice

Fig. 26.—End Elevation of Alternative Form of Vice

the vice with the carrying nut; it is secured to the post with two stout coach-screws. The runner guide extends half-way along the lower rail, a strip 3½ in. by ½ in. being attached to the rail, as the latter does not come flush with the post (see Fig. 23). The vice shown by Figs. 25 and 26 requires the addition of a side plank, 1¾ in. by 6 in. or 7 in. deep, screwed to the top. It is secured at the back with blocks, more particularly near the vice, but, of course, kept clear of the screw and runner. A vice is sometimes fitted at the opposite diagonal.

The wedges securing the top of the bench are shown projecting ½ in. or more above, merely to indicate their position more clearly. They should be flush excepting the one next to the vice, which may be used as a bench stop. The vice runners and wedges should be of some hardwood, such as beech, ash, or teak the remainder of the bench can be of deal A suitable height for the bench would b 2 ft. 10 in. from the ground to the under side of the top, which should be of 1⅞ in stuff.

BENCH WITH SIDE AND TAIL SCREWS

The bench fitted with side and tail vice shown by Fig. 27 is extremely useful fo cabinet-making and similar work, wher it is desirable to hold pieces of materia that may have to be planed, moulded chamfered, mortise-grooved, etc., withou using a bench knife or similar method o fixing. The dimensions on Figs. 28, 29 and 30, of course, can be altered to mee requirements. The whole may be con structed of hardwood, such as beech o birch, and in any case it will be best t have hardwood for all the parts formin the top, side cheeks, and cheeks of screws these being the main parts of the bench the framing of the legs, rails, etc., migh be of red deal. Fig. 30 is a section on A (Fig. 28).

Having sawn out the pieces, next plan them true. Then the legs and rails shoul be set out, the latter for mortising, an the former for tenons. The mortises g right through, producing a much firme result than when the tenons are onl stubbed in half way. The haunche mortise and tenons between the top rail and legs, with the tenons of the cross rail through the legs, are shown in Fig. 31 The side rails are dovetailed, mortised, an tenoned together, as in Figs. 31 and 32 where it will be seen that the tenon of th rail is firmly held in position by a wedge which must be released, and the tenon o the rail lifted up before it can be with drawn. The side rails have a bare-face tenon, that is, have a shoulder on th inside only. When these joints fit satis factorily, the legs and cross rails shoul be glued together and cramped up an the tenons fixed with wedges, which should be glued before insertion.

The top should be planed to breadth and thickness, and then the ends cut off and planed square and to length. The front of the back and end cheeks (Fig. 29) should next be carefully set out and worked. At the front end of the side cheek B (Figs. 28 and 29) the thickness for dovetailing is not the full 2 in., but is less by $\frac{3}{4}$ in., the breadth of the pin hole, as shown at Fig. 29. After the side cheeks have been dovetailed and fitted together, the front cheek should be grooved on the back for receiving the stop (see Figs. 29 and 33). The inside edge of the top should be rebated as shown at Fig. 30 to receive the well board. This should fit just tight between the end cheeks, the front side and back cheeks being firmly secured to the top plank and well board. Four-inch screws may be used for the front and side cheeks and $2\frac{1}{2}$-in. screws for the back, the heads being sunk a little below the surface. It will be found advantageous to glue the side cheeks to the main board of the top. The cheeks and ends of the runners should be mortised and tenoned together, as shown by Fig. 34, the top of the runner being kept at the same distance from the top of the cheek as the thickness of the top plank ; two tenons may be more difficult to make ; but the result will be stronger than when one tenon only is used. These joints should be firmly glued and wedged together with the runner at right angles to the cheek.

The construction of the guide boxes for the runners is clearly shown in Figs. 30 and 33, the pieces, a trifle deeper than the thickness of the runner, being firmly fastened to the top plank with $3\frac{1}{2}$-in. screws. The bottom is formed of $\frac{3}{4}$-in. boarding screwed to the guides. The box for the tail runner extends from the top rail to the inner surface of the end cheek. Wrought-iron bench screws about 18 in. by $\frac{7}{8}$ in., having split collars, will be found most satisfactory, and in fixing them into their places, the cheek and runner should be pushed in and firmly held in position ; then the centre of the hole for the screw in the cheek should be marked, sufficient room being allowed for the flange of the

Fig. 27.—Bench with Side and Tail Screws

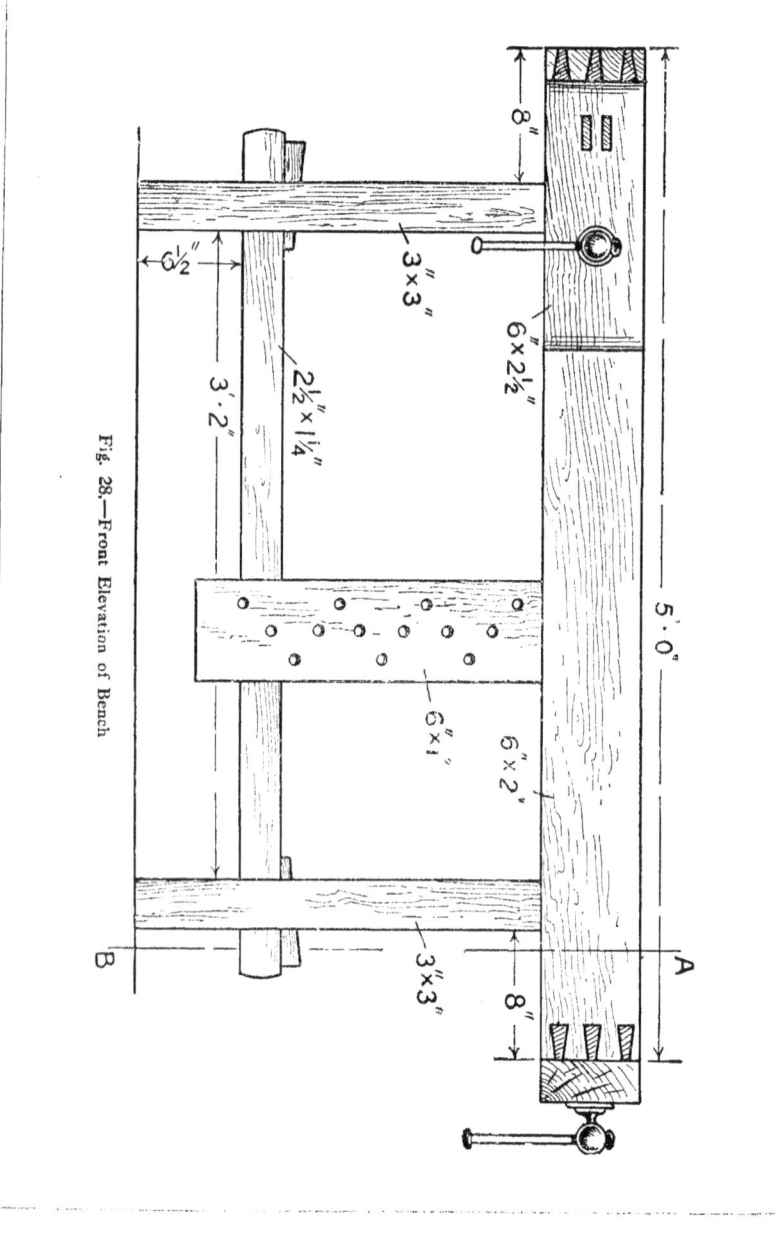

Fig. 28.—Front Elevation of Bench

WORK BENCHES

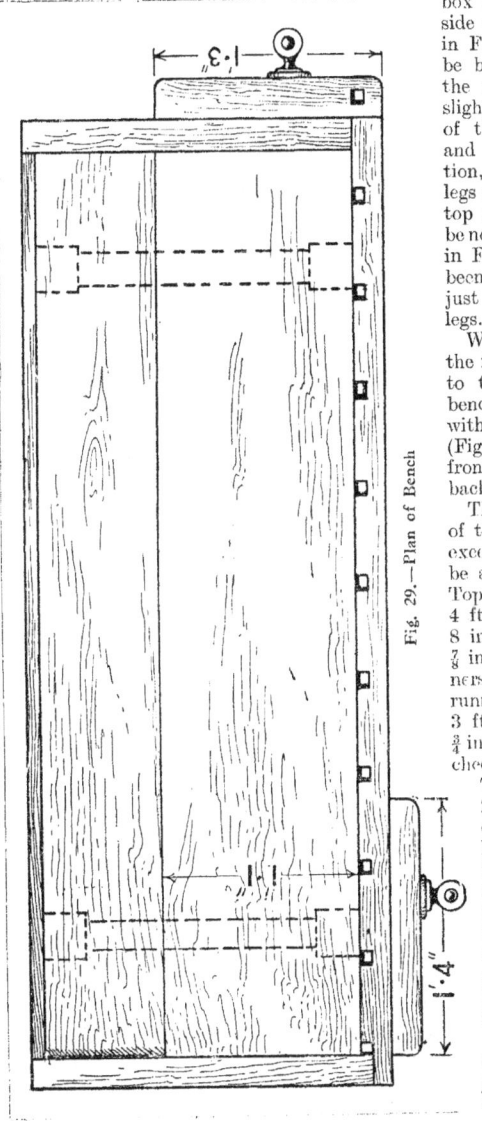

Fig. 29.—Plan of Bench

box (or nut) or screwing to the side check of the bench, as shown in Fig. 33. The hole should next be bored through the cheeks of the screw and bench with a bit slightly larger than the diameter of the screw. Then the collars and boxes can be fixed in position, and the framework of the legs and top fitted together. The top rail of the back legs should be notched for the runner, as shown in Fig. 31, and if the work has been done accurately the top will just slide on the upper part of the legs.

When the parts are adjusted, the front cheek should be secured to the legs and the top of the bench to the top rails of the legs with $3\frac{1}{2}$-in. screws. The peg board (Fig. 28) should be screwed to the front of the bottom rail and the back of the front cheek.

The following are the net sizes of the pieces required; a little in excess of these dimensions should be allowed for waste in working. Top board, 2 in. by $13\frac{1}{4}$ in. by 4 ft. 8 in.; well board, $\frac{3}{4}$ in. by 8 in. by 4 ft. 8 in.; peg board, $\frac{7}{8}$ in. by 6 in. by 1 ft. 9 in.; runners, 2 in. by $2\frac{1}{2}$ in. by 2 ft. 3 in.; runner guides, $1\frac{1}{2}$ in. by 2 in. by 3 ft. 2 in.; guide box bottoms, $\frac{3}{4}$ in. by $5\frac{1}{2}$ in. by 1 ft. 7 in.; screw cheeks, $2\frac{1}{2}$ in. by 6 in. by 2 ft. 7 in.; front and end cheek, 2 in. by 6 in. by 9 ft.; back cheek, 1 in. by 6 in. by 5 ft.; legs, 3 in. by 3 in. by 9 ft. 8 in.; top rail (front end), 2 in. by 4 in. by 1 ft. 9 in.; top rail (back end), 2 in. by $4\frac{1}{4}$ in. by 1 ft. 9 in.; bottom rails (ends), 2 in. by 2 in. by 3 ft. 6 in.; and bottom rails (front and back), $1\frac{1}{4}$ in. by $2\frac{1}{2}$ in. by 8 ft. 2 in.

It will, of course, be understood that the above are the *finished* sizes, hence the need for the allowance mentioned.

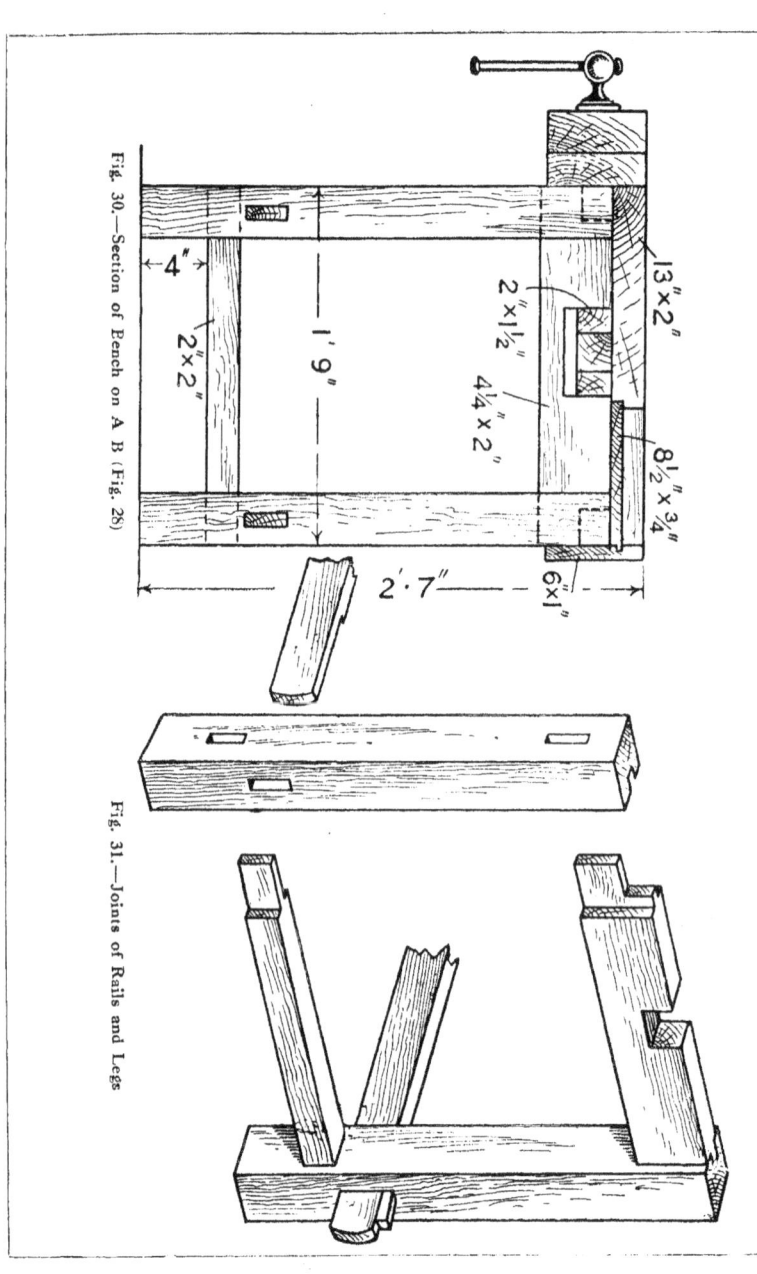

Fig. 30.—Section of Bench on A B (Fig. 28)

Fig. 31.—Joints of Rails and Legs

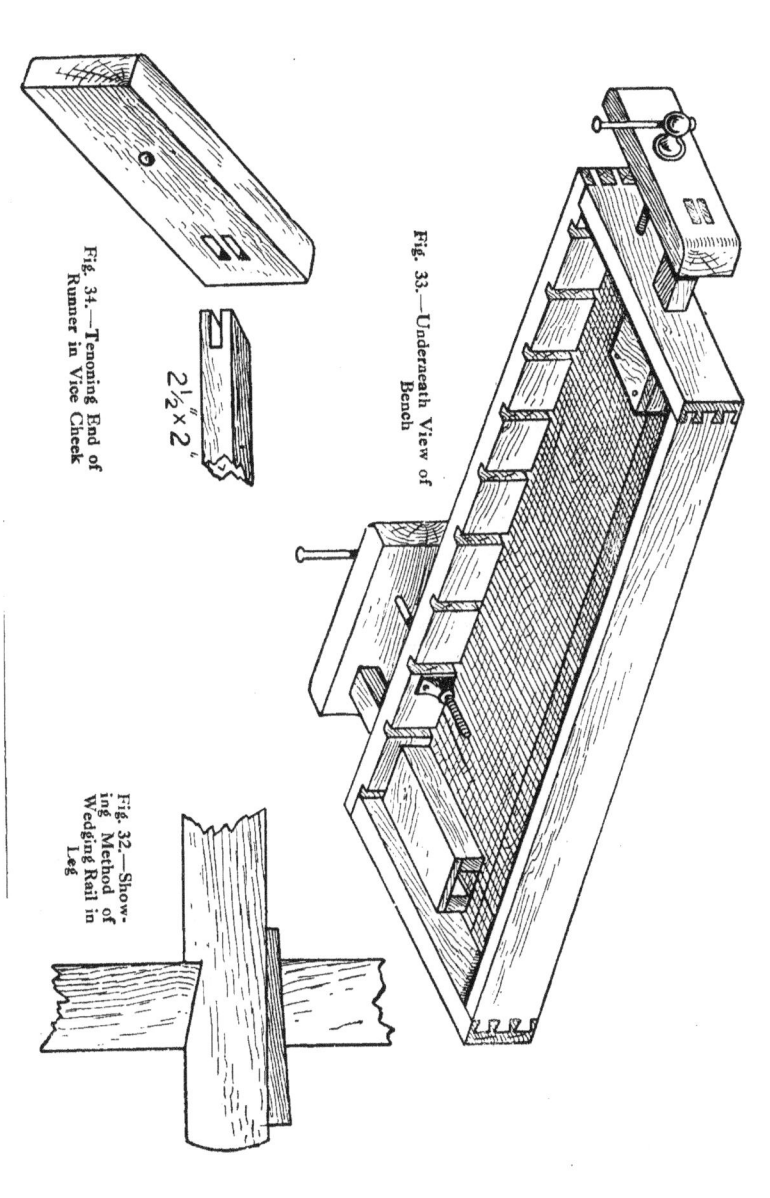

Fig. 33.—Underneath View of Bench

Fig. 34.—Tenoning End of Runner in Vice Cheek

Fig. 32.—Showing Method of Wedging Rail in Leg

2½" × 2"

ALTERNATIVE DESIGN FOR BENCH

The illustration Fig. 35 shows a carpenter's bench 6 ft. long, 2 ft. wide, and 2 ft. 6 in. high, which has a side vice and an end vice. The latter is especially useful in holding any piece of work securely on the bench, for it can be gripped between stops or wooden pins, one of which occupies one of the holes in the top of the bench, and the other a hole in the upper edge of the end-vice cheek (see Figs. 35 and 36). With the exception of the vice cheeks, which must be of hardwood, such as beech, all parts may be constructed of red deal.

The top consists of two boards, 5 ft. 9 in.

The side and end cheeks or boards are also of 1½-in. stuff. The former are 6 ft. long, the latter 1 ft. 9 in., while the width of all is 9 in. (The measurements given in this article are those of the boards after planing; therefore ⅛ in. must be added to the thicknesses to allow for finishing.) Before these four cheeks are secured to the top and to each other, a hole for the vice screw must be cut in that of the front, and two holes are to be cut in an end piece for the tail vice screw and runner. The screw nuts can then be attached. The screws for both these vices are the common wooden screws (Fig. 39). If iron ones are preferred, the necessary alteration in the fitting of these parts is easily accomplished.

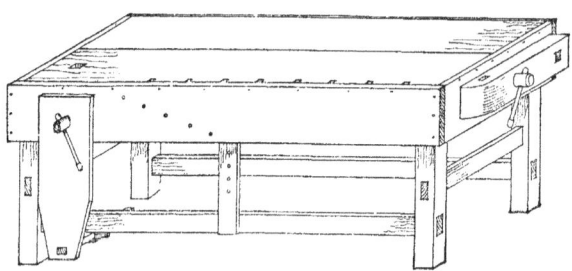

Fig. 35.—Alternative Design for Bench

long, 1½ in. thick, and 10½ in. wide, which are joined by two rails screwed across their under surface, as shown in Fig. 37. These rails are 1 ft. long, 1 in. thick, and 3 in. wide, and are secured at a distance of one-third of the length of the top boards from each end. Notches are cut in the front edge to provide the holes for the stop, as shown in Fig. 33. They are 1 in. square, and are situated at intervals of 6 in. To give greater depth, glue and screw a 3-in. wide strip of 1½-in. stuff, 5 ft. 9 in. long, to the under surface, to be flush with the front edge. Fig. 38 shows this detail. Mark with the square the positions of all the notches on the double edge, carry the ends of each line over the board, and strip to the extent of 1 in., and connect the terminations of each couple. Then cut out with a saw and chisel.

At the distance of 9½ in. from the left-hand end of the front cheek, and 2¼ in. from the bottom edge, place one leg of a pair of compasses, and describe a circle equal to the diameter of the screw, say 2 in. With a keyhole saw cut out the stuff, first boring a hole large enough to admit the blade. The screw should fit the hole easily. Fig. 40 shows the nut of the front vice screw fixed in position on the inside of the board. To obviate the necessity for using long screws, the thickness of the nut is reduced one-half at each corner as shown. The screw-hole for the tail vice is of similar diameter. Its centre is 6 in. from the front extremity of the right-hand end of the top, and 4 in. from the upper edge. At a distance of 11 in. from this end make the hole for the casing of the vice runner. It is 3½ in.

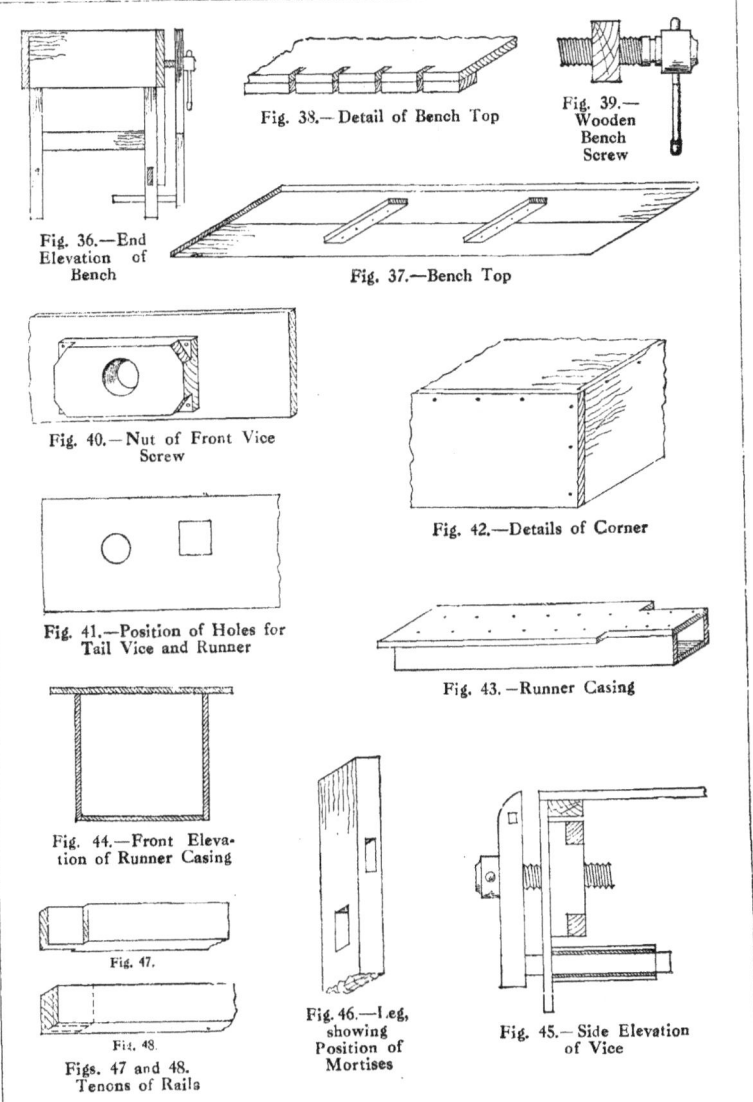

Fig. 38.—Detail of Bench Top
Fig. 39.—Wooden Bench Screw
Fig. 36.—End Elevation of Bench
Fig. 37.—Bench Top
Fig. 40.—Nut of Front Vice Screw
Fig. 42.—Details of Corner
Fig. 41.—Position of Holes for Tail Vice and Runner
Fig. 43.—Runner Casing
Fig. 44.—Front Elevation of Runner Casing
Fig. 47.
Fig. 48.
Figs. 47 and 48. Tenons of Rails
Fig. 46.—Leg, showing Position of Mortises
Fig. 45.—Side Elevation of Vice

square, and is 1½ in. from the upper edge. Fig. 41 shows the appearance of the board when these holes have been made. Screw the parts together. Fig. 42, which is a detail of one of the corners, shows that the front board (and consequently the rear board) is screwed to the edges of the end boards. Dovetail joints can be used if desired.

Next arrange the runner casing, which is a long square tube attached to the under surface of the bench top, and designed to ensure the runner of the vice cheek moving in and out in a straight line. Fig. 43 gives a general view of the casing, and Fig. 44 a front view. The casing is composed of four pieces of ¾-in. stuff. The upper is 5½ in. wide, except for 1½ in. at one end, where it is 3½ in., so that it can pass into the hole in the end board for the casing. Two of the other pieces (those for the sides) are 2¾ in. wide, and 2 in. is the width of the bottom length. All are 1 ft. long. Before they are screwed together, place the runner in the tube while the sides are being secured to the top. The runner is 1 ft. 6 in. long and 2 in. square, and should fit the casing freely. The projecting edges of the upper length enable the casing to be screwed to the top of the bench as shown in Fig. 45, which represents the vice in a state of completion; that is, with the addition of the vice cheek and runner, the top of the bench being supposed to be removed. It will be seen that the front of the casing enters the hole of the end board, and is flush with its outer surface. As the nut of the screw is 8 in. long, it will be seen that between it and the front there is a space of 2 in., which will provide room for one of the legs.

The legs should next be cut out and fixed in place. They are about 2 ft. 4½ in. long, 3 in. wide, and 2 in. thick. The rails connecting them near the lower end are tenoned into them. Each leg requires a couple of mortises made in it, one for the end and the other for the front or back rail tenon. At a distance of 5 in. from one end of a leg, square a line across all faces, and repeat 3 in. distant. Connect those crossing the narrow or 2-in. wide faces by a couple of lines, each ⅝ in. from the edge. This indicates the position of the mortise. The other mortise is situated 3 in. distant from, or above, the first, and is made in the wide faces of the wood; it is 3 in. long and ¾ in. wide. The remaining legs should be treated in the same way. Fig. 46 shows the lower part of one of them.

The front and back rails are 5 ft. 9 in. long, the end rails being 1 ft. 9 in. The tenons of the front and rear rails are exactly similar, while those of the end rails differ only in the fact that they are 1 in. shorter. Fig. 47 shows one of them, and Fig. 48 the method of setting out the work. For a front or back rail run a pencil line round the stuff 3 in. from the end. Mark two other lines between one of the lines crossing the 2 in. face and the end, and let them be parallel with, and ⅝ in. from, the edge of the wood. Repeat on the opposite side and connect the lines over the ends, as shown in Fig. 48. Then with a saw make the four cuts necessary to produce the tenon, which should fit its mortise firmly, but not so tightly as to split the wood. The end rail tenons are similarly set out, but the shoulder line is 2 in. from the end instead of 3 in. Glue the tenons in the mortises, and add a nail or a wood peg. Then screw to the bench top, letting the latter be turned upside down during the operation.

Before cutting out the cheeks for the vices, complete the immovable parts of the bench. One only remains to be done; this is the peg board, the strip of wood that contains the holes for the wooden peg designed to support in the vice boards which need such assistance. This board is 1 ft. 4 in. long, 3 in. wide, and 1½ in. thick. It reaches from the lower edge of the front board to the lower edge of the front rail, to which it is screwed. To make a firm joint between the upper extremity and the bench, a piece of 1-in. wood, 3 in. wide and 8 in. long, should be screwed across the joint at the back, as shown in Fig. 49. Midway between the ends of the bench is about the best position for the peg board. Bore holes in it and in the front cheek of the bench to take a wooden peg ½ in. in diameter.

WORK BENCHES

Fig. 35 suggests the number and position of these. Fig. 50 is a view of the cheek and runner of the tail vice. The cheek is 1 ft. 5 in. by 7 in. by 3 in., and one end may be rounded as shown.

The hole for the bench screw is just large enough to admit the screw; its centre is 7½ in. from this rounded end and 4 in. from the top edge. From the bottom edge bore a ½-in. hole through to the screw aperture, so that a hardwood key A may be driven to fit into the collar on the bench screw (Fig. 51). The object of the key is to ensure the vice cheek moving out with the screw when the latter is twisted to the left. The runner and edge of the cheek for the peg is on a line with the holes of the bench top. It should be at least 3 in. deep, and is 1 in. square. The cheek for the other vice is 2 ft. 4 in. long and 1½ in. thick, its width at the top extremity being 8 in. and at the bottom 4 in. The hole for the screw has its centre 6½ in. from the upper end, and midway between the side margins.

The runner is 1 ft. long, 2 in. wide, and 1 in. thick, and is pierced with ¾-in. holes at close intervals from a point 1¾ in. from the front end. It is mortised into the cheek, so that it is in contact with the lower edge of the front rail. The widest surface is horizontal. The mortise

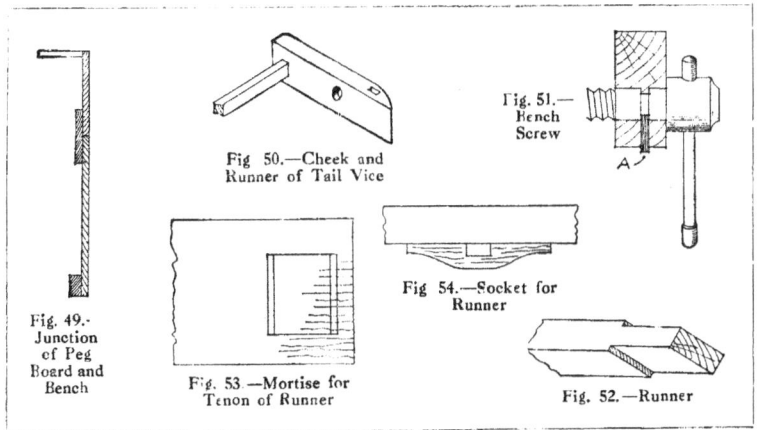

Fig. 49.—Junction of Peg Board and Bench

Fig. 50.—Cheek and Runner of Tail Vice

Fig. 51.—Bench Screw

Fig. 53.—Mortise for Tenon of Runner

Fig. 54.—Socket for Runner

Fig. 52.—Runner

cheek are united by tenon and mortise. Accurately measure the position for the mortise on the vice cheek, indicating it by drawing a 2-in. square in pencil on both sides. As the end of the runner has a tenon 2 in. by 1½ in. (see Fig. 52) the mortice must correspond. Therefore two lines are drawn parallel with, and ¼ in. from, the sides of each square (see Fig. 53), and the mortise is made accordingly. The tenon is long enough to occupy the mortise from the front to the rear surface of the cheek, and care must be exercised to ensure a good fit. The hole in the upper is 1 in. square, and passes through the cheek. Therefore the tenon of the runner has its width reduced one-half, ½ in. being taken off each edge to the extent of 1½ in.

A socket for the runner to work in is provided and nailed to the lower rail, as shown in Fig. 54. It should be flush with the front surface. A peg 2 in. long is provided for the runner, and two stops, each 4 in. long, are prepared for the bench and the tail vice. About 10 in. from the front of the bench, and 4 in. from the left-hand end, is a suitable position in

THE PRACTICAL WOODWORKER

which to fix a bench stop to hold a board during the operation of planing.

WATCHMAKERS' BENCH

The watchmakers' bench shown by Figs. 55 to 59 is 3 ft. 6 in. long by 3 ft. 3 in. high by 1 ft. 9 in. deep. It contains eleven various size drawers and a sliding tray. The top is in solid mahogany 1 in. thick, with a rim along the front and ends, the latter diminishing to the front. Figs. 60

Fig 55.—Watchmakers' Bench

and 61 are elevations of the parallel front to the bench and of the panelled end.

The front and ends are framed and panelled in American whitewood, and are 1 in. thick. Fig. 62 is a detail of the angle of the panelled framing. Fig. 63 is a section through the bench top. The tray for jewellers' work rests on runners, as shown in Fig. 64. The standard at the end of the nest of drawers, also the shelf immediately above the tray (Fig. 65), may be either in whitewood or pine, prepared from 1-in. material. The rails and drawer runners are prepared in mahogany, and the dustboards (see Fig. 58) either of deal or pine. The front and sides and side slips of the drawers are in mahogany, and the bottoms may be either of whitewood or pine. The fronts of the drawers are raised as shown in the detail (Fig. 66). Fig. 67 is a detail of the drawer side, showing the grooved slip with tongued bottom, and Fig. 68 is an enlarged detail of the bench top. The panels in the end framing at the right hand of the nest of drawers are flush on the inside.

A foot-wheel for a lathe may be used at the left hand of the bench, with band holes at A (Fig. 55).

The materials required for the construction of the bench are given in the following list of quantities:

For the top, one piece of mahogany 3 ft. 7 in. by 1 ft. 10½ in. by 1 in.; one piece 3 ft. 9 in. by 4 in. by 1 in.; two pieces 1 ft. 11 in. by 4 in. by 1 in.; and one piece 3 ft. 7 in. by 1½ in. by ½ in. For the framing stiles, four pieces of whitewood 3 ft. 3 in. by 2¾ in. by 1 in.; and two pieces 3 ft. 3 in. by 2¼ in. by 1 in. For the muntins, four pieces of whitewood 2 ft. 11 in. by 2⅜ in. by 1 in. For the rails, one piece of whitewood 3 ft. 6 in. by 5¼ in. by 1 in.; two pieces 1 ft. 9 in. by 5¼ in. by 1 in.; one piece 3 ft. 6 in. by 2¾ in. by 1 in.; and two pieces 1 ft. 9 in. by 2¾ in. by 1 in. For the panels, three pieces of whitewood 2 ft. 7 in. by 11¼ in. by ½ in., and two pieces 2 ft. 7 in. by 7¼ in. by ½ in. For the base, one piece of oak 3 ft. 7 in. by 1 ft. 10 in. by 1 in. For the standard, one piece of whitewood 3 ft. 2 in. by 1 ft. 8 in. by 1 in. For the shelf, one piece of whitewood 2 ft. 2 in. by 1 ft. 8 in. by 1 in. For the divisions, two pieces of whitewood 6 in. by 1 ft. 8 in. by 1 in., and one piece 1 ft.

ADJUSTABLE BENCH STOP

All who are used to working at the bench know what it is to be troubled with a bench stop so firmly inserted, that it requires considerable persuasion with the hammer when it is to be properly readjusted. The contrivance shown in Fig. 69 obviates all force and is simply adjusted by means of a form of cam A, which, when turned clockwise, gradually raises the stop above the surface of the bench top.

The cam should be made of some close-grained hardwood such as oak or beech, and is fixed to the rail between the legs

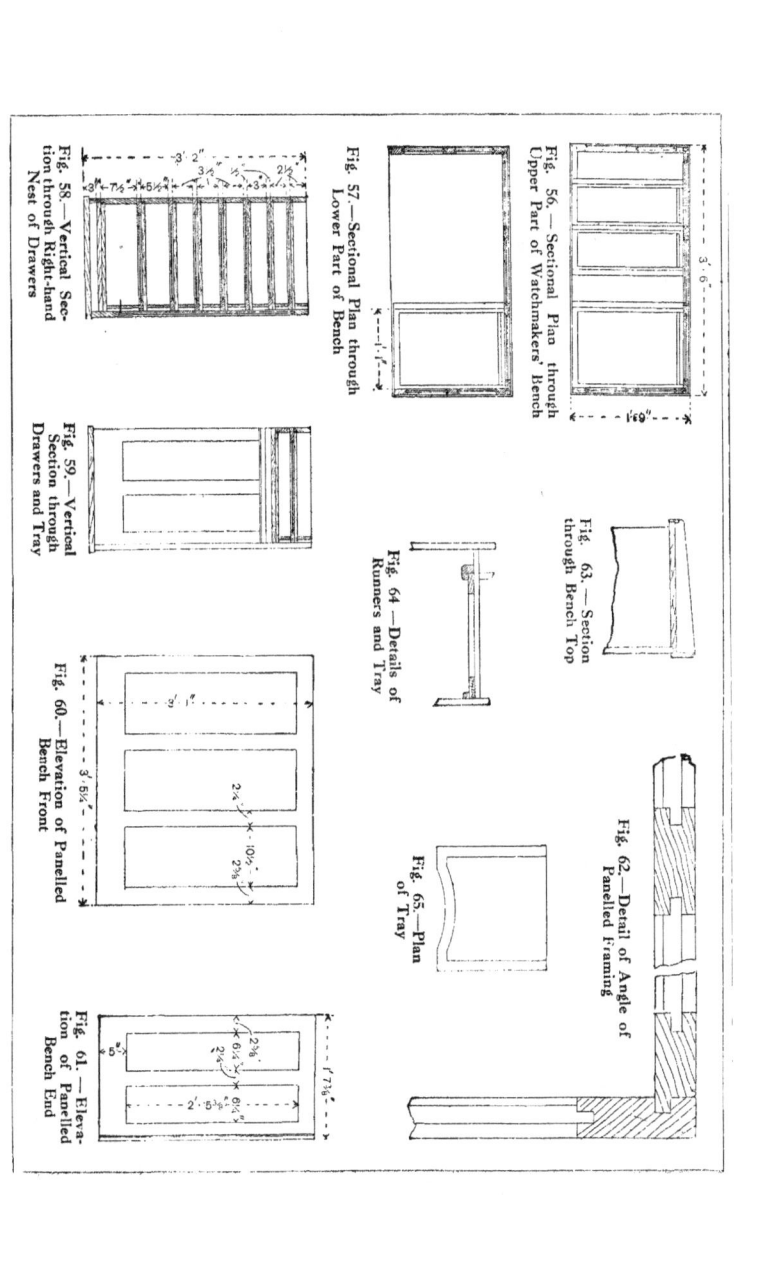

THE PRACTICAL WOODWORKER

of the bench by means of a screw, which should be driven in just sufficiently tight to enable the cam to be turned; a metal washer should be inserted between the cam and the rail.

An easy method of setting out the shape of the cam is as follows: Divide the circle into a number of equal parts as B to N (Fig. 70), and draw radii as shown. Divide one of the radii into twelve parts, the same number as the circumference is divided the stop in position, the top being level with the surface of the bench, and hold the cam under the end of the stop, so that the latter is resting on the part where the line D (Fig. 70) crosses. Then drive the screw in the cam. By slowly turning the wheel forwards, the stop can be raised, or by turning backwards, lowered, to such a nicety, that it can be easily adjusted to $\frac{1}{16}$ in. The stop fits quite easily in the mortise in the bench top, and is kept

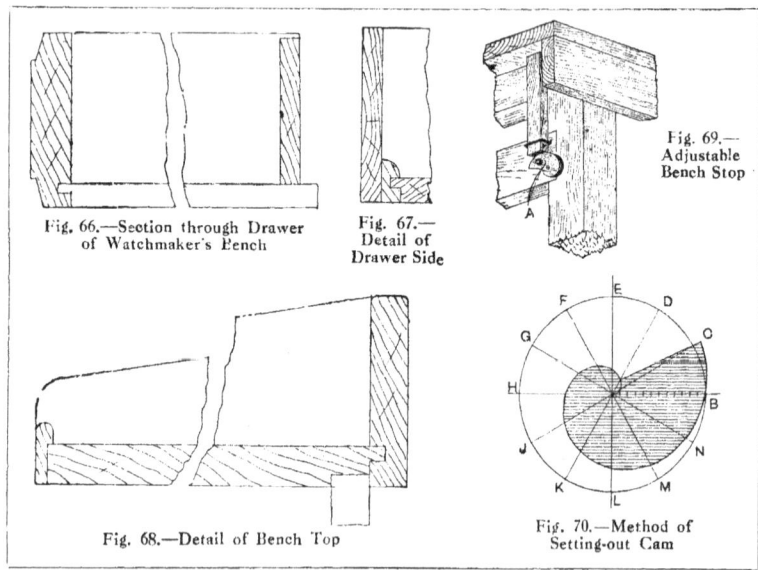

Fig. 66.—Section through Drawer of Watchmaker's Bench

Fig. 67.—Detail of Drawer Side

Fig. 69.—Adjustable Bench Stop

Fig. 68.—Detail of Bench Top

Fig. 70.—Method of Setting-out Cam

into. Then, starting the curve from the centre, on C mark one of the divisions of the radius, on D two, on E three, on F four, and so on, until the outside is reached; then trace the curve through the points. The twelfth division finishes on B, but mark one more division on C outside the circle, and from this point draw a line as shown to the point where the curve crosses D. The scored part is the cam to be cut out in wood, the centre being the point where the screw is inserted.

To fit the cam to the bench, first place vertical by means of an iron guide, which could be made from a piece of stout wire.

IMPROVISED BENCH VICES

In cases where a cabinetmaker's or carpenter's bench is not available, a table has to serve. For light work which has to be held vertically, such as cutting dovetails or ornamental shapes with the bow-saw, and so on, a handy contrivance is a hand-screw fixed to a table as shown in Fig. 71. One chop A (Fig. 71) of the

WORK BENCHES

handscrew is secured with two screws driven from the underside of the table top, as in Fig. 72. The chop A should be

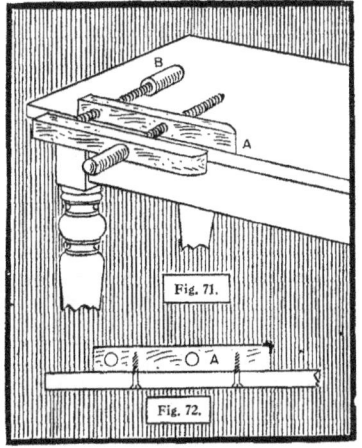

Figs. 71 and 72.—Improvised Bench Vice

exactly level with the table edge, so that the surface for the work to rest against is increased. Should the handle B of the handscrew be thicker than the chop A, and thus prevent it from turning freely, a thin piece of $\frac{1}{4}$-in. or $\frac{1}{2}$-in. stuff may be placed between the chop and the table, the iron screws passing through it, of course.

When the handscrew has served its purpose it can be taken from the bench in less than a minute, and the table can then be used for planing, etc.

Another Improvised Vice.—Another simple device is shown in Figs. 73 and 74.

A piece of quartering A, $1\frac{1}{2}$ in. square by 2 ft. 6 in. long, is taken, and a short piece cut with one end rounded is fixed to one end of the long piece to form a foot B. The length of this foot is determined by the distance which the top of the table overlaps the leg, the idea being to keep the piece A as vertical as possible, in side view, so as to grip the material square,

to prevent its slipping when being cut. Next a short piece of quartering is cut and recessed to take the foot B and secured firmly to the table leg, as shown at C; this forms a step for the foot B. A couple of Bowden-brake springs are next fastened to the table leg and also to each side of the upright piece A.

It is important that these springs should slope towards the table, so as to keep the foot piece B from riding up out of the step, and, of course, the tighter these springs are stretched the tighter the vice will grip.

A thin piece of wood D is tacked to the top of the table to prevent the saw from cutting through, and a thicker piece E placed on top to form a stop. This last piece may be adjusted to suit the thickness of wood to be cut. A piece of wood in position for cutting is shown at F. It may also be placed vertically between the edge of the table and the piece A, for cutting end joints, etc.

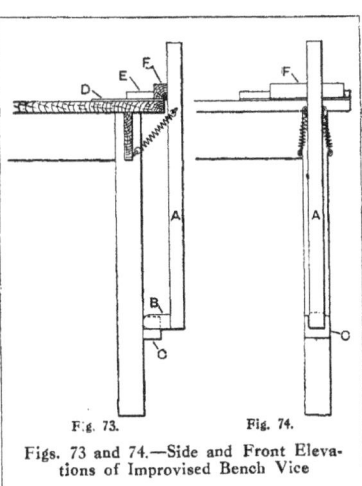

Figs. 73 and 74.—Side and Front Elevations of Improvised Bench Vice

The whole device may be rigged up in about ten minutes and the cost, largely determined by the amount of material to hand, in any case is small.

EASILY-MADE BACK AND FRONT VICES

The front and back vices shown by Figs. 75 to 78 are constructed chiefly of wood. The only metal parts in the front vice are the screw, nut, and handle, while in the back vice, in addition to the screw, nut, and handle, an iron stay is fitted between the vice and bench ; the jaws of the vice are protected with iron plates. Beech or ash should be used for the construction of it.

In the front vice (Figs. 75 and 76) the front leg of the bench acts as the back jaw of the vice. The front jaw A (Fig. 76) is 2 ft. long by 4 in. wide by $1\frac{1}{2}$ in. thick at the top, tapering to 3 in. wide by $1\frac{1}{4}$ in. thick at the bottom. The guide B is $1\frac{1}{4}$ in. wide by $\frac{3}{4}$ in. thick, mortised into the front jaw 3 in. up from the bottom, and is fixed with wedges. A mortise is cut in the leg through which the guide passes, and a number of holes are bored in the guide, into which an iron pin fits, for regulating the width of the vice at the bottom to correspond with the width at the top.

An enlarged section through the vice, showing the screw and its fittings and method of fixture, is shown by Fig. 79. The nut D, a front view of which is shown by Fig. 80, is fixed to the back of the leg with two screws. An iron plate (*see also* Fig. 81), $\frac{1}{2}$ in. thick by 3 in. in diameter, is fixed to the front of the jaw with two screws, and an iron washer E (Fig. 81) interposes between the plate and the head of the screw. The handle G is $\frac{5}{8}$ in. in diameter and 11 in. long ; one end is made in the solid, while the other is screwed on, as shown at Fig. 79. The distance from the top of the bench to the centre of the screw should be about 6 in. Bench screws fitted with a nut and handle, similar to the one shown at Fig. 79, can be obtained from tool dealers.

The back vice shown by Figs. 77 and 78 has two wood jaws H (Fig. 78) 1 ft. 9 in. long by $3\frac{1}{2}$ in. wide by $1\frac{1}{2}$ in. thick. The jaws are protected at the top with iron plates J (*see also* Figs. 82 and 83), 3 in. deep by $\frac{1}{4}$ in. thick, let in and fixed with screws. The guide K is $1\frac{1}{2}$ in. wide by $\frac{3}{4}$ in. thick, mortised into the front jaw, and fixed with a bolt. The screw and its fittings are similar to that used for the front vice.

The method of fixing the vice to the bench is shown in Fig. 82. A nut is mortised into the bench from the bottom, about 2 in. in from the end, and a $\frac{1}{2}$-in. bolt with a square head passes through the back jaw and the bench, screwing into the nut. The vice is further secured with the iron stay L, of $\frac{1}{2}$-in. diameter, the ends of which are screwed to the jaw of vice and bottom of bench top.

TOOL RACK FOR BENCH

The tool rack shown in Fig. 84 will hold all the tools most commonly used by woodworkers, it rests on the top of the bench and can be adapted if necessary to serve two benches placed back to back. Figs. 85 and 86 are elevation and plan respectively. The tools provided for are : Trying, jack and smoothing planes ; foot rule; tenon saw; 1 in., $\frac{3}{4}$ in., $\frac{1}{2}$ in., $\frac{3}{8}$ in., $\frac{1}{4}$ in., and $\frac{1}{8}$ in. firmer chisels ; pair of wing compasses ; hammer, screwdriver, marking gauge, mallet, try-square, and marking knife. Space is left also for other tools, such as files, mortise gauge, bevel, spokeshave, etc.

The quantity of material required for the single rack is as follows ; back 5 ft. $1\frac{3}{4}$ in. by 1 ft. 3 in. by $\frac{7}{8}$ in. ; top shelf 5 ft. $1\frac{3}{4}$ in. by $4\frac{1}{8}$ in. by $\frac{5}{8}$ in. ; bottom shelf 2 ft. $4\frac{1}{8}$ in. by $4\frac{1}{8}$ in. by $\frac{5}{8}$ in. ; middle shelf 1 ft. $10\frac{7}{8}$ in. by $4\frac{1}{8}$ in. by $\frac{5}{8}$ in. ; two partitions 9 in. by 4 in. by $\frac{5}{8}$ in. ; and two ends 1 ft. 3 in. by $4\frac{1}{4}$ in. by $\frac{7}{8}$ in. For the double rack this quantity will have to be doubled.

It will be noticed that the ends of the single rack just fit over the ends of the bench, to which they are secured by screws. The back should be first taken in hand, as it is the foundation upon which the rest is built. The top shelf is ploughed into this $\frac{1}{8}$ in. deep and is housed into the two ends, which in turn fit into a rebate cut $\frac{1}{4}$ in. deep into the ends of the back (*see* Fig. 90). The bottom shelf, on which the jack plane rests, is housed and screwed into the ends and dovetailed into the

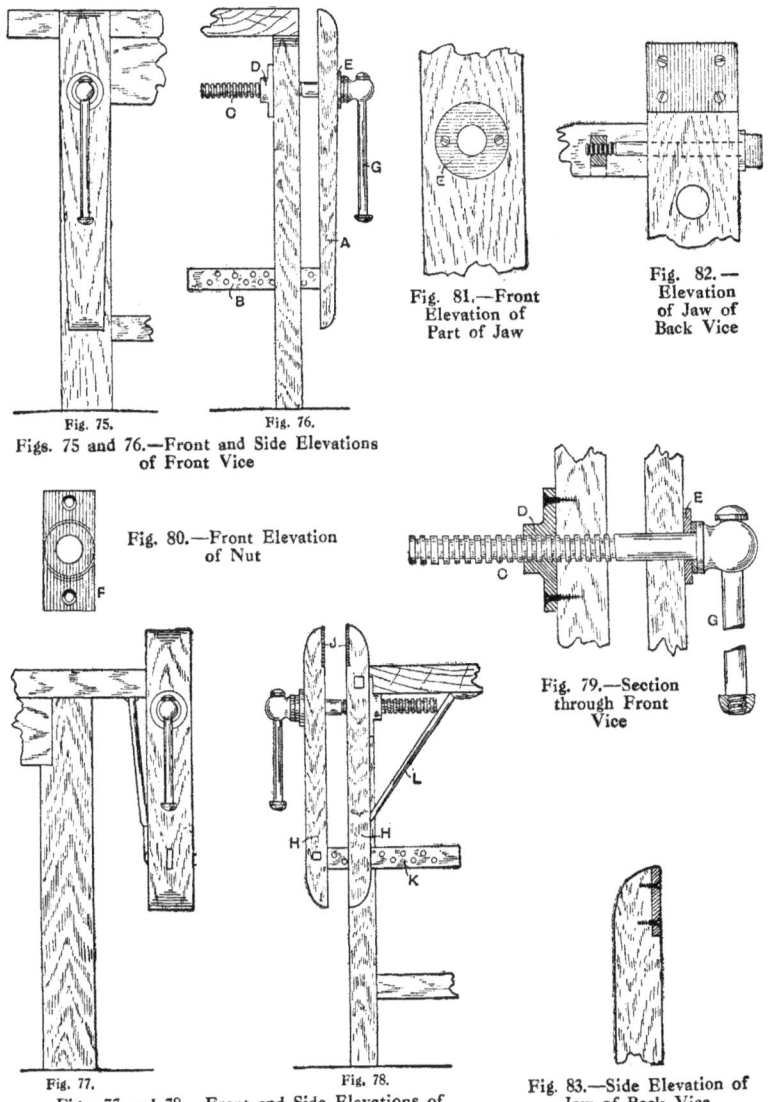

Fig. 75. Fig. 76.
Figs. 75 and 76.—Front and Side Elevations of Front Vice

Fig. 81.—Front Elevation of Part of Jaw

Fig. 82.—Elevation of Jaw of Back Vice

Fig. 80.—Front Elevation of Nut

Fig. 79.—Section through Front Vice

Fig. 77. Fig. 78.
Figs. 77 and 78.—Front and Side Elevations of Back Vice

Fig. 83.—Side Elevation of Jaw of Back Vice

THE PRACTICAL WOODWORKER

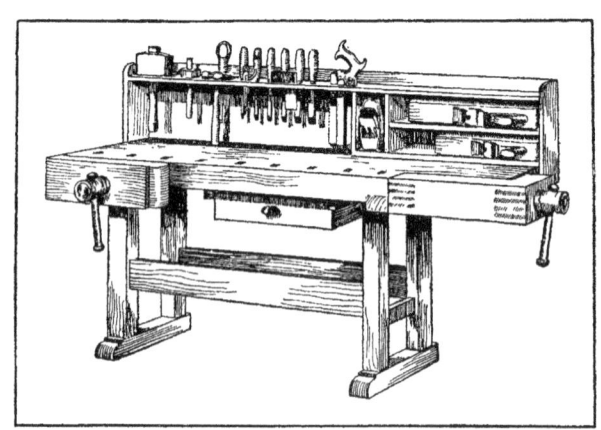

Fig. 84.—Tool Rack for Bench in Position

middle partition. This partition is also housed and screwed into the underside of the top shelf, and fastened to the back with screws. The middle shelf and the inner partition are housed together and are connected in the same way to the other pieces. Provision is made for the marking knife in the inside of the left-hand end, under the shelf, a metal staple being screwed on to receive it, as shown in Fig. 91.

The construction of the double rack is slightly different, as will be seen in Fig. 89. Here the back becomes a division

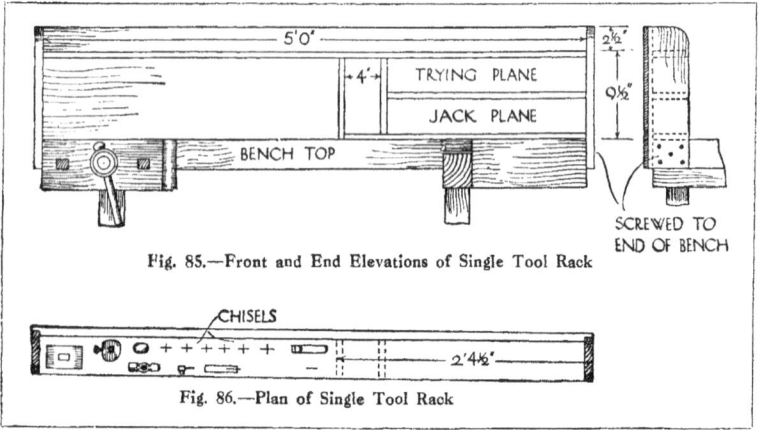

Fig. 85.—Front and End Elevations of Single Tool Rack

Fig. 86.—Plan of Single Tool Rack

WORK BENCHES

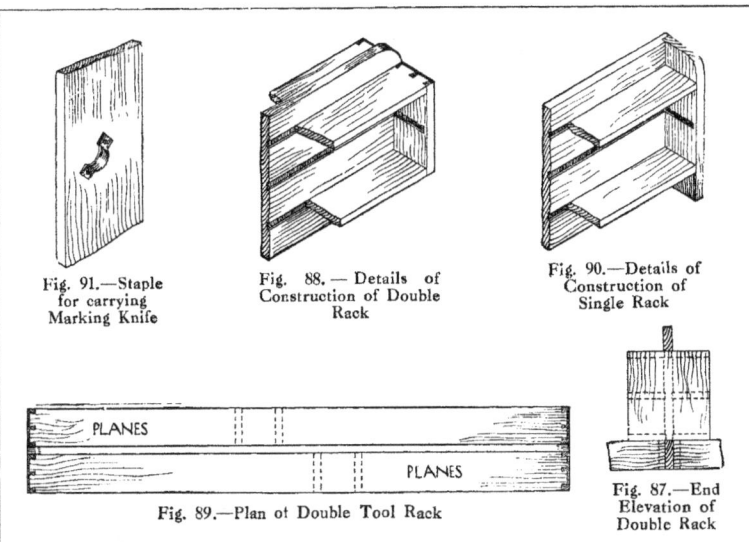

Fig. 91.—Staple for carrying Marking Knife

Fig. 88.—Details of Construction of Double Rack

Fig. 90.—Details of Construction of Single Rack

Fig. 89.—Plan of Double Tool Rack

Fig. 87.—End Elevation of Double Rack

between the racks and goes through from top to bottom and is housed into the ends by means of plough grooves ¼ in. deep. In this case the ends are 8⅞ in. wide, and the top and bottom shelves are lap dovetailed into them (Figs. 87, 88 and 89). Otherwise the construction is the same as for the single rack. It will be seen that the back of the double rack projects down between the backs of the bench wells (*see* Fig. 88). This arrangement enables the rack and the benches to be bolted or screwed together. The rack may be made in yellow deal, pine, or whitewood, and if varnished, it will not only look better but can be kept cleaner.

PORTABLE FLAP BENCH

The portable bench shown ready for use by Fig. 92 and folded by Fig. 93 is very suitable where a bench is required occasionally. Figs. 94 and 95 are front and end elevations of the bench. When the bench is not in use, the screw, screw cheek, and runner can be taken out, the legs folded to the wall, and the top and side folded and let down, as shown in Figs. 93 and 96. The construction is so clearly shown in the illustrations that only the leading points need description.

A simple method of jointing the legs and rails is lap-dovetailing, which is described in an earlier section. The top should be at least 1½ in. thick, and is formed of two boards jointed ; to keep it true, it should be clamped and tenoned. The top should be hinged to the rail A, and the side of the bench hinged to the top as shown at B (Figs. 95 and 96), 3-in. butt hinges being used for this purpose.

The wall-piece C should first be firmly screwed to the rail of the top A. The legs should be hinged at the top to this piece, and also at the bottom to the strip D, which should be sufficiently thick to project from the wall to the thickness of the wall-piece C. The piece D can be attached to the skirting-board with a few screws. The wall-piece C, if against a lath-and-plaster partition, can

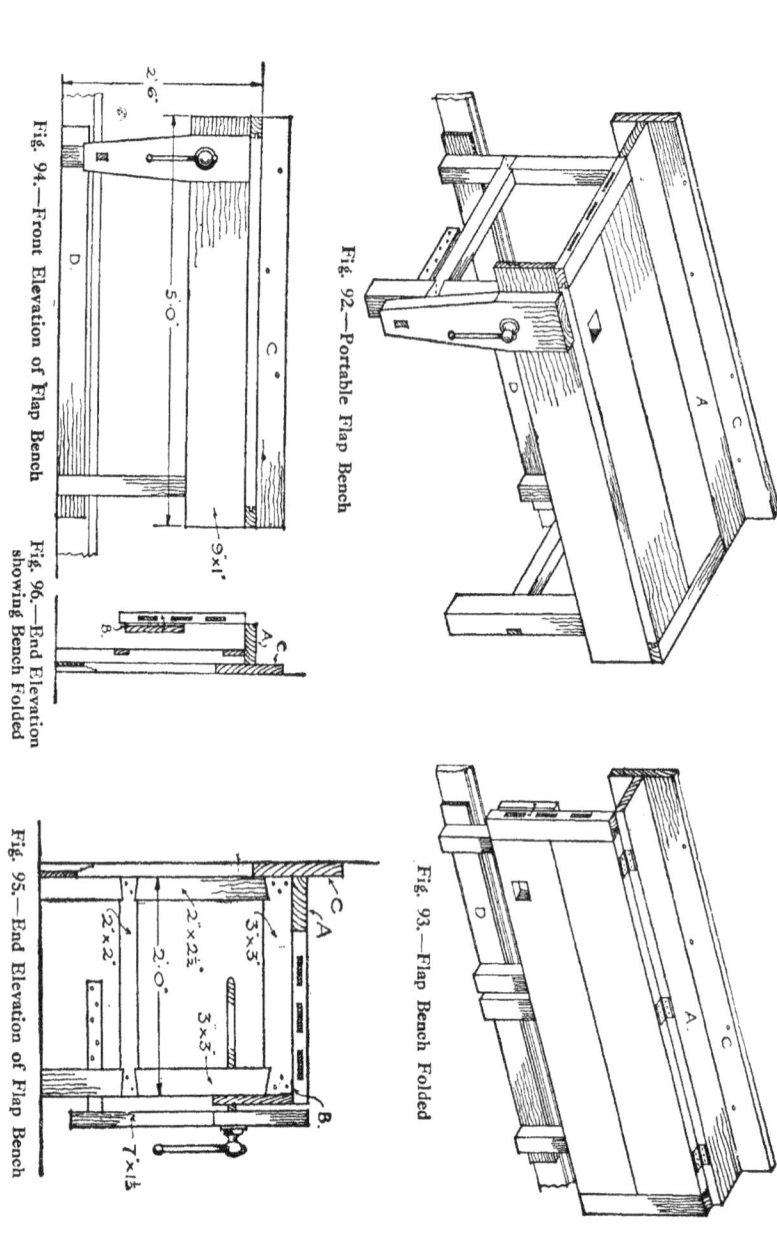

Fig. 92.—Portable Flap Bench

Fig. 93.—Flap Bench Folded

Fig. 94.—Front Elevation of Flap Bench

Fig. 95.—End Elevation of Flap Bench

Fig. 96.—End Elevation showing Bench Folded

WORK BENCHES

be firmly and easily fixed to two or three of the studs of the partition with half a dozen screws. If it is against a brick wall, drill a few holes into the wall and drive in hardwood plugs; or, better still, with a long fine bradawl probe the wall until the joints are found, and then with a steel chisel cut square holes about $\frac{3}{4}$ in. side and about 3 in. or 4 in. deep. These holes may then be fitted with hardwood plugs, into which screws are inserted through the wall-piece.

The fitting up of the screw, cheek, and runner (the last-named being of hardwood) will present no difficulty. The leg to which the screw is attached is of a larger size than the others. The side and top of the bench when folded up can be kept in position by a hook and eye as shown. A convenient form of bench stop will be one of the improved iron stops which require letting in.

This bench may be made additionally firm by inserting a few screws through the side into the legs, and through the top into the rails. To remove the bench, withdraw these screws.

BENCH FOR NAILING PICTURE FRAMES

Cramps are rarely, if ever, used by the professional picture framer, as the method would be too slow and costly. Instead, a special form of bench is used, as shown by Figs. 97 to 105.

On the average framer's bench there is fixed a block of hardwood with one edge shaped a true mitre, as shown at A (Fig. 97). Against this mitred block the first mitred length of moulding is placed with its outer edge lying on the bench. The adjacent length of moulding, which has been previously bored with a bradawl, is held firmly against the mitre of the first length on the bench. The bradawl (a 3-in. pattern-maker's) is inserted into the previously bored hole, and when the mitres are fair and match evenly, the awl is forced into the second moulding about $\frac{1}{4}$ in. to $\frac{1}{2}$ in. as a guide for the nail. The nails are special small round wire ones with very small heads. As a rule, one is sufficient in each corner, but before nailing the mitre is brushed with glue. The glue should not be brushed within $\frac{1}{4}$ in. of the front faces, because in nailing up the surplus glue would be squeezed out over the gilt, making it look unsightly, and wasting time required in cleaning it off. After the two pairs of mitres have been nailed up against the mitre stop A, a loose block B (Fig. 98) is inserted to form a square face or stop, against which the square corner of the frame is supported while the other two sides are joined up.

Sometimes a separate fixed square edge stop block is attached close to the mitred stop block shown in Fig. 97. These two blocks are all that are used by many framers. The method is quite elementary, and considerable care must be exercised to keep the upright piece in line with its fellow while nailing together. Also, it may be noticed, on referring to Fig. 98, that there is a tendency (in theory, at least) while nailing up the third and fourth corners for the brads at C to have a sheering strain placed on them, and at the same time the lower angle of the moulding to have its extreme point bruised against the square stop block. To overcome the first of these difficulties, a vertical fence about 1 ft. 4 in. high, and capable of sliding in or out to suit the varying sizes of frames, has been introduced. By its adoption, if the bottom length of moulding is close to the fence and the vertical pieces resting against the fence also, the operator can be certain that the frame will be nailed up and lie flat when finished. This will also save the trouble of looking to see if each length is being held vertically while joining up the frame.

The fence is shown in use in two positions in Figs. 97 and 98; an end view is given in Fig. 99, and the plan is shown by Fig. 100. The block is locked in the desired position by either a winged nut or, for speed, an eccentric lever acting on the T-shaped bolt in the groove formed in the bench. A guide fillet is also attached to the fence, and slides in the groove. The fillet is shown by dotted

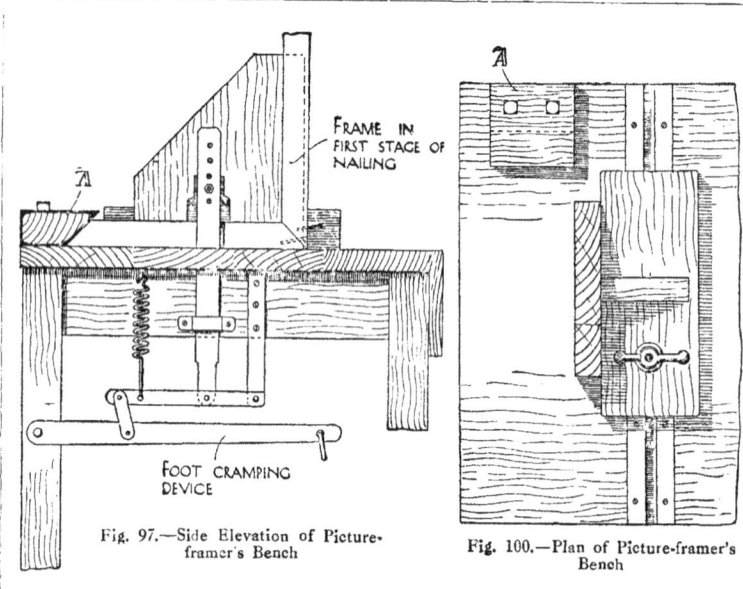

Fig. 97.—Side Elevation of Picture-framer's Bench

Fig. 100.—Plan of Picture-framer's Bench

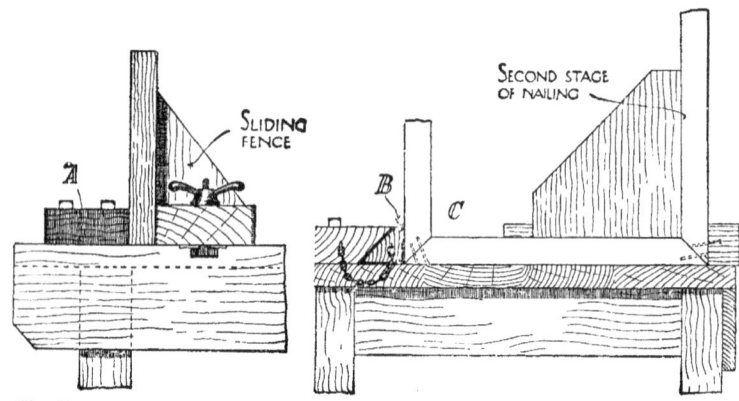

Fig. 99.—End Elevation of Sliding Fence

Fig. 98.—Showing Picture Frame in Second Position for Nailing

WORK BENCHES

lines in Fig. 100. By the adoption of the vertical cramping bar actuated by a foot lever, much of the strain of hammering is taken off the stop blocks, and the partial section is given in Fig. 101. The foot lever engages in a fine-toothed rack similar to the brake handle on horse-drawn vehicles; thus the foot is relieved from

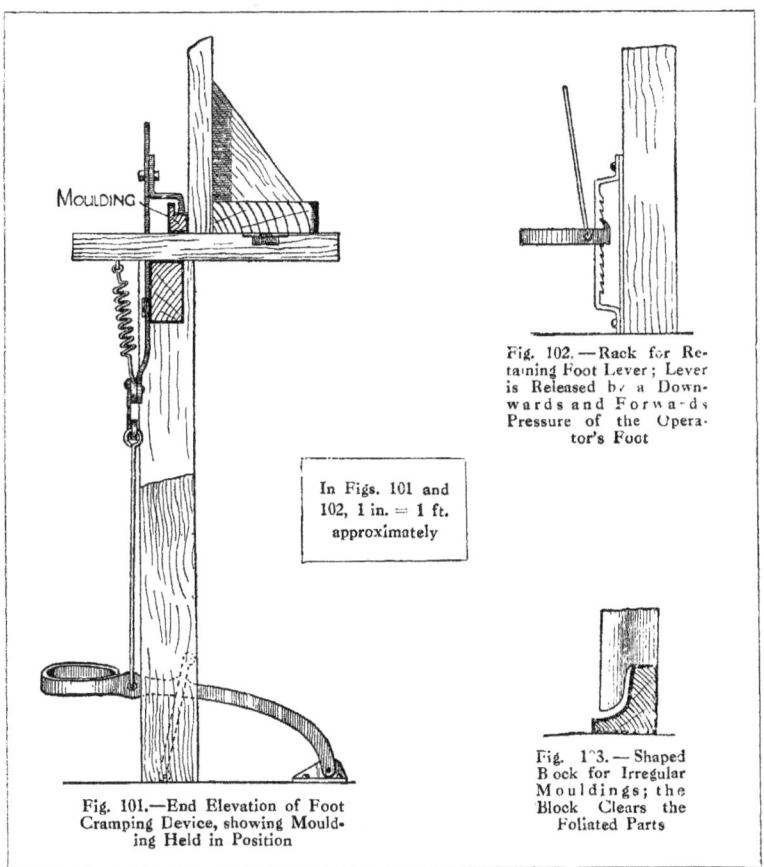

Fig. 102.—Rack for Retaining Foot Lever; Lever is Released by a Downwards and Forwards Pressure of the Operator's Foot

In Figs. 101 and 102, 1 in. = 1 ft. approximately

Fig. 103.—Shaped Block for Irregular Mouldings; the Block Clears the Foliated Parts

Fig. 101.—End Elevation of Foot Cramping Device, showing Moulding Held in Position

danger of damage or sheering previously mentioned is greatly minimised.

A side view of the clamping arrangement with its adjustable clamping grip and helical spring for quick lift or release is shown in Fig. 97. The end view in pressure as long as desired. To release, it is only necessary to press down and also towards the post or away from the rack (see Fig. 102), when the spring will cause the whole arrangement to rise up quickly. The iron work in connection with the foot cramping gear is simple to make, and is within the capabilities of any blacksmith.

When dealing with fancy-edge moulding, by $\frac{3}{4}$ in. deep to receive the head of the T-bolt. On each side of the centre groove, rebates are formed to receive the $\frac{3}{16}$-in. by $1\frac{1}{4}$-in. strips of metal attached

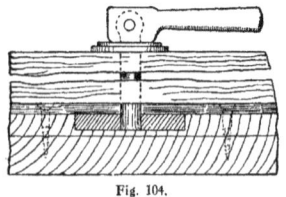
Fig. 104.

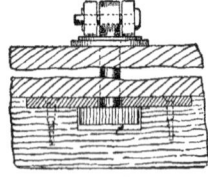
Fig. 105.

Figs. 104 and 105.—Two Elevations showing Details of Cramping Lever and Bolt of Picture-framer's Bench

it will be necessary to make parallel blocks of wood to suit the shape of the particular moulding. Fig. 103 shows a block suitable for florentine moulding. The block clears the outer foliated part, and supports the inner plain edges only.

Details of the T-groove for the sliding fence are shown in Figs. 104 and 105. The bench is grooved about $1\frac{1}{4}$ in. wide to the bench with stout countersunk screws. A quick clamping action is effected by the eccentric lever shown in Fig. 105. When the handle is in a vertical position, it lifts the T-bolt tightly against the metal plates, because of the eccentricity of the pin in the lever. Adjustment is made by inserting washers of varying thickness until the right tension is obtained.

Garden Carpentry

SEED DRILLS

A HOE is commonly used to make the drills for seeds, but the correct implement is a seed drill as shown by Figs. 1 and 2.

It consists of a block of wood, into which It is chamfered at the back as shown, and is rounded at the top and pointed at its lower end. Fig. 3 gives a separate inside view of the head, showing how it can be marked to get the varying depths for

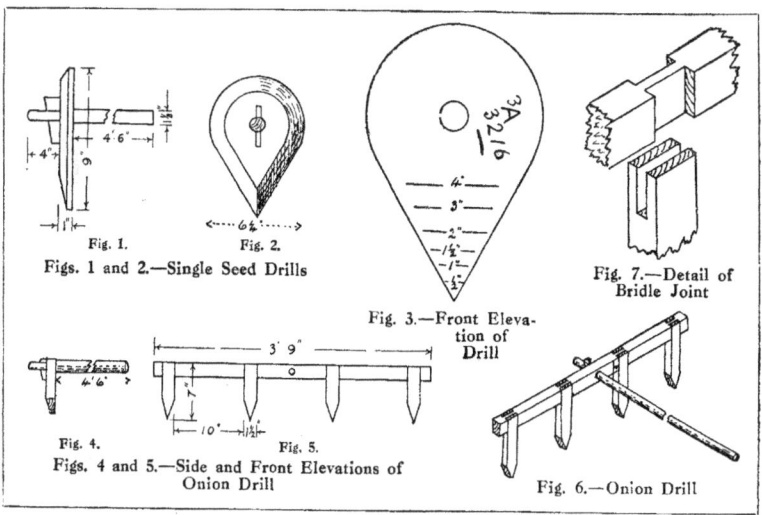

Fig. 1.
Fig. 2.
Figs. 1 and 2.—Single Seed Drills

Fig. 3.—Front Elevation of Drill

Fig. 7.—Detail of Bridle Joint

Fig. 4.
Fig. 5.
Figs. 4 and 5.—Side and Front Elevations of Onion Drill

Fig. 6.—Onion Drill

is mortised a long shaft. The shaft is made, preferably, out of a hayfork shaft, which, being of ash or hickory, is strong and pliant, and capable of withstanding hard blows and shocks. The block of wood is made of birch, ash, oak, or sycamore. seeds. The joint is a round mortise. The shaft is shouldered, as shown in Fig. 1, and a wedge is driven in at the back.

Figs. 4, 5, 6 and 7 show a drill for onion seeds which require parallel rows. The shaft again is best made from a hayfork

THE PRACTICAL WOODWORKER

shaft or a piece of ash, and is fixed to the cross-piece in the same way as for the drill. The teeth or drills are fixed to the cross-piece by means of a bridle joint, shown by Fig. 7. All these joints can be glued if the drill is afterwards to be painted or the ground when planting out young seedlings.

Figs. 8 and 9 give front and side elevations of a dibber made from the broken shaft of a spade. The measurements are given. If a broken shaft is not available

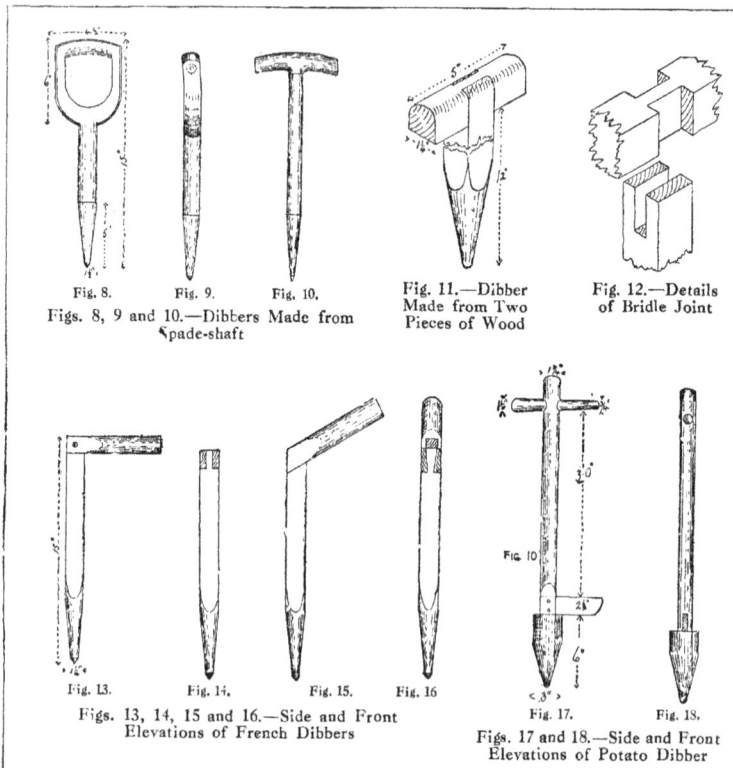

Fig. 8.   Fig. 9.   Fig. 10.
Figs. 8, 9 and 10.—Dibbers Made from Spade-shaft

Fig. 11.—Dibber Made from Two Pieces of Wood

Fig. 12.—Details of Bridle Joint

Fig. 13.   Fig. 14.   Fig. 15.   Fig. 16
Figs. 13, 14, 15 and 16.—Side and Front Elevations of French Dibbers

Fig. 17.   Fig. 18.
Figs. 17 and 18.—Side and Front Elevations of Potato Dibber

varnished, but if not it is better to use white-lead paint in the joint and to fasten with oak pins.

GARDEN DIBBERS

These are sometimes known as dibbles. They are used for making the hole in then a piece of birch, ash, beech, or sycamore can be used to make one similar. Some gardeners point the dibber with sheet iron or other metal, to prevent the point becoming worn, or rotted by alternating damp and dryness. A spade handle of the type shown in Fig. 10 is also very suitable. A dibber made from

GARDEN CARPENTRY

material whose section is 1¼ in. by 1¼ in. finished size is shown by Fig. 11. The joint between the handle and the shaft is sometimes driven into the end to prevent undue wearing, although this rusts, and in time causes rotting of the wood. The

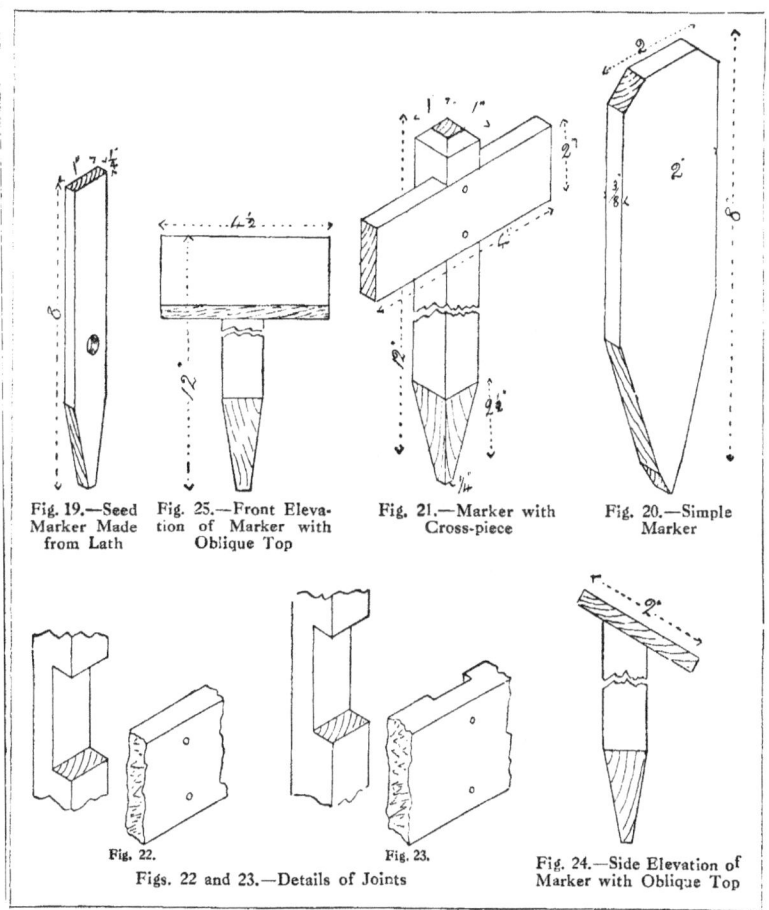

Fig. 19.—Seed Marker Made from Lath

Fig. 25.—Front Elevation of Marker with Oblique Top

Fig. 21.—Marker with Cross-piece

Fig. 20.—Simple Marker

Fig. 22.

Fig. 23.

Figs. 22 and 23.—Details of Joints

Fig. 24.—Side Elevation of Marker with Oblique Top

is known as a bridle joint, and is shown separately by Fig. 12. The pointed portion is rounded and tapered. It is better not to taper it to a point, but to let the end be about ¼ in. A boot hobnail joint should be fixed with white-lead, and not glue. The top of the handle is rounded to fit the hand.

A better form of dibber is shown by Figs. 13 and 14. The handle only extends on one side of the shaft, and enables the whole hand to grasp it. It also is rounded in both shaft and handle. The joint is a dovetailed bridle joint. Figs. 15 and 16 show a still better form. This is similar to Fig. 13, but it has its handle fixed to the shaft at an obtuse angle. This enables the handle to be grasped more easily, as will be realised when a dibber like this is once used. An angle bridle or an angle dovetail bridle may be used as the joint, as in Figs. 14 and 16.

It is not necessary that these dibbers should be short, so that too much back bending is induced. They may have longer shafts, long enough to make the holes without stooping too far. Figs. 17 and 18 give views of a potato dibber such as is often used to plant potatoes. The base is made out to about 3 in. in diameter, and the shaft is about $1\frac{3}{4}$ in. It is long enough to work without stooping, and the side step is for resting the foot on to drive the dibber into the soil, and at the same time guide its distance into the ground to get the correct depth for the potato. To make it, paint and screw to a central shaft four pieces of $\frac{3}{4}$-in. stuff to make the lower end thicker. Then round both the shaft and head, and point the head. Bore a hole near the top of the shaft to receive the handle. Mortise, before rounding, the foot-rest into the shaft, and paint and screw tightly.

SEED MARKERS

Often a piece of stick, a piece of broken plaster lath, or a twig is used for marking the resting-place of seeds. A little time spent in making some presentable seed markers is well worth while, and these, with care and a little attention, will last for more than one season.

Fig. 19 shows a seed marker that is only a slip of wood, but it has a little handicraft in it. Seed markers like this can be made from prepared trellis laths. They are cut to length, and pointed with a chisel, and the top end pared end-grainwise with a chisel also. Do not cut the point dead sharp, but leave it about $\frac{1}{8}$ in. or $\frac{3}{16}$ in. wide. A hole drilled through each with a centre bit will enable them to be tied together and hung up when not in use. Fig. 20 shows a wider marker. This is thicker too, and enables more particulars regarding the plant to be placed on it. It is planed up, set out, and then cut by means of a chisel.

Fig. 21 shows a seed marker that is made of two pieces of wood. The joint between the two can be a housed joint, as shown by Fig. 22, or a half-lap, as shown by Fig. 23 ; in the latter case wood is taken out of each piece. The cross-piece is screwed to the upright, after well painting the joint. The upright can be any length, and to prevent undue stooping a length of about 2 ft. would be very convenient.

Another type is that shown by Figs. 24 and 25. This is to meet the need spoken of already. The board is fixed at an angle to the upright, so that the name may be presented at right angles to the line of vision. It is not necessary to do more than nail the name-board to the upright, painting the joint first to prevent as far as possible decay due to weather. All the boards can be made to any shape desirable.

All the markers should be painted with a thin coat of white or light-coloured paint. This keeps them from perishing too soon by alternate dry and wet, and also enables the name of the seed to be written on them more easily.

Strips of tin can be used as cross-pieces instead of wood. Painted black and lettered white, they are quite good. It is well to "tin" the cut edges of the tinplate to prevent the rusting of the mild steel which forms the base of the tinplate.

SEED GUARD

A most useful guard for seeds and young plants, which are often destroyed by birds when left without any protection, is shown by Fig. 26. The guard consists of two wood ends fixed in the desired position with stakes, the guard being formed with twine wound round the heads of nails which are driven into the edges of the wood ends at frequent intervals. The ends for the guard are shown in Figs. 27

GARDEN CARPENTRY

and 28. They are cut to the dimensions given in Fig. 28, from wood ¾ in. or 1 in. thick, and two stakes are nailed across

Wood from old boxes and packing-cases could be used very largely in constructing these pieces of garden equipment.

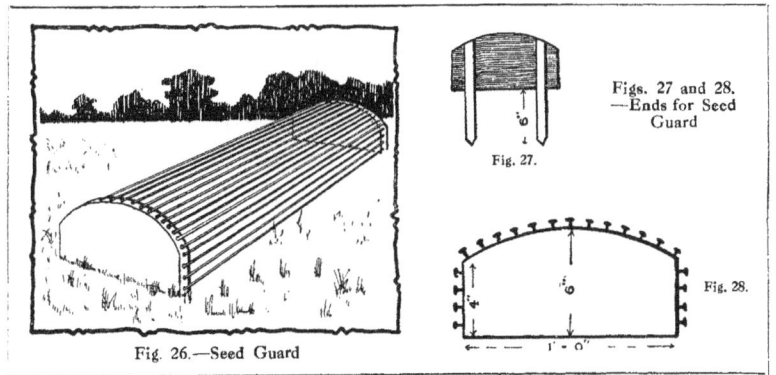

Fig. 26.—Seed Guard

Fig. 27.

Figs. 27 and 28.—Ends for Seed Guard

Fig. 28.

each end, the stakes being about 1½ in. wide and pointed at the ends. Nails are

Too much attention cannot be paid to painting any of the objects described,

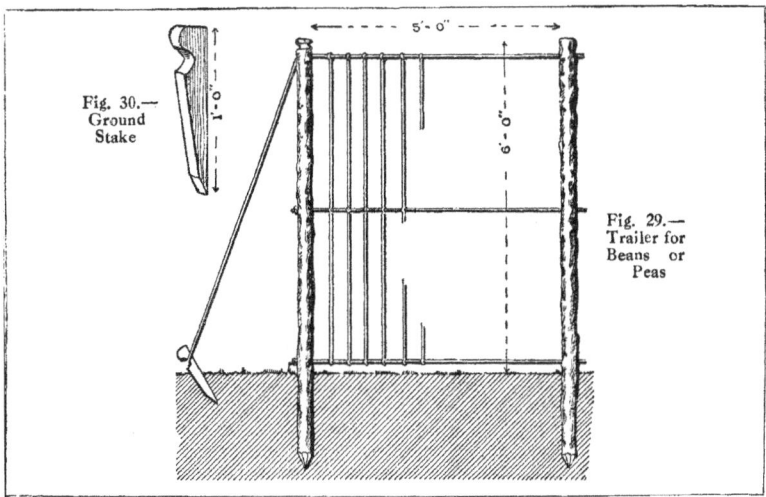

Fig. 30.—Ground Stake

Fig. 29.—Trailer for Beans or Peas

driven into the edges of the ends at frequent intervals, as shown in Fig. 28, and the guard string wound round the nails.

and special care should be taken to see that all the joints are well painted before fixing.

TRAILER

A trailer for beans and peas is shown by Fig. 29, and with the aid of this trailer the usual bean and pea sticks can be dispensed with; when once made it will last for years. It consists of wood poles driven into the ground at intervals. Fairly stout wires are fitted across the top, in the middle, and at the bottom of the poles, these wires being connected by other upright wires or strings up which the beans and peas climb. The end poles are secured with stays and stakes as shown.

The poles for the trailer should be 8 ft. long by 2½ in. or 3 in. in section, driven

Fig. 31.—Garden Tool-box

into the ground about 2 ft. The horizontal wires fit through holes in the poles, and are knotted or twisted to keep them in place. The top wire could be continued to the ground, and fixed with a stake as shown in Fig. 29. Side stays of wire should also be arranged between the tops of the end posts and the ground, being secured with wood stakes. A suitable wood stake is shown by Fig. 30. The upright wires or strings should be arranged at intervals of 3 in., being twisted or tied to the horizontal wires.

GARDEN TOOL-BOX

A tool-box is a great convenience in a garden, and even the most enthusiastic gardener will welcome the seat formed by the top of the tool-box. The tool-box and seat shown by Fig. 31 is of fairly simple construction, and considering its usefulness the cost is trifling. Figs. 32, 33, and 34 show elevation, end view and plan.

It is proposed that ordinary deal should be used, the boards being grooved and tongued together; but there is no reason why any ordinary boards which one may have on hand should not be used if desired. Suitable dimensions are given in the illustrations, but they may be altered as desired, as the size to which the box is made will depend on the size and number of tools which it is intended to hold. It will be noticed that the ends of the box are sunk into the ground, but this is optional, the object being to prevent the box being moved.

There are two ends made, as shown by Fig. 36, consisting of boards cut 2 ft. 5 in. long, and made up to 1 ft. 6 in. wide. The boards are held together with battens A and B, which are 1 ft. 3 in. long by 3 in. deep by 1 in. thick, nailed on the inside in the positions shown. A batten 1 ft. 6 in. long by 2 in. deep by 1 in. thick is also nailed across the bottom edge on the outside of each end. The ends are connected by four rails C (see Fig. 35), which are 3 in. deep by 1 in. thick in section. These rails are framed into the ends in the positions shown, the inner faces being kept tight against the ends of the battens A and B, so that the outer faces will stand ½ in. in from the edges of the ends. It will be best to tenon the rails C into the ends, and a joint, as shown in Fig. 37, may be used, whilst mortises are cut in the ends, as shown in Fig. 36. To strengthen the joints between the rails and the ends, angle-plates could be fitted in the corners, as shown in Figs. 35 and 38. The plates could be of iron 3 in. wide by $\tfrac{1}{16}$ in. thick, and may be about 3 in. long each way, each being fixed with four screws.

The bottom may be covered with ½-in.

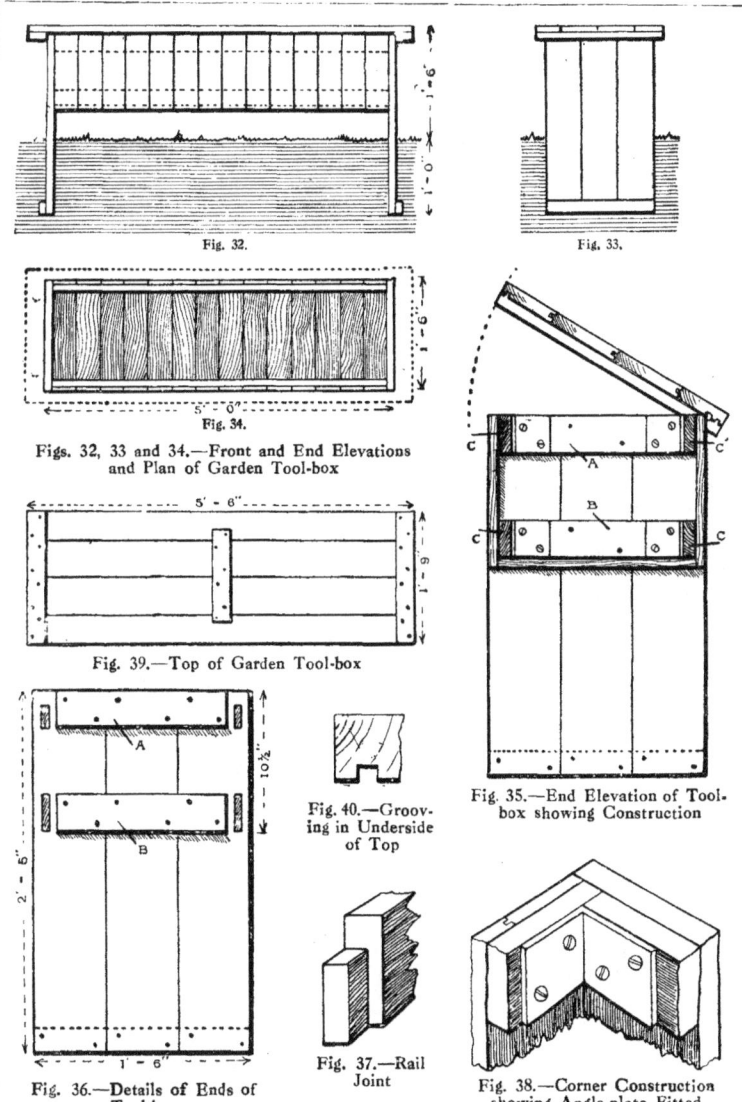

Fig. 32.

Fig. 33.

Fig. 34.

Figs. 32, 33 and 34.—Front and End Elevations and Plan of Garden Tool-box

Fig. 39.—Top of Garden Tool-box

Fig. 40.—Grooving in Underside of Top

Fig. 35.—End Elevation of Tool-box showing Construction

Fig. 36.—Details of Ends of Tool box

Fig. 37.—Rail Joint

Fig. 38.—Corner Construction showing Angle-plate Fitted

grooved-and-tongued matchboards, fixed with the joints running from front to back, as shown in Fig. 34, and nailed to the bottom rails C. The front and back of the box may be covered with similar boards nailed to the faces of the rails C, as shown

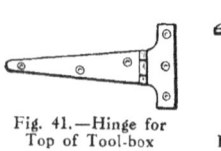

Fig. 41.—Hinge for Top of Tool-box

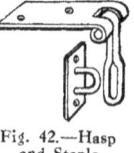

Fig. 42.—Hasp and Staple

in Figs. 32 and 35. The cover of the box should be formed from 1-in. grooved-and-tongued matchboarding, and should be made to overhang 3 in. at the ends and 1½ in. at the front and back (Fig. 39). If small grooves are cut along the front and back edges of the underneath side of the cover, as shown in Fig. 40, this will prevent water from running back under the cover. The cover is held together with battens 3 in. by 1 in. in section, two being fixed across the ends and one in the middle, the latter being cut so that it will fit between the sides of the box. The cover is hinged at the back with a pair of T-hinges similar to that shown by Fig. 41, and for fastening the cover a hasp and staple similar to that shown by Fig. 42, which may be secured with a padlock, will be very suitable. To make the cover quite watertight it will be well to cover it with a piece of canvas tacked round the edges, and well painted underneath.

In fixing the seat, the earth must be removed so that the ends may be sunk into the ground. The portions sunk into the ground should be tarred or coated with thick paint, and when the seat has been set level the earth should be well rammed in. Some would, perhaps, prefer to set the ends in concrete. It is needless to add that the tool-box and seat would be improved by an annual coating of paint, the first coat consisting of red lead, oil and a large proportion of turpentine, the later coats containing white lead, boiled oil and less turpentine.

COMBINED GARDEN SEAT AND TOOL-BOX

A seat which also provides a lock-up for tools is shown in part front elevation, end elevation and part plans by Figs. 43, 44 and 45.

The carcass should preferably be made from 1-in. tongued-and-grooved flooring but any odd timber or packing-cases which may be available could be utilised The height, length, and width, inside should be decided by the space required for the spade, rake, hoes, fork, waterpot etc., which have to be accommodated The dimensions given will probably be found suitable for average needs. The timber should be cut to size, and given a coat of priming before assembly. The boards forming the sides and the ends should be arranged with the tongues uppermost and grooves beneath, so as to prevent the entry of any moisture. The joints should "break" at the corners which should be grooved as shown, and the sides secured to the ends with 3-in cut nails driven askew. The bottom should be secured with 2½-in. No. 10 screws.

When assembling, give each joint a coat of white-lead and red-lead in boiled oil and any cracks or defective joints should be stopped with the same mixture stiffened with putty. The underside of the bottom the cross-bearers of quartering, the foot rest laths, and the buried portion of the ground stakes should be treated with two coats of carbolineum or creosote.

The top, or seat, should be of good sound stuff 1¼ in. thick, with tongued-and grooved joints well leaded as above described, and braced with three battens screwed on the inner side. The front edge should have a nosing deep enough to carry off any water. The arm supports serve to stiffen the seat and support the back, the rails of which are of flooring with front edges rounded. They are screwed to uprights of 2-in. by 1½-in stuff tenoned into the lid, the centre one being also bracketed at the back. The arms themselves need not necessarily be more than about 3 in. wide.

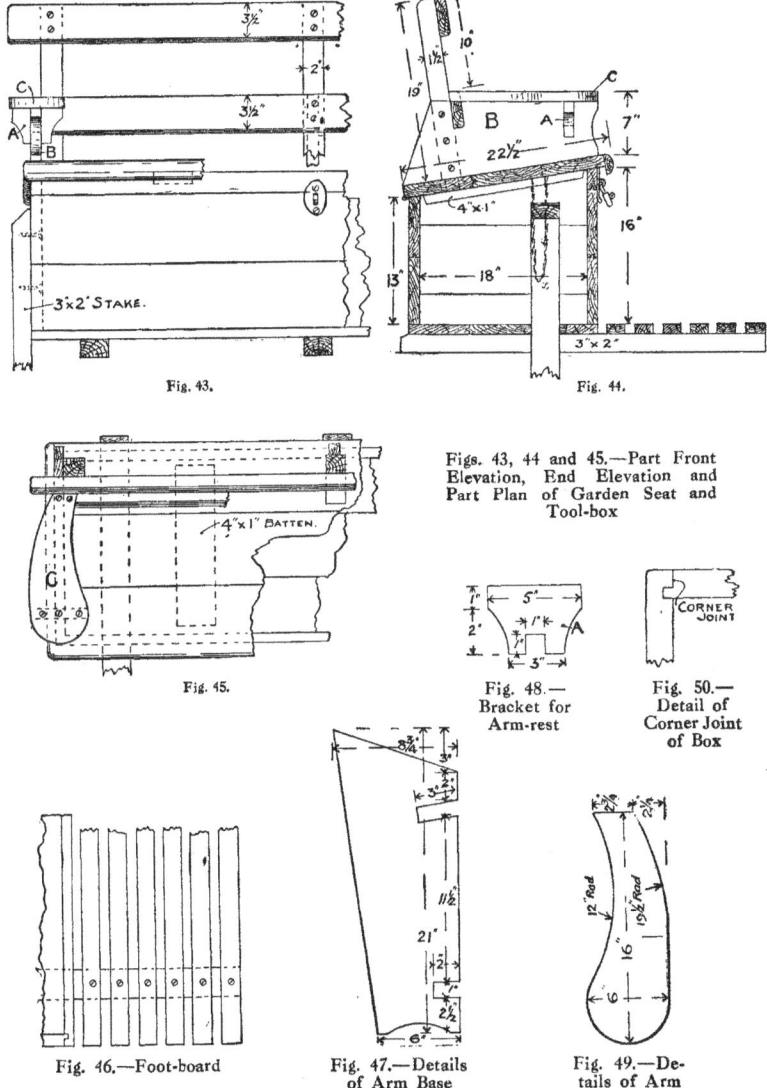

Fig. 43.

Fig. 44.

Figs. 43, 44 and 45.—Part Front Elevation, End Elevation and Part Plan of Garden Seat and Tool-box

Fig. 45.

Fig. 48.—Bracket for Arm-rest

Fig. 50.—Detail of Corner Joint of Box

Fig. 46.—Foot-board

Fig. 47.—Details of Arm Base

Fig. 49.—Details of Arm

The hinges, of the box type, must be set back to allow the seat to overhang about ½ in. The top can be fastened with a stout staple padlock and hasp, and prevented from falling back when opened by a suitable length of chain or sash-cord, attached as shown in Fig. 44. Details of the joints, etc., are shown in Figs. 47 to 50. Fig. 47 gives the dimensions for base of the arms; Fig. 48 is the supporting bracket for the arm-rest; Fig. 49 and Fig. 50 is the corner joint of the tool-box. The construction of the foot-board is shown in Fig. 46.

Unauthorised removal is prevented by stout stakes driven into the ground, one at each end of the box, which is screwed to them from inside. The entire seat and box should, when completed, be given three coats of good oil paint, the last one being improved by the addition of a little copal varnish well mixed in.

GARDEN SEAT WITH CANOPY

The seat shown by Fig. 51 folds into small compass when not in use, and is very light. It has a canvas canopy, which, besides being useful in a strong sun, also acts as a draught screen. Figs 52 and 53 show an elevation and section of the seat respectively, and also give the principal dimensions to which it may be made, while Figs. 54 to 57 show details of the construction. In making the seat, first prepare a full-size section (Fig. 53).

The legs A (Fig. 53) are 6 ft. 9 in. long, and the legs B are 6 ft. long, each being 1½ in. wide by 1 in. thick. The top cross rails C, which connect the top ends of each pair of legs, are 3 in. by ¾ in. in section, and the bottom cross rails D are 2 in. by ¾ in These cross rails are screwed in

Fig. 51.—Garden Seat with Canopy

position, the top rails being level with the top ends of the legs, while the bottom rails are fixed 2 in. up from the bottom ends Each pair of legs is kept rigid by fixing two diagonal rails E to them, as shown in Figs. 51 and 52. These rails are 1¼ in by ½ in. in section, and are fixed with screws. Fig. 54 shows the method by which the legs are hinged together. A ⅜-in. rivet passes through the legs, iron washers are fitted under the heads of the rivet, and a ¼-in. washer is placed between the legs. The legs are hinged so that when opened out they correspond with the dimensions given in Fig. 53. A rule joint G is used for keeping the legs in position when open, and this is made from two pieces of ⅜-in. by ⅛-in. mild steel, riveted in the centre and screwed to each leg (Fig. 53).

The back rails F are 1½ in. by 1 in. in section, and they are hinged at the top to the legs B with rivets as shown in Fig. 55 A block J, which is 6 in. long by 1½ in wide by 1¼ in. thick is screwed to the top end of the legs, and a ¼-in. washer is placed between each block and the back rail. The seat rails K, which are three in number, are 1½ in. deep by 1 in. wide, and are shaped as shown in Fig. 53. The end seat rails are hinged to the back rails H, while the middle seat rail is hinged to the middle back rail L (see Fig. 52), which should be of a similar section as the rails H.

Two bolts similar to that shown in Figs. 56 and 57 are fitted to the end seat rails, and these slide in the slot rails M The bolts are ½ in. in diameter; a ¼-in washer is fitted in the centre, while the square portion which fits into the seat rail is ⅜ in. square, and the end is screwed and fitted with a nut and washer for fastening

GARDEN CARPENTRY

purposes. The slot rails M are 1½ in. by 1 in. at the ends, and are shaped out where the slot is cut to 1 in. square. The rails should be long enough to allow the seat to fold, and they are fixed to the legs B with screws at each end. The seat battens are eight in number, and the five back battens, which are each 2 in. wide by ¾ in. thick, are fixed in position with screws.

The canopy covering should be of a light striped tent duck. For the back, top, and overhanging portion at the front two widths of material will no doubt have to be employed. The shaped sides are cut, and the whole is strongly sewn together round the edges, and ornamented with lace.

SEAT ROUND A TREE

There is no more desirable position for a seat in the open air than under the spreading foliage of a large tree. The drawings (Figs. 58 to 62) show a simple method of fitting up a suitable bench with the minimum of labour. The sizes must depend entirely on the tree it is intended to encircle, and the dimensions given varied accordingly; but the principle involved will remain exactly the same.

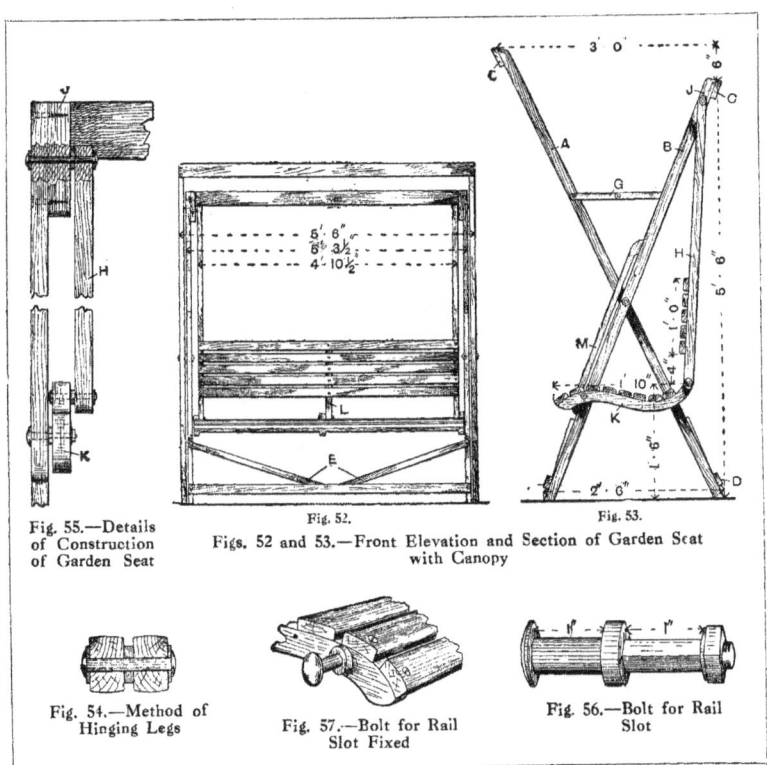

Fig. 55.—Details of Construction of Garden Seat

Fig. 52.

Fig. 53.

Figs. 52 and 53.—Front Elevation and Section of Garden Seat with Canopy

Fig. 54.—Method of Hinging Legs

Fig. 57.—Bolt for Rail Slot Fixed

Fig. 56.—Bolt for Rail Slot

First of all the surface immediately round the base of the trunk should be made up approximately level, and a number of uprights bedded firmly in the ground by means of long tarred ends. (Fig. 61). They need to stand about 14 in. or 15 in. high, and may be of any reasonable size from 2 in. by 2 in. upwards, or unwrought sections of stout branches might be employed. They are set out, avoiding any roots, in the positions indicated by the eight small squares marked with crosses in Fig. 60, and carefully arranged in order to see that proper alignment is secured, and that all the tops are as nearly as practicable dead level.

Horizontal bearers as A, B, C, and D in the same figure, two of which are 5 ft. 9 in. and the other two 2 ft. 10 in. long, and each about 2 in. by 1½ in., with ends rounded or splayed, as in Fig. 62, are then spiked strongly down to the uprights, and will afford a level surface on which to nail a series of battens, say 1½ in. by ¾ in. or thereabouts, spaced out with not more than ⅛-in. intervals between. These battens should be rounded or at least chamfered along their upper edges, and nailed once only over each bearer. They should be cut to fit as closely as possible to the outline of the tree where they butt against it, and the outer ends had better be left a little longer than necessary, and sawn off to the exact outline after the whole series has been fixed in position. It is wise to make such seats very slightly sloping inwards for comfort and drainage purposes.

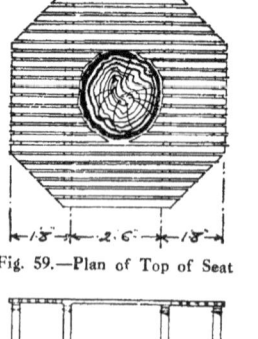

Fig. 58.—Seat Round Tree

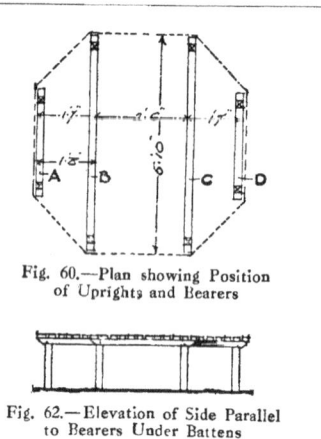

Fig. 59.—Plan of Top of Seat

Fig. 60.—Plan showing Position of Uprights and Bearers

Fig. 61.—Elevation of Side Parallel to Top Battens

Fig. 62.—Elevation of Side Parallel to Bearers Under Battens

GARDEN SEAT OF MODERN DESIGN

A substantially constructed seat, quite modern in style and calculated to stand any amount of exposure to the weather, is shown in the perspective sketch Fig. 63. It would look extremely well painted white, or it could have some more serviceable finish. A width of 5 ft. between the arms as drawn will probably be sufficient; but this might be increased if desired, provided that a central support is added. With reference to any simplification in the work the stuff used might be a trifle lighter in section, although the design depends for success largely on the use of fairly large parts; but the four shaped uprights shown in the sketch might be kept plain, and the turning to the front legs could be omitted. The seat also, instead of being made up all in one piece, could be composed of narrow battens with rounded edges and spaces between.

The seat consists of four vertical legs each $2\frac{3}{4}$ in. square, shown at the outer corners of the half-plans in Figs. 66 and 67. The back legs are each 3 ft. 8 in. long, and shaped to a slightly segmental outline at the head, while the front ones are 1 ft. $11\frac{1}{4}$ in., with $1\frac{1}{2}$ in. extra for a tenon as dotted at A (Fig. 69), where a length of $4\frac{1}{2}$ in. is shown round-turned to a quaint stumpy outline. Each front leg is connected to the one behind by a $2\frac{3}{4}$-in. square rail as at B (Fig. 65) 3 in. above the ground, showing 1 ft. 3 in. long, tenoned and secured with oak pegs at the ends, as are all the joints in the job. A central rail is similarly fixed between these short ones from one end to the other C (Fig. 64)

Fig. 63.—Garden Seat of Modern Design

and D (Fig. 66), and might be $2\frac{3}{4}$ in. by only $1\frac{1}{2}$ in. wide. With its bottom edge 1 ft. $\frac{1}{4}$ in. up from the ground, another $2\frac{3}{4}$-in. rail is tenoned between the short legs to take the front of the seat, and at the back another splayed off as at E (Fig. 69) is tenoned in place $\frac{1}{2}$ in. below the front one. At the ends, short rails are fixed connecting the two, and consequently sloping downwards slightly towards the back. Mortised for the front, leg and tenoned into the back, the arm is square except for a cut outline to the front as in Fig. 69, and is intended to be fixed horizontally, not parallel to the sloping

THE PRACTICAL WOODWORKER

seat, to take which latter four transverse bearers are fixed from front to back, their ends being dotted under the seat in Fig. 64.

The seat itself can be ¾ in. thick, composed of two or three pieces crosstongued together, and having projecting seat, which can then shift slightly without risk of splitting.

The framing of the back is of a lighter character than the rest of the work, and will be observed to slope back as much as possible within the limits of the 2¾-in. end posts. It is all 1¼ in. thick, and com-

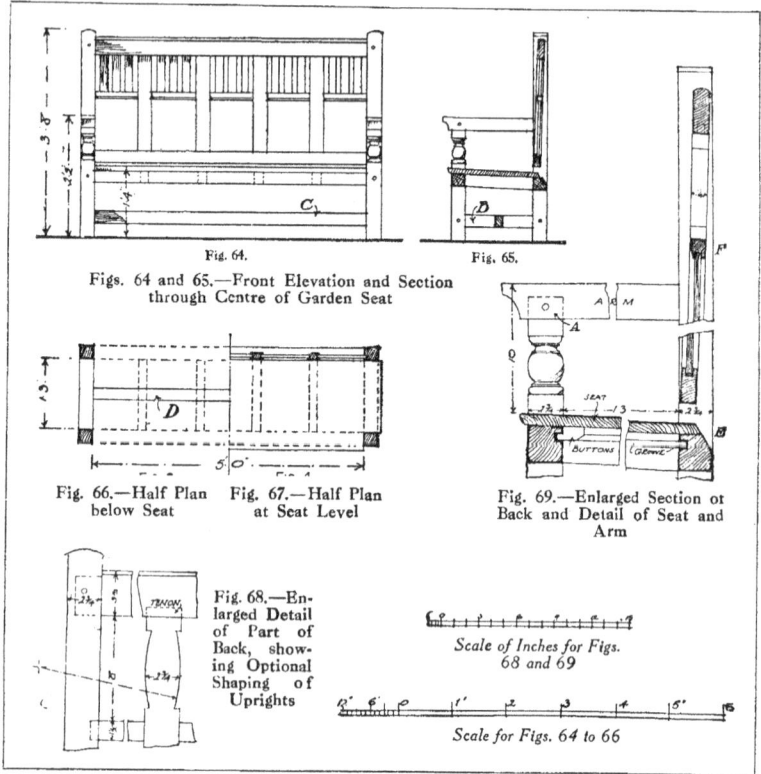

Figs. 64 and 65.—Front Elevation and Section through Centre of Garden Seat

Fig. 66.—Half Plan below Seat

Fig. 67.—Half Plan at Seat Level

Fig. 69.—Enlarged Section of Back and Detail of Seat and Arm

Fig. 68.—Enlarged Detail of Part of Back, showing Optional Shaping of Uprights

Scale of Inches for Figs. 68 and 69

Scale for Figs. 64 to 66

rounded edges except at the back, which can be splayed, as at E in Fig. 69. The seat should not be fixed direct to any of the supports; but the outside bearers should be grooved and arranged with loose wood "buttons," as in Fig. 69, fixed 6 in. or so apart and screwed to the prises a 3½-in. top rail with rounded upper edges, 2¾-in. bottom rail to be fixed about 1½ in. above the seat, and four intermediates 2¾ in. wide, their tops either plain or cut to the simple outline indicated, the curve of which is part of a circle of 11¼-in. radius (Fig. 68). These parts will

GARDEN CARPENTRY

all be tenoned together and to the end posts and filled in with five oak panels fitting in grooves previously prepared, and finished on top with strips of grooved moulding $1\frac{1}{2}$ in. high as at F (Fig. 69), the front being very flatly moulded, because any pronounced projection would be annoying to those leaning against it. Between the rail just mentioned and the top is a space of 8 in., which is intended to be filled in with thin strips $1\frac{1}{2}$ in. or more in width, leaving open spaces between.

It will be well to take the actual sharp arris off all exposed angles of the work, and no glue should be used for joinery required to stand in the open, white-lead being more suitable, if something additional to the pegged joints already mentioned is desired.

TWO RUSTIC SEATS

Much of the commercial " rustic " garden furniture is open to adverse criticism concerning its design and general suitability. The first is frequently extremely poor, and, being devoid of originality, has tended to bring this class of work into a considerable amount of disfavour. At the same time, however, rustic construction is supposed to harmonise with garden surroundings better than other classes of work, and it certainly has the advantages of being easily prepared from material which is often already on hand, or, at all events, material easily obtainable.

A design less liable to reproach on these scores than some is shown by Fig. 70, and consists principally of perfectly straight poles (which may be of larch or some similar variety) arranged in a much simpler manner than is usually encountered. In this design the main uprights are continued upwards, in order to receive an awning or other shelter when desired ; or they could, of course, be kept down sufficiently to leave the arms and back of ordinary heights. For a shady position where provision for an awning is superfluous, Fig. 71 may prove of interest, showing as it does a sketch for a very similar seat with the addition of curved arms and back.

For either seat the construction would be much the same, and, as is usually the case with such work, it need only be of the simplest, not to say crudest, description. The main framework should be of comparatively heavy stuff selected for its straightness, and when cut to sizes suiting the dimensions shown in Figs. 72, 73, and 74, should be carefully fitted so that one piece butts closely against the curved contour of another, and the whole then spiked or screwed very securely together. The minor filling-in pieces can next be readily settled, and they should be fitted in position in such a way as to brace and stiffen the larger parts throughout. As a whole, the construction does not call for an explanation in detail ; but a proposal for the arrangement of the seat is explained by Fig. 75, which is a section of the front bearer of the seat showing it as one-half of a stout circular pole having a fillet spiked on it at the back in order to receive small wrought slats, as at A in Fig. 74, which, of course, rest on a similar bearer and fillet along the back of the seat. These wrought fillets will be found much more satisfactory than any rustic pieces in such a position, and they should slope down a little to the rear, and be rounded off on top to avoid any sharp angles.

As regards the seat shown in Fig. 71, the only special remark is that the top rail of the back to it should be selected curved naturally to a suitable outline, and in both instances it is strongly advised to keep the seat low and wide, and also if practicable to slightly slope both the actual seat and the upright back.

HIGH-BACKED GARDEN SEAT WITH SCREEN

Given for a background a well-matured garden, the model shown in the sketch (Fig. 76) should prove very effective, and repay the labour involved in its construction. It would probably appear to the best advantage if placed at the end of a long central path, and it will be all the better for a raised platform of concrete finished with pebbles and having a brick edging, which might be curved out in a sweeping line as shown by the plan, while if, say, three wide steps up could be tapered slightly, if possible, towards their tops, which are tenoned into a light horizontal head with shaped ends projecting 9 in. beyond the posts. Under this i

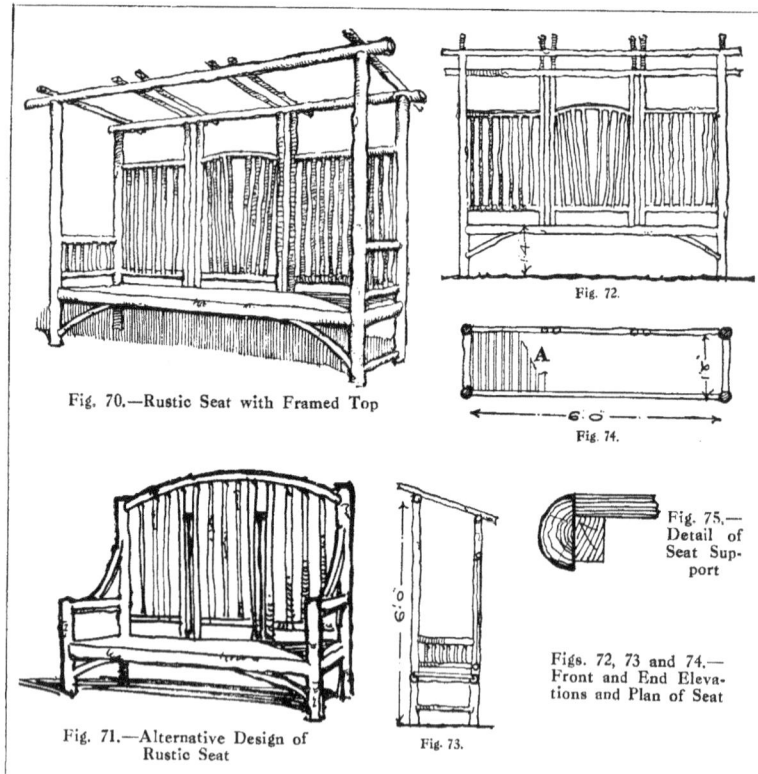

Fig. 70.—Rustic Seat with Framed Top

Fig. 71.—Alternative Design of Rustic Seat

Fig. 72.

Fig. 73.

Fig. 74.

Fig. 75.—Detail of Seat Support

Figs. 72, 73 and 74.—Front and End Elevations and Plan of Seat

arranged to follow this line, the result would be correspondingly enhanced. Figs. 77, 78, and 79 are part elevation, section through centre and plan respectively.

The design will readily be seen to consist of an angle seat with high back, over which a light sort of screen or arbour is erected. This latter is standing 7 ft. 3 in., composed of two posts above the platform or ground level, at least 3 in. square and fixed an upright 1-in. board, having its lower edge shaped to a flat hollow curve as shown. This completes the front part, which should be erected with the posts securely bedded in the ground, preferably with concrete round their ends. The back supports can next be attended to. They stand 3 ft. 3 in. to the rear, and constitute practically a reduced copy of the front, two smaller posts standing 6 ft.

GARDEN CARPENTRY

high and 5 ft. 6 in. apart, supporting a head with shaped ends, the upper surface of which (as also that of the one first described) is taken off to the required angle to suit a number of laths arranged on the slope in a radiating fashion, to take climbing roses or creepers. The back is filled in with trellis, which might be made up in a square form, rather than to use the common diagonal pattern, and the sides could be enclosed in a similar way if desired.

The seat is independent of the surrounding work, and will be found rather more difficult to construct, the reader being particularly referred to the enlarged details shown. Incidentally it may perhaps be as well to mention that the angles for the setting out on the plan are all drawn with the ordinary 60° set-square,

also that the front edge of the central part of the seat is 3 ft. long, while the sides are each 2 ft. 3 in. clear in front.

Taking first the half plan (Fig. 79) to the left of the centre line, this shows the four main uprights of this half of the framing (A, B, C, and D), the two back ones being 4 ft. 9 in. high with rounded tops, and the exact heights of the others being shown

Fig. 76.—High-backed Garden Seat with Screen

on the details. The first three are each 2 in. by 2 in. square, while D should be 3 in. by 2 in., or at least 2½ in. by 2 in., in order to properly take the other parts which will have to be jointed into it; B and C are connected up to form the end framing by the arm E and bottom rail F shown on the detail (Fig. 80), while between them at the distance figured above the ground is a bearer G (reduced from 3 in. by 2 in. in front to 2 in. by 2 in. at

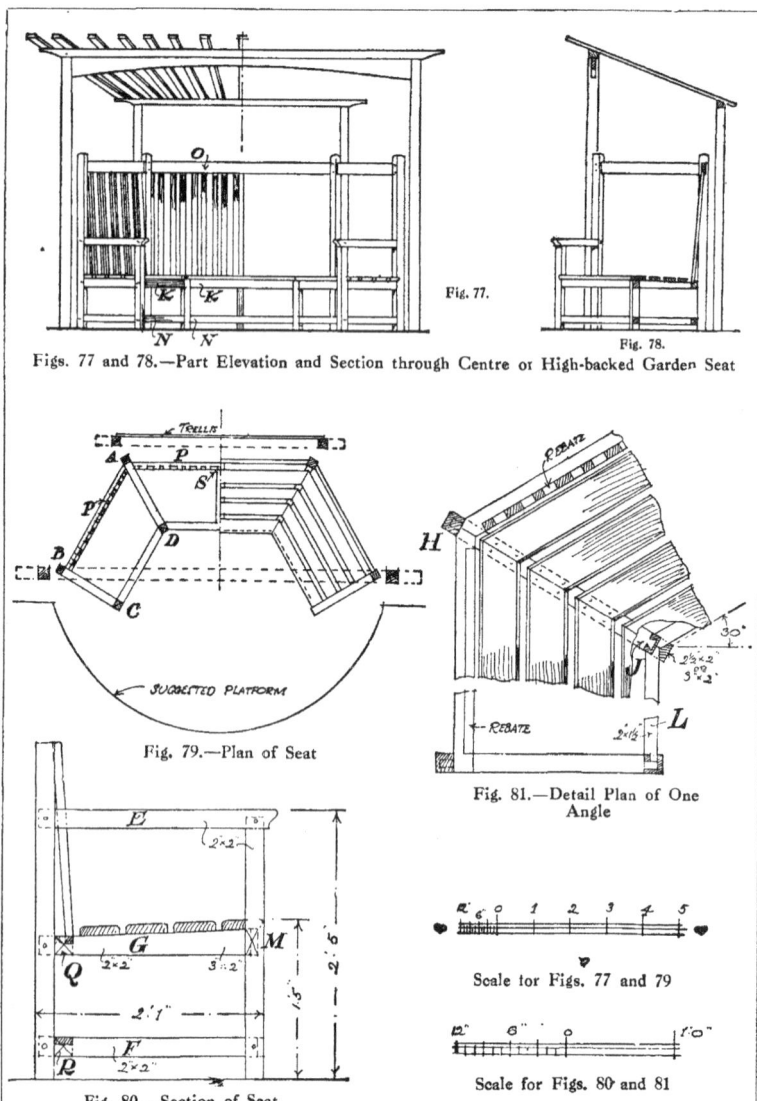

Figs. 77 and 78.—Part Elevation and Section through Centre or High-backed Garden Seat

Fig. 79.—Plan of Seat

Fig. 81.—Detail Plan of One Angle

Fig. 80.—Section of Seat

Scale for Figs. 77 and 79

Scale for Figs. 80 and 81

GARDEN CARPENTRY

the back end), which is framed into B and C. All these six joints are simple tenons, and it is suggested that they be secured with oak pegs driven through the centres.

Uprights A and D are connected in a somewhat similar manner, omitting the arm rail; but being on the skew, as compared with the end framing, their distance apart will be a little greater, and must be decided by exact setting out of the work. A detail plan of this part is given (Fig. 81), which shows at H the bearer tenoned into the back upright and dovetailed into the front one at J. This joint will make the best job, although a tenon could be substituted. These two parts of the framing are then joined to each other and to the corresponding parts of the other half of the seat by means of the following: (a) 2-in. by $1\frac{1}{2}$-in. rails under the front edges of the seat, as K K on front view, and L on the detail plan, which shows an ordinary tenon at one end and a special form at the other (J), to suit this particular case. The object is to cut away as little as possible of the upright, consistently with producing secure work. These rails are only $1\frac{1}{2}$ in. wide to allow $\frac{1}{2}$ in. for a rounded edge to the front board of the seat, without this projecting beyond the line of the uprights (see M on detail of end).

(b) 2-in. by 2-in. bottom rails (N) tenoned in a similar manner at each end.

(c) $4\frac{1}{2}$-in. by $1\frac{1}{4}$-in. heads (as O, front view) housed into the back uprights.

(d) 2-in. by 2-in. back bearers (as P on the plan and Q on the detail of the end). These are fixed in position as indicated at Q, by halving with the seat bearers G, and they have a rebate $\frac{3}{4}$ in. wide to take the laths forming the filling in to the back, which also fit into a rebate worked along the front lower edge of the top piece O. These laths are alternately $1\frac{1}{4}$ in. and 2 in. wide or thereabouts, with 3-in. spaces between, and only require careful fitting and nailing into the rebates just described.

(e) The last connection between the framings at A and B will be a 2-in. by 2-in. rail, similar to Q, and halved in the same way over the bottom rails as at R on the detail of the end.

When the seat has been formed with $4\frac{1}{2}$-in. by 1-in. boards with rounded angles, nailed in position at equal distances, and mitred as shown on the detail plan, the work will have been completely specified, with the possible exception of a short upright, which it may be found advisable to introduce to stiffen the back bearer in the centre, at S on plan.

Paint or some preserving stain may be adopted as a finish, and it will be as well to keep always in mind the need of solidity for work of this character, which has to stand forsaken through long periods of rain that severely test the quality of both material and workmanship.

ORNAMENTAL SEAT FOR GARDEN

The garden seat shown by the photograph (Fig. 82) is of a convenient yet uncommon design, and the utilisation of the ends as seats economises space. The seat is shown painted and enamelled white. The working drawings Figs. 83, 84 and 85 are to the scale shown on page 527.

The material required is as follows: 3-in. by 3-in. legs—eight 3 ft. 6 in. and four 2 ft. 6 in.; 6-in. by 2-in. rails—two 2 ft. 8 in. and four 5 ft. 6 in.; 4-in. by 2-in. rails—two 4 ft., four 1 ft., and four 10 in.; $3\frac{1}{2}$-in. by 2-in. rails—four 1 ft. and two 4 ft.; 2-in. by $2\frac{1}{2}$-in. arms—four 1 ft.; $2\frac{1}{2}$-in. by 1-in. laths to seats and back—ten 5 ft. 6 in., ten 4 ft., and forty-six 1 ft. 6 in.; 3-in. by 1-in. front laths—two 5 ft. 6 in. and two 4 ft.; 6-in. by 1-in. panels—four 9 in.; 5-in. by 1-in. feet—four 5 in. and four 1 ft. 1 in.; 3-in. capping—two 2 ft. 6 in., one 2 ft. 2 in., two 1 ft. 8 in., and eight 1 ft.; 3-in. by 2-in. cross rails under the seats—six 1 ft. 5 in.; 1-in. by $\frac{1}{2}$-in. false ends—four 8 in. and four 10 in.; 3-in. by 2-in. muntins in the seat backs—two 1 ft. 9 in.; 2-in. by 2-in. muntins in the seat backs—two 1 ft. 9 in.; $1\frac{1}{2}$-in. by 1-in. bearers for seat-lath ends—eight 1 ft. 3 in.

Fig. 83 is a sectional end elevation; Fig. 84 a front elevation, and Fig. 85 a plan of one half and a cross horizontal section of the other half, omitting the laths to show the arrangement of the rails under. Figs. 86 and 87 give enlarged details of two joints used in the construction of the seat. Most of the joints are based on the ordinary mortise-and-tenon joint. The cross rails supporting the seat laths and binding the seat together are fixed with a stop dovetail joint (*see* Fig. 86). The corner rails are fixed with a mortise-and-tenon joint as in Fig. 87, being necessarily arranged differently to the mortise-and-tenon joint that is cut in the direction of the grain. The back framing is crowned with a capping, as shown in section by Fig. 88. The panels in the end seats under the arms are fixed in grooves cut in the arm (underside) and the rail at the bottom. The front legs of the end seats are tapered to 2 in. square at the top end.

The legs of wooden seats of this description are subject to wet rot, due to standing with their exposed ends in the ground, and thereby absorbing moisture, with no opportunity of drying by ventilation. This is guarded against by fixing 1-in. pieces, chamfered on the edge, to the ends of the legs, thereby not only saving

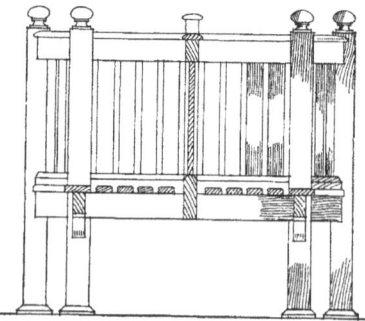

Fig. 83.—Sectional End Elevation of Seat

the ends of the legs, but at the same time introducing a neat and ornamental feature to the general appearance of the seat. The panelling on the back framework is of 2¼-in. by 1-in. laths, fixed ½ in. or so apart.

In arranging the woodwork of outdoor work, account should be taken of the fact that when wood is joined in any way, decay begins there first; therefore as few

Fig. 82.—Ornamental Garden Seat

GARDEN CARPENTRY

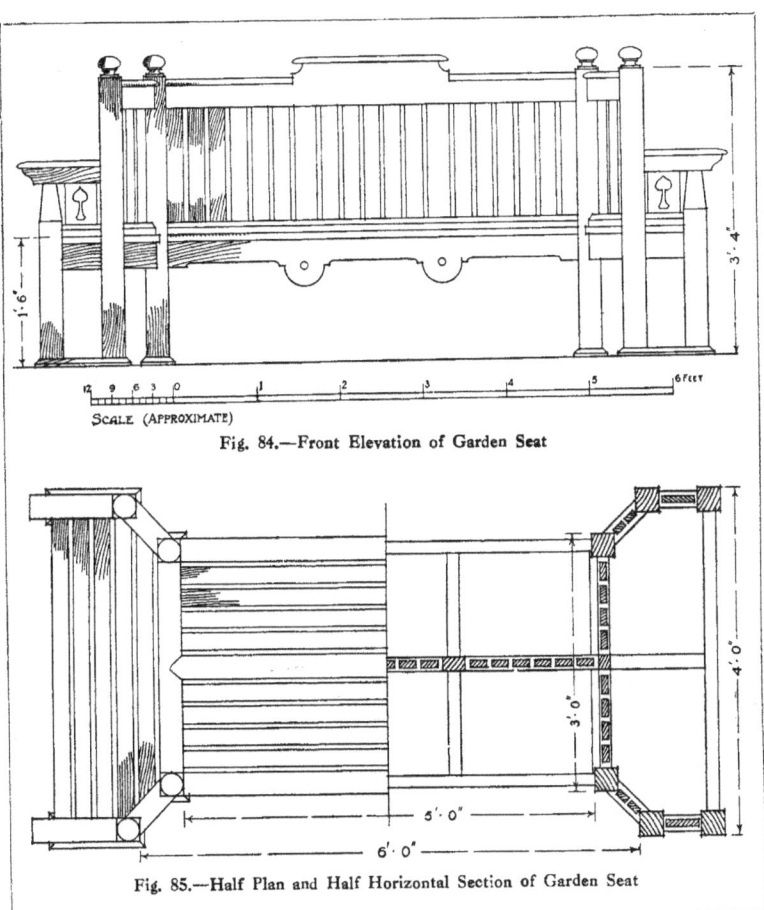

Fig. 84.—Front Elevation of Garden Seat

Fig. 85.—Half Plan and Half Horizontal Section of Garden Seat

joints as possible should be used. If it is possible to get the wood exposed on all its sides, so much the better. This is so in the present case. The laths forming the back panelling touch wood only at each end, and as all joints made are painted together with white-lead, and the whole seat is given four coats of paint and one of white enamel, the chances of decay due to exposure are reduced to the lowest possible minimum. The only nails used are in fixing the seat laths, and they should be punched in and well puttied with oil putty after the first or priming coat. The mortise-and-tenon joints, which in most cases cannot be wedged (except by a hidden or fox wedge), are pinned with wooden pins. The top rail, which is

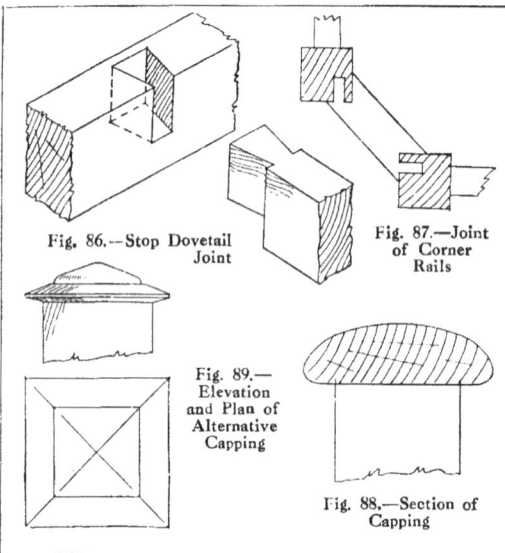

Fig. 86.—Stop Dovetail Joint

Fig. 87.—Joint of Corner Rails

Fig. 89.—Elevation and Plan of Alternative Capping

Fig. 88.—Section of Capping

raised in the centre, is made all in one piece. It could, for the sake of economising timber, be made in two pieces, the top and shorter piece being screwed down to the longer rail; but the objection to this is that a joint is thereby formed, which if water once gets in causes decay.

For this reason the exposed top ends of the legs are a source of weakness, although the turning of the ends reduces this, because of the pressure of the turning tool compressing and hardening the end.

The turning should be as fat and solid as can be obtained; no project-

Fig. 90.—Hooded Garden Seat and Table

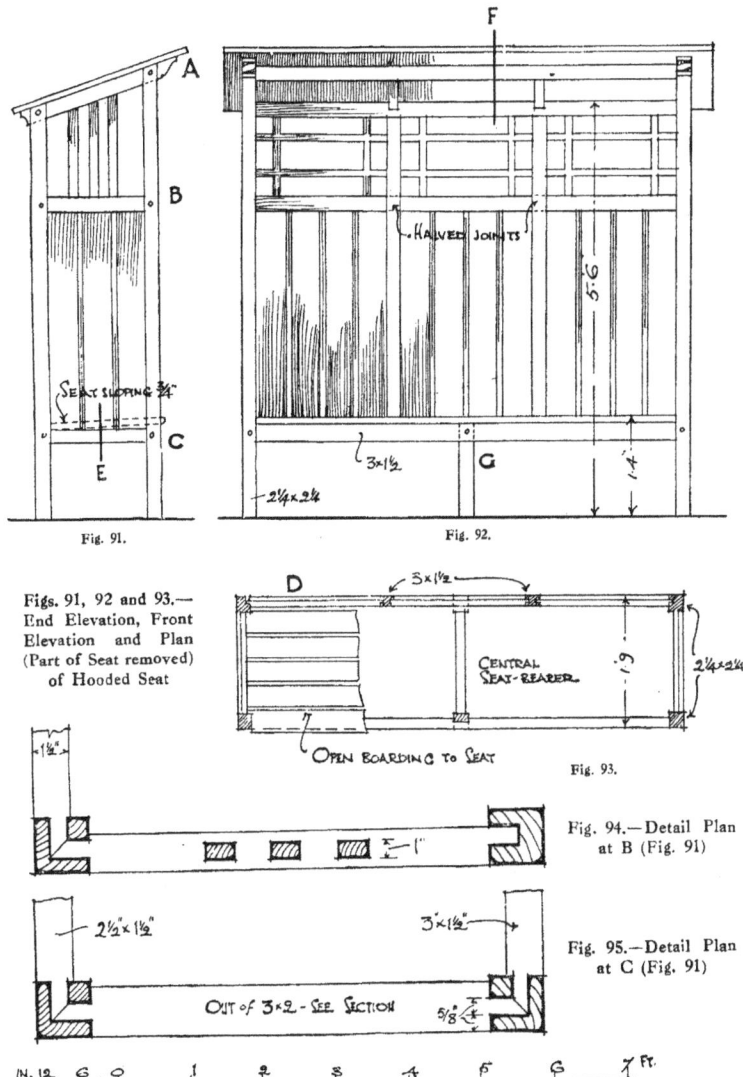

Figs. 91, 92 and 93.—End Elevation, Front Elevation and Plan (Part of Seat removed) of Hooded Seat

Fig. 94.—Detail Plan at B (Fig. 91)

Fig. 95.—Detail Plan at C (Fig. 91)

Scale for Figs. 91–93 and 98

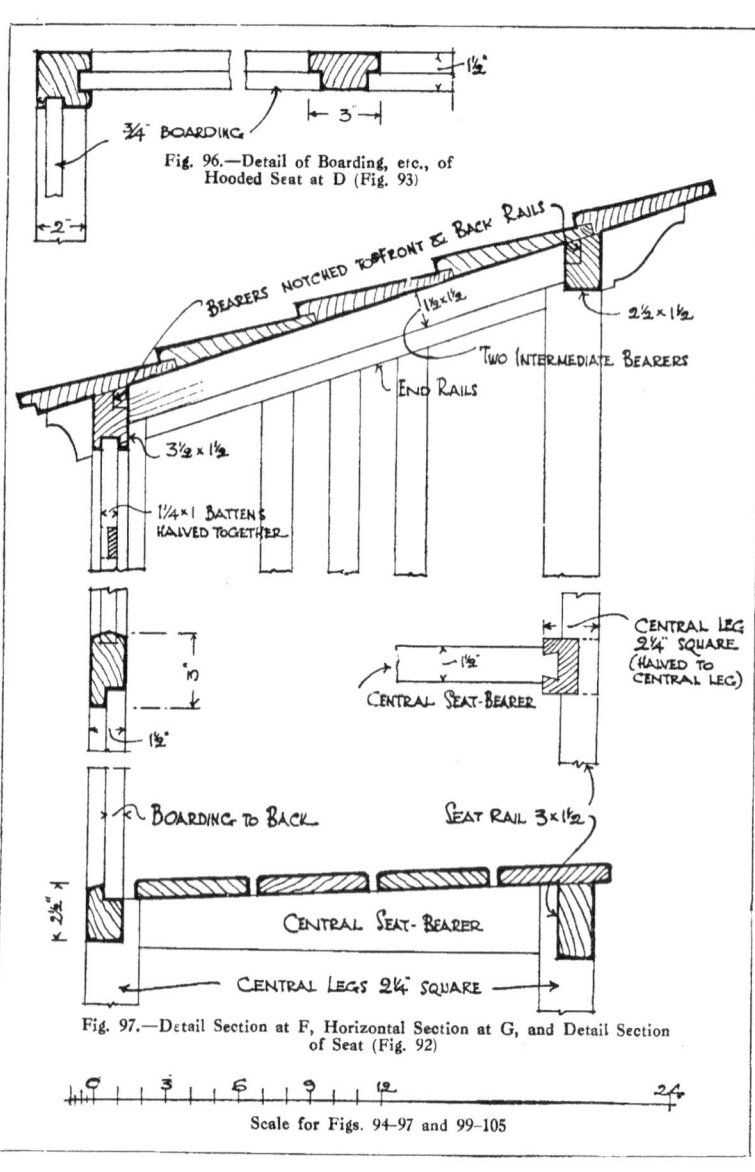

Fig. 96.—Detail of Boarding, etc., of Hooded Seat at D (Fig. 93)

Fig. 97.—Detail Section at F, Horizontal Section at G, and Detail Section of Seat (Fig. 92)

Scale for Figs. 94–97 and 99–105

ing members that would easily be broken off by the weather should be introduced. An alternative method is to cap the ends, as shown in Fig. 89. In putting the seat together, it is a good plan to paint all the separate parts first—tenons, dovetails, and mortises; the mortises should be especially well painted. Then next day put the seat together, again using paint for the joints. In this way the joints are protected from decay as far as is possible. If a double seat is too large, a single-fronted seat can be made by omitting one side and drawing up the ends.

HOODED SEAT AND TABLE

The hooded seat and table shown in Fig. 90 (p. 528) are of simple construction and are for garden or outdoor use. The end elevation, front elevation and plan of the seat are shown in Figs. 91, 92, and 93; various details are given in Figs. 94 to 105.

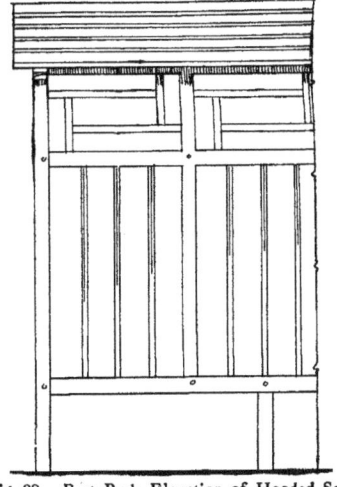

Fig. 98.—Part Back Elevation of Hooded Seat with Alternative Arrangement of Bars at Top

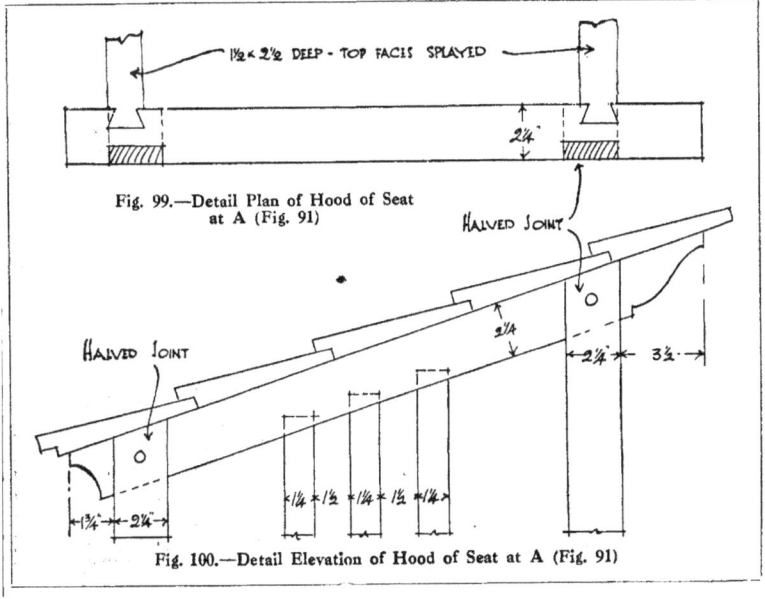

Fig. 99.—Detail Plan of Hood of Seat at A (Fig. 91)

Fig. 100.—Detail Elevation of Hood of Seat at A (Fig. 91)

The seat is composed of four boards with open joints supported by the two end rails and a centre bearer. Note that owing to the slope of the seat the rails and bearer are tapered in width (Figs. 94 and 95). The back and sides are boarded at the bottom and filled in with open bars at the top. An alternative arrangement of the bars is shown in Fig. 98. Two pieces $\frac{1}{2}$ in. by $1\frac{1}{2}$ in. in section are dove-

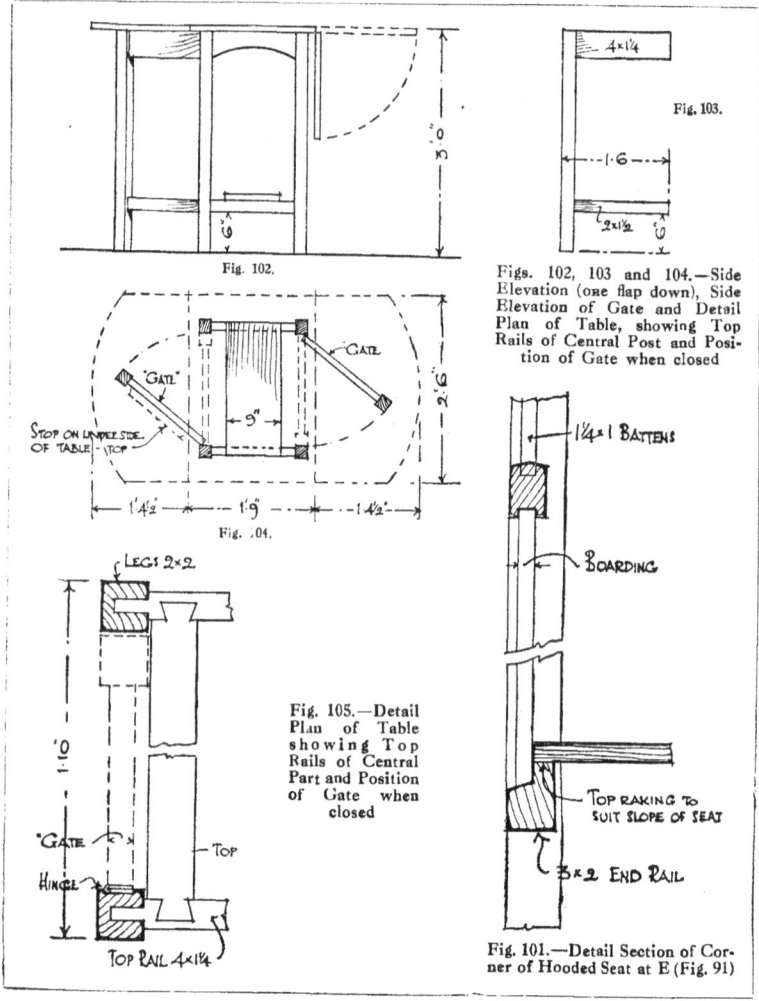

Figs. 102, 103 and 104.—Side Elevation (one flap down), Side Elevation of Gate and Detail Plan of Table, showing Top Rails of Central Post and Position of Gate when closed

Fig. 105.—Detail Plan of Table showing Top Rails of Central Part and Position of Gate when closed

Fig. 101.—Detail Section of Corner of Hooded Seat at E (Fig. 91)

GARDEN CARPENTRY

tailed (Fig. 99), between the top rails to give rigidity to the roof, and to afford adequate bearing for the rebated and weathered roof boarding. Details of the construction of the sides are given in Figs. 99 and 100. A detail of a back corner showing the boarding is shown in Fig. 102.

Hinged Table.—The table (Figs. 102 to 105) consists essentially of a rectangular fixed portion having four legs; between the legs on each of the long sides of the firmer foundation, and counteracts any tendency of the swing to overturn. If the four posts are allowed to enter the ground about 6 in., the swing frame can be made a temporary fixture, and should any alteration of position be desired, no great difficulty will be experienced in removing it.

The whole is made of good quality deal scantlings, and should be constructed as follows : Figs. 107 and 108 are the side and front elevations of the swing, and

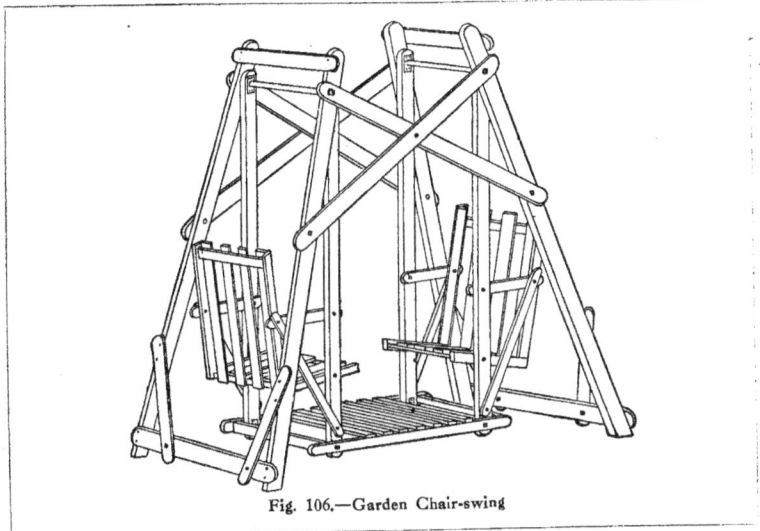

Fig. 106.—Garden Chair-swing

table a " gate," or auxiliary leg, is hinged. Each of these folding legs supports a flat (or extending) leaf hinged to the centre table top. The " gates " are hinged so that when they are closed they allow the hinged flaps to drop.

GARDEN CHAIR-SWING

The two swinging chairs are supported in a large trestle-like frame, as shown in Fig. 106. This method of spreading the posts outwards gives the framework a show the lengths of all the pieces before the chairs are fixed in position. All the pieces should be prepared by planing to the sizes given. The $\frac{3}{8}$-in. bolt holes are bored with a pin bit, and bored so that the bolt has a free fit so as not to split the wood when it is driven in. The ends are cut off with a bow-saw a sufficient distance away from the bolt holes, so that it is not likely to split when the strain is on the framing. The ends are then finished off with a spokeshave. The holes at A are bored large enough to receive two long bolts having a thread at each end to receive the nuts. As these bolts take the weight of the swing, it is necessary to have them made of ⅝-in. round iron.

The cross braces strengthen the side frames, and these frames are held together by pieces at the top and bottom. These are screwed on the edges of the long posts each side, as shown at B and C in Fig. 108. The struts in the lower corners are bolted on to the lower cross bearers and screwed on the edges of the posts. These are necessary to prevent the frame distorting sidewise. Fig. 109 shows the platform on which the chairs are fixed. It consists of two side pieces into which are mortised

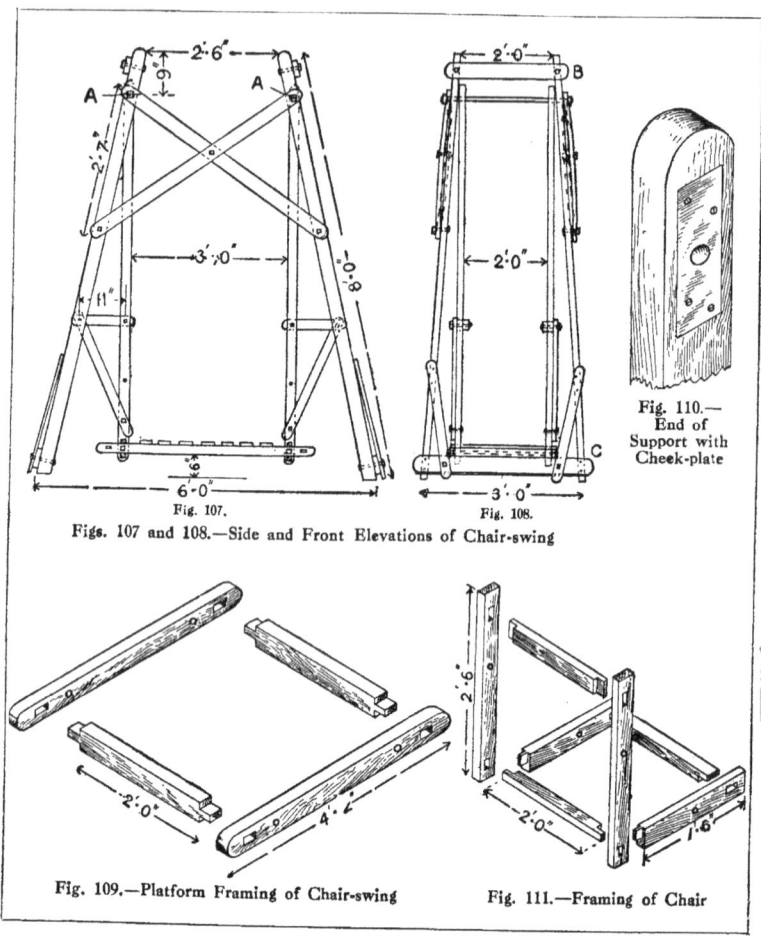

Figs. 107 and 108.—Side and Front Elevations of Chair-swing

Fig. 110.—End of Support with Cheek-plate

Fig. 109.—Platform Framing of Chair-swing

Fig. 111.—Framing of Chair

GARDEN CARPENTRY

and tenoned two cross pieces; these joints are held securely together by pinning. About 2 in. away from the cross pieces holes are bored in the side pieces to receive the long bolts, the same as those at the top. Strips or battens are then screwed on to the top of the side pieces. To ensure the full working of the upright supports, these strips should not be fixed too close to the same. The holes in the supports should be bored about $2\frac{1}{2}$ in. or 3 in. from each end, so as to fit freely on the long bolts. Sixteen small cheek-plates will be required for the four supports. These are made of $\frac{1}{8}$-in. hoop iron, 4 in. long and $1\frac{1}{2}$ in. wide, as shown in Fig. 110. The holes should be drilled large enough to fit freely on the long bolts. Fig. 110 shows an end of a support with a cheek-plate screwed on.

The chairs are bolted on to the upright supports by triangular framing. The arms of the chairs are fixed to the supports in front, and the back ends are supported by a strut which takes its thrust from a bolted joint lower down the support. The back and seat of the chair are bolted on to this triangular framing, as shown in Fig. 110. Two pieces are carried across the back of the chair and one across the seat of the chair. On these are nailed the laths to form the back and the seat. All the chair bolts are $\frac{5}{16}$ in. in diameter, and should be washered before they are screwed up. Fig. 111 shows the mortise-and-tenon joints before they are driven together and pinned.

All the pieces should be painted before they are bolted together. The sizes of all the pieces required are: Slanting posts, $2\frac{1}{2}$ in. by $\frac{7}{8}$ in.; cross braces, $2\frac{1}{2}$ in. by $\frac{7}{8}$ in.; corner struts, 2 in. by $1\frac{1}{4}$ in.; top and bottom cross bearers, $2\frac{1}{2}$ in. by $\frac{7}{8}$ in.; platform framing, $1\frac{3}{4}$ in. by $1\frac{1}{4}$ in.; platform strips, $1\frac{1}{4}$ in. by $\frac{3}{4}$ in.; upright supports, $1\frac{3}{4}$ in. by $1\frac{1}{4}$ in.; chair framing, $1\frac{1}{4}$ in. by $\frac{7}{8}$ in.; and chair laths, $1\frac{1}{4}$ in. by $\frac{1}{2}$ in.

ERECTING A GARDEN SWING

The general idea of a simple swing is given in Fig. 112, and also shows the construction below the ground which is necessary to keep the posts from shaking loose by the action of swinging. Figs. 113 and 114 give front and end elevations of the swing. The timbers with which the swing is to be made may be of oak, ash, or pitch-pine; but if these are not available and a cheaper material is desired, good red deal might be used.

The dimensions of the swing are 8 ft. 11 in. high from the ground, and 5 ft. between the posts, the ends of which, with the sill, are sunk 3 ft. 6 in. in the ground. It will be as well to first give a list of the timbers, as from this it may

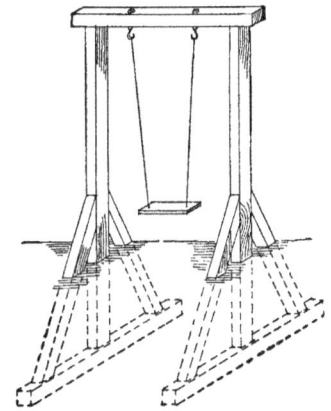

Fig. 112.—Garden Swing showing Construction Below Ground

be seen at a glance all the pieces that will be required, and so facilitate matters in the cutting up and in the ordering of the stuff. Two pieces 11 ft. 10 in. by 1 in. by 4 in. for the posts; one piece 6 ft. 8 in. by 7 in. by $5\frac{1}{2}$ in. for the head; two sills 6 ft. 6 in. by 6 in. by 6 in.; and four struts 6 ft. by 4 in. by 4 in.

To begin, first take the two posts, and at both ends of each cut a stub tenon 4 in. by 3 in., which should fit tightly and squarely into the mortise in the headpiece and sill. The posts are further secured to the head with $2\frac{1}{2}$-in. by $\frac{1}{4}$-in. iron straps, hammered to shape and fastened with screws; but this fixing is best left until

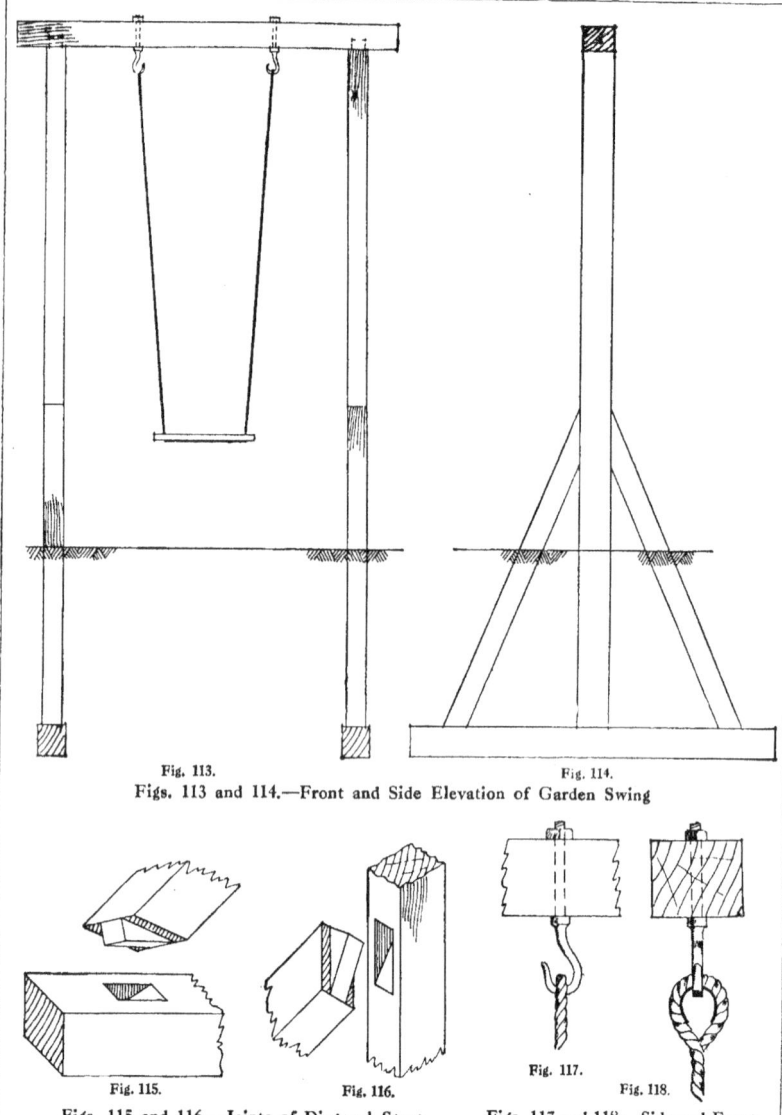

Fig. 113. Fig. 114.
Figs. 113 and 114.—Front and Side Elevation of Garden Swing

Fig. 115. Fig. 116. Fig. 117. Fig. 118.
Figs. 115 and 116.—Joints of Diagonal Strut   Figs 117 and 118.—Side and Front Elevations of Suspension Hook

GARDEN CARPENTRY

all is ready for erection. The diagonal struts are jointed to the posts and sill in the manner shown by Figs. 115 and 116, and the struts should be additionally strengthened with ½-in. bolts. The suspension hooks are shown enlarged by Figs 117 and 118, and if facilities are not at hand for making them, they may be procured from a local ironmonger. The hooks are fixed in the head 2 ft. 6 in. apart with a nut, and care must be taken to have a good-size iron washer between the nut and the wood. Good stout manilla rope or galvanised-iron strand wire must be used to suspend the seat, and it is important to have galvanised-iron thimbles to work in the hooks. Over these thimbles the rope should be properly spliced. For the seat, cut a piece 2 ft. long and 10 in. wide from a ¾-in. board, and after planing, screw a piece of ½-in. stuff 5 in. wide on the underside at each end to strengthen the board. The seat should be suspended so that it is about 1 ft. 9 in. above the ground; all edges and corners should be rounded off.

The posts and struts should now have the corners taken off or chamfered, and the parts of the framework that are to be below the ground must be well tarred or creosoted. The upper portions should be given two or three coats of paint. After making the excavation, the trenches should have a 6-in. broken brick foundation, which must be well rammed and levelled, and the swing is placed in position and the trenches filled with stones and small material.

FOLDING SEE-SAW

A see-saw is much safer than a swing, and while the latter can only be used by one child at a time, two or even more may use a see-saw. The folding see-saw shown by Fig. 119 is not difficult to make, and requires but a small amount of material. It is made with a top frame, which is fitted

Fig. 119.—Folding See-saw

with a middle and two end seats, the latter being fitted with folding backs. The top is hinged to a folding stand, which may easily be adjusted at three different heights.

Fig. 121 shows the see-saw folded. In making, it is essential that a hardwood should be used, say, ash or birch, finished with stain and varnish.

The sides A (Figs. 120 and 122) are 9 ft. long by 4 in. deep in the middle, and 2½ in. deep at the ends by 1 in. thick. The end seats B and the middle seat C are 1 ft. 6 in. long by 8 in. wide by ¾ in. thick, dovetailed into the sides, as shown by Fig. 123, and fixed with screws. The two connecting rails D are 1 ft. 6 in. long by 1 in. in diameter, and are framed into the sides,

THE PRACTICAL WOODWORKER

for which purpose the ends of the rails are cut, as shown in Fig. 124. The folding seat backs are made as shown in Figs. 125 and 126, each having two sides (E, Fig. 120) connected by three battens (F, Fig. 120). The sides are 10 in. long by 1½ in. wide by ¾ in. thick, and the battens are 1 ft. 7¾ in. long by 2 in. wide by ¾ in. thick. The backs are hinged to the sides of the top frame by means of rivets (see Fig. 131). Care must be used in boring the holes for the rivets, to see that the backs will fold flat, and when open will stand a little out of the perpendicular. Rivets about ⅜ in. in diameter should be used. Iron washers ⅛ in. thick are placed between the frames, and similar washers are placed under the heads of the rivets.

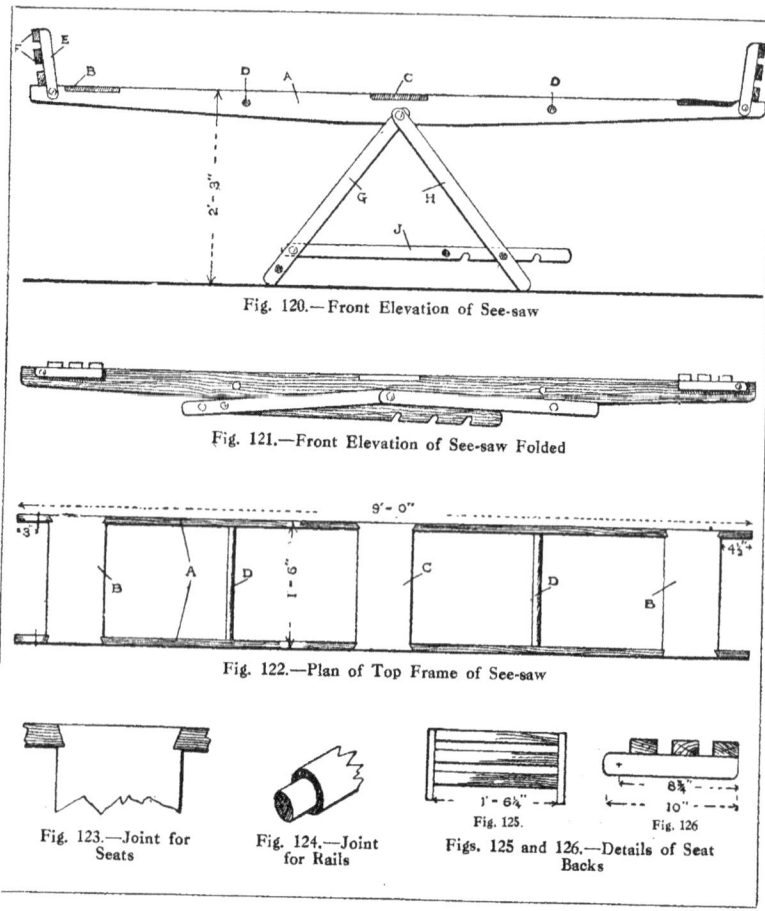

Fig. 120.—Front Elevation of See-saw

Fig. 121.—Front Elevation of See-saw Folded

Fig. 122.—Plan of Top Frame of See-saw

Fig. 123.—Joint for Seats

Fig. 124.—Joint for Rails

Figs. 125 and 126.—Details of Seat Backs

GARDEN CARPENTRY

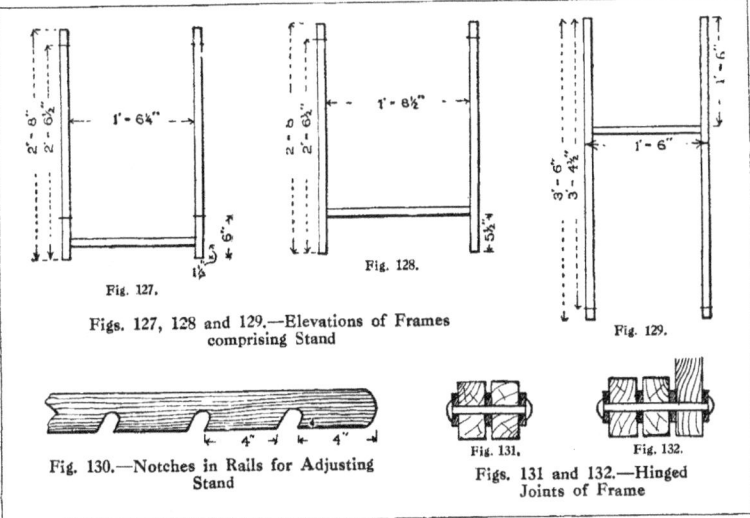

Fig. 127.

Fig. 128.

Fig. 129.

Figs. 127, 128 and 129.—Elevations of Frames comprising Stand

Fig. 130.—Notches in Rails for Adjusting Stand

Figs. 131 and 132.—Hinged Joints of Frame

The stand is made with three frames G, H, and J. The frame G is shown by Fig. 127, and is made with two side rails, which are 2 ft. 8 in. long by 2 in. wide by 1 in. thick, and a cross rail 1 ft. 8¼ in. long by 1 in. in diameter. The cross rail is framed into the side rails with joints, as shown in Fig. 124. The frame H is shown by Fig. 128, and consists of two side rails 2 ft. 8 in. long by 2 in. wide by 1 in. thick, and a cross rail 1 ft. 10½ in. long by 1 in. in diameter. The frame J is shown by Fig. 129, and consists of two side rails 3 ft. 6 in. long by 2 in. wide by 1 in. thick, and a cross rail 1 ft. 6 in. long by 1 in. in diameter. Holes ⅜ in. in diameter for hinging the frames together are bored in the positions shown in Figs. 127, 128, and 129, and notches 1 in. wide and quite ¾ in. deep are cut in the side rails of the frame L, in the positions shown by Fig. 130. The frames G and H are hinged to the sides of the top frame with rivets which pass through all three frames, as shown in Fig. 132, ⅓-in. washers being placed between each. The frame J is hinged to the frame G with rivets, as shown in Fig. 131. The notches in the side rails of the frame J engage with the cross rail of the frame H when fixing or adjusting the see-saw.

Garden Baskets

GARDENER'S TRUG OR BASKET

THE word "trug" will not probably have any meaning for a great many readers, but when they see the photograph the case will be altered. The above is the name given to what is called a garden basket in a good many parts of the country, although the former name is that used by the makers themselves. But as these are localised in a small village in Sussex the name has not gained so wide a reputation as the goods themselves. The wood generally used in making trugs is willow for the boards and ash for the rims and handles; but there is no reason why they cannot be made entirely of ash, except that it is harder to work, and, on the other hand, small trugs are often made of the willow throughout. The variety of willow most sought after for the purpose is a special soft kind called sallow willow.

The tools needed are very few indeed, the saw, hammer, and draw-knife being the principal ones. In addition to these there is required an appliance for holding the wood while it is manipulated, and one for steaming the rims and handles to make them bend to shape. The former cannot very well be dispensed with, but as it is extremely handy for a variety of uses besides the one now being dealt with, the time and material used in the making of it will not be thrown away, even if only one or two trugs are made. In the case of the steaming apparatus, use can be made of hot water only for a small job, and the whole arrangement can easily be fitted up if it is preferred to do so later on, and as the cost is not much, instructions on fitting up the entire plant are here given. The trugs are, as a rule, made double the length in relation to the width, and the one used as an illustration for this article is 27 in. long by 13½ in. wide, while the handle is shaped so that it is the same depth as it is wide; but the upper or handle part is bent slightly different from the lower part which forms the bottom of the trug.

For a trug of the above size the rim will have to be 7 ft. long and the handle 4 ft.,

Fig. 1.—Gardener's Trug

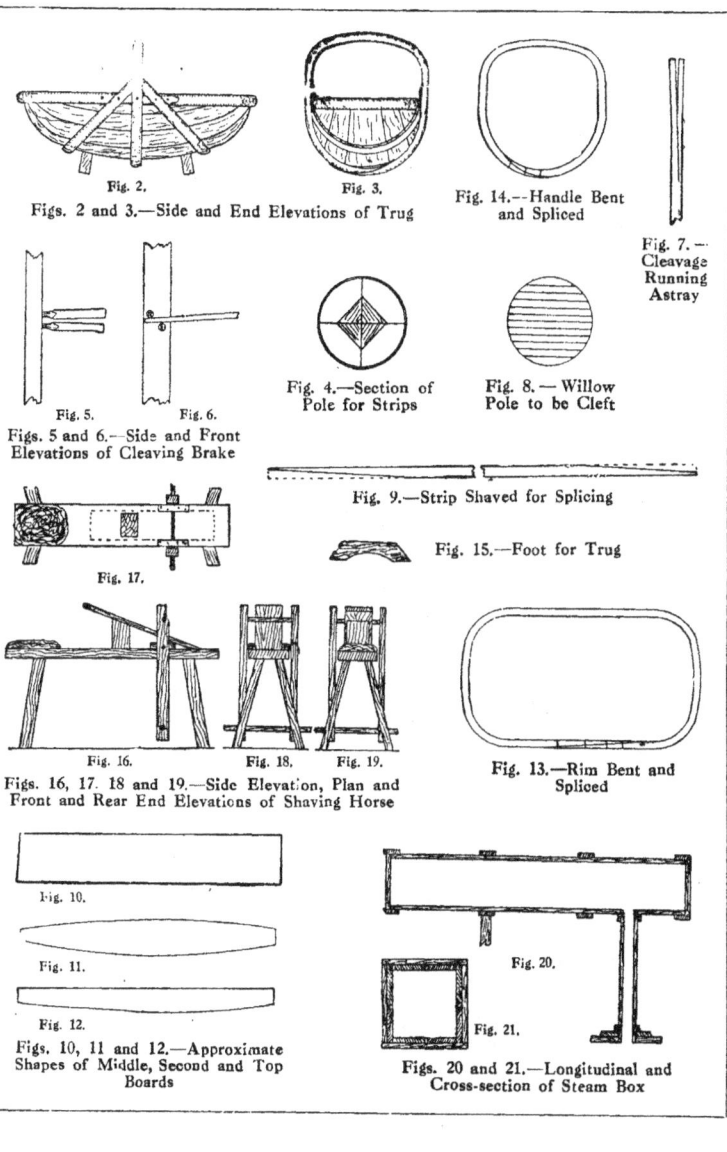

these lengths including sufficient wood for the lapped splicings, as shown in Fig. 13. These strips, which, as stated above, should be of ash, are formed in their rough state by cleaving an ash pole some 2½ in. in diameter into quarters, and then shaving off the sharp corners with the draw-knife, also making the tapered-off ends for the splicings at the same time. The boards are cleft out as thinly as possible from the lengths of willow pole, which may be from 3 in. to 4 in. in diameter for this size of basket, and must be cut into lengths of 34 in.

Begin with the rims and handles, the forming of which will be made easier by means of the photograph of the finished trug (Fig. 1) and the side and end elevations (Figs. 2 and 3). Fig. 4 shows the section of the ash pole from which the rim and handle are to be made, the shaded portions showing the waste, which will eventually be cut away with the draw-knife. The correct tool for cleaving out the pole is a cleaving axe; but for present purposes the ordinary handbill can be used, driving it in at the proper place with a piece of wood, and splitting the wood by using the tool itself as a lever. It will be found that in the hands of a novice the wood will tend to split unevenly, although the theory is that it should follow the pith. This is what it should do, but it will only do so if handled properly, and Figs. 5 and 6 show the necessary appliance to carry this out. The two pegs are driven into a convenient post as shown, at a height of about 4 ft. from the ground, one being slightly higher than the other. The pole being cleft is placed between them, as in Fig. 6, when by putting a slight pressure on the end the cleavage will run downwards. Thus if the work is proceeding as in Fig. 7, the bottom piece will run out to a thin edge; but if the pole is placed in the "brake" (Figs. 5 and 6) with the *thicker* part downwards, and this part slightly bent down, then the split will right itself, and the two pieces finish equal in size.

The strips must now be "shaved" to shape with the draw-knife, the ends being sloped off for a length of about 8 in. to form the splice, and at the same time the rough parts left in cleaving must be trimmed off. With the exception of the one sloped end, *the bark must be left intact*, otherwise it will be difficult to form the bends successfully. The boards will be cleft out in the same way, but as there is not the same chance of guiding the cleavage in this case, it is best not to attempt to cleave them too thin, especially at the first attempt. Fig. 8 shows the end of the length of willow ready for cleaving out, and Fig. 9 shows how the ends of the rim and handle strips must be sloped off to form the splicing. The boards will have to be finished in width to suit the position they will occupy in the finished trug, thus the middle board should be almost or quite parallel, as in Fig. 10, the next boards at each side will come more like Fig. 11, and the next something like Fig. 12. That is providing there are five boards only, but it is best in a trug of the size being dealt with to use seven boards. In all cases the number of boards must be an odd one, so that the first one to be fixed comes flat in the bottom.

To put the rims together after steaming the strips, they must be bent over a pole or something equally convenient so that the corners are as symmetrical as possible, and so that the splice comes in the middle of one side, as in Fig. 13, and in bending them the bark must be on the *outside*. The splicings are nailed at once, driving the nails through from the outside, and resting them on an old flat-iron or something similar, so that the nails are clinched firmly at the same time as they are driven.

The handle is put together in the same way, noting that while the bottom part (where the splicing must be) is bent to a semicircle, the upper (or handle) part is bent more sharply at the corners, thus giving a better hand-grip. Although these rims and handles are bent and put together by the eye only by those who are making them regularly, it is advisable for the novice to use a board shaped to the inside of each, so that the strips can be bent round the edges; and if an iron plate is inserted where the nails will come in fixing the splicings together, the clinching

GARDEN BASKETS

will be done at the same time, the same as though the operations were done in the regulation manner. Fig. 14 shows the handle bent and spliced.

After the rims and handles are formed, the two need nailing together at right angles, and then the frame is ready for the boards. The middle one of these is fixed first by a single nail in the middle into the bottom part of the handle portion. The board is then bent down with the hands to the required curve, and nailed at the ends, driving the nails through so that they are clinched on a piece of iron. Each board is put in in the same way, bending them so that they bed evenly on the one previously fixed, and nailing them first in the middle and then to the rim at the ends. After all the boards are fixed, the ends which project above the rim are trimmed off with a sharp knife. It will be noticed that the trug in the photograph is fitted with diagonal braces, while that in Fig. 2 has both braces and feet. This latter is done to show both styles in one illustration. In practice, the trug being dealt with would have braces only, the smaller sizes having these omitted, but feet being fixed instead.

The braces consist of strips prepared in the same way as the rim strips, nailed to the rim and tucked inside the handle and nailed there. The boards are also nailed to them from the inside of the trug. The feet are shaped like Fig. 15, and are fixed by nailing into them from the inside.

A brief description of how the special shaving horse and steaming apparatus are made will now be given. The former is shown in side elevation by Fig. 16 and in plan by Fig. 17, while Figs. 18 and 19 show end elevations from the front and seat ends respectively. The main part consists of a stool some 4 ft. 6 in. long, about 1 ft. 8 in. high, and some 9 in. wide at the top. At one end is formed a padded seat for comfort's sake, and at the other is fixed the sloping board as shown, also the swinging frame. This latter is pivoted to the seat by the iron bolt shown, which is held in place by the two fillets of wood shown in Fig. 17. The frame has a cross-bar near the top end and another near the bottom end, the latter projecting 3 in. at each side. These bars answer the double purpose of holding the frame together, and the upper one of holding the work while using the draw-knife, and the lower one by the user placing his feet on the projecting ends and thrusting that end of the frame from him, causes the top bar to grip the work on the sloping board. It will be seen that the more pressure needed in the use of the draw-knife the more pressure is put on the work to hold it firm.

The steaming apparatus is shown in longitudinal section by Fig. 20, and in cross-section by Fig. 21. At the bottom of the illustration is shown the lid of a copper used for washing purposes. This has a hole cut in the middle some 3 in. square, and from this rises a hollow shaft, which supports a box of sufficient length to take any length of strip likely to be required. This box may be 9 in. square on the inside, and may be made quite roughly, the boards being held together by ledges as shown. One end is a fixture, but the other must be removable, being fixed in place with two buttons while the steaming operations are taking place. The front of the box must be supported by an upright of some description as shown.

The steaming is carried out as follows: The copper is filled with water and boiled up in the usual way, and while this is being done the box may be filled with the strips to be steamed, when as soon as the water boils the steam, instead of escaping, passes up into the box and thoroughly softens the wood, so that it will bend anywhere and in any way as required. The strips only need to be steamed, the boards will bend without it, and it may be mentioned that they must be shaved very thin, especially at the ends, so that they bend freely without fracture. Three-ply wood is not suitable for trug-making. It might do to a certain extent as regards the actual making, but at the first exposure to damp the trug would fall in pieces in no time. Flat-headed nails must be used; any other kind would pull through the soft wood-

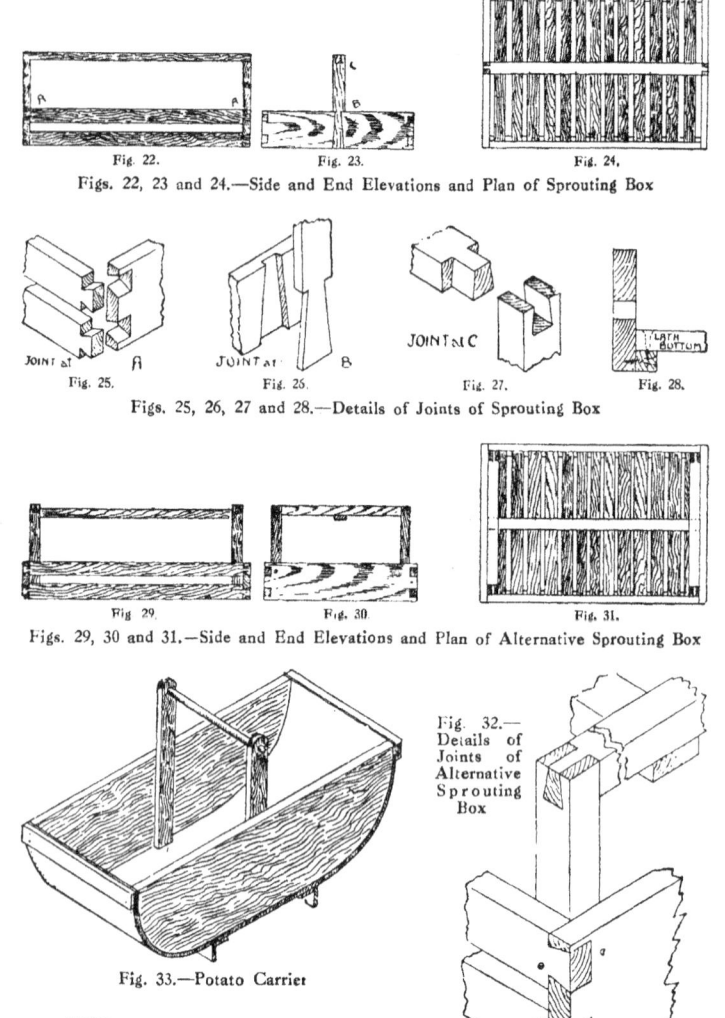

Figs. 22, 23 and 24.—Side and End Elevations and Plan of Sprouting Box

Figs. 25, 26, 27 and 28.—Details of Joints of Sprouting Box

Figs. 29, 30 and 31.—Side and End Elevations and Plan of Alternative Sprouting Box

Fig. 32.—Details of Joints of Alternative Sprouting Box

Fig. 33.—Potato Carrier

GARDEN BASKETS

POTATO CARRIERS

Figs. 22, 23, and 24 give elevations and plan of a sprouting box and collector, most of which is made of strips of wood, roofing tile laths $1\frac{1}{4}$ in. by $\frac{3}{4}$ in. in section being useful for this purpose. To make a box of strips is to make it light and to save material. It also allows a current of air all round the tubers.

When using comparatively small strips of wood, great reliance has to be placed on the joints. In the instance here given dovetail joints are used, these being the most suitable for strength and durability. It will be noticed that the bottom is so arranged as to secure the greatest resistance to the downward pressure of any weight of potatoes that may be placed on it. The bottom rests on side laths which are screwed to the sides, and the bottom laths are placed across the box to gain the greatest strength. Figs. 25, 26, and 27 give the details of the joints at A, B, and C respectively. Fig. 28 is a cross-section of the side, showing the lath supporting the bottom screwed to the side.

One drawback to this box or carrier is that if several are needed they cannot be packed one on another and so save space. Figs. 29, 30, and 31 give elevations and plan of a box made so that they can be so placed. The ends of both boxes are not made of laths, but all the rest of the box consists of laths alone. In Fig. 32 is given an enlarged detail showing the construction of the box.

The potato and general carrier shown by Fig. 33 is very useful. The bottom is of strong linoleum nailed or screwed to the sides. It is especially useful for gathering a daily supply of vegetables.

The scale to which Figs. 22, 23, 24, 29, 30, 31, and 33 are made is given, so that little difficulty will be experienced in getting the sizes. It can be understood that these sizes can be varied to meet individual requirements, although the weight that can easily be carried will limit the size in its outward dimensions.

Trellises, Porches and Arches

MAKING AND FIXING TRELLIS WORK

SAWN laths, such as are used for plaster work, are very suitable for the construction of treillage. These laths are sold in bundles of 500 foot lengths and are obtainable from any builders' merchant. The size of trellis work panels is optional, but convenient sizes are as follow. The square mesh (Fig. 1) 2 ft. wide and of any length required; 45° mesh (Fig. 2) in panels 5 ft. by 2 ft. 6 in.; 60° mesh panels 4 ft. by 2 ft. 6 in., and 70° mesh 6 ft. by 2 ft. 6 in.; the longest laths required in each panel being in order 3 ft. 6 in., 4 ft. 6 in., and 6 ft. 6 in. For a quick method of construction obtain four well-seasoned and thoroughly dry boards, the size of the panels, and not less than 1½ in. thick. Cut them quite square and set out the meshes on the face to Fig. 1, allowing 3 in. spaces apart. Grooves are now sunk to the transverse line ⅜ in. deep; cut into the lines to allow a little play for the lath. The longitudinal

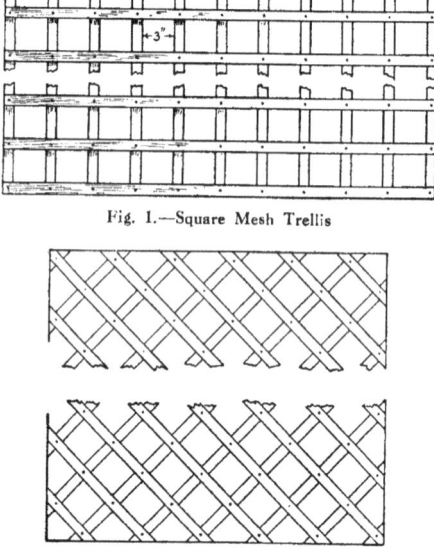

Fig. 1.—Square Mesh Trellis

Fig. 2.—Diamond Mesh Trellis

TRELLISES, PORCHES AND ARCHES

grooves are sunk $\frac{3}{16}$ in. only. Fill in the transverse grooves with $\frac{7}{8}$ in. hoop-iron drilled, countersunk and screwed to the woodwork. Then place the laths in transverse grooves and follow with the longitudinal ones above them. Nail each centre with $\frac{1}{2}$ in. trellis pins. The hoop-iron underneath the laths serves to clinch the pin as it is driven home. The projecting laths at the end and sides may now be cut off and the panel removed and folded up. Panels of each kind of mesh may be set out in a similar manner.

Trellis work is erected on a garden wall by providing a suitable framework of desired length and height. To make the framework obtain some pieces of red deal about 3 in. by 2 in. and fix same to the wall about 6 ft. apart by means of wall hooks, as shown in Fig. 3. A top rail of the same size wood is fixed to the posts by bolts. A plough groove on the underside of this rail, as shown in Fig. 4, will be an advantage. For the lower part of the framework a piece of wood about 2 in. by $1\frac{1}{2}$ in. will do to fix on the top of the wall (see Figs. 3 and 4).

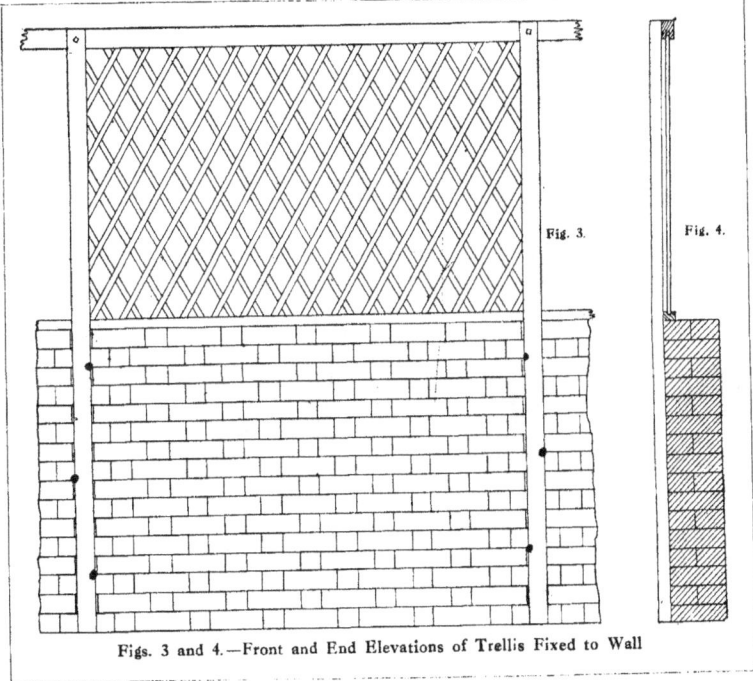

Figs. 3 and 4.—Front and End Elevations of Trellis Fixed to Wall

GARDEN ARCH

It may be worth while to point out the rather meaningless nature of very many garden arches of every type which are constantly seen standing isolated from all immediate surroundings and serving no real purpose, and it is contended if such arches can be made part of some feature in a more or less comprehensive scheme, the effect is likely to appear more coherent and complete.

The central arch portion of the one under consideration (Fig. 5) consists first of all of four upright posts 1½ in. square and 8 ft. 10½ in. long, one end of each being pointed and well tarred ready for bedding in solid ground. The top end has a "notch" 1 in. wide and 1½ in. deep taken out of it, as figured in Fig. 6. This notch is intended to receive the end of one of the two cross-pieces c (Fig. 6) and D (Fig. 7) 2½ in. deep and 1½ in. wide, with their ends cut to the outline suggested at E in Fig. 8. The dotted line in this figure indicates the end of the upright where partly cut away to receive the cross-piece, under the overhanging end of which is fixed a shaped bracket cut out of ⅞ in. stuff 12 in. long and 3 in. wide, as at F in Fig. 8 and as dotted in Fig. 6, this being merely firmly bradded in the position there shown.

Fig. 5.—Garden Arch and Dwarf Screen

The couple of upright posts on each side of the arch are kept at a distance of 12 in. in the clear, by means of three short rails, G, H, and J in Fig. 9, 1½ in. square, and notched and splayed at their ends, as shown in plan by Fig. 10, where the shaded squares, of course, represent the posts. This is probably the very easiest joint possible to form, although quite efficient in such a case when properly nailed or screwed. It will be readily gathered from Figs. 7 and 9 that the rail G is about 4 ft. 6 in. above the ground level, J only about 6 in., and H midway between the two others. Either one or both of the lower rectangular spaces to the sides of the arch may appropriately be filled in with trellis, if possible of the square rather than the diagonal variety. This square treillage can be made from plasterers' laths, and will complete the arch with the exception of a series of six light strips fixed across the two cross-pieces on the top, as indicated on the various figures.

Dealing next with the simple screens at the sides of the arch, it is proposed to adopt for these an even more elementary form of construction. They are intended to consist of uprights some 5 ft. 6 in. long arranged in pairs 3 in. apart, except next the arch, where a single upright will be observed, and they will be set out at about 3-ft. intervals right across the garden. They can be made of practically any very light stuff, and should have three horizontal rails of the same size running across them, as in Fig. 7. level with the rails G, H, and J (Fig. 9). The fixing here depends not even on a simple joint such as that previously described for the arch, but entirely on the nailing or screwing at these points of crossing. On the lower portions of this framework it should be found quite straightforward to fix trellis such as that indicated.

TRELLISES, PORCHES AND ARCHES

A curved member at the top, as at K in Fig. 7, is a distinct improvement. It can be contrived with a length of pliable cane bound in position with wire, and will help to carry the climbing roses, etc., round to the top bar or rail.

The whole of the work should be thoroughly protected from the effects of sun

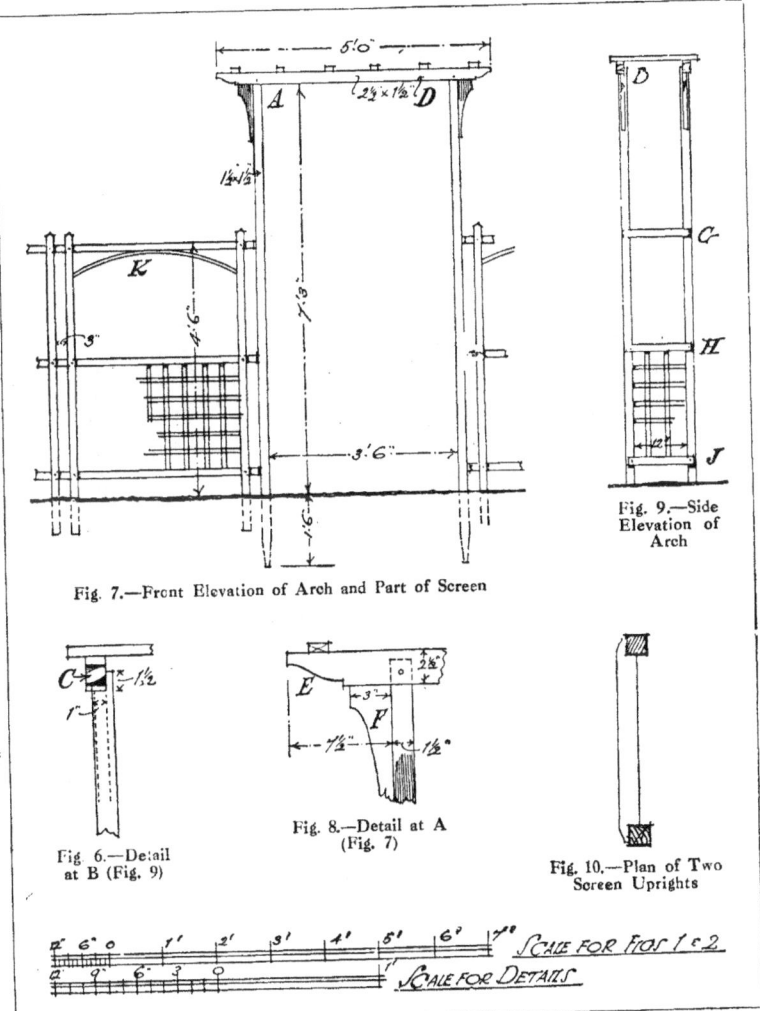

Fig. 7.—Front Elevation of Arch and Part of Screen

Fig. 6.—Detail at B (Fig. 9)

Fig. 8.—Detail at A (Fig. 7)

Fig. 9.—Side Elevation of Arch

Fig. 10.—Plan of Two Screen Uprights

THE PRACTICAL WOODWORKER

and rain by a sufficient coating of paint or creosote.

TRELLISED ARBOUR

The line drawing (Fig. 11) shows a scheme for a simple structure which can be kept merely as a trellised arbour, as shown, or developed into a summer-house, by filling in the sides with boarding and putting a felted roof. Most of its effectiveness depends on the flanking arches with which it is combined, and the whole will poles, stout for the framework and small for the filling-in; or the whole would look well in squared and painted or stained stuff for the framework with planed trellis between. Carefully fixed together at the various joints, it will be found that no halving, etc., is necessary.

Figs. 12 and 13 are respectively skeleton elevation and plan to show the proposed arrangement of the work, while the suggested sizes can be obtained from Figs. 14 and 15, these being a half plan and cross-section. Fig. 14 gives lengths enabling

Fig. 11. - Trellised Arbour

afford opportunities for a fine display of roses or other climbers. A device of this sort is especially suitable for the comparatively narrow garden plot, which is always increased in apparent extent by transverse screens; or the same idea could be introduced in several other positions.

It is not essential that the two arches should be especially made for this scheme; they can equally well be of the ordinary wire, trellis, or "rustic" types, and either round or pointed. Their distance apart will, of course, depend on the total width of available ground, the dimensions given in the figures being in the nature of suggestions. The arbour itself also can be of either larch or other straight unwrought the sloping sides to be set out, and also the main uprights A and B, which should be very firmly bedded in the ground, with concrete or bricks round them if necessary. They are splayed at the top to receive a head as at C (Fig. 15), which will later serve to take a series of light horizontal battens to form the roof. A sill D and rail E are also fixed along the sides and back, and filled in with uprights from top to bottom. The lower panels are finished with lattice work of some description, and the whole requires very thoroughly painting or treating with some efficient preservative.

The seat introduced could be based on one of the numerous designs shown and described on other pages of this work.

TRELLISES, PORCHES AND ARCHES

and it will be found a great improvement if the floor of the arbour is paved with concrete or gravel, arranged slightly sloping so that water will not accumulate, and brought out to a curved step or riser along the front, which could be finished with bricks set on edge

have a striking effect in any garden, even if it was not erected for either of the definite objects mentioned. The screen could be altered and adapted to meet individual requirements. For instance, the arch and gate could be omitted, or the arch could be included and the gate omitted,

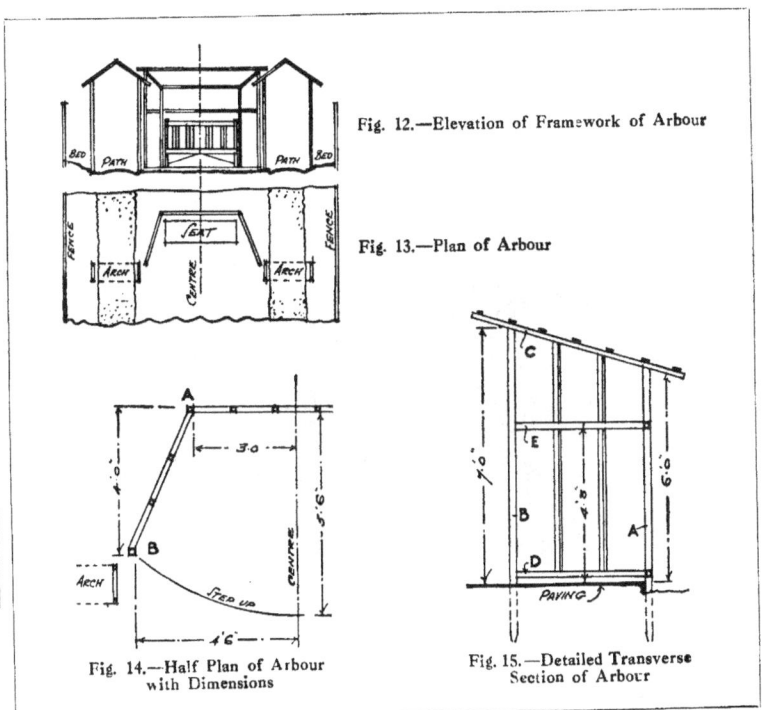

Fig. 12.—Elevation of Framework of Arbour

Fig. 13.—Plan of Arbour

Fig. 14.—Half Plan of Arbour with Dimensions

Fig. 15.—Detailed Transverse Section of Arbour

TRELLIS ARCH AND SCREEN

The trellis arch and screen shown by Fig. 16 could be used for many purposes in the garden, such as for hiding an unsightly part, and when covered with climbing plants would prove an effective screen. Or it could be used to divide the flower and kitchen gardens, while a piece of ornamental woodwork of this description would while the dimensions which are given could be varied. Oiled or varnished oak could be used in making the screen; but painted deal could be used if desired, and would give a very fine effect if painted white.

The upright posts for the side portions of the screen (Fig. 17) are 7 ft. 6 in. long, this allowing a length of 1 ft. 6 in. for sinking into the ground by 2½ in. thick by 2 in. wide. The upper connecting rails are 3 ft. 10 in. long by 2½ in. thick by 2 in. deep, and they are shaped as shown, being compassed about 4 in. The lower connecting rails are 3 ft. 10 in. long by 2 in. deep by 1½ in. thick. The upper connecting rails are mortised and tenoned into the uprights, as shown by Figs. 18 and 19, and the lower connecting rails are mortised and tenoned into the uprights, as shown by Figs. 18 and 20. These joints when they are finally fixed should be well painted and secured with wood pins. The rails which form the be about 4 in. square by ½ in. thick. Small tenons are formed at the top ends of the uprights, suitable mortises being cut in the caps, and by this means the caps are fixed in position.

The uprights for the arch are of a similar section to the uprights at the sides. The upper cross rail is 3 ft. 10 in. long by 2¼ in. thick by 2 in. deep, and is shaped as shown, while the lower cross rail is 3 ft. 1 in. long and of a similar section. The lower cross rail is tenoned into the uprights, and the uprights are tenoned into the upper cross

Fig. 16.—Trellis Arch and Screen

trellis are 1 in. wide by ½ in. thick in section, and the horizontal rails are fixed 8 in. apart, the perpendicular rails being fixed 4 in. apart. The horizontal rails are mortised into the uprights, as shown by Fig. 21, the outer faces of the rails being kept level with the outer faces of the lower connecting rails. The perpendicular rails are mortised into the upper connecting rails, as shown by Fig. 22, and are nailed to the lower connecting rails, while the horizontal and perpendicular rails are nailed together, as shown by Figs. 21 and 22. The tops of the uprights should be finished with wooden caps, which should rail, as shown by Fig. 18. The small upright rails which are framed between the upper and lower cross rails are 1 in. wide by ½ in. thick in section, and they are mortised into the upper and lower cross rails, as shown by Fig. 18.

The gate is framed up with two sides rails and top and bottom rails (Fig. 23). The side rails are 3 ft. 4½ in. long by 2¼ in. thick by 2 in. wide. The top rail is 2 ft. 9 in. long by 2¼ in. thick by 2 in. deep, and is compassed about 4 in., and the bottom rail is 2 ft. 9 in. long by 2 in. deep by 1½ in. thick. The top and bottom rails are framed into the side rails with mortise-

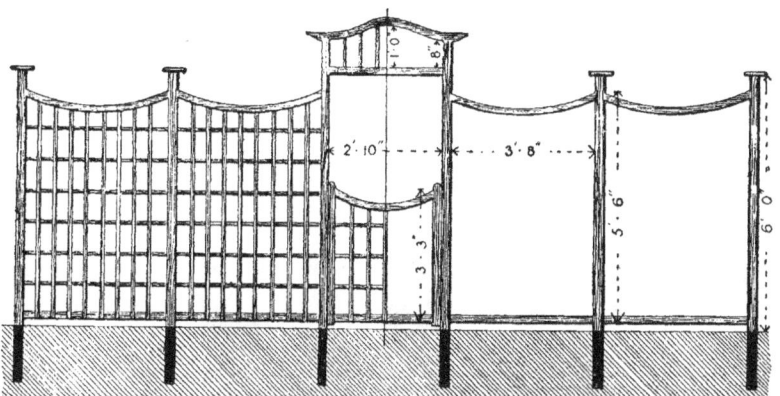

Fig. 17.—Front Elevation of Trellis Arch and Screen

Fig. 18.—Detail of Framing of Arch

Fig. 19.—Method of Fixing Upper Rails

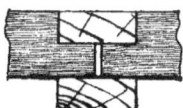

Fig. 20.—Method of Fixing Lower Rails

Fig. 21.

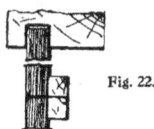

Fig. 22.

Figs. 21 and 22.—Method of Mortsing Horizontal and Perpendicular Connecting Rails

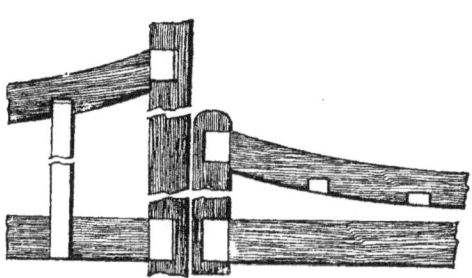

Fig. 23.—Detail of Framing of Screen and Gate

and-tenon joints, as shown by Fig. 18, and the small rails which form the trellis are fixed in a similar manner to those in the sides of the screen. The gate should be hung with butt hinges, and fitted with a suitable latch of the garden gate variety.

In fixing the screen, holes must be prepared in the ground for the reception of the lower ends of the uprights, and when the screen is in position the earth must be well rammed in round the uprights. It will be well to give the parts of the uprights which are sunk into the ground a coat of tar or thick paint.

SIMPLE COTTAGE PORCH

In the choice of a design for a porch there are many from which to choose, such as the close porch with glass sashes, the rustic porch, and the open porch with wrought timber. The porch here shown (Fig. 24) is entirely made of wood, and covered with a piece of waterproofing material on the top. Front and end elevations and plan are shown by Figs. 25, 26 and 27 respectively.

Any kind of wood is suitable for this piece of work. Red, yellow, or even white pine might be used for cheapness. Hardwood would be very suitable; but, as a rule, it is difficult to work, and is expensive. Of course, if there is no objection to the cost, a teak, mahogany, or oak, varnished, porch would look very well. The material required is: Two front posts, 7 ft. by $2\frac{1}{4}$ in. by $2\frac{1}{4}$ in.; two back posts, 7 ft. 3 in. by $2\frac{1}{4}$ in. by $2\frac{1}{4}$ in.; four rails, 1 ft. 4 in. by $2\frac{1}{4}$ in. by $2\frac{1}{4}$ in.; two top rails, 2 ft. 3 in. by $2\frac{1}{4}$ in. by $2\frac{1}{4}$ in.; one bracket, 1 ft. by 6 in. by 1 in.; six pieces for lower panels, each 3 ft. 3 in. by 1 in. by 1 in.; for the lattice panel, 44 ft. of $1\frac{1}{4}$ in. by $\frac{3}{8}$ in.; and for the roof, 4 ft. 3 in. by 2 ft. 3 in. by 1 in. Six holdfasts about 5 in. long, as shown in Fig. 28, and a piece of tarred felt to cover the roof are also required.

Fig. 24.—Cottage Porch

Plane the wood on the face and edge, and then gauge for the thickness and breadth. The planing should now be completed, taking care that each piece is perfectly square and that the surfaces are true. The piece for the top should be planed on both sides, but it is just possible that it will only be procurable in two pieces 15 in. fully wide, when it would require to be jointed where the two pieces meet. Plane up the four edges, and fit together the two parts forming the joint. Put two dowels $\frac{3}{8}$ in. in diameter in the joint. These circular pins are 3 in. long, and are fitted in for $1\frac{1}{2}$ in. into corresponding holes bored in the edge of the joint. The dowels should fit tightly, as

TRELLISES, PORCHES AND ARCHES

the firmness of the joint between the two boards depends on that for the holding together.

If a long flooring board can be procured, the top part of the roof could be formed out of this, and would save the making of special joints. Plane the flooring board on the face, and make small chamfers on the joints, which will give the underside of the roof a very pleasing appearance.

The parts of the framing should be marked off in pairs. This is best done by marking the face of each piece and also the inner edge. Bring together the two pairs of posts, and mark off the positions of the bottom and middle mortises. Square the marks on both edges, and mark the thickness of the tenons on the mortise spaces. Lay one of the front and back posts on the top of the bench, as if in position to form

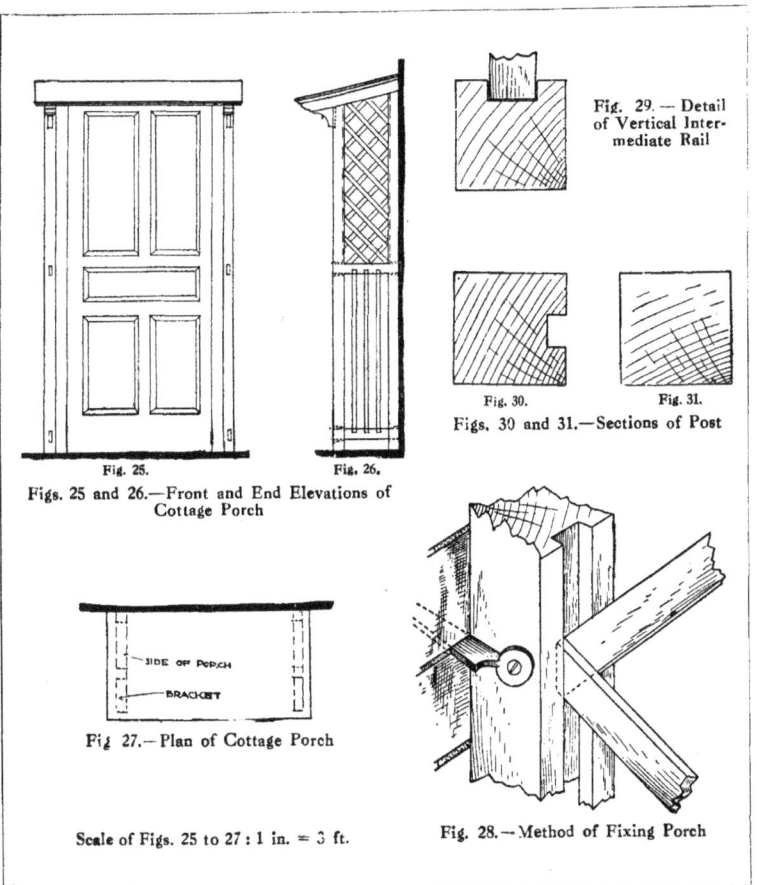

Fig. 29. — Detail of Vertical Intermediate Rail

Figs. 30 and 31.—Sections of Post

Figs. 25 and 26.—Front and End Elevations of Cottage Porch

Fig. 27.—Plan of Cottage Porch

Scale of Figs. 25 to 27 : 1 in. = 3 ft.

Fig. 28.—Method of Fixing Porch

the side of the porch. Lay the top rail in position at the head of the posts, and mark off the position of the tenons on the ends of the posts and the two mortises on the top rail. The lengths of the mid and bottom rails are marked off in the same way as the post, with the addition that the mortises are set out for the small posts in the lower panel.

The mortises can now be cut out. The mortises on the lower mid and top rails are only cut halfway down. In tenoning cut the shoulders of the joint first, then form the tenon on the cross rails. The vertical intermediate rail has no tenons, these being housed in both ends, as shown in Fig. 29. The next part of the work is the cutting of the groove for the lattice panel and the shaped bracket at the top of the post. A section of the post below the lattice pattern is shown by Fig. 31, and a section with the groove by Fig. 30. These grooves are only cut out on the posts, the mid and top rails being left plain. Mark off the grooves with a scratch gauge, and mortise out with a chisel, and finish with a rebate plane. There is no reason why a plough should not be partly used to form this work.

The top rails having been already mortised are now marked off for the ornamental end. Set off from the outer mortise the breadth of the shaped bracket, then ½ in. for a projection beyond the bracket, and add 3 in. for the moulded end. The curved edge is cut with a fine bow-saw, after which it is pared and glasspapered. The cutting of the shaped brackets is shown, the marking off having been done on both sides of the wood. Finish the curved edge with the spokeshave, and rub with glasspaper.

In fitting together the framing, each of the inner edges of the posts should be cleaned off and glasspapered, after which the edges of the rails and the vertical division pieces can be planed all round. In putting together, fit the division pieces into the rails. Then turn this part into a horizontal position, and fit into the post as shown. The outer post is then placed in position, when the two posts are drawn close together, and are fixed by driving wedges into the mortises at each side of the tenons. The top rail for the roof is now fitted on to the ends of the posts, and the bracket nailed in position. All these joints should be put together with paint, each part being well coated, and the wedges dipped into the paint before being driven into the joint.

In fitting the lattice panel, arrange the frame of the side of the porch on the bench, then place the strips of wood for the panel in position. Mark the length of each piece by drawing a line on both sides top and bottom, using a wooden straightedge as shown. The various strips for the panel are now cut to the lines set off, when each is fitted into the grooves in the posts and nailed.

In fitting up the porch, the wood framework should be fixed to the wall of the house with three holdfasts on each side. Of course, the positions of the side frames depend very much on the width of the door; but a very good plan for a small porch is to set up the side frames 3 in. back from the side of the door. Cut out the mortar joint for a depth of 3 in. at the holdfast, fill up with a piece of wood, and drive the holdfasts in position in one vertical line from top to bottom. Each side frame is now fitted to the wall, and the wall post is screwed to the holdfasts.

The roof boarding is then cut to its proper length, cleaned smooth on the ends, and chamfered on the lower arris on the front and both ends. In nailing the boards in position, see that the side frames are at right angles to the wall, and that the projection of the roof boarding is the same on both ends. Cover the roof with a piece of natural asphalt or felt roofing, and if the house front is a brick one, scrape out the first horizontal joint above the porch roof. Put the edge of the felt into the joint, then fold down to form a flashing along the roof to where it is to be tacked along the edges. In painting the porch, rub all the wood well with a piece of glasspaper. Then cover all the knots with knotting, and give the priming coat. Allow it to stand at least one day, then rub down again. Putty all the nail holes, and coat with paint. For the finishing

TRELLISES, PORCHES AND ARCHES

coats, rub well with glasspaper and coat evenly with white enamel. This may be repeated; but in each case allow plenty of time for the succeeding coat to harden.

COVERED COTTAGE PORCH

The working drawings given comprise front and side views (Figs. 32 and 33), plan above the ground level (Fig. 34), plan looking down on the top (Fig. 35), and enlarged details of the construction (Figs. 36 and 37), which has been kept as simple as possible. The various sizes given can be varied somewhat, but if adhered to the effect will be similar to that shown by the small sketch of the completed porch (Fig. 38).

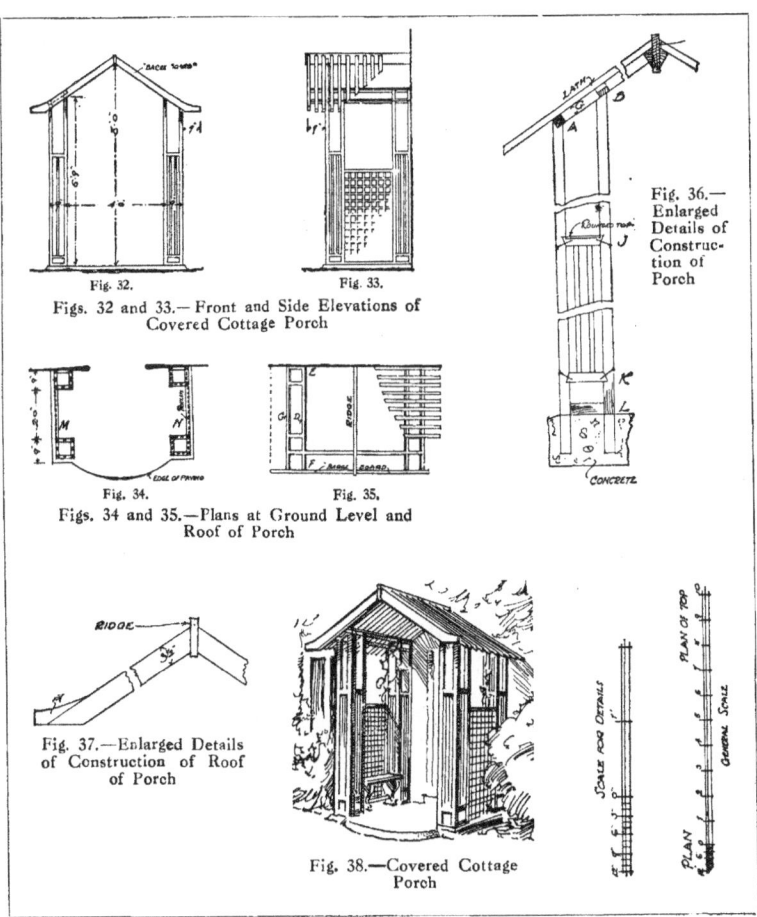

Figs. 32 and 33.—Front and Side Elevations of Covered Cottage Porch

Fig. 36.—Enlarged Details of Construction of Porch

Figs. 34 and 35.—Plans at Ground Level and Roof of Porch

Fig. 37.—Enlarged Details of Construction of Roof of Porch

Fig. 38.—Covered Cottage Porch

To ensure stability it is advisable to bed the uprights in a layer of concrete a few inches in thickness, which can be finished smooth on top or with a gravel surface, as preferred. The main structure is composed of four groups of posts, one at each angle, and each formed by four uprights from 1 in. to 1½ in. square. These are shown on the plan (Fig. 34) and the front of one group in detail in Fig. 36, from which it will be seen that the tops are cut out to take two horizontal bearers, as at A and B on the detail and C and D on the plan of top. From the latter illustration it will be gathered that they start from the wall face at E and continue to F, at which point they project 9 in. in front of the uprights below. The short cross-pieces (G on the detail, and which will readily be found on the plan of top) are spiked in position where shown, to keep the bearers at the correct distance apart, while next the front a fourth cross-piece is not stopped against the bearer B like the others, but is halved with it, and continued up to meet the ridge as shown on the detail. This ridge may be 6 in. by ¾ in., and is fixed against the wall at one end, and at the other projects about 1½ in. in advance of the bearers described, being supported by the fourth cross-piece on each side. Two rafters or barge boards about 3½ in. by ¾ in. are firmly fixed to the ends of the bearers and against the ridge. The detail shows how it is suggested to shape the feet of this portion, by adding a small curved piece as at H.

The roof will eventually be formed either with ordinary trellis or very light laths as shown, to take the upper ends of which triangular pieces should be fixed on the sides of the ridge. Horizontal pieces as at J and K (Fig. 36) should be fitted into the uprights on all sides, the upper ones being 4 ft. 6 in. above the paving and rounded off on top if desired. These will be filled in with square strips, either one or, for preference, two to each side, which will not require mortising, a nail driven in on the slant at each end being sufficient. A sill piece may be inserted next the cement (see L), and the sides at M and N (Fig. 34) similarly filled in with a couple of rails to take pieces of trellis as noted, forming a recess on each side of the porch. The trellis may be of the diagonal variety or specially built up of laths at right angles to each other as shown, which would make a superior style of finish.

It should be understood that this is a very light method of construction, not suitable for anything heavier than trellis, for which it is well adapted. There will be no difficulty in arranging the same design to take, for instance, a boarded roof. Rafters about 2 in. by 1 in. may be fixed on top of the bearers A and B.

TRELLISED PORCH WITH GABLE ROOF COVERED WITH WEATHER-BOARDING

The porch shown in Fig. 39 is of picturesque but economical construction. Half front elevation, side elevation, plan and section are shown by Figs. 40, 41, 42 and 43 respectively. The base is composed of a layer of concrete having a slope towards the front so that water will drain off the floor. The corner and door posts are of 3 in. by 3 in. material, and are grooved in the lower portions to receive the panels, which latter are made of grooved-and-tongued boarding, as indicated in Fig. 46.

The sills are held in position either by holding down bolts as shown, or by iron dowels. Fig. 47 shows a detail of sill and boarding.

The top of the sides and the front wings are composed of square bars halved together, thus forming open trellis work. The rafters over the front are strengthened by cross bracing, as shown in Figs. 40 and 45. The roof is covered with rebated weather boarding.

The top rails of the sides are continued and bracketed (see Figs. 43 and 44) to give support to overhanging gable. A detail of the barge boards is shown in Fig. 48. Seats are formed on each side of the porch, the construction of the supports being indicated in Fig. 42. The porch may be made of any suitable timber, red deal being preferable.

RUSTIC ARCH AND ESPALIER

The resident in a country district will often find ready to his hand a variety of woods, pear, apple, larch, oak, etc., suitable for rustic carpentry; whereas the city dweller may have difficulty in obtaining just what he wants. Whilst almost any wood will answer for temporary work, the best for permanent work is probably larch (*Larix europœa* D.C.: Order *Abietineœ*), whose straight growth specially fits it for the carrying out of decorative designs; it lasts longer in exposed situations than any other ordinary wood—heart of oak only excepted—and probably ten times as long as those portions of the oak that are generally available for garden carpentry. Larch, too, is plentiful; for larch plantations now abound in most districts, and when they are thinned the rustic carpenter should look out for his supply. The poles grown in thick plantations are better for rustic work than those that grow singly, as the former taper more gradually, and have fewer branches. The wood of spruce and other firs which have the same symmetrical growth, has almost as good an appearance, but it has not the lasting properties of

Fig. 39.—Trellised Porch

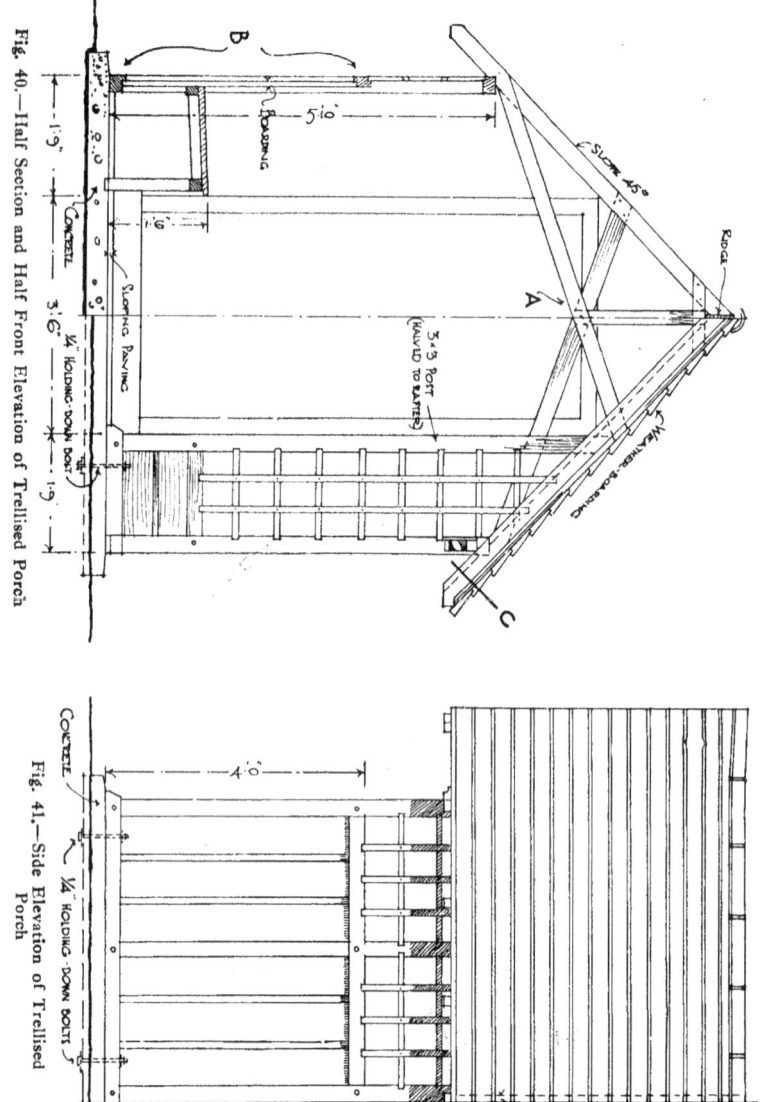

Fig. 40.—Half Section and Half Front Elevation of Trellised Porch

Fig. 41.—Side Elevation of Trellised Porch

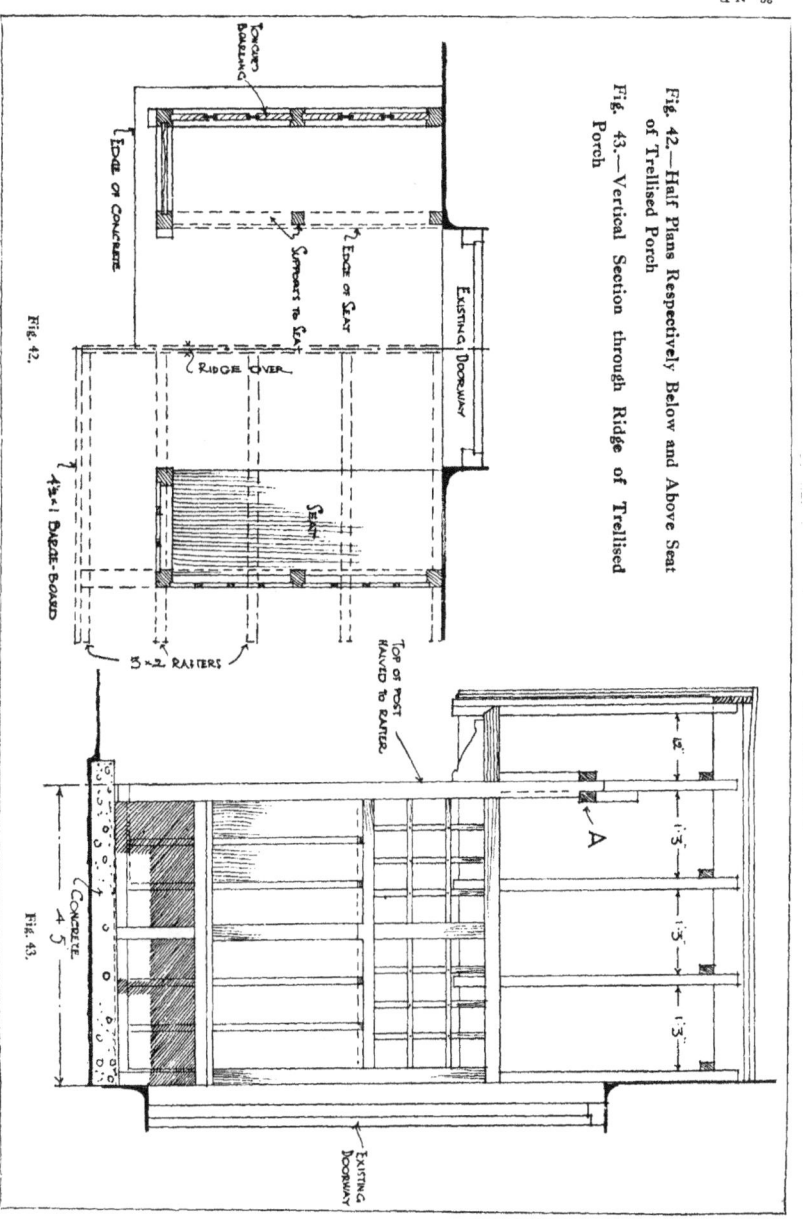

Fig. 42.—Half Plans Respectively Below and Above Seat of Trellised Porch

Fig. 43.—Vertical Section through Ridge of Trellised Porch

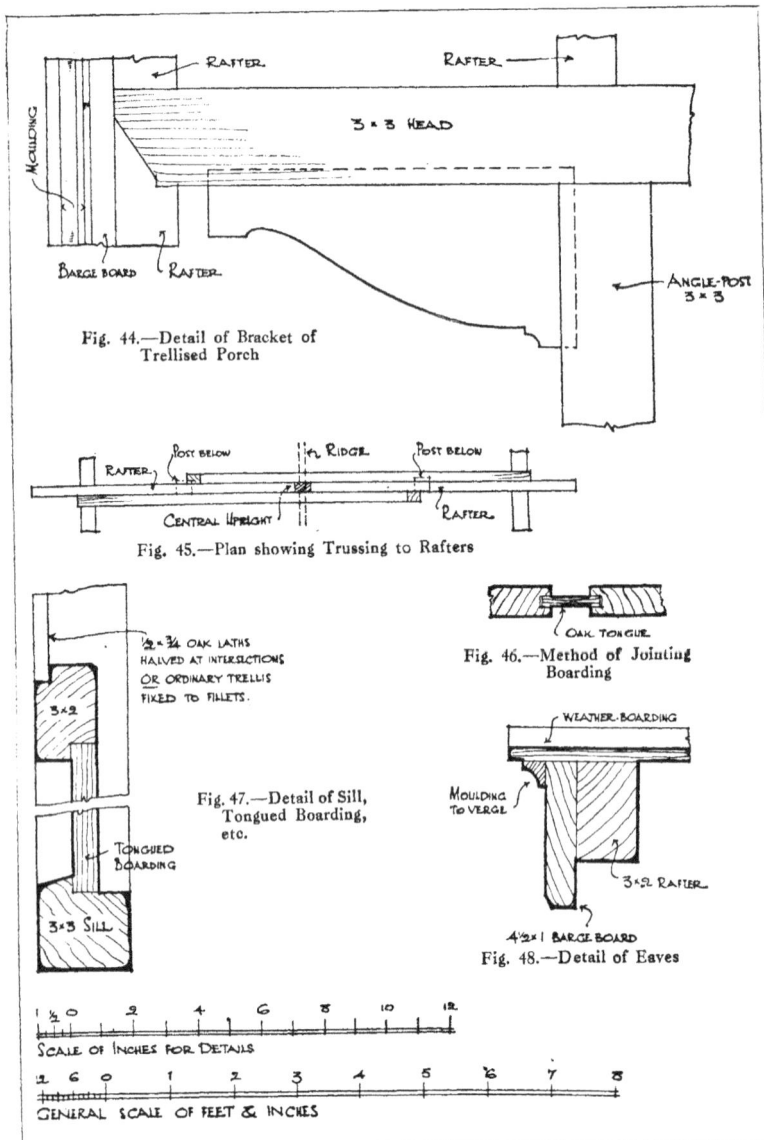

Fig. 44.—Detail of Bracket of Trellised Porch

Fig. 45.—Plan showing Trussing to Rafters

Fig. 46.—Method of Jointing Boarding

Fig. 47.—Detail of Sill, Tongued Boarding, etc.

Fig. 48.—Detail of Eaves

larch. The timber of the larch is not subject to knots, as are the other members of the pine family; but its chief advantage is its non-liability to rot, even in damp places. It frequently happens that the larch poles are erected when in a green state; and it is then necessary to remember that there is considerable shrinkage in the course of drying.

of perhaps 1 ft. 6 in. The plan (Fig. 51) and perspective sketch (Fig. 49), however, show it to be square, presenting the same general appearance on all four sides.

It can be built up entirely of unwrought larch or similar poles, with small stuff for the filling-in at the sides and in the upper parts. Substantial lengths of a fairly heavy section should be obtained for the

Fig. 49.—Rustic Arch and Espalier

The wood of the larch is yellowish-white in colour, and, whilst generally straight and even, it is frequently coarse in grain and liable to split.

The arch illustrated in Fig. 49 is an elaboration of a type fairly often encountered, as will be seen on reference to the front elevation (Fig. 50), from looking at which it might very easily be taken for a rustic arch of the kind having a depth

main uprights, with their ends well tarred if possible, and bedded, say, 2 ft. in the solid ground. In erecting larch or other posts for arches, screens, etc., one of the best methods is to make a narrow hole with a crowbar, and then drive in the pole by means of blows from a heavy mallet or beetle. By the method of digging holes with a spade for the insertion of the posts the solidity of the earth is destroyed, and the posts may prove to be loose in their holes. The main horizontal pieces at the top should be lighter, but still fairly solid, the cross-pieces above them being much smaller in section, and the balustrade or railing at the sides might be of similar light material.

The bracket pieces shown across the upper corners on each face should be selected branches of as nearly the required shape as possible, with their ends cut on the splay to suit. Or these can be varied in a number of ways that will readily occur to the worker, who will doubtless also be able to vary the diamond shape and the uprights in pairs shown as filling in at the top of the framework. The whole of the work is intended to be secured together with stout nails driven in on the slant, while for some of the smaller parts, binding round with several strands of copper wire is likely to be found a very efficacious mode of fixing.

The espalier forms a pleasing feature when continued across a garden, lending interest, and dividing it up, but without any appearance of hemming it in. Similar material to that for the arch can be employed, or, if preferred, planed stuff or cane, the latter easily bending to form the semicircular part shown for each bay.

RUSTIC SCREENS AND ARCHES

These screens and arches may be varied and modified in a number of ways. The

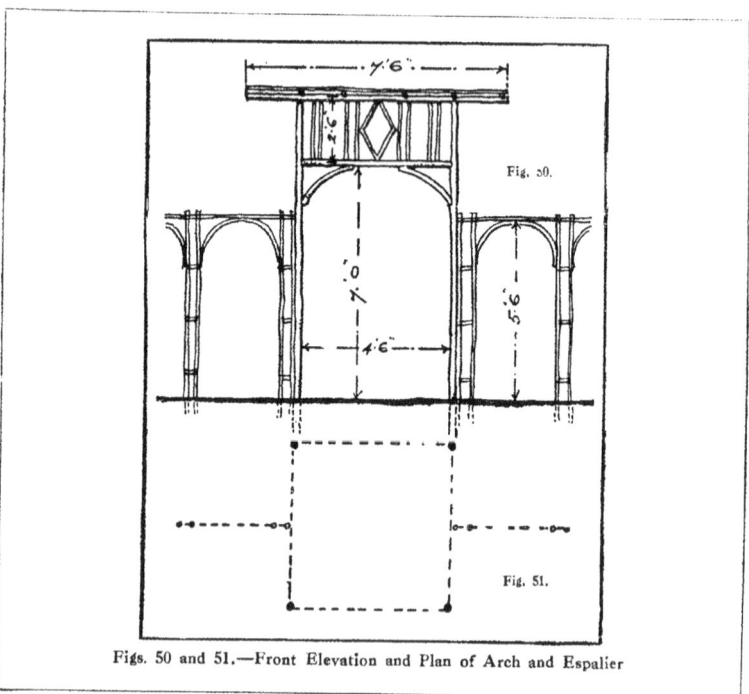

Figs. 50 and 51.—Front Elevation and Plan of Arch and Espalier

TRELLISES, PORCHES AND ARCHES

main framework in each case should be of stout rustic poles strongly nailed together, and let well into the ground to ensure stability; while the filling-in may be of much lighter unwrought branches, slightly towards the top. These square supports should be repeated at intervals of 5 ft. or so. The second (Fig. 53) is the only design without the supports just mentioned, and will need sloping props

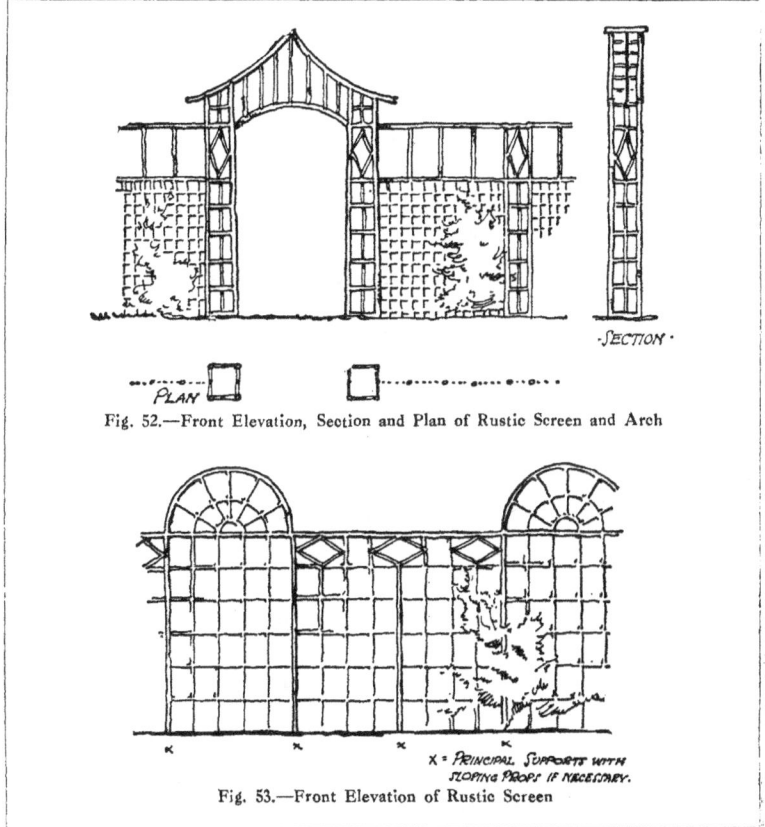

Fig. 52.—Front Elevation, Section and Plan of Rustic Screen and Arch

Fig. 53.—Front Elevation of Rustic Screen

etc., or of planed laths or trellis. Such work should be treated with rot-proof stain or coarse varnish.

In Fig. 52 each side of the arch is a square framework or standard, as indicated on the plan, and the sides taper on each side of the main posts to withstand wind pressure. Fig. 54 would be suitable for the edge of a terrace or bank.

Alternative Design.—Another screen illustrated in Fig. 55 is of the very sim plest construction, the most primitive material and tools, together with the least possible knowledge of carpentry, constituting all that will be required in order to carry out the design.

Larch poles are very suitable for the main framework and bean-sticks, etc., for the minor parts. The various slightly curved pieces shown should be selected with the outline naturally bent, and ample

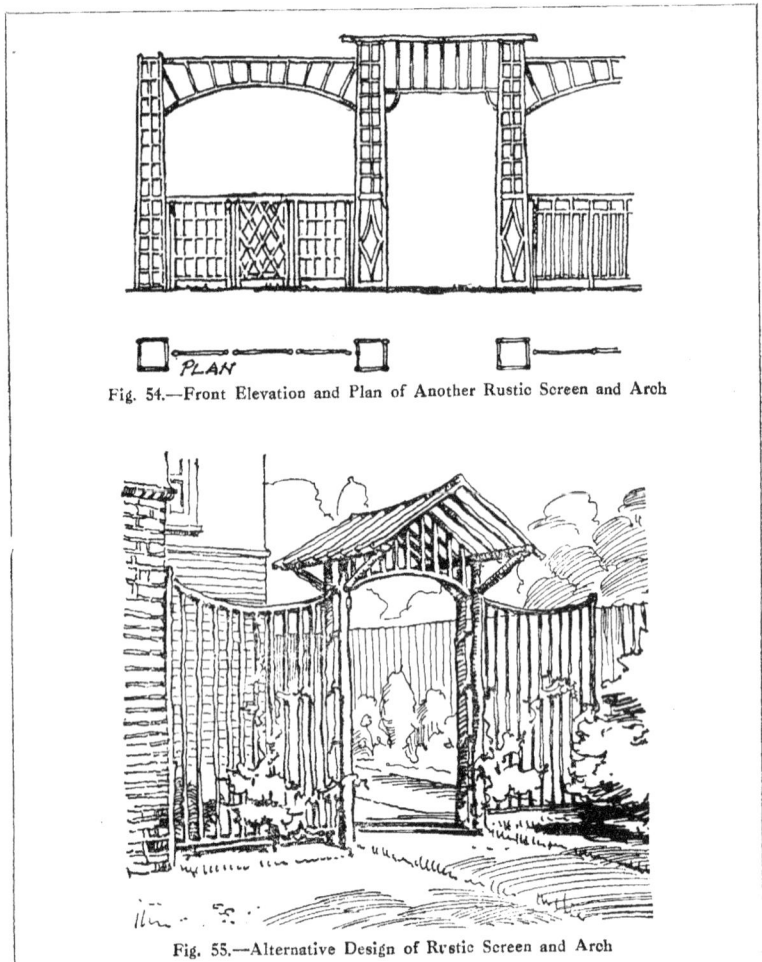

Fig. 54.—Front Elevation and Plan of Another Rustic Screen and Arch

Fig. 55.—Alternative Design of Rustic Screen and Arch

TRELLISES, PORCHES AND ARCHES

length should be allowed where required for bedding the ends in the ground. In doing this it will be found better to drive the uprights in with a mallet than to dig up the earth; 1 ft. 6 in. or 2 ft. should be plenty for ordinary soils, and if tar is handy an application to the ends intended to be buried will act as a preservative.

It is thought that the construction will be apparent from the illustrations. Briefly, and taking the arch first, this consists of in the side view, and connected to the plates by an odd number of pairs of sloping pieces (kept odd in order to have a pair in the centre to take the ends of the small uprights shown above the opening). The sloping members just mentioned should butt against the ridge, and overlap the plate at their lower ends by about 1 ft., being strongly nailed, as, of course, are all the other joints. The actual curved piece for the head of the arch should have fairly stout thickness, and

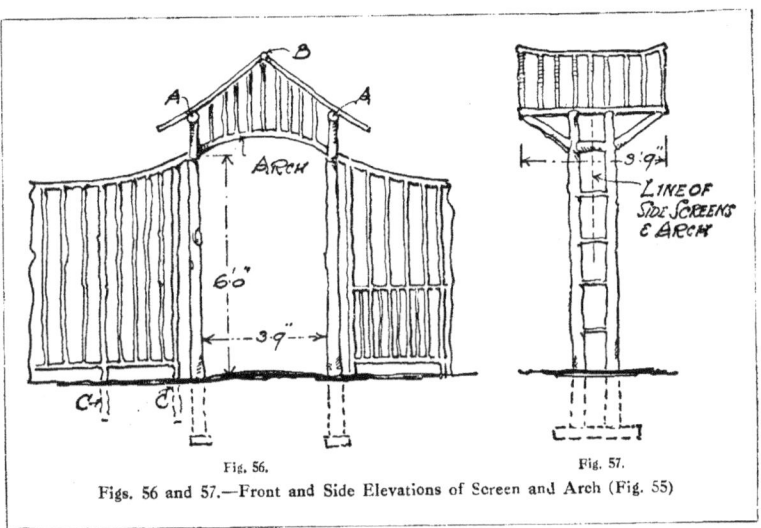

Figs. 56 and 57.—Front and Side Elevations of Screen and Arch (Fig. 55)

four extra stout uprights standing about 7 ft. 6 in. above the ground, supporting horizontal "plates" (as at A) 3 ft. 9 in. long, having sloping pieces under to form brackets.

The lower ends of the pair of main uprights on each side of the opening should go down about 2 ft., and may be fixed to a horizontal "sole-piece," as shown by dotted lines (Figs. 56 and 57), for additional stability.

A thin piece will need to be used as a ridge (B, Fig. 56), selected if possible with its ends turned upwards as shown have a series of thin uprights to fill in the space above it.

The screens at each side of the arch have naturally curved heads, and main uprights or standards, say, four to each bay, counting the end ones (C, Fig. 56), with short sills fitted in between just above the ground with smaller intermediate poles at the desired spaces; but should these be rather wide apart, or if the passage of animals is to be guarded against, a secondary filling in with thin stuff, as shown to the lower part on the right-hand side of Fig. 56.

RUSTIC PERGOLAS

Many large modern gardens can be more suitably ornamented and beautified by the skilful constructing of a prominent and judiciously arranged "pergola," either along a garden walk or sometimes placed to screen the domestic or vegetable portion of the ground from that devoted to ornamental purposes, namely, flower and lawn surfaces. When erected in an artistic manner and adorned with suitable "climbers," they well repay the amount of labour and cost of erecting same.

In beginning the work, assuming the allows the knee to be placed on the material. If the stuff is rather green or wet, the blade will require a fair amount of set to get round the curve without sticking or catching in the cut. After the tops are cut, the splices on the runners or plates should be cut to a fixed line marked by means of a cutting box, which is similar to a mitre box, but having a longer bevel cut. It will be found when putting splice end to splice that it (the splice) will require a saw run through the joint to make a neat, clean fit to exclude the rain. Also, it should be a good rule to always mock the splice joints where

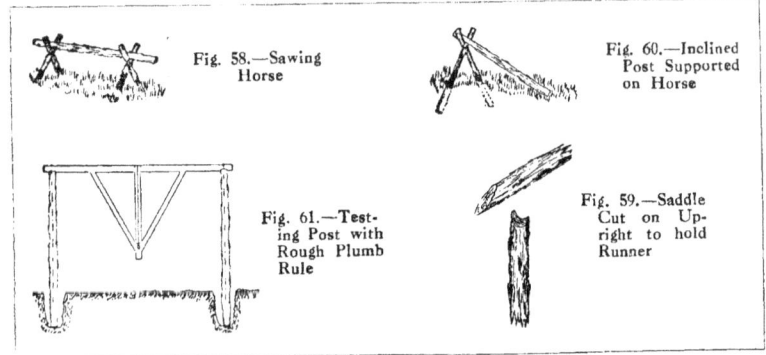

Fig. 58.—Sawing Horse

Fig. 60.—Inclined Post Supported on Horse

Fig. 61.—Testing Post with Rough Plumb Rule

Fig. 59.—Saddle Cut on Upright to hold Runner

job worth the extra trouble, construct a couple of portable "saw horses," or instead drive a couple of pieces of larching with pointed ends crosswise into the ground with a "mall" or "beetle," and spike well together where they cross (see Fig. 58). For a very large job two or more can be erected midway between the ends of the pergola, and in pairs, say, about 6 ft. or 5 ft. apart, to lay the larching in for cutting same. The "saddles" on the uprights or posts should be cut out as shown in Fig. 59, to hold the runners. Some lay the posts horizontal, as in Fig. 58; others cut them whilst the top end rests in the notch inclining upwards, as in Fig. 60. The latter way is just as convenient, but a little awkward at first to get the bow saw blade square in the cut. This way possible. The rafter pieces can be all nailed on and cut roughly to length, or to a chalk line stretched along the tops.

Premising that the stuff has all been cut within a little, proceed to get the first post into the required or stated height above the ground and well rammed up solid all round. If it is desired to keep the spacing equal all through mark a cord line by winding it round a couple of nails driven in a length of larching the required spacing apart, and marking the cord at the nails with some black paint. Then on stretching the marked line along over the post holes it will give the spacing very easily, and save time as well. To level the posts within a little on a flat location, make a rough plumb rule to hang up in the "saddles" (see Fig. 61), and thus

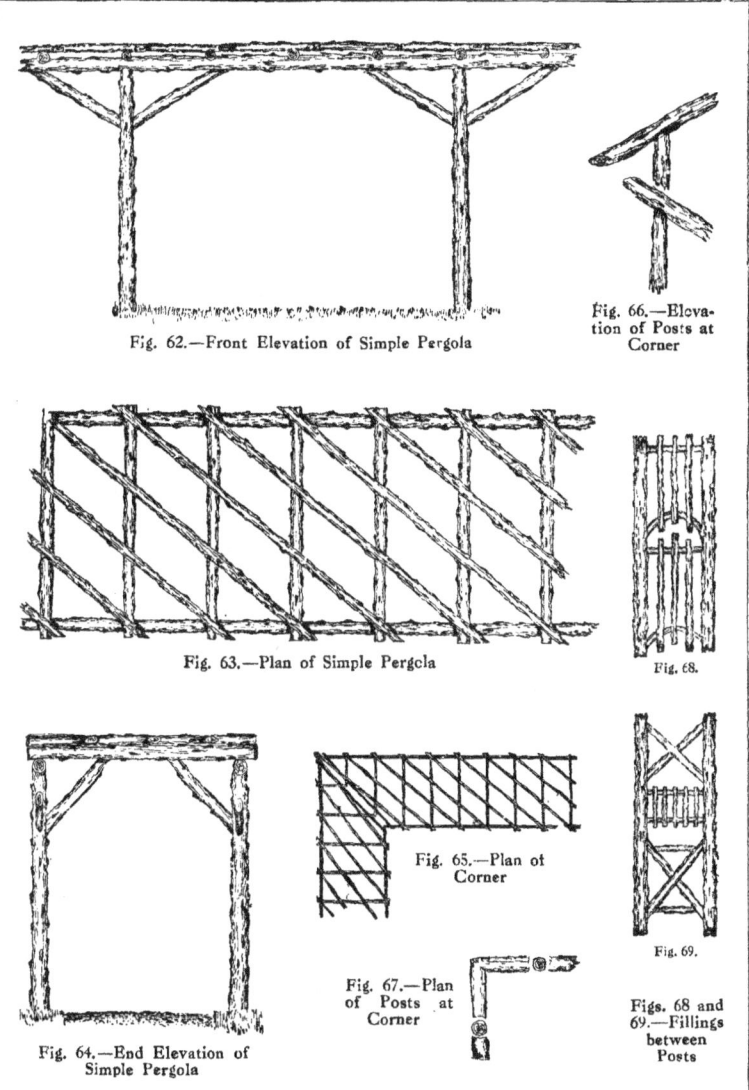

Fig. 62.—Front Elevation of Simple Pergola

Fig. 66.—Elevation of Posts at Corner

Fig. 63.—Plan of Simple Pergola

Fig. 68.

Fig. 64.—End Elevation of Simple Pergola

Fig. 65.—Plan of Corner

Fig. 67.—Plan of Posts at Corner

Fig. 69.

Figs. 68 and 69.—Fillings between Posts

raise or lower each succeeding post to a nicety. It is a good plan to put a large stone or brick in the hole on which to stand the post if the soil is loose and loamy; the nailing drives the posts down. The posts, as a rule, can be plumbed up with the eye.

The plates should be nailed between the posts carefully, as the jarring tends tion or run of same. To prevent winding, it is a good plan to erect and ram up the extreme end posts, and stretch the chalk on same at the top and bottom for the intermediate ones, thus obtaining a good guide with little difficulty. The ramming should be done fairly well above the ground line, so that no water will stand in a pool round the posts.

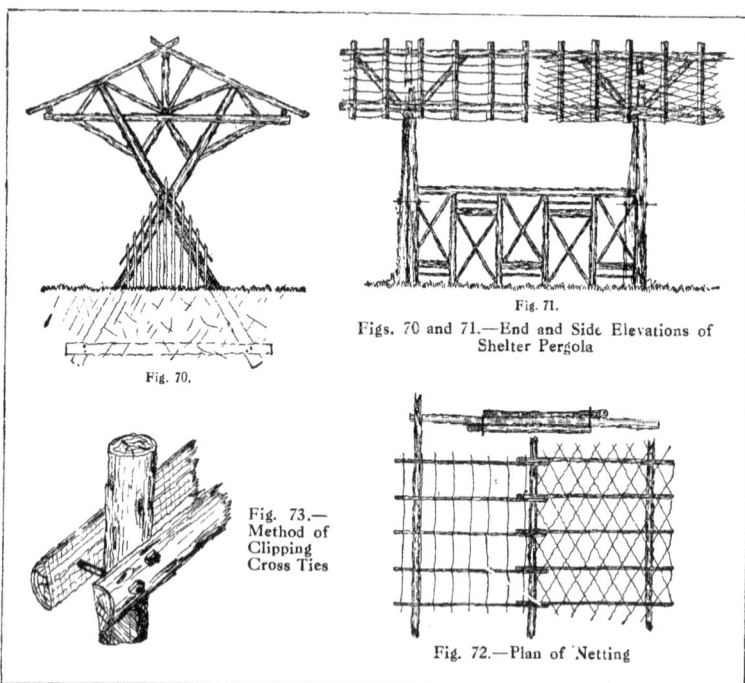

Fig. 70.

Fig. 71.

Figs. 70 and 71.—End and Side Elevations of Shelter Pergola

Fig. 73.—Method of Clipping Cross Ties

Fig. 72.—Plan of Netting

to loosen the other parts already nailed. The braces especially require sound nailing, without unduly splitting the stuff, otherwise the structure will weaken from wind causes later on in stormy weather if much exposed. If the pergola has to follow up or down a declivity, the tops will rake the same or follow the ground line, but be level crosswise to the direc-

Figs. 62, 63, and 64 show a simple design for a pergola, presenting no trouble even to the amateur carpenter. Care should be exercised in keeping the diagonal rafters fairly close, so that the "climbers" can run along without requiring a lot of training. In some cases, if the small branches are left on they form an excellent means for enabling this to be obtained.

TRELLISES, PORCHES AND ARCHES

otherwise long willows can be weaved in and out, just securing the ends with a piece of galvanised wire.

In Fig. 65 will be seen the plan of the pergola showing the manner of working a corner detail. Here double posts should be arranged (*see* Figs. 66 and 67); the diagonal runners meet and hang over the mitre corner, whilst the cross bearers mitre together, and lay on two inserted carrying diagonal bearers. This arrangement lends itself to great variation, and the diagonal bearers could also be made flush with the runners. These methods will equally apply to any angular corner other than square. Curved braces can be cut if obtained, and fixed here and there in pairs, whilst in Figs. 68 and 69 are shown alternative filling in between the posts.

More Simple Designs.—A simple form of pergola that differs from the previous one is shown in Figs. 70 and 71, and forms, more or less, a charming shelter which could be easily made rainproof by waterproof cloths or coverings, or else close-laid boarding with water grooves in same. Thus their erection is more suitable to public gardens, pleasure grounds, and similar places. It will be seen in Fig. 70, which is an end elevation, that the roof is umbrella-shape in section, whilst in Fig. 71, which is a front elevation, the filling in between the cross standards is clearly shown, and can be in alternate bays, or two or more bays filled and then one missed to allow of passing from side to side. Fig. 72 is a plan of the netting, either diagonal or rectangular mesh, laid over roof spars for the foliage of the "climbers." The detail (Fig. 73) shows how the standards are clipped between the earth-buried cross ties, and bolted up with galvanised bolts and nuts or otherwise spiked on with galvanised French or rose-headed gate nails.

An alternate design is given in Fig. 74, whilst Fig. 75 shows a different filling for the panel. These should not be always slavishly copied, but should serve as examples to be thoughtfully improved on, and serve as guides to sound construction. Rough tenons and mortises will consider-

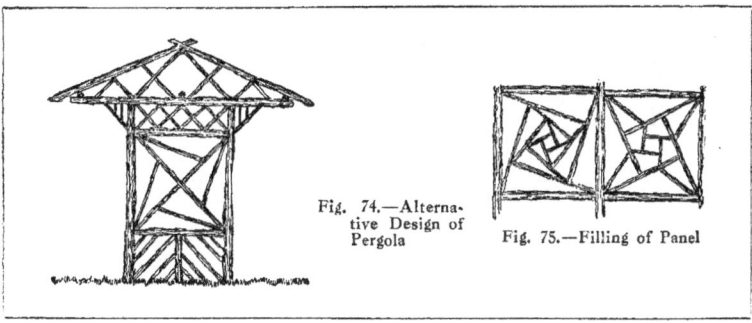

Fig. 74.—Alternative Design of Pergola

Fig. 75.—Filling of Panel

ably strengthen any intricate detail of filling. The type shown in Fig. 70 could be easily made into a square-form shelter, by having another crossing set of tied standards at right angles. The vertical lower cross filling would in this case be omitted, and the roof made out from a central spar, bored at the top end to receive a small flag-pole.

Single Pole Type.—In the front elevation view (Fig. 76) is shown a shelter of the single-pole or standard type. This would act as a divisional screen or fence, and a sunshade when placed in a position facing north. It is simply constructed, and should be strong and substantial to avoid undue pressure from wind force acting on the top portion, with a consequent leverage due to the height. Fig. 77

is a side view, whilst Figs. 78 and 79 show alternate methods of laying the roof spars, either splicing same, or else running the ends by taking care that the joints "mock" or otherwise do not come all on one inclined supporting spar.

The standards are firmly braced and tenoned into sole-plates (Fig. 80), which clearly seen that to get the dowel pins in correctly, a beginning must be made at one end as follows : Support the first bay runners in position, and then bore from the opposite sides of the standards into the runners. Then remove these, and place No. 2 bay runners in correct position, bore into same through the already bored

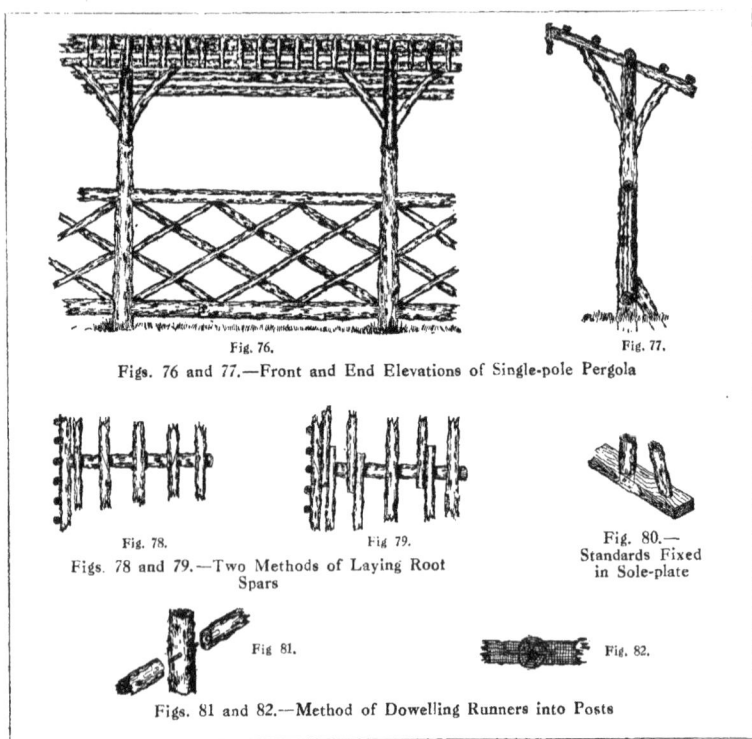

Fig. 76.
Fig. 77.
Figs. 76 and 77.—Front and End Elevations of Single-pole Pergola

Fig. 78.
Fig. 79.
Figs. 78 and 79.—Two Methods of Laying Roof Spars

Fig. 80.—Standards Fixed in Sole-plate

Fig 81.
Fig. 82.
Figs. 81 and 82.—Method of Dowelling Runners into Posts

are placed in rectangular trenches with a well-rammed bottom, fairly level to maintain a plumb position of the standards, whilst the re-turned soil is being rammed round same. The horizontal runners are cut right between the posts or standards, and are held in place with dowels, as in Figs. 81 and 82. It will be holes in the standard next to No. 1, and then right through the other standard into the farther or opposite end. Next take these away, place No. 1 bay runners with the sawn joints creosoted in the final position, and drive dowels into same until they project about 2 in. or 3 in. out of the standard. Then the runners of No. 2 bay

TRELLISES, PORCHES AND ARCHES

are knocked on the projecting dowel ends, the other end driven down into place, and so on. Otherwise, to facilitate or expedite the work where possible, the centre bay can be done first, then working away from same to each end.

be noticed how securely braced this design is, and should be soundly constructed and strongly nailed. The dowel method is shown here in preference to mortise and tenon, as these would unduly weaken the standards.

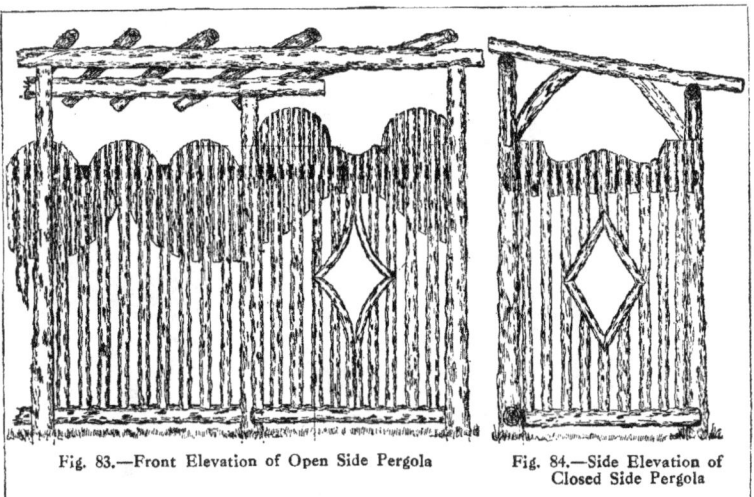

Fig. 83.—Front Elevation of Open Side Pergola

Fig. 84.—Side Elevation of Closed Side Pergola

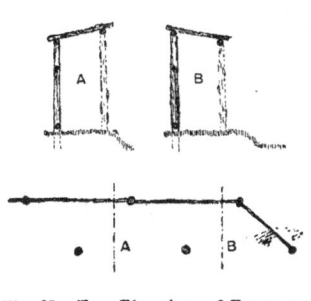

Fig. 85.—Two Elevations of Frames and Plan of Promenade Pergola

Promenade Pergolas.—The pergolas shown by Figs. 83 and 84 are of the open and screened side type, forming pleasant promenades and seat walks, and are more elaborate than the ordinary post and rafter type. In Fig. 85 is shown a plan of the two types, and a side view of each (A and B), the difference only consisting in the rake of the roof spars. Observe that the posts or standards are not in front of one another on a transverse plane, but zigzag in plan (see Fig. 85), one plan serving for both side views.

The filling in of the screened sides may be split fence larching, which is usually sawn down the centre. They are nailed to sawn top rails, which are tenoned into the posts and pinned. The over-lapping top and bottoms of the profile pieces or short pales are secured at the back by nailing on galvanised hoop iron, with holes

Along the front edge of the top a horizontal spar is well spiked or nailed to the inclined top bracing spar, and along on this front short pieces are nailed as shown, to form a bordering or fascia. It should

punched in same to receive the nails. They are usually cut to shape by nailing them on temporarily, and then marking them by chalking round a template placed correctly over the ends. It should be observed that the pales stand on a runner rail at the bottom, which clears the ground to prevent rot or decay.

In Fig. 86 is shown a pergola that possesses a feature of relieving the ordinary type by altering the outline of the roof spars on each side, by alternating the position of same, and giving at the same time twisting surfaces to the planes of the roof spars, which are clearly shown in Fig. 87 (side view) and the plan (Fig. 88). The

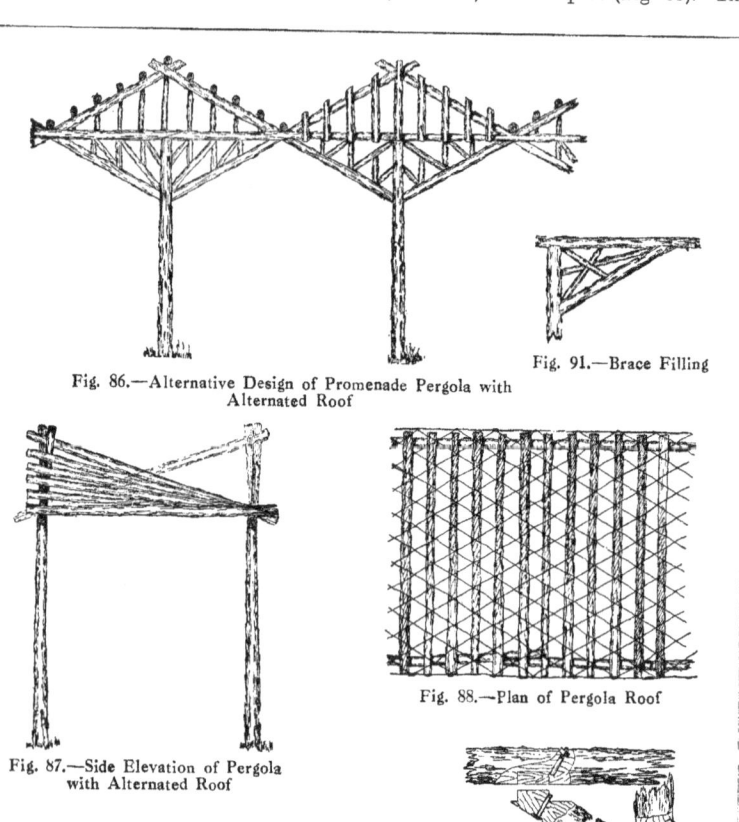

Fig. 86.—Alternative Design of Promenade Pergola with Alternated Roof

Fig. 91.—Brace Filling

Fig. 88.—Plan of Pergola Roof

Fig. 87.—Side Elevation of Pergola with Alternated Roof

Fig. 89.—Detail of Bracing

Fig. 90.—Detail, showing Position of Post Bolts

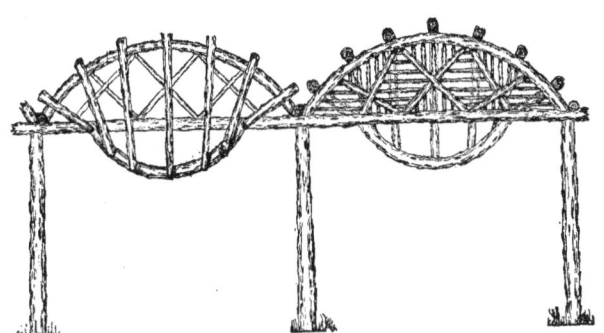

Fig. 92.—Design of Pergola with Alternating Segmental Roof Spar

Fig. 93.—Showing Winding of Roof Spars

Fig. 95.—Detail of Joint of Curved and Horizontal Pieces

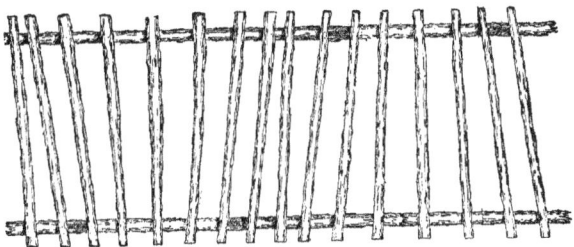

Fig. 94.—Plan of Roof

spars are approximately parallel to one another; but as will be seen, they lay up on the gable spars, the centre one resting in the cross intersection at the top. This arrangement occurs on each side alternatively, and will produce a novel and pleasing effect. The detail (Fig. 89) shows the bracing secured with mortised-and-tenoned joints bolted up, whilst Fig. 90 shows how the post bolts must pass one another for clearance purposes where two braces occur. Fig. 91 is a detail of brace filling.

The design shown by Fig. 92 gives variety by alternating the segmental roof spar with a reverse curve dip on the other side, thus producing a pleasing outline. Fig. 93 shows quite clearly how the roof spars wind, and the plan (Fig. 94) shows also how they radiate on each side to a centre point caused by the reverse curved plate or runner spar. A detail of the joint is shown by Fig. 95. The wrought iron strap should be well screwed at the joint, whilst the dowel pins will prevent sag. Careful bracing underneath the roof spars, with an angle iron here and there, will thoroughly tie the sides together.

Summerhouses

OPEN-FRONTED SUMMERHOUSE

A SUMMERHOUSE of modern design, which will be found to entail practically no complicated work in its erection, providing that the directions given are carried out, does remarkably primitive ideas, and being quite at variance with modern ideas. Rustic (that is, unworked) material is well enough in its place, and is permissible for arches and similar erections; but for larger work it has little to com-

Fig. 1.—Open-fronted Summerhouse

is shown by the sketch Fig 1. Its design is in opposition to the so-called "rustic" type of work which would seem to have been rather overdone, exhibiting as it mend it. In such cases, the main framework should be of properly wrought stuff, while any filling-in and minor details generally may properly be carried out with lengths of branches, if desired, as is suggested in the present instance.

Front and end elevations, cross section and plan are given by Figs. 2, 3, 4, and 5.

Briefly describing the summerhouse in detail, the plan shows the assumed dimensions, which are liable to be varied in order to meet particular requirements, projecting ends at the bottom) firmly to suitable wood fixing-blocks, bedded in a layer of concrete over the whole area involved.

Referring to the sketch of the construction (Fig. 6), this shows in perspective the main framing of one-half of the summerhouse, and this would

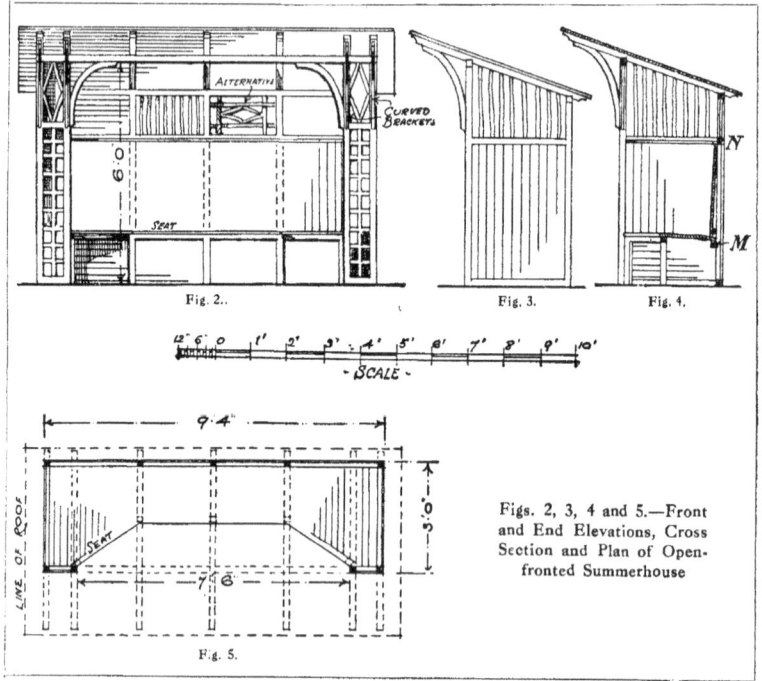

Figs. 2, 3, 4 and 5.—Front and End Elevations, Cross Section and Plan of Open-fronted Summerhouse

always endeavouring, however, to preserve as low and wide an effect as possible, for which purpose the opening on the front is kept down to 6 ft. high as the absolute minimum. The work will most probably be secured in position by bedding the ends of the upright members in the earth, either tarred or bedded in concrete. An alternative method would be to screw the framework (without any make a substantial job in 2-in. by 2-in. stuff, or a little smaller section could be used. The main uprights consist of A and B about 8 in. apart in front, and C at the back corner, these being all bedded in the ground if this method is adopted. Between them, and of such lengths as to keep them at the correct distances to make up the dimensions given, are sill-pieces D, E, and F, tenoned

SUMMERHOUSES

into the uprights. (Notice that F runs the whole length of the back.) Heads G and H are fitted along the front and back, jointed to the uprights, as shown on the enlarged details (Fig. 7) and three intermediate uprights, two of which show at J and K, are fitted between the back head and sill. Notice that these do not divide the whole width of the back into four equal parts, being set out to equally quarter up the space between B and its counterpart on the other side (marked 7 ft. 6 in. on the plan), the reason for doing which will be apparent when the roof is dealt with. Intermediate horizontal rails, as at L, are notched between the uprights, in the manner indicated in the enlarged details, at a height of about 4 ft., to take the boarded back to the seat, the short length in front between A and B being kept a little higher to reduce the length of the top panel thus formed.

The sloping rafters, with shaped or plain ends projecting 2 ft. or more in front and 6 in. behind, are set out directly over the uprights as shown, to receive a boarded and felted or some similar roof. They should be notched to fit over the heads; or for a simpler method the upper faces of the latter may be splayed off to the required angle, and the rafters then firmly spiked on without any other connection.

Thus far advanced the skeleton should be quite rigid; but if leaving anything

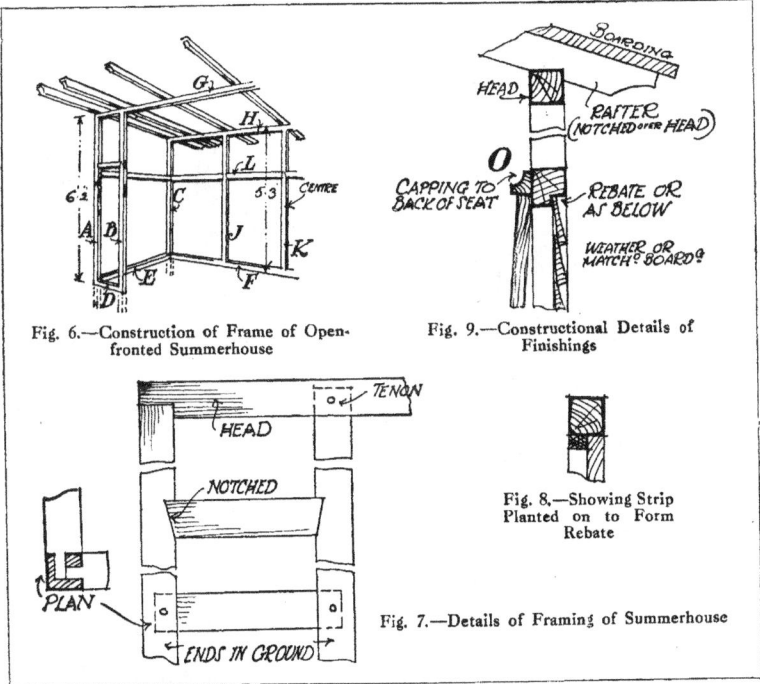

Fig. 6.—Construction of Frame of Open-fronted Summerhouse

Fig. 9.—Constructional Details of Finishings

Fig. 8.—Showing Strip Planted on to Form Rebate

Fig. 7.—Details of Framing of Summerhouse

to be desired, diagonal braces might be fitted across the openings of the lower part to stiffen the whole.

As regards the finishings. the outside can readily be covered in where shown with matchboarding or feather-edged weather-boarding fixed on the face of the work, or into rebates, previously worked to receive it. (Both this method, and an alternative in which a small strip is planted on to form a rebate, are shown on the enlarged details, Figs. 8 and 9.) The open panels can be filled in with laths or rough branches in the diamond or lattice forms shown. The six curved brackets should be at least 1 in. thick, cut to good continuous curves and strongly secured. They will complete the work except the seat, on which a certain amount of care should be expended if the whole is to be a success. for unless it is thoroughly comfortable this result cannot be attained. Uprights will be required along the front, either with or without a sill next to the ground, and support horizontal bearers, another being fixed across the uprights at the back (see M on cross section), slightly lower than the front, which might suitably be 1 ft. 4 in. high, so as to obtain a slope. Light strips having their upper angles rounded off and of sufficient strength to span the increased distance at each end where the seat widens, are fixed across at close intervals, and should stop short of the front edge of the front bearer, and be finished with a rounded nosing fixed on top of the latter and projecting slightly.

The back of the seat is formed of matchboarding nailed to a small fillet just above M, and to the intermediate rail at N (see cross section), with a small moulding as a capping as shown at O on the enlarged details. To keep the work simple it will be quite satisfactory to make the seat backs at the ends vertical instead of sloping.

It is probably superfluous to urge in conclusion the necessity for properly painting or otherwise preserving the structure. Any preservtive will suit.

Fig. 10.—Another Open-fronted Summerhouse

ANOTHER OPEN-FRONTED SUMMERHOUSE

To the average worker the summerhouse shown by the perspective sketch (Fig. 10) and by the drawings Figs. 11 to 14 should present but few difficulties, all these having been as completely as possible eliminated in the planning. It is quite unpretentious, deriving its effect from the treatment of the sloping angles, over which the roof projects, thereby forming suitable positions for hanging baskets as shown, the whole having a certain character never to be attained

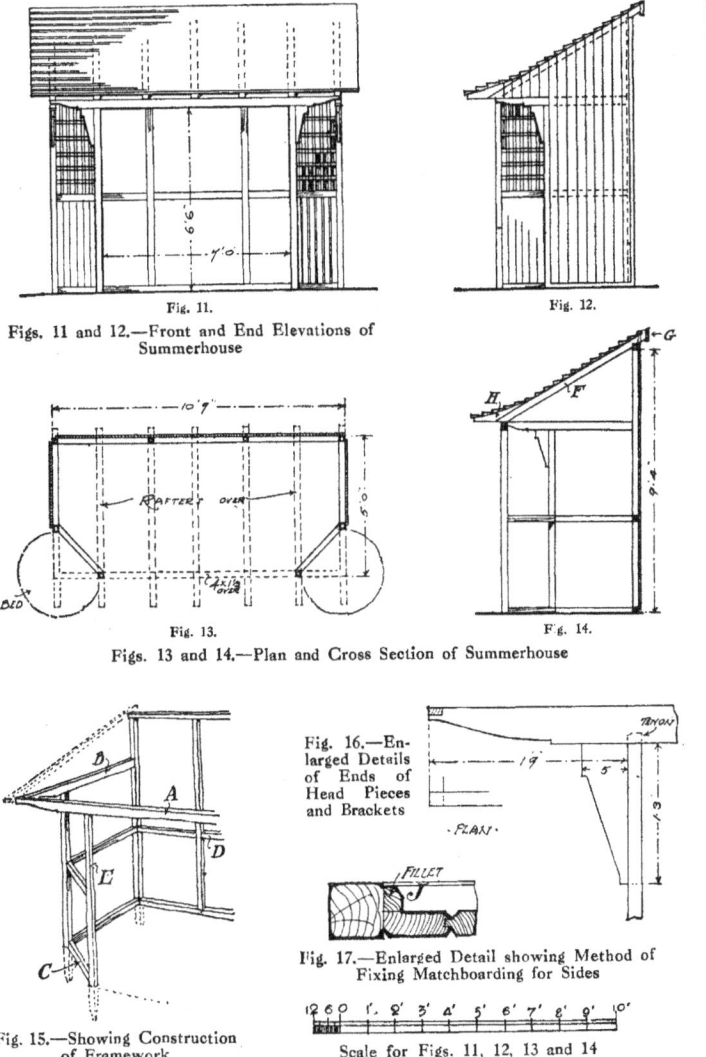

Figs. 11 and 12.—Front and End Elevations of Summerhouse

Figs. 13 and 14.—Plan and Cross Section of Summerhouse

Fig. 15.—Showing Construction of Framework

Fig. 16.—Enlarged Details of Ends of Head Pieces and Brackets

Fig. 17.—Enlarged Detail showing Method of Fixing Matchboarding for Sides

Scale for Figs. 11, 12, 13 and 14

by summerhouses of the usual "rustic" variety.

The principle of the work is explained by Fig. 15, a rough diagram of one-half of the framework, all the parts being of stuff about 1½ in. square, with the exception of the heads A and B, which might with advantage be 3½ in. or 4 in. deep. It is all fixed together and made up in accordance with the dimensions given, or to suit any special requirements. The main uprights have for preference tarred and spiked ends bedded in the ground, unless there is any likelihood of removal, in which case the sills might be anchored down to pegs driven into the ground. Should a boarded floor be wanted, it can be contrived to rest with the necessary bearers or joists on the sills, the total height of the structure being increased accordingly.

All the angle-posts should be tenoned into the heads, and the ends of the sills similarly fitted into the angle-posts, although an exception might be made in the case of the sill across the angle at C, this being merely butted and strongly nailed in place, the intermediate uprights at the back and the middle horizontal rail D receiving similar treatment. The ends of the head A overhang the front posts E for 1 ft. 9 in., as does also the end of the part B the post below it. These parts A and B are halved together at their extreme ends, shaped to the given curve, and finished with brackets 1 in. thick below, all according to the enlarged detail in Fig. 16.

Rafters as at F (Fig. 14) are spaced out equally, spanning the width between the front and back heads, splayed off at their feet, and notched to fit over the back, unless it is preferred to slope the top of this portion to the same angle as the whole roof, and then simply nail the rafters on it, in either case letting them project about 4 in. and finishing with a small fascia board as G. To get a good effect, the feet of the rafters should have "sprockets" (that is, pieces shaped as at H to lessen the slope of the roof next the eaves) fixed on top, and arranged to project horizontally about 1 ft., the curved line thus imparted to the roof greatly improving its general appearance.

The roof can be covered with any of the usual materials, preferably feather-edged weather-boarding, while the same covering or matched and V-jointed boarding, fixed vertically, can be used for the sides and back, either fixed on the face of the framing, or, for a good-class finish, fixed on small fillets planted round, as at J in Fig. 17. The latticed parts at the sides can be easily built up of laths regularly spaced out, and, of course, the entire work will need thorough treatment with paint, etc., to ward off rot and decay.

With regard to the position of this summerhouse and the treatment of the surrounding garden, it is difficult to write anything of general application; but the small circular beds shown at the corners might be worth considering, while, if at the end of a plot, the little building might serve as a screen for a frame-ground, or for the various garden impedimenta of a more or less undesirable appearance. It might very easily be extended during the months of summer and autumn by means of a canvas awning hooked to the head A (Fig. 15), and carried to suitable upright poles with any guy ropes found to be necessary. Apart from this idea, and without affecting it either way, should it be thought desirable to enclose the summerhouse, a pair of suitable doors could be formed of rectangular trellis on light wooden frames. Any fixed seating in the interior can very easily be arranged for.

GABLE-FRONTED SUMMERHOUSE OR SHELTER

Another example of a summerhouse of a better style than can be produced by the use of the ordinary "rustic" material is shown by Fig. 18. Though this is composed entirely of worked stuff, endeavour has been made throughout to scheme it in such a way that only the minimum amount of labour will be involved, consistent with a presentable appearance. The design has been kept free from the fussiness and attempts at ornament so often encountered, the effect aimed at being that of a substantial and durable shelter. To this end the framing of the front portion more especially should be made of as heavy material as is reasonably possible, although for actual considerations of strength much lighter posts, etc., than those advocated could be made to serve the purpose equally well. With care it will be understood that some of the tenons, etc., often employed in such a case could be omitted; but anyone at all conversant with the use of carpenter's tools will be in a position to settle these points of procedure to suit his own views. A front elevation section and plan are shown by Figs. 19, 20, and 21.

The base of the summerhouse consists of a rectangular frame of sill-pieces as outlined by A, B, C, and D (Fig. 21), say $3\frac{1}{2}$ in. wide and 2 in. high, halved together at the four angles. This frame can be well tarred and bedded in earth or gravel, or spiked firmly down to suitable wooden blocks embedded in a layer of concrete spread over the site. Later, when the structure has been completed, the space inside the frame can be filled in with either concrete finished cement-face, gravel or other paving, or a boarded wood floor can be laid across it from one side to the other, all necessary intermediate sleepers or plates to support it in the centre being supplied as found to be required.

Upright square posts $3\frac{1}{2}$ in. by $3\frac{1}{2}$ in., as at D and C (Fig. 21), are prepared and stub-tenoned into the angles of the sill, as shown in detail by Fig. 22. They will be about 4 ft. 9 in. high from the top of the sill, and if preferred could be of $3\frac{1}{2}$-in. by 2-in. stuff with the greater width

Fig. 18.—Gable-fronted Summerhouse or Shelter

towards the front, a remark equally applicable to posts E and F (Fig. 21). These latter have their feet tenoned into the front sill, and will be about 6 ft. long. At their heads they are tenoned into a horizontal piece G (Fig. 19) of the same thickness and measuring about apex of the front gable, no ridge-board being required in such a case as the present. The lower ends of the rafters will simply be cut to the required angle and firmly spiked down to the top of the corner posts, and their upper faces bent out to a flatter slope by means of

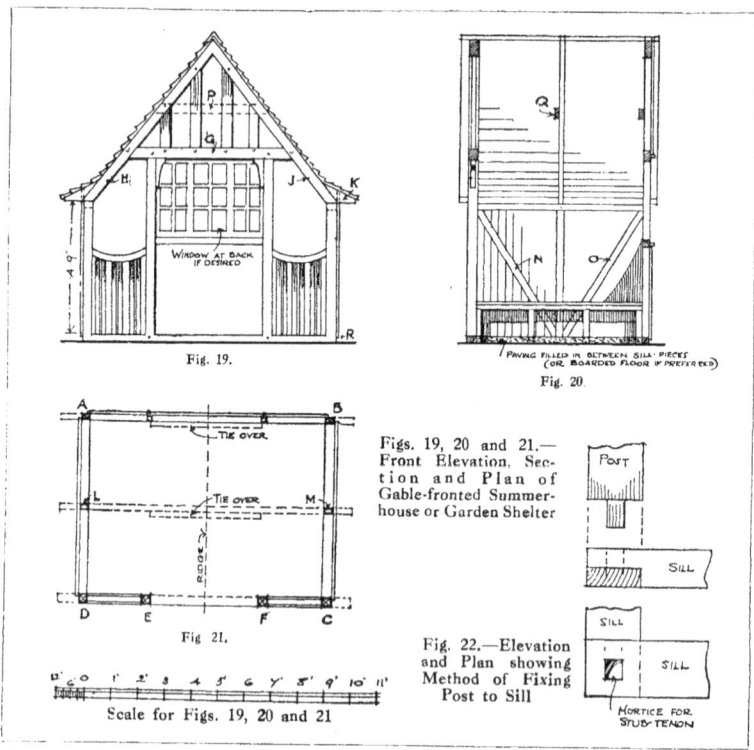

Fig. 19.

Fig. 20.

Figs. 19, 20 and 21.—Front Elevation, Section and Plan of Gable-fronted Summerhouse or Garden Shelter

Fig 21.

Scale for Figs. 19, 20 and 21

Fig. 22.—Elevation and Plan showing Method of Fixing Post to Sill

4 in. on the face. This in turn should have splayed ends tenoned into rafters, as at H and J in the same figure, although, as a matter of fact, a small piece of iron as a strap screwed across the joint on the inner face makes a passable substitute. This method of jointing is also suitable for the junction of the two rafters at the triangular "sprockets," as at K (Fig. 19), projecting about 9 in. beyond the sides. The four upright members in the gable-end can be prepared from boards of about 4 in. by 1¼ in. or 1 in., spaced out at equal intervals and having their ends merely butted into position. The two curved brackets, cut out of pieces 12 in. by 4 in.

by, say, 1½ in. thick, can be planted on without jointing, and the plain square handrail weathered on top and either straight or slightly curved as shown, together with the plain square balusters under set out in pairs, can all be fixed simply with butted and nailed ends.

The framing of the other parts of the summerhouse is quite rudimentary, and can be composed of rather lighter stuff if desired. For each side is required a back post, as at A or B (Fig. 21), fixed as in Fig. 22 to the angle of the sill, an intermediate upright L or M (Fig. 21), and a head fixed between the angle-posts. The back will be formed in much the same way, with two intermediate uprights taken up to meet the rafters, which are similar to the front ones but rather lighter. A couple of horizontal rails will be required if it be decided to introduce a window as shown, which can be glazed or of the trellis variety.

Should any part of the structure appear at all lacking in steadiness at this stage (as there is always a tendency for rectangular framing without diagonals to do), it should be stiffened with braces fixed across the spaces in the framework, as at N and O (Fig. 20). Two rafters will be needed in the centre over the two intermediate uprights in the sides, butted together at the ridge and stiffened with a "collar" spiked on, as at P (Fig. 19)

Fig. 23.—Gable-roof Summerhouse with Pigeon Cote

and Q (Fig. 20), suitable also for the back rafters.

The roof can be covered with weather-boarding or plain boarding to take felt or Willesden paper. The sides and back can also be filled in with weather-boarding, or matched and V-jointed boarding, with its edges vertical, care being taken to keep this clear of the ground as far as possible (R, Fig. 19), and fitting it close up to the underside of the roof-boarding as indicated at K (Fig. 19). The boarding round the window at the back will require to be finished with a bead or moulding, and a number of projecting pegs, either constructional or mere shams, on the front will tend to add interest to the general effect, and are indicated in Fig. 19.

The interior can be lined with thin matchboarding if desired, and seats fitted where required.

GABLE-ROOF SUMMERHOUSE WITH PIGEON COTE

The claims to originality in the design of the summerhouse shown by Fig. 23 are based in the main on little differences in the detail of the finishings.

Front and end elevations, cross section and plan are shown by Figs. 24 to 27.

Broadly, there are two ways in which it is possible to set about the erection of such a house, one being to leave projecting ends on the main uprights, and bed them solidly in the ground, the horizontal rails being previously framed into them; and the other, and generally preferable method, consists of the use of a set of sill-pieces of a substantial size, halved at the angles, and having the uprights stub-tenoned into them, as shown in Fig. 28. With this latter system it is usually essential to spike the sill-pieces down to stout wooden pegs buried firmly in the ground.

Assuming the house to be built in this latter way, the main framework might well be as shown in Fig. 29, the various dimensions being as figured on the other illustrations, or adjusted to meet special requirements. In the figure are shown 3-in. by 3-in. sill-pieces, and 2-in. by 2-in. uprights, one at each corner, stub-tenoned at the bottom into the sills and at the top into 3-in. by 2-in. heads set with their 3-in. sides upright and about 10 ft. long, as at A and B. Shorter heads measuring about 2 in. by 2 in. are filled in at the ends, as at C and D, without tenoning. Two pairs of rafters, 2 in. by 2 in. or any other convenient size, are then prepared to slope rather more than 45°, notched to fit over the heads and cut to a splay at their tops to fit against a ridge piece about 4 in. by 1 in. and 11 ft. 6 in. long, as in Fig. 30, which also indicates how the slope of the roof-boarding is intended to be flattened out a little for effect by means of a small piece or "sprocket" E on each rafter, which, however, is not essential. Intermediate rafters should subsequently be fitted, as at F and G in Fig. 24, and had better be stiffened and held in position by horizontal "collars" spiked on their sides, as at H in Fig. 26. If at this stage the framework be found at all lacking in rigidity, this defect can be entirely obviated by filling in diagonal "braces" as indicated by the dotted lines in Figs. 24 and 25.

Uprights about 2 in. by 2 in. or a little less will be required, as at J, K, and L in Fig. 27, and an intermediate horizontal rail, as at M (Fig. 24), should be filled in all round the back and ends, which can then be covered with vertical boarding nailed on the outer face of the framework, the two small spaces, as at N (Fig. 25), being only filled in with two pairs of plain square balusters each as shown, a treatment which could also be partially continued along the front if desired. An appearance of finish is imparted by the introduction of six shaped brackets of the outline shown in Fig. 31 and 1 in. thick, where shown on the uprights.

The roof and gable-ends can easily be filled in with feather-edged weatherboarding on the framework, either with or without the turned terminal shown added in the centre of the ridge, and overhung to form dovecotes or not as desired. As a matter of fact, the additional projection shown at the apex will be found a great help to the general effect, whether intended to be fitted up for birds or not. Details of the cotes will be found in Figs. 32, 33, and 34, where it will be observed that the horizontal shelves are fixed, while the fronts can be taken out in order to obtain access to the interiors for cleaning purposes; they can easily be fastened by means of small turn-buckles.

The site should be rendered as dry as possible, and the whole of the wood

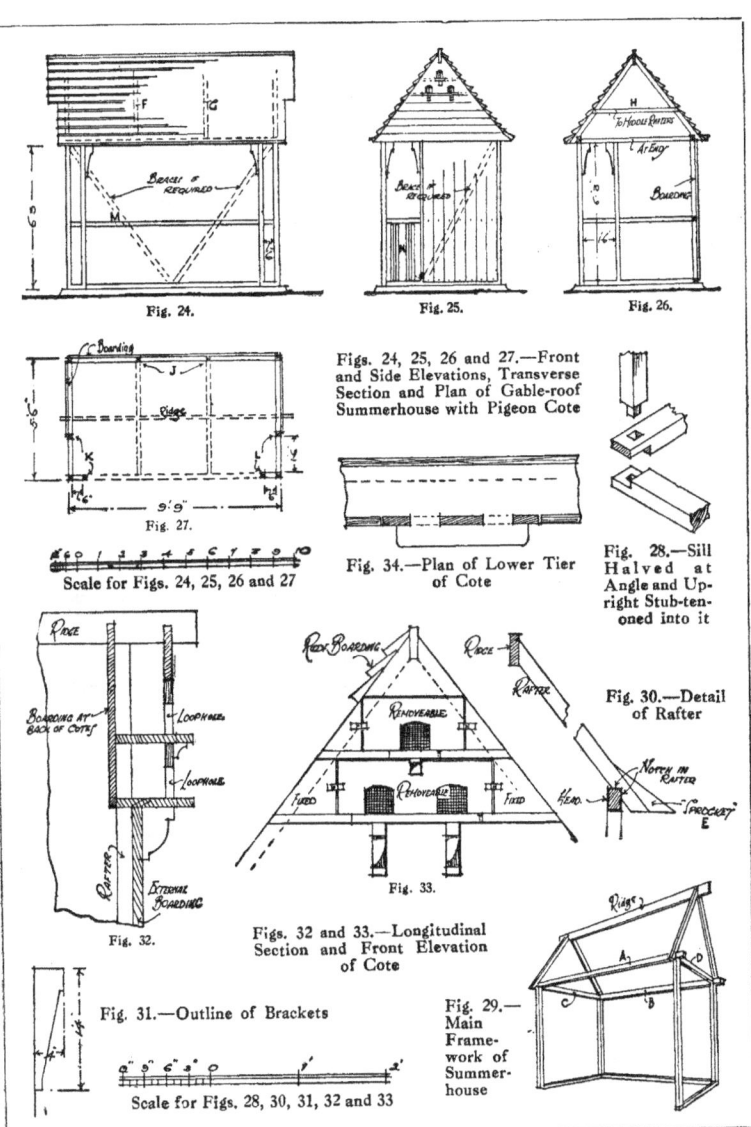

THE PRACTICAL WOODWORKER

thoroughly painted or protected by means of stain or varnish.

GABLE-ROOF SUMMERHOUSE WITH DOOR AT END

A summerhouse with gable roof, and of a different style from those previously described, is shown by the illustration (Fig. 35).

same as shown. If machine-prepared, the backs of the boards should be smoothed off. The curved piece at the top of the opening should be cut to shape and framed to the uprights. The rafters should be of 3-in. by 2-in. stuff, spaced about 1 ft. 4 in. apart if the top ends of the rafters are fixed to a ridge board about 1 in. thick. The roof should be of 1-in. feather-edged boarding. Some

Fig. 35.—Gable-roof Summerhouse with Door at End

Figs. 36, 37, and 38 show front and end elevations and plan respectively.

The dimensions given will meet ordinary requirements, but can be altered as desired.

The posts and rails of the framework should be of 3-in. by 3-in. stuff, with 3-in. by 2-in. intermediate uprights, and after being planed to size should be set out and mortised and tenoned together. The lower part of the framework can be covered with 1-in. feather-edged boarding, with either fillets to cover the corners or the corner posts rebated to receive

light sashes, made to fit the openings and to fasten to the posts, will be useful in windy weather.

When finished, two coats at least of wood-preserving stain should be applied.

EXTENSIBLE SUMMERHOUSE

The type of summerhouse shown in front elevation by Fig. 39 and in section and plan by Figs. 40 and 41 fulfils a dual purpose. Thus for the hot weather the comparatively large size, for a shelter, of 19 ft. by 7 ft. can be obtained (assuming that

SUMMERHOUSES

the dimensions given on the illustrations are adhered to), and in cooler weather the structure can be reduced to quite an ordinary size by lowering the side pieces.

Reference to the illustrations will show section as the uprights, are tenoned into them in the ordinary way on all four sides, and at the top three pairs of 2-in. by 1½-in. rafters and a light ridge board are nailed in position. The ridge should project 8 in. or 9 in. at each end. Next,

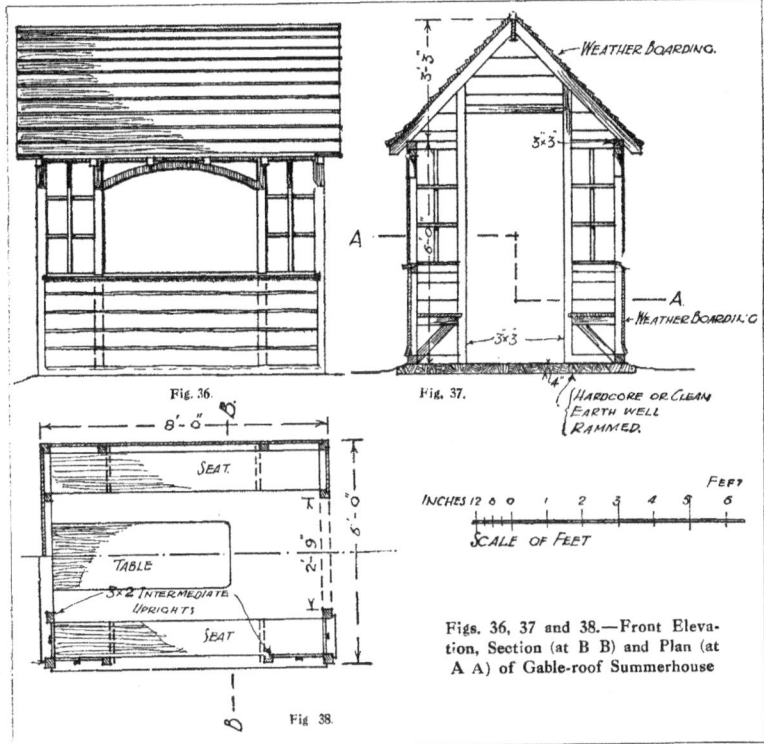

Figs. 36, 37 and 38.—Front Elevation, Section (at B B) and Plan (at A A) of Gable-roof Summerhouse

the main dimensions suggested, and the construction may be briefly described as follows :—Fig. 42 is a rough sketch of the framework, of which the four uprights (shown on plan at A, Fig. 41) can be 3 in. by 2 in. or a little less. These should have their ends tarred and bedded in concrete if possible. A sill B (Figs. 39 and 42) and head C (Fig. 42), of the same in order to add an effect of solidity to the two front uprights, two other pieces about 2 in. by 2 in. or 1½ in. by 1½ in. are fixed against them in the manner shown at D in Figs. 39 and 41. These should butt tightly against sill and head, and between them immediately under the head is fixed a 1-in. board, cut to about the arched outline shown in Fig. 39.

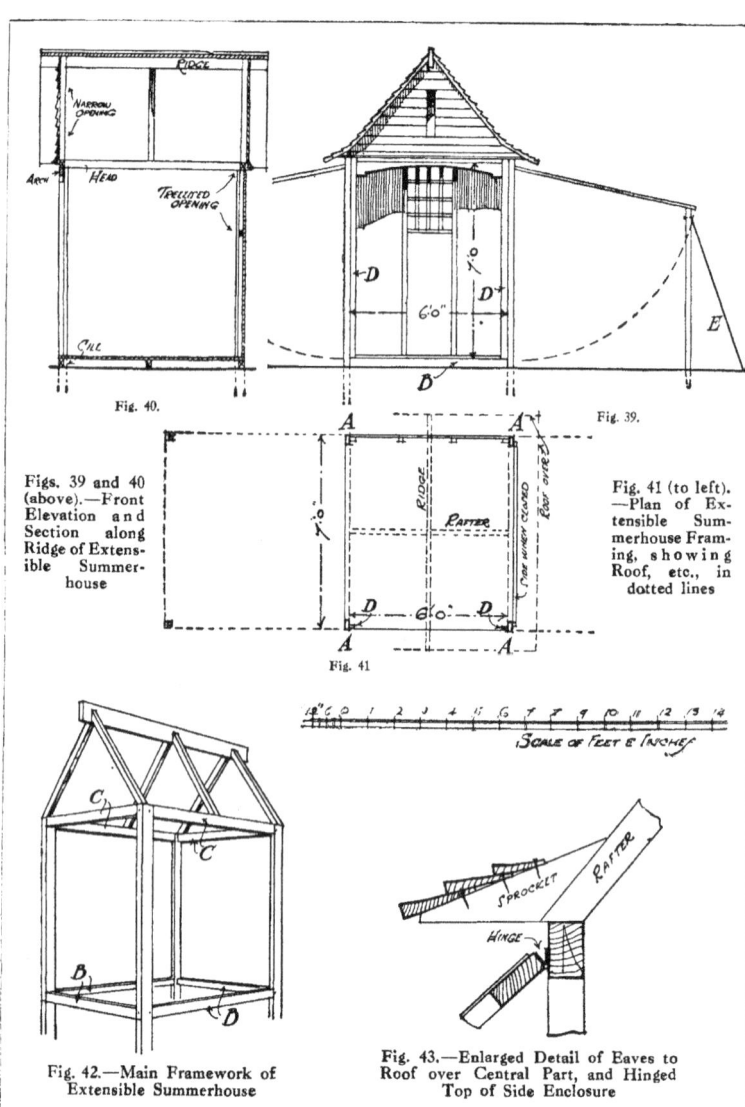

Figs. 39 and 40 (above).—Front Elevation and Section along Ridge of Extensible Summerhouse

Fig. 41 (to left).—Plan of Extensible Summerhouse Framing, showing Roof, etc., in dotted lines

Fig. 42.—Main Framework of Extensible Summerhouse

Fig. 43.—Enlarged Detail of Eaves to Roof over Central Part, and Hinged Top of Side Enclosure

SUMMERHOUSES

This should be placed about ¼ in. back from the face of the pieces D, which should in turn be another ¼ in. back from the face of the 3-in. by 3-in. angle-posts.

The back of the structure is fitted with two intermediate uprights and two small fillets against the angles to take boarding, either feather-edged or matched; but should the latter be decided on, the intermediates should be arranged horizontally. The effect will be improved if a rectangle in the back is filled in with strips or laths to form a sort of trellised opening or window, fairly high up.

A couple of uprights should be fitted in the gable-ends, which can then be covered in with weather-boarding, tilted out a little on small triangular fillets along the bottom edges, in order to prevent a flat effect, and leaving a small lancet opening in the centre (Fig. 42). The feet of the rafters are splayed off to the correct angle, so that they may butt against the head on which they are supported, as in Fig. 43; but the roof should be curved out along the eaves by means of triangular "sprockets" fixed on the rafters as in the same figure. A strip of moulding should also be fixed along the inside of the junctions between the boarding on each side and the ridge, to break the joint.

It will be necessary to make the sides as light as possible in order to simplify the handling of them when in use; 2½-in. by 1-in. stuff would be suitable for the frames, halved together at the angles, and with any necessary cross-pieces to take the covering, which it is suggested might, for the sake of the lightness, be of Willesden or similar material, or indeed of stout canvas. Three hinges will be advisable for each side, and the joint need not be particularly close-fitting, as it is well over-lapped by the projecting eaves of the central part. Of course, the chief trouble likely to be encountered is that of the side portions twisting in the sun, and to prevent this, well-seasoned wood should be obtained. The uprights to support the opened sides may be of any light section, and should have projecting pins at their top ends, fitting into sockets in the frames, and in exposed positions it may be found advisable to have guy-ropes to pegs in the ground, as at E (Fig. 39).

The boarded floor to the central part, if adopted, should be laid on the sills already mentioned, with any additional bearers found necessary added between, unless it is preferred to have the floor in removable sections, when it might be in three divisions held together at the back with battens or ledges. The flooring will require cutting to fit round the angle-posts.

It will hardly be necessary to insist on the imperative need of proper protection for such a structure, by thoroughly painting it, or treating it with some efficient tar stain, or other preservative.

REVOLVING SUMMERHOUSE

A summerhouse that can be turned according to the direction of the wind makes it very comfortable and pleasant to sit in, even well into the autumn. The one about to be described is large enough to accommodate a reclining chair, or two or three persons at tea. It is constructed of ordinary deal and such materials as are readily bought at any neighbouring woodyard.

Figs. 44 and 45 show an elevation and section. The method of building is as follows:—A hole 1 ft. 6 in. square by 1 ft. deep is first dug at a suitable place, and in this a 2-in. iron pipe is placed standing upright. Concrete is now poured round the pipe and then left for several days to dry.

In the meantime the track on which the wheels carrying the house will have to run may be taken in hand. Fig. 46 is a plan of the track. A 1-in. board 11 in. wide is placed on the floor of an available room, and a nail temporarily driven into the floor to represent the centre on which the house revolves. A piece of string is then attached by one end to the nail, and at the correct lengths of the string a bradawl attached to the other end, by which as much of the inner and outer curvature of the track as the 11-in. board will permit is scribed on the board, the ends of the segment being marked off radially with the nail. This forms the template for cutting out the remainder of the segments for the track, sixteen being required. The segments are then placed in their proper positions, relatively one to the other, taking care that the radial joints at the ends of the segments in the top course break joint with the radial joints of the segments of the lower course. The courses are then nailed together piece by piece, using 2½-in. french nails, and turning the points well over the underside of the lower course.

The track when finished should be very rigid. It is now placed on the lawn, the pipe centre standing approximately in the centre of the track. To get this truly central, a piece of string or wire looped at one end and passed over the pipe serves to measure the distances diametrically from the pipe to the outside edge of the track, say, across two imaginary diameters to get four measurements. The track is then moved about until all four measurements are equal and the track central with the pipe centre. Four holes the size of an ordinary broomstick are next bored through the track, and four pegs cut from a broomstick driven down through these holes into the lawn below, thus retaining the track in its central position.

The next part to be dealt with is the large square framing forming the foundation of the house, and to which the upright posts are to be attached, also the flooring and the wheels, which have to take the whole weight of the house.

Fig. 47 is a plan of the framework under the floor. The sides, at their ends, are dovetailed into the ends as shown, the dovetails then being spiked or screwed. Two beams running from the front to the back are next halved into the top edges of the main frame, and between these two beams a block of wood with a 2-in. hole is fitted. This forms the bearing and keeps the house rotating in its proper position when turned. These two beams perform the double function of supporting the floorboards, and also of keeping the house in its proper position

relatively to the track. The wheels and their supports are next fitted. Cast-iron wheels of 8 in. in diameter are suitable. They are fitted between two diagonal beams, which are let into the underside edges of the main frame.

The four corner posts may be next erected and secured inside, the corners of the main frame having first been mortised for the middle string and checked back for the top string. The rafters are cut at one end to the proper angle, and notched near the other end to give proper landing on to the upper corner edge of the top string. The purlin is then put temporarily in position, and the rafters secured thereto, one by one. The posts forming the entrance to the house and their horizontal framings are now secured, the former being fastened to the inside of the main framing, and the latter being tenoned into the corner posts of the house. This completes the framing, and it is ready for planking.

The floor should be first laid and well secured by nailing to the main framing and the various beams. The back and sides should then be planked, taking care to get the plank edges well together before permanently driving in the nails. As shown, provision is made in the house sides for four windows, which are hinged at the top. These are made out of the same material as the sides of the house.

The roof is next put on, and, after planking, should be well painted. Whilst the paint is wet, stout canvas is well stretched on and given two coats of paint. The gable is now put in position, and the house being finished, the inside may be treated with best copal varnish, and the outside given three coats of oil paint.

The scantlings of the material necessary are as follows :—Roof : grooved-and-tongued boarding, 5 in. by ⅜ in. ; rafters, 2½ in. by 2 in. ; gable A, 5¼ in. by ¾ in. Framing : top string B, 3 in. by 3 in. ; middle string C, 3 in. by 2 in. ; corner posts D, 3 in. by 3 in. Flooring : side and end planking, 5 in. by ⅝ in., grooved and tongued ; nosing round entrance framing E, 4 in. by ¾ in. ; beams under flooring carrying centre block 5½ in. by

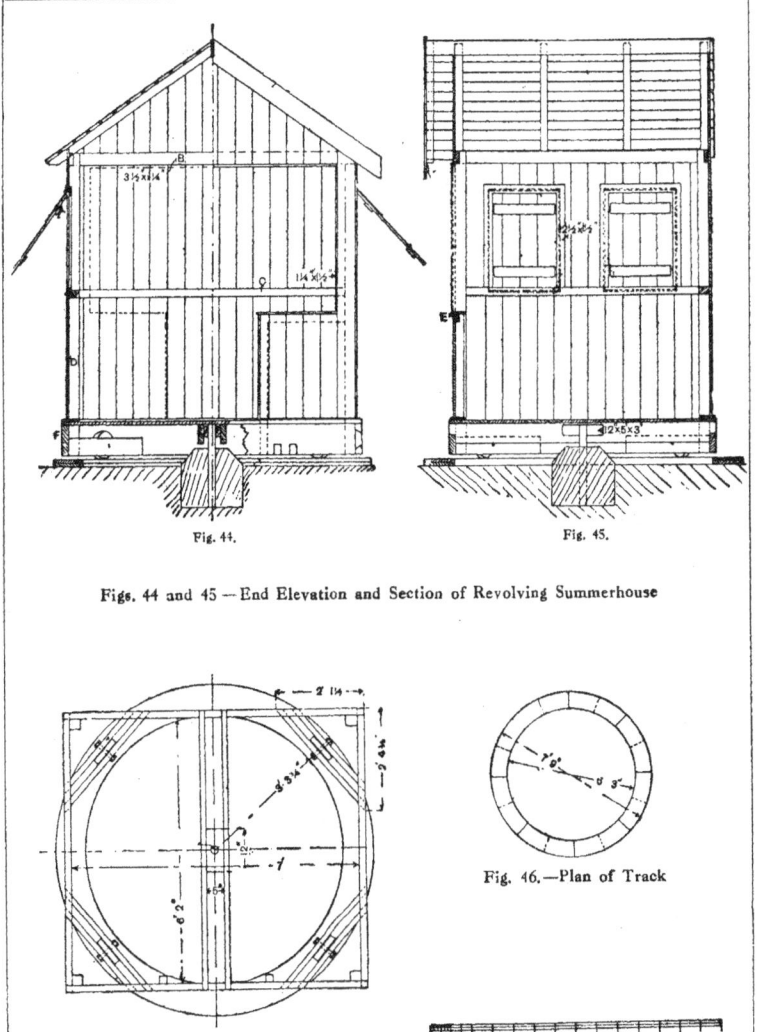

Figs. 44 and 45—End Elevation and Section of Revolving Summerhouse

Fig. 46.—Plan of Track

Fig 47.—Plan of Framework under Floor

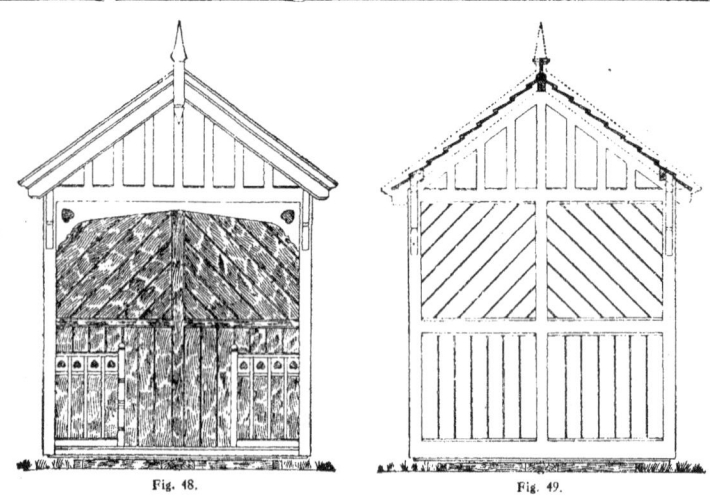

Figs. 48 and 49.—Front and Back Elevations of Portable Revolving Summerhouse

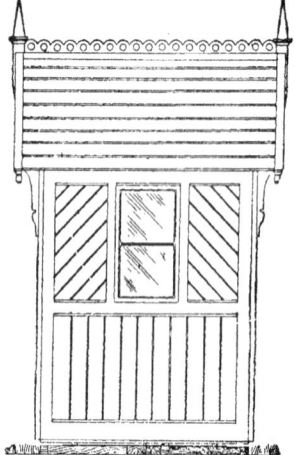

Fig. 50.—Side Elevation of Portable Revolving Summerhouse

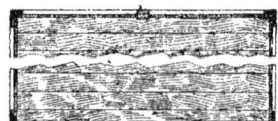

Fig. 51.—Part Plan of Roof

Fig. 52.—Floor Framing with Rollers Attached

SUMMERHOUSES

1½ in.; main framing round base of house F, 8½ in. by 2 in.; wheels of cast-iron, 8 in. in diameter; bolts for wheels, 1 in. in diameter; and beams for wheel centres, 5 in. by 2 in.

PORTABLE REVOLVING SUMMERHOUSE

Another design for a revolving summerhouse is shown by Figs. 48 to 51.

Pine or deal are suitable woods for construction, and the inside lined with 1-in. or ¾-in. matchboarding. The latter is arranged with the joints as showing outwardly, and where the perpendicular and angular pieces meet, strips of ½-in. stuff may be nailed on, as shown in Fig. 48. The outer framing may be made of 1½-in. or 1¼-in. stuff, tenoned and mortised together, and the horizontal rails bevelled to carry off the rain. The panels in the gables may be inserted in grooves ploughed in the framing. As a portable structure is desired, the roof with the gables should be made in one part, allowing the ridge and wall-plates and the outer rafters to butt against the barge-boards, and thus form a groundwork for fixing the latter. The wall-plates should be arranged to drop inside the upright framing, the latter being notched to receive the rafters. Instead of the rafters being cut away to receive the feather-boards of the roof as shown, the feather-boards may be simply laid on the top of the rafters. To make a good weathertight roof, roofing felt should first be nailed across the rafters, and then the feather-boards on the top. The framing for the floor (see Fig. 52) may be made of 3-in. planks, with 1-in. floorboards. The rollers are fixed on the cross-bars. A thick iron plate with a hole in the centre is fixed to receive the centre bolt, say, 1 in. in diameter. The latter is fixed in the lower framing (made of 3-in. stuff), on which is fixed stout sheet iron to form the roller track (see Fig. 53).

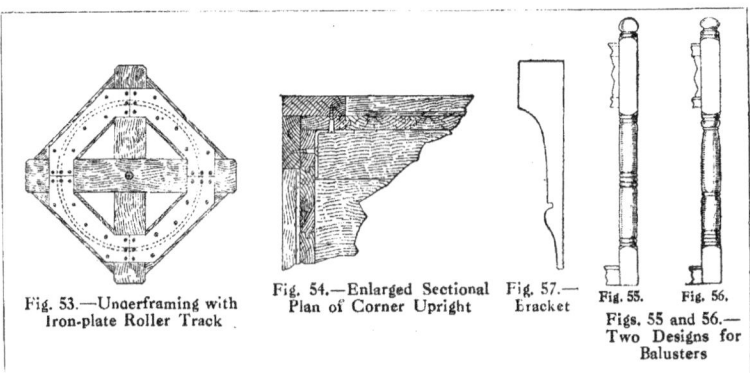

Fig. 53.—Underframing with Iron-plate Roller Track

Fig. 54.—Enlarged Sectional Plan of Corner Upright

Fig. 57.—Bracket

Fig. 55.   Fig. 56.

Figs. 55 and 56.—Two Designs for Balusters

These plates, if desired, may be made in sections of a circle. It will be seen that the outer upright framings fit against the floor framing, and the inner matchboarding rests on the floorboarding. Instead of the corner iron brackets being fixed with screws as shown, bolts may be used; but in this case the bolt heads will show outside. Fig. 54 gives an enlarged sectional plan of a corner upright, Figs. 55 and 56 give alternative designs for the balusters, and Fig. 57 shows the brackets fixed to the corner posts.

The inside matchboarding may be varnished, and as an alternative for the outside the panels in the gables may be white, and the matchboarding alternating pale green and white.

Garden Rooms or Bungalows

GARDEN ROOM

To what extent this type of garden room or bungalow can be erected depends on the garden, and the requirements of such an erection.

hygienic condition. It consists of a room 15 ft. by 10 ft. 6 in., with glass doors opening on to a small veranda enclosed by treillage, and it should be so placed as to command the sunniest outlook

Fig. 1.—Garden Room

The illustration (Fig. 1) shows how a modern type of summerhouse can be adapted to the cult of the open-air life. In its arrangement it has been made as far removed as possible from the haunts for spiders, so often encountered, and it is capable of being kept in a perfectly available, and be in a fairly dry situation. It is thought that although the design and construction may be varied to suit particular circumstances, the following description and notes will be found generally useful.

Front and end elevations are shown

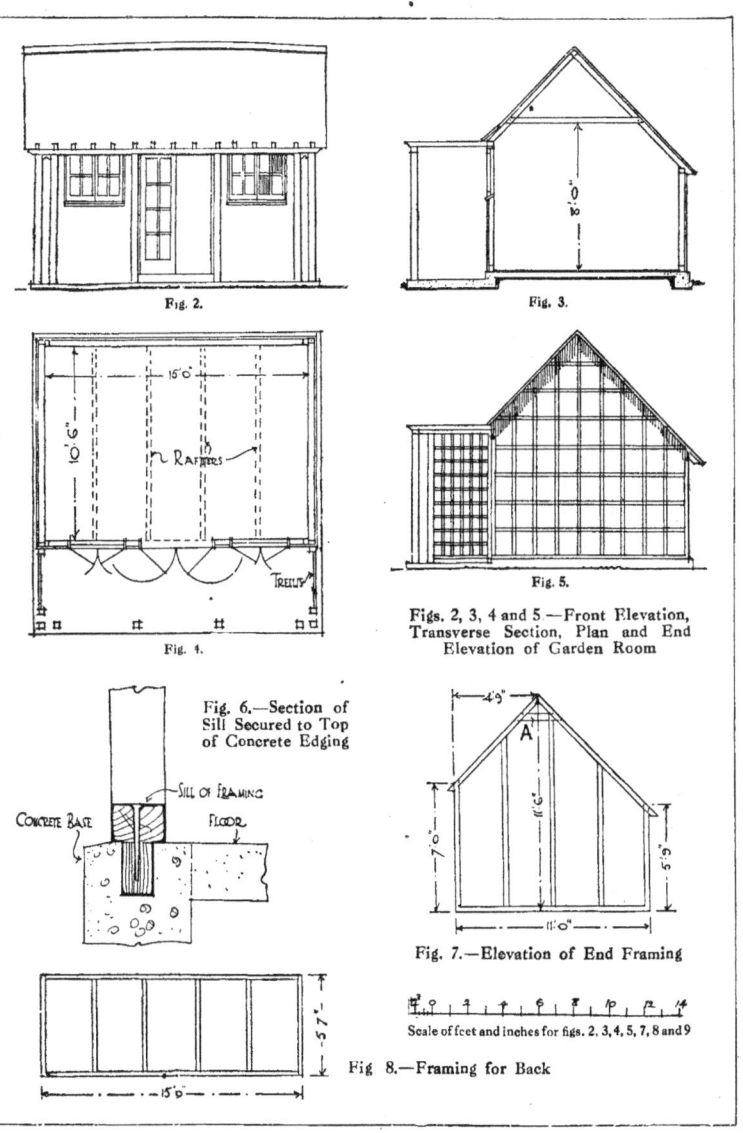

Fig. 2.

Fig. 3.

Fig. 4.

Fig. 5.

Figs. 2, 3, 4 and 5.—Front Elevation, Transverse Section, Plan and End Elevation of Garden Room

Fig. 6.—Section of Sill Secured to Top of Concrete Edging

Fig. 7.—Elevation of End Framing

Scale of feet and inches for figs. 2, 3, 4, 5, 7, 8 and 9

Fig 8.—Framing for Back

by Figs. 2 and 3, and a plan and transverse section is shown by Figs. 4 and 5.

As a foundation, in some cases it may be sufficient to use a layer of well-rolled gravel, ashes, or broken brick, to ensure being ultimately finished with tar or cement, and perhaps boarding nailed to small bearers about 2 ft. apart bedded on the layer. For permanence the undersides of the boarding, as well as of the

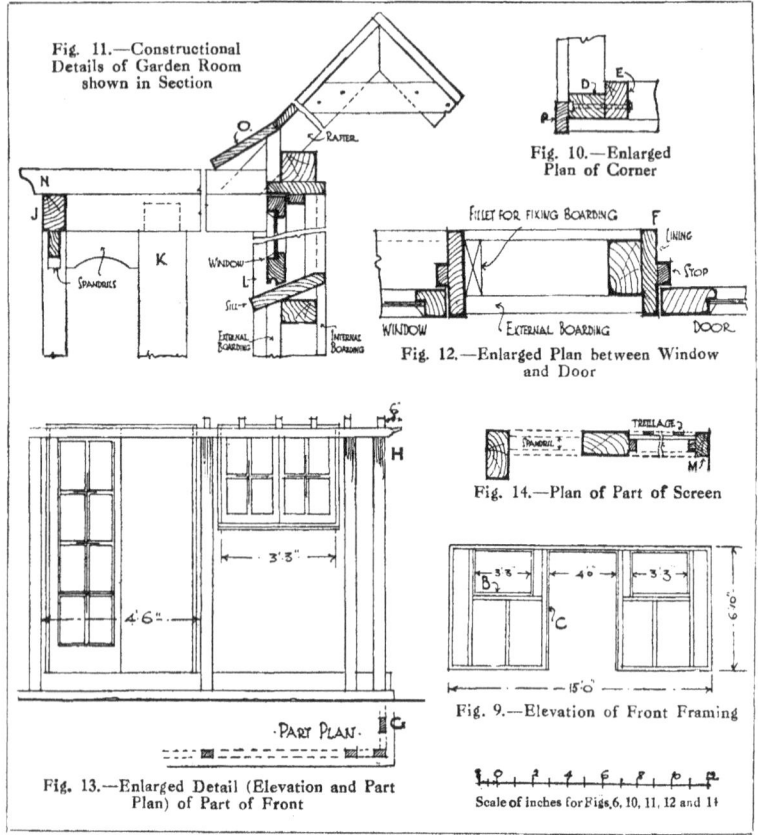

Fig. 11.—Constructional Details of Garden Room shown in Section

Fig. 10.—Enlarged Plan of Corner

Fig. 12.—Enlarged Plan between Window and Door

Fig. 14.—Plan of Part of Screen

Fig. 9.—Elevation of Front Framing

Fig. 13.—Enlarged Detail (Elevation and Part Plan) of Part of Front

Scale of inches for Figs. 6, 10, 11, 12 and 14

comparative dryness under the structure. In this event, the top soil should be removed, stout pointed stakes driven well in and sawn off level to serve as fixing for the sides, and a good dry layer substituted for the top soil, its top surface hidden woodwork, should be well tarred. A better foundation could be formed by clearing the top soil as before and forming a rectangle of about 11 ft. by 15 ft. 9 in. with boards, held in position with pegs in the ground. With

GARDEN ROOMS OR BUNGALOWS

these as a guide, a base of rough concrete about 6 in. wide, and, say, 9 in. above the ground, could be readily formed, the woodwork being afterwards fixed to it by screwing or spiking to wooden blocks bedded in the top of the concrete at intervals round the sides, as in Fig. 6. Another method would be to bed about ten long bolts in the concrete, and to drill holes in the bottom of the framing to suit these, this method requiring considerable precision. At a later stage, the centre between the concrete edges might be filled in with tarred ashes, etc., or preferably about 3 in. of concrete finished to a smooth cement face by trowelling.

The floor should be level with the top of the concrete edging, the outside of which can be finished with cement or old tiles, etc., as a facing, and a step at the entrance being also treated in a similar manner. The paving to the veranda can be of concrete, or gravel bound with tar or cement, and should slope a little away from the doors.

In beginning the main structure the first things to consider are the sides, consisting of two ends (Fig. 7), a back (Fig. 8), and front (Fig. 9). These can be framed up very suitably with 3-in. by 2-in. rough-sawn timber, the outer parts halved together at the angles, and the intermediate uprights either tenoned or more probably merely spiked in position, their purpose being to stiffen the outer portions and to provide fixing for future boarding, etc. Note in Fig. 7 how the sloping rafters are held together by a piece of board nailed on at A, and how their lower ends project about 6 in., thus giving strength to the joints with the uprights. The dimensions shown in these three figures should be carefully worked to; the inner lines, as at B and C in Fig. 9, will be referred to later. The side in this figure could obviously only be put completely together when in its ultimate position.

Having prepared these skeleton sides they should be placed in position on the base already prepared, being supported by temporary sloping struts, and spiked,

screwed or bolted through the bottom rails or sills. The angles should have two of the uprights coming together, as at D and E in Fig. 10, these when bolted and screwed fairly closely forming a very sound job, and tying the work together. Next, four sets of rafters exactly similar to those in Fig. 7 should be prepared, and birdsmouthed over the tops of the front and back, as in Fig. 3, and to a larger scale in Fig. 11, their tops being halved (Fig. 3) or merely mitred and secured as before (Fig. 11). The rafters are spaced out equally, as dotted in Fig. 4, and can be stiffened by means of light horizontal pieces nailed on to one side of each pair, 8 ft. above the floor, as clearly shown in Fig. 3.

The door opening can be treated with 1-in. planed linings about $4\frac{1}{2}$ in. wide, as at C in Fig. 9 and F in Fig. 12. To these $\frac{1}{2}$-in. stops can be fixed, to suit $1\frac{1}{2}$-in. doors of the ordinary type, which can be made or bought. They should be hinged flush with the outer edge of the linings in order to open back flat on occasion. The same remarks apply to the small windows with the exception of their sills, which, as seen in Fig. 11, consist of boards about $6\frac{1}{2}$ in. wide, fixed sloping on small triangular blocks.

Dealing next with the small pergola in the front, its posts need to be fairly wide for the sake of appearance; but if square would be rather heavy and costly. A compromise is accordingly suggested in Fig. 13 and Fig. 14, where 4-in. by 2-in. uprights are indicated, while even 3-in. by 2-in. might be allowed. Those on the return G (Fig. 13) could be omitted. All the uprights used should have well-tarred ends bedded in the ground, their tops being tenoned into a head about 3 in. by 2 in., having shaped projecting ends, as at H (Fig. 13). It is seen in section at J in Fig. 11, which shows also a similar head at the end, taking the top of the optional post K, and resting on a 2-in. by 1-in. upright L, seen on plan at M (Fig. 14). The heads should have their tops level with those of the windows, and are intended to support a series of crosspieces about 2 in. by $1\frac{1}{2}$ in., spaced out as shown on the various illustrations, and shaped and projecting slightly. as at N in Fig. 11, which also shows 4-in. by 1-in. shaped spandrel pieces intended to be fixed as a finish between the tops of the adjacent posts.

The roof should be covered in with feather-edged weather-boarding, or ordinary boarding covered with stout inodorous felt, tarred and sanded when in position. The roofing is intended to overhang well all round, and at the front to be slightly tilted, as at O (Fig. 11). The sides can also be covered with boarding, stopping against an upright batten at the angles, as at P (Fig. 10); or it would be an excellent idea to get a builder's man to lath and roughly cement-render them. Internally the whole can be lined with ½-in. matched and V-jointed boarding, any necessary fixing fillets being added, as noted in Fig. 12. where it will be noticed that the linings to the door and windows project sufficiently to stop the inner and outer coverings. the former having mouldings fixed over the joints if desired. Externally. the treillage screens at each end of the veranda can be formed with stout plasterers' laths on small fillets, as in Fig. 14 while the larger work on the ends (and back if desired) can be composed of battens about 1½ in. by ¾ in. crossing at right angles, the horizontal ones being applied last; if against the boarding they would form a lodgment for moisture.

Two thorough coatings of some recognised wood-preservative should be applied throughout, the interior being varnished in addition. There are several such preservatives on the market which are well worth the expenditure.

Fig. 15.—Garden Bungalow

GARDEN ROOMS OR BUNGALOWS

GARDEN BUNGALOW FOR OPEN-AIR LIFE

For the most part the bungalow shown by the photograph (Fig. 15) is designed for permanent occupancy, although to most people it would appear to be something built for use only during a portion of the year. No doubt the climatic conditions of this country are such that the difference in purpose would involve something being done for the warmth of the apartment during the winter months.

For an open-air cure, or for an ideal apartment for open-air life, no heating apparatus is required, and for that reason the construction of the bungalow only will be described.

The illustration (Fig. 15) gives a general view of the finished structure, which is shown built on a wood staging raised from the ground about 2 ft. Figs. 16, 17, 18, and 19 show front and side elevations and plan and cross section respectively.

The treatment of the ground can be

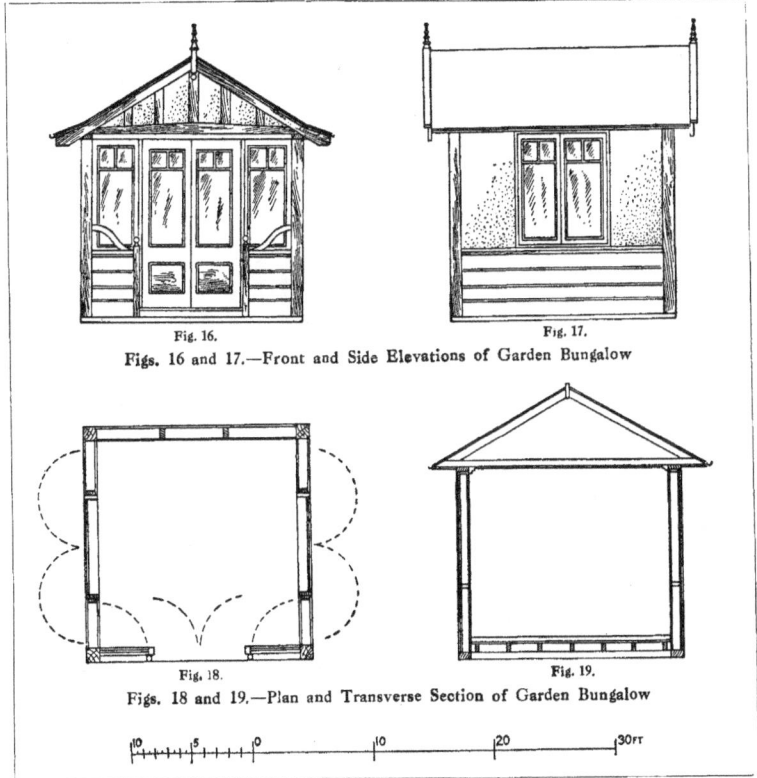

Figs. 16 and 17.—Front and Side Elevations of Garden Bungalow

Figs. 18 and 19.—Plan and Transverse Section of Garden Bungalow

similar to that for the preceding erection. The internal size of the room is 8 ft. by 8 ft., just sufficient to hold a single bed, a dressing-table, and two chairs. The plan shows the front arranged with folding doors which open to the inside, and two opening sidelights which can be folded

corners. This in turn receives the wall framing. The corner posts are 4 in. square, and are checked, as shown in Fig. 21, to receive the weather-boarding. The other vertical posts and the top horizontal rail are cut from 4-in. by 2-in. stuff, and the lower horizontal rail is 5 in. by 2 in., for the reason that the outer edge is finished flush with the boarding. The framework as shown is complete ready to receive the windows and finishings.

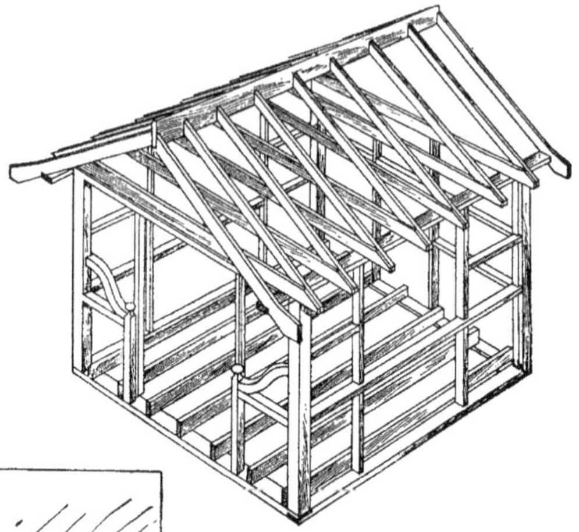

The timbers for the roof are 3-in. by 2-in. spars and ceiling joists, 6-in. by 2-in. barge, and a 5-in. by 2-in. ridge. These are fitted up in the

Fig. 20 —Framework for Garden Bungalow

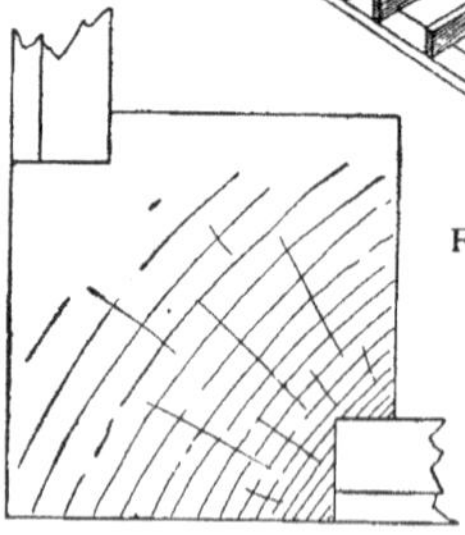

Fig. 21.—Enlarged Detail of Corner Post

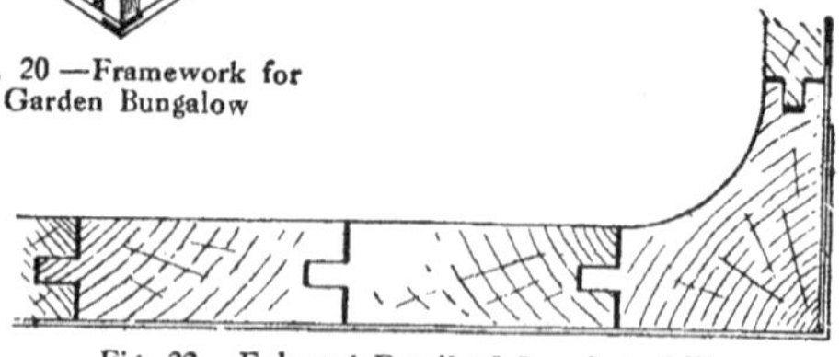

Fig. 22.—Enlarged Detail of Junction of Floor and Wall

round against the side walls. Thus when the doors are open and the windows folded round, for all practical purposes the front might be considered as entirely open. On both sides are double-casement windows which open to the outside, and are arranged so that they fold completely round. The framework, which is shown by Fig. 20, is of red pine and consists of a 6-in. by 2-in. frame half-checked at the

usual way to receive the ¾-in. matchboarding, which is covered with Ruberoid. The floor is laid with 5-in. by 2-in. joists, which are covered on the top with Willesden paper and laid with 1½-in. flooring. Fig. 22 gives a detail of the floor at the junction with the wall linings. Paper similar to that placed under the floorboards is fitted behind the walls and ceiling linings.

Garden Lights

SIMPLE GARDEN FRAMES

THE simplest form of cold frame is a small box or packing-case with a sheet of glass over it. These are useful enough, and have the merit of convenience and mobility, and a specially suitable reference to individual plant requirements. But the garden creates problems that these useful makeshifts do not touch.

box by means of butt hinges, and the whole thing is complete.

A window sash has no means of clearing its upper surface of water because the glass is surrounded by a raised wooden border; in other words, the stiles and rails. Therefore a properly-constructed sash for a cold frame should have one rail finishing under the glass; and further, the sash should have a fall, as in a roof,

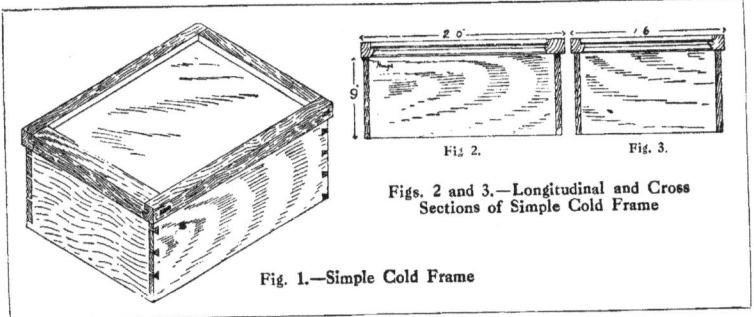

Fig. 1.—Simple Cold Frame

Figs. 2 and 3.—Longitudinal and Cross Sections of Simple Cold Frame

Cold frames can be of all sizes and shapes. Old sashes can be used in making them. To do this, a box can be made as shown in Figs. 1, 2, and 3, which give particulars of how to fit up a box for a single-light sash. It is not necessary that this box should be made to take to pieces, as it is small enough to be easily portable. The sash can be hung to the

to enable water to run off. Figs. 4, 5 and 6 show such a small frame. The bottom rail finishes on its upper surface just at the beginning of the glass rebate.

The joint at the junction of the top rail and stile is shown by Fig. 7, and the joint at the junction of the stile and the bottom rail by Fig. 8. Dowels should be used for fixing the joints, white-lead paint being used as a binding medium.

Sometimes it is required to have the sash so that it can be taken off, and in this case a slide arrangement is necessary.

When the sash is loose it is apt to be caught by the wind and blown off. This is easily guarded against by fixing wooden buttons on the frame, as shown in Fig. 10. In the case of a frame with a hinged

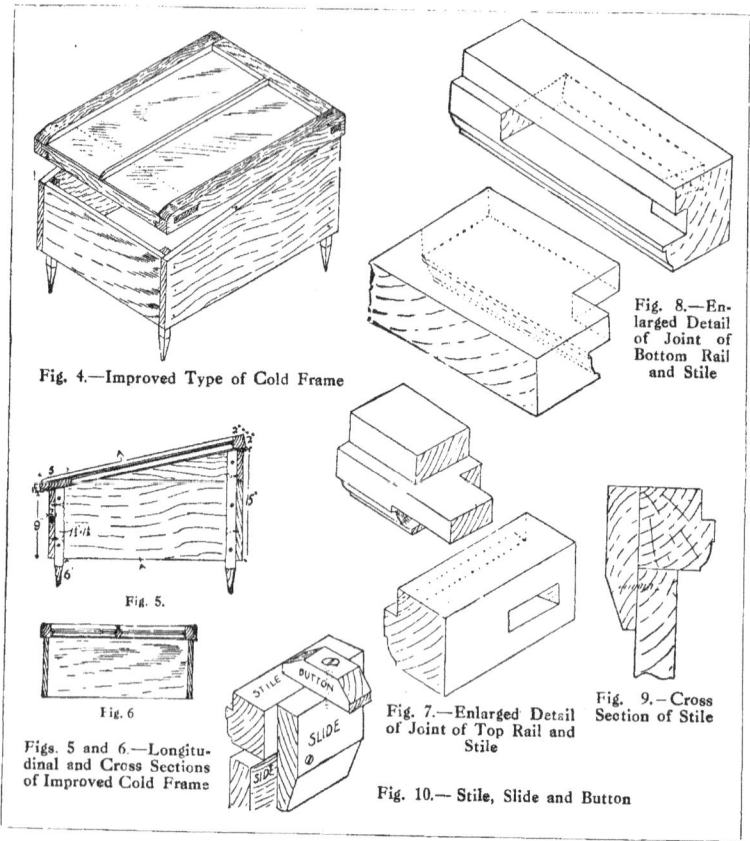

Fig. 4.—Improved Type of Cold Frame

Fig. 8.—Enlarged Detail of Joint of Bottom Rail and Stile

Figs. 5 and 6.—Longitudinal and Cross Sections of Improved Cold Frame

Fig. 7.—Enlarged Detail of Joint of Top Rail and Stile

Fig. 9.—Cross Section of Stile

Fig. 10.— Stile, Slide and Button

This is shown by Fig. 9, which is a section of the stile of the sash, side of the frame and slide piece. It as an advantage to have this slide piece even if the sash is hinged, because it makes the cold frame more air-tight, and consequently warmer.

sash a stick is needed to keep the sash raised when necessary. For a larger cold frame the sash will require bars.

In glazing a frame, each succeeding upper square of glass should overlap the next lower one by about $\frac{3}{4}$ in., and each

GARDEN LIGHTS

pane should be tacked at its lower end to prevent slipping. The sash, if of any size, should have a handle fixed on the top rail to assist in moving it. To protect the glass from stones, wire-netting of ¾-in. mesh may be stretched across.

For fixing the cold frame, stakes are driven into the ground so that they lie in the angles of the frame, and the latter is screwed to them.

light, 3 ft. long by 4 ft. wide; two lights, 6 ft. long by 4 ft. wide; and three lights, 9 ft. long by 4 ft. wide. With the larger lights: One light, 4 ft. long by 6 ft. wide; two lights, 8 ft. long by 6 ft. wide; and three lights, 12 ft. long by 6 ft. wide.

The lights are made as shown in Fig. 12. It will be noticed that the bottom rail is thinner than the stiles and top rail, this being to allow the glass to come over it, so that the water will run away, while

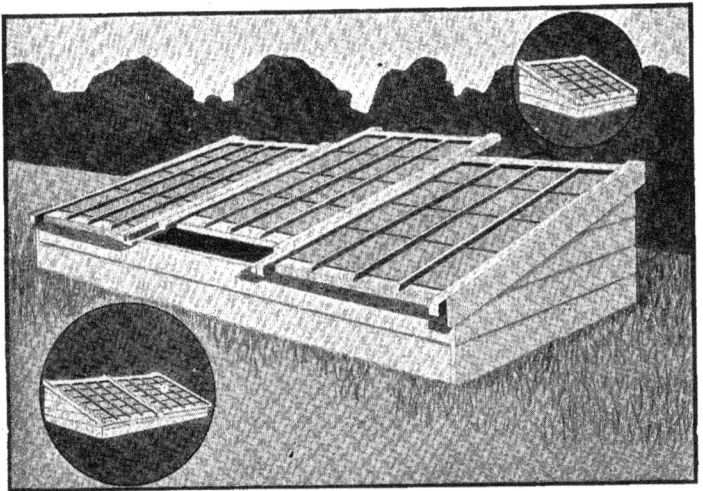

Fig. 11.—Three-light Garden Frame (Inset, One- and Two-light Frames)

GARDEN FRAMES OF SPECIAL CONSTRUCTION

Specially constructed garden frames are usually made with one, two or three lights. A three-light frame is shown by Fig. 11, and the insets in this figure show frames with one and two lights. The constructional work of these frames is of a fairly simple character.

The frames shown have sliding lights, and prove very satisfactory in use. The lights may be either 4 ft. by 3 ft. or 6 ft. by 4 ft. With the smaller lights frames can be made to the following sizes: One

a throating should be cut in the underside to prevent the water running back and into the frame. A tie rod of ½-in. round iron, fixed across the light, as shown in Fig. 12, will greatly strengthen it.

The body for a three-light frame is shown in Fig. 13; but the construction in the case of a one-light or two-light frame is almost identical. A section through the frame is given by Fig. 14, and the sectional dimensions for a frame to suit either the smaller or larger lights are given in Figs. 15 and 16. Grooved-and-tongued boards not less than 1⅛ in. thick should be used. Those for the

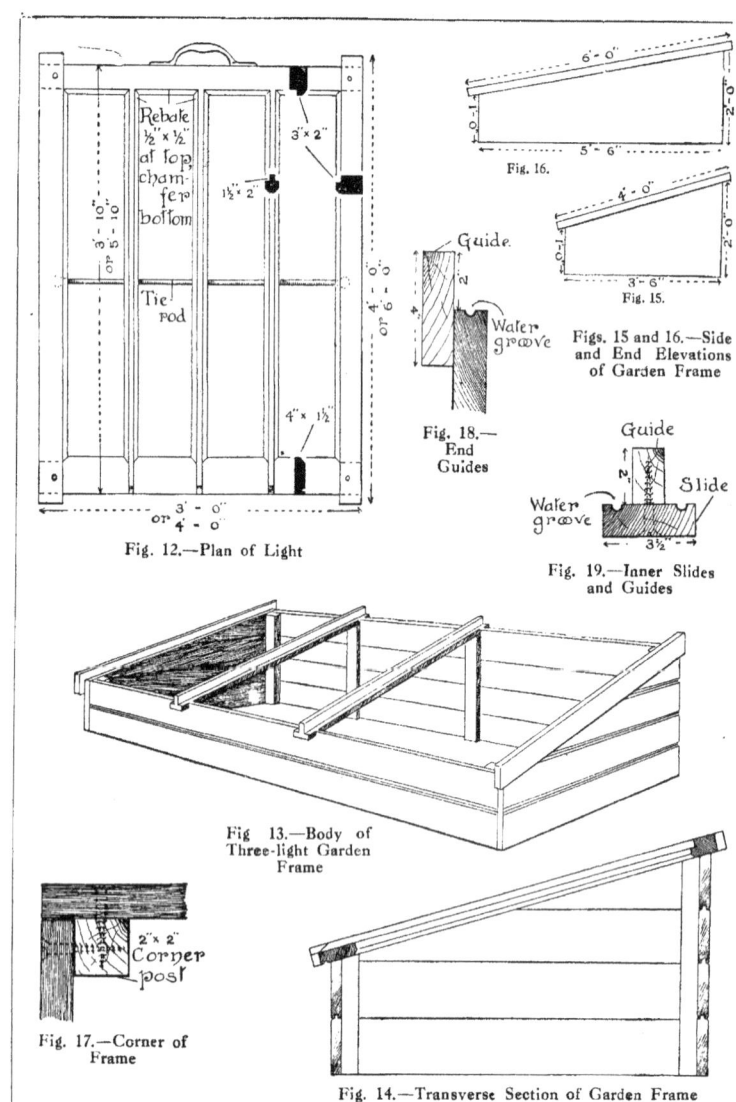

GARDEN LIGHTS

sides are cut to shape, and 2-in. corner posts are screwed 1⅛ in. in from the ends, as shown in Figs. 14 and 17. Water grooves could be cut at the top edges of the sides, as clearly shown in Fig. 18. The front and back boards are screwed to the corner posts which have been previously fixed to the sides, as shown in Fig. 17. In two-light or three-light frames the front and back could be strengthened with cross-battens, as shown in Fig. 13.

In two-light or three-light frames the inner slides and guides are formed as shown in Figs. 13 and 19, water grooves being cut in the slides. For the guides at the ends see Fig. 18.

Deal may be used in constructing the frames; but being exposed to the weather all the joints should be put together with white-lead paint.

corners of the ends and frames. The frames of glass measure 1 ft. 6 in. square, and the length of the frame could be extended according to the number of frames available.

Fig. 21 shows the sectional dimensions of the frame to which the ends and inner frames should be made. The ends (Fig. 22) are of ½-in. boards, preferably grooved and tongued, and held together with two battens 1 in. square nailed in position. Two wood stakes 1 in. square are fitted to each end for fixing in the earth; they are pointed, and project about 6 in. The inner frames (Fig. 23) are of wood 1 in. square, half-lapped and screwed together at the top, as shown in Fig. 24, and kept from spreading by a cross batten, which should be 1 in. deep by ½ in. thick, screwed in position. The bottom ends of the frames are cut to a point as shown. The metal clips could be of either thin iron or steel 1 in. wide, and shaped as shown by Fig. 25. The clips are let in flush with the edges of the ends and frames, each being fixed with two screws.

The wood and metal parts of the frame should be kept well painted.

EXTENSIBLE GARDEN FRAME

An extensible garden frame of simple construction is shown by Fig. 20. The frame is made in parts, and could be fitted up on any desired spot. There must be two wood ends, and a number of inner frames, which are covered with loose sheets of glass. The glass is not fixed in any way, but simply rests on the ends and frames, and is held at the bottom by small metal clips, which are fitted at the

Fig. 20.—Extensible Garden Frame

HAND LIGHT

A hand light has many advantages over the larger garden frame, and by its use seeds may be raised on the site they are

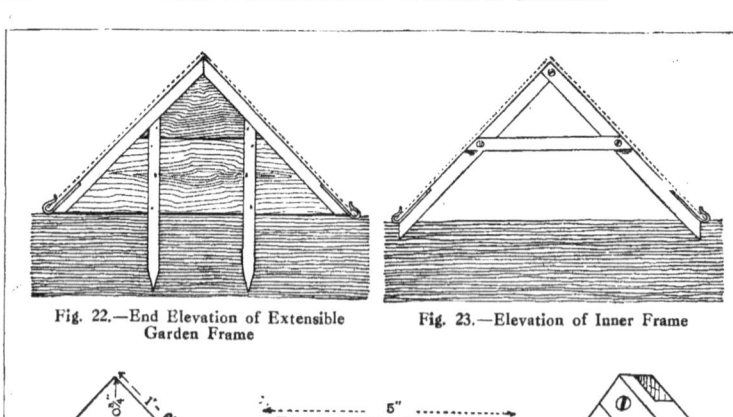

Fig. 22.—End Elevation of Extensible Garden Frame

Fig. 23.—Elevation of Inner Frame

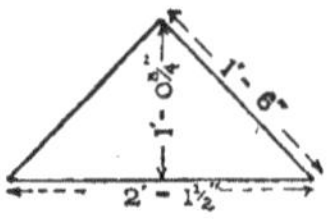

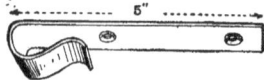

Fig. 21.—Sectional Dimensions

Fig. 25.—Metal Clip

Fig. 24.—Joint at Apex of Frame

permanently to occupy. It may be used for forcing vegetables and small salads in their permanent positions, and with glass on each side the contents of the light receive a maximum amount of heat and sunshine which is very beneficial.

Fig. 26 is a general view of the light, and Figs. 27 and 28 are side and end elevations. A cross section is shown by Fig. 29. The ends A (Fig. 30) are made from ½-in. boards to the sizes given in Fig. 31. The boards should, preferably, have grooved-and-tongued edges, and they are held together with two battens B. The battens are 2½ in. wide by ½ in. thick, and the upper edges project ½ in. above the

Fig. 26.—Hand Light

edges of the ends to form rebates for the glass. Two small battens C (Fig. 31), which are 4 in. long by 1½ in. wide by 1 in. thick, are fixed to the ends 1 in. in from the edges to carry the side rails D. The side rails are 2 ft. 5 in. long by 4 in. deep by 1 in. thick. The top edges are bevelled to match the ends, and they are fixed to the battens C. Small angle-plates fixed in the corners between the battens C and the side rails D would greatly strengthen the work. The top rail E is 2 ft. 10 in. long by 2½ in. deep by 1 in. thick. Notches are cut in the underside to fit over the ends of the light, and the ends of the rail are rounded.

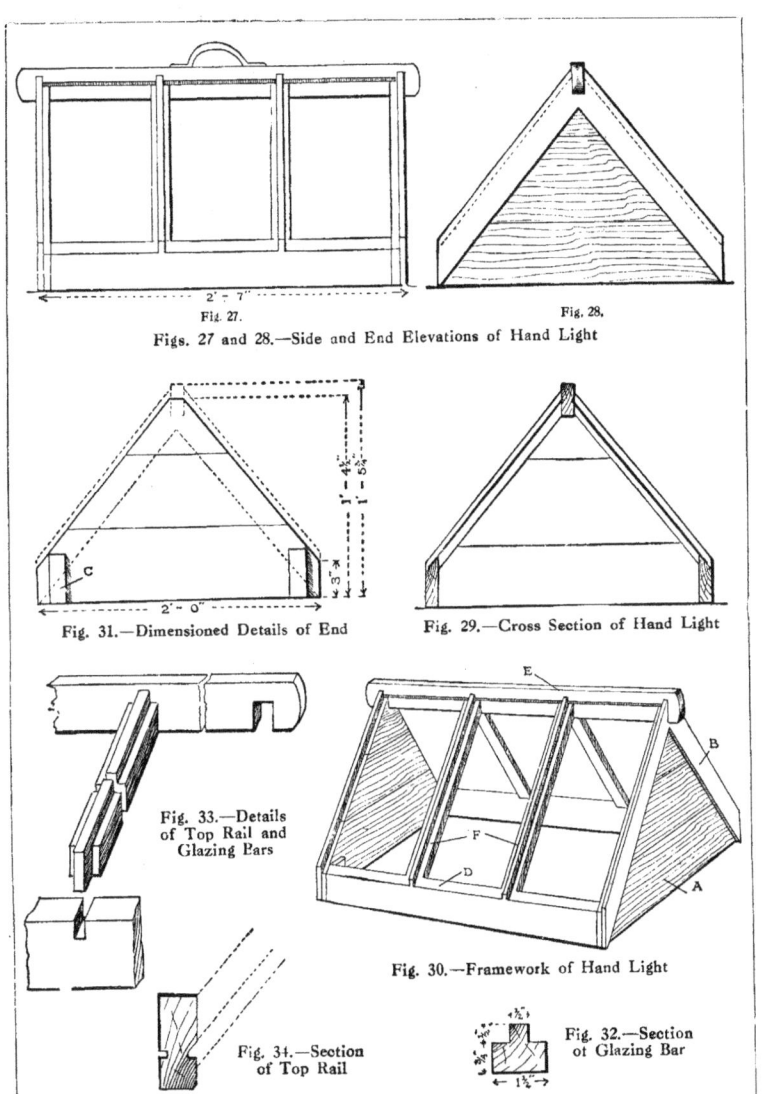

Figs. 27 and 28.—Side and End Elevations of Hand Light

Fig. 31.—Dimensioned Details of End

Fig. 29.—Cross Section of Hand Light

Fig. 33.—Details of Top Rail and Glazing Bars

Fig. 30.—Framework of Hand Light

Fig. 34.—Section of Top Rail

Fig. 32.—Section of Glazing Bar

The glazing bars F, two of which are fitted at each side of the light, are of a section similar to that shown by Fig. 32. These bars simply butt against the top rail, and are notched into the side rails, as shown in Fig. 33. Grooves are cut in the top rail in a line with the rebates in the glazing bars and ends to form a fixing for the glass. A square groove is first cut, and this is then bevelled at the bottom edge to correspond with the slope of the glazing bars and ends, as shown in Fig. 34.

raising plants and bringing them on as soon as possible. The one shown by Fig. 35 can easily be put together at quite a trivial cost. In appearance it resembles a miniature garden frame on legs, with a slanting glass roof, which can be raised or moved as required. It is heated by a paraffin-oil lamp, and is so constructed that no noxious fumes can reach the seedlings. The outside dimensions of the propagator are 2 ft. 7½ in. wide by 1 ft. 10¼ in. deep, and it stands 3 ft. 1 in. high at the back and 2 ft. 8½ in. at the front.

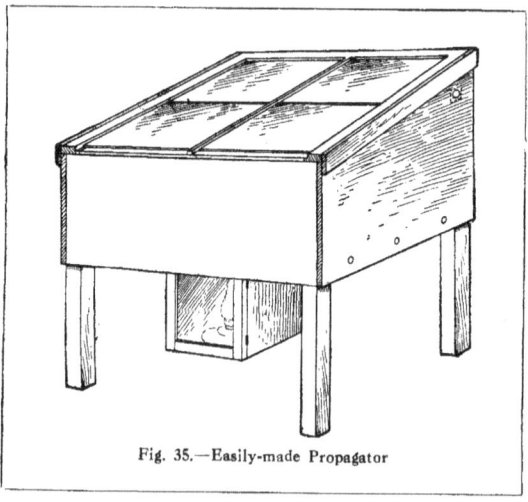

Fig. 35.—Easily-made Propagator

The glass used in glazing the light should be 21 oz., sprigged and bedded in oil putty, care being taken to paint the rebates before glazing. An iron handle similar to that shown in Fig. 26 is screwed to the top rail, and will be found useful for moving the light. When complete the light should be painted with not less than two coats of good oil paint.

EASILY-MADE PROPAGATOR

Where a greenhouse or hotbed is not available, a propagator is very useful for

As will be seen on reference to the cross section (Fig. 36), the water tank, which measures 2 ft. 6 in. by 1 ft. 9 in. by 1½ in. deep, rests on the top of the legs, and thus gives the propagating chamber a depth of about 1 ft. 2 in. at the back and 10 in. at the front.

To begin the construction, first cut four legs from a length of 2-in. quartering, and square them off to each 1 ft. 8 in. long. These should be then connected at the top by rails 2 in. wide by 1 in. thick, which should be dovetail-keyed into the legs, as in Fig. 37. The rails should be

GARDEN LIGHTS

brought flush with the outside face of the legs, and the dovetails worked parallel on the front face and made only ⅞ in. long into the thickness of the latter. The legs and framing, which should now resemble Fig. 38, are next covered in on the under-

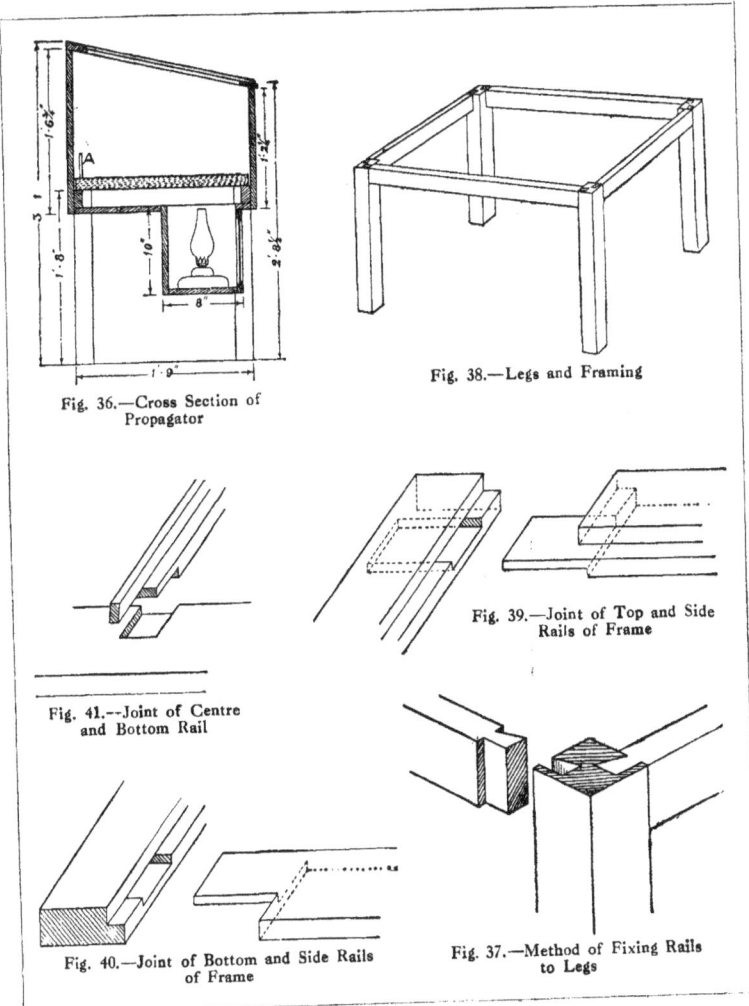

Fig. 36.—Cross Section of Propagator

Fig. 38.—Legs and Framing

Fig. 39.—Joint of Top and Side Rails of Frame

Fig. 41.—Joint of Centre and Bottom Rail

Fig. 40.—Joint of Bottom and Side Rails of Frame

Fig. 37.—Method of Fixing Rails to Legs

side of the rails with ¾-in. grooved-and-tongued boarding, leaving an opening 8 in. square at the centre of the front for the reception of the lamp chamber. This should be made 10 in. high of the same thickness boarding, nailed together at the angles and all round at the top to the edge of the opening in the bottom of the propagator. A glass panelled door should be hinged at the side of the front of the lamp chamber for the purpose of attending to the lamp, and a few ¾-in. holes made in the sides to allow air to enter and the fumes to escape.

The sides of the propagator are next cut from ¾-in. grooved-and-tongued boarding, the front measuring 1 ft. 2¼ in. high and the back 1 ft. 6¾ in. These are nailed together at the corners, and also to the framework at the top of the legs. It is of great importance to have well-seasoned boarding, and to see that the tongues are not broken away in places, causing bad joints, or the heat will escape at any gaps and cause trouble with draught to young seedlings.

The glass-framed top is of 1-in. stuff, and the top and two side pieces should be planed to 2½ in. wide, and rebated throughout their length to a depth of ½ in. each way. The front piece need only be ½ in. thick and 2½ in. wide. The four pieces should now be mortised and tenoned together, the top into the two sides as in Fig. 39, and the bottom piece as in Fig. 40. A centre rail 1 in. square and rebated on each side should be tenoned into the top and let in the bottom as in Fig. 41, and when the joints are ready, glued up and wedged in tightly between two lengths of batten, so that the joints come up quite close. With the addition of a couple of runners nailed to the top of the sides, this will complete the woodwork of the propagator. The rebating should receive a coat of white-lead prior to bedding the glass in soft oil putty, or the latter will not stick properly, after which the whole should be painted with three coats of good oil colour to preserve the wood.

The tank to contain the water should be made of stout zinc well soldered together at the angles, and to prevent the top sagging in the centre, a few short pieces of zinc tubing should be soldered on the inside at intervals. A short length of tubing A (Fig. 36) should also be soldered at one of the sides, by which the tank may be emptied or filled. A good paraffin-oil lamp capable of holding sufficient oil to last at least a full day without requiring to be refilled will be needed to heat the tank, and the top of the glass chimney should be quite 2 in. or 3 in. clear of the bottom of the tank.

The best material with which to cover the top of the tank is undoubtedly cocoa-nut-fibre refuse; but if this is not procurable or is too expensive, fresh sawdust will answer the same purpose. Whichever is used, it is imperative that the material be kept thoroughly moist throughout the entire depth. A thermometer should be fixed to one of the sides of the propagating chamber, so that it can easily be seen from without, and for general purposes an even temperature of about 60° should be maintained. The lamp should be first turned up as for giving light, and when once the heat is diffused throughout the propagating material it should be turned low. The chamber will then keep up an even temperature and the lamp will burn all night and day without needing replenishing or altering.

Greenhouses

PORTABLE GREENHOUSE: TENANT'S FIXTURE

A SPECIAL feature of the greenhouse shown by Fig. 1 is its portability. It is of simple construction, being formed of four principal parts, namely, top, side, and two ends, and these being connected together with screws, very little fixing to the wall is required. By this means the greenhouse would be a tenant's fixture, and, for removal, could be taken apart by undoing a few screws. Front and two end elevations are shown by Figs. 2, 3 and 4.

Good quality red deal will be the most suitable wood, and it will be more economical to buy it ready sawn to the following sizes: Bars for side, ends, and roof, 2 in. by 1 in., 120 ft. run; stiles, rails, etc., for sides and ends, 3 in. by 2 in. 120 ft. run; stiles and rails for roof and

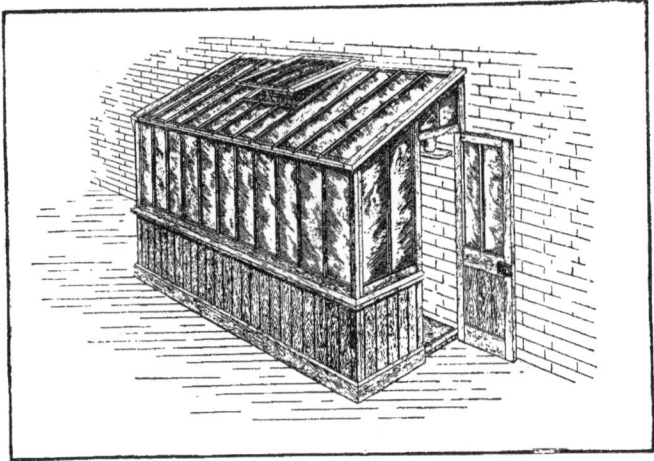

Fig. 1.—Portable Greenhouse

THE PRACTICAL WOODWORKER

middle rail of side and ends, 4½ in. by 2 in., 50 ft. run; bottom rail of roof, 4½ in. by 1¼ in., 13 ft. run; ventilating skylight, 3 in. by 1½ in., 14 ft. run; hinged sash in end, 2 in. by 2 in., 14 ft. run; matchboarding for lower part of framing including plinth, ⅞ in. by 6¼ in., 130 ft. run; middle and bottom rail for door, 7 in. by 2 in., 5 ft. run; weathering strip, and stout bars in end and roof, 1½ in. by 2 in., 50 ft. run. The foregoing sizes are for the wood in the rough, the dimensions marked on the illustrations being those of the wood when planed. To prevent waste, care must be taken to purchase such lengths of wood as will cut up to the best advantage.

Saw the wood off to lengths; all vertical parts such as stiles should be cut off 2 in. longer than required; for the rail-pieces having tenons allow about ½ in. longer at each end. All the pieces should be planed true on one side, then an edge planed at right angles, after which they should be gauged, and planed to the thickness and breadth indicated in the illustrations. It is advisable to set out and complete one piece before attempting the second, so as to avoid mistakes through the pieces becoming mixed.

The principal parts lettered in Figs. 5, 6, and 7 are as follows: A, bottom rail; B, middle rail; C, top rail; D, bottom rail of roof; E, trimming bar; F, top rail of roof; G, wall-piece; H, top rail of ventilating skylight; M, fillet to hinge same to; J, bottom rail of skylight; K, plinth; L, weathering strip or sill; N, stile of side; O, P, and T, stiles of end; R and S, stiles of door; U, matchboarding; V, stop round door opening; W, bar.

The setting-out and subsequent operations for the side will now be described. The two angle stiles should be placed

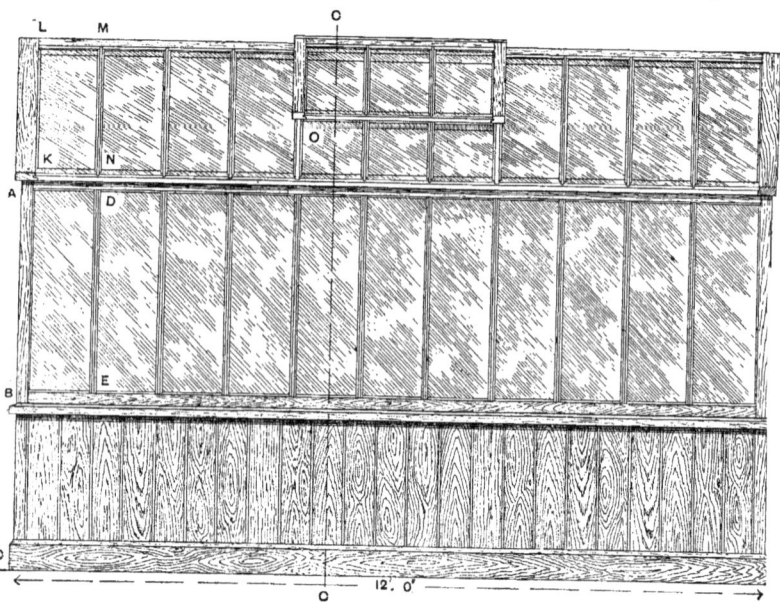

Fig. 2.—Front Elevation of Portable Greenhouse

together in pairs, the positions for mortises being shown in Figs. 8 and 9, and a halved joint (Fig. 10) should be marked across the edges; as the mortises are to be made right through, the lines must be continued to the opposite edges. The top, middle, and bottom rails can next be placed together, and marked out for shoulders at each end (see Figs. 8, 9, and 10). They should also be set out for the mortises for the bars (Figs. 11 and 12). By referring to Figs. 8 and 9, it will be seen that the outer shoulder has to fit to the rebate, and therefore must be set out to the depth of the rebate longer than the inner one. The mortise gauge should now be set to suit the chisel that is to be used (one about ⅝ in. will be the most suitable), then gauge the pieces for the mortises and tenons. Next make the mortises in the stiles and rails; in the former they go through, and in the latter they should be about 1¼ in. deep, as indicated in Figs. 11 and 12. The tenons can now be cut; not the shoulders. The bars should next be set out and gauged, and the tenons cut. Each piece should now be gauged for the rebates. The rebating can be done with a side fillister; but if this tool is not available, a rebate plane can be very easily adapted for the purpose. Three pieces of wood are screwed to the plane; one to only allow it to work a fixed distance "on," and two other pieces to prevent it going below the desired depth. Care must be taken to keep the iron projecting a little beyond the side of the plane, in order to produce clean rebates.

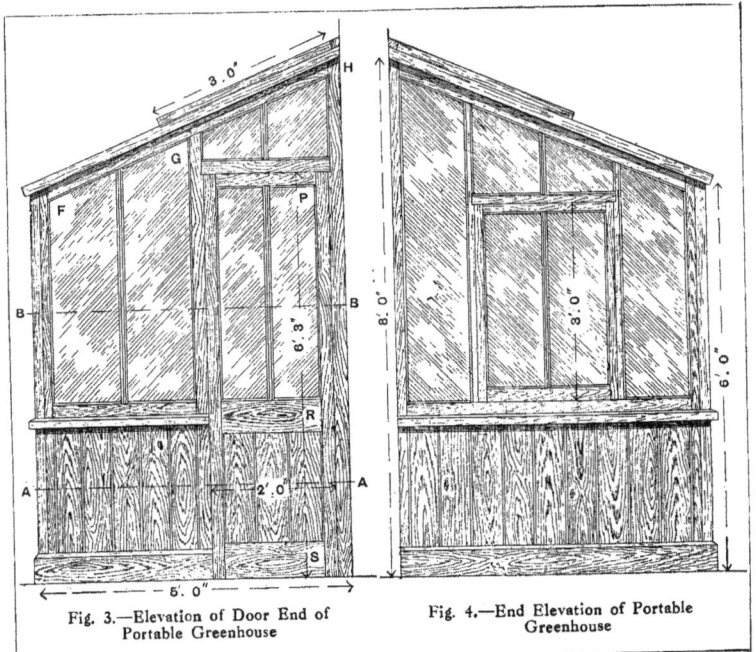

Fig. 3.—Elevation of Door End of Portable Greenhouse

Fig. 4.—End Elevation of Portable Greenhouse

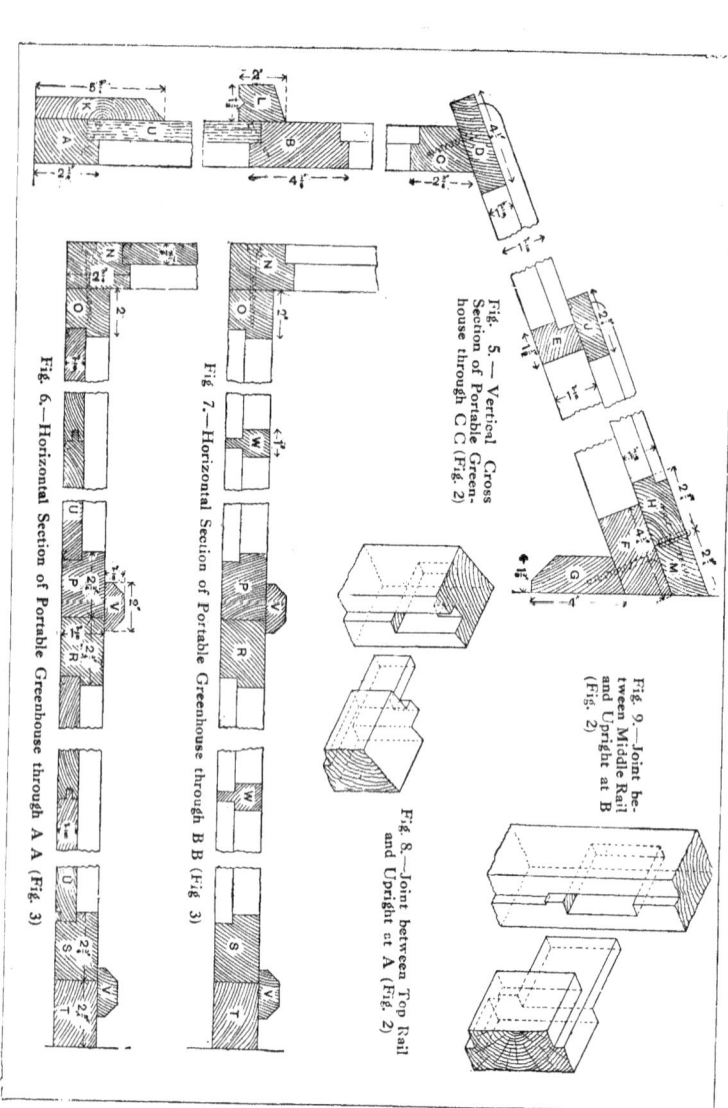

The shoulders of the tenons can now be cut. The tenons of the top and middle rails must be reduced to the shape shown in Figs. 8 and 9, forming a haunch. The under edge of the middle rail and the top edge of the bottom rail require to be rebated for boarding (see Figs. 5, 10, and 12). Now plane the upper edge of the top rail to the angle shown at Fig. 5. The rebate of the lower part of the stiles must be made deeper, so as to receive the edge of the board (see Fig. 5). Each tenon must now be fitted in its respective mortise, after which the whole should be put together and any necessary easing done. Then take two pieces, paint the joints, and put together. The tenons of the top and middle rails must next be

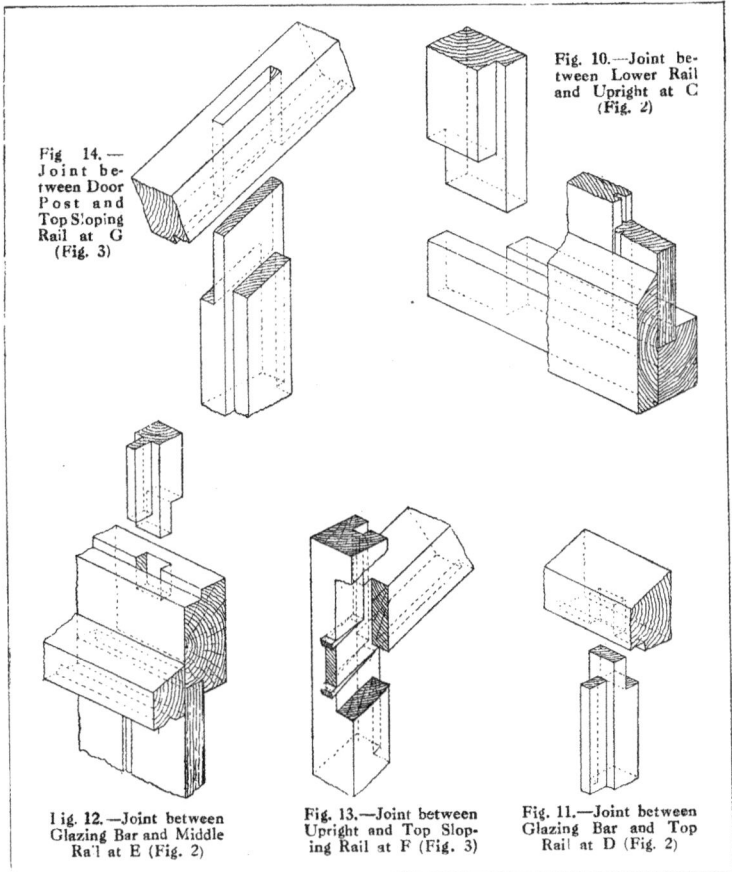

Fig. 14.—Joint between Door Post and Top Sloping Rail at G (Fig. 3)

Fig. 10.—Joint between Lower Rail and Upright at C (Fig. 2)

Fig. 12.—Joint between Glazing Bar and Middle Rail at E (Fig. 2)

Fig. 13.—Joint between Upright and Top Sloping Rail at F (Fig. 3)

Fig. 11.—Joint between Glazing Bar and Top Rail at D (Fig. 2)

wedged in the mortises, as indicated at Fig. 13. The bottom rail and stiles can be connected with two or three screws. Any unevenness between the surfaces of the stiles and top and middle rails should be planed away. It is important to keep the frame square until the boarding is fixed in the lower part; that is, the stiles and rails must be held at right angles to each other. This can be done by temporarily nailing two strips of wood across the top angles. The matchboarding for the lower part can now be cut off to lengths and secured to the middle and bottom rails with 2-in. nails driven in obliquely, as indicated in Fig. 5. The top of the stiles should be sawn and planed level with the top of the rails, and the ends of the tenons and wedges planed flush to the edges of the stiles.

Next prepare a board long enough to form the plinth (see K, Fig. 5). carefully mitre the ends, and secure by nailing to the boards and bottom rail. The weathering strip, or sham sill, L (Fig. 5) should be planed to the form shown; the V-groove can be made with the rebate plane. The ends of the sill should now be mitred; then nail the sill to its position as shown Secure the bars

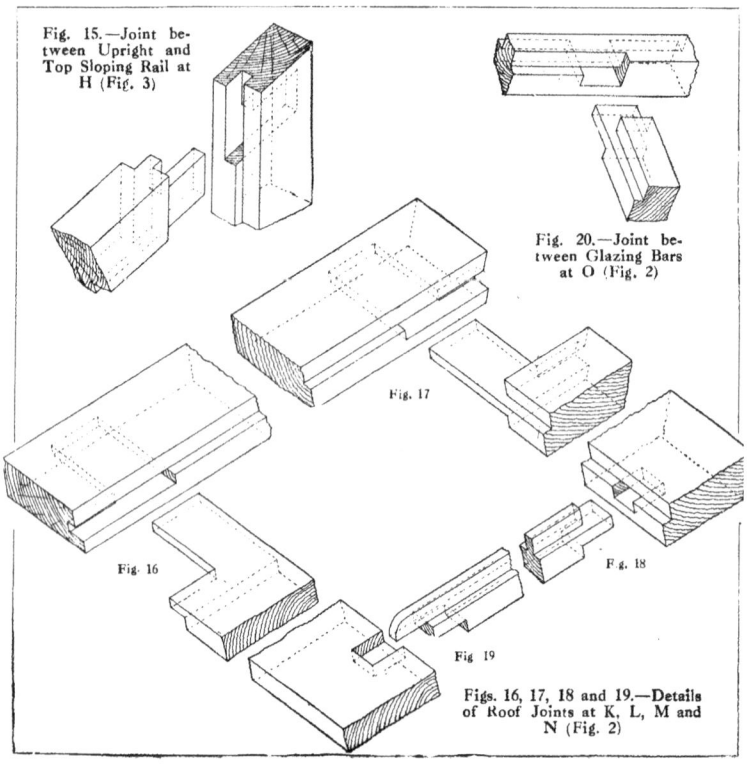

Fig. 15.—Joint between Upright and Top Sloping Rail at H (Fig. 3)

Fig. 20.—Joint between Glazing Bars at O (Fig. 2)

Figs. 16, 17, 18 and 19.—Details of Roof Joints at K, L, M and N (Fig. 2)

GREENHOUSES

to the top and middle rails with a small nail.

The lower parts of the ends are prepared in a similar way to that described for the side. But two points that must be kept in view are, that the mitre of the sill piece and the plinth must be made to project beyond the edges of the stiles of ends, a distance equal to the thickness of the stiles of the side framing (*see* Figs. 3 and 4). It will be found easier to make the joints for the lower part and fit them together first. The top rail can then be placed in position, and the shoulders marked on it at each end, and also the position of the mortises in the stiles can be determined, after which the pieces may be gauged and the mortises and tenons made ; the form of these is shown in Figs. 13, 14, and 15. The mortises for the bars in the top rail, also those for the pieces forming the top of the doorway and the hanging sash, should be set out and made. The ends can now be put together, and each bar laid on and marked for shoulders, then gauged ; the tenons and shoulders can then be cut, and the bars fitted into their respective positions. The method of completing each end will be almost exactly the same as described for the side. A good plan is to procure a piece of oak about 2 in. square for a threshold, and to connect the stiles that form the doorway, as shown in Fig. 1.

The making of the roof and skylight should present little difficulty. The wood for the bottom rail should be planed up to dimensions, noting that the thickness of this is less than the stiles by the amount of the rebate. The several pieces should be set out for the joints, etc., which are shown by Figs. 16, 17, and 18, the one for connecting the stiles to the bottom rail requiring special notice. The form of joint between the bars and the bottom rail is shown by Fig. 19. By referring to Fig. 2 it will be seen that the bars supporting the ventilating skylight require to be rebated their whole length on one side, and only as far as the trimming piece on the other. It should also be noted that they are stouter than the other bars, and it will be as well to let their tenons pass through the top rail. The joint connecting the bars and the trimming pieces is shown by Fig. 20.

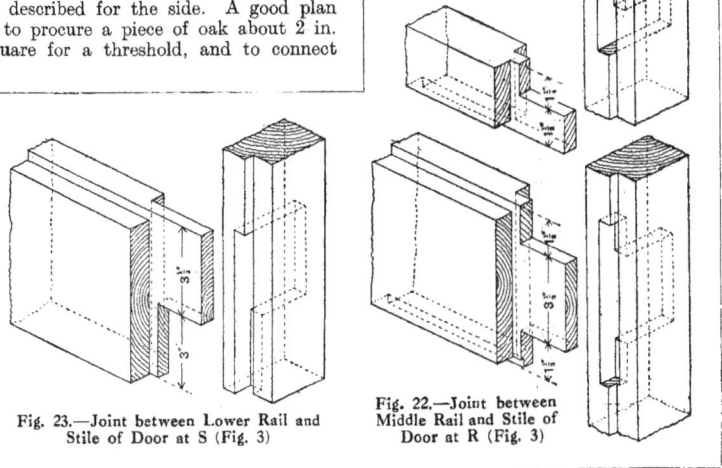

Fig. 21.—Joint between Top Rail and Stile of Door at P (Fig 3)

Fig. 23.—Joint between Lower Rail and Stile of Door at S (Fig. 3)

Fig. 22.—Joint between Middle Rail and Stile of Door at R (Fig. 3)

The tenons of the bars should be fixed to the top and bottom rails with a small nail, and the whole completed in a manner similar to that described for the other parts. The joints of the door are shown by Figs. 21, 22, and 23.

The method of fixing will now be described. The ground where the ends and a side are to stand should be levelled, and very suitable foundation would be formed by a course of bricks. One end and the side should be placed in position, and temporarily stayed until screwed together; the other end should be fixed to the side in the same manner. The wall piece G (Fig. 5) should be prepared and cut off to the exact length. This should next be placed in position and firmly secured to the wall with 4-in. nails driven into the brickwork. The roof can now be lifted on and secured to the wall piece, ends, and side with 3½-in. screws, as indicated in Fig. 5. The stiles abutting to the walls should be secured by two or three holdfasts. Then plane the edges of the door and sash to fit into their respective openings and hinge them, and also the skylight on the top. A chamfered fillet, as shown in section at v (Figs. 6 and 7), should be prepared and fixed round inside the door opening and window in the opposite end.

The greenhouse will now be ready for a first coat of paint, after which it should be glazed and finally finished with two more coats of paint of any colour desired.

SMALL SPAN-ROOF GREENHOUSE

The matter of keeping the cost as low as possible has been consistently borne in mind when designing the span-roof greenhouses shown in side and end elevations by Figs. 24, 25, and 26. and to further this object in the actual construction it is not advised that the timber should be purchased in so many pieces cut to the lengths required, or it will cost more; but rather that it should be bought in bulk, the worker cutting it up himself. The quantities required, with the various sizes and sections are given later.

The greenhouse is 12 ft. long by 7 ft. wide, the height being 5 ft. to the eaves. The roof is of square pitch, that is, the rafters form a right angle at the top, and the whole structure stands on a foundation consisting of a single row of bricks as shown. The lower portion is boarded with 1-in. tongued-and-grooved boards, the upper part and the roof being glazed. The door is placed in the middle of one end of the house, thus leaving room for a stage down each side. Ventilation is provided for by the two ventilators at one side of the roof, and one at the other, thus forming a through current of air, which can be regulated as desired.

The necessary setting out and framing together is very simple. Figs. 27 and 28 show the framing of the door end and one side respectively. In these latter illustrations the posts A are the same. The corner posts must be mortised as in Fig. 29 to take the sills, the middle rails, and the top rails or plates. The whole of the mortises must be kept back from the face sides (that is the outsides) the thickness of the boarding to be used in the lower part, which will be ⅞ in. This will facilitate the making of the rebates to take the glass and the boarding, and also simplify the tenons on the various rails, etc., which have to fit to the posts. The intermediate posts in the sides and ends will be mortised to take the middle rails, as shown in Fig. 30, these mortises passing straight through. They will also be tenoned to fit into the top rails (plates), and cut as shown at the bottom to fit the sills. The reason of this latter cut, instead of an ordinary tenon, will be given later. The two door posts will be similar to the last mentioned, with the exception that instead of the tenon to fit into the top rails, mortises must be made instead, as shown in Fig. 31. These mortises must not be allowed to pass through the wood, or it will show in the doorway. Other similar mortises must be made higher up and on the opposite sides to take the door head, and the posts should be left to run up so as to cut off afterwards to fit the rafters when these are fitted and fixed.

The sills will need cutting, as in Fig. 32,

GREENHOUSES

being kept less in width to allow the board to run down beyond them. The mortises take the form of slots, which accounts for the shape of the tenon at the bottom of the intermediate posts (Fig. 30). The tenons at the end of the sills, which fit into the corner posts, must be "barefaced": that is, with a shoulder on the inside only, as shown on the left in Fig. 32. The top rails will be tenoned as in Fig. 33, to fit the corner posts; also mortised to take the intermediate posts. These mortises should not go through the wood. The rail is shown wrong way up in the illustration, so as to show the mortises. The outside upper corner of them stronger, they are each made nearly long enough to reach through the post, and each halved on to its fellow. Thus the rails will not only be pinned to the post, but will also be pinned together through the halving. The corner posts will need rebating to take the glass and boards at each side on the outside corners; the intermediate posts will need rebating in the same way at each of the outer corners; also the top rails on the underside, and the middle rails both on the under and the upper sides. The rebates in all cases should be ⅜ in. deep, and reach to the mortise or tenon, as the case may be. Thus Fig. 33 is shown ready

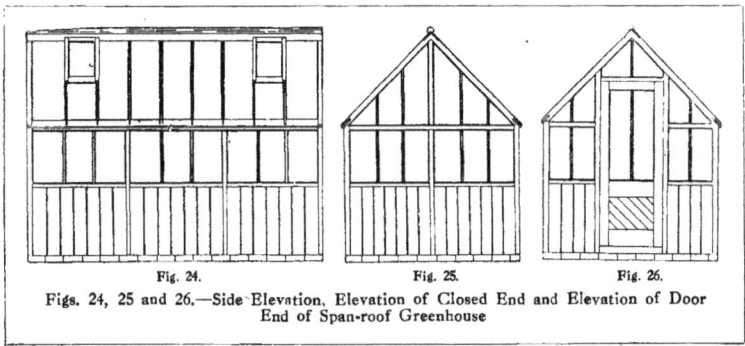

Figs. 24, 25 and 26.—Side Elevation, Elevation of Closed End and Elevation of Door End of Span-roof Greenhouse

these rails must be chamfered off to an angle of 45°, as shown in Fig. 28, to form a bed for the eaves board, and when the framing is put together the chamfers will be continued on the ends of the posts as shown. Fig. 34 shows the top rail for the end opposite the door (Fig. 25). The ends of the tenons are shown mitred so as to fit up to the tenons of the side rails in the corner posts, thus giving more hold for the pins when fixing together. The mortise for the middle post must, in this case, pass through the wood to take the continuation of the post. In the middle side rails (see Fig. 25) the tenons would be very short where they come to the intermediate posts, if cut in the ordinary way, therefore, to make for rebating, and Figs. 34 and 35 are shown with one rebate made. The door posts will need rebating as above at one side; but the door side will either need a deeper and wider rebate to take the door, or slips may be nailed on to answer the same purpose; probably the latter will be found the better way. In all cases where a tenon comes to a mortise in a post or other part that has to be rebated, the outer shoulder must be left longer to fit into the rebate. Fig. 36 is a section of one side of the greenhouse.

When all the parts are cut correctly, the whole frame may be put together, carefully painting each mortise and tenon as it is fitted; also the pins as they are driven in. The frame will then be ready

THE PRACTICAL WOODWORKER

for the roof, a section of which is shown by Fig. 37. Fig. 38 is an enlarged section at the eaves.

The outside rafters must be cut as in Fig. 39 and the intermediate ones as in Fig. 40; and the roof being of square outside rafters may be tenoned together; or, if preferred, they can be halved, and fixed with screws; or they may be mitred. The intermediate rafters will, as a matter of course, be mitred, and no ridge board is necessary. At the upper

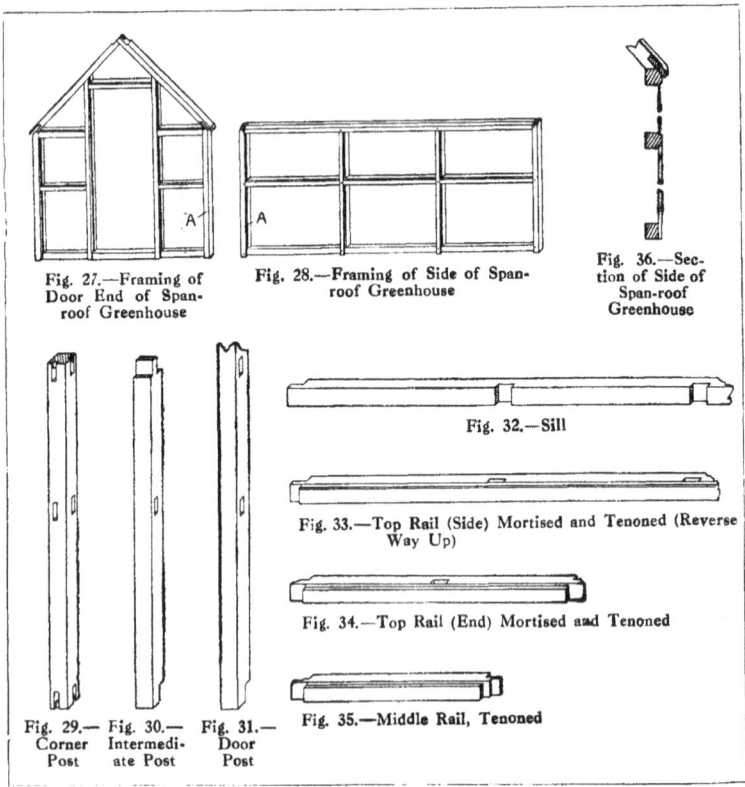

Fig. 27.—Framing of Door End of Span-roof Greenhouse

Fig. 28.—Framing of Side of Span-roof Greenhouse

Fig. 36.—Section of Side of Span-roof Greenhouse

Fig. 32.—Sill

Fig. 33.—Top Rail (Side) Mortised and Tenoned (Reverse Way Up)

Fig. 34.—Top Rail (End) Mortised and Tenoned

Fig. 35.—Middle Rail, Tenoned

Fig. 29.—Corner Post   Fig. 30.—Intermediate Post   Fig. 31.—Door Post

pitch, it follows that the angle at the bottom will be one of 45°. The point at A must come to the edge of the chamfer on the top rail, so that the plain surface B and the chamfer are continuous when the rafters are fixed, and form a bed for the eaveboard C. At the upper end the ends the tongues of the rafters must be cut away down to within about $\frac{3}{16}$ in. of the rebate, to take the boards D, which will fix to each pair of rafters on both sides of the roof, and the glass will fit up under them, as in Fig. 41. These roof boards may be anything from 3 in. to

5 in. wide by ¾ in. thick. They are nailed one on the other at the apex of the roof, the ridge roll E covering the joint. In fixing the boards, take care that the rafters are kept the correct distance between.

The two ventilators take the form of in a small house like the one being described, the top rail can be fitted and hinged to the ridge roll. The opening of the ventilators is done by means of a curved iron bar fixed to the bottom rail of the ventilator, and a cord passing over a pulley fixed in the cross trimmer

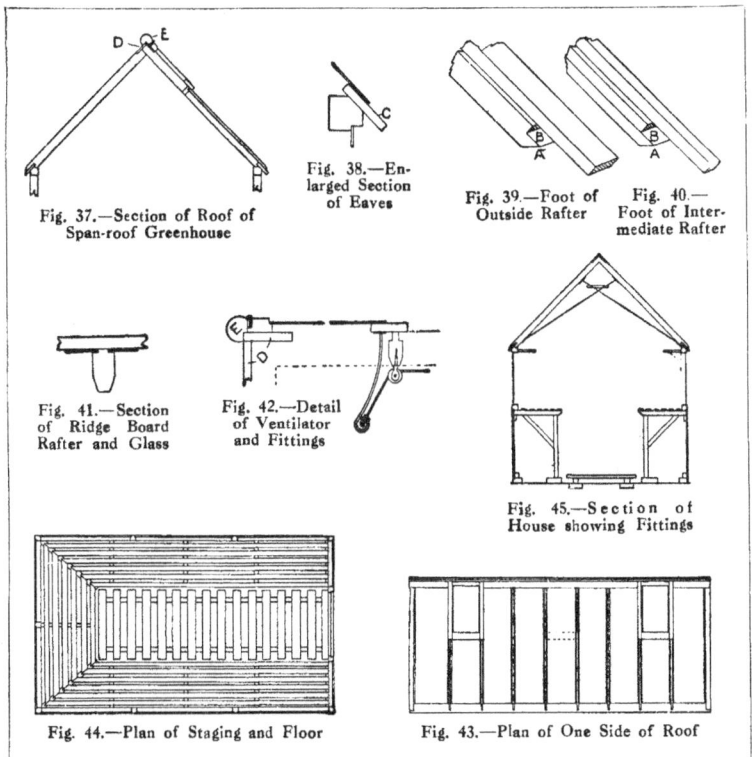

Fig. 37.—Section of Roof of Span-roof Greenhouse

Fig. 38.—Enlarged Section of Eaves

Fig. 39.—Foot of Outside Rafter

Fig. 40.—Foot of Intermediate Rafter

Fig. 41.—Section of Ridge Board Rafter and Glass

Fig. 42.—Detail of Ventilator and Fittings

Fig. 45.—Section of House showing Fittings

Fig. 44.—Plan of Staging and Floor

Fig. 43.—Plan of One Side of Roof

small sashes, made so as to cover one pair of rafters in width, and to reach about halfway between the ridge and the eaves in the length. A piece of rafter material is fixed between the pair of rafters, in the correct position for the bottom rail of the sash to rest on. When closed, and between the rafters. A section of the whole arrangement is shown by Fig. 42. The plan of one side of the roof (Fig. 43) shows the position of the two ventilators on that side; the dotted lines also show the position of the single ventilator on the opposite side. The bars in the sides

THE PRACTICAL WOODWORKER

and ends of the greenhouse, apart from the actual framing, may be cut to fit tightly and fixed with brads; or they may be tenoned into the middle rail and bradded to the top rail, if preferred. The fixing of the boarding round the greenhouse will present no difficulty, and the door can be simply framed up with mortise-and-tenon joints or halving joints. The door will be fixed with butt hinges, and should be fitted with a lock and key.

A plan of the inside fittings is shown by Fig. 44. The staging along each side is 2 ft. wide, and that across the end is 6 in. wider. It consists of battens 2 in. wide by 1 in. thick fixed to the bearers, as shown in the section (Fig. 45), with a space of about 1 in. between. The ends of the bearers which come to the outside of the greenhouse rest on fillets screwed to the outer boarding as shown, the inner edge of the staging being supported by the braced legs. These latter should stand on a brick laid in the ground or firmly on it, and should be painted on the end grain before they are fixed. The floor, as shown, may be dispensed with if preferred; but the greenhouse will be found much more comfortable with it. It consists of two pieces of scantling 2 in. square resting on bricks at intervals in their length, the floor proper being slats 3 in. or 4 in. wide, spaced out as shown.

The whole should be kept down in width sufficiently to allow of the complete floor being turned up and taken out through the door when required. Shelves may be fixed along the top rail, supported by brackets, as shown in Fig. 45, and another one may be fixed in the top part of the roof. Solid shelves are shown as being more convenient for fixing; but if formed of laths in the same way as the staging, they will last longer. Iron tie rods, as shown in Fig. 45, should be fixed across the house in the middle lengthwise.

In conclusion, a specification of the materials required to build the greenhouse is here given, the various sections being shown by Figs. 46 to 56. Top rail (Fig.

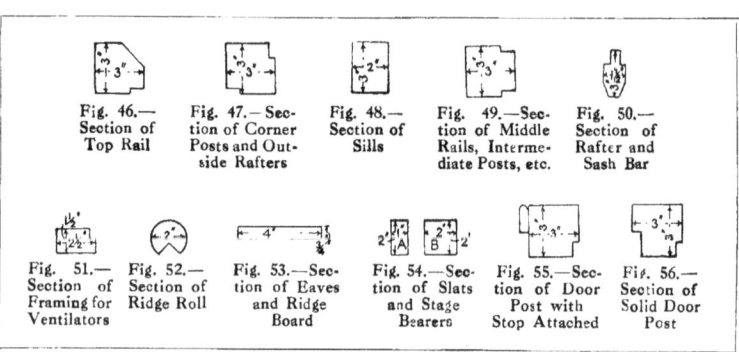

Fig. 46.—Section of Top Rail
Fig. 47.—Section of Corner Posts and Outside Rafters
Fig. 48.—Section of Sills
Fig. 49.—Section of Middle Rails, Intermediate Posts, etc.
Fig. 50.—Section of Rafter and Sash Bar
Fig. 51.—Section of Framing for Ventilators
Fig. 52.—Section of Ridge Roll
Fig. 53.—Section of Eaves and Ridge Board
Fig. 54.—Section of Slats and Stage Bearers
Fig. 55.—Section of Door Post with Stop Attached
Fig. 56.—Section of Solid Door Post

46), 24 ft. required; corner posts and end rafters (Fig. 47), 50 ft.; sills (Fig. 48), 40 ft.; intermediate posts and middle rails (Fig. 49), 70 ft.; intermediate rafter for glass 15 in. wide (Fig. 50), 120 ft.; stiles and top rails of ventilators (Fig. 51), 24 ft.; ridge roll (Fig. 52), 12 ft.; eave and ridge boards (Fig. 53), 52 ft.; slats and bearers for stage and floor (Fig. 54), 400 ft. for A and 100 ft. for B; door post (stop nailed on) (Fig. 55), 14 ft.; door post solid (alternative) (Fig. 56), 14 ft.; 1¼ squares of 1-in. tongued-and-grooved boarding; 14 ft. of 9-in. by 1½-in. for the door; 60 ft. of sash bar (as Fig. 50, but smaller); 300 ft. of horticultural glass; putty, paint, nails, screws, etc.

Tents

PORTABLE SUMMERHOUSE TENT

A STRUCTURE having the advantages of a summerhouse combined with the portable character of a tent, capable of being taken from one house to another, or of being packed away in a small space, has several points in its favour. Such a shelter provides a very fair garden room for rest cures or other purposes.

A perspective sketch of the tent is shown by Fig. 1, and another sketch (Fig. 2) shows the construction generally. It will be seen that it is composed of a light wooden framework screwed together, or preferably put together with one small galvanised thumbscrew and nut through each joint. Each end is supported by a framework of the dimensions shown, consisting of two 3-in. by 2-in. rafters and a 3-in. by 2-in. horizontal sill with shaped ends. These are connected by two sloping standards, also 3 in. by 2 in., fixed on the inside, while on the outer side are screwed two upright planks, 5 in. by 1 in., to stiffen the whole. Side and end elevations are given by Figs. 3 and 4. At the apex the rafters are held together by a small iron plate, screwed on as shown in the isometric drawing, Fig. 5, of one end of the ridge, and are notched out to take the end of a 4-in. by $1\frac{1}{2}$-in. ridge piece, which is also notched out as shown, so as to fit over the rafters.

The ridge is of such a length as to keep the standards 10 ft. apart and to overhang about 7 in. It has a wedge-shaped fillet 12 in. long fixed at each end for appearance. At the lower ends of the rafters 3-in. by 2-in. pieces of the same length as the ridge are screwed, and these complete the framework, which should be found to be fairly rigid. Two lengths

Fig. 1.—Portable Summerhouse Tent

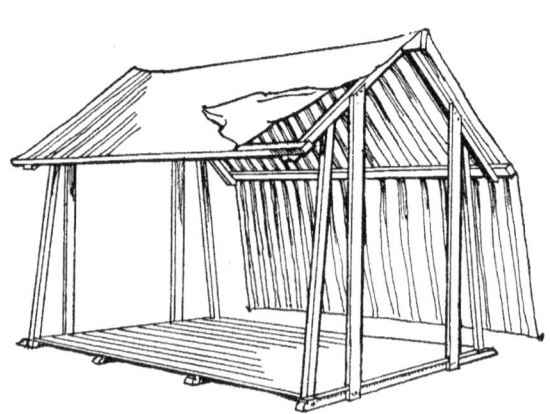

Fig. 2.—Portable Summerhouse Tent showing Construction of Framework

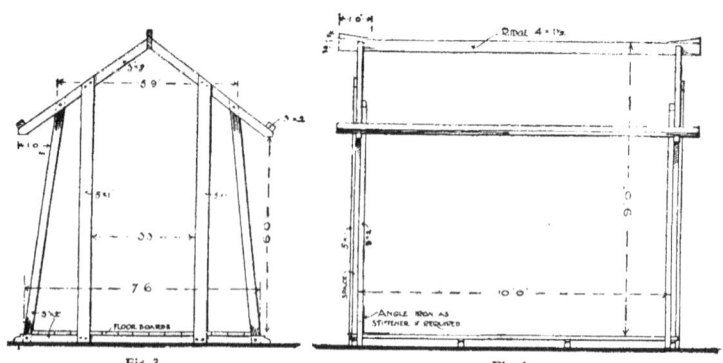

Fig. 3. Fig. 4.
Figs. 3 and 4.—End and Side Elevations of Framework of Tent

SCALE OF FEET AND INCHES

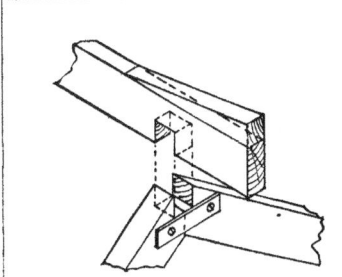

Fig. 5.—Joints at Apex of Rafters of Summerhouse Tent

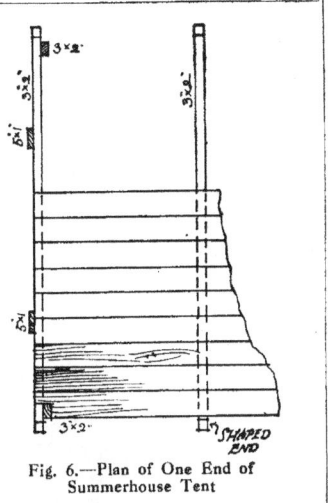

Fig. 6.—Plan of One End of Summerhouse Tent

similar to the sill pieces can be laid on the ground between the ends, and a light boarded floor laid across them, as partly shown on the plan (Fig. 6). These boards need not all be fixed, for if a light fillet be screwed across them at each end this will keep the whole in position. Should there be any slight lack of steadiness when completed, a plain flat angle bracket can be fixed at each end, as shown in the front view.

The drawings fully explain the nature of the summerhouse, and also show how it is intended to be covered with strong striped blind-canvas fixed to the woodwork with rings and hooks. One broad piece will be tied to pegs in the ground at the back, and come up over the ridge and down to the front as shown, and side pieces the shape of the ends will need to be fitted in position. At this stage it may be left, or the awning may be continued on cords and two upright poles to shade a distance of 6 ft. or more in front of the summerhouse, as suggested by the smaller of the perspective views.

GARDEN TENT WITH EXTENDING CANOPY

A garden tent of simple construction and which may be made at a small cost is shown by Fig. 7.

The framework, as will be seen on referring to Fig. 8, consists of a number of upright rods, which are connected by other horizontal rods, while the roof is formed with four rods, which are connected in the centre. The tent may be made to any size which will best meet individual requirements, although a convenient size would be a body 8 ft. square by 6 ft. high, with an extending canopy 8 ft. long, the roof of the body having a rise of 1 ft. 6 in. in the centre. It will be found advisable to make the rods of ash, each being $1\frac{1}{4}$ in. in diameter. The upright rods are cut to a length of 6 ft., and a metal ferrule is fitted at each end to prevent splitting. Small iron spills are fitted at each end of the upright rods, as shown in Figs. 9 and 10. These may be formed from long wire nails by simply removing the heads. The spills are driven into the ends of the rods, those at the top ends projecting about 2 in. and those at the bottom ends about 3 in. The horizontal rods which connect the upright rods are next prepared. Metal ferrules are fitted to the ends, and an iron screw-eye, similar to that shown by Fig. 11, is screwed into each end. The horizontal rods are fitted to the upright rods by means of the screw-eyes, which fit over the projecting spills on the upright rods as shown in Fig. 9.

The roof rods are cut long enough to give the required rise in the centre, and metal ferrules are fitted at the ends. Screw-eyes are fitted at each end of the roof rods, with one exception, in which case a spill and fly-nut is fitted in place of the screw-eye. The spill and fly-nut is shown by Fig. 12, and it provides a means of connecting the roof rods in the centre. The screwed spill is $\frac{5}{16}$ in. in diameter, and is fitted with a fly-nut; a taper spill is also provided at the top, and this is driven into the end of the rod. Six guy-ropes are required for keeping the tent rigid, and one of these is fitted to each of the upright rods. A metal eye-piece is spliced, or securely tied, to the top end of each rope, as shown in Fig. 13. A suitable peg is shown by Fig. 14; each peg should be about 8 in. long by $1\frac{1}{4}$ in. wide by $\frac{3}{4}$ in. thick, and shaped as shown. The toggles (Fig. 15), by means of which the guy-ropes are tightened, should be about 4 in. long by $1\frac{1}{4}$ in. wide by $\frac{3}{4}$ in. thick. They are shaped as shown, and holes are provided at each end through which the ropes pass.

A striped tent cloth would be very serviceable for the covering. The sides and back should be separate from the roof covering, and the roof is fitted with a valance about 4 in. deep. The material is cut to shape, and the various portions are strongly sewn together. The covering is held in position by small looped tapes

Fig. 7.—Garden Tent with Extending Canopy

which are sewn at intervals round the edges, the tapes being threaded over the rods. Small turned wood caps, similar to that shown by Fig. 16, may be fitted to the top ends of the upright rods to give a finished effect. The caps fit over the metal spills, and they should be placed in position after the guy-ropes are fixed.

Brass curtain-rod ends, which may be obtained with a screwed shank, can be used as a substitute, and in this case the spills would not be required.

TENTS

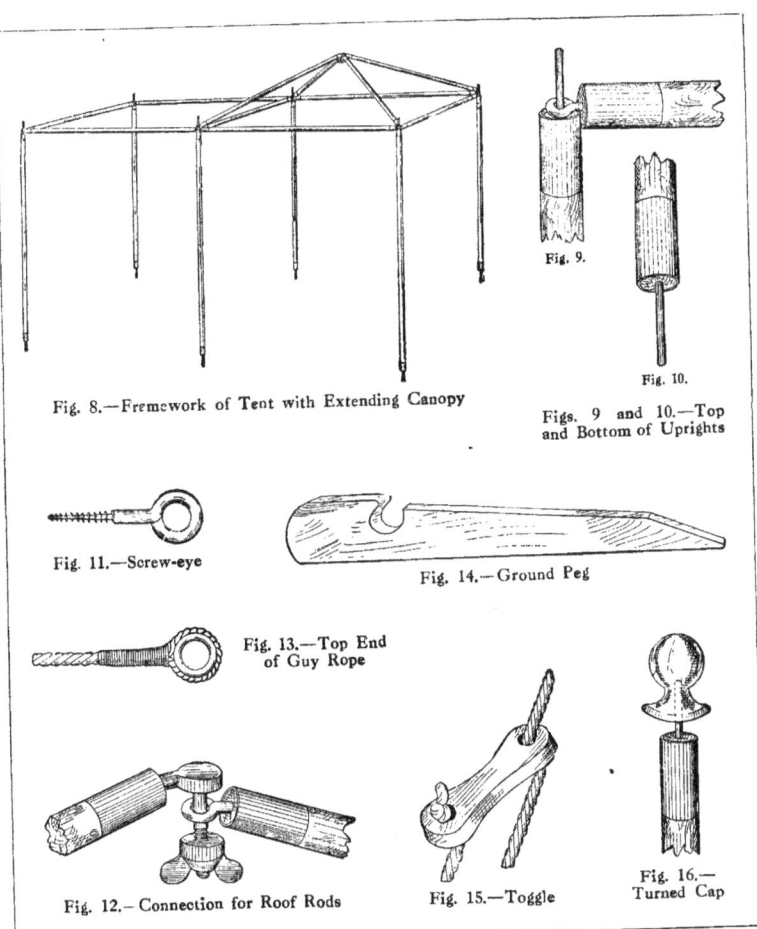

Fig. 8.—Framework of Tent with Extending Canopy

Figs. 9 and 10.—Top and Bottom of Uprights

Fig. 11.—Screw-eye

Fig. 14.—Ground Peg

Fig. 13.—Top End of Guy Rope

Fig. 12.—Connection for Roof Rods

Fig. 15.—Toggle

Fig. 16.—Turned Cap

PORTABLE FISHING TENT

The framework of a light portable waterproof shelter or tent, large enough to cover two people and useful when fishing on the river-bank, is shown by Fig. 17. The tent is rectangular in shape and open in the front, the frame being of bamboo. The minimum size for two people to sit side by side would be: width, 3 ft.; depth from front to back, 2 ft. 6 in.; height at front, 5 ft.; and height at back, 4 ft. 3 in. The four uprights A (Fig. 17) have the bottoms plugged with pointed hardwood ends for inserting in the ground. The tops are notched, plugged, and dowelled, as shown at B (Fig. 18), and the side rails D (Fig. 17) are plugged and bored to receive the dowels, as shown at C (Fig. 18). The back rail E (Fig. 17) is dowelled into the side rails, which project at the back far enough to allow the dowels to miss those of the uprights, and the front rail F should project about 9 in. in front of the uprights; and to allow of this, the side rails D are lengthened.

The covering may be of unbleached calico, of which the roof piece only need be waterproof. This should be 6 in. prevent the tent blowing over, cords are used. These pass over the top frame, being secured to the sides by a hitch to the rails, and are fastened into the ground with tent pegs.

The roof should be painted with a mixture of boiled linseed oil and gold-size; 1 pint of oil to 1 gill of size. If desired, the tent could be easily fitted to a boat. The uprights could be fitted into staples driven into the gunwale, and four cleats used for securing the cords.

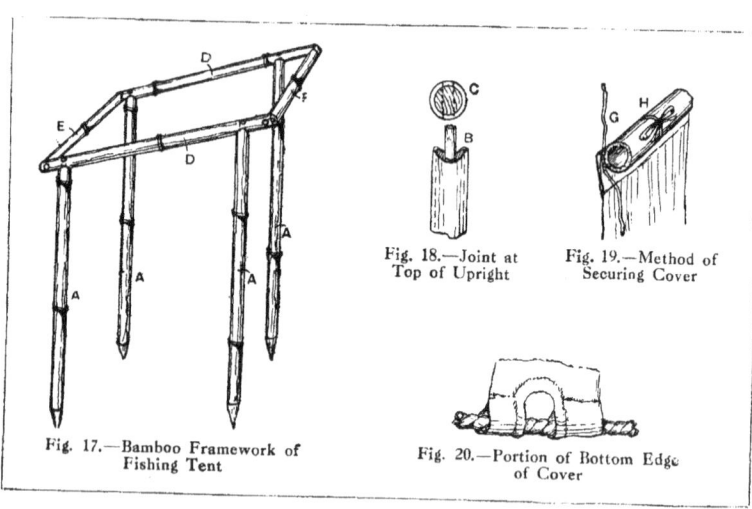

Fig. 17.—Bamboo Framework of Fishing Tent

Fig. 18.—Joint at Top of Upright

Fig. 19.—Method of Securing Cover

Fig. 20.—Portion of Bottom Edge of Cover

larger all round than the size of the roof frame to form a valance, and this margin may be turned down and sewn at the corners. Tapes, about 6 in. apart, can be sewn to the cover about 7 in. in from the edges for tying the top on to the frame. The sides and back may be in one piece, tapes being sewn on at the edges, as shown in Fig. 19, G showing a tape loose and H a tape tied to the frame. The bottom should be hemmed and have a cord run through; pieces can then be cut out at intervals (see Fig. 20) for pegging the sides to the ground. To

OCTAGONAL WOOD FLOOR FOR BELL TENT

The floor for use in a bell tent may be either temporary or permanent. A temporary floor would be constructed with a few joists and floorboards, but one to be used permanently as a portable floor would require to be constructed on different lines.

Supposing that the diameter of the tent is roughly 13 ft., the floor to make it convenient for handling and packing should be in eight sections. Fig. 21 shows

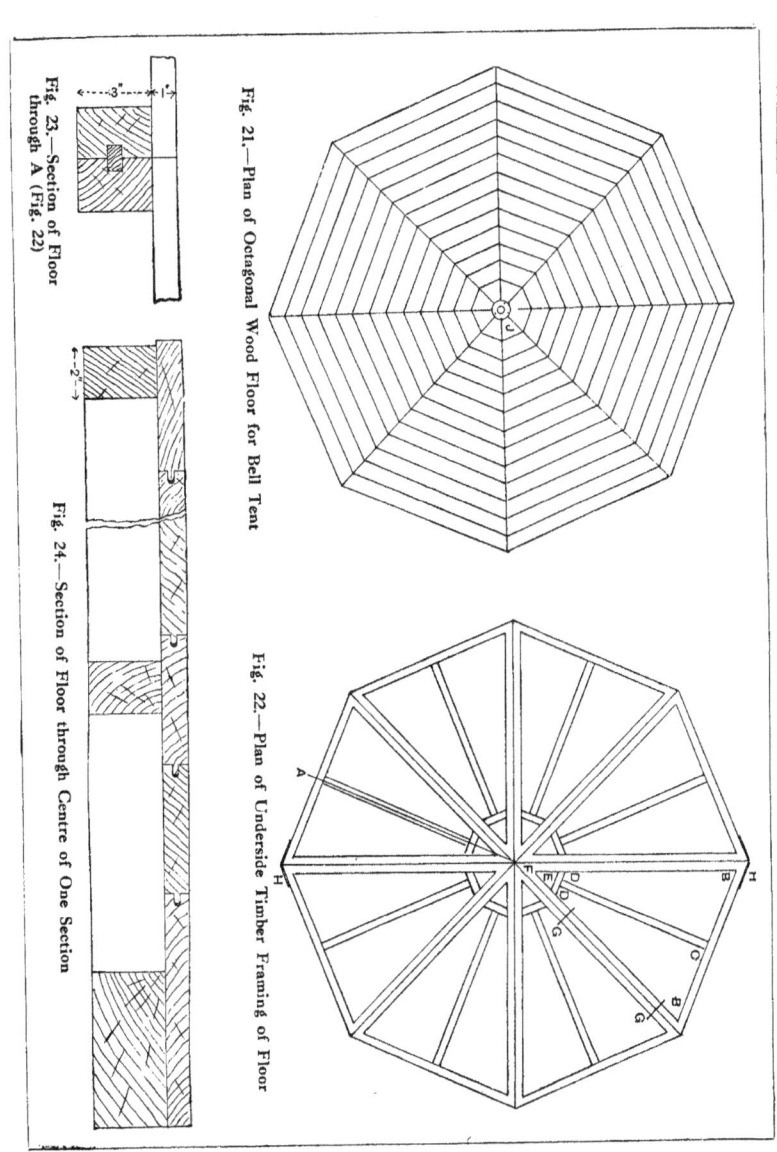

Fig. 21.—Plan of Octagonal Wood Floor for Bell Tent

Fig. 22.—Plan of Underside Timber Framing of Floor

Fig. 23.—Section of Floor through A (Fig. 22)

Fig. 24.—Section of Floor through Centre of One Section

the floor as finished, and Fig. 22 shows the underside timber framing. The shape of the floor is consequently octagonal, each section being a triangle. The under framing consists of 3-in. by 2-in. deal framed together, as in Fig. 22. The angles B are dovetailed, mortised and tenoned at C, D, and E, the whole of these joints being pinned through with oak pins. The mitred joint at F is well screwed together. Each section is constructed in the same way, and should be built from the same lines. When finished, the sections are covered with 5-in. by 1-in. tongued-and-grooved flooring, screwed to the framing, as shown in Fig. 21. Fig. 23 is a section through A (Fig. 22).

The outer edge of each section of the framing is grooved to receive a hardwood tongue, one side being glued and fixed. This tongue keeps the floor level (see Fig. 24). Each joint should be marked with a chisel where the sections come together in the same place. When being put together, each half of the floor is bolted together at the radiating joints (see G, Fig. 22), and turned over on to some rough sleeper joists, leaving a space to enable the air to pass beneath. The two half sections may be kept together by means of iron angle brackets screwed on the outer edge at H (Fig. 22). At the centre J (Fig. 21) is an iron plate and socket to receive the centre pole.

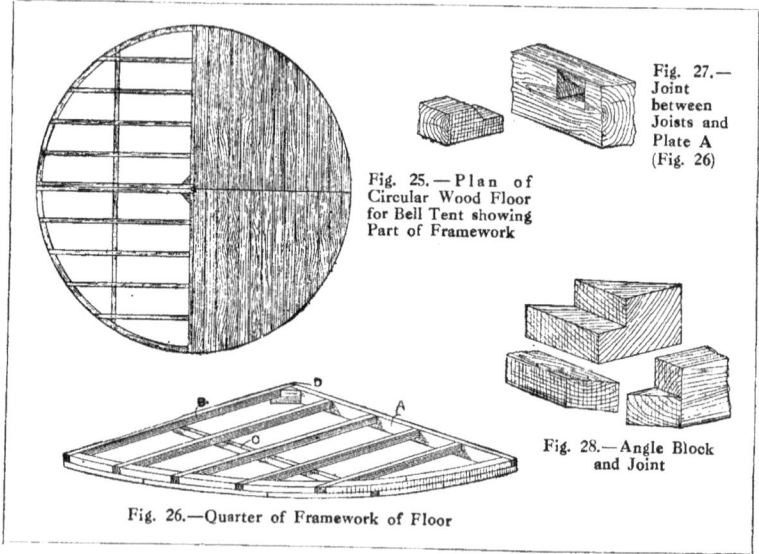

Fig. 25.—Plan of Circular Wood Floor for Bell Tent showing Part of Framework

Fig. 27.—Joint between Joists and Plate A (Fig. 26)

Fig. 28.—Angle Block and Joint

Fig. 26.—Quarter of Framework of Floor

CIRCULAR WOOD FLOOR FOR BELL TENT

Another floor constructed on rather different lines is shown by a half plan each of both floor and framework in Fig. 25. This floor is made so as to separate in four pieces when not in use. Fig. 26 is a conventional view of one-quarter of the framework. The plate A should be made of 4-in. by 2-in. stuff, the main joist B and the other joists being of 2-in. by 2-in. stuff. A suitable form of mortise-and-tenon joint for connecting the joists to the plate A is shown at Fig. 27. The rim is formed of two thicknesses of 2-in. stuff, as shown at Fig. 26, where it will be seen that the joists rest on the lower thickness, to which they are nailed. The spaces between the joists are filled in with strips cut to the curve as shown. The two thicknesses of the rim should be well nailed together. A sleeper C is nailed to the underside of the joists, thus strengthening and stiffening them. The internal angle of each piece having to be partly cut away, it should be strengthened by a block, as shown at D. The block and form of joint is shown to a larger scale at Fig. 28. The floorboards should be grooved and tongued, $\frac{3}{4}$ in. by 4 in. to 6 in. wide, the narrow widths being preferable. They should be nailed to the framing in the usual manner. The curved edges of the floorboards and framing may be cleaned off with a spokeshave.

The whole of the wood should be of good red deal, and the underside treated with a coat of tar. Each quarter should be secured to the two adjacent ones with a couple of $\frac{1}{2}$-in. bolts and nuts, the wing form of nut being very suitable for this purpose.

Poultry Houses

POULTRY HOUSE WITH SHELTERED SCRATCHING-PLACE

A FEATURE of the poultry house (illustrated by Fig. 1 and shown in detail and for forty birds 9 ft. 6 in. by 7 ft. The eaves should be kept to the same height in every case, and the roof should be at the same angle, which will make the centre higher in the larger, and lower in

Fig. 1.—Poultry House with Sheltered Scratching-place

by Figs. 2 to 6) is the provision of a sheltered scratching-place under the roost. The house, as shown, is designed for the accommodation of twelve birds; for twenty birds it should be 7 ft. by 5 ft.; the smaller, houses. It is not proposed to enter into the constructional details of these houses very fully, for the work is largely of the nature of that necessary for shed and outhouse erection which

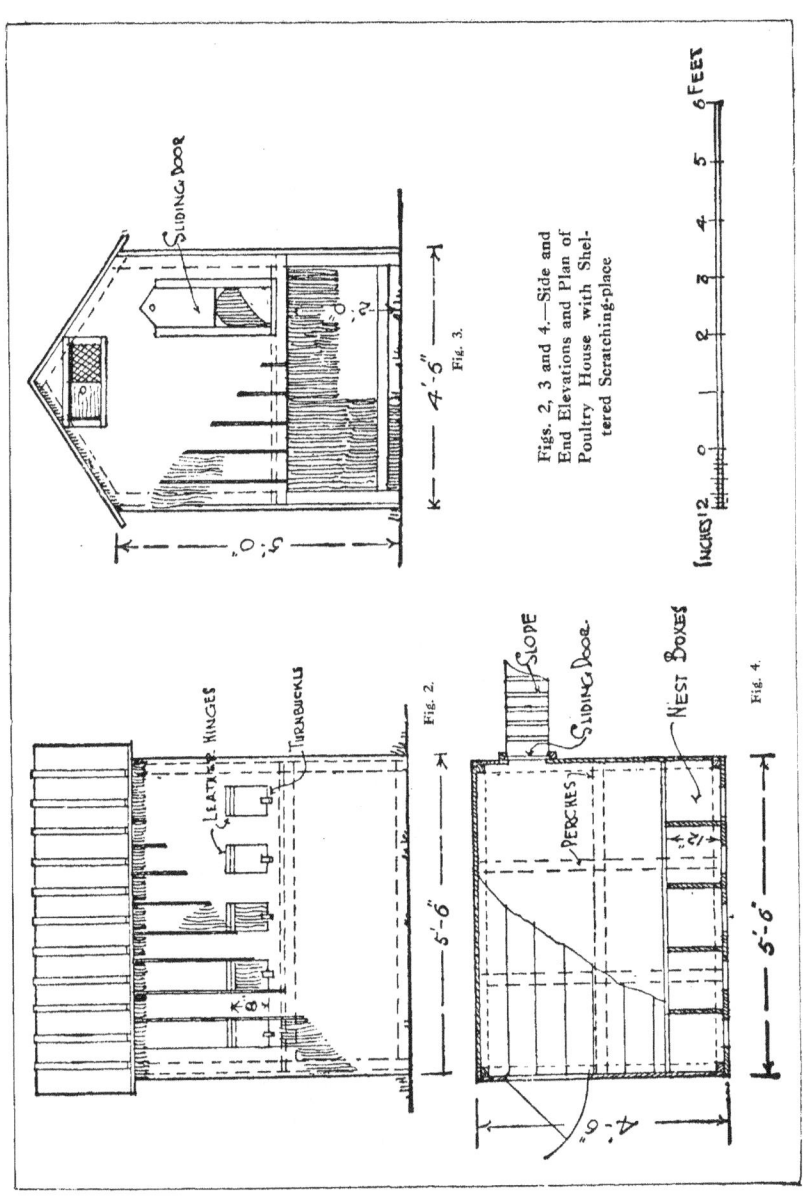

Figs. 2, 3 and 4.—Side and End Elevations and Plan of Poultry House with Sheltered Scratching-place

THE PRACTICAL WOODWORKER

has been fully dealt with in preceding pages.

To construct the house, first prepare a simple framework on the usual lines, as shown dotted in Figs. 2, 3, 4, and 5. Each joint should be notched and then secured with a couple of 2-in. No. 14 wood screws. Make sure that the frame is square, and then nail on the boarding. Five spaces are to be left on one side in the position shown (Fig. 2), which may be fitted with doors hinged with a strip of leather at the top and fitted with a button at the bottom, Fig. 6. A doorway is provided at this end, and the boards are brought down to the ground, but the bottom rail is kept up $3\frac{1}{2}$ in., so that the notches in the cornerposts for this rail and the side sills do not come opposite each other. The object in keeping the front end 2 ft. above the ground, as shown in Fig. 3, is to provide a dry run for the fowls, and this should have dust-baths or should be covered with a few inches of ashes. The floor is covered with 1-in. matchboarding, supported on two or three joists, 4 ft. 4 in.

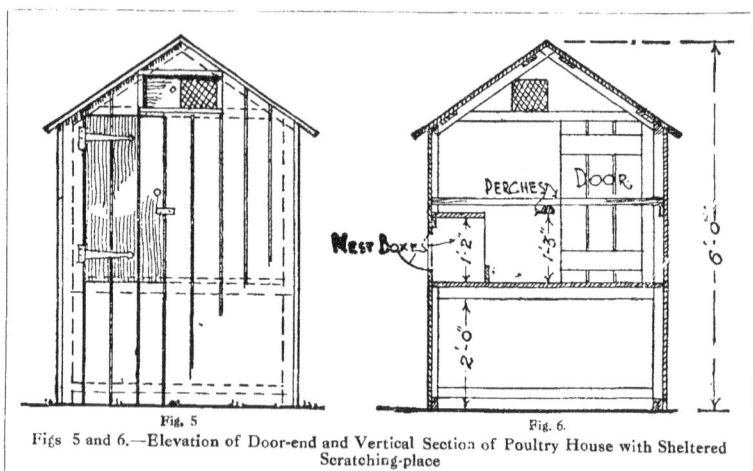

Figs 5 and 6.—Elevation of Door-end and Vertical Section of Poultry House with Sheltered Scratching-place

for the purpose of gathering eggs from the nest-boxes. A doorway 12 in. by 8 in. is cut in the front end in the position shown (Fig. 3), and slide pieces are nailed on each side of this to enable the door to be lifted, an iron pin being used to hold it in position, or it may be hung with a pulley and cord. At the top a large opening is cut at each end and filled in with $\frac{3}{4}$-in. mesh wire for the purpose of ventilation, a sliding shutter, as shown at the top of Figs. 3 and 5, being used to regulate the amount of air for cold or warm weather if the position be very exposed.

The inside of the back end is shown in long by $2\frac{1}{2}$ in. by 2 in., to which the boards may be nailed. The floor at the ends rest on the end rails, but should not be nailed if the house is built to take apart. In fitting up the inside, five fixed nest-boxes are provided. To make these, fillets $1\frac{1}{2}$ in. by 1 in. are nailed to the inside of the house, to which a shelf 1 ft. 2 in. above the floor and the full length of the house is fixed. The space under this is divided into compartments, as shown in Fig. 4, an outside door being provided for each (Fig. 2), and a strip (Fig. 4) $2\frac{1}{2}$ in. wide nailed along the front. Three perches are used, two being across the house and one

POULTRY HOUSES

running lengthways in the centre. These may be made by sawing a pole 2½ in. or 3 in. in diameter through the centre, the ends resting on fillets nailed to the ends and sides of the house. The top of the perches should not be more than 1 ft. 6 in. above the floor. A ladder, made by nailing strips across a 7-in. by 1-in. board, must be provided to enable the fowls to enter the house from the run.

POULTRY HOUSE WITH HOOD

A type of house suitable for extension by a simple repetition of the parts to any desired length is shown by Fig. 7. End and part front elevations and plan are shown by Figs. 8, 9, and 10. One of its bays is shown in section in Fig. 11, where the usual dropping-board is seen supported on an end-rail. The top front has a wooden hood similar to that in the last example, shielding an open space (see also Fig. 9). Below this in the centre of the 6-ft. bay is an opening, covered in with wire and capable of being closed when necessary by means of frames filled in with glass or canvas, hinged at the bottom, as in Fig. 11. These latter are kept in position when closed by means of turn-buckles at the top. Alternatively they could slide up and down in rebated guides. Doors should be provided in the ends, as in Fig. 8, and can be furnished with small hen-doors at the bottom as shown, closed when necessary by means of a hinged flap. The fronts of the intermediate units of the house will be similar to those of the end portions in every way, unless it be desired to arrange a door in one of them instead of at the ends, which might then be reserved for runs. A long house of this description could be separated into two distinct divisions by

Fig. 7.—Poultry House with Hood

means of a central partition, or there are other variations capable of introduction. One upright (Fig. 10) is decentralised to suit the door, for which it forms a rebate, as it projects a little beyond the boarding, whereas the other upright is in the centre of the piece of framing.

POULTRY HOUSE WITH COVERED RUN

This is another pattern in which a covered run is provided under the hen-roost. The house (Fig. 12) is drawn to

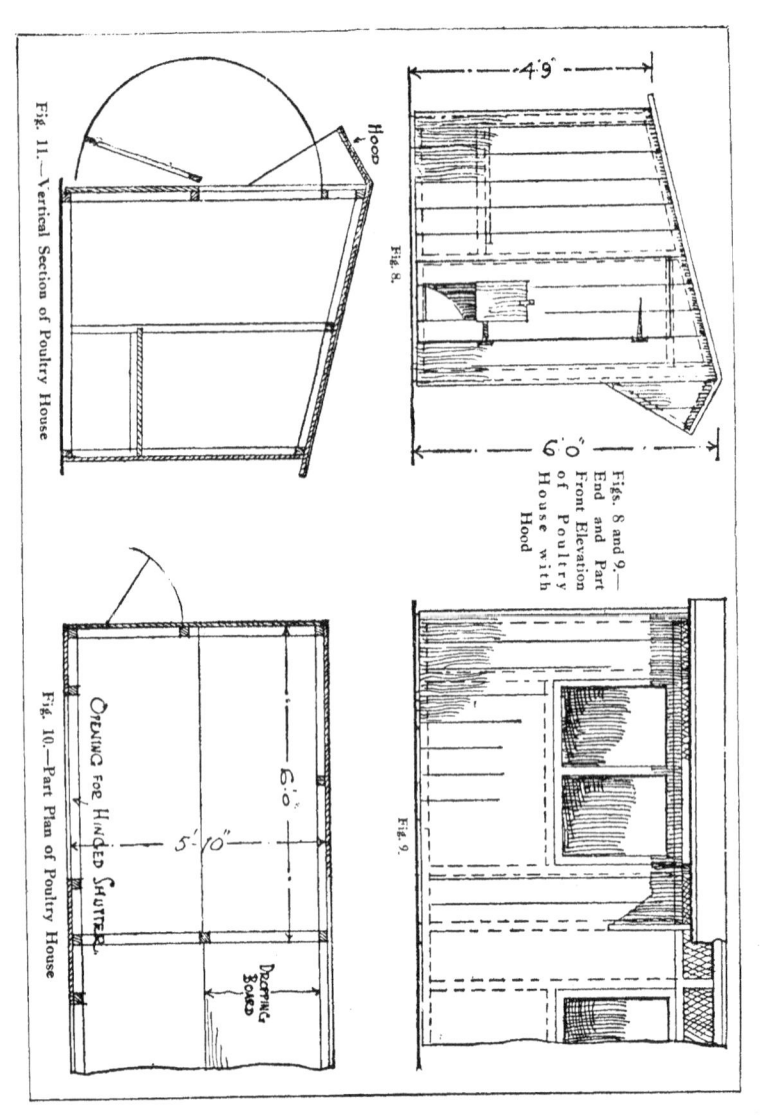

Figs. 8 and 9.—End and Part Front Elevation of Poultry House with Hood

Fig. 10.—Part Plan of Poultry House

Fig. 11.—Vertical Section of Poultry House

POULTRY HOUSES

the size of 9 ft. by 5 ft., and if built to these dimensions would accommodate comfortably from twenty to thirty fowls. The arrangement of the framework will be gathered from the scale drawings in which the positions of the uprights as well as of two intermediate bearers used to stiffen the floor are shown. The boards of the latter run longitudinally. Two sloping struts will be required to stiffen the front rail, as in Fig. 13, and these can be framed in position, or secured with small blocks or cleats as shown. A hen-door with sloping plank is required (Fig. 13), above which an arrangement of sliding ledged shutters is employed, as in previous cases, whereby the centre of the front can be thrown entirely open or wholly or partially closed at will. The left-hand shutter is shown fully open, and the right-hand one completely closed. Above these again is a narrow, continuous ventilating strip, permanently open and sheltered by the projected boarding of the roof, as in Fig. 14, and also by the triangular pieces at the ends, seen in Fig. 16. At one end the necessary door only leaves room for two projecting sitting-boxes, but there is just sufficient room for four at the other end. A plan of the house showing part of the floor is shown by Fig. 15.

INTENSIVE POULTRY HOUSE

The new system of poultry keeping now receiving great attention is one by which the fowls are kept in small houses, to which no runs need be attached, the floors being raised well off the ground. Every

Fig. 12.—Poultry House with Covered Run

care is taken to keep the interiors of the houses as dry as possible, and over the floor is spread a litter of chaff or similar material 3 in. or 4 in. deep. An interesting feature of the system is that the houses do not need frequent cleaning out, and that a house of given dimensions can accommodate many more birds than under the old system.

The size of the house shown by Fig. 17 is 18 ft. long by 14 ft. deep, 7 ft. high at the front, and 5 ft. at the back, but this size may be varied according to the space available. It should be remembered that deep houses are preferable to shallow ones. This house has a partition in the centre,

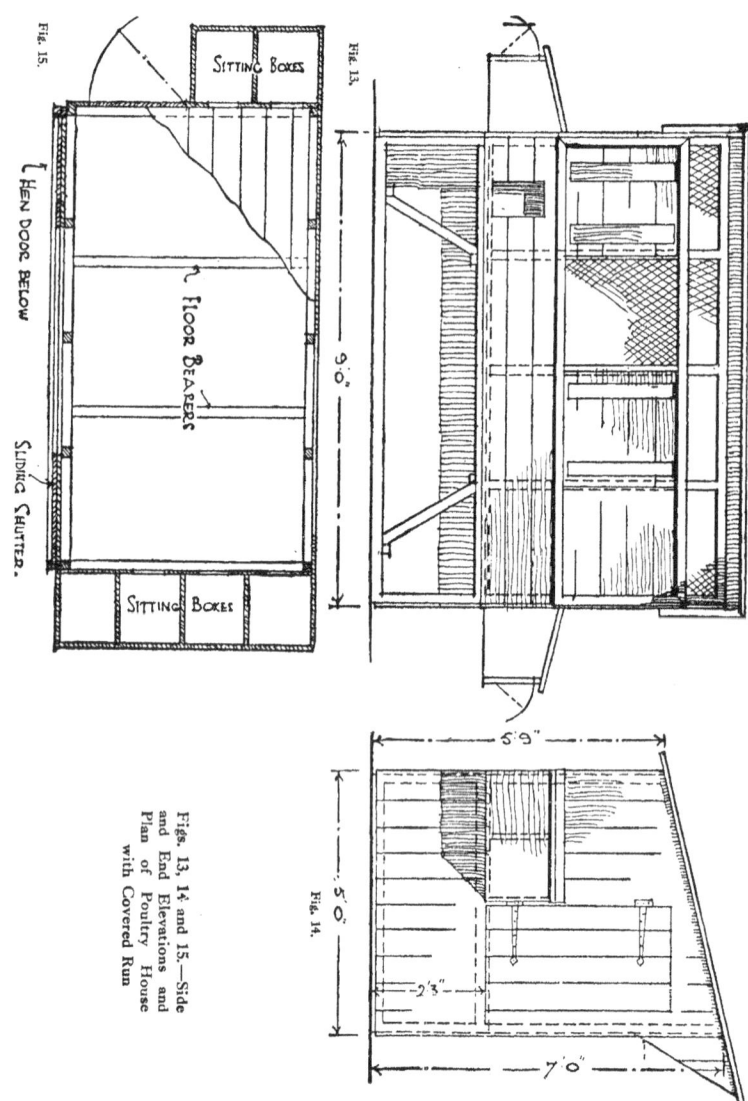

Figs. 13, 14 and 15.—Side and End Elevations and Plan of Poultry House with Covered Run

POULTRY HOUSES

partly boarded and partly covered with wire netting, thus allowing two breeds to be kept separate, that is, two houses in one, each 9 ft. long or wide and 14 ft. deep. For the foundations, eight railway sleepers or similar pieces of timber are placed in four rows about 3 ft. 6 in. apart, with five 9-in. brickwork piers under each row, due care being taken over the levels. If the ground is sloping, an extra course or two of bricks will be required at the back or the front, and it will be better for the drainage. The house should face south or southwest. On the sleepers place thirteen pieces of scantling, 3 in. by 2 in., for the floor joists, one flush with each end, the remainder at equal distances. All the joints in this house are halved, being much simpler and quicker than mortise and tenons, and allowing longer pieces of timber to be used.

Fig. 18 is a general view of the framework of the front, and Fig. 19 the framework of one end. For the front, eight pieces, 9 ft. 6 in. by 3 in. by 2 in., are required if the halving joint is made in the centre as shown by Figs. 20 and 21, or four pieces 18 ft. long without the joining, and four pieces 7 ft. long for the uprights, as shown by Fig. 20. For the back, four pieces 9 ft. 6 in. long are joined, the same as for the front, and three uprights 5 ft. long. The framework of the front and back is made with the 3-in. side to rest on the floor joists; but the ends are made with the 2-in. side downwards. The advantage of this will be found, as the corners when bolted or screwed together make 4-in. by 3-in. corner posts. The framework of the ends consists of one piece 14 ft. long for the bottom; one piece for the top 14 ft. 3 in. long; and for the uprights pieces 5 ft., 5 ft. 6 in., 6 ft. 6 in., and 7 ft. long; also one piece about 5 ft. 6 in. by 2 in. by 2 in. to support the dropping board. Note the front and back uprights are 3 in. above the top bar; this allows for the rafters A (Fig. 19). The two inner uprights are flush, so that two of the rafters can be directly over these. The rafters should project 6 in. over each end, as shown in Fig. 17.

Having got the foundations and floor joists in position, next fit up the front and back framework, and place them on the ends of the joists, nailing to each joist. The ends are not supported on the joists, but on two or more pieces nailed to the

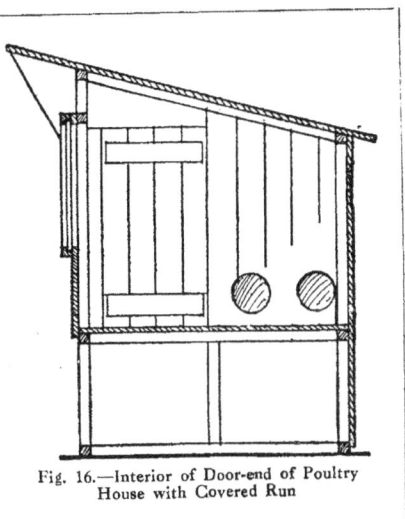

Fig. 16.—Interior of Door-end of Poultry House with Covered Run

outside joists; also to the front and back upright pieces, thus making the 4-in. by 3-in. corner posts. The floorboards can then be nailed in. Then a framework similar to the ends will be required to support the rafters in the centre. This can be covered with netting to form a division in the house if required. The back and ends, also the lowest section of the front, can now be covered with ¾-in. matching. It will be found convenient not to board up too much of the ends until after the roof is finished, as it facilitates getting in and out. The two upper sections of the front should be covered with fine-mesh wire netting fixed on the inside.

41—N.E.

Framework doors with fine-mesh netting are fixed inside to allow the wooden doors to be opened in fine weather for extra ventilation. At the back of the house, about 2 ft. from the floor, fix the dropping board c (Fig. 19). This should be 3 ft. wide, and about 6 in. above this place the perches. The nest boxes can be placed where desired. For the six upper divisions of the front make frames of 1½-in. square stuff, to be covered with white calico. The upper three are hinged at the top, and an iron stay secured to fix them open at various angles according to the weather. The lower three can be fastened with buttons, to be taken away in the summer months, or kept fastened in the winter. This house will accommodate sixty birds, thirty in each compartment.

About 550 ft. of 3-in. by 2-in. material will be required for the framework, rafters, and floor joists; nearly three squares of boards for the roof; just over two and a half squares for the floor; and four squares of matchboarding for outside and

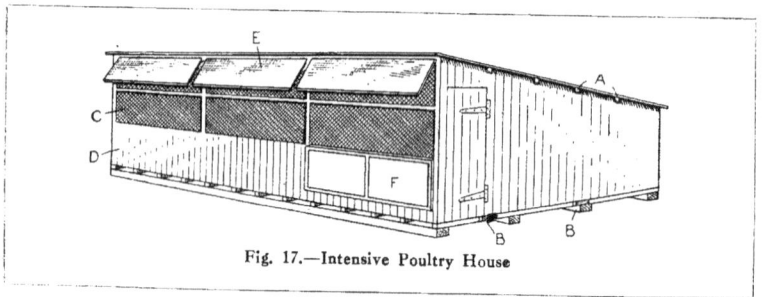

Fig. 17.—Intensive Poultry House

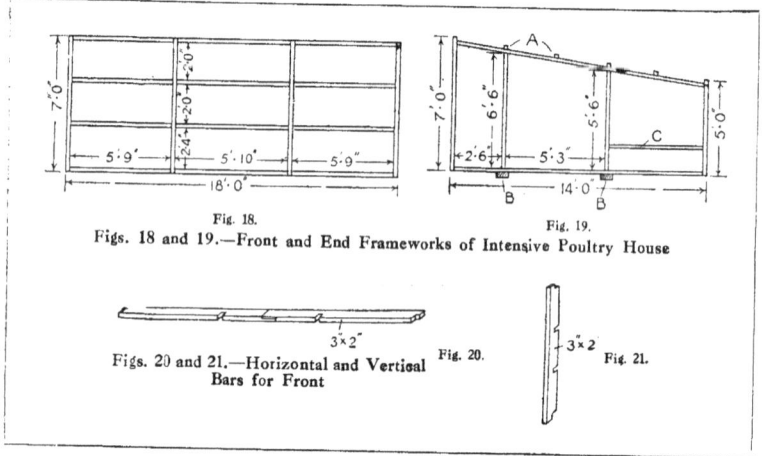

Fig. 18.   Fig. 19.
Figs. 18 and 19.—Front and End Frameworks of Intensive Poultry House

Figs. 20 and 21.—Horizontal and Vertical Bars for Front   Fig. 20.   Fig. 21.

POULTRY HOUSES

dropping boards. The roof should be covered with sarking felt well tarred; about one and a half rolls being required.

The following are particulars of the letter references in the illustrations (Fig. 17): A represents the ends of the rafters; B the 3-in. by 2-in. blocks nailed to the outer floor joists to support the ends of the house (the ends are bolted to the back and front, and these are to keep the ends from sagging); C the wire netting for the six upper sections of the front; D the matchboarding for the three lower sections; E the shutters covered with white calico, hinged at the top, and fastened at the desired angle with casement stays; and F the shutters for the lower sections (one only shown), hinged at the bottom, hanging down over the matchboard D.

THREE-TIER INTENSIVE POULTRY HOUSE

For erecting the intensive poultry house shown in front elevation and cross section by Figs. 22 and 23, almost any wood at hand can be utilised. The pens to be erected not being large, expensive long lengths of timber are not necessary. Bacon boxes can be had cheaply, and would provide ideal floors. There are some readers who, doubtless, have a shed, where the intensive pens can be erected. If so, the compartments can be constructed to suit the size of the house. Others, with no shed available, can possibly erect a lean-to building against a wall, and thus save erecting the whole back of a house.

To proceed to erect the house first provide five uprights of 2-in. by 2-in. stuff for the front, and fix one at each end. The assistance of a plumb-line will ensure that they are exactly perpendicular. Next take two pieces of 3-in. by ¾-in. stuff. Nail one to the top of the two posts, on the front of the upright, close to the roof, and the other level along the floor at the bottom, on the front of the posts. Now fix the remaining three uprights, one in the centre and one each side at equal distances behind the 3-in. by ¾-in. piece.

Fig. 22 shows their positions. Five more 2-in. by 2-in. uprights are now required for the back. Fix them on the wall and exactly behind the front posts. Ten pieces of 2-in. by 2-in. stuff the width of the house are now cut, and fixed by halving them on to the uprights, from the back to the front. These will form the joists or supports for the two floors. Where the ends of the joists come at the front nail two lengths of 3-in. by ¾-in. stuff. The height of the front is now divided into three equal distances. Next lay the floors. Timber from bacon boxes will be found 1 in. thick, grooved and tongued. This is cheap, and the joints will prevent dust falling below. The floor can be fixed lengthwise or across the house, according to the suitability of the timber. Now nail 3-in. by ¾-in. stuff on the uprights at the front, so as to level everything up to the four long lengths already fixed. It may be stated that the 3-in. by ¾-in. timber is always kept cut to this size by any timber merchant. It is called "wall plate," and is sold by the 100-ft. run. The next wood to use is 1½ in. by ¾ in., called "pantile battens." They cost very little, and are tied in bundles of almost any length.

Fix exactly in the centre of the 3-in. by ¾-in. stuff, with which the front is covered, the 1½-in. by ½-in. battens. This will form a rebate ready for fitting the doors. Put in the divisions before placing doors over the front. These partitions can be a frame covered with wire, or all wood and fixed with or without exit holes cut in them, with movable doors, for the poultry to pass through. Another kind of division (Fig. 24) is made of wood, with an exit hole (not shown) 7 in. by 10 in. at the bottom, hinged to the floor above or roof, so that it can be lifted up and suspended with a button or hook-and-eye arrangement.

The floor of the bottom tier can be dealt with at any time, requiring, as it does, ashes and cement, or sand and cement. Proceed by levelling the ground roughly. Lay some ashes an inch deep or more, and see that they are down tight. Make a dry mix of sifted ashes, or cement

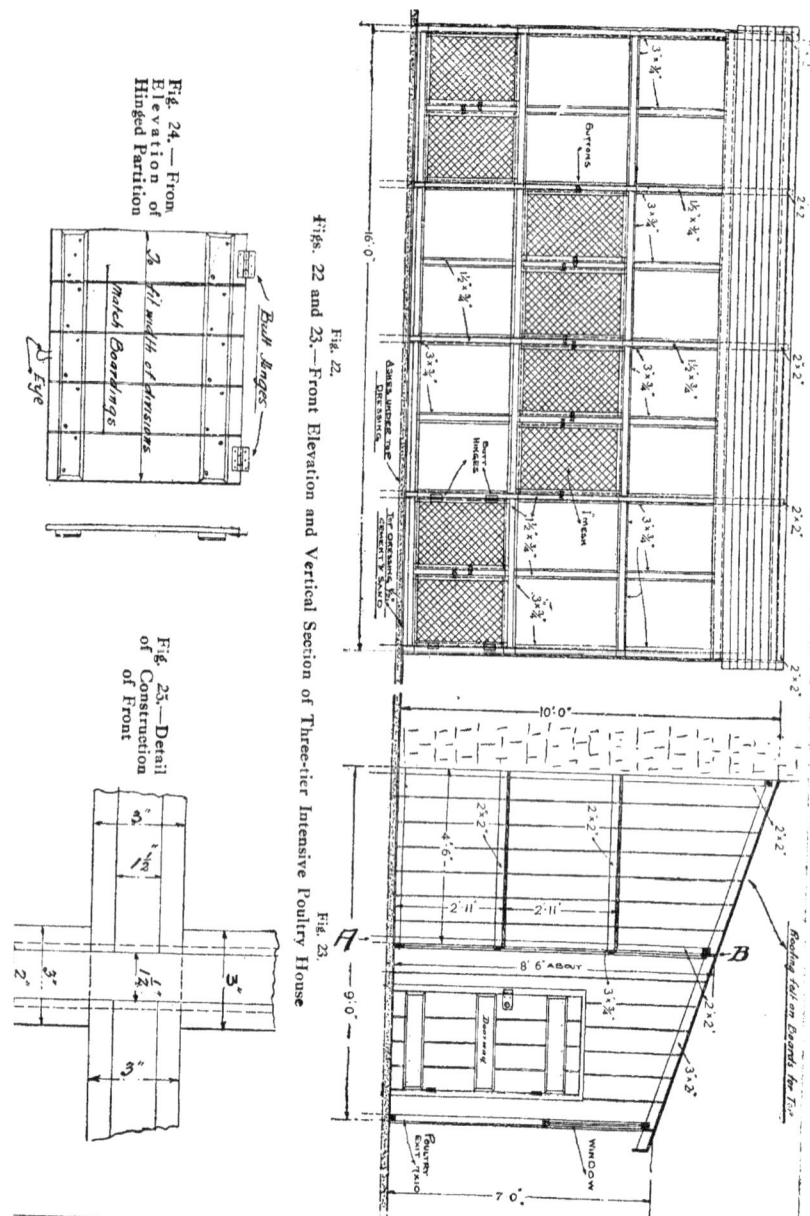

Fig. 24.—Front Elevation of Hinged Partition

Figs. 22 and 23.—Front Elevation and Vertical Section of Three-tier Intensive Poultry House

Fig. 25.—Detail of Construction of Front

and sand, 2 parts of sand to 1 part of cement. When well mixed, add water to make into a plaster, and trowel a layer, say This will dry almost as hard as rock. The floor can be made to slope to the front, if desired.

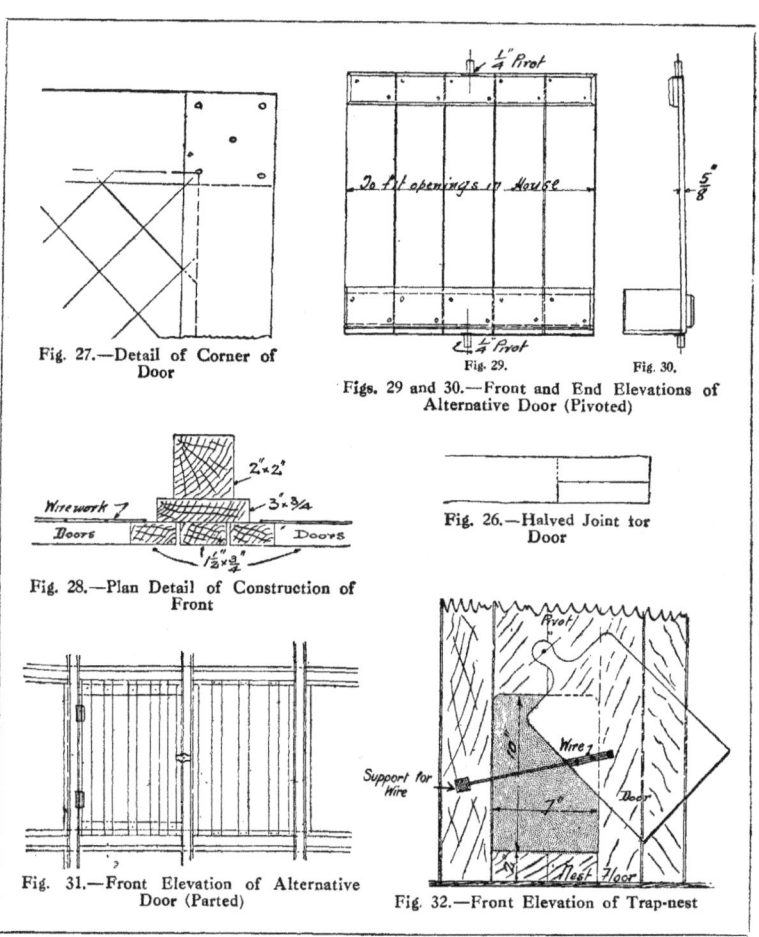

Fig. 27.—Detail of Corner of Door

Figs. 29 and 30.—Front and End Elevations of Alternative Door (Pivoted)

Fig. 28.—Plan Detail of Construction of Front

Fig. 26.—Halved Joint for Door

Fig. 31.—Front Elevation of Alternative Door (Parted)

Fig. 32.—Front Elevation of Trap-nest

½ in. thick, all over the floor, doing one pen or compartment at a time. It can be made smooth by using a wet trowel, or brushing over gently with a wet brush.

The fitting of the doors for the pen fronts or compartments can be a matter of individual taste. The style of door as shown in Fig. 23 is suitable. To fit them up, fix in a length of the 3-in. by ¾-in. stuff down the centre of the opening, and on this nail some 1½-in. by ¾-in. material. The pen front is now divided into two equal parts. A detail of the house front is shown by Fig. 25. This shows the 3-in. by ¾-in. timber, and fixed on it is the 1½-in. by ¾-in. batten. Note the rebate this forms for the doors to be fitted loosely into. Measure across the rebate, cut off four lengths for the top, bottom, and two sides. Halve these together into a frame, covering with wire netting, the inch mesh being a suitable size. Fig. 26 shows the method of halving, and Fig. 27 the finished door corner. The halved ends are held together with screws, which should go just through. If they are too long, file down level. Next screw a pair of butt hinges on the door; with the door centred, screw the other part of the hinge to the frame. Fig. 28 shows the 2-in. by 2-in. front upright, the 3-in. by ¾-in. stuff fixed to it, and on this again is the 1½-in. by ¾-in. batten. The rebate is shown with the doors fitted, and the wire netting tacked to the back. Figs. 29 and 30 show another style of door large enough to fill the entire front, or it can be made the size of half the pen front. Strap together enough matchboard or other wood to fill the opening; drive a piece of ¼-in. rod into the centre of the top and bottom, forming pivots, as shown, and fit them into sockets in the front. A receptacle like a shelf, to hold food, water, grit, shell, or what is required, can now be placed at the bottom. Prevent any trough being upset by nailing on a band of tin-plate or galvanised iron. The door inserted in its sockets can be revolved, with food inside, to feed the stock; or outside, to have a fresh supply of food put ready for the next meal. Still another very useful door is shown in Fig. 31. It is so simple that no description is necessary, the front being parted, as described before, but instead of covering it with wire netting, use spars, or lengths of the batten fixed with nails. A shelf fixed below will hold a trough of food, water, or anything required, the birds feeding through the bars.

A nest-box and perch combined can be made simply by nailing a couple of uprights at the centre and up the sides of the nest-box. Cut off a length of perch to fit in between these and nail it in. It will be like the handle of a coal-box. Now, if a top is made removable from between strips of wood, dirt or droppings can be removed very easily.

A suitable type of trap-nest is shown by Fig. 32. It is easy to set, costs little to make, its fall makes no noise and the bird is not hit with violence into the nest-box. Make a front, of any wood, to an ordinary nest-box, and cut an opening as shown. Make the door out of thin wood, 8 in. by 11 in., and fasten the top with a screw as a pivot. The wire seen across the opening is flattened at one end and nailed to the door, a fixture. A support or rest is placed where shown, and this keeps the door from falling down. To enter the nest, the fowl presses in under the wire, lifting up its loose end, causing the thin movable front to fall into place behind her, shutting the bird inside. The outer door can easily be cut out of tin-plate by means of metalworker's hand shears.

COOP FOR BROODY HENS

Broody hens are a constant source of trouble to the poultry keeper, but the trouble may be greatly minimised by providing a few coops of the pattern here described and shown in perspective by Fig. 33.

The coop may be roughly framed together, as shown by Fig. 34, with deal scantling about 1½ in. square. If the maker has the necessary tools and skill, the joints may be mortised and tenoned; if not, a few wire nails to hold the joints together until the boards are fixed will do quite well, as the boards when in position and nailed will hold the framing together. A piece of ¾-in. mesh wire netting A is strained across the top of the middle frame, as shown in Fig. 35, and secured with small staples. Three-quarter-inch matchboarding can be used for covering the sides, back, and top, and the front can be made up with vertical strips of 2-in. by

POULTRY HOUSES

¾-in. deal, as shown in Fig. 33, the middle strip being passed through a slot in the roof boards at the top and secured by by 3 in. by 3 in. is secured to the front of the bars, as shown in Figs. 33 and 35, and is made from ¾-in. stuff.

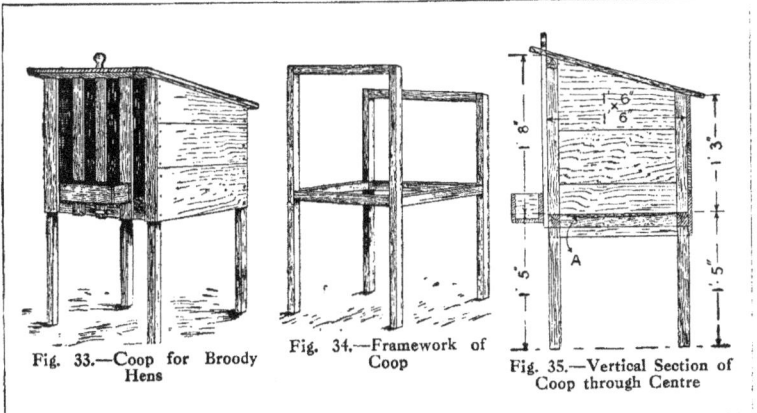

Fig. 33.—Coop for Broody Hens
Fig. 34.—Framework of Coop
Fig. 35.—Vertical Section of Coop through Centre

means of a hoop-iron socket at the bottom, thus providing one of the simplest forms of opening for putting in and taking out the broody hens. To complete the coop, a feeding trough about 12 in. long

The coop is dimensioned 1 ft. 6 in. by 1 ft. 6 in. by 1 ft. 3 in. to 1 ft. 8 in. high; but if a very large breed of fowl is kept, it is desirable to increase the sizes somewhat.

Incubators and Chicken Rearers

HOT-AIR INCUBATOR

The 60-egg hot-air incubator shown by Figs. 1 and 2 has been designed with a view to simplicity of construction, butt joints being used throughout, so that anyone with but an elementary knowledge of carpentry, and few tools, need not be afraid to tackle it.

The wood is of three sizes only, simplifying matters still more. It consists of 25 ft. run of 1 in. by 1 in., either rough or planed (dahlia sticks would do); 50 ft. of stop bead about $\frac{5}{8}$ in. by $\frac{7}{8}$ in. (used for holding window sashes in place, so will be ready planed); 21 ft. super of $\frac{1}{4}$ in. three-ply wood. This is sold in sheets, 3 ft. by 4 ft., so two would be required; or two or three good tea chests would do equally well.

The necessary fittings are obtainable from firms who specialise in poultry appliances. A brief description of them and their functions is here given. The heater, drop-bottom pattern, shown in section by Fig. 3, is the most important. The lamp fits up against the lower end of the flue A, and its heat passes upwards and out at the vent B, and down below the level of the jacket C. It is most important that the vent B is quite smoke-tight, so that there is no possibility of the fumes from the lamp getting into the fresh-air tube D. The heat of the flue induces a current of air to flow upwards through the space D, and so into the incubator through the lug E. A damper F, worked by the regulator, controls the amount of hot air passing into the machine by allowing the surplus to escape at the vent G. The heater is built up of galvanised iron and iron castings, and is lagged with a thick jacket of asbestos H. It is fixed with screws through the flange J to the side of the incubator. The hot-air pipe (Fig. 4) is made out of stout tinplate 15 in. long and 2 in. in diameter, with a flange about $3\frac{1}{2}$ in. square soldered $1\frac{1}{2}$ in. from one end. The pipe should be lap-seamed. Another piece of tin $3\frac{1}{4}$ in. square and a piece 17 in. by 3 in. are also required. A piece of asbestos board, say 6 in. square by $\frac{1}{8}$ in. thick, will be required to go under the flange and round the tin tube. The thermometer should be of the hanging variety, and is hung from the centre bar of the upper diaphragm by two screw-eyes. The bulb should be 2 in. above the egg-trap bottom. The lamp (Fig. 5) is 6 in. in diameter, and 2 in. deep, and is fitted with a $\frac{7}{8}$-in. burner. With the usual burner a chimney will be required.

A bi-metal regulator is shown by Fig. 6. The thermostat A, which is suspended by the connecting tube B just above the egg tray, is made of two metals having unequal expansion, such as aluminium and steel, or zinc and steel. When the heat in the egg chamber reaches about 100°, owing to the unequal expansion of the two metals, the thermostat has a tendency

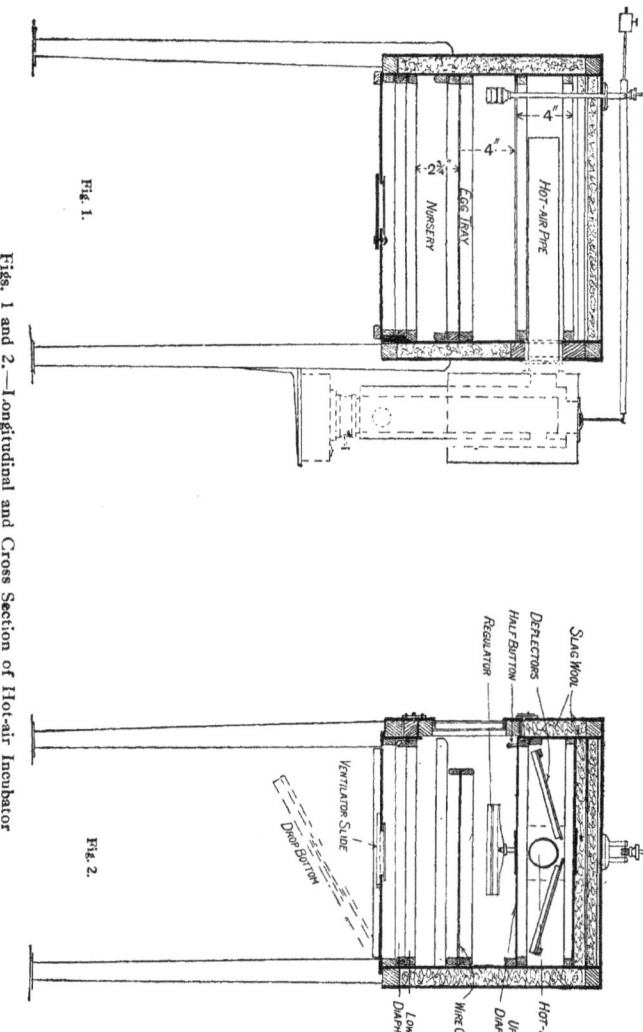

Figs. 1 and 2.—Longitudinal and Cross Section of Hot-air Incubator

to buckle and exerts a pull on the pull rod C, which in turn is connected to the beam end D. This beam is pivoted to the base-plate E, so that the pull working through the beams lifts the damper F off the heater top, and allows the surplus heat to escape until the heat of the egg chamber goes down. The thermostat regains its original position and drops the damper again. This action is almost imperceptible and quite automatic. The base-plate E is screwed to the top of the incubator, and the connecting tube is 7 in. long. The counterpoise G is adjusted to balance the beam, so that the slightest movement takes effect. Although the bi-metal regulator is the one used in most hot-air machines, the capsule regu-

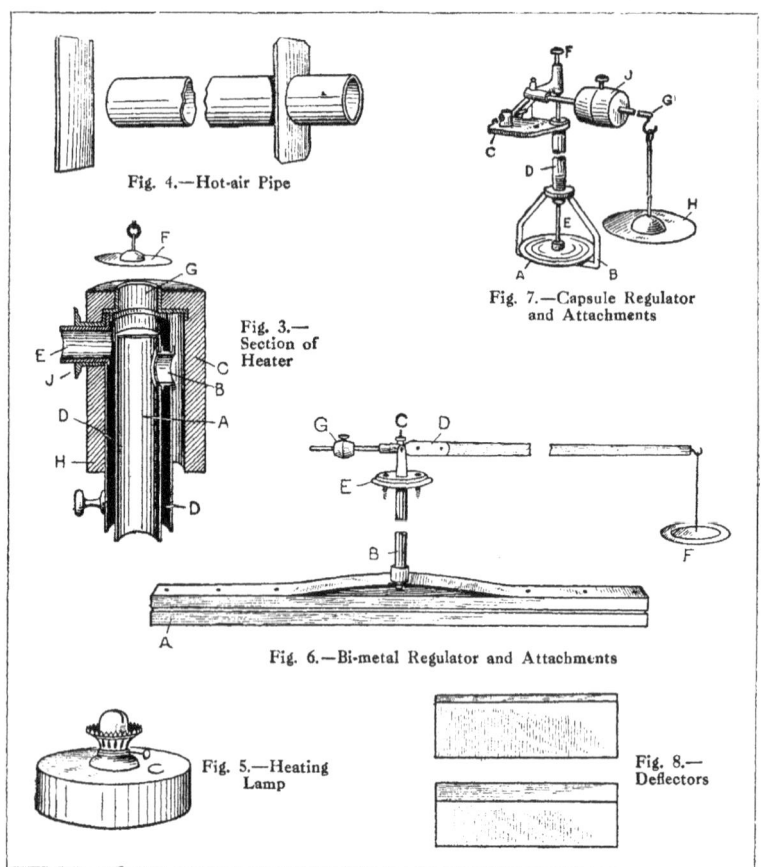

Fig. 4.—Hot-air Pipe

Fig. 3.—Section of Heater

Fig. 7.—Capsule Regulator and Attachments

Fig. 6.—Bi-metal Regulator and Attachments

Fig. 5.—Heating Lamp

Fig. 8.—Deflectors

INCUBATORS AND CHICKEN REARERS

lator (Fig. 7) is equally as good, and considered by many better. A capsule A rests on the holder B, which in turn is connected to the base-plate C by the tube D. The capsule, which is composed of two pieces of brass soldered together at their edges, contains a liquid which boils, and therefore expands, at a temperature of about 100°, bulging out the capsule. This movement is communicated through the needle E to the adjusting screw F

strawboard $17\frac{1}{2}$ in. by $5\frac{1}{4}$ in., and the upper edge, that is, the one nearest to the hot-air pipe, is edged with tin 1 in. on the underside, with $\frac{1}{2}$ in. turned over the top edge. Two strips of stop bead $17\frac{1}{2}$ in. long are cut for each, and the deflectors nailed to them, one at the lower edge and the other up against the tin, both strips on the upper side. Other requirements are: one piece of wire cloth $17\frac{3}{4}$ in. by 13 in. for the egg tray, and one

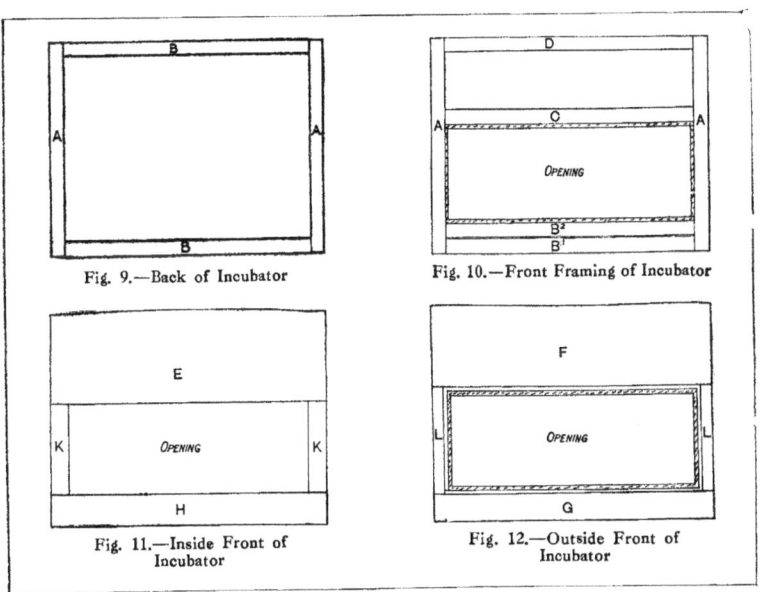

Fig. 9.—Back of Incubator

Fig. 10.—Front Framing of Incubator

Fig. 11.—Inside Front of Incubator

Fig. 12.—Outside Front of Incubator

and lever end. This lifts the lever rod G and the damper H, the weight J in this case exerting a downward pressure on the capsule, making its action more steady. If it is desired to use gas, the base-plate is replaced by one containing a gas valve controlled by the end of the lever rod. The damper is not connected to the lever end, but is placed loosely over the heater vent. The valve turns down the gas automatically. A pair of deflectors (Fig. 8) will also be required. They are of

piece about 4 in. square for the ventilator; three pieces of canvas 18 in. by 15. in. for the diaphragms (fairly close woven, that used for baling cloth is suitable); two pieces of felt 18 in. by 15 in. of not too close a texture; three pieces of strawboard 18 in. by 15 in.; 4 lb. of cotton batting, cotton-wool, or wadding for the top packing; two pieces of glass, 16 in. by 5 in. bare, for the door; two pairs of $1\frac{1}{2}$-in. brass back flap hinges; two pairs of brass buttons; 1 pair of brass half-buttons; one brass knob; one pair of 3-in. shelf brackets; and one set of legs or 10 ft. of 2-in. by 2-in. stuff.

The back (Fig. 9) should be made first. Cut two pieces of three-ply wood 20 in. by 15 in., two pieces A of 1 in. by 1 in. 15 in. long, and two pieces B of 1 in. by 1 in. 18 in. long. Nail one piece of three-ply to these battens, putting the pieces A at each end with the outer edge flush, and the pieces B in between and flush with the other edges. This forms a box 1 in. deep, and is filled with some non-

20 in. by $1\frac{3}{4}$ in.; one piece of three-ply H 20 in. by $2\frac{1}{4}$ in. Place the five pieces of batten in the positions shown in Fig. 10, and nail the piece E to them, keeping the edges flush with D and at each side A, but allowing it to overlap C by $\frac{1}{4}$ in. Nail the piece H to B^1 and B^2, the sides A overlapping B^2 towards C for $\frac{1}{4}$ in. On the sides A nail two pieces K $1\frac{1}{4}$ in. by $6\frac{1}{2}$ in. coming in between E and H (Fig. 11). Then turn the frame over. There is now a frame partly covered, with an opening 7 in. by 18 in., having a $\frac{1}{4}$-in. rebate inside, which is for the door (see Fig. 14). The insides of these battens are best planed. Now fill in the space between D and C with the non-conductor, and nail on the piece of three-ply F, keeping it flush with the edge D, and it will fall short

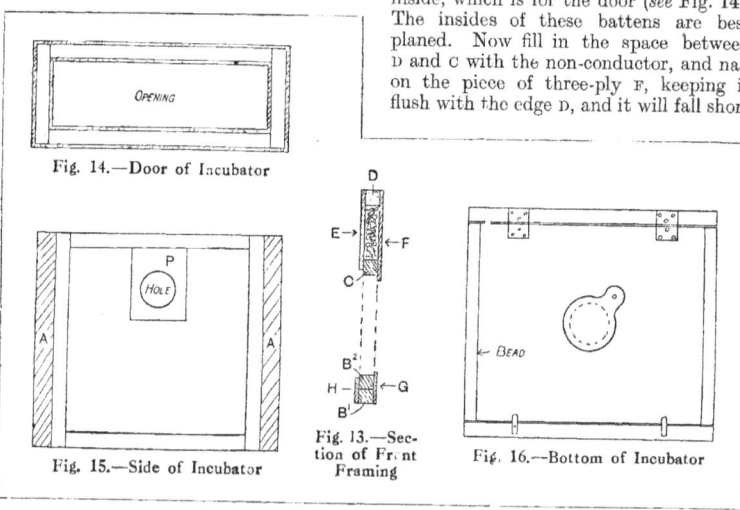

Fig. 14.—Door of Incubator

Fig. 15.—Side of Incubator

Fig. 13.—Section of Front Framing

Fig. 16.—Bottom of Incubator

conductor, such as sawdust, flock, cotton-wool, or better still slag-wool, which, although more expensive, is one of the best non-conductors. Upon these double walls depend the success of the machine. When the packing is done, nail the other piece of three-ply on the top, and the back is complete.

For the front (Fig. 10), cut two pieces A of batten 1 in. by 1 in. 15 in. long; four pieces, B^1, B^2, C and D, 18 in. long; one piece of three-ply E (Fig. 11) 20 in. by $6\frac{1}{4}$ in.; one piece of three-ply F (Fig. 12) 20 in. by $5\frac{3}{4}$ in.; one piece of three-ply G

of the edge C by $\frac{1}{4}$ in. (see section, Fig. 13). Nail on to B the piece G, keeping it flush with the outside edge of B^1. Two pieces of three-ply L are now cut to nail on A, $\frac{3}{4}$ in. by $7\frac{1}{2}$ in. between F and G, keeping them flush on the outside edges. This forms another rebate $7\frac{1}{2}$ in. by $18\frac{1}{2}$ in. This side forms the outside of the incubator (Fig. 12).

The door must now be made to fit the opening. Cut two pieces of 1 in. by 1 in. 7 in. long, and two pieces 16 in. long. These being in sight are best planed; but do not take too much off, or the door will not fit close. Cut a piece of three-ply 18½ in. by 7½ in., to be an easy fit in the outside rebate formed by F, G, L, L (Fig. 12). A piece is cut out of this 15½ in. by 4½ in., leaving a frame 1½ in. wide. Nail this to the battens in position, as shown in Fig. 14, leaving a ¼-in. rebate both inside and outside the frame. The corner of the frame should be nailed with a couple of 2-in. oval wire nails, making the holes with a bradawl first to prevent splitting. Fit this into the opening, making as good a fit as possible without the door binding; hang with 1½-in. brass hinges to G, and fit turn buttons on F (Fig. 12).

For the left-hand side cut two pieces 1 in. by 1 in. and 15 in. long; two pieces 1 in. by 1 in. and 13 in. long; one piece of three-ply 15 in. by 15 in.; and one piece of three-ply 15 in. by 17½ in. Make up and pack the same as for the back; but allow the longer piece of three-ply to project at each side 1¼ in. (see A, Fig. 15). This is the outside.

The right-hand side is made in a similar way, but a piece of 1-in. wood P, 5 in. by 4 in., is put in the position shown in Fig. 15. A hole 2¼ in. in diameter is cut through the two pieces of three-ply and the block P to take the hot-air intake, the centre being 3¾ in. from the top and midway from the sides.

The case may now be put together, the sides going in between the back and front, and the 1¼-in. piece of three-ply that overhangs on the sides covering the edges of the front and back. They may be screwed or well nailed. Nail pieces of the stop bead all round the inside, with their top edges 1¾ in. from the top of the case, the square edge upwards. Other pieces of the stop bead are nailed all round the inside flush with the bottom edge, square edge upwards. The bottom frames will rest on these. Two pieces of stop bead 15 in. long are nailed to the two sides, the top edge being 11½ in. from the top of the case. These are the runners for the egg tray. Another piece of stop bead 17½ in. long is nailed to the back inside, with the upper edge 6¼ in. from the top edge of the case; on this will rest the back edge of the upper diaphragm. A piece of stop bead is also nailed to the front inside, with its lower edge 5½ in. from the top edge of the case, square edge downwards.

The drop bottom is made of a piece of three-ply 14 in. by 18 in., with a 3-in. hole in the centre and two pieces of stop bead 14 in. long nailed to its edges (see Fig. 16), and is hinged to the back by small hinges. A piece of three-ply 1 in. by 16½ in. is nailed to the back, to take the hinge, and a piece the same size to the front, to take turn buttons that keep the bottom in place. Cut a 4-in. circle of three-ply wood, having a lug of the shape shown in Fig. 16, and fasten to the bottom with a screw or small nut and bolt, so that it covers the 3-in. hole and can be adjusted so as to make the opening more or less. The egg tray is made of stop bead, and is 13 in. by 17⅜ in. outside measurement. The corners need only be butted and nailed with 1¼-in. oval wire nails. Nail to this frame a piece of ¼-in. mesh wire cloth 13 in. by 17⅜ in., and nail other pieces of stop bead on the top with the round edge upwards. This will make a strong and easily made frame.

Now make two frames, 15 in. by 17½ in., of the stop bead, and cover them with fairly close-woven canvas. These are the bottom frames, and should be an easy fit in the bottom of the incubator, where they go one on top of another. Two pieces of felt are placed between these frames to regulate the ventilation. Another frame the same size is made, with a centre bar of three-ply 3 in. wide set longwise—that is, the 17½ in. way. This is covered with canvas as the others. It rests on the strip nailed to the back, and fits up against the strip on the front, canvas side downwards, being kept in place by buttons secured to the two sides. Cut two pieces of glass 16 in. by 5 in., and put one piece in the door, bedded with a little white-lead or putty. Nail a bead ½ in. by ¼ in. on the frame, and putty the other piece of glass on them; put in a few brads, and finish off with putty. This leaves a dead air space of ½ in. between the two glasses.

The heater, which is screwed to the side with the hole in it, can now be fitted. Next the hot-air tube is nailed by its flange inside, with the small hole upwards.

Put the upper diaphragm in place, and fix a small block to support the hot-air tube at its extreme end. Fix the deflectors in place in the position shown in Fig. 2, using the stop bead for supports. They should be 1¾ in. apart at the top, and start 3 in. below the top edge of the case and slant 2 in. downwards. Cut a piece of strawboard 15 in. by 17½ in.; nail to it in the centre and longwise a piece of three-ply 3 in. wide, and to the wood a piece of tin the same width. This is to protect the strawboard from the incoming heat. Put this in the top of the incubator, tin side downwards and resting on the ledges 2¼ in. from the top. Fix a block 2 in. square by 3 in. long on the left-hand side above this, through which will be drilled a hole to take the connecting tube for the regulator. The space left is filled with alternate layers of thin strawboard and cotton-wool. Then cut a piece of three-ply to cover the top, and screw down. Bore a ½-in. hole in the top 3 in. from the left-hand side and midway back to front. Mark where this hole should come in the upper diaphragm; remove the diaphragm and bore the hole. Put the diaphragm in position again, push the connecting tube of the regulator upwards, and screw on the top work and the baseplate to the top of the incubator. When ordering, state that the distance between the diaphragm and the top of the case is 6¼ in., and the distance from the centre of the thermostat to the end of the case is 7½ in.

The legs are now to be fitted. These may be made of 2-in. by 2-in. stuff 2 ft. 6 in. long, tapered to 1½ in. at the bottom, with a piece cut out 1 in. deep and 6 in. long. Screw a leg to each corner of the sides, so that the incubator rests on the shoulder formed by taking out the piece. A pair of shelf brackets are screwed to the legs on the heater side, and a three-ply shelf, 7 in. by 18 in., screwed to them. They are fixed at such a height that when the lamp is in position in the heater there is room for a piece of wood, say, 1 in. thick between the shelf and the lamp bottom, thereby holding it in place. This block is withdrawn when the lamp is to be attended to, and the shelf forms a useful support for this purpose. Fix the screw eyes for the thermometer into the centre of the upper diaphragm, so that the bulb is 2 in. above the wire cloth of the egg drawer. Give the machine a good rub down with glasspaper, punch all the nails and stop with putty. A good stain is made with brunswick black or cycle japan diluted with turpentine. Finish with a coat of varnish.

Any cellar or downstairs room away from draughts, direct sunlight, and slamming doors is the best place to set the machine. Thoroughly warm the machine up, and leave running for a couple of days before putting in the eggs.

HYDRO OR HOT-WATER INCUBATOR

The hydro or hot-water incubator now about to be described has served as a model for very many makes, and has been of substantially the same design since about 1881.

The illustrations, Figs. 17, 18 and 19, show two elevations and plan of a 50-egg incubator with drying box. Three sections are shown by Figs. 20, 21 and 22.

The outer case is made of ¾-in. yellow pine, in the form of a square box 20 in. long, 20 in. wide, and 17½ in. from the top of the base-board to the underside of the top, dovetailed at the corners. Both base and top are also of pine, with the edges rounded, the base being in one piece. The top—apart from the glazed lid at the front—is in narrow widths, secured by round-headed brass screws, with washers under their heads. The opening for the drawer, 15½ in. long and 5 in. high, is cut in the front of the case, 1 in. above the top of the base-board. On a level with the bottom of this opening is fixed the inner floor, on which the drawer slides. As shown, there is a ½-in. space between the inner bottom and the base for ventilation purposes, the air passing in through four holes bored in the corners of the base, and finding its way into the egg chamber through a central hole in the inner bottom. The water

INCUBATORS AND CHICKEN REARERS

tank is 17 in. square and 4 in. deep, and is made of copper; it is traversed by a flue $1\frac{3}{4}$ in. in diameter and 13 in. long from the outside of the water jacket, which extends to the outside of the case. The return flue is $\frac{5}{8}$ in. from the other, and the two are arranged to occupy a central position, widthways, in the tank. Where they pass through the woodwork of the case and the packing, the flues are encased in a water jacket $4\frac{3}{4}$ in. wide, $2\frac{3}{8}$ in. deep, and $1\frac{1}{2}$ in. long, the upper corners of which are quadrant shaped. There is a false bottom, which may be of perforated zinc, arranged about $\frac{3}{4}$ in. from the bottom of the tank. Between

In Fig. 17 three tiers of ventilation holes are shown, each hole being furnished with a $\frac{1}{2}$-in. brass eyelet; those in the lower row serve as outlet ventilators for the egg chamber—the inlets being through the base, as previously mentioned. A similar row of holes is provided at the back of the case. The middle row of holes serves as inlets for fresh air, which is warmed as it passes over the tank, and passed between the partition and the $2\frac{1}{2}$-in. upright piece, through the perforated zinc, into the drying box, finally escaping, laden with the moisture from the drying chicks, through the upper row of holes. The glazed lid, forming the

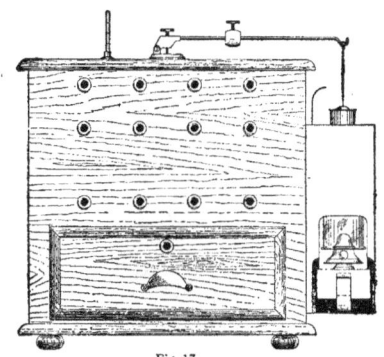
Fig. 17.

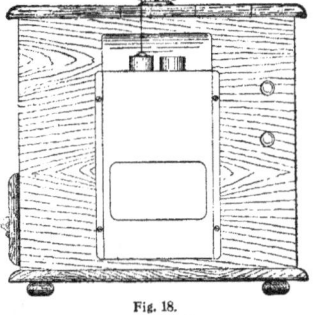
Fig. 18.

Figs. 17 and 18.—Front and End Elevations of Hot-water Incubator

the top of the tank and the underside of the lid there is a space of $4\frac{3}{4}$ in., and, $8\frac{3}{4}$ in. from the inside of the front of the case, this space is partitioned off by a $\frac{5}{8}$-in. board running right across the case, and this forms a drying box for the newly hatched chickens. As seen in Fig. 20, a floor, $\frac{3}{8}$ in. thick and $7\frac{3}{4}$ in. wide, is fixed, distant $3\frac{1}{2}$ in. from the underside of the lid; this allows a space of about $\frac{7}{8}$ in. between the lower side of the floor and the top of the tank; to the edge of this floor a $\frac{1}{2}$-in. upright, $2\frac{1}{2}$ in. wide, is fixed, and along the upper bank edge of this upright piece a strip of coarsely perforated zinc is tacked.

front portion of the top, by which the chickens are introduced and removed, fits over the drying box, and is not fixed, but is kept in position by small fillets tacked to the underside.

The opening which takes the egg drawer is $15\frac{1}{2}$ in. wide, $17\frac{3}{4}$ in. from the front of the case to the partition supporting the tank, and $7\frac{3}{4}$ in. high from the surface of the inner floor to the bottom of the tank. The egg drawer is an easy fit in the $15\frac{1}{2}$-in. by 5-in. hole cut in the front of the case, and is $17\frac{1}{2}$ in. long from inside the false front, which, as will be seen, overlaps the drawer opening about $\frac{5}{8}$ in. all round. The inside measurement of the drawer is 14½ in. square. The wood frame, which is covered with perforated zinc, and forms the bottom upon which the eggs rest during incubation, allows a space of 1⅞ in. round the sides of the drawer, and the concavity of this zinc bottom allows the eggs in the centre of the drawer to be ⅞ in. lower than those at the extreme sides. For noting the temperature of the egg drawer, a hole is bored through the drawer front; outside it is bushed with a brass eyelet, and inside it is fitted with a pasteboard tube of about ⅜ in. internal diameter, which projects 2½ in. inside the drawer. The centre of this hole is ½ in. below the

Over this zinc support a double thickness of coarse canvas is used, and dips all round in the water contained in the tray, so all air passing into the incubator is filtered through the wet canvas and moistened in its passage. A single thickness of the dry canvas is used under the eggs in the egg drawer.

The apparatus for regulating the heat includes a metal capsule (to be obtained from fittings manufacturers). The bottom of the tripod upon which this capsule rests is 2⅞ in. from the bottom of the tank, and the needle tube which supports the tripod is arranged in the centre of the egg drawer. Heating arrangements

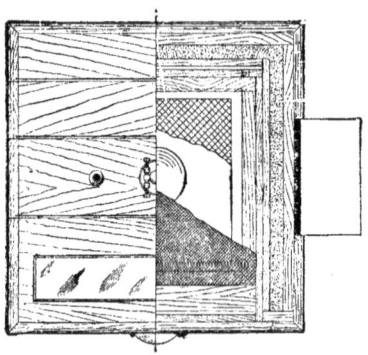

Fig. 19.—Part Plan of Lid and Part Horizontal Section through Egg Chamber

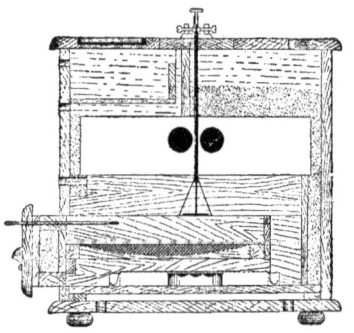

Fig. 20.—Vertical Cross Section through Centre of Incubator with Drawer partly Open

drawer top, and when in use the thermometer bulb projects slightly beyond the inner end of the paste-board tube, and is thus in the correct position for recording the heat reaching the whole of the eggs, the concavity of the bottom of the egg drawer compensating for differences of temperature which exist between the centre and the outsides of the egg chamber.

The zinc water tray beneath the egg drawer is 12½ in. square, with sides 1 in. high and a hole 4 in. diameter in the centre. The inner inverted tray of coarsely perforated zinc which supports the damping canvas is 11 in. square and 1 in. high.

consist of a lamp box, 13 in. high 8 in. wide, with a projection of 5 in., of which ⅛ in. consists of an air space between the lamp box proper and the side of the case. The upper portion of the lamp box to a depth of 6¼ in. contains in the front portion a ⊣-shaped inlet flue, and in the back portion a ⌐-shaped outlet flue, both 1¾ in. in diameter. The flues in the lamp box are embedded in some nonconducting composition to connect them with the flue traversing the tank, a couple of nipples or connectors are employed, 2¼ in. long, and of such diameter that they are a good fit in the flues, a reeded band being raised about the centre of each

INCUBATORS AND CHICKEN REARERS

connector to prevent it being pushed wholly into one portion of the flue. Both inlet and outlet flues extend 1 in. above the lamp-box casing; and, to protect the woodwork of the incubator, the back of the lamp box is extended upward $2\frac{3}{4}$ in. to form a shield, and the upper end is bent outwards to the extent of 1 in. The lamp that supplies the heat is a rectangular vessel made of tinplate, 8 in. long, 4 in. wide, and 2 in. deep, mounted on and hinged to the back of a U-shaped casing of similar dimensions, but 3 in. deep.

Beneath the lamp at the front end, and front of the lamp box, on the bottom of which the lamp slides. When the lamp is pushed quite home the spring is released, and the glass cylinder then beds itself against the bottom of the upper portion of the lamp box so that the burner is immediately below the opening of the inlet flue, whilst the spring exerts its influence to keep the glass tightly in place. For packing between the egg chamber and the case, and also round the tank, ordinary sawdust is employed. The illustrations are strictly to scale, and all minor measurements may be taken from them.

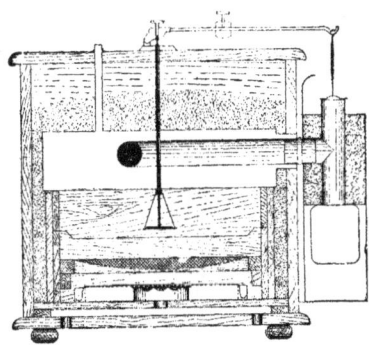

Fig. 21.—Longitudinal Section through Centre of Incubator

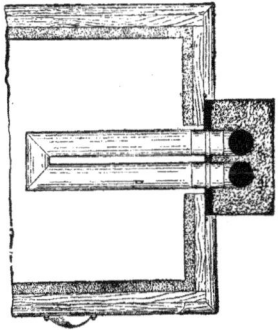

Fig. 22.—Part Sectional Plan of Incubator through Tank

fixed to the bottom of the casing, is a spiral spring; in order to keep the spring in check, a square wire loop is hinged to the casing and passes over a catch soldered to the lamp reservoir. The burner is of the flat-wick type, but of somewhat special construction, obtainable from dealers in incubator fittings; it takes a $\frac{3}{4}$-in. wick, and is fitted with a gallery to accommodate a glass cylinder chimney, about 3 in. long and $2\frac{1}{2}$ in. diameter, which serves as a connection between the lamp burner and the inlet flue in the lamp box.

To place the lamp in position, the spring is depressed so as to allow the glass cylinder to pass into the opening in the

HOT-WATER CHICKEN REARER

While other methods of heating chicken rearers require less expensive and carefully adjusted fittings, the hot-water system, properly installed, provides certain advantages. With it the whole sleeping compartment can be maintained at a uniform temperature, and there is no possibility of the chicks coming in contact with gases or vitiated air from the heater. There is also the added advantage that, if by accident or negligence the lamp should go out at any time, the water would maintain practically the same temperature for a considerable period, whereas any hot-air or direct system of heating would cool off very quickly. Added to this is the fact that, once the water has attained the requisite temperature, only a tiny flame will be necessary to maintain it at a fairly constant level.

The rearer shown by Fig. 23 is mounted on a framework of legs, in order to facilitate attendance and cleaning operations. When it is desired to work the rearer in conjunction with a run on the grass a lower arrangement is necessary; but in such a case it would be quite simple to provide a table or stand, on which the whole could be placed when brought under cover. Figs. 24, 25, and 26 show front and end elevations and plan respectively.

This rearer will accommodate at least sixty chicks, and consists (as shown on plan in Fig. 26) of a sleeping-place insulated by means of double walls, and heated by an overhead tank, a lamp compartment for heating the tank, and also indirectly warming the next division or "scratching compartment" a little. This latter compartment is divided from the run by means of a removable partition, beyond which the rearer is well sheltered, but has no source of heat. In use, the chicks are at first confined to the sleeping chamber. Later they can be allowed also in the partially warmed compartment during the day, and still later in all three, the partition being finally removed and the top raised to admit sunlight. For this purpose wire guards on wood frames should be substituted for the solid roof.

To construct the rearer a framework of deal about 2½ in. by 1½ in. will be required, the arrangement of which can best be gathered from Fig. 23. There are six uprights (three of which are shown in Fig. 24), three cross-rails 6 in. above the floor level, a long one notched over these, and two other long rails for the front and back, as at A in Fig. 24 and in section at B and C in Fig. 28. Short rails from front to back will not be required for the upper part of the framing, as this will be securely held by the floorboarding fixed across the rails B and C, and also by the

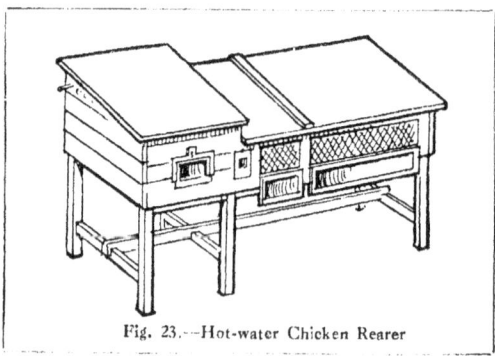

Fig. 23.—Hot-water Chicken Rearer

end boarding nailed horizontally across, as in Figs. 25 and 27. The whole of the framing should be halved together and screwed. The boarding should be tongued together, and is shown 6 in. wide wherever practicable, that for the black being perfectly plain, and the front arranged with openings as shown. The two outer compartments should have fine wire mesh filled in to their fronts, fixed between wood, as at D in Fig. 26, to cover the cut ends of wire, and in these openings there should be fitted small glass windows consisting of rebated and mitred frames, hinged at the bottom to hang down when not required, as in Fig. 23, and closing on occasion as dotted at E in

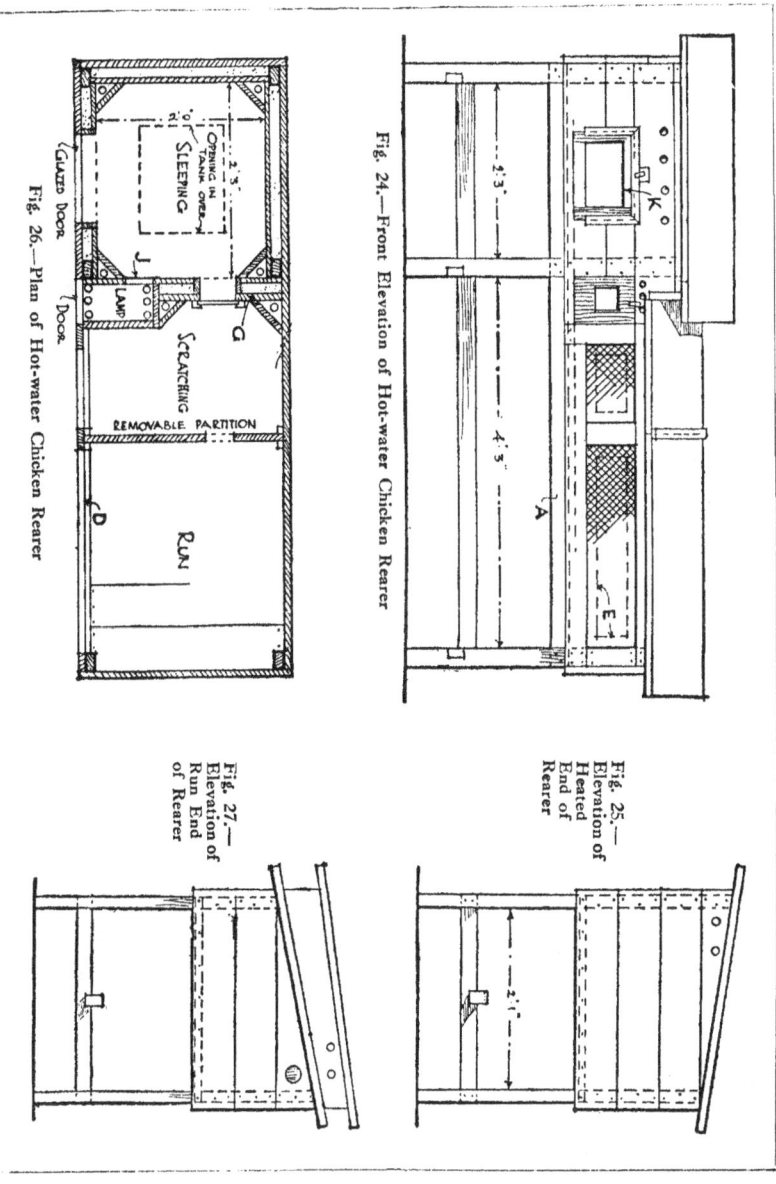

Fig. 24.—Front Elevation of Hot-water Chicken Rearer

Fig. 25.—Elevation of Heated End of Rearer

Fig. 26.—Plan of Hot-water Chicken Rearer

Fig. 27.—Elevation of Run End of Rearer

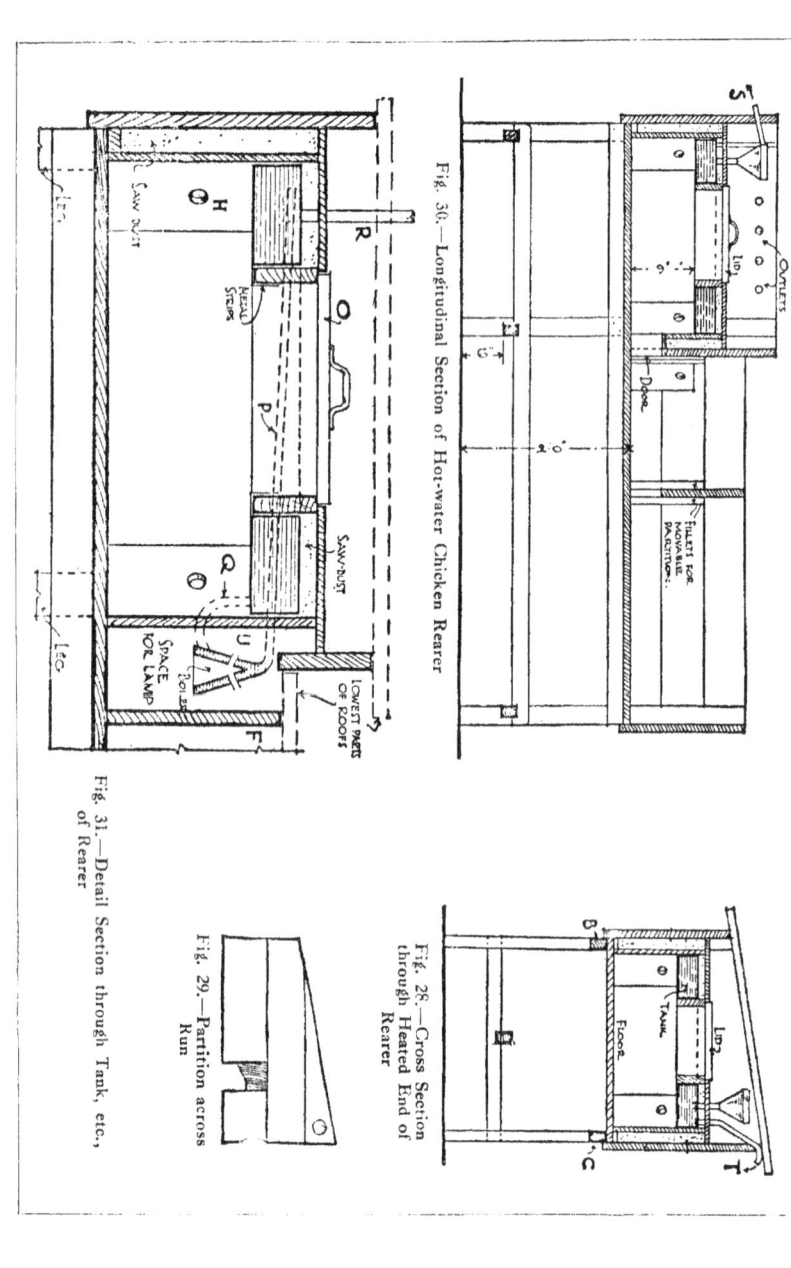

Fig. 30.—Longitudinal Section of Hot-water Chicken Rearer

Fig. 31.—Detail Section through Tank, etc., of Rearer

Fig. 29.—Partition across Run

Fig. 28.—Cross Section through Heated End of Rearer

INCUBATORS AND CHICKEN REARERS

Fig. 24. The movable partition should be made as in Fig. 29, sliding between fillets as in Fig. 30, with a small opening (with sliding door), and a circular vent cut at the top, a similar one being arranged in the end of the run (Fig. 27).

The construction of the roof is intentionally omitted; but it should be in two portions, each to hinge or take right off, and composed of boarding on ledges either inside or outside the front and back upright boarding, the whole being felted in the usual way.

Dealing next with the sleeping compartment and 6 in. wide, arranged with holes near the top H (Fig. 31) and in the floor, to serve as inlets for fresh air. The corner pieces in the sleeping chamber support the tank. Air inlets to feed the lamp should be bored in the floor of the lamp space at back and front (see Fig. 26), as if in the upright front they might allow a draught to extinguish the flame. On the left a piece of glass should be inserted as at J (Fig. 26), to slightly illuminate the sleeping compartment at night. It should be on the side away from the lamp.

In severe weather the sliding door might

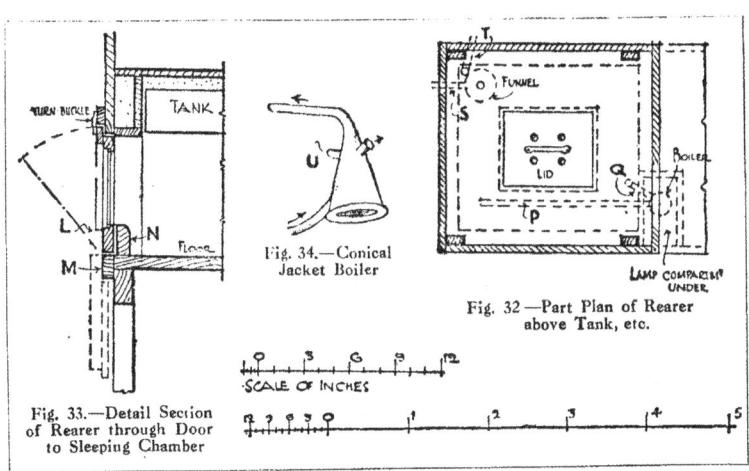

Fig. 34.—Conical Jacket Boiler

Fig. 32.—Part Plan of Rearer above Tank, etc.

Fig. 33.—Detail Section of Rearer through Door to Sleeping Chamber

ment, this should be fitted up with double walls, as shown in Fig. 26, the inner divisions being either ordinary wood, three-ply, or stout millboard, fixed to the necessary small fillets, and the cavities packed with sawdust rather than left empty. There need be no cavity next the lamp space, the division on the right of which should be of thicker boarding. It is carried up to the underside of the sloping roof to the outer compartments as at F in Fig. 31, as is also the division at G in Fig. 26. In this latter a sliding door will be required. Six corners should be cut off with sloping pieces 9 in. high have a piece of baize cut into strips to keep off the cold air when the door is raised, and careful fitting is necessary for the cleaning and observation door K (Fig. 24). This is hinged at the bottom and secured at the top with a turn-buckle or other fastening as shown. It might be made double; but a good draught-excluding arrangement is explained by the section in Fig. 33. Here the dotted indication of its position when open shows that the fillet mitred round the top and sides (to cover the joint, as in Fig. 24) cannot be taken below the point L, because of the boarding at M. To compensate for this a piece N is fixed across the opening, and rounded slightly at the top. There is nothing special about the door, into which the glass might be puttied. For the lamp space the door need not fit so tightly. It can be arranged flush with the boarding, hinged as before, and should have a small pane of glass inserted, so that the condition of the lamp flame can be seen from without.

The tank is a hollow rectangle, constructed of stout zinc or preferably copper. It measures 2 ft. 3 in. by 2 ft. by 3. in., has a central opening 1 ft. 3 in. by 1 ft., and is boxed in with a top packing of sawdust, a central frame and lid O (Fig. 31), with a handle for lifting, all as before, and as shown by Figs. 28, 30, 31, and 32. Holes as outlets for foul air should be bored in the lid, as in Fig. 32, and the space above (see Fig. 28) should be ventilated by means of a series of holes quite near the top (see Fig. 30).

Briefly, the heating installation consists first of a conical "jacket boiler" (Fig. 34), seen in section in Fig. 31. The inner cone which is placed over the burner is 2 in. wide at the bottom and $3\frac{1}{2}$ in. high, and the outer one $\frac{1}{2}$ in. wider all round, thus allowing just sufficient space for the water, which as it becomes heated flows along the tube P (Figs. 31 and 32), taken nearly to the top of the tank, and held there with wire, displacing colder water which immediately flows to the boiler via the tube Q, which should have a slight curved drop below the boiler as shown, thus completing the necessary circulation. For filling purposes there is required a tube as at R, taken 1 in. below the top of the tank, fitted with a large funnel, which should always be kept filled in order to ensure that the tank is not running dry. An overflow, as at S in Figs. 30 and 32, is advisable, and an outlet T (Figs. 27 and 32) is essential. This latter should start quite flush with the underside of the top of the tank, and be taken 1 in. above the funnel; it allows the air to escape when the tank is being filled. They both serve to throw escaping water free of the interior. All the tubes employed should be copper and $\frac{1}{2}$ in. in diameter. The woodwork must be cut away for the insertion of the pipes, etc., and made good when the whole has been satisfactorily adjusted. Note that outlets, as at U (Figs. 31 and 34), must be provided for the escape of the products of combustion from the underside of the boiler, and holes cut above the lamp door, as in Fig. 24, for the same purpose.

The lamp might be bought ready made or fitted with a special oil container, rectangular in shape and of the largest possible capacity to suit the space. Those fitted with a rim round the flat top to contain water and thus prevent the oil from overheating are desirable.

The chimneyless burners often used for rearers would not suit this particular case, as the flame would be too confined; but a $\frac{5}{8}$-in. "Queen Anne" type of burner would suit. It should be quite near the bottom of the boiler, and fitted with a glass or preferably mica chimney. To work efficiently it must be cleaned at intervals, especially the gauze perforations, which should be thoroughly brushed. Care is also necessary to see that the inlets and outlets to the lamp space are adequate, as otherwise the flame is sure to become sooty.

A thermometer should be placed about half-way between the centre and one side, and with the bulb about 3 in. above the floor.

Tubs and Churns

WASHING KEELER

A KEELER is a round tub about 2 ft. in diameter, tapering down to 15 in. at the bottom, and about 16 in. or 18 in. deep. It is made specially for use in the washing of clothes.

Anyone who can use tools fairly well can make one of these useful articles quite as easily as he can turn out the washing trough; in fact, it is easier to make the round keeler watertight than it is the oblong trough. Fig. 1 shows a keeler as seen from immediately above, and Fig. 2 is an elevation of the same article. It is made up with a series of taper pieces of wood jointed together and held tightly by four iron hoops. The bottom fits into a channel formed in the tapered pieces (technically "staves"), and provided that the joints are made true the keeler cannot help being watertight. The size of the keeler is governed by the number and width of the staves. For one of the size mentioned above there will be required twenty-four staves 3 in. wide at the top and $\frac{1}{8}$ in. under 2 in. at the bottom. Fig. 3 shows a board 11 in. wide by 6 ft. long with these twenty-four pieces marked on it, ready for cutting out. After cutting out is completed comes the most important part of all, the jointing up of the staves, and this is only difficult as regards the angle to which the edges have to be planed so that they will fit closely when assembled into the perfect circle. This angle can only be found by setting out the number of staves round a circle and drawing radiating lines from the centre. The angle will vary according to the number of staves being used to make up the whole, therefore it is necessary to set out the number correctly. The correct angle for the present example is 9°, and a section of one of the staves with the edges planed to this angle is given by Fig. 4.

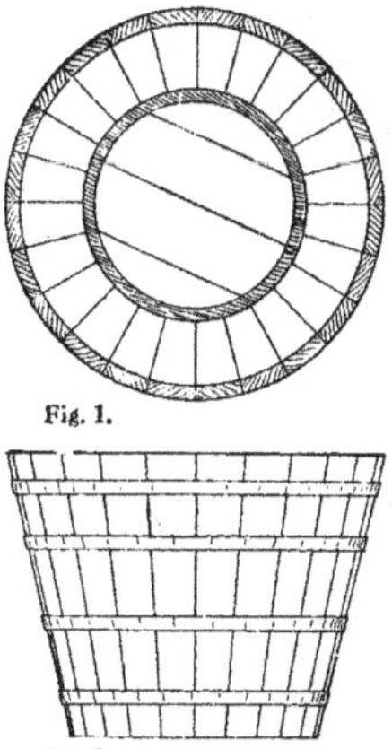

Extreme accuracy as regards the width of any or all the staves is not necessary, but the correct angle on the edges is essential. After the jointing up is finished each stave must be squared off

Fig. 1.

Fig. 2.

Figs. 1 and 2.—Plan and Elevation of Washing Keeler

at the small end, not squared from one edge but from a centre line so that the cut-off end is at the same angle from each edge, and from this "squared" end the position of the channel to take the bottom is marked with a gauge. The width of the channel should be about ⅜ in. It should be **V**-shaped, and it must be on the narrow side of the stave. One stave with the channel cut is shown by Fig. 5, and an isometrical sketch of the same is shown by Fig. 6. For convenience in putting the keeler together it is as well to insert two short dowels in each joint, and Fig. 6 shows the holes bored for these. Needless to say, these must be made truly as regards distance from the bottom end of the staves, or the dowels will do more harm than good.

The bottom is made up of fairly narrow pieces of wood jointed up truly, the joints dowelled, and the whole cut correctly to the size required. To ascertain this it is as well to put the whole together, and take the actual measurement across the channel; the bottom can then be cut to a true circle, and the edges bevelled off to fit. In this connection it is necessary to remember that the joint should be a close one inside the keeler, and though the angle of the chamfers on the bottom should be the same as those which form the channel, yet it is better to err as shown in Fig. 7 rather than as in Fig. 8; the former would be a passable job, but the latter would not. The complete bottom ready for putting in is shown in plan and section by Figs. 9 and 10 respectively.

The hoops for holding the keeler together are now required. These are made out of ordinary hoop-iron riveted together and made to the correct "dish" by hammering round one edge on an anvil. The correct length for the hoops can best be ascertained by passing a string round the keeler at the places where the hoops are to be fixed, remembering that they will drive up considerably during the act of tightening. The two ends of the hoop-iron punched to take the rivets are shown by Fig. 11, and a section of the joint after riveting by Fig. 12. The heads of the rivets should be on the inside of the hoops so as to avoid as much friction as possible in the driving on. The hoops will now be absolutely straight and parallel, and require hammering round on the inside to form the dish to fit the tapered sides of the keeler. This is given by hammering round the inside as stated above, and has the effect of expanding the iron and bending it edgewise, as in Fig. 13, where the upper illustration shows it straight as originally purchased, and the two other illustrations successive stages as the hammering proceeds. Care must be taken not to overdo it, but to stop when the hoop will just fit the sides of the keeler. In putting together, the upper hoops should be placed in position first, gradually tightening them up until the bottom will just drop in from the inside, when the bottom hoop can be put on and the whole tightened up. The hoops are driven on best by holding a solid piece of iron on them horizontally, and striking this with a hammer; gentle taps and plenty of them is the correct way, rather than any violent hammering, which would only result in a distorted and ugly result.

A section of the finished keeler is shown by Fig. 14, where the ends of the staves both top and bottom are cut off in a straight line across. This can now be done, and will finish the job. By leaving two of the staves at each side of the keeler some 3 in. longer at the top end, and cutting a grip in them, as in Fig. 15, handles are formed for lifting purposes.

Keelers of an oval shape can be formed in the same way, as in Figs. 16 and 17. The former is struck out with the compasses from the square as dotted lines, the latter from a diamond as shown in the same way. The only difference in making the oval and round keelers is, whereas in the latter the staves are all required to be planed to the same angle on the edges in jointing up, the latter must be varied in the angles. There is, however, no difficulty in this, as the joints have to radiate from the centre from which this particular portion is struck; they will then be certain to fit. In like manner the hoops will require to have more "dish" in the quicker curves, otherwise

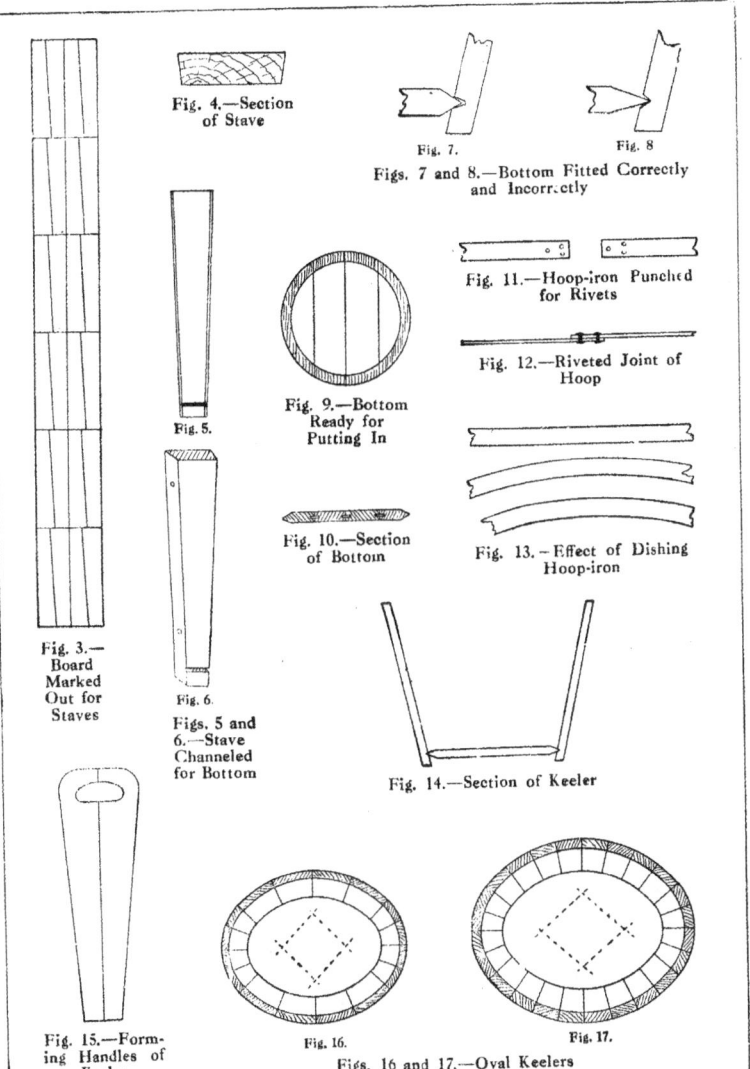

Fig. 4.—Section of Stave

Figs. 7 and 8.—Bottom Fitted Correctly and Incorrectly

Fig. 11.—Hoop-iron Punched for Rivets

Fig. 12.—Riveted Joint of Hoop

Fig. 5.

Fig. 9.—Bottom Ready for Putting In

Fig. 10.—Section of Bottom

Fig. 13.—Effect of Dishing Hoop-iron

Fig. 6.

Figs. 5 and 6.—Stave Channeled for Bottom

Fig. 14.—Section of Keeler

Fig. 3.—Board Marked Out for Staves

Fig. 15.—Forming Handles of Keeler

Fig. 16.

Fig. 17.

Figs. 16 and 17.—Oval Keelers

THE PRACTICAL WOODWORKER

the making of the oval and the circular is identical.

Deal of good quality is quite suitable for the making of these keelers, but it must be free from knots and shakes; or they may be made of non-resinous sapwood to prevent stain-formation on the clothes to be washed in them. For a keeler of large size use 1-in. wood, but for a small one up to 12 in. in diameter ¾-in. stuff will be sufficient.

WOODEN BUCKETS

Wooden buckets are constructed in practically the same manner as the keeler just described. In the first place it is advisable to make full-size working drawings similar to Figs. 18, 19, and 20. The dimensions are a matter of individual requirements, but a medium-size bucket would be about 12 in. high and 12 in. in diameter at the top, with a bottom diameter of 10 in. and staves ⅝ in. thick. The staves should not exceed 3 in. in width at their tops, and lines drawn from the centre, as in Fig. 19, give the correct angle for the joints of the staves. Any kind of wood can be used providing it is well seasoned and free from knots and sap.

The number of staves required should be set out with a pair of compasses round the greatest diameter at the top. These can now be finished to size and section, as in Fig. 19. Templates should be made of the end sections of the staves at the top and bottom, as in Fig. 18, and applied to the staves after they have been wrought to size, and bevelled for joints, as in Fig. 19. The outsides of the staves are easily wrought to the required diameters, but their insides present a difficulty which can be got over by using suitable round-sole planes.

To produce the three hoops of the correct shape lay out on a large board or floor the shape of the bucket, as shown in Fig. 21; draw the centre line, and produce the sides until they meet in point A. Then with A as centre and B and C as radii, describe two arcs of circles as shown by dotted lines, and repeat for each hoop. This will give the correct shape of the hoop-iron when flat. The length required for the hoop will be three and one-seventh times the diameter of the tub at the place where the hoop is to go, with the addition of 2 in. for a lap joint. Take a piece of hoop-iron of this required length, lay it flat

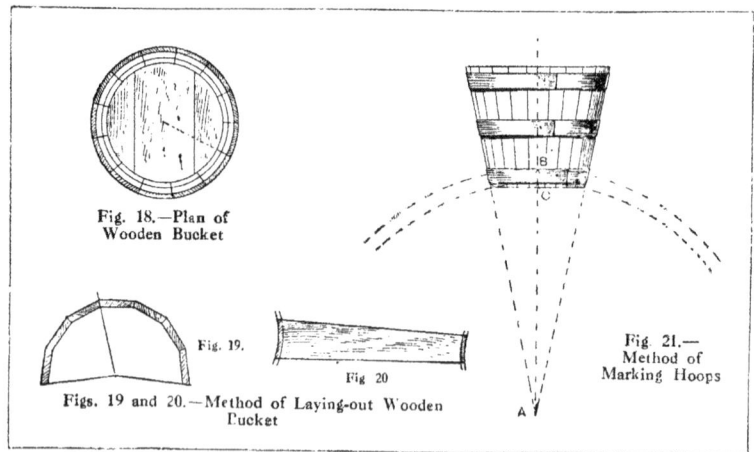

Fig. 18.—Plan of Wooden Bucket

Fig. 19.

Fig 20

Figs. 19 and 20.—Method of Laying-out Wooden Bucket

Fig. 21.—Method of Marking Hoops

TUBS AND CHURNS

on an anvil or iron weight, and hammer it with even blows along one edge, when it will be found to curve away from the hammered edge. Turn over and hammer on the other flat to prevent curling up, and apply frequently to the curve until it is of the required shape. Then

SMALL BUTTER CHURN

A simple household churn that will make ½ lb. of butter at a time, taking for the operation ten minutes, is shown by Fig. 22.

The container is an ordinary preserved-

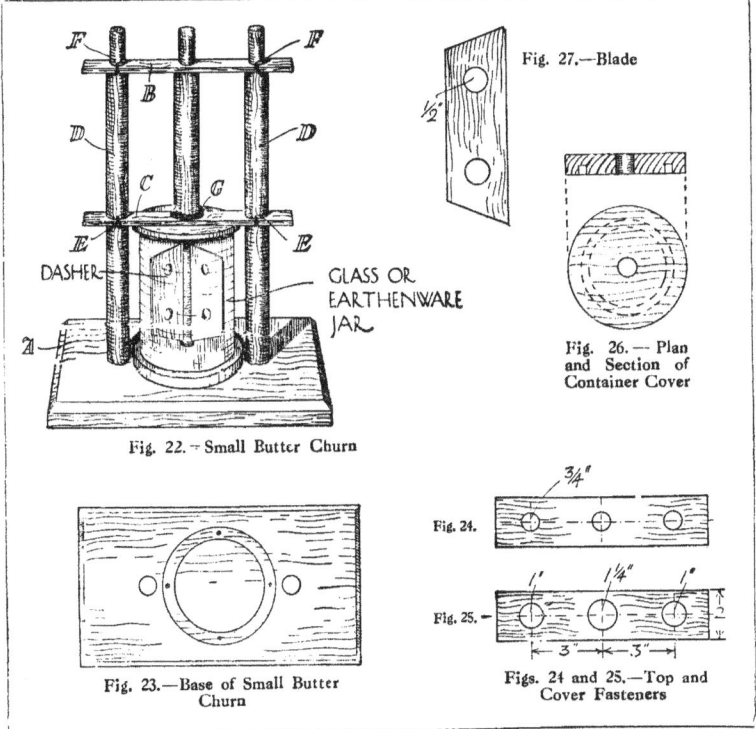

Fig. 22.—Small Butter Churn

Fig. 23.—Base of Small Butter Churn

Fig. 27.—Blade

Fig. 26.—Plan and Section of Container Cover

Figs. 24 and 25.—Top and Cover Fasteners

bend round the bucket, pinch and rivet the joint, and the hoop will be ready to drive on.

The instructions given for assembling the keeler are equally applicable in the case of a bucket, and therefore need not be repeated other than to point out that the pinching process must be well done.

plum jar about 6¼ in. by 3¾ in. Of course, any vessel of similar size may be used, and earthenware or tin might be employed, but a glass bottle is much the best, as the process may be watched. The bottom portion of the dasher (below the collar) should be grooved out to fit the dasher blades, ¼ in. deep; the grooves should be a fit with the dasher blades, so that when wetted and swelled they are fixed tight. When the dasher is ready, slip the container cover on from the bottom (the hole in the cover is $\frac{3}{4}$ in.), slide the dasher blades into their grooves, and drop the whole into water for an hour, when the blades will be found quite tight. The base A is 1 ft. long, 6½ in. wide, and 1 in. thick, with a $\frac{3}{4}$-in. projecting ring $3\frac{7}{8}$ in. internal diameter (see Fig. 23). The top fastener B (Fig. 22) and cover fastener C (see Figs. 24 and 25) are $\frac{3}{8}$ in. thick. The standards D (Fig. 22) are 1 in. in diameter and 1 ft. long, exclusive of 1-in. ends $\frac{3}{4}$ in. in diameter, with a hole in the centre of each for pins E, and others in $\frac{3}{4}$-in. ends for the pins F. These pins are made from No. 16 B.W.G. brass wire, 3 in. long, exclusive of the head. Fig. 26 shows a plan and section of the container cover. It is 1 in. thick and 5 in. in outer diameter,

with a $\frac{1}{4}$-in. groove, $\frac{1}{2}$ in. from the edge, and a central $\frac{3}{4}$-in. hole.

The dasher has three blades, 1¼ in. wide, 4 in. maximum and 3 in. minimum length, and $\frac{1}{2}$-in. holes. Fig. 27 shows the shape of one of the blades. The centre spindle is 1 in. in diameter at the top, with a $\frac{1}{2}$-in. pin 1 in. long, the diameter of the spindle being reduced to $\frac{3}{4}$ in. for the

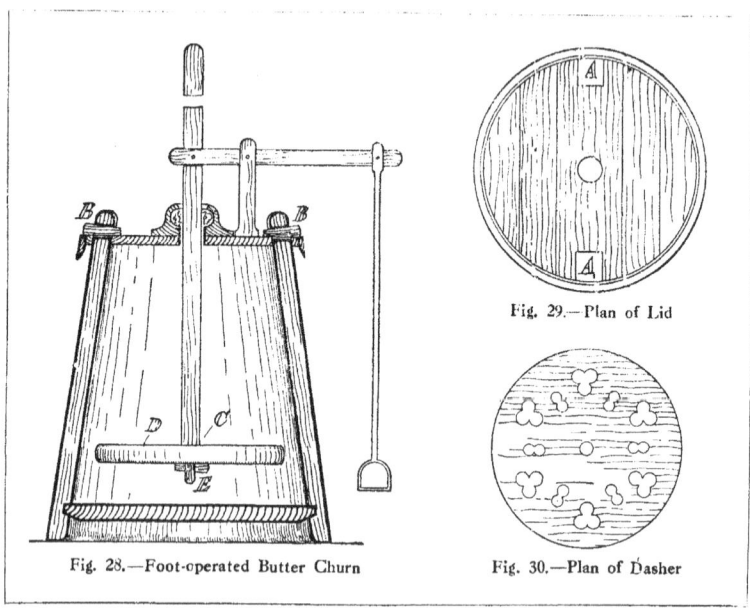

Fig. 28.—Foot-operated Butter Churn

Fig. 29.—Plan of Lid

Fig. 30.—Plan of Dasher

blades. The collar G (Fig. 22) is 1 in. thick and 1¼ in. in diameter.

To use the machine, slip the container into the bottom ring (see Fig. 23), fill it three-quarters full with cream, put in the dasher, fix the cover on the bottle, slide the cover fastener on from the top, and fix it hard down on the cover by means of the two pins, which should fit tight into the holes in the standard just level with the top of the cover. Now slide on the top fastener and fix it similarly with two pins, fasten the churn by a clamp to a

TUBS AND CHURNS

table top, take half a dozen turns with string round the dasher stem above the collar, and pull it sharply to and fro. To prevent losing the pins they should be fastened to the standards by means of small staples and strings.

The woodwork should be teak, which will stand the wetting and drying, and does not taint the butter.

FOOT-OPERATED BUTTER CHURN

An upright churn that can be worked by the foot is shown by Fig. 28. It is made like an ordinary straight tub, the bottom being perfectly level inside—that is, the usual bevel is taken from the outside only. Two of the staves, exactly opposite each other, project 4 in. above the others at the top, passing through a mortise hole A (Fig. 29) cut in the lid, also being themselves mortised to allow of a wedge B (Fig. 28) being inserted to keep the lid in position. A kind of packing-box is fastened on the lid, in the hollow cavity of which a cloth is packed during the operation of churning to prevent splashing and leakage. The upright shaft has a shoulder c turned on its bottom end (Fig. 28), against which the dasher D (Fig. 28) is fixed by a wedge E passing through the lower end of the shaft. Trefoil holes, $\frac{3}{4}$ in. in diameter, are bored in the dasher (Fig. 30). The dasher should be made in one piece if possible. The lid (see Fig. 29) may be made in several pieces, pegged together and placed tightly inside a wooden hoop and secured with screws.

The butter is produced by alternately raising and lowering the central shaft in quick succession.

The churn may be made of 1-in. oak, teak, or ash.

Doors and Windows

DOORS

Ledged and Battened Doors.—The simplest type of door is the ledged and battened door as shown in Fig. 1. The boards or battens should be tongued, grooved and beaded, or V-jointed.

It is usual to select the boards so that the width will build up to the required size. In Fig. 1 six 6½-in. boards are suitable. Cut the boards to length and cramp together. Measure the surplus width and divide it between the two outside boards. Cut away the surplus width. If the boards are not a convenient width, it may be necessary to make each board narrower and re-plough the groove to receive the tongue.

Prepare the ledges as shown. The top ledge is suitable for inside work, the middle and bottom ledge show two methods for outside work, the latter being better because the throating throws off the water.

Construction.—Take one of the outside boards and mark on the back the positions for the ledges. Nail on the ledges firmly, taking care to have them at right angles to the edge.

Turn the ledges and board over so that the ledges lie flat and "out of twist" on the bench. Place the remaining boards in position and cramp up. Rule pencil lines where the nails are required. Nail every board securely and punch the nails.

Screws in the outside boards prevent them curling off, and paint should be applied between the ledges and boards.

Ledged and Braced Door.—This door (Fig. 2) is similar to the previous one with the addition of the braces, which prevent the door from

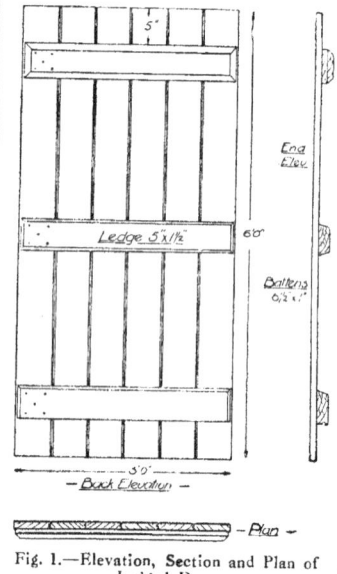

Fig. 1.—Elevation, Section and Plan of Ledged Door

DOORS AND WINDOWS

dropping at the outer edge and rubbing on the floor.

The simplest method is to make the door exactly as Fig. 1, and then "let in" the braces; these must be placed so that the bottom end is on the same side as the hinge.

The chamfers on the ledges and braces will require mitreing where they meet. Two ways of letting in the braces are shown. Keep the end of the brace about 3 in. away from the end of the ledge or the portion receiving the thrust will shear off.

Framed and Ledged Doors.—This makes an excellent door for hard wear.

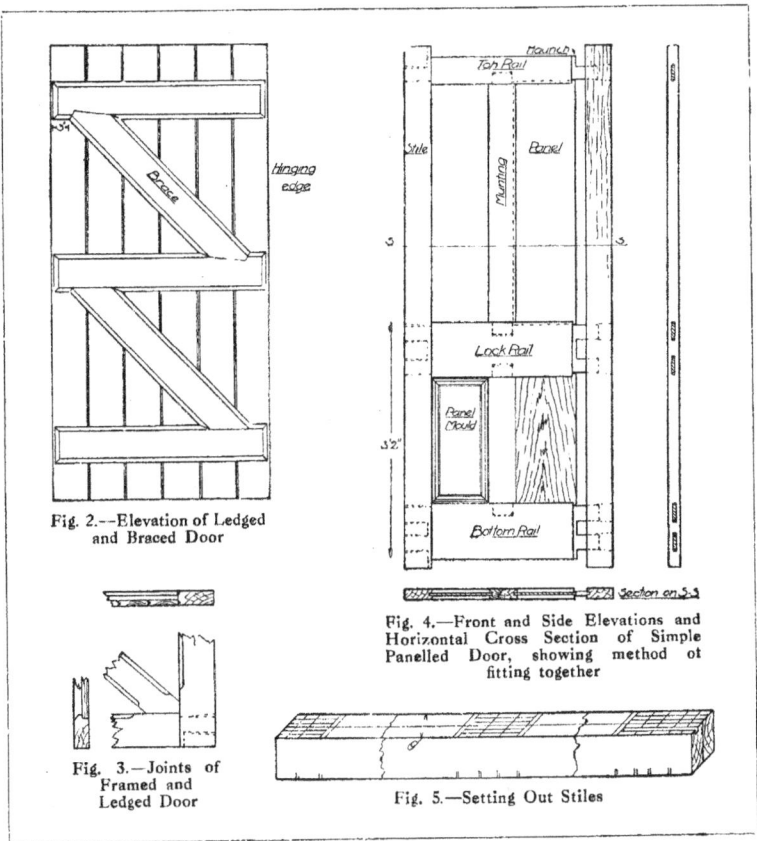

Fig. 2.—Elevation of Ledged and Braced Door

Fig. 3.—Joints of Framed and Ledged Door

Fig. 4.—Front and Side Elevations and Horizontal Cross Section of Simple Panelled Door, showing method of fitting together

Fig. 5.—Setting Out Stiles

It consists of stiles, head, ledges and boards. The stiles and head are equal in thickness to the ledges and boards together.

The ledges and head are tenoned into the stiles and the head is rebated for the boards, which run from the head to the floor line (see Fig. 3).

It is better to stop-chamfer the stiles, and run the chamfer through on the rail and ledges. The boards are flush with the stiles and head on the face side, and all the members of the framing are flush on the back.

The stiles are sometimes rebated for the boards, but generally grooved to receive the tongue. Very often the width of the boards available decides which method is to be used.

Braces may be added if required. It is then advisable to stop-chamfer all the members of the framing as shown.

Panelled Doors.—These consist of framing which is grooved, and panels of thinner material inserted, or the groove may be formed by planting beads as for glass.

The variety and style depend upon the individual ideas of the designer, but the principles of construction are similar in most cases. Fig. 4 shows the simplest form of panelled door, with one stile partly removed to show the construction. The names of the various members are shown on the drawing. The following is a table of approximate sizes for a 6 ft. 8 in. by 2 ft. 8 in. by 1¼ in. door.

CUTTING LIST

Material	Length	Breadth	Thickness
2 Stiles	6' 10"	4½"	1½"
1 Munting	3' 6"	4½"	1½"
1 ,,	2' 0"	4½"	1½"
1 Top rail	2' 8½"	4½"	1½"
1 Lock ,,	2' 8½"	9"	1½"
1 Bottom ,,	2' 8½"	9"	1½"
2 Panels	3' 4"	11"	½"
2 ,,	1' 10"	11"	½"
Panel Mould	54' 0	1½"	½"

The extra length on the stiles is to provide horns, to protect the corners until the door is hung.

Setting Out.—Set out one stile, marking the position of the rails and mortises on the face edge. Square the mortises over to the back edge and allow for wedge room. Note that the mortises are the depth of the panel groove from the inside edges.

Place the two stiles together, with face sides on the outside and the face edges together, thus pairing them. It is necessary to pair the stiles, etc., in all framing. Square all the marks on to the second stile (Fig. 5). Set the mortise gauge so that the mortise is one-third the thickness of the material, and in the middle; then gauge all the mortises from the face side.

In all the preparation and assembling, work from the face side. Next set out the rails. First set out one rail and then transfer to the others as with the stiles. Allow ⅛ in. over the finished width for cleaning up the edges. The muntings are set out from the stiles.

Prepare all the mortises and tenons, and groove the edges for the panels ⅜ in. deep. Also plough a piece of waste stuff for a mullet; this is to test the panels for thickness, as shown in the chapter on planing.

Haunches are necessary on the outer edges of top and bottom rails to allow for wedging the rails; also between the tenons on the wide rails. These haunches are equal in length to the depth of the panel groove less ₁⁄₁₆ in.

Prepare the panels, allowing ₁⁄₁₆ in. clearance all round. Common sense must be used if the material is not seasoned, and allowance made for shrinkage.

To assemble the parts, when prepared, and everything has been fitted, commence with the lock rail and muntings, place the panels in position, then the head and bottom rails, and lastly the stiles.

Prepare a level surface on the bench for cramping up, to prevent the door from being twisted when finished. When the joints are satisfactory, knock the stiles partly off (see Fig. 4). Glue the tenons and drive the stiles back. Cramp up quickly, glue and drive in the wedges. Avoid any glue getting on to the panels, as they must be free to expand or contract. The top rail is wedged down and the bottom rail up, to tighten the joints between muntings and rails. Clean off, smooth and sandpaper.

DOORS AND WINDOWS

The panel moulds must be nailed to stiles and rails only otherwise the nails will fix the panels.

Take the sharp corners off the panels and tenons before assembling. The bottom panel (Fig. 4) shows the correct way to arrange the grain. Fig. 4 shows how to set out and gauge the stiles, also one stile prepared for the bottom rail. The panel groove is omitted for clearness.

Doors with Diminished or "Gun-stock" Stiles.—The upper panels of these doors are of glass. The intention is to provide the maximum of lighting; also it allows more scope for ornamentation and design, and often this is the only reason for its adoption. Fig. 6 shows a familiar type. The material is prepared as for the previous door. In setting out the difficulty is with the joint between the lock rail and the stile.

Set out the stiles as shown in Fig. 7. The diminishing takes

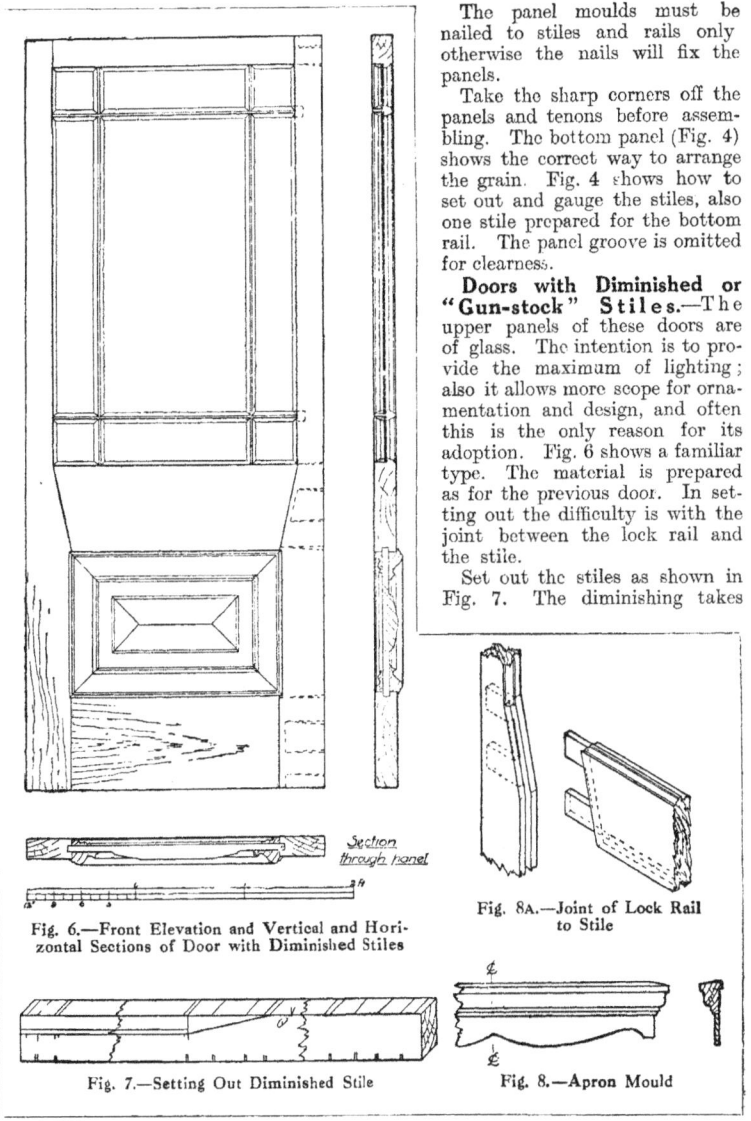

Fig. 6.—Front Elevation and Vertical and Horizontal Sections of Door with Diminished Stiles

Fig. 8A.—Joint of Lock Rail to Stile

Fig. 7.—Setting Out Diminished Stile

Fig. 8.—Apron Mould

place in the width of the lock rail, less the mould. It is important to guard against error, as it is impossible to rectify a mistake without making the door narrower. Fig. 7 shows clearly what is required, also the construction.

If the mould is planted on after the door is finished, the work is simplified throughout.

Leave the preparation of the bars until later. The door is usually allowed to stand, after framing together, for further seasoning, so that it is useless to fit the joints and prepare the bars until it is intended to wedge up.

The bars should be halved where they cross, and tenoned at the joints; the thickness of the tenon depends upon the form of the mould. The horizontal bars should run through on the rebate side. The mould on the bars should be mitred with the rails and stiles. In machine joinery they are scribed.

It is usual to scribe the lock rail on to the stile to allow for shrinkage (*see* Fig. 7). The raised panel entails a lot of labour, unless the raised portion is planted on and screwed from the back.

The bolection moulds are often built up in panels, by slips and screws, before placing in position; this prevents the mitres from opening. Generally the moulds are driven in tightly and slot-screwed from the back of the panel, to allow for expansion or contraction of the panel. The panel mould at the back covers up the screws.

An apron mould (Fig. 8) can be placed on the lock rail if desired; its length is equal to the lock rail (*see* Fig. 8A).

Bookcase Doors.—This type of door comes under the heading of cabinet-making rather than joinery, and the construction differs slightly from the preceding doors, owing to the lightness and delicacy required.

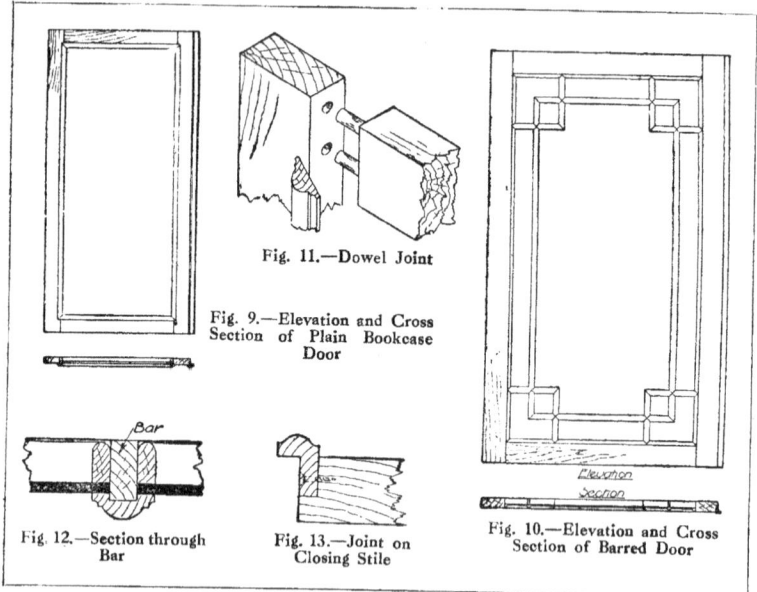

Fig. 11.—Dowel Joint

Fig. 9.—Elevation and Cross Section of Plain Bookcase Door

Fig. 12.—Section through Bar

Fig. 13.—Joint on Closing Stile

Fig. 10.—Elevation and Cross Section of Barred Door

DOORS AND WINDOWS

Two examples are shown (Figs. 9 and 10). One is extremely simple in construction, and the other of the type known as a barred door, used in Chippendale and similar styles.

The rails may be joined to the stiles by the ordinary mortise-and-tenon joint, a stump tenon with fox wedges, or by dowels (Fig. 11). The latter is generally adopted by the cabinet-maker. The rebate for the glass is formed by planting the mould on the face of the door (Fig. 11).

In the barred door (Fig. 10), the bars are formed in two parts, the bar itself being formed of rectangular pieces, and the mould being planted in afterwards. It is grooved on to the bars and held in position by glue (Fig. 12).

It is necessary to set out a portion of the door to full size and work from the drawing. The bars are halved together where they cross. In delicate work, narrow tape is glued on the back to strengthen the joints. For the stiles and rails, half the mould is planted on. Fig. 13 shows the best method of forming the joint on the closing stiles.

In a large amount of cabinet-work the ornamentation is laid on to the face of the glass. This cuts out a lot of labour, but entails much work if the glass is broken. If curved ornamentation is used, the curved portions are steamed and bent on a saddle to the required shape. Such steaming is best undertaken by a firm equipped with a steam-chest.

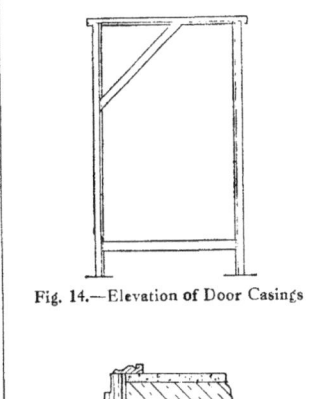

Fig. 14.—Elevation of Door Casings

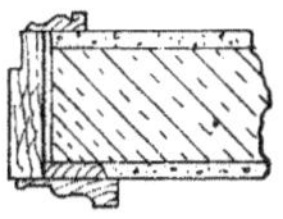

Fig. 15.—Section through Stile of Door Casings

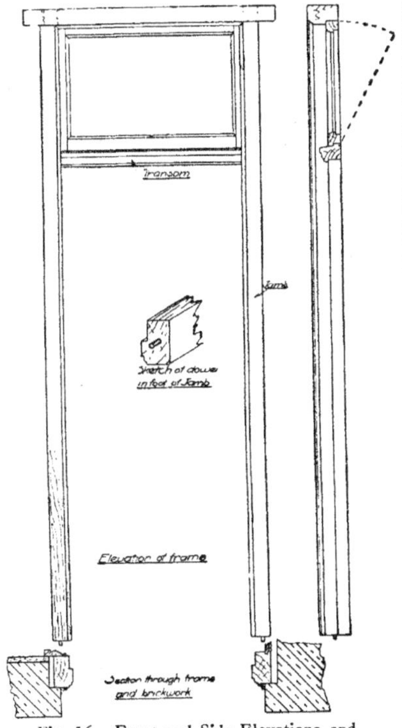

Fig. 16.—Front and Side Elevations and Sections of Door Frame

THE PRACTICAL WOODWORKER

the casings is increased, and often framed and moulded panels are formed.

Frame for External Door.—For outside walls a much stronger frame is required, such as Fig. 16. It is formed of about 5 in. by 3 in.

In construction the stiles or jambs are tenoned into the head, which projects at each end to build into the wall in new work. The transom is shown prepared for an opening light. The fixing is done by wedging at the top and transom and by iron dowels driven into the foot of the jamb (Fig. 16). These dowels fit into corresponding holes drilled in the stone or concrete. The sectional plan shows the method of finishing for a 9-in. wall, and also for a thicker wall.

Garden Door.—The garden door shown in Fig. 17 is both simple and effec-

Fig. 17.—Trellised Garden Door

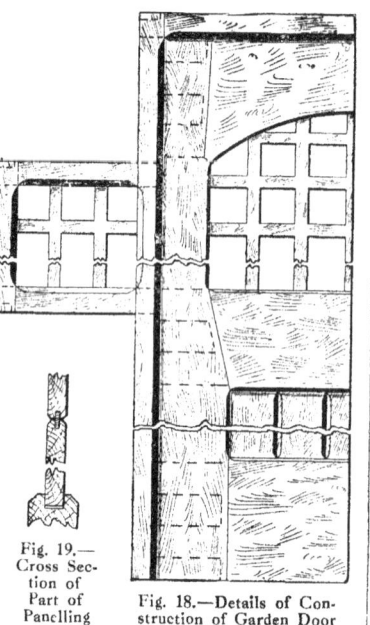

Fig. 19.—Cross Section of Part of Panelling

Fig. 18.—Details of Construction of Garden Door

DOOR FRAMES

The form of a door frame depends upon the position in which it is placed. Fig. 14 is a common type used for inside work. It is formed of 6-in. by 1¼-in. casing stuff, which is stocked by most builders. The section Fig. 15 shows the method of fixing for a 4¾-in. wall. The wall is plugged and the casings nailed to the plugs. For better-class work, grounds are fixed to the brickwork (as shown), and the woodwork fixed to the grounds.

The stiles are housed into the head to the depth of the rebate. The horizontal and diagonal stays are to keep the casings square until they are fixed.

If the wall is more than 4½ in. thick, the width is made up by wood linings or by plaster. In good work the width of

DOORS AND WINDOWS

tive, and is especially suitable for reproduction in oak. The framework is framed up with an opening on each side of the door; the door is framed together, and the lower portion is panelled, while the upper portion of the door and the openings at the sides are filled with an open trelliswork. It is suggested that the opening for the door be 7 ft. high by 3 ft. wide, and the openings at the sides 2 ft. 6 in. high by 1 ft. wide, and 3 ft. 6 in. above the ground level.

The door framework is $3\frac{1}{2}$ in. by $2\frac{1}{2}$ in., framed together with mortise-and-tenon joints; it is rebated to receive the door and the edges are stop-chamfered. The trelliswork at the sides is composed of bars 1 in. square in section, which are half lapped together and stump-tenoned in position. The door consists of two stiles and three rails. The stiles are 4 in. wide at the top, increasing to 6 in. in width at the bottom, by $1\frac{1}{2}$ in. thick; the top rail is 10 in. deep at the ends and 6 in. deep in the middle by $1\frac{1}{2}$ in. thick; the middle rail is 8 in. deep by $1\frac{1}{2}$ in. thick, and the bottom rail is 10 in. deep by $1\frac{1}{2}$ in. thick. The rails are tenoned into the stiles with joints similar to those indicated in Fig. 18. The panelling at the bottom is $\frac{1}{2}$ in. thick, and is in about five portions. The edges of each portion are slightly chamfered, and are tongued together, as shown by Fig. 19, and the panelling is rebated into the edges of the door frame as shown in the same illustration. The trelliswork at the top is made up in a similar manner as that in the openings at the sides, and the edges of the door framework are slightly chamfered.

The door should be hung with three 3-in. butt hinges or with a pair of long flap wrought-iron hinges, and a suitable lock and handle should also be fitted.

WINDOWS

Windows are primarily intended to give light, but, in addition, it is nearly always necessary to arrange for ventilation, and sometimes for ornamentation. Very little guidance can be given with regard to the position or size, other than what may be found in any Local Bye Laws. It must be remembered, in designing, that there is a minimum size, dependant upon the size of the room in which the window is placed. Only the types of window which the average woodworker and amateur are likely to have to contend are dealt with here.

Fast-Sheet Windows.—Fig 20 shows

Fig. 20.—Section and Elevation of Fixed-sash Windows

in elevation and vertical section a fast sheet, such as is used in positions where ventilation is not required or has been otherwise provided for. The material generally used is known as sash stuff and may be obtained ready prepared to the following sizes, 3 in. by 2 in., 2 in. by 2 in. and 2 in. by 1 in. bar stuff, the latter being moulded and rebated on both sides. Very often thicker stuff, or a special mould, is required, in which case it is necessary to prepare the stuff in the ordinary way as explained in the section on doors.

Also, the bar stuff is often considered too thin, and 2 in. by 2 in. substituted and moulded on both sides.

The drawing shows the window fixed in position, with a portion of the linings on the inside, and the scotia on the outside. The window is divided into squares according to the size of glass required. The reason for having small squares is to diminish the cost of breakages, but it will be understood that the inclusion of bars adds very much to the labour of making. The stiles are mortised for the rails and bars. The mortise is not necessarily in the middle of the stuff, but depends upon the moulding. It should be placed on the square of the mould. The usual form is shown in Fig. 21, which also shows the method of making the joint between rail and stile. The dots show the easier method when making by hand, and it will be observed that instead of the mould being scribed through, only a small portion is scribed and the shoulder is left square; therefore the haunch is on the stile instead of on the rail. If the stiles are 3 in. or more the usual haunch may be used exactly as described for the top rail in making a gunstock door. If there are several bars it is better to put them together by halved joints and mitre the moulding. The horizontal bar should run through on the rebate side, otherwise the rebate will probably break off.

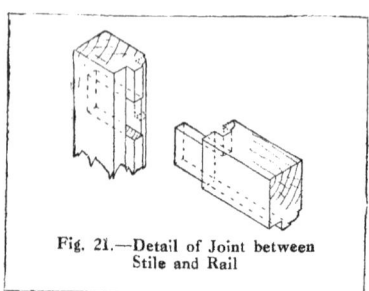

Fig. 21.—Detail of Joint between Stile and Rail

The window is fixed by means of the wedges at the top and bottom, and by holdfasts up the sides. An oak lath about 1 in. by ½ in. is shown in the sill, bedded in white-lead and oil. This preserves the wood. The linings may be mitred at the angles, but the usual method is as

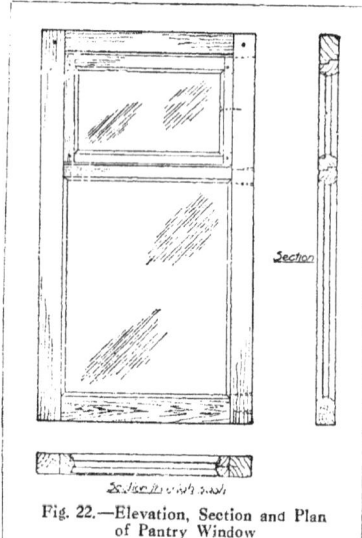

Fig. 22.—Elevation, Section and Plan of Pantry Window

shown. The scotia is mitred on the outside. If the window is beaded for the glass, then the mould is placed on the outside of the window, as this obviates the difficulty of glazing the windows from the outside. When the mould has to stand the weather, the horizontal members should have the top edge bevelled instead of moulded to throw off the water. The tenons on the bars should run through the stiles and rails, then the bars can be straightened when wedging up. When driving in the wedges cast the eye along the bar and tap the wedges to keep the bar straight until it is all right, then drive in the wedges tightly. For outside windows use paint when putting together, for inside windows use glue

Pantry Windows.—Fig. 22 shows a small window, with top portion opening

DOORS AND WINDOWS

for ventilation, generally called a pantry window. The same type of window, but much larger, is generally used in mills and warehouses. The construction is the same as for the fixed sheet, but the stiles are slot mortised for the head, so that when the sash is hung, or pivoted, the head is regulated to the correct position, and then pinned instead of wedged. The transom is rebated on the top edge for the sash, and the stiles, above the transom, have the mould taken off. The sash is pivoted, very often by an ordinary screw at each side, and opened by a length of picture cord which is attached to eyes in the top and bottom rail of sash. Pivots must be used for larger sashes. The pivots or screws must be slightly above the centre and then the sash will close of its own accord. This method gives an open joint between the window stile and sash stile. If this is objected to, it is necessary to have rebates; then it is easier to hinge the sash to the transom and open with a quadrant or fanlight opener. The same general principles of construction apply to any size of window, the only difference being the addition of bars.

Sash and Frame Windows.—Fig. 23 gives the details for a sash and frame window of the simplest form such as is usually found in cottage property. The window consists of a built-up frame and two sashes which slide up and down. The sashes are

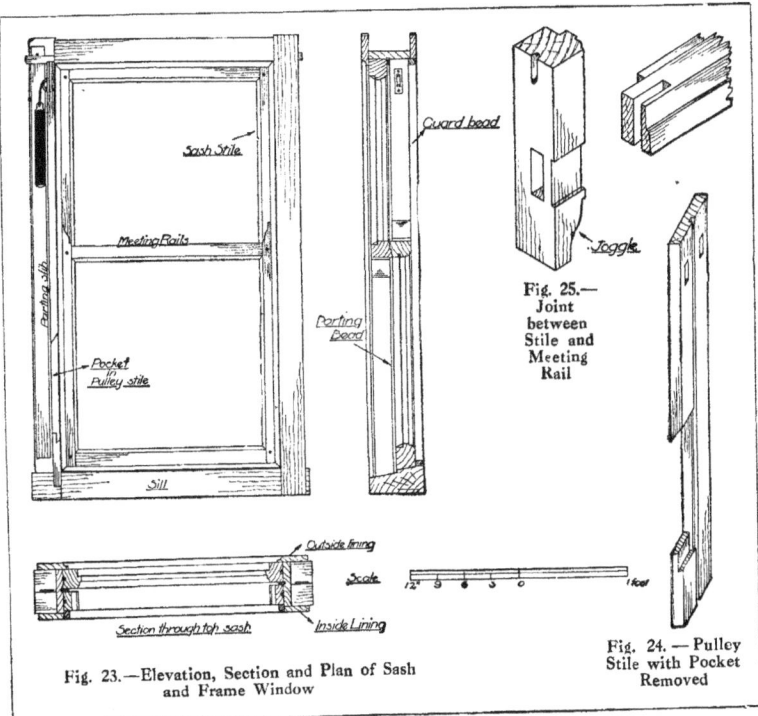

Fig. 23.—Elevation, Section and Plan of Sash and Frame Window

Fig. 25.—Joint between Stile and Meeting Rail

Fig. 24.—Pulley Stile with Pocket Removed

balanced by means of weights attached to the sashes by pieces of cord which pass over pulleys let into the sides of the frame. The weights run in boxes formed at the sides of the frame, and the two weights to each sash should together approximately equal the weight of the sash. In order to ensure that the sashes keep in position, the weights of the bottom sash should be a little lighter than the sash, and those of the top sash a little heavier.

The frame should be constructed first. This consists of sill, $5\frac{3}{4}$ in. by 3 in.; pulley stiles and head, $4\frac{1}{2}$ in. by $\frac{7}{8}$ in.; outside linings, about $3\frac{1}{2}$ in. by $\frac{5}{8}$ in.; inside linings, $\frac{5}{8}$ in. narrower than the outside linings; guard-beads, $\frac{7}{8}$ in. by $\frac{3}{8}$ in.; parting beads, $\frac{7}{8}$ in. by $\frac{3}{8}$ in. or $\frac{5}{16}$ in. The above are finished sizes. It is usual to have parting slips to separate the weights; these are rough pieces about $1\frac{1}{2}$ in. by $\frac{1}{16}$ in., hanging loosely from the head to within a few inches of the sill. Also, back linings are nailed on the back edges of the linings to keep the boxes free from mortar, etc. The sill is trenched to receive the pulley stiles, which are wedged and nailed; it is also shouldered to receive the outside and inside linings, which finish flush with the sill. The head is trenched about $\frac{1}{4}$ in. deep, to receive the stiles, and secured by nails. A slot is also made at each end to receive the parting slips. The stiles are cut square to the necessary length and then prepared for the pocket pieces. Fig. 24 shows one method of preparing the pockets, but there are many ways in which this may be done. The pockets must be large enough to put the weights through. To prepare the pocket, as shown in Fig 24, commence with the bottom, and cut in half the thickness from the front with the sash chisel. Note that the cut is bevelled inwards. Then turn over and saw as deeply as possible to half the thickness with a dovetail saw, and finish off with the sash chisel. Saw down the groove for the parting bead with a pad saw, and then make the bevelled cut at the top with a dovetail saw. The top is then forced out until the pocket splits off at the bottom, when it is replaced, screwed in position and cleaned off with the smoothing plane. The sash chisel, which has a very thin and wide blade, should be dipped in water before using.

The pulleys must be let in on the centre line of the sash run, and about 3 in. from the top of the stile. Mortise for the body of the pulley and then let in the plate flush with the face of the stile. Everything is now ready to assemble. Commence with the sill and stiles. Wedge and nail the stiles firmly, taking care to have them out of twist, then put on the head. Lay the frame on a level surface, square, and fix temporarily. Then nail on the inside linings, avoiding nailing into the pockets. Turn the frame over, test again for squareness, and put on the outside linings. These project $\frac{5}{8}$ in. inside for the sash to run against. If they are moulded it is necessary to mitre for the mould. Make a gauge for the $\frac{5}{8}$-in. projection and use it whilst nailing on the linings.

The sashes present no difficulties, except at the meeting or middle rails, and Fig. 25 shows the method of making the joint. The rails are $\frac{1}{16}$ in. (the thickness of the parting bead) thicker than the rest of the sash. This increased thickness should be rebated as shown, to exclude the dust, etc., and to prevent the sash fastener being opened from the outside. The sash is much stronger if provided with joggles and also looks better in appearance.

The stiles are mortised in the ordinary way, and, in addition, are cut out about $\frac{1}{16}$ in., to receive a corresponding portion of the meeting rail, as shown in Fig. 25. Care should be taken that the wrong side of the stile is not cut out. For the top and bottom rail proceed in the ordinary way, as shown in Fig. 21. Wedge up and pin the sashes, clean off, then plough the groove for the sashcord, about two-thirds the length of the stile, as shown in Fig. 25. Fit the sashes into the frame, and at the same time put in the parting and guard-beads.

The sashes are hung, of course, after the frame is fixed, and the sashes glazed. They should be weighed after glazing in order to find what weights are required. Take out the beads and pockets. A ' mouse ' is necessary (this is a piece of

DOORS AND WINDOWS

chain, lead or even a nail, bent to go through the pulley and attached to a piece of twine). Tie the twine to the sashcord, pass the mouse over the pulley, take hold of the mouse through the pocket, and draw the cord through. Then attach the weight securely, and pull the cord outside, until into position. This is a usual source of trouble at first. Replace the beads for completion. Special nails known as clout nails are used for nailing on the cords. Fig. 24 shows the pulley stile mortised for the pulleys and with the pocket removed. Fig. 25 shows the joint between the meet-

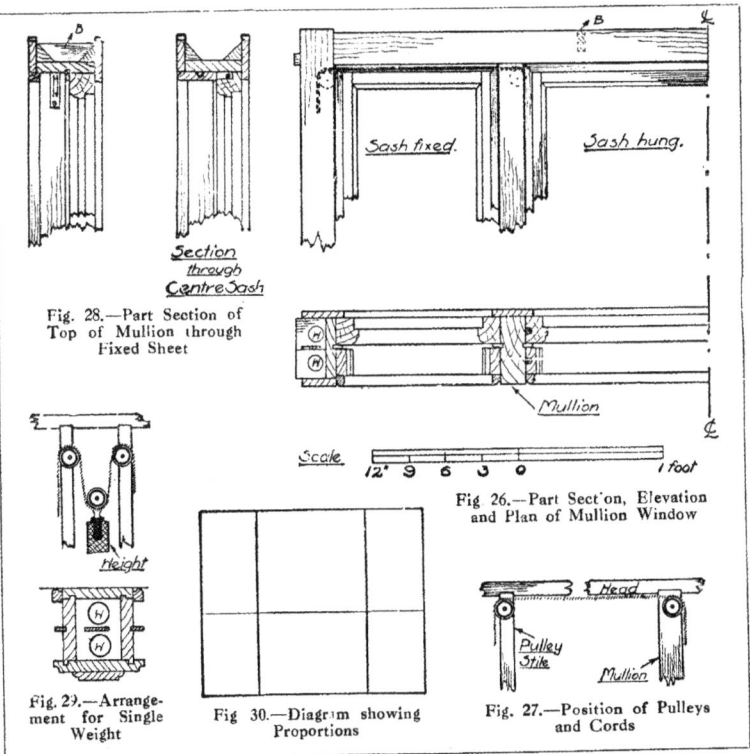

Fig. 28.—Part Section of Top of Mullion through Fixed Sheet

Fig. 29.—Arrangement for Single Weight

Fig. 30.—Diagram showing Proportions

Fig. 26.—Part Section, Elevation and Plan of Mullion Window

Fig. 27.—Position of Pulleys and Cords

the weight is near the top of the box, and temporarily nail the cord in this position to the frame. When all the cords are in position they may be cut to the correct lengths and nailed to the sides of the sashes. See that the cords for the bottom sash are long enough and the top cords short enough for the sashes to go ing rail and stile, also the method of preparing the joggle and the groove for the cord.

It is necessary to draw the section and plan to full size, otherwise it is impossible to set out the stuff correctly for the sashes. The size of the window generally refers to the brickwork opening, so that when setting out the opening is marked first and then the outside lining is set out to the margin required.

Mullion Windows.—Fig. 26 shows the simplest type of mullion window. The chief advantage is that the narrow mullion does not exclude much light. Only the centre sashes are hung, the outside sashes being fixed. The constructional work procedure is similar to that of the sash and frame window, except for the arrangement of the pulleys, an extra pulley being required for each cord. It is necessary that the cord should run over the outside sashes owing to the weights being on the outside of the frame, and this necessitates the pulleys being at the top of the pulley stiles and mullions. Figs. 27 and 28 show the method of arranging the pulleys in the mullion. The mortise does not go any deeper than is necessary for the pulley and a narrow groove is made for the cord to pass through the remainder of the thickness. The ordinary pulleys may be used with the top flange broken off. The head holds the pulley securely at the top, so that the screw at the bottom is sufficient. Instead of breaking off the flange it may go into the head, or, if preferred, special pulleys may be purchased. The top fixed sash is rebated for the cord to pass over, and a wide guard-bead is used to cover the cords. The bead is removed in elevation to show the cord passing over the sash. This guard-bead is screwed so that it is easily removed for rehanging the sashes when required. The mullions are cut square to the same length as the pulley stiles. Triangular blocks are glued to the head and top linings as shown in section to strengthen the linings and also two strengthening blocks (B Fig. 26). Fig. 27 shows the arrangement of the pulleys and cord. If all the sashes have to be hung, the mullions must be framed for the weights, as on the outsides. The objections to this window are the labour it entails and the light it excludes, as the mullions have to be of sufficient width to take the four pulleys. Fig. 29 shows an alternative method, where one weight acts for two sashes, but this is very troublesome for rehanging. The weight is cast with lead and may be square or circular. A special pulley is inserted and a rivet passed through. Fig. 30 is a line diagram to show the proportions.

Yorkshire Light.—This window (Fig. 31) is easy to make and very satisfactory in every sense. The frame consists of two stiles, head and sill, formed of 5 in. by $2\frac{1}{4}$ in., and an upright bar in the centre of 2-in. by 2-in. sash stuff, or $2\frac{1}{2}$ in. by 2 in. specially prepared as in Fig. 32. One half of the frame is rebated for glass, and the other half is arranged for a sliding sash.

Both the sill (which should be of hardwood) and head run through, and the stiles are tenoned into them. Double tenons may be used if desired, but they entail a lot of labour; and one big tenon, say $1\frac{1}{2}$ in. with two large nails to assist it, is quite good enough. The head is shown rebated for the sash to slide in, and the sill is ploughed for an oak or wrought-iron lath to act as a runner. An oak lath may be used at the top also in place of the rebate. In that case the guard-beads only serve to keep out the draught, and may be dispensed with if desired. That would mean a narrower frame. The sash is formed of 2 in. by 2 in., or one stile may be prepared, as shown in Fig. 32. The stiles run through, and the top and bottom rails are tenoned into them in the ordinary way. The bottom rail should be of hardwood, as there is considerable wear between the sill and bottom rail. Very often small pulleys are let into the bottom edge of the rail to ease the friction, the pulleys running on a strip of hoop-iron. Metal shoes are sometimes used running on a strip of wrought iron. If a lath is used at the top instead of the rebate, it is necessary to put the sash and lath in together, and then screw the lath to the head whilst regulating the sash for easy running. Bars may be used according to the size of glass required. The sash is secured by a thumb-screw, which passes through the loose sash and into the fixed upright bar. Fig. 32 is a section through bar of frame and stile of sash showing alternative methods.

DOORS AND WINDOWS

Casement Windows.—These windows consist of the frame and one or more sashes, opening on hinges. If the casements or sashes come down to the floor, so that they may be used as doors, they are called French casements. With regard to details and design, no windows are as subject to variation as casement windows, often the sashes are all made to open inwards, but this generally gives trouble with the bottom rail of the bottom casements, owing to the rain beating in. Patent metal water bars are obtainable for the purpose of keeping out the wet. Sometimes the top sashes are arranged to open inwards and the bottom ones

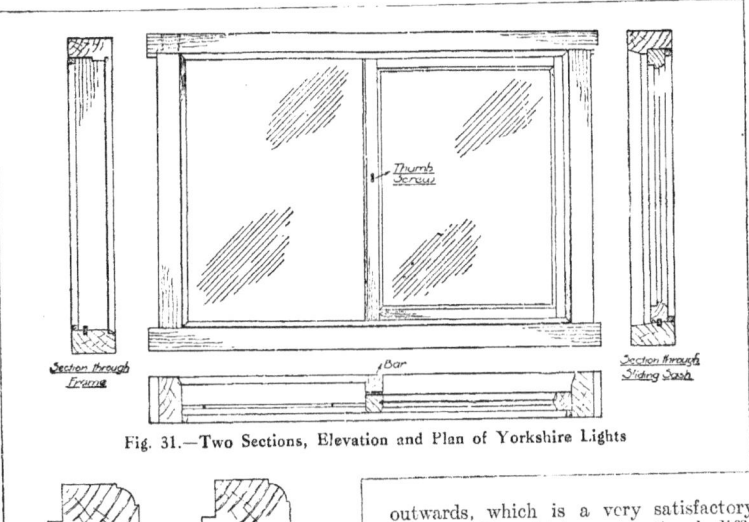

Fig. 31.—Two Sections, Elevation and Plan of Yorkshire Lights

Fig. 32.—Two Constructions of Sliding Bar and Stile of Yorkshire Light

dows, so that these makes are largely a question of individual taste.

Fig. 33 shows a simple type with a centre mullion. Four casements are shown, but it is not necessary for all of them to open. All the sashes in this window open outwards, and this necessitates the top ones being hinged to the head. Very outwards, which is a very satisfactory method. The chief constructional difficulty with casement windows is the preparation of the various sections, especially the transom. It is an easy matter if machines are available, but entails a lot of hard work by hand. It is usual to partly cut for the shoulders and tenons, and do the mortising before the moulding and rebating. If the tenons are finished completely before the rebating and moulding, it is difficult to get a seating for the planes, also the shoulders get bruised. This refers to making by hand. Casement stays are placed on the bottom rail of bottom casements, to prevent them blowing open, and also to fix them into any desired position. Casement fasteners are used to fasten them when closed. The top sashes are hinged to the head and a

684 THE PRACTICAL WOODWORKER

quadrant fixed at the transom. Leaded lights are usually put in the top sashes and are very effective. The drawings show plaster. It is usual to plough grooves for this purpose. The right-hand stile in plan (Fig. 33) shows an alternative method of

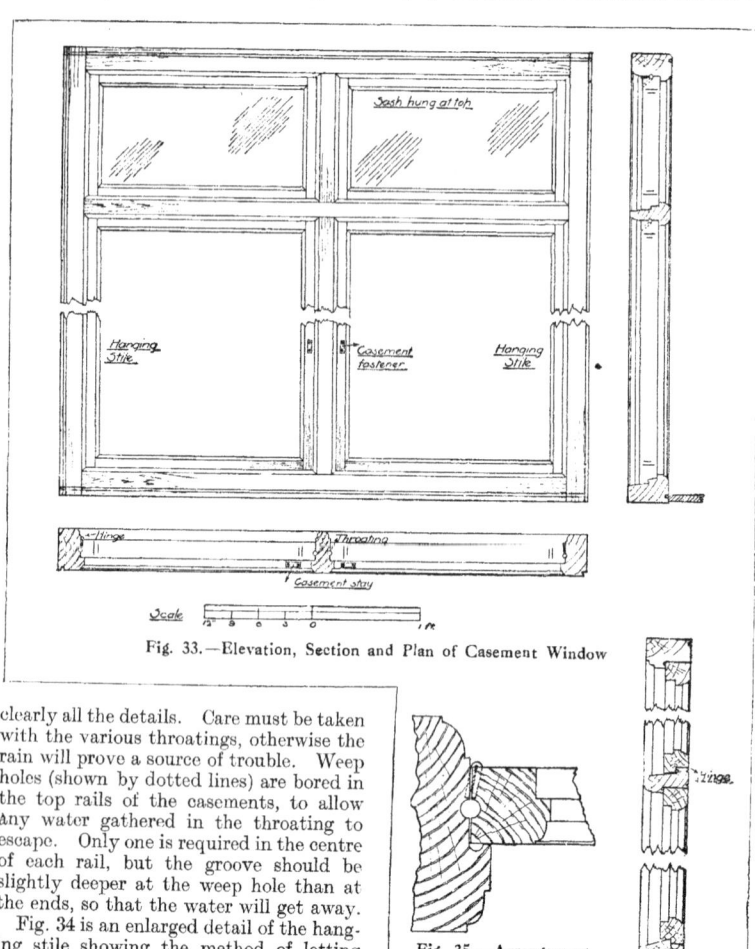

Fig. 33.—Elevation, Section and Plan of Casement Window

Fig. 35.—Arrangement of Hinging for Window to Open Inwards

Fig. 34.—Detail of Hinging Stile to Casement

clearly all the details. Care must be taken with the various throatings, otherwise the rain will prove a source of trouble. Weep holes (shown by dotted lines) are bored in the top rails of the casements, to allow any water gathered in the throating to escape. Only one is required in the centre of each rail, but the groove should be slightly deeper at the weep hole than at the ends, so that the water will get away.

Fig. 34 is an enlarged detail of the hanging stile showing the method of letting in the hinges, and also the throatings, either or both of which may be used. The inside of the frame should be prepared for the window bottom and the linings or

DOORS AND WINDOWS

forming a key for the plaster. If it is required to open the sashes inwards, the details necessary to make a satisfactory window are shown in Fig. 35. The water is certain to get through at the bottom rail, but the section of the sill will allow it to run out at the weep holes. The weep holes are bored with brace and bit, and then the holes are charred with a red hot iron, or filled in with brass tubing. In these details the top sashes are hung at the transom and opened by a quadrant at the top.

Circular Framing.—When building up circular framing, it is generally better to build up by dividing the thickness into layers and crossing the joints, then gluing and nailing or screwing the several layers together. Fig. 36 shows this method very clearly. The section of the sash stuff is divided into two parts. The division is arranged according to the members. It should be as near to the centre of the stuff as possible, but the first consideration is the ease in sticking the mould. For instance, in Fig. 37 if the section is

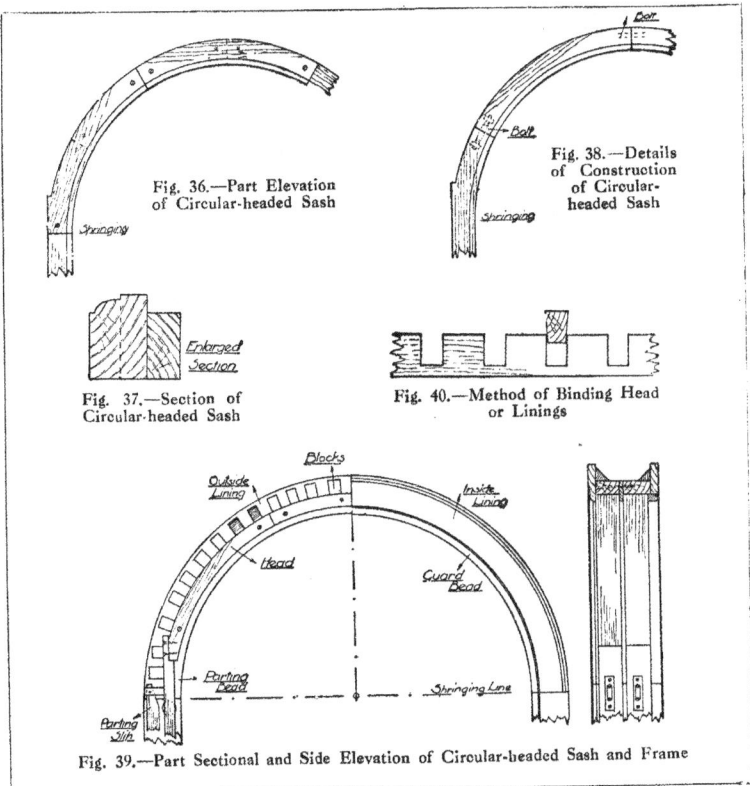

Fig. 36.—Part Elevation of Circular-headed Sash

Fig. 38.—Details of Construction of Circular-headed Sash

Fig. 37.—Section of Circular-headed Sash

Fig. 40.—Method of Binding Head or Linings

Fig. 39.—Part Sectional and Side Elevation of Circular-headed Sash and Frame

divided into two layers it is much better to divide as shown by the full line than by the dotted line, as the latter would entail the sticking of the mould on one piece and the rebate on the other, whereas the full line only requires a narrower ring to form the rebate. The number of the joints depends upon the radius of the circle and the width of the material available. The success of the work depends upon an intelligent division of the joints.

If the framing has to be cut out of the solid, the method of making the joints is by hammer-headed keys or by handrail bolts, sometimes assisted by dowels, as shown in Fig. 38. The latter is preferable for small work. The joints should radiate to the centre for striking the curves. In all circular work it is necessary to set out the work to full size and to cut thin templets for the various members required, so that they can be applied when cutting out the planks or boards. If the radius is not too small it is better to steam and bend any small section that is permanently fixed, such as the guard-bead in Fig. 39, which shows the circular part only of a circular-headed sash and frame. The lower portion is as already described for a sash and frame.

The chief difficulty is the circular head to the pulley stiles. Two methods are available. First by means of layers built up of three layers, the parting bead forming one layer. This method has been described already. The second method is very good and is more favoured by the majority of craftsmen. That is, to bend the head to the required shape. This may be done in two ways. If it is a large radius, the usual way is to cut out as shown in Fig. 40. Then bend to the required shape and fill in the notches with wedge-shaped pieces of pine, the length of which is equal to the width of the head. These pieces are well glued and driven in tightly, and the whole allowed to dry before being disturbed. It is necessary to prepare a temporary drum or saddle to bend the work round. For a semi-circular head or any work with a small radius it is better to commence with a piece sufficiently thin to bend round the drum and then glue blocks on the back, afterwards gluing on canvas. The point where the bending commences is called the springing, and a few inches of material should be left on below the springing to secure to the stiles and to fix to the drum. With the second method the parting bead should be planted on, instead of arranging for a groove. Tongues entail a lot of labour and are not worth the increased cost. Glue and nail on the inside and outside circular linings, and then block well inside the head. In Fig. 36 one half of the inside lining is omitted to show the joint between the stile and the head. The stile runs up and screws are put through from the back. The method of fixing the parting slip is shown. A block is fitted in tightly between the linings, and slotted or mortised for the slip. It is necessary to prepare a stop on the sash and the frame, otherwise the sash would bang on the head at the crown and break the glass. This is shown on the elevation of the sash (Fig. 38), which is drawn separately for clearness. The sash may be prepared in concentric layers, as in Fig. 33, or by cutting the material out of the solid and jointing by means of handrail bolts or hammer-headed keys, as in Fig. 38. Concentric layers construction is easier for hand work.

For a segmental head the preparation would be the same for the frame, except for the joint between pulley stiles and head. In this case it is better to trench the head for the stiles as if it were a straight head. Also on the sash, the joint between head and stile would be an ordinary open mortise-and-tenon joint and pinned. For a very flat segmental arch, as is commonly found in cottage property, it is usual to keep the head to the pulley stiles straight, and follow the curvature of the brickwork with the outside lining only. This necessitates the top rail of the sash being wide, and the under edge cut to the same curvature as the lining.

Bull's-eye Windows.—This term is applied to small circular windows the sash of which opens as a whole on pivots (Fig. 41). The building up of the frame and sash is as previously described for circular work.

DOORS AND WINDOWS

Both frame and sash should be divided into two thicknesses. The beads will be cut out of the solid. Prepare a board the same thickness as the width of the bead. Cut out the inside of the bead to the correct sweep, then work the bead by means of a router and cut off with a bow saw, or band saw if available. Part of the bead on each side fixes to the sash and the other part to the frame. The sash will open in at the top so that the bead at the top should be on the inside, and the bead at the bottom on the outside. The drawing shows the method of cutting the beads. Set out the sash and beads when open horizontally, as shown by dotted lines, then draw the line A A through the intersections of the two drawings. The cut for the beads is at right angles to the line A A, and from the points of intersection. The pivoting is rather a difficult operation. First it is necessary to have a plane surface on the frame at the centre, equal to the thickness of the window. The plane surface will be a square. For good work, the best method is to cut pieces off the sash and beads, to give the required size, and glue them on to the frame.

If a straight surface is left on the frame when preparing, and the corresponding portion cut off the sash and beads when fitting, it is better for outside work as the small pieces glued on are apt to get broken off in time. Fix the pivot to the frame and the eye to the sash, then the groove, necessary to slip the sash into position, can be made in the bead so that it will not show when the sash is closed.

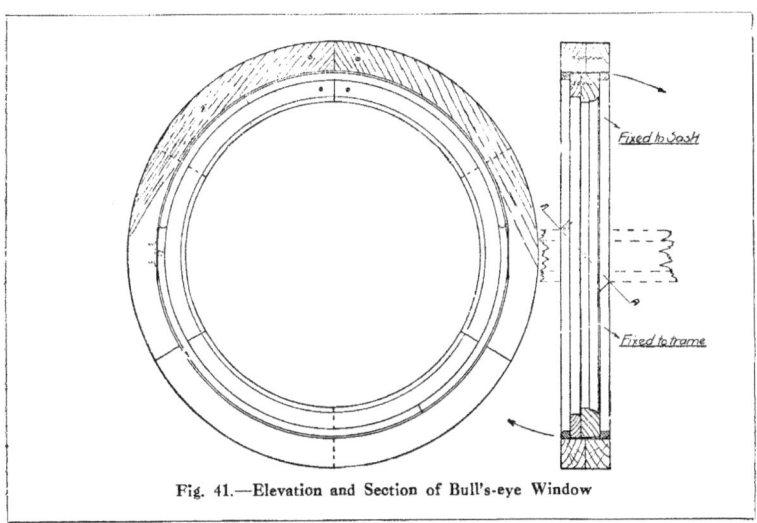

Fig. 41.—Elevation and Section of Bull's-eye Window

Circular Louvre or Ventilator.—Fig. 42 gives the section and elevation of a circular ventilator. The frame should be prepared as in the previous example, either by cutting out of the solid and using handrail bolts or hammer-headed keys, or by building it up in two layers and crossing the joints.

The setting out for the louvres and the cutting of the louvres is an interesting geometrical exercise. The drawing shows the top surface of the top louvre developed, or the true shape to which the louvre is cut. Consider the front edge A A as an axis, and

THE PRACTICAL WOODWORKER

revolve the louvre about this axis until it is perpendicular.

In the section, this revolving is shown by the edge A 2, 3, 4, 5. It is turned vertically to A 5'. In the elevation the point 5, when revolving, will follow a path at right angles to the axis until it reaches the same height as in the section. So from point 5 draw a vertical line, and the place where a horizontal line from 5' in the section cuts this vertical line will be the point required. Repeat for points 2, 3, and 4, and draw a curve through these points. This gives the true shape of the louvre.

By this method it is necessary to repeat for each louvre, which is very tedious, the practical method described below being much simpler. For this method set out two rods or boards, with the edges of the louvres marked on the edges of the rods. These rods will be exactly alike. Put the frame together temporarily, fix the rods one on each side, and with a straightedge mark the positions of the louvres both on the face and the back of the frame. The rods B B, and the method of applying them,

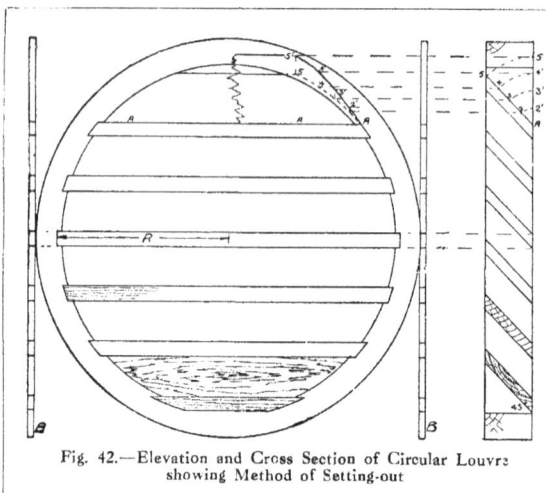

Fig. 42.—Elevation and Cross Section of Circular Louvre showing Method of Setting-out

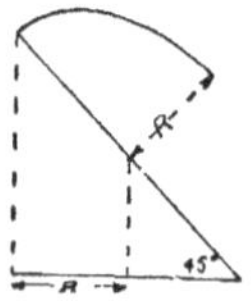

Fig. 43.—Method of Setting-out Louvres

are shown in Fig. 42. Next, take a piece of cardboard, equal in width to the thickness of the louvres, set it to the marks on the front and back of the frame. Mark on each side of the cardboard, and this gives the cuts for the louvres. Take the frame asunder and cut out to the marks to a depth of half an inch. Now put the frame together permanently. To cut the louvres, set out a quarter ellipse as shown in Fig. 43.

To obtain the axes, set out a line equal to R in Fig. 43. Draw a right-angled triangle with the hypotenuse at 45°, because the louvres are inclined at 45°. The hypotenuse is the major axis, and the base R is the minor axis. Draw the ellipse. Apply this templet in the grooves for the louvres until a portion is found to fit. Mark this portion and apply it to the louvre. Get the edge cut by means of a bevel for both front and back.

Fixing Woodwork to Walls

The fixing of woodwork depends largely upon circumstances, the position of the work, what strain it will have to stand, and the kind of wall, etc., to which it is fixed.

In America, Swedish putty is often used and the results are very satisfactory. The woodwork is smeared round the edges with the putty where it comes in contact

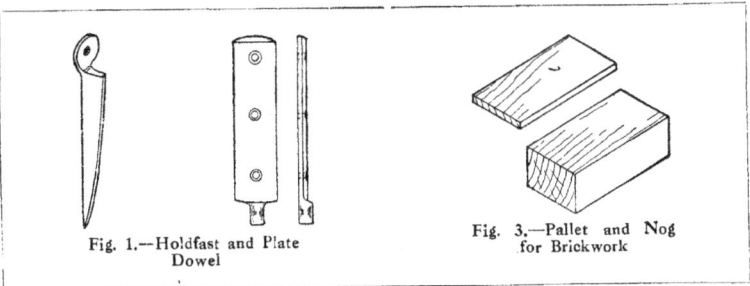

Fig. 1.—Holdfast and Plate Dowel

Fig. 3.—Pallet and Nog for Brickwork

The usual method is to plug the walls, but there are other methods equally good such as holdfasts and plate dowels (Fig. 1), building-in slips, wood bricks, breeze blocks, etc., during the course of erection.

with the wall. The fixture is then pressed into its position and two or three light rails driven in, or any other method used that will hold the fixture in position until the putty is set. The surplus putty,

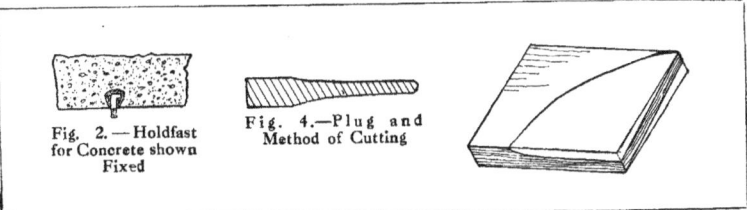

Fig. 2.—Holdfast for Concrete shown Fixed

Fig. 4.—Plug and Method of Cutting

which has been pressed out, is cleaned off as soon as possible, as it sets quickly. Many workmen assert that this is an excellent method. It is certainly clean, labour saving, requires little skill, and is efficient.

A good method in concrete is to cut out the concrete to the required size, and wider at the back of the hole. Fill in with quick-setting cement or plaster-of-paris, and quickly insert any fastening required (Fig. 2). If an ordinary screw is used, grease before insertion for easy removal. This method is used because wood plugs are of very little use in concrete walls or ceilings.

The nog is exactly the size of a brick. The latter is not always satisfactory owing to shrinkage, but the slip is excellent if the required positions are known. Plugging is generally adopted, because the plugs can be placed just where they are required, but this method entails more labour and often disturbs the brickwork.

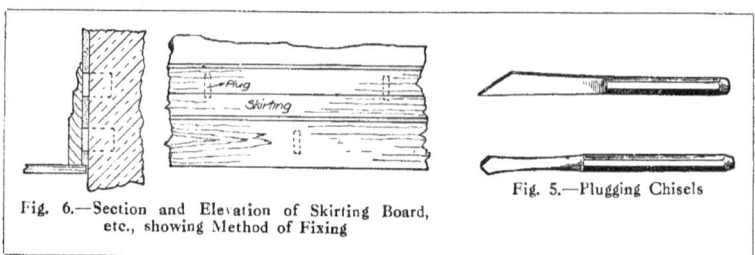

Fig. 6.—Section and Elevation of Skirting Board, etc., showing Method of Fixing

Fig. 5.—Plugging Chisels

It is usually against the local bye-laws to put timber in chimney flues, so that metal fastenings are used, such as holdfasts and wire hooks instead of plugging.

After the completion of a building, if it is desirable that the walls should not be damaged, plugs and metal fixings are nearly always adopted.

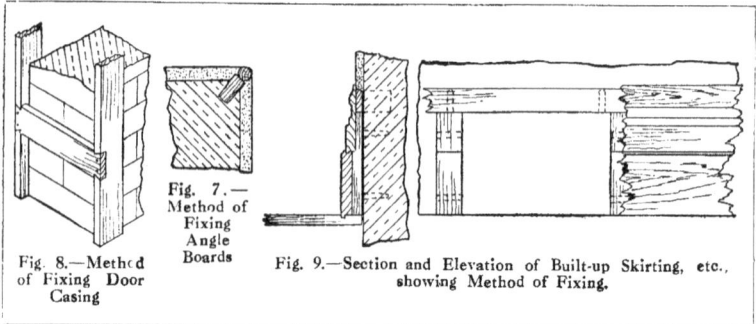

Fig. 7.—Method of Fixing Angle Boards

Fig. 8.—Method of Fixing Door Casing

Fig. 9.—Section and Elevation of Built-up Skirting, etc., showing Method of Fixing.

Fig. 3 shows the wood slip or pallet and nog which are built in as the building proceeds. The slip is the size of a brick (9 in. long by 4½ in. wide), with the thickness equal to the joints in the brickwork.

There are various methods of plugging. By raking out the mortar from the joints of the brickwork and driving in a plug made as shown in Fig. 4 (see page 72 for photograph of the operation).

FIXING WOODWORK TO WALLS

If the joints are difficult to find, or the wall is built of masonry blocks, drilling a circular hole with some form of steel drill and driving in a square or circular plug is a better method.

There are several patents on the market, similar to the latter method but with some form of improvement. One of them is to insert lead plugs, which are split at one end. The plug is hollow, similar to small lead piping, and as the screw is screwed into position, the split end opens and grips tightly in the hole. These plugs are very good in hot rooms where timber would shrink.

Fig. 4 shows the method of cutting the plug, also a section through the centre. It will be noticed that the end driven into the wall is nearly parallel like the joint which it has to fill. Also it is slightly twisted by chopping more off one edge than the other, similarly on both sides.

Sawn plugs are often used if a large quantity is required, but they are never so satisfactory; they are wedges rather than plugs, and so can only grip at the outer edge of the joint, whereas it is more important to grip at the back of the joint.

Fig. 5 shows two common types of plugging chisels. Plugs should be split from straight grained yellow pine, and tapered by means of the axe. The square or circular plugs are prepared with the chisel.

Plugging in New Work.—The distance apart of the plugs depends on what has to be fixed to them, and the strain to which the work will be subjected. They are usually driven in the horizontal joints for vertical fixtures, and in the vertical joints for horizontal fixtures.

For narrow skirting, picture rails, dado moulds, etc., the plugs should be about every three bricks apart. Rake out the mortar to a depth of 2½ in., drive in the plug firmly, and cut off ¾ in. away from the brickwork to allow for the thickness of the plaster. Wide skirtings and built-up skirtings require two rows of plugs and they should be in triangular form, as shown in Fig. 6 in section and elevation.

When fixing door casings the opening is plugged up the sides. Three plugs are sufficient on each side for a 6-ft. 8-in. frame, but if there is no fixing to the floor and lintel, then four plugs are necessary.

The external angles of brickwork when plastered are generally provided with "angle beads" running from floor to ceiling. The plugs are driven in the joints, as shown in Fig. 7, about every 2 ft. in height. They are cut off, so that the bead finishes flush with the plaster on both faces of wall.

Fixing High-class Work.—In better-class work "grounds" are fixed to the plugs and the finished work is fixed to the grounds, sometimes by means of slotted screws. If the fixtures are polished hardwood this latter method is only used in first-class work and would prove very difficult for the amateur.

If grounds are being fixed, the same procedure is necessary for the plugging, but the plugs are cut off level with the brickwork, and the grounds finish level with the plaster. Fig. 8 shows how to prepare the grounds for a door casing. The angle at the top of the door opening should be halved.

Fig. 9 shows section and elevation of grounds for a built-up skirting, consisting of a horizontal ground and short vertical grounds about 2 ft. 6 in. apart. The groove on the floor board for the skirting is seldom done owing to the amount of labour it entails.

In all this work it is necessary to be straight, plumb, and generally level. The chalk line is useful to ensure a straight length. This is a length of twine well chalked and pulled taut across the plugs. It is fastened at each end to the correct position, then raised in the centre and released suddenly (see photograph on page 32). Or the plugs may be marked separately, direct from the line, by means of a foot square placed with a stock on the floor, and a pencil; this at once gives a plumb line and the position for cutting.

The plumb bob and rule are used for vertical surfaces (see Fig. 10 for method of using the rule). The bob, which is of lead or brass, swings freely, and the work is regulated until the string covers the centre line of the rule.

For plumbing small work, the level resting on the stock of a foot square is all that is required, the blade being used in the same way as the plumb rule.

Fixing to Plastered Walls.—Fixing in finished buildings necessitates slightly different methods. It is desirable that the walls should not be damaged, hence it is difficult to find the brick joints. The drill is therefore used more than the plugging chisel. There are many forms (see Fig. 5), but they are all used in the same way. Give the drill a circular motion in the hand whilst striking with the hammer. When the square or circular plug is driven in, cut off level with the plaster, then give another hit with the hammer. The plug should be just under the surface of the plaster, so that the fixture will pull tightly on to the plaster when being fixed.

Various Fixing Devices.—Fig. 11 shows a method adopted by electricians, etc., in mills and warehouses. The pieces of bent metal, about 1 in. by ¼ in., hang on to the flange of the girders. They are tapped to receive a set-screw, which passes through anything it is required to fix on to them.

The holdfast is very convenient for fixing windows, door frames, or any kind of frame in brickwork openings (reveals). It is a rough method of fixing but very efficient. The holdfast is driven into the brickwork joint, and a screw put into the fixture (see Fig. 1).

Dowels are cylindrical pieces of iron, about 3 in. by ½ in., used in the feet of posts, etc., which have to sit on stone or concrete. The application is shown in the section on doors and frames.

Plate dowels serve the same purpose as the dowels, but they are used after completion, and where the first fixings have failed. They are the especial friend of the property repairer. The stone or concrete is drilled to receive the dowel and the plate is screwed on to the face of the woodwork (see Fig. 11).

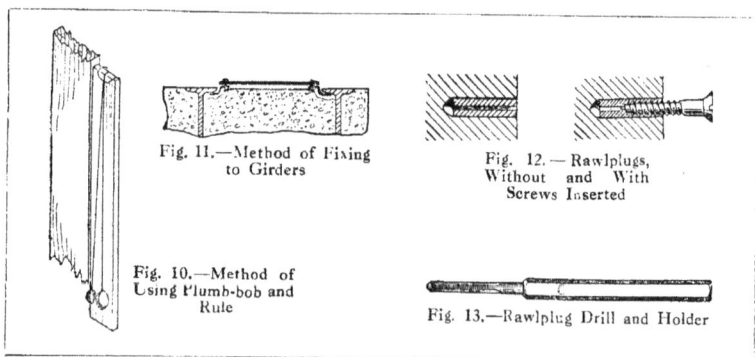

Fig. 11.—Method of Fixing to Girders

Fig. 10.—Method of Using Plumb-bob and Rule

Fig. 12.—Rawlplugs, Without and With Screws Inserted

Fig. 13.—Rawlplug Drill and Holder

The Rawlplug outfit is useful and cheap, whether for the use of the skilled craftsman or of the amateur. The plug consists of a tube of stiffened fibres which expand when the screw is driven into them, thus making a secure fixing (see Fig. 12).

The drilling tool consists of the drill and the holder (Fig. 13). The drills and plugs are in various sizes. Probably the most suitable size for average work is number 12 or 10, with plugs of assorted lengths. No skill is required, and when completed gives a strong and very neat fixing. It is extremely useful for marble, glazed tiles and other materials that require great care when driving in ordinary plugs owing to the brittle nature of the material.

FIXING WOODWORK TO WALLS

Methods of Fixing after Plugging.—Any fittings or fixtures standing on the floor must be fitted to the irregularities of the floor. Very often the fixture is not fitted, but only the plinth which is fitted on afterwards.

The following description of scribing a skirting to the floor is typical of other fittings.

Cut the skirting to length, then tack temporarily to two of the plugs, aiming to get as level as possible, and also considering the skirtings on the adjacent walls. Thickness a small piece of wood to the greatest irregularity. Then, with a pencil

If the floor is very irregular it is wise to cut the skirting for all round the room, and test for any exceptional hollows in the floor, then some idea can be formed as to the amount to be scribed and cut off.

Picture Rails, Shelving, etc.—Above the picture rail is generally an ornamental frieze which differs in depth considerably according to taste. If the frieze is paper it is necessary to ascertain the depth from the decorator.

Cut two strips of wood equal in length to the depth of the frieze, and use these as distance pieces whilst nailing the mould on to the plugs. If the ceiling is not

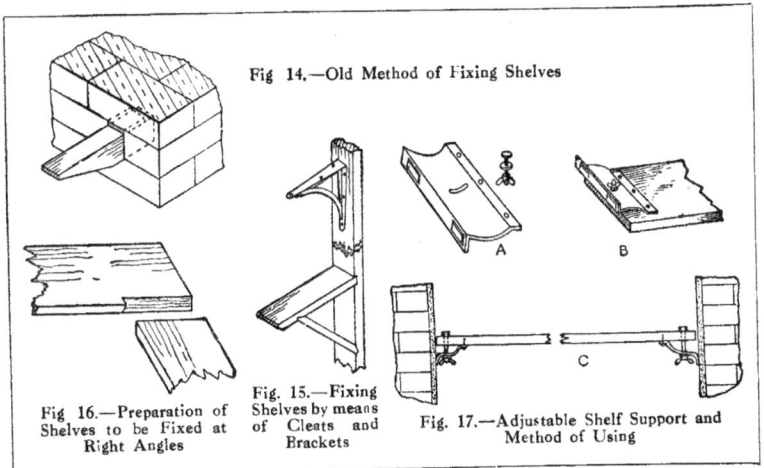

Fig 14.—Old Method of Fixing Shelves

Fig. 16.—Preparation of Shelves to be Fixed at Right Angles

Fig. 15.—Fixing Shelves by means of Cleats and Brackets

Fig. 17.—Adjustable Shelf Support and Method of Using

lying flat on the piece of wood, run it along the floor, marking the skirting along its whole length. Scribing compasses are better for the purpose if they are at hand. Cut to the pencil mark by means of axe or saw.

The internal angles or corners of the skirting are scribed, because the skirting is apt to drive in further than expected when nailing on to the plugs. In any case scribing gives a more satisfactory internal angle. The external angles are mitred.

straight, the mould must be kept straight, and the greatest distance between ceiling and mould should be equal to the depth of the frieze. The chalk line is used to get the straight line on the wall.

The corners are treated in the same way as for the skirting.

As a temporary or movable rail, circular rods about 1 in. in diameter, and enamelled white, are very effective. These simply rest on brass fittings plugged and screwed to the wall about every 4 ft. apart.

Shelving.—The old-fashioned method of fixing shelves was to cut out a portion of a brick and wedge in the wall a 3-in. by 2-in. shelf nog (Fig. 14) about every 4 ft. apart. A much better method, especially if there are more than one row of shelves, is to plug and fix cleats on to the wall; then screw cast-iron or steel brackets on to the cleats (Fig. 15). The brackets may be formed of timber, if desired, as shown.

Where the end of a shelf butts up to a wall, horizontal cleats are fixed on the wall to carry the end of the shelf. The cleat should be about 2 in. by 1 in., and chamfered. When one shelf is fixed at right angles to another shelf they are prepared as shown in Fig. 16. If this is too much trouble a strip of wood may be screwed on the underside of the shelf running through to the wall for the end of the second shelf to rest upon.

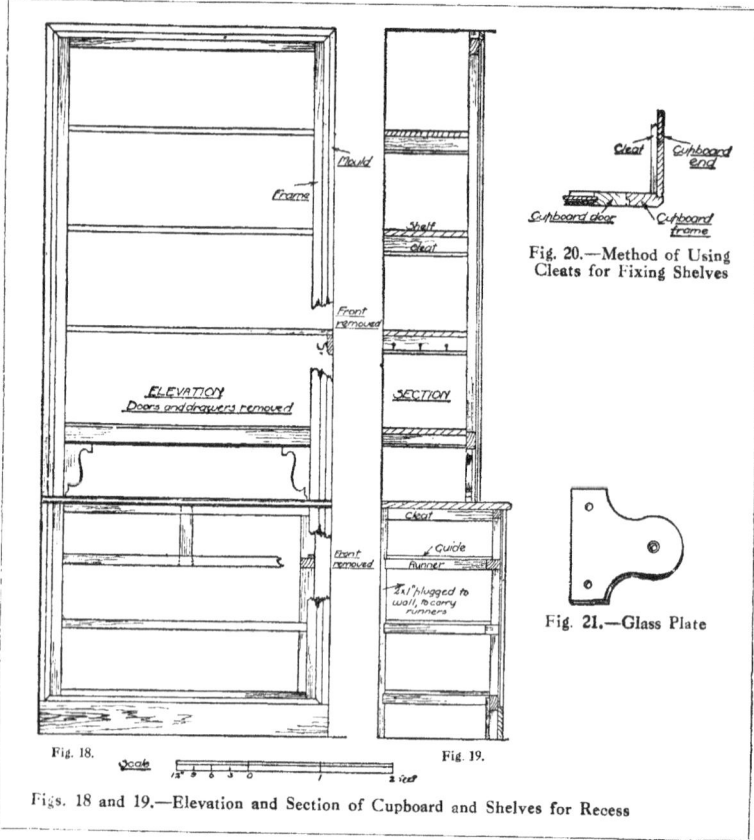

Fig. 20.—Method of Using Cleats for Fixing Shelves

Fig. 21.—Glass Plate

Figs. 18 and 19.—Elevation and Section of Cupboard and Shelves for Recess

FIXING WOODWORK TO WALLS

Many forms of adjustable shelves are now on the market, and the advantages are obvious, as they can be regulated to any height required.

Fig. 17 shows the Ford patent shelf support. This is a very good device to prevent any damage to the walls. The shelf is cut $\frac{1}{8}$ in. shorter than the distance between the walls. Then the attachments are screwed on each end, and the thumb-screw which passes through both shelf and bracket is tightened up. This presses the attachments into the wall. It is claimed by the inventor that the greater the weight the greater the security. In Fig. 17 A shows the support, B the support screwed on a shelf, and C when the shelf is fixed in position.

Cupboard with Shelves.—First fix horizontal cleats, level, and to the required heights. They should be about 3 in. deep, then cup hooks may be screwed into them (see Figs. 18 and 19). The shelves are nailed to the cleats.

For cottage property in course of erection the shelves are fixed before the plastering is done. Two plugs at each end are considered sufficient for the shelves to rest upon, and the plaster does the rest. Often nails take the place of the plugs in "jerry" building.

The front edges of the shelves are kept plumb, and the cupboard frame is nailed to the shelves, the bottom shelf forming a rebate for the doors. An architrave or lining, fixed round the frame to break the joint between frame and plaster, completes the fixing. This description applies to a cupboard between two walls. Where there is only one wall it is necessary to have an end to the cupboard. This carries the shelves by screwing on cleats (Fig. 20). The end and shelves must be securely fixed to the wall and, if possible, the end should be run through the plaster ceiling and nailed to the ceiling joist unless it runs to the floor, and a bottom cupboard formed. If the end does not go to the floor, cleats should be fixed along the wall to carry the back of the shelf.

If there are drawers to the lower portion, then the cupboard and the drawers are two separate pieces of framing ; Figs. 18 and 19 give details of a fixture of this description for a recess, with drawers omitted. To the housewife this is one of the most useful pieces of furniture about the house, and should be included in every cottage.

In the case of overmantels, mirrors, hanging bookcases, etc., which are fixed

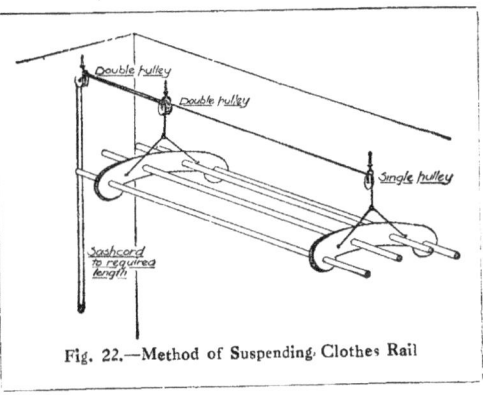

Fig. 22.—Method of Suspending Clothes Rail

flat on to the wall, small brass plates, known as glass plates, are used (Fig. 21). These are screwed on to the back of the fixture, the fixture is placed in position on the wall, and the screw holes marked on the wall. The exact position is drilled, and a small plug driven in. Leave as little of the plate showing as possible.

If it is desired to have the fittings movable, the plates may be purchased with slotted holes.

Clothes Rails.—In some parts of the country these are considered necessary for drying and airing the clothes. The method of fixing is very simple. The pulleys are screwed into the joists and the cords fix on to the rail, run over the

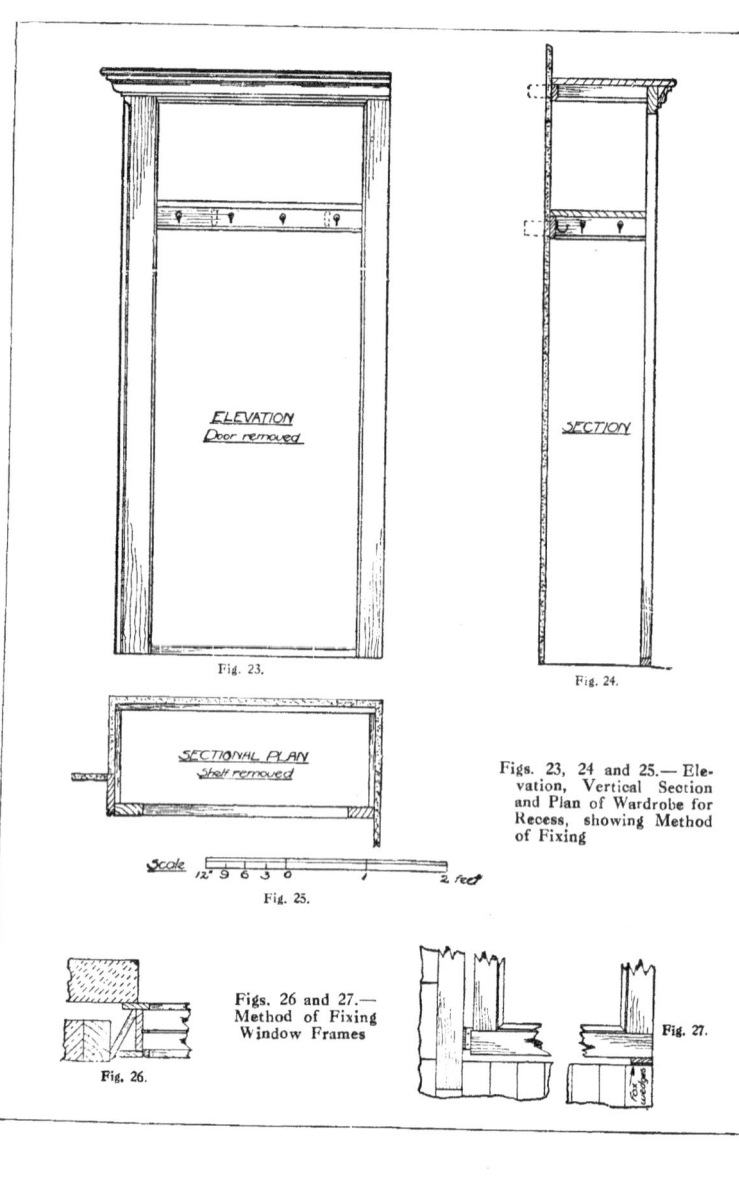

Fig. 23.

Fig. 24.

Figs. 23, 24 and 25.—Elevation, Vertical Section and Plan of Wardrobe for Recess, showing Method of Fixing

Fig. 25.

Figs. 26 and 27.—Method of Fixing Window Frames

Fig. 26.

Fig. 27.

FIXING WOODWORK TO WALLS

system of pulleys and down the wall, where the cord can be manipulated to raise or lower the rail.

Difficulty in locating the joists is sometimes experienced. If the ceiling has not been decorated for some time, the lines of the joists are easily seen. If not, go into the room above and look for the nails in the floorboards. This will give the direction of the joists, then select the joists you require, measure the distance from the wall, and mark the same distance on the ceiling below. By gentle tapping with the hammer on the ceiling the joist is easily found. Then bore with brace and bit into the joists, and screw up the pulleys. Fig. 22 shows the rail in position with the pulleys taken out of the ceiling.

Wardrobe.—This is a very simple piece of furniture for the amateur to construct. The method of procedure is similar to the cupboard. The cleats into which hooks may be screwed should be 3 in. wide, and run round the ends and back. There is generally only the one shelf, and the top. As the recess is usually not as deep as the wardrobe, a wood lining is added to make out the width. Figs. 23, 24 and 25 show the usual type for cottages. The cleats are first plugged to the walls, then the shelf is fixed and then the frame, which consists of stiles and head only. The top is placed on afterwards, and any moulding required for ornamentation. A strip of wood is nailed on the floor in the door opening. This prevents any trouble with the door and the carpets, and also prevents the dirt being swept into the wardrobe. The door frame may be prepared for an ordinary 6-ft. 6-in. by 2-ft. 6-in. panelled door. Screw revolving wardrobe hooks may be fixed on the underside of the shelf.

Windows.—Only two types of windows are dealt with as coming within the scope of this section. First, the fast sheet (*see* section on windows); this may be fixed by wood slips, plugs, or holdfasts. The latter are very good for this purpose if covered by linings. The frames must be bedded on the bricks with mortar, with a little cement or hair added. This sill is generally bedded in thick white-lead and boiled oil. Plugs are driven in at the top and bottom to get equal margin outside.

The sash and frame requires different treatment. Secondly, there may be a wood lintel above the opening and short pieces of wood about 3 in. or 4 in. by 1 in. are pressed against the outside linings, one at each side of the frame. The other end of the 3-in. by 1-in. piece is nailed to the lintel. The sill is fixed by driving in fox wedges between the end of the sill and the brickwork. This fixing at top and bottom is quite sufficient, unless the frame is an unusual height, when holdfasts should be driven in the brickwork up the sides. Figs. 26 and 27 show the method of fixing.

In many of the concrete block systems breeze blocks are used on the inside, and as these give secure holding to nails, etc., much of the laborious preparation is done away with, to the great satisfaction of the workman, and especially so to the amateur.

This section has only dealt with the general principles of fixing and their application to a few typical woodwork examples. Numerous other examples of shelves, cupboards, etc., are given in other sections.

Bevelled Work and Curved Work

THERE is no difficulty in setting out bevels for work that is splayed in only one direction. Consider, for example, the box shown in Fig. 1. The long sides are inclined but the ends are upright. The box is also shown in front view in Fig. 2 and end view in Fig. 3.

To make the box the two sides are shaped to the exact section as shown in the end view (Fig. 3), the edges being splayed and tested with a bevel; the length of the sides is given in the front view. The end pieces have to be cut to fit between the splayed sides, and the correct shape of the ends is obtained direct from Fig. 3. It should be noted that the ends of these end pieces are only splayed in one direction, that is, the side of an end must be tested for accuracy with a bevel, but the edge is square and must be tested with a try-square. All the bevels required to make this example are obtained straight from the front and end views of the box.

OBLIQUE WORK

If all four sides of the box were sloping (*see* Fig. 4) the bevels for the sides cannot be obtained direct from the drawings, but must be specially obtained. Work of this kind is called oblique work; the sides of barrows, knife boxes, troughs, wash-tubs and hoppers are usually of this type.

Fig. 4 shows a simple example of a double splayed box (without bottom) having butt joints and level edges. The plan, front, and end views are shown in Figs. 5, 6, and 7 respectively. In this

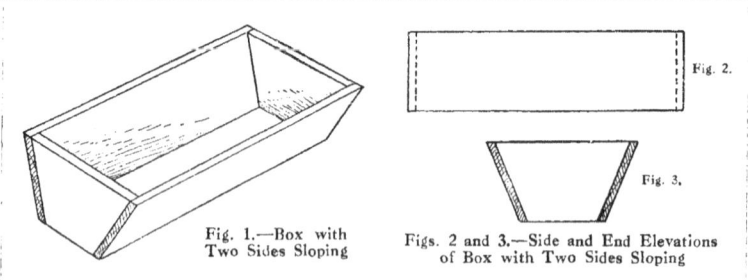

Fig. 1.—Box with Two Sides Sloping

Figs. 2 and 3.—Side and End Elevations of Box with Two Sides Sloping

BEVELLED WORK AND CURVED WORK

example the sides all slope at the same angle and the pieces are all of equal thickness. The sides and ends can therefore be cut from the same piece—which should is more important, the width of the surface looks smaller in plan than it actually is.

To get the true shape of the end surface A, imagine the bottom edge to be a hinge

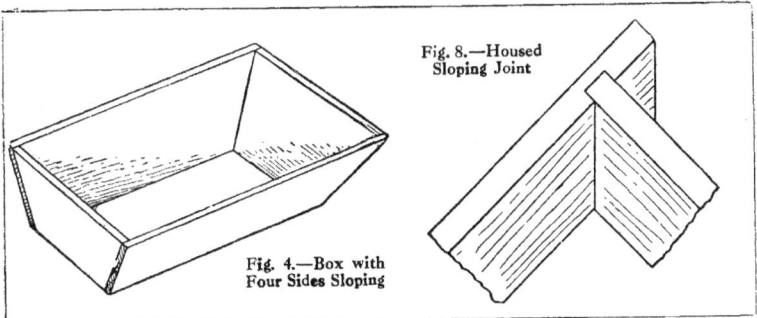

Fig. 4.—Box with Four Sides Sloping

Fig. 8.—Housed Sloping Joint

be made to the section as given in the end view, and the edges tested with a bevel.

The *true* shapes of the ends or sides are not given in the drawings. Consider the

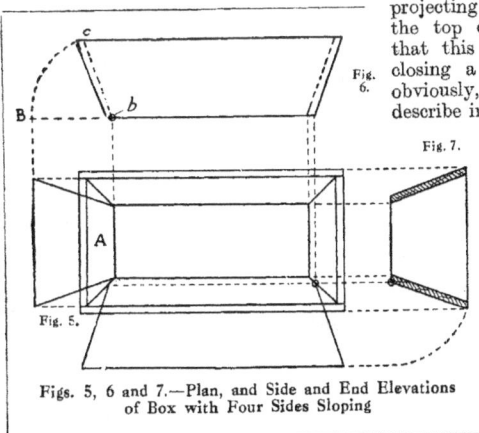

Figs. 5, 6 and 7.—Plan, and Side and End Elevations of Box with Four Sides Sloping

inner surface an end; the top and bottom edges, being level, are seen at their true length in plan, but the sloping edges are not seen at their true length; and, what

and the surface rotated about the hinge until it lies level or flat. When it is level its true shape will be seen in plan. This is accomplished in the drawing by describing an arc with b as centre and $b\,c$ as radius, thus giving point B, and then projecting downwards to meet lines from the top corners of the surface. Note that this operation is very similar to closing a trap-door in a floor, when, obviously, points on the door would describe imaginary lines in plan at right angles to the hinged side, and circular arcs in elevation.

The shape of the ends being obtained the bevel can be transferred to the surface of the piece of wood. The "cut" on the edges is marked with a try-square, and the pieces are then sawn. As the sides and ends slope at the same angle the bevel for the sides is the same as for the ends. To make the example geometrically complete the true shape of the outer surface of a side is shown, the method of hinging or "developing" being the same as for the end. If the joints were housed

THE PRACTICAL WOODWORKER

as in Fig. 8, the bevels would not be altered and the edge "bevel" would still be square.

Irregular Splayed Box.—Figs. 9, 10 and 11 show the plan and two sections of a splayed box or hopper. The sides are of equal thickness. The sections should be drawn first and the plan projected from them, in order to get the width of the edges in plan. The edges are level, and therefore the bevels for cutting the mitres can be obtained directly from the plan. Two of the joints are shown butted, in which case the edge cuts are square. The bevels for the sides are obtained by rotating the sides about their bottom edges as before. Note that the four inner surfaces are developed and also that the adjacent edges that join together must be the same length.

Edge Bevels.—If the edges of the box are not level they have to be developed like the sides. Figs. 12 and 13 show the corner of a square-edged box with mitred joints, the thickness of edge being exaggerated for clearness. The edge is hinged about its top corner until it becomes level, and the true width of the edge and the edge bevel for cutting the

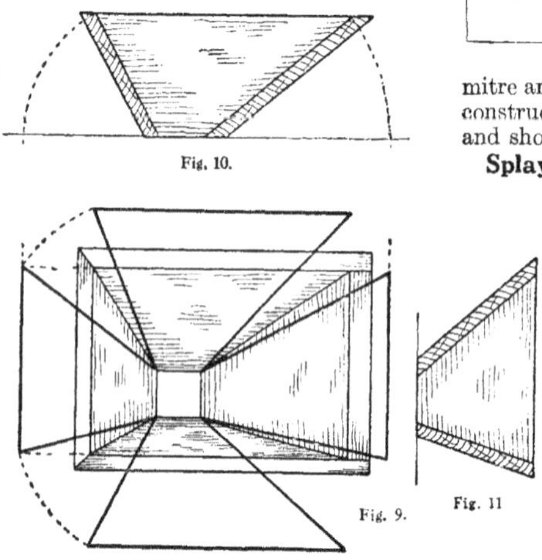

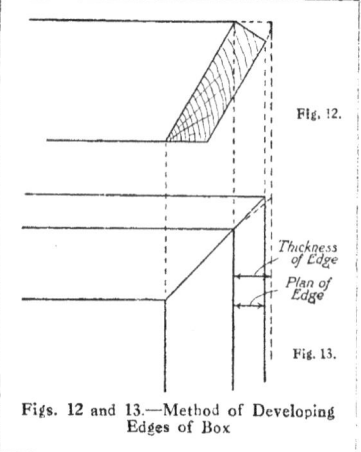

Figs. 12 and 13.—Method of Developing Edges of Box

Fig. 10.

Fig. 9. Fig. 11

Figs. 9, 10 and 11.—Plan, and Side and End Elevation of Irregular-splayed Box

mitre are shown in plan. The geometrical construction is as for developing the sides and shown in Figs. 12 and 13.

Splayed Linings.—Fig. 14 shows the elevation and vertical section of the splayed linings for a window or door. The left-hand half shows the elevation of the edges of the linings.

In order to obtain the bevels for the joints the inside surfaces of the linings must be developed. The top lining is hinged back about its lower edge until its true shape is seen in elevation. The right-hand lining has been dealt with in a similar manner. The geometrical construction is similar to the last example, and should be obvious from the drawing.

Inclined Tube.—Fig. 15 shows an inclined tube, horizontal sections of which are rectangles. The method of develop-

BEVELLED WORK AND CURVED WORK

ment should be obvious from previous examples.

Louvre Boards.—Figs. 16 and 17 show the elevation and vertical section of a circular louvre frame. In order to cut the louvre boards to shape their surfaces post. Imagine the strut to be covered with paper which is joined along the top edge of the strut. Consider an edge of the paper to be held in position along the top edge of the strut and the paper unwrapped from the strut. Draw dotted "path"

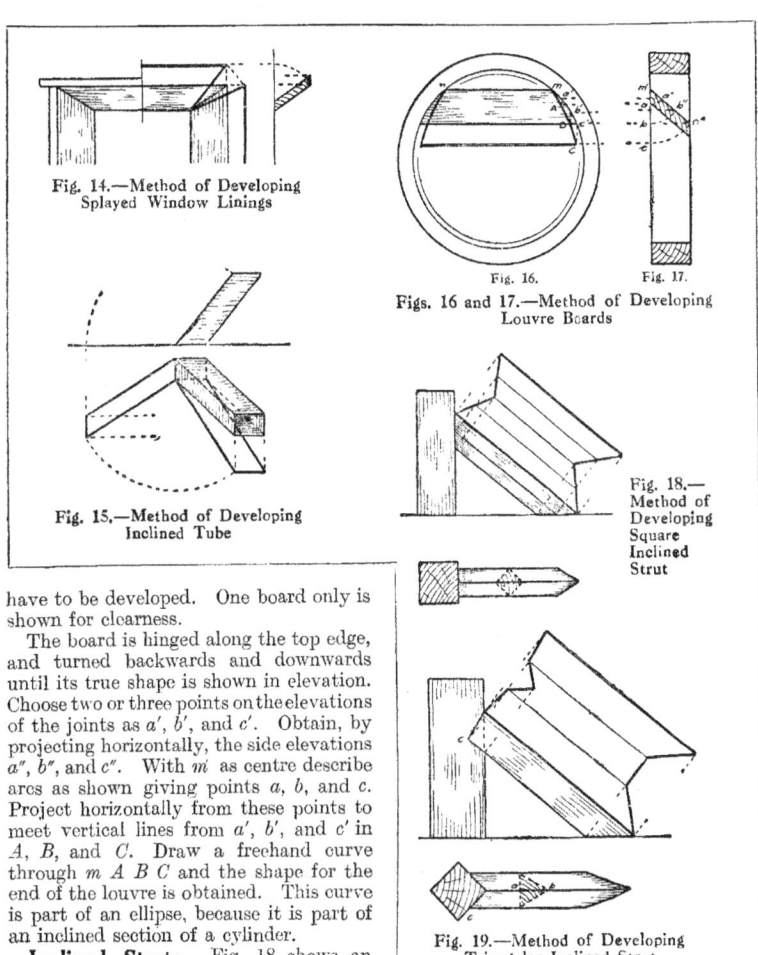

Fig. 14.—Method of Developing Splayed Window Linings

Figs. 16 and 17.—Method of Developing Louvre Boards

Fig. 15.—Method of Developing Inclined Tube

Fig. 18.—Method of Developing Square Inclined Strut

Fig. 19.—Method of Developing Triangular Inclined Strut

have to be developed. One board only is shown for clearness.

The board is hinged along the top edge, and turned backwards and downwards until its true shape is shown in elevation. Choose two or three points on the elevations of the joints as a', b', and c'. Obtain, by projecting horizontally, the side elevations a'', b'', and c''. With m as centre describe arcs as shown giving points a, b, and c. Project horizontally from these points to meet vertical lines from a', b', and c' in A, B, and C. Draw a freehand curve through $m\ A\ B\ C$ and the shape for the end of the louvre is obtained. This curve is part of an ellipse, because it is part of an inclined section of a cylinder.

Inclined Struts.—Fig. 18 shows an inclined square strut abutting against a

THE PRACTICAL WOODWORKER

lines as shown in elevation intersecting the edges of the strut in the development—note that the distance of the edges apart is obtained from the small dotted section in plan and is equal to the width of the sides of the strut.

Fig. 19 shows an inclined strut fitting against a square post fixed cornerwise. The strut is an equilateral triangle in section, as shown in the plan. Note that the elevation of the strut is equal to ab (plan). The point c' on the elevation of the joint is obtained by projecting up from c in plan. The development is obtained as before, and should present no difficulty.

It will be a great advantage in each of the examples given to cut out the developments in paper and fold into shape. By this means the reason for the geometrical methods used will be easily understood and better remembered.

CURVES

After the constructional side of a piece of woodwork has been designed and considered, the ornamental or decorative features receive attention. First the useful, then the artistic. In this section utilitarian and artistic curved work will be dealt with as far as is generally practical. The simplest case that can be taken is the ring of wood, as in a circular

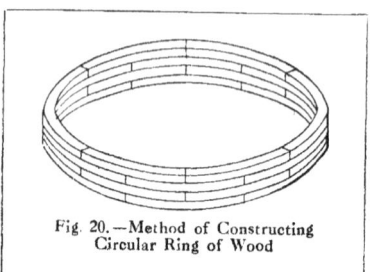

Fig. 20.—Method of Constructing Circular Ring of Wood

louvred ventilator, the rail of a circular table, or as in the rim of a cart-wheel. These three being articles, serving various purposes, are differently constructed; the rings are built up, and their parts joined together in different ways. The first has been dealt with in the section on windows.

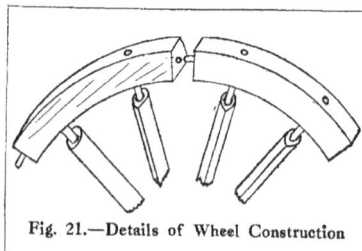

Fig. 21.—Details of Wheel Construction

The rail or rim of a circular table built up of a series of pieces is shown by Fig. 20. The series of layers, when finished, are veneered on the outside. Take, for example, a rim 3 ft. in diameter, 4 in. wide, and $\frac{7}{8}$ in. thick. It would be formed with a series of layers five or six in number, each being $\frac{5}{8}$ in. or $\frac{3}{4}$ in. thick, each layer to form a ring of five or six pieces. The joints of the pieces must not coincide in the layer above or below. Proceed to make a pattern to the shape and length required, and then mark out on a $\frac{3}{4}$-in. board. Cut out with a bow saw, and finish with a spokeshave. The gluing up should be done on boarding on which are drawn the rings showing the plan of the rim. The boarding must be conveniently small enough to allow the pieces to be cramped. Pieces forming the first ring are cut and fitted on the plan, the ends being cut to the pattern, the bevel of which has been obtained by the method previously explained. It is not essential in this case that all the pieces should be of the same length, providing they are approximately the same length and are cut to fit the plan.

There are two methods of gluing the first ring. One is by chalking the board thoroughly all round, so that the glued joint will more readily separate when the rim is finished. The other is by gluing paper on to the board, on which the plan must be drawn, and then gluing the work

BEVELLED WORK AND CURVED WORK

to the paper. When the glue is dry, true the surface with a plane, and fit the pieces on for the next ring in the same way. Then glue again, cramp the pieces down

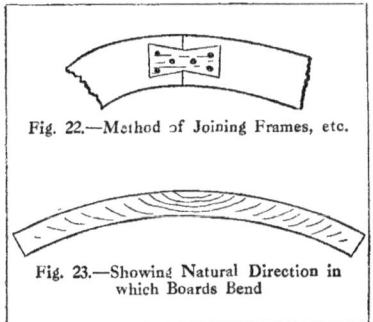

Fig. 22.—Method of Joining Frames, etc.

Fig. 23.—Showing Natural Direction in which Boards Bend

all round, using one or two brads or pins for the ends if necessary. When dry, level off and repeat the process until the right depth is obtained. The rim is then released from the board when finished, the inside is cleaned up with a compass plane and spokeshave, and the outside also rounded to a good surface ready for veneering.

The rim of a cart-wheel is divided up into pieces known as felloes, each being long enough to receive two spokes. They are prepared from a pattern which is a part of a circle larger than the wheel, so as to make the rim higher at the joints. The joints are not fitted close, as in the other cases, but are made slightly V-shaped. These are two important matters to allow for the cramping up by the contraction of the tyre. The felloes, after being shaped to pattern, are placed round the shoulders of the spokes of the wheel and the holes marked to receive same. The felloes are joined to one another by means of dowels. After the felloes are shaped and chamfered they are driven on the spokes simultaneously. Fig. 21 is an illustration of same. Some kinds of carriage wheels have the rims in two semicircular pieces, but these are bent by steam at special steambending works.

Ash or hickory is generally used for this purpose.

A ring of wood often takes the shape of an ellipse, as in frames for looking-glasses, etc. This requires two or three patterns of different shapes. The method of fixing the joints is shown by Fig. 22. A piece of hardwood, $\frac{1}{4}$ in. or $\frac{3}{8}$ in. thick, of double dovetail shape, is recessed in at the back of the joint, glued and screwed in. After the joints have been cleaned off the mouldings are worked on by means of routers.

The shaping of wood to cylindrical form, as in desk-tops, piano fronts, carriage panels, curved footboards, etc., is done in various ways. Boards can be bent by steam to this shape, and are used where they can be permanently secured by other framework or by iron fastenings. This method of bending is largely adopted in the carriage-building trades, where glued joints, as would be used by other constructions of curved boards, would soften and jar apart in the exposure to the weather and the vibration of the vehicle.

Another method often adopted by carriage and wagon builders in bending a board, when only a slight curvature is required, is by heating the concave side

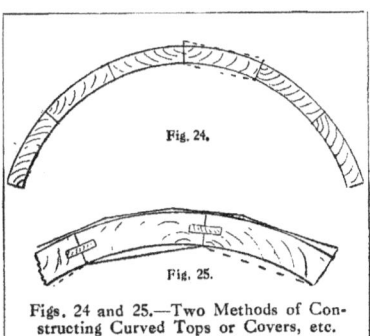

Figs. 24 and 25.—Two Methods of Constructing Curved Tops or Covers, etc.

and continually wetting the other side of the board. This can be done by moving the board to and fro over a fire or forge. Advantage should be taken of bending the board in the direction of its natural tendency, that is, the convex or outer side should be nearest the centre of the tree. This can be ascertained by the annual rings. Fig. 23 shows how a board warps or bends naturally away from the centre of the tree unless otherwise prevented. An end view of the board is given, and the annual rings indicate the side nearest the centre of the tree. If the planing is done before the bending, a good finished surface can be obtained with scraper and glasspaper.

thick, the width should be about 3 in. If the curve is of smaller radius the pieces should be narrower. Hardwood should be used, mahogany being especially adapt-

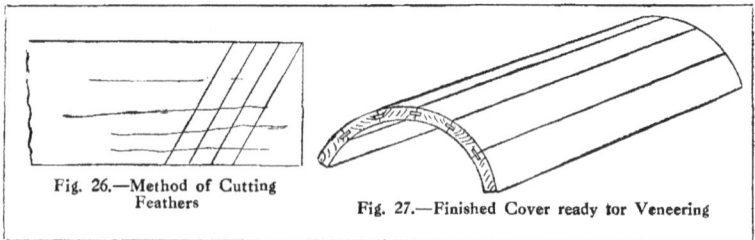

Fig. 26.—Method of Cutting Feathers

Fig. 27.—Finished Cover ready for Veneering

The course adopted for making circular desk-tops and such like articles, which are generally veneered as required, should be as follows. First draw the end view of the boards full-size, as in Fig. 24, showing the width of the pieces of which it is made. Supposing the boarding is to finish ¾ in.

able for such work. The thickness of the board can be ascertained by drawing a line from the corners inside, and another line parallel to it and tangential to the outer curve, as shown by the dotted lines. If the curve is circular, the angle for the edges will be equal, and should be taken by the bevel from the drawing. Care is required in shooting the edges to the correct angles, and after testing with the bevel they should be tested on the drawing to make sure of obtaining the correct

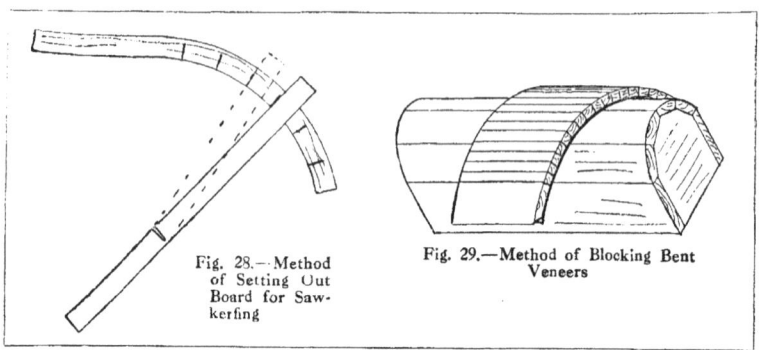

Fig. 28.—Method of Setting Out Board for Sawkerfing

Fig. 29.—Method of Blocking Bent Veneers

shape. The joints are rubbed when gluing, which should be done in two or three operations, giving the joint time to harden before being weighted by the extra piece.

BEVELLED WORK AND CURVED WORK

When ready for rounding off, the ends should be marked with a pattern obtained from the drawing. The inside curve should be worked with a "round" plane

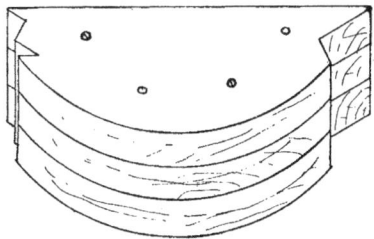

Fig. 30.—Blocks for Bull-nose Step

as wide as obtainable; or if many boards of this shape are to be made, an old jack plane might be rounded to fit the curve, and the cutting iron ground accordingly. A scraper could be ground to fit the curve for finishing before the glasspaper is used.

A stronger method of shaping by grooving and feathering the joints is shown by Fig. 25. After shooting the edges, plane a tangential surface at right angles to the joint sufficiently near to allow for finishing. Then plough the grooves as indicated about ½ in. or more in depth on each edge. Now cut off a number of feathers, obliquely, from a board the thickness of the grooves, as in Fig. 26. Cutting the tongues as feathers in this fashion allows the grain to cross the joint instead of longitudinally

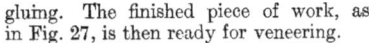

Fig. 31.—Riser for Step Shaped for Binding

with the joint, which would be a source of weakness. The feathers should be shot sufficiently narrow so as not to bind and prevent the joint being rubbed close when

gluing. The finished piece of work, as in Fig. 27, is then ready for veneering.

The curved work in connection with furniture is chiefly of an artistic character rather than geometrical, as in building construction. It consists of work composed of a number of curves which cannot always be set out geometrically, but are symmetrically constructed from a freehand design to one's artistic taste. Examples of such work can be seen in the art of chairmaking. There should be no difficulty in preparing a pattern of any fancy shape and making the required article, providing the piece is of the same thickness as the plank from which it is made. Should there be a double curvature on the piece to be made, the worker should ascertain the width and thickness from the drawing, showing the two views of the article. In the case of pieces forming the back of a chair, some will resemble pieces like the circle on circle, or, to be more correct, circle on cylinder, so that many

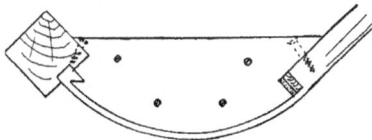

Fig. 32.—Bent Riser Fixed in Position

pieces have to be cut of cylindrical form for such work, and then the required circle or other pattern marked. The second curve or pattern is not always definitely marked on these cylindrical pieces until they have been approximately dressed to shape, fitted, and joined up temporarily by dowelling. Then the pieces are dressed to shape before gluing up.

The tools required for such work are the bow saw, spokeshave, smoothing and compass planes, the firmer chisel for paring the small convex surfaces, and the half-round file for finish-

THE PRACTICAL WOODWORKER

ing. Two or three routers may be wanted for grooves, beads, and mouldings.

Saw-kerfing, as a method of bending boards, can be done in cases where there is no great strain or stress on the board, and where these methods are pursued the board needs support from the adjacent fixings. Saw-kerfing on the concave side of a board for a convex or external finish requires care in making the cuts regular in depth and equidistant. Fig. 28 illustrates a method of approximating the distance apart of the saw cuts. A piece of wood, the same thickness as the board to be bent, is sawn nearly through or until it is sufficiently flexible to close in, and is then placed to the centre of the curve required. The movement round the circumference, in the operation of closing the cut, gives the space between the cuts on the board. The same saw must be used, and cuts to the same depth as in the test piece.

Veneers can be bent over a built-up cylinder or other shape, and blocks or strips of wood are fitted to the veneer and glued on, as in Fig. 29. This method is carried out in making the concave well hole of a staircase, in which instance the whole work is bound and strengthened by gluing canvas over the fillets or strips.

Reducing a board almost to the thickness of veneer, and by the aid of steam bending it round a block of wood, which is built up and made the required shape to give an external or convex curve, is a method sometimes employed. The lower

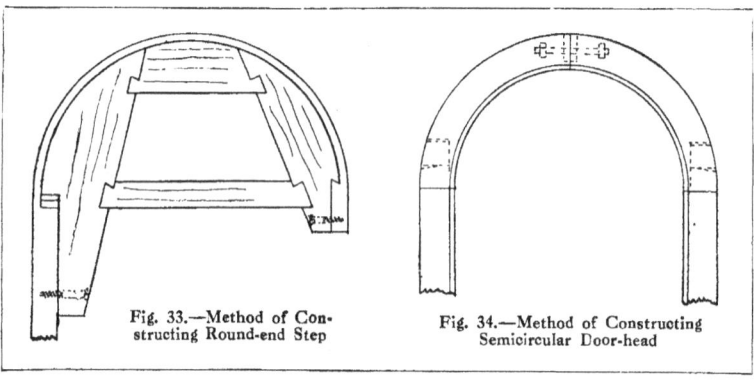

Fig. 33.—Method of Constructing Round-end Step

Fig. 34.—Method of Constructing Semicircular Door-head

risers of a staircase, such as a bull-nose, round end, or curtail step, are good examples of such work. For a bull-nose step, three or four pieces of thick boarding to

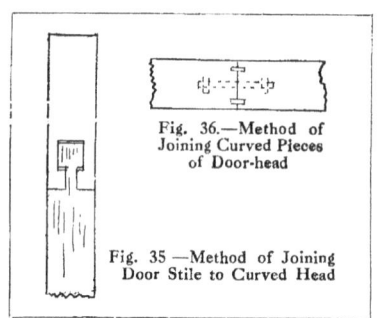

Fig. 36.—Method of Joining Curved Pieces of Door-head

Fig. 35.—Method of Joining Door Stile to Curved Head

the depth of the step are cut out reverse ways of the grain, glued, and screwed together (Fig. 30). The board for the riser, of about $\frac{7}{8}$ in. in thickness, is reduced to $\frac{3}{16}$ in. in thickness, in the portion to be bent, by planing. A splayed fillet of hardwood, to form a hook, is well secured by gluing and screwing, as in Fig. 31. After

BEVELLED WORK AND CURVED WORK

the block has been fitted, the portion of the board for bending is well steamed, folded round, and secured by folding wedges. Screws are then fixed through the block to the thicker portion of the board. This is shown with the end housed into the newel post (Fig. 32). The block for a round-end step is sometimes made of four parts dovetailed together, and rounded off with saw, smoothing plane, and file. The wedging and screwing are performed in the same manner as the bull-nose step (Fig. 30).

An example of work where straight and curved pieces are joined together is shown by the semicircular head of a doorway (Fig. 34). Methods of joining the pieces together, and also on to the straight portion, are shown by Figs. 35 and 36.

In the first a hammer-headed key is worked on the door stile in the solid, as shown in the side view. It is recessed to about three-fourths of the depth of the wood, and two wedges are required. This joint could be secured in the same way as the top joint (Fig. 36). The bolt has two nuts, one at each end, one being an ordinary nut and the other a circular one with notches on the edge, and these notches enable it to be tightened with a small cold chisel. The holes are bored in the end of each piece forming the joint; the nuts are let in from the top side and a washer must be used with the circular nut. The joints are kept flush by means of two cross tongues, as shown in the plan of the joint (Fig. 36). These methods are the most common practice in curved work.

Cramps and Cramping

WHEN assembling work, especially furniture, it is often necessary to have recourse to mechanical aid for the purpose of forcing the joints together, or for holding them during such time as the glue is setting, or nails, screws, pins or wedges etc., are being inserted. Appliances used for this purpose are termed cramps, and they are made in a very extensive range of patterns which gives them a wide field of application. Not only are they of use during the fitting together of work, but frequently also whilst it is being shaped.

Improvised Cramps.—Formerly it was the custom to improvise wooden cramps, but now most workshops are equipped with a good supply of the various kinds of metal cramps, which saves the time of making wooden cramps, though to the amateur or the craftsman in a small way of business improvised cramps often supply a temporary need which would not warrant the purchase of a metal cramp.

Fig. 1 shows a cramp improvised for the purpose of holding together strips of wood that have been glued. It is made by driving two stout nails—or, better for

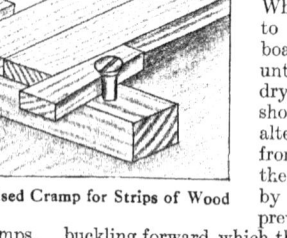

Fig. 1.—Improvised Cramp for Strips of Wood

most purposes, screws—into a strip of wood at a distance apart which is rather more than the width of the two pieces of wood that are to be held together. A wedge is then driven tightly to hold the joint together as indicated in the illustration.

It often occurs that a strip of hardwood has to be glued to a softwood piece. After being glued the two can be held firmly together until the glue sets by small cleat cramps and wedges at frequent intervals as clearly shown by Fig. 2. When it is desired to hold several boards together until the glue is dry, the cramps should be arranged alternatively on the front and back of the boards, as shown by Fig. 3, so as to prevent them from buckling forward which they tend to do.

Fig. 4 shows a good method of forcing together the edges of floorboards ready for nailing. A batten is nailed or screwed to two or three joists, and a piece of wood is placed against the edge of the front floorboard as shown. Wedges are then driven until the joints of the boards are up close. When it is required to glue and "wedge up" a number of sashes or light doors, a pair of wooden cramps may be made and fixed

CRAMPS AND CRAMPING

to a bench, as shown in Fig. 5. In making this cramp it is important that the back of the mortise and the splayed end of the cleat should be in the same plane so that the edge of the wedge may fit close to them. This will be understood from Fig. 6.

Another improvised cramp is shown by Fig. 7. This is a very simple and well-known form of cord or rope cramp, and is suitable for holding together the mitred joints of a frame until the glue has become properly set. The same principle of the twisted rope will suggest itself to a number of other applications, such as the holding together of boards placed edge to edge, etc. A piece of iron rod should be used to twist the rope in such a case as the latter, and when this is sufficiently taut the rod can be tied in position.

Wooden Screw Cramps.—Fig. 8 shows a very useful form of small wooden screw cramp suitable for holding together small work. The head and shoe is double-tenoned and mortised to the back, and to give further strength an iron rod provided with a nut at each end passes right through as shown. This cramp is the prototype of the common form of iron G-cramp, and which has largely taken its place

A long bar cramp made of wood, and which used to be very largely used, especially by cabinet-makers, is shown by Fig 9. This also has been almost entirely superseded by the light steel sash cramp described later on. Two methods of attaching the screw head firmly to the bar are shown by Figs. 10 and 11. In Fig. 10 it will be seen that a metal strip that embraces the screw head is used. The alternative method (Fig. 11) is by means of a bolt and nut. As is clearly shown, the nut is let into the bar from the top, a hole having previously been drilled longitudinally to meet it.

When cramping up thin flat work it is usually necessary to provide some means of support or stiffener in order to prevent the stuff buckling and doubling up. In addition to a support being necessary it is essential that the jaws of the cramp should work parallel to each other. A cramp that fulfils these conditions is shown by Fig. 12. It can be suitably used for thin panel material or light framing. Adjustment for large

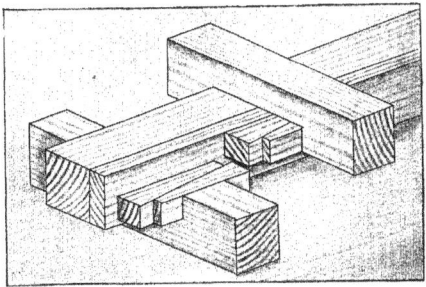

Fig. 2.—Another Form of Improvised Cramp for Strips

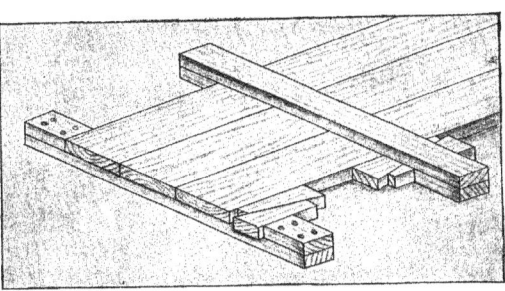

Fig. 3.—Improvised Cramp for Boards

or small work is provided by the series of peg holes in the longitudinal bars.

Probably the form of wooden screw cramp most commonly used at the present

THE PRACTICAL WOODWORKER

day is the double-jaw hand-screw shown by Fig. 13. This form of cramp lends itself to such a variety of purposes and is so simple of application that it has never been ousted by the metal cramps. A modification and improvement of this type of cramp is the Jorgensen hand-screw snown by Fig. 14. This is so made that the jaws can be operated at various angles, a feature extending the scope of its application to cramping surfaces whose edges are not parallel.

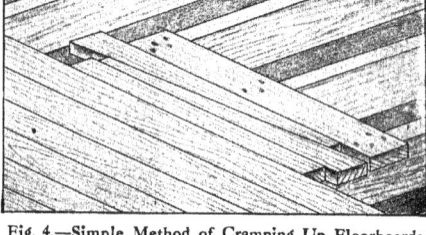

Fig. 4.—Simple Method of Cramping Up Floorboards

A very good form of gig cramp for use when it is required to have curved parts built up of two or more thicknesses of wood is shown by Figs. 15 and 16. The thin layers of material are glued and bent, forced into and held in position, as shown in Fig. 16. The bent piece of work is shown by Fig. 17. It will be noticed that the bolts are long and have screw threads on for at least half their length.

Metal Cramps.—The most commonly used metal cramp is the ordinary G-cramp shown by Fig. 18. This type is so well known that it needs no description. A couple of instances of its use are given later, and as it can be adapted to such a variety of situations, further suggestions are unnecessary. The same remarks also almost apply with regard to the bar or sash cramp. Three patterns of this type of cramp are shown by Figs. 19, 20 and 21. The first has a T-section bar, and one jaw of the cramp is made adjustable by means of a metal peg which can be inserted in holes drilled at intervals in the bar. Adjustment of the other two forms is provided by means of a toothed bar and wedge and the difference between these two latter lies in the section of the bar. Fig. 22 shows an extension piece suitable for fitting on a cramp provided with a T-section bar and peg-holes. A pair of fittings, which are so designed that they can be fitted on a bar of wood and thus make a useful bar cramp, are shown by Fig. 23.

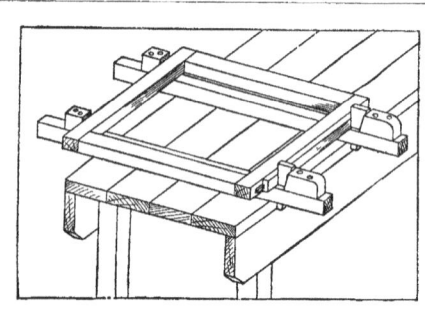

Fig. 5.—Application of Wedge Cramp for Light Framing

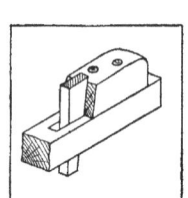

Fig. 6.—Wedge and Cleat

CRAMPS AND CRAMPING

Figs 24 and 25 show two forms of bench holdfast primarily intended for holding work down on the bench, though various other uses for them will suggest themselves according to the nature of the work in hand. In each case the post of the appliance is inserted in a hole in the bench, and a binding action, due to side pressure which results when the work is clamped, holds it firm. It will be seen that the arm of Fig. 25 has a variable reach.

When glue jointing short boards of $\frac{3}{4}$-in. and upwards thickness, iron dogs, as they are usually called, are very useful. As will be seen by Figs 26 and 27 the ends are tapered inwards so that as they are driven in they draw the joint together. They have to be used carefully as they tend to split the wood. Fig. 28 clearly shows the manner in which they are used. Fig. 29 shows an ordinary kind of mitre cramp much in favour. The principal

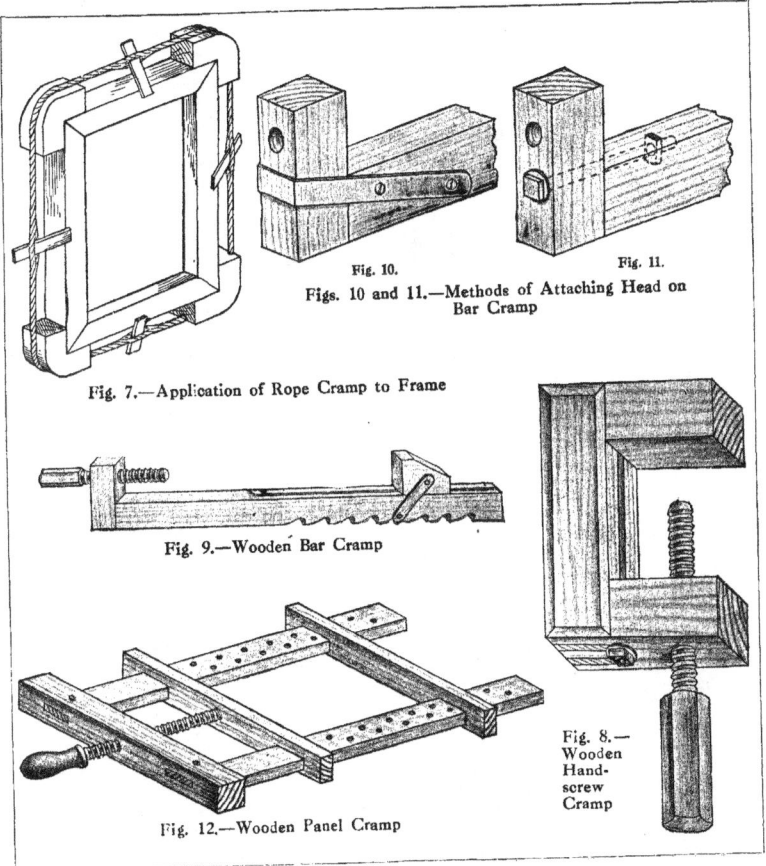

Figs. 10 and 11.—Methods of Attaching Head on Bar Cramp

Fig. 7.—Application of Rope Cramp to Frame

Fig. 9.—Wooden Bar Cramp

Fig. 8.—Wooden Hand-screw Cramp

Fig. 12.—Wooden Panel Cramp

THE PRACTICAL WOODWORKER

advantage of this form of cramp is that the joint can be screwed or nailed whilst being firmly held together by the cramp. The manner of its use is shown by Fig. 30. Fig. 31 illustrates a good kind of cramp of cramps are so obvious that no useful purpose would be served in detailing them, but a few examples are given here of methods which perhaps would not readily suggest themselves. In addition to the

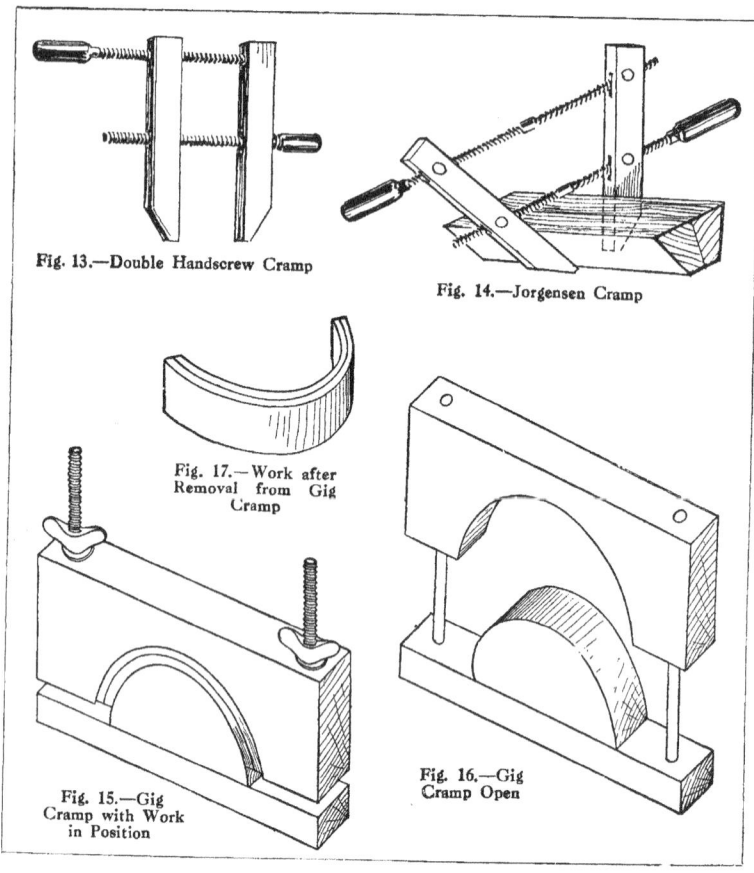

Fig. 13.—Double Handscrew Cramp

Fig. 14.—Jorgensen Cramp

Fig. 17.—Work after Removal from Gig Cramp

Fig. 15.—Gig Cramp with Work in Position

Fig. 16.—Gig Cramp Open

now on the market for cramping up the four mitres of a frame at once. It can be quickly adjusted to any size frame within its limits.

Cramping.—The simpler applications cramp itself it is sometimes necessary to employ improvised accessories for a particular piece of work. Such a case is illustrated by Fig. 32, which shows an ordinary G-cramp being used to cramp the

CRAMPS AND CRAMPING

joints between the curved rails and legs of a small table or stool. Two hardwood cleats are made of a shape similar to that shown in Fig. 33. Then a piece of hoop-iron of the proper length is drilled and countersunk for screws at each end, and then fixed to the cleats as shown. Somewhat similar is the method of cramping up the end of a couch or article of like form by means of a hoop-iron band and

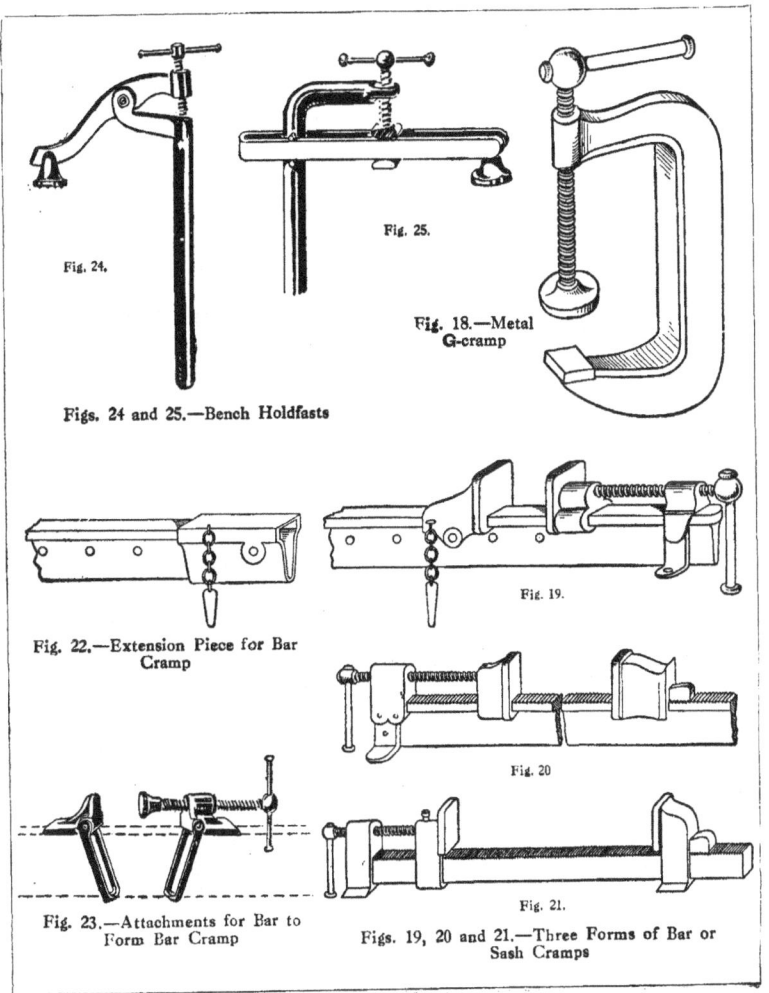

Fig. 24.

Fig. 25.

Fig. 18.—Metal G-cramp

Figs. 24 and 25.—Bench Holdfasts

Fig. 22.—Extension Piece for Bar Cramp

Fig. 19.

Fig. 20

Fig. 23.—Attachments for Bar to Form Bar Cramp

Fig. 21.

Figs. 19, 20 and 21.—Three Forms of Bar or Sash Cramps

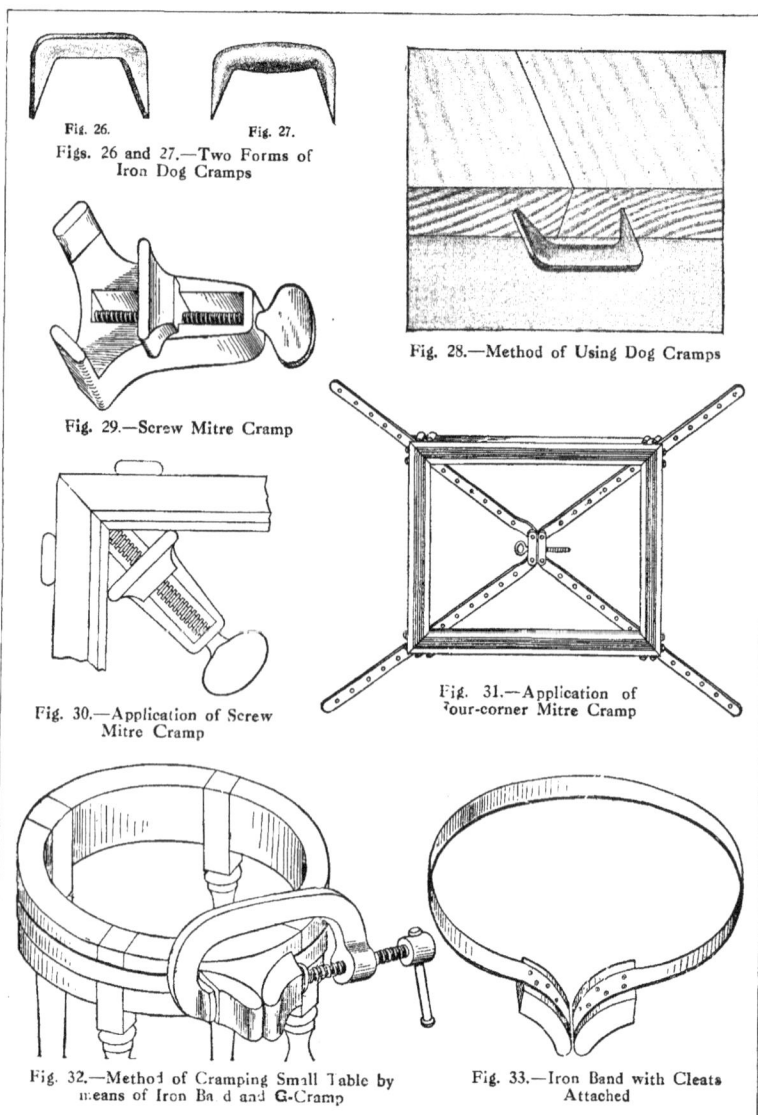

Fig. 26. Fig. 27.
Figs. 26 and 27.—Two Forms of Iron Dog Cramps

Fig. 28.—Method of Using Dog Cramps

Fig. 29.—Screw Mitre Cramp

Fig. 30.—Application of Screw Mitre Cramp

Fig. 31.—Application of Four-corner Mitre Cramp

Fig. 32.—Method of Cramping Small Table by means of Iron Band and G-Cramp

Fig. 33.—Iron Band with Cleats Attached

CRAMPS AND CRAMPING

cleats which are held by a long iron or wooden cramp fastened on each side as illustrated (Fig. 34). Flexible iron bands are also useful under conditions such as are illustrated by Fig. 35. The band should be a piece of hoop-iron 1 in. to 1½ in. wide. The shanks of a couple of ½ in. bolts are filed partly flat or sawn down for

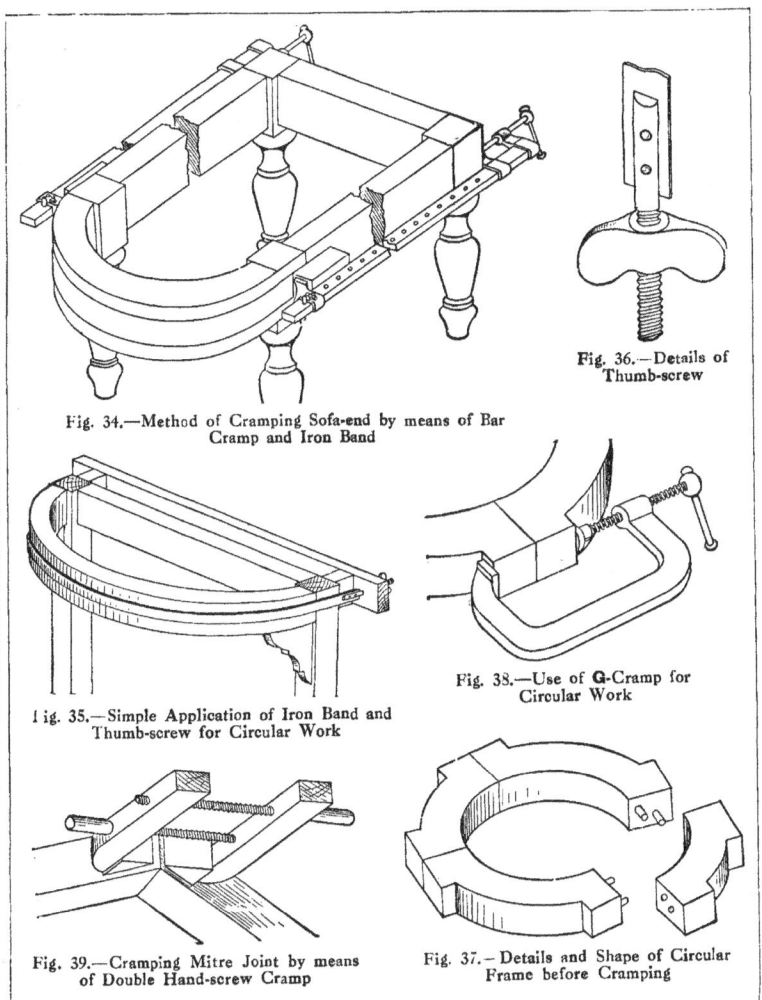

Fig. 34.—Method of Cramping Sofa-end by means of Bar Cramp and Iron Band

Fig. 36.—Details of Thumb-screw

Fig. 35.—Simple Application of Iron Band and Thumb-screw for Circular Work

Fig. 38.—Use of G-Cramp for Circular Work

Fig. 39.—Cramping Mitre Joint by means of Double Hand-screw Cramp

Fig. 37.—Details and Shape of Circular Frame before Cramping

about two inches with a hacksaw. These are placed on to the ends of the hoop-iron and holes are drilled through each and rivets inserted ; this will be understood by reference to Fig. 36. Ordinary nuts with a spanner may be used, but good size wing nuts will be found more convenient.

When jointing up circular pieces of framing, similar to that shown by Fig. 37, it is a good plan to cut out the pieces with projecting horns as illustrated. Then the joints should be made and dowelled, after which they can be glued and held firmly by means of G-cramps as shown by Fig. 38. When the glue is set the horns can be cut off and the frame finished.

Fig. 39 shows a good method of cramping up a mitre by means of a hand-screw ; two blocks of wood are cut to shape and glued on and allowed to stand for a few hours ; the joint is then glued and cramped up close and held until the glue is properly set.

Simple Book-racks and Book-shelves

COLLAPSIBLE SLIDING BOOK-RACK

A USEFUL book-rack suitable for table use, and designed to accommodate varying numbers of books and at all times to keep sides, 2 ft. by 9 in. by $\frac{3}{4}$ in. thick; four brass cabinet hinges 1 in. wide; two dozen $\frac{1}{2}$-in. brass screws; a piece of 1-in. by $\frac{1}{16}$-in. strip brass 1 ft. long, similar to that used for bent metalwork.

To make the book-rest, the piece of

Fig 1.—Collapsible Sliding Book-rack

them in an upright position, is shown by Fig. 1.

The choice of the kind of wood to use is a matter of individual taste, but preferably it should be hard. The quantities of materials required would be as follows: Base, 1 ft. 10 in. by 10 in. by 1 in. thick; wood 1 in. thick is sawn into three strips, two of which should be 2½ in. wide and one 5 in. wide. These will be seen on reference to Fig. 2. They are then planed true to the finished dimensions, and the two pieces forming the sides grooved, as shown in Fig. 3. The centre portion or slide is

THE PRACTICAL WOODWORKER

rebated four times or sunk at each of its edges (*see* Fig. 3). These operations are carried out usually with tenon saw, chisel, mallet, and rebate plane. The pieces should fit tightly but easily into each other. However, should they stick or jar, a little ordinary blacklead (as used in the cleaning of fire-grates) applied to the grooves and slide will help matters considerably.

It can be cut out by means of a bow saw, finished on the outside with a spokeshave, and pared down on the perforation and small parts with a chisel all kept true or square to the surface.

The preparation of the sides for the other style consists simply of planing the wood true to the sizes given, perforating the diamond pattern with the brace and centre-bit and paring down with a sharp

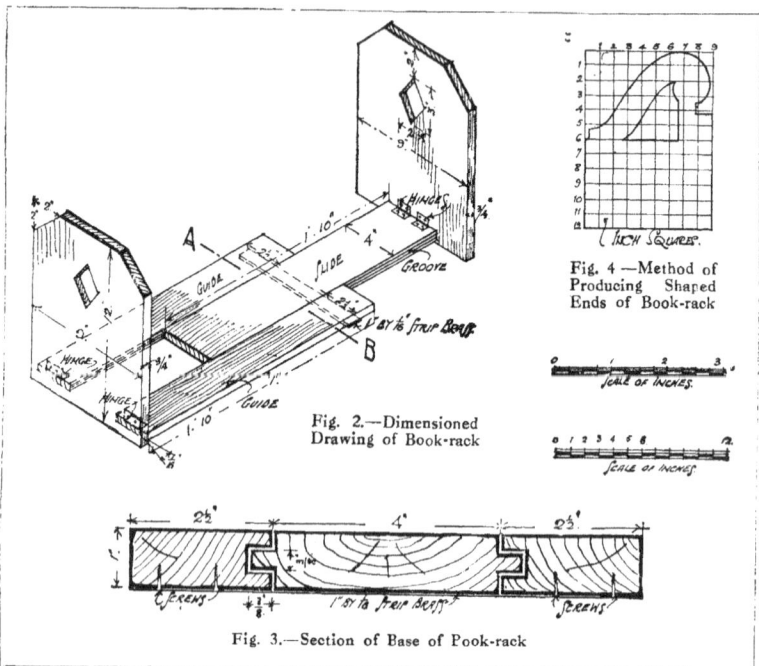

Fig. 2.—Dimensioned Drawing of Book-rack

Fig. 3.—Section of Base of Book-rack

Fig. 4.—Method of Producing Shaped Ends of Book-rack

Alternative designs for the end pieces are shown, one style being that shown by the photograph, and the other in the dimensioned drawing (Fig. 2). The first design for the ends is shown by Fig. 4, and it will be seen that it is produced in a series of 1-in. squares to enable it to be drawn in outline on the piece of wood by following the intersections of the curves on same.

bevelled-edge chisel. The corners are cut off to 2 in. each way. The hinging of the sides to the guides and slide is shown in Fig. 2, and it will be noticed that they project $\frac{1}{16}$ in. below the base to compensate for the thickness of the strip of brass introduced to prevent the guide from spreading or getting out of position. Obviously this allows the rest to stand evenly. The brass is drilled and screwed to the underside of the guides, the former being done with an archimedean drill. For convenience of packing away, the dimensions of the sides are so arranged that they will fall exactly on to the base, and so occupy the least possible space.

EASILY-MADE HANGING BOOK-RACK

The book-rack shown by Fig. 5 has been specially designed to accommodate the ordinary low-priced pocket novel. Its construction is simple, and makes but moderate demands in the way of skill and tools, and if neatly made will form a useful article of furniture for the wall or mantel-shelf.

The top is of $\frac{5}{8}$-in. stuff; the sides, shelf, and brackets are of $\frac{1}{2}$-in. stuff (finished thicknesses); and the back is of three-ply or fretwood $\frac{1}{8}$ in. thick. It may be made of pine or clean sound deal, and painted and enamelled any colour; or any furniture hardwood, such as oak, walnut, or mahogany, may be used, and the job either left clean or french-polished as desired.

All dimensions are indicated on the working diagrams (Figs. 6 to 10). The material required for the job is as follows: Top, 2 ft. 6 in. by $6\frac{3}{8}$ in. by $\frac{5}{8}$ in.; shelf, 2 ft. 3 in. by $5\frac{1}{2}$ in. by $\frac{1}{2}$ in.; sides (to cut two), 1 ft. $10\frac{1}{4}$ in. by $5\frac{1}{2}$ in. by $\frac{1}{2}$ in.; brackets (to cut four), 1 ft. by 9 in. by $\frac{1}{2}$ in.; back (including slight allowance for trimming), 2 ft. by 1 ft. by $\frac{1}{8}$ in. There will also be required a few $1\frac{1}{2}$-in. and $\frac{5}{8}$-in. wire brads, and four 1-in. No. 6 screws. The four ornamental side brackets (Fig. 9)

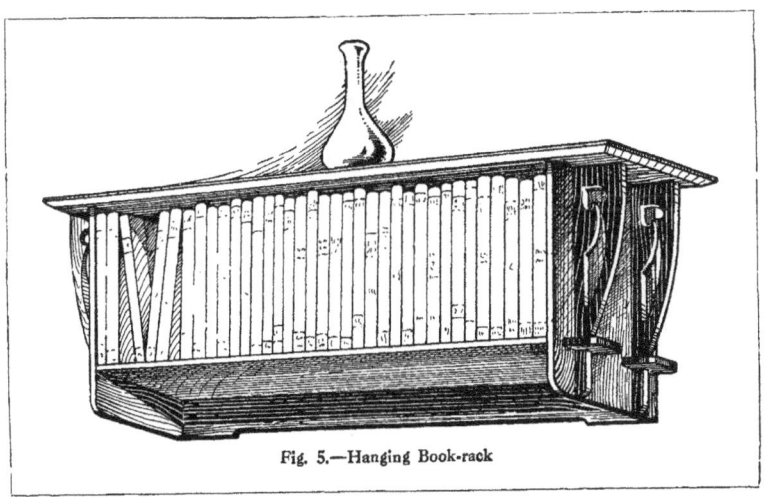

Fig. 5.—Hanging Book-rack

should be fret-sawn to shape and perforated, and the lower or wedge part left rather more than the figured size of $\frac{5}{8}$ in. wide to allow for subsequent fitting. Two tenons are formed at each end of the shelf as shown, and these project through corresponding mortises cut in the sides of the book-shelf, to which the shelf is secured by means of the bracket wedges passing through the slots made in the shelf tenons. The dimensions for these tenons and slots are given on the plan and side views (Figs. 7 and 8), and in fitting the brackets the lower portion should be slightly tapered, so that when gently tapped home in the slots they will act as wedges and draw the shelf and sides tightly together. If this fitting is carefully done no other fixing at this part will be necessary. One 1-in. No. 6 screw placed in each bracket where indicated in the front view (Fig. 6) will completely secure these useful overmantel members in position after they are well home in the slots.

driven through the top into each bracket, a hole being first bored with a bradawl for these particular brads, to avoid the risk of splitting the brackets. Of course, the top can only be put on after the shelf, sides, and brackets are all assembled. This done, the only part of the job remaining is the preparing and fixing of the back, and before beginning this take a try-square and see that the book-rack is "square," that is, the shelf and top must form a right angle with the sides. Then lay the book-

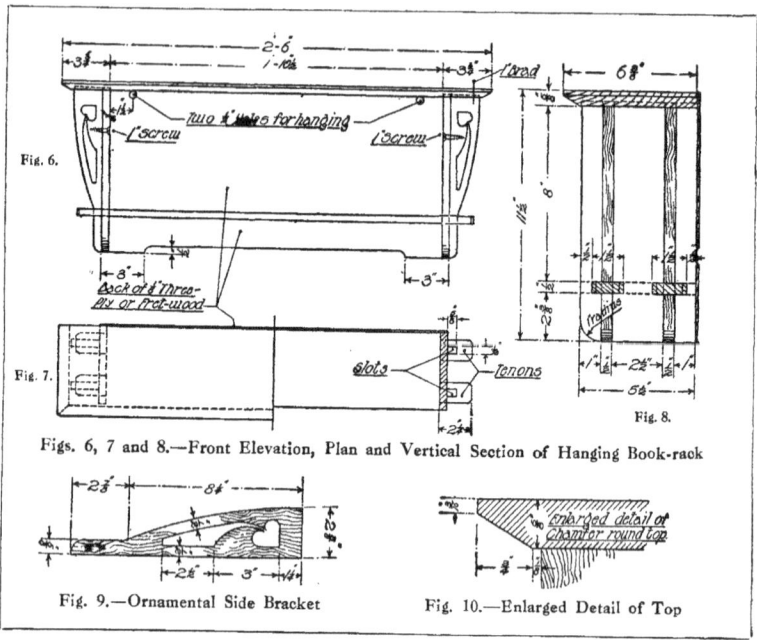

Figs. 6, 7 and 8.—Front Elevation, Plan and Vertical Section of Hanging Book-rack

Fig. 9.—Ornamental Side Bracket

Fig. 10.—Enlarged Detail of Top

The top of the book-rack is chamfered off on the front edge and two ends (see enlarged detail, Fig. 10). The upper ends of the two sides and of the four brackets should be housed (let in) to the top to a depth of ¼ in. (see dotted lines in the front and side views, Figs. 6 and 8), and secured by means of glue and some of the 1½-in. wire brads. One of these brads should be

rack down with its back edges flat on the ⅛-in. three-ply or fretwood, mark with a pencil round the outside of the sides and top to get the exact outside size ; also mark off the positions of the two ½-in. holes for the nails on which the book-rack is to hang, and the simple shaped piece at the bottom edge. Cut the back to the pencil lines, bore the two holes, and saw

BOOK-RACKS AND SHELVES

out the shaping, and fix the back in position on the back edges of top, shelf, and sides with the ⅝-in. brads spaced about 2 in. apart. The whole will then be perfectly rigid.

If it is decided to finish off with paint and enamel, the brads in the top should be punched about ⅛ in. below the surface, and these brad-holes stopped with putty after the first coat of paint has been applied. Two coats of paint, followed by a coat of enamel, will give a very satisfactory finish, except in the case of white or cream being

house, or for the purpose of keeping a few favourites close at hand, is shown by Fig. 11. Front and end elevations and plan are shown by Figs. 12, 13 and 14 respectively.

The shelves and the four upright members are finished ⅜ in. thick, the top is ⅞ in. thick, and the back panel is of ¼-in. fretwood. The three shelves are housed, glued, and bradded to the uprights, the housings being stopped ⅜ in. from the front edge of the latter. A detail of the central shelf is given (Fig. 15), from

Fig. 11.—Small Partitioned Book-rack

selected, in which case the enamel should be preceded by three coats of paint. It is advisable to omit the enamel from the inside of the book-rack, as books are always inclined to stick on enamelled surfaces.

SMALL PARTITIONED BOOK-RACK

Another book-rack suitable for the accommodation of the smaller-sized odd volumes which frequently lie about the

which it will be seen that it is shaped and moulded on its front edge. The moulding is similar to that detailed for planting on the side shelves and is returned on to the edge of the uprights. Housings are formed in the top to receive the ends of the uprights, these housings being stopped 1⅞ in. back from its front edge, which together with the two ends is moulded as detailed. The back edge is rebated for the back panel, as are also the two outside uprights, and is attached to all the back

THE PRACTICAL WOODWORKER

edges of the bookcase with brads. The top rail, finished with a ¼-in. bead, is let in flush with the front edge of uprights, and here it should be noted that the joint where this rail is let in should be so arranged as to be concealed by the cornice moulding when this is in position. A portion of the cornice moulding is shown broken away in the front view to make this point clear.

the exact length of the front and ends, but they should be approximately ½ in. wide with spaces ¼ in. wide between. The spandril piece under the central shelf (Fig. 16) is ¼ in. thick, and is fixed ⅜ in. back from the front edge of the upright with glue and pins and some small angle-blocks. There are, in addition, spandrils under the side shelves, but they are only ⅛ in. thick and are set back ⅛ in. only, and

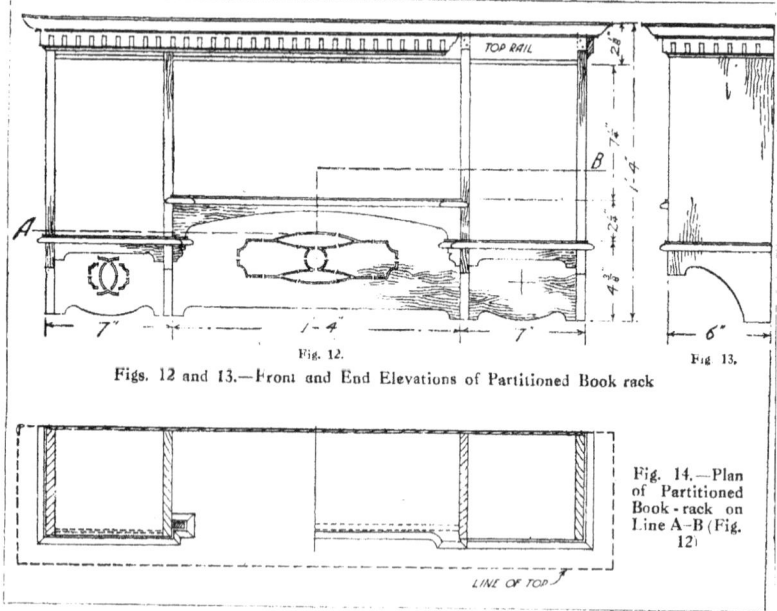

Figs. 12 and 13.—Front and End Elevations of Partitioned Book rack

Fig. 14.—Plan of Partitioned Book-rack on Line A–B (Fig. 12)

On reference to the detail of the top and cornice moulding (Fig. 17), it will be seen that the latter is made in two pieces. The dentils are formed on the 13/16-in. by 5/16-in. strip by first rebating out and moulding the lower portion, and then cross-cutting the upper part with a fine saw, removing the spaces between the blocks with a ¼-in. chisel. The 5/16-in. by 3/16-in. slip c is then glued on to complete the moulding. Care must be taken to set the dentils out to suit

are glued and pinned in place as before. A small moulding, as detailed (Fig. 18), is glued and pinned to the front edge of the side shelves, and is carried round the ends of the bookcase and mitred round the lower portions of the central spandril piece, as shown in the sectional plan.

The curved parts and fretwork are given in a detail (Fig. 16) set out on ½-in. squares. The design in the back panel is formed by perforations ⅛ in. wide, and is

BOOK-RACKS AND BOOK-SHELVES

afterwards backed with red silk. For convenience in fretting out the design, the back panel should be made in two pieces, stuff to use; preferably it should be stained black with ebony stain and wax-polished, the grain being left open and not

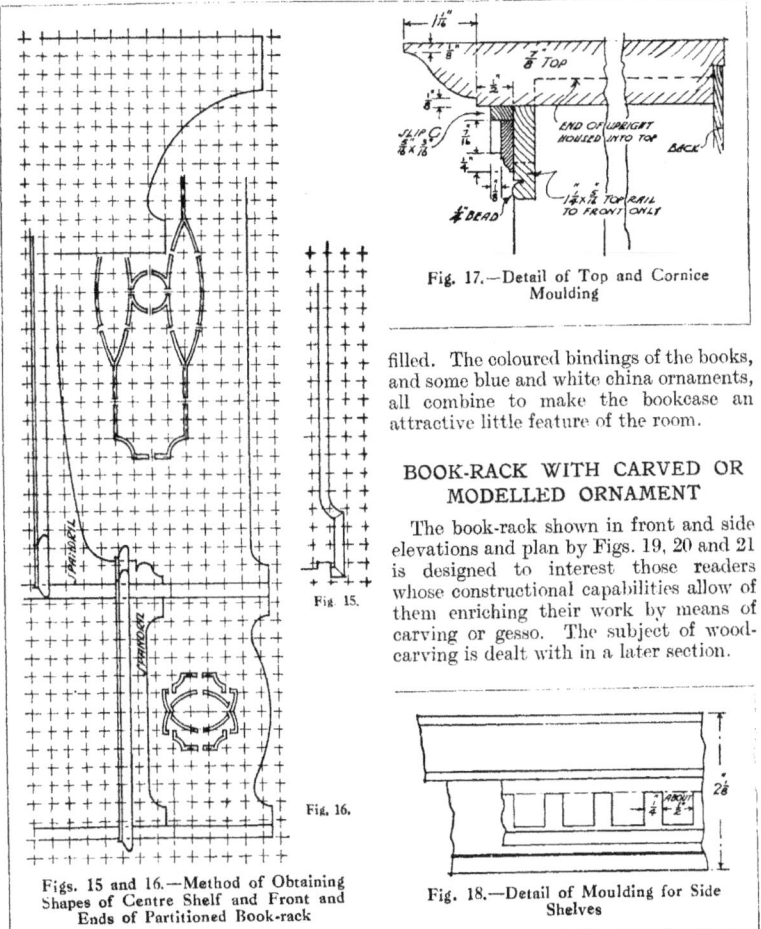

Fig. 17.—Detail of Top and Cornice Moulding

Fig. 15.

Fig. 16.

Figs. 15 and 16.—Method of Obtaining Shapes of Centre Shelf and Front and Ends of Partitioned Book-rack

Fig. 18.—Detail of Moulding for Side Shelves

filled. The coloured bindings of the books, and some blue and white china ornaments, all combine to make the bookcase an attractive little feature of the room.

BOOK-RACK WITH CARVED OR MODELLED ORNAMENT

The book-rack shown in front and side elevations and plan by Figs. 19, 20 and 21 is designed to interest those readers whose constructional capabilities allow of them enriching their work by means of carving or gesso. The subject of wood-carving is dealt with in a later section.

the joint being arranged to come behind the central shelf.

Figured oak would be very suitable

The shelves comprise sides, a thin back shaped at the bottom, as at A (Fig. 19), a top with moulded projecting edges, a

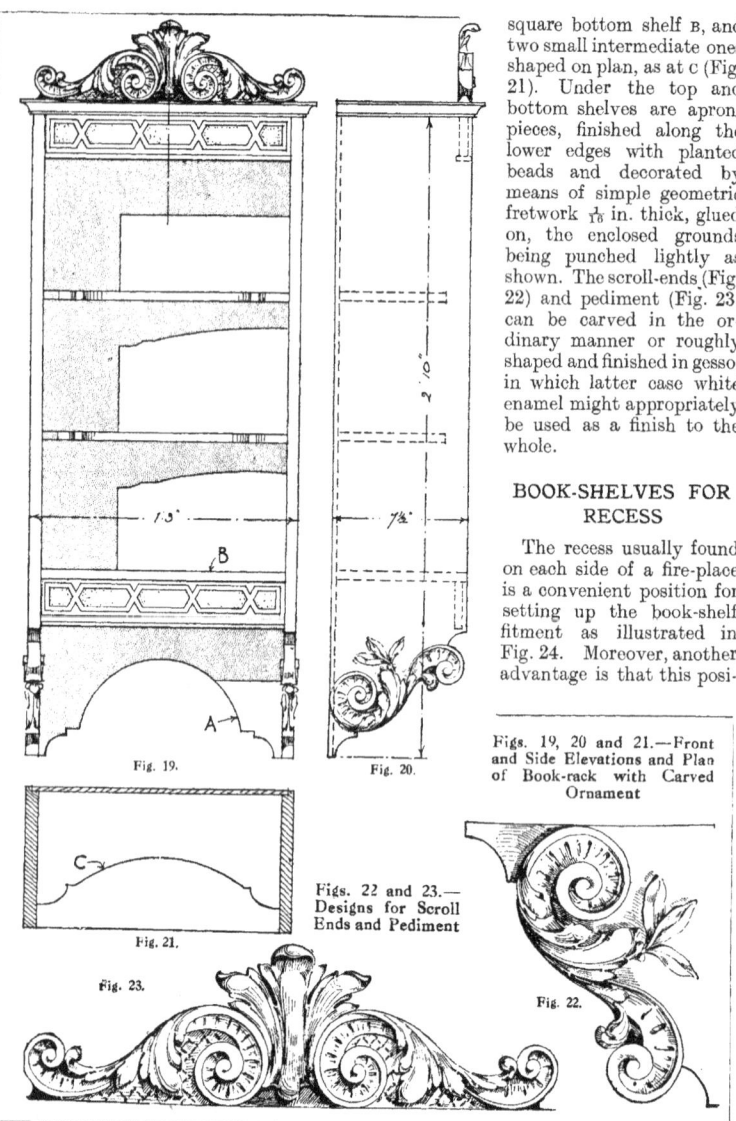

square bottom shelf B, and two small intermediate ones shaped on plan, as at C (Fig. 21). Under the top and bottom shelves are apron-pieces, finished along the lower edges with planted beads and decorated by means of simple geometric fretwork $\frac{1}{16}$ in. thick, glued on, the enclosed grounds being punched lightly as shown. The scroll-ends (Fig. 22) and pediment (Fig. 23) can be carved in the ordinary manner or roughly shaped and finished in gesso, in which latter case white enamel might appropriately be used as a finish to the whole.

BOOK-SHELVES FOR RECESS

The recess usually found on each side of a fire-place is a convenient position for setting up the book-shelf fitment as illustrated in Fig. 24. Moreover, another advantage is that this posi-

Figs. 19, 20 and 21.—Front and Side Elevations and Plan of Book-rack with Carved Ornament

Figs. 22 and 23.—Designs for Scroll Ends and Pediment

tion is generally the driest in the room. The design given is of quite a simple character, for the entire construction can be made without mortise-and-tenon or dovetail joints, enabling the whole to be readily taken apart for removal. The timber suggested is American whitewood "faced up" with walnut or some other hardwood, such as oak or mahogany.

Fig. 25 is a front elevation of the fitment in a recess 3 ft. 9 in. wide and 1 ft. 2 in. deep, with a total height of 6 ft. 9 in. from the floor to the top of the cornice; but these dimensions may be modified to suit a larger or smaller opening. If the room has a picture moulding, a good plan is to make the top of the cornice to line with the under edge of the moulding. It will be clear from the sectional view (Fig. 26) that the fitment is arranged in two parts. The lower portion, which is $11\frac{1}{2}$ in. deep and 3 ft. 3 in. high, terminates at the moulded shelf, and provides accommodation for large bound volumes, atlases, etc. The upper portion is made $7\frac{1}{4}$ in. deep for the smaller books. For the lower sides, prepare two pieces of whitewood each 3 ft. 2 in. by $10\frac{7}{8}$ in. by $\frac{7}{8}$ in., and proceed to tongue and groove to the front edge of each a strip of walnut $1\frac{3}{4}$ in. wide and $\frac{7}{8}$ in. thick, as indicated in Fig. 27. This piece of walnut, besides improving the appearance, facilitates the fitting of the sides to any irregularities in the walls. The pilasters cause a space of 1 in. between the sides and the walls, which is easily filled by screwing two battens each $10\frac{1}{2}$ in. by $1\frac{1}{2}$ in. by 1 in. to the back of each side.

For the moulded shelf, which forms the division between the upper and lower portions, plane a piece of walnut 1 ft. $\frac{1}{2}$ in. wide and $\frac{7}{8}$ in. thick, and, after moulding the front edge, glue and screw to the underside a 2-in. strip of walnut to form an under moulding. Carefully cut this shelf to fit between the walls, and notch a piece from each of the upright sides to make room for the under moulding; a detail is shown by Fig. 28.

The sides of the upper portion are made in a similar manner to the lower sides, the whitewood being cut to 3 ft. $5\frac{5}{8}$ in. long and $6\frac{7}{8}$ in. wide before being tongued to the pilasters. It will, however, be observed, as shown in Fig. 29, that the whitewood sides project $3\frac{3}{8}$ in. above the tops of the pilasters, in order that the tongues may receive the cornice front. This cornice

Fig. 24.—Book-shelves for Recess

consists of a length of whitewood $3\frac{3}{8}$ in. deep by $\frac{5}{8}$ in. thick, "faced up" by gluing on lengths of walnut moulded to the section given in Fig. 30. Notice that the top moulding projects $\frac{3}{8}$ in. above the whitewood, thus forming a rebate, into which a $\frac{3}{8}$-in. dust-board is afterwards screwed. Fig. 31 shows the position of the groove that is cut at each end of the cornice back, to fit the tongues on each side, as indicated in Fig. 31. Make all the shelves of whitewood to finish a full $\frac{7}{8}$ in. thick, facing the front edges with $\frac{3}{8}$-in. walnut. The finished width for the upper shelves is $6\frac{3}{4}$ in., and for the lower ones $10\frac{7}{8}$ in. Fig. 32 is a detail of the $2\frac{3}{4}$-in. by $\frac{1}{2}$-in. curved piece, which is tongued to

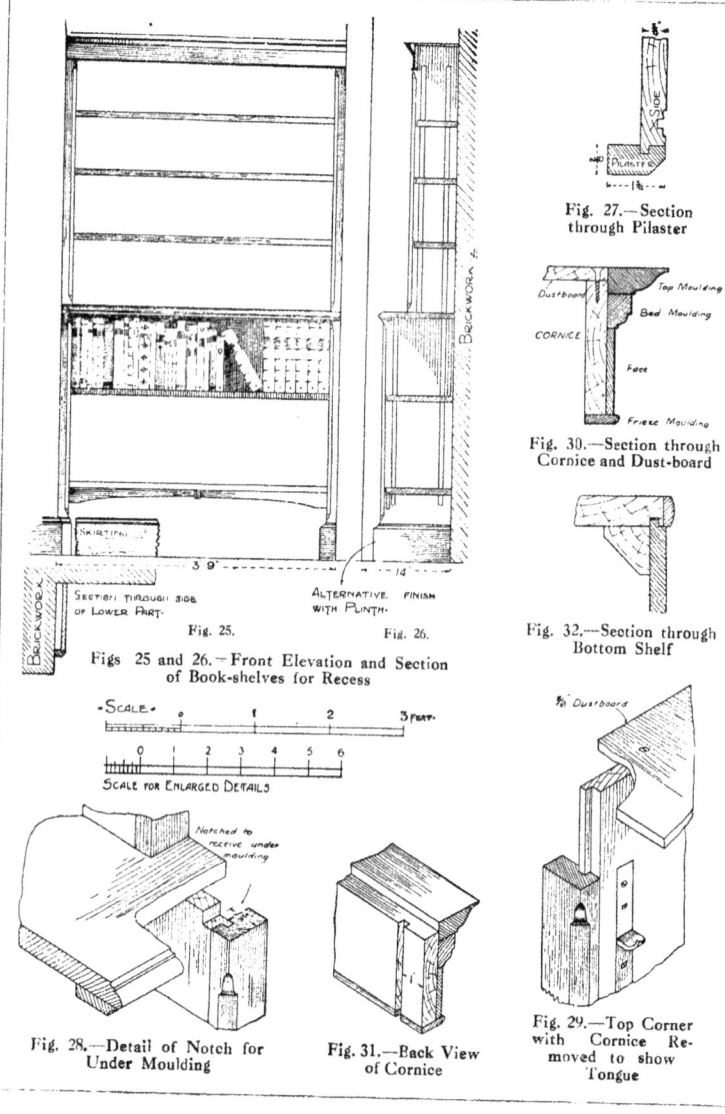

BOOK-RACKS AND BOOK-SHELVES

the underside of the bottom shelf, and strengthened with blocks which may be glued at the back. The moulded shelf, a

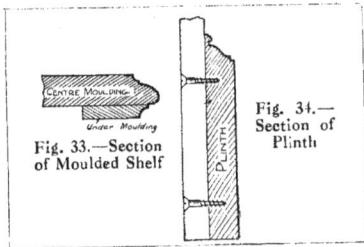

Fig. 33.—Section of Moulded Shelf

Fig. 34.—Section of Plinth

section of which is shown by Fig. 33, and which forms the division between the upper and lower portions, is, of course, a fixture; but all other shelves (including the bottom one) are adjustable. For supporting the shelves strips of metal, called ladders, are screwed into grooves shaped as shown in Fig. 27, which are ploughed in the side pieces. These ladders are pierced with small holes at regular distances of about 1 in., and small metal supports are inserted for the shelves to rest upon, as illustrated in Fig. 29.

If the room has a **skirting** board, the pilasters should be scribed over it, and a finish obtained by working, moulding, and mitreing a length of skirting along the sides. Should there be no skirting board, a neater finish can be made by mitreing and screwing (from the back) a 6-in. plinth of walnut, details of which are shown by Fig. 34. The appearance of the pilasters is improved by working a ½-in. stop-chamfer on the edges, and when this is accomplished the whole will be ready for finishing prior to finally setting up the parts in position. After staining the whitewood to match the walnut, finish the whole with either french or wax-polish, according to choice.

Proceed to set up in position as follows: First place the lower sides against the walls, and screw down the wide moulded shelf to them. The screw-heads will be covered by placing the upper sides into position, after which fit the cornice on to the tongues, and screw the 7¼-in. by ⅜-in.

dust-board into the cornice rebate and also into the top of the upper sides. Finally insert the metal supports into the ladders, and place the shelves as required. If the work has been carried out as described there should be no need to screw the sides to the walls. The position and number of shelves is a matter of choice, for any shelf not in use can be placed on the top of the dust-board. The fitment can be quickly taken to pieces for removal in the following order: (1) Remove all shelves and metal supports; (2) unscrew and remove the dust-board and the cornice; (3) remove the upper sides; (4) unscrew and remove the moulded shelf and, lastly the lower sides.

MOVABLE SHELVES FOR BOOKCASES

In making bookshelves or cases it is always an advantage to have the shelves adjustable to any size of books. There are various methods of doing this.

Figs. 35 to 38 show a very simple way. This is done by boring two rows of small holes (about ⅜ in.) up the inner sides of the case ends, about 1½ in. from the front and back edges, to take iron pins (see Figs. 37 and 38). Instead of the iron pins, fillets of wood 1 in. wide by ¼ in. thick, with two wood dowels, are sometimes used (see Fig. 39). It is seldom necessary to have

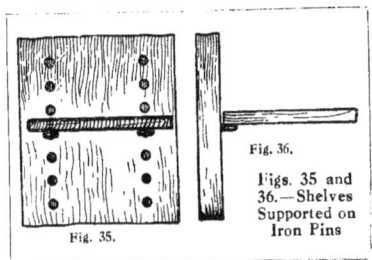

Fig. 35.

Fig. 36.

Figs. 35 and 36.—Shelves Supported on Iron Pins

a shelf nearer than 7 in. from the top and bottom. This system is easily carried out, but is only advisable when the case ends are of hardwood and suitable thickness.

THE PRACTICAL WOODWORKER

Another method is shown by Figs. 40 and 41. For this, four slips of wood are prepared the length of the inside ends, by 1¼ in. wide and ½ in. thick. They are placed together evenly and square, to be temporarily nailed for marking and cutting all of the steps at the same time. Mark square across the four edges at 1¼ in. apart, leaving 7 in. plain at each end. Run a ⅜-in. gauge line on both sides from the marked edges, cut the marks with a fine saw to the gauge lines, and with a sharp chisel make the steps. In fixing to the case sides, one of the shelf supports should be used to get the slips the correct distance apart. Fig. 42 shows a more expeditious way of making the slips. Two lengths must be got out 2½ in. wide by ½ in. thick, placed evenly together, and temporarily nailed. A gauge line is run along each side exactly central; then with a pair of compasses set to 1¼ in., mark along the gauge line. At these points bore holes with a ⅞-in. clean-cutting centre-bit (see Fig. 43), then divide at the gauge line. In fixing the slips in open bookcases, the front ones should be rounded as shown in Fig. 44; or if left square, the case ends should have a bead run on to break the joint (see Fig. 45).

Figs. 46, 47 and 48 show different methods of fixing the leather edging to shelves. In Fig. 46 are shown slips of wood ½ in. square in section, which are nailed on the underside, about ⅛ in. from the corner of the rounded edge, the leather edging being fixed with glue. Fig. 47 shows the upper edge of the leather held between the shelf and the slip, which is screwed on, no glue being required. Fig. 48 shows the shelves grooved, the edging being wedged in with the slip.

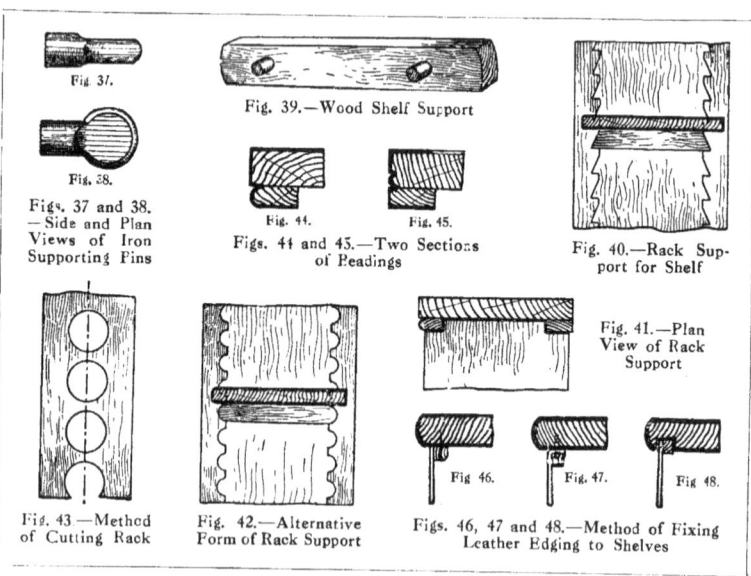

Fig. 37.
Fig. 38.
Figs. 37 and 38.—Side and Plan Views of Iron Supporting Pins

Fig. 39.—Wood Shelf Support

Fig. 44.
Fig. 45.
Figs. 44 and 45.—Two Sections of Beadings

Fig. 40.—Rack Support for Shelf

Fig. 41.—Plan View of Rack Support

Fig. 46.
Fig. 47.
Fig. 48.

Fig. 43.—Method of Cutting Rack

Fig. 42.—Alternative Form of Rack Support

Figs. 46, 47 and 48.—Method of Fixing Leather Edging to Shelves

Dwarf Bookcases

DWARF BOOKCASE WITH GLAZED DOORS

The bookcase as shown in the half-tone reproduction (Fig. 1) is of a quiet design that is not likely to clash with furniture of any period, and in the details and instructions which follow the whole of the work has been made extremely simple. Front and side elevations and plan are shown by Figs. 2, 3 and 4.

The making of the doors presents the only difficulty, and these are open to modification if required. For instance, the diamond arrangement of the glazing bars could be altered to a series of rectangular panes of quite pleasing proportions, by means of one vertical and two horizontal bars to each of the two doors; or, of course, all the bars could be omitted. This would, however, deprive the bookcase of most of its interest as a design, and it is suggested as an alternative that the glazing might be of leaded glass, either in some fairly ordinary decorative manner, or perhaps divided with very broad lead cames into such a simple design as that shown on the right-hand side of Fig. 2.

Fig. 1.—Dwarf Bookcase with Glazed Doors

It is not desired to advocate "short-cut" methods in joinery or cabinet-making; but as it is felt that an inexperienced amateur might hesitate to tackle a piece of work requiring such careful and comparatively minute work as the tenoning together of the doors for this bookcase, the following suggestion may show him a way of circumventing the obstacle. It is simply to mitre the four sides of the doors together, as might be done with a picture-frame; securely done, this does not make a bad job; but, of course, it is far inferior to the traditional method of framing up.

Any material can be used, although, naturally, a hardwood is desirable for any furniture of this class, and the main parts of the construction are given in Fig. 5. Here are seen two upright sides A and B, $9\frac{1}{4}$ in. by 1 in. and 2 ft. $10\frac{1}{2}$ in. long, having a $\frac{1}{2}$-in. by $\frac{1}{2}$-in. rebate down their inner back edges as at C. Two and a quarter inches up from the bottom each upright has a groove $\frac{3}{8}$ in. deep and $\frac{1}{2}$ in.

THE PRACTICAL WOODWORKER

high to receive the tongued end of a bottom shelf 9 in. by 1 in. and 2 ft. 1¾ in. long, as at D (Fig. 6), this joint being afterwards strengthened by means of angle-

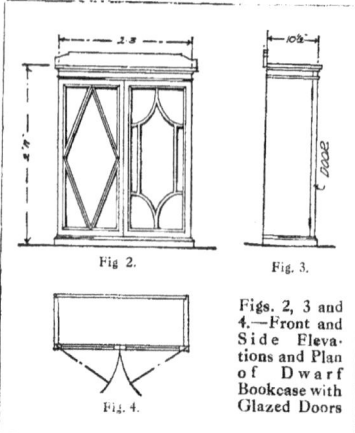

Figs. 2, 3 and 4.—Front and Side Elevations and Plan of Dwarf Bookcase with Glazed Doors

blocks underneath as there shown. Note that the front edge of this piece comes out to the same face as the front edges of the sides, and therefore its back edge should correspond with the front edge of the rebate C. The top shelf, 2 ft. 4¾ in. long and 11⅜ in. by 1 in., has its back edge coinciding with that of each side; but the lower part of this edge is rebated ½ in. by ⅜ in. to receive the back, as in Fig. 7 at G. At a later stage all its sharp angles should be rounded off. At present, however, to obtain a good durable job, the top of each piece should be rebated, so as to leave a tongue ½ in. by ⅜ in. high, which should be let into a groove in the underside of the top, as at E (Fig. 6). This will complete the main structure of the bookcase, and the smaller parts can next be dealt with.

First of all, a light back might be fixed into the rebates in the top and sides, and butted against the back edge of the bottom shelf, as shown at F (Fig. 7). This back might be of ¼-in. stuff, tongued together if possible, and if well fixed it will add a good deal of rigidity to the work as a whole.

The back of the top will ultimately be finished with an upright piece 3½ in. by ½ in. or so and 2 ft. 4¾ in. long, applied as at G (Fig. 7), and shaped at each end to some such contour as the ogee curve indicated at the top of Fig. 6, this piece being, of course, to help fill in the gap next the wall usually caused by the thickness of the skirting board. Any intermediate shelves required across the interior should be about 9 in. by ¾ in., with their ends not fixed, but merely resting on small fillets fixed against the sides, as at H (Fig. 6).

For the front of the bookcase, pieces 2¼ in. by 1 in. and 2 in. by 1 in., as at J and K in Fig. 7, and both 2 ft. 3 in. long, should be fitted against the front faces of the side pieces at the top and bottom, as suggested by the dotted lines at L (Fig. 5). The joint at the top should be carefully secured to avoid its opening subsequently, and it might be fixed by means of small triangular blocks on the inside where out of sight. The top is intended to be finished with a small ovolo moulding under the edge of the projecting shelf, and a very small bead, approximately a quadrant in section, planted on just above the bottom edge of the piece J (Fig. 7). The base is

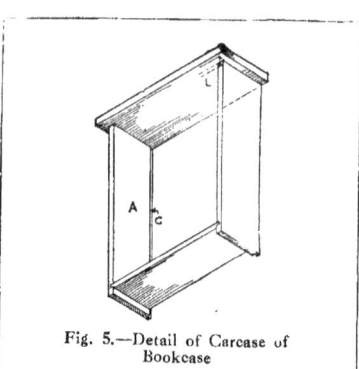

Fig. 5.—Detail of Carcase of Bookcase

finished with a 1¾-in. by ½-in. skirting slightly moulded, and mitred round as shown just a shade above the floor-level.

The doors should be fitted as tightly as

DWARF BOOKCASES

possible in order to exclude dust, and are 1 in. thick, hinged as shown on plan in Fig. 8, which also indicates a small fillet M fixed along the edge of the left-hand door for the other leaf to butt against. A similar fillet will be advisable, as at N (Fig. 7), fixed along the bottom edge of the piece J, and presenting a width of about ⅜ in. to stop the doors. The latter, subject to the remarks previously made, should be possible. For the diamond treatment they should be set out with the points Q and R (Fig. 9), each in a line with the inner edges of the frame. The bars will need very carefully fitting as shown, and it will be best to arrange their ends with neat little projecting tenons let into the frame, as dotted at S and T, and bradded in addition. Without these tenons there is a risk of the bars working loose in time.

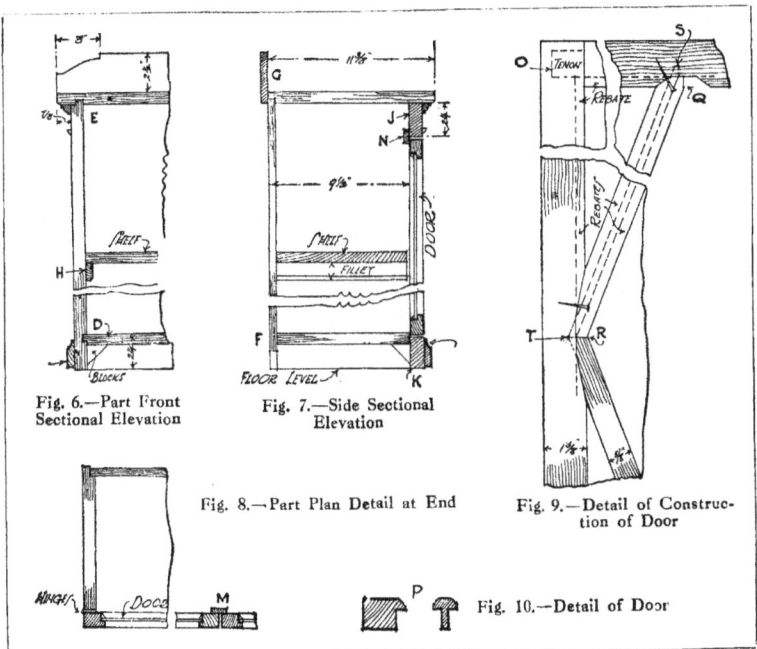

Fig. 6.—Part Front Sectional Elevation

Fig. 7.—Side Sectional Elevation

Fig. 8.—Part Plan Detail at End

Fig. 9.—Detail of Construction of Door

Fig. 10.—Detail of Door

framed up with 1-in. by 1⅜-in. stuff tenoned at the angles, as at O (Fig. 9), and rebated at the back to receive the glazing. If desired, they can be moulded along the front, but it is suggested that any moulding be dispensed with in favour of a square edge slightly rounded off, as at P (Fig. 10). This would also apply to the wooden glazing bars, if these are adopted, in which case they should be kept as light as If a moulded section is preferred, it must be mitred with great care at the intersections, and when the glass is ready to be inserted in the panes, it may be simpler to use putty than fixing-beads.

SMALL BOOKCASE WITH RACK

A bookcase of rather more elaborate design and yet of simple construction is shown by Fig. 11. The illustrations, Figs. 12 to 16, show two elevations, two sections, and plan of the case.

The work could be carried out in any desired wood, and might be elaborated with inlay by the expert cabinet-maker. If preferred, the glazed doors could be omitted. If used, the doors can be rendered decorative by either of the arrangements of glazing bars shown in Fig. 12.

The sides of the main case should finish about 3 ft. 2⅝ in. by 7⅞ in. and 1 in. thick. At a height of 2½ in. above the floor they are connected by a ⅞-in. bottom shelf 8⅝ in. wide, as at A (Fig. 17), 2 ft. 1¾ in. long, and stop-housed into the uprights, leaving ⅜ in. for a back as at B. Later, the bottom will be finished with stout longitudinal bearers, as at C and D, secured with screws and angle-blocks, and a 2¾-in. by ⅝-in. moulded skirting mitred round the ends and front as shown. The sides are stop-housed ⅜ in. deep into a top shelf E (Fig. 17) 2 ft. 3½ in. by 9¾ in., slightly rounded on the exposed edges, overhanging ¼ in. on the ends and the front, but ½ in. at the back, where it is slightly rebated to receive the ⅜-in. back filling, which is fixed horizontally in ⅜-in. by ⅜-in. rebates in the sides, as at F in Fig. 16.

Fig. 11.—Small Bookcase with Rack

The doors are 1⅛ in. thick, or less if hard wood be employed, ovolo moulded and tenoned together in the usual manner, the glass being secured on the inside with small wood fillets. Hinges should be arranged for the doors, as in Fig. 13, and a fillet at the top and rebate at the bottom G and H (Fig. 17) to exclude dust, for which purpose small fillets might also be fixed on the insides of the doors, as at J in Fig. 15, to form a fairly tight joint when closed, these fillets being fixed from the back before it is filled in. The same figure shows a strip at the meeting of the two doors; it should be fixed on the left-hand one to form a rebate. The upper part of the work consists of two ⅞-in. uprights, 11¾ in. long and 6 in. wide, dowelled to the main top shelf, and housed into a smaller shelf K 1⅛ in. thick, and moulded on the solid, as shown in Fig. 17. The whole should be rebated for a back L similar to that below, but overhanging it to the extent of ½ in. At the front is fixed a rail M 1½ in. by ⅝ in., finishing with a thin bead on the underside. A part longitudinal section is given by Fig. 18, and this renders the reading of Fig. 17 easier.

DWARF INLAID BOOKCASE

The dwarf bookcase shown by Fig. 19 is intended to be made in mahogany, and inlaid with boxwood lines and circular corners on the two doors.

The shelves are movable, and can be adjusted to any height (*see* Fig. 20). A

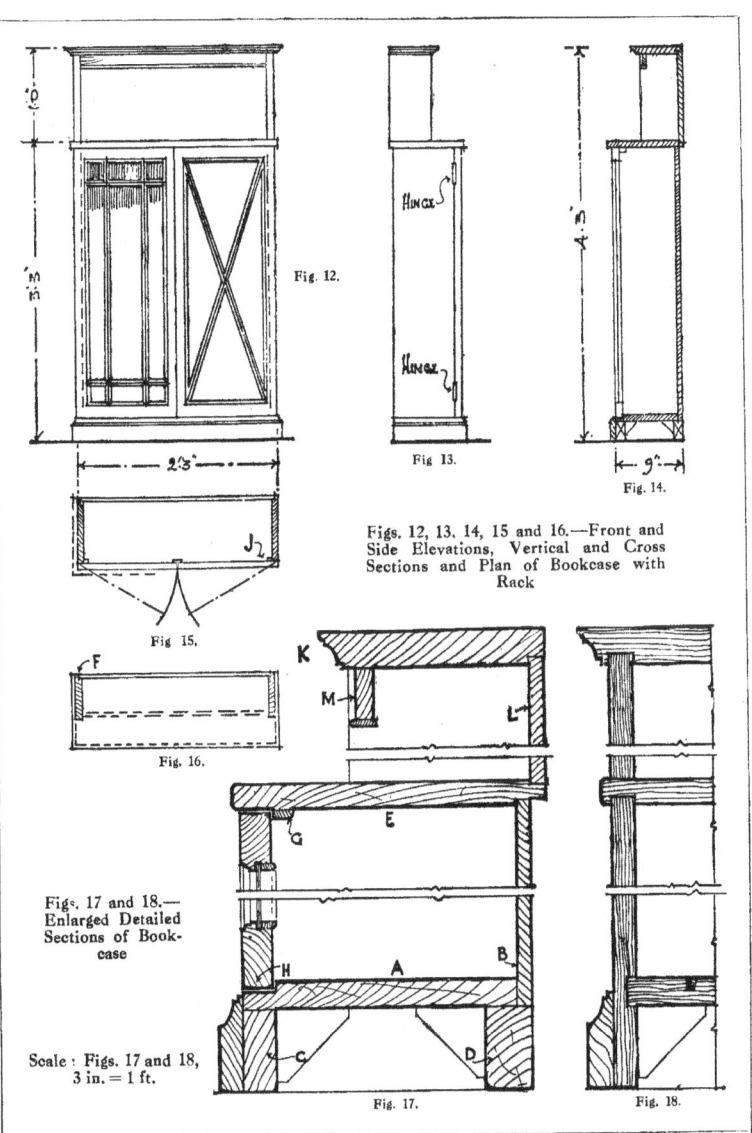

Figs. 12, 13, 14, 15 and 16.—Front and Side Elevations, Vertical and Cross Sections and Plan of Bookcase with Rack

Figs. 17 and 18.—Enlarged Detailed Sections of Bookcase

Scale: Figs. 17 and 18, 3 in. = 1 ft.

middle gable divides the carcase in two, making the shelves stiffer, and giving a more compact arrangement for the books. The length of the bookcase over the doors is 3 ft. 3 in.; height from floor to top, 3 ft.; depth over gables, including doors, 11 in., which gives an inside depth of 9¼ in., allowing ½ in. for the back and 1 in. for the doors. The splayed plinth gives character to the bookcase, and is easily made. Fig. 21 shows the method

dovetail them to receive the top and bottom, which are ⅝ in. thick (see Fig. 23). Rebate the back edges of the gables ½ in. deep for the back. The middle gable is 9½ in. wide by ⅞ in. thick, and is fixed to the top and bottom with square pins mortised through and wedged.

Before gluing the carcase together, the holes should be bored in the end and middle gables for the brass studs which support the movable shelves. Bore them at

Fig. 19.—Dwarf Inlaid Bookcase

of making it up. A pine frame 4 in. deep by ¾ in. thick is dovetailed together, bevelling the front and ends about ½ in. from the perpendicular. Clamps of oak, ¼ in. thick, are glued on the front and ends, mitreing them at the corners, afterwards cutting the front to the shape shown in Fig. 19. Mitre the moulding (Fig. 22) 2½ in. wide by ⅝ in. thick to the top edges of the plinth at the front and ends, and put a few blocks inside to strengthen it. Plane up the two outside gables, 10 in. wide by ⅞ in. thick, and lap-

intervals of 1 in. between the centres. The studs (Fig. 24) are sunk flush with the underside of the shelves to prevent the latter shifting. The edge of the shelf is finished with a moulding. In boring the holes in the middle gable, alter the distance from the edges sufficient to allow the studs to clear each other on the opposite sides. The carcase back shown in the plan (Fig 23) is ½ in. thick, and consists of three muntins grooved to receive the tongues on the panels. Work a small bead on the edges of the panels

DWARF BOOKCASES

to break with the flush joint. The middle muntins should be 5 in. wide and the two end ones 3 in. wide. The top is ¾ in. thick, the finished size over the moulding being 3 ft. 4½ in. long by 1 ft. 1 in. wide. It projects ¾ in. over the ends and front and 1¼ in. over the back. A moulded clamp (Fig. 25) is mitred and glued to the underside of the top. Screws only should be used to fix the ends, so as to allow the top freedom to shrink. The stiles and rails of the two doors (see Fig. 26) are 1½ in. wide by 1 in. thick, except the right-hand stile of the left-hand door, which is kept about ¼ in. wider to underlap the dividing bead. They are mortised and tenoned together, and a small ovolo moulding is worked on the inner edges. Rebate the edges to receive the glass. Work the rebates the same distance on the edges as the moulding, so as to form a square shoulder for the mortise-and-tenon joints (see Fig. 27). The boxwood lines on the doors, as in Fig. 27, are inlaid in the following manner: File a piece of broken saw-blade to the width of the line, and insert it in an easily made router (Fig. 28). Work

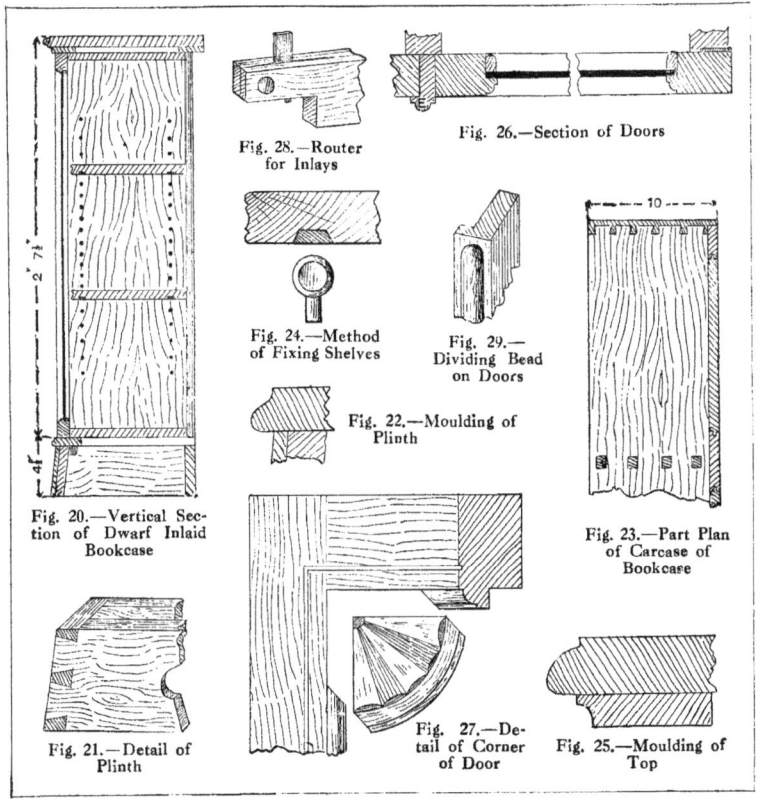

Fig. 28.—Router for Inlays

Fig. 26.—Section of Doors

Fig. 24.—Method of Fixing Shelves

Fig. 29.—Dividing Bead on Doors

Fig. 22.—Moulding of Plinth

Fig. 20.—Vertical Section of Dwarf Inlaid Bookcase

Fig. 23.—Part Plan of Carcase of Bookcase

Fig. 21.—Detail of Plinth

Fig. 27.—Detail of Corner of Door

Fig. 25.—Moulding of Top

the router with a forward motion till the required depth is obtained. Then glue in the lines and mitre them at the corners.

The circular corners shown in Fig. 27 are first turned with the same moulding on the edges as the doors, and the inlay made up of angular strips of boxwood and mahogany veneers. After gluing the corners in position, a piece of cotton glued to the back will strengthen the joint.

The closing bead (Fig. 29) is glued to the edge of the stile on the right-hand door (*see* Fig. 26). It need not be re-

Fig. 30.—Dwarf Bookcase with Shelf

bated until fixed on the door. Fig. 29 shows the finish of the bead at the ends. Use 2½-in. brass butt hinges for the doors. A flush bolt for the left-hand door and a lock for the other door complete the fittings. The glass panels should be thinly bedded in with putty coloured to match the mahogany, and fixed with beads mitred and bradded to the rebated edges of the doors.

All the internal parts of the bookcase (shelves, top and bottom, back and middle gable) may be of pine with slips of mahogany glued to the front edges. In

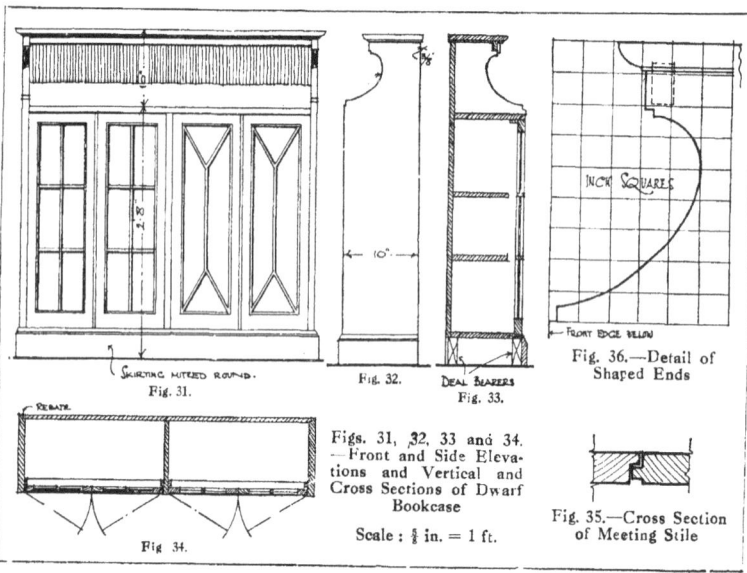

Figs. 31, 32, 33 and 34. — Front and Side Elevations and Vertical and Cross Sections of Dwarf Bookcase

Scale : ⅜ in. = 1 ft.

Fig. 36.—Detail of Shaped Ends

Fig. 35.—Cross Section of Meeting Stile

DWARF BOOKCASES

polishing the bookcase care should be taken to keep the inlays as clear as possible.

Fig. 37.—Curtained Bookcase with Central Glazed Cupboard

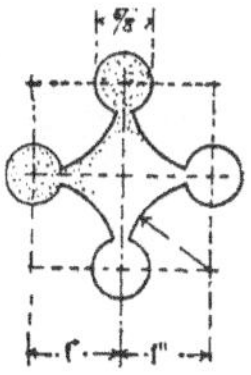

Fig. 43.—Detail of Pierced Ornament

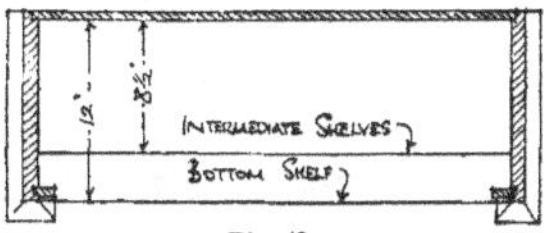

Fig. 42.

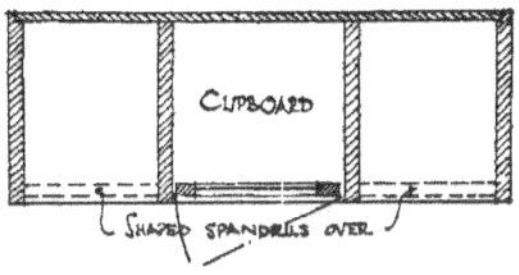

Fig. 41.

Figs. 38 and 39.—Front and Side Elevations
Fig. 40.—Vertical Section
Figs. 41 and 42.—Cross Sections

Scale : $\tfrac{3}{8}$ in. = 1 ft.

Fig. 40.

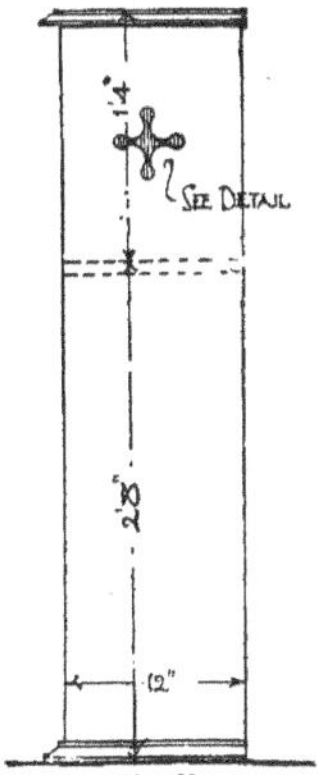

Fig. 39.

Fig. 38.

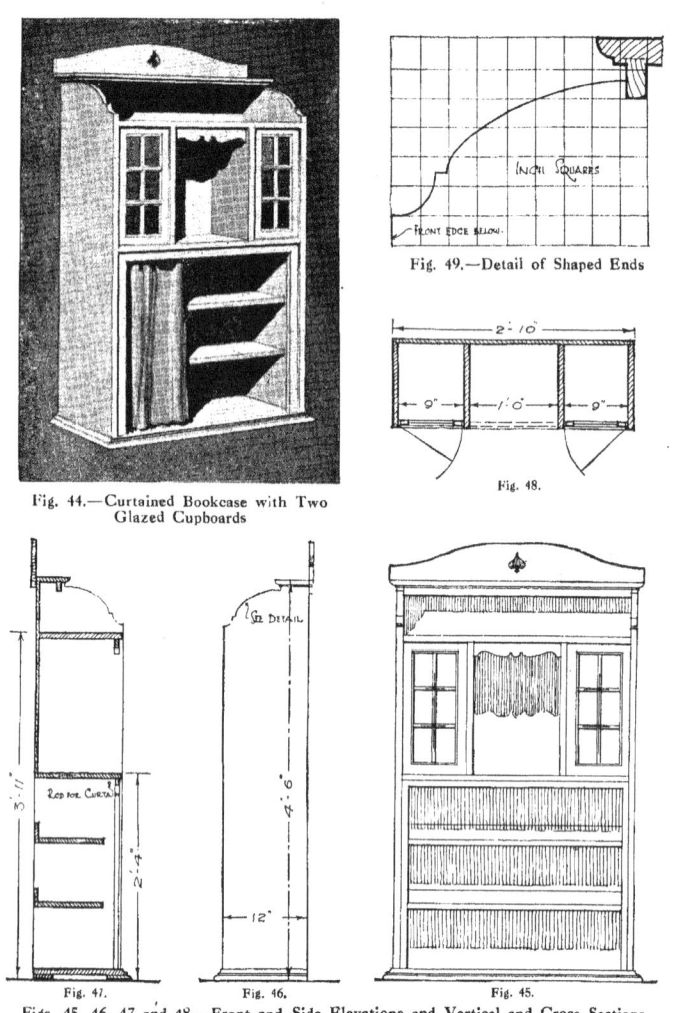

Fig. 44.—Curtained Bookcase with Two Glazed Cupboards

Fig. 49.—Detail of Shaped Ends

Fig. 48.

Figs. 45, 46, 47 and 48.—Front and Side Elevations and Vertical and Cross Sections
Scale : ⅝ in. = 1 ft.

DWARF BOOKCASES

DWARF BOOKCASE WITH SHELF

Constructional details of the remaining examples of bookcases in this section follow so much upon the same lines as those already described that it has not been thought necessary to treat of them fully. The design and working scale drawings given in each case, together with a few notes on the outstanding features, will be quite a sufficient guide for their construction.

The bookcase shown by the reproduced photograph (Fig. 30), and in front and side elevations and vertical and cross sections by Figs. 31 to 34 respectively, has two pairs of doors with wood glazing bars arranged

Fig. 50.—Open Bookcase with Central Glazed Cupboard

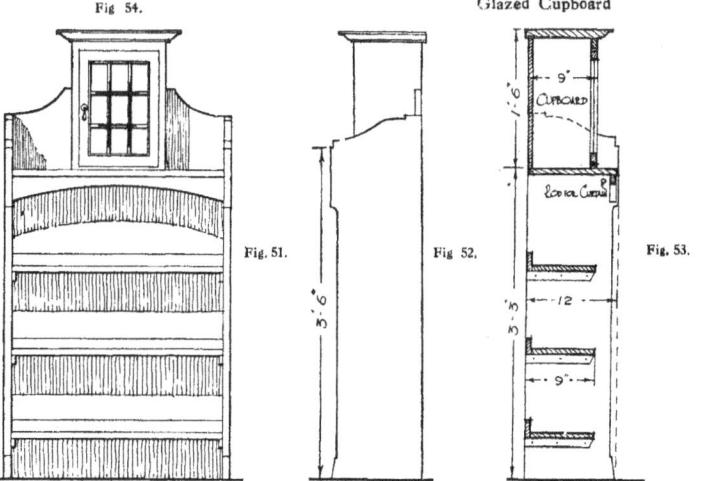

Figs. 51, 52, 53 and 54.—Front and Side Elevations and Vertical and Cross Sections
Scale : ⅝ in. = 1 ft.

in plain rectangles, or in accordance with some simple geometric pattern, as on the right of Fig 31. These narrow doors are much more convenient for access than wider ones, and the meeting-stiles can be sunk and rebated as in Fig. 35. The shelves should be adjustable, preferably with metal strips and pins let in at the upright ends of the case, or otherwise in accordance with one of the other methods given on an earlier page. The method of producing the curved tops of the side pieces is shown by Fig. 36.

CURTAINED BOOKCASES WITH GLAZED CUPBOARDS

The design in Fig. 37 is rather less akin to the conventional bookcase, having a small cupboard flanked by open recesses at the top, and some shelves screened by a curtain sliding on a small rod below. Figs. 38 to 42 show front and side elevations, vertical section and two cross sections. An alternative to the draped curtain would be a spring-roller and blind to draw down from the top of the lower portion. The diagonal bars to the cupboard door are in wood. A detail of the side ornaments is shown by Fig. 43.

Similar in general idea to the last example, Fig. 44 has two open shelves at the top, two glazed cupboards and a central recess below them, and at the bottom a series of curtained shelves. Particular attention should be paid in this—as also in the other designs—to the mouldings, pierced ornaments and shaped portions. As with the two preceding cases, the illustrations (Figs. 45 to 49) are deemed sufficiently explanatory.

OPEN BOOKCASE WITH CENTRAL GLAZED CUPBOARD

Another bookcase on similar modern lines to the three last described, but varied somewhat in detail and arrangement, is shown by Fig. 50. Front and side elevations and a vertical section and plan are shown by Figs. 51 to 54. The small panes to the cupboard should be in leaded glazing. If wood bars are used, four panes only would be suitable.

Revolving Bookcases

MINIATURE REVOLVING BOOKCASE

The small bookcase shown by the half-tone reproduction (Fig. 1) is of a very suitable size for general purposes, and the construction is such that it could easily be adapted for two tiers of books if required.

Such a bookcase of the revolving type should naturally be built to suit the volumes for which it is intended.

The design can be varied by different treatments of the four upright sides, which are shown relieved by a simple line of inlay. This might be made more elaborate, or a moulding substituted to give a panelled effect, or the sides could be shaped or fretted if desired. A more personal interest than that resulting from the precise reproduction of someone else's design can be infused into the work by means of such modifications.

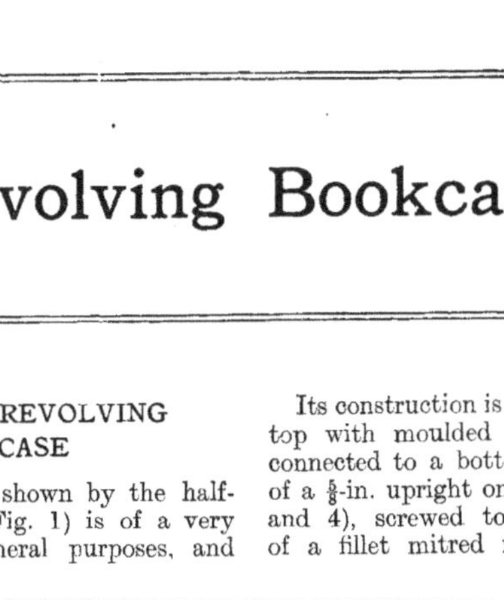

Fig. 1.—Miniature Revolving Bookcase

Its construction is as follows : A square top with moulded edges A (Fig. 2) is connected to a bottom shelf B by means of a $\frac{5}{8}$-in. upright on each side c (Figs. 3 and 4), screwed to the top by means of a fillet mitred round the underside D (Fig. 5), and notched into the bottom, screwed and finished with a mitred moulding, as at E in Fig. 5. In the centre is a square pillar F (Fig. 2), sub-tenoned at the top and having its lower end rounded $1\frac{1}{4}$ in. in diameter and projecting $1\frac{3}{4}$ in. below the bottom shelf. Fillets G in Fig. 4 should be fixed on the bottom, as guides for the books.

The base consists of a 1-in. board H (Figs. 2, 3, and 4), with shaped feet framed in along its diagonals. These feet are seen in true elevation in Fig. 3 and foreshortened in Fig. 2. Four small friction-rollers should be fitted in slots, as at I in Fig. 4, the rounded end of the central pillar fitted loosely through a circular hole in the middle of the base, and secured with a metal or hardwood disc screwed on, as at J in Fig. 2, thus completing the bookcase.

tions and sections being presented by Figs. 7 to 10. The inner case is shown by Figs. 11, 12 and 13, while Fig. 14 is a sketch more clearly showing its construction. Fig. 15 illustrates a detail

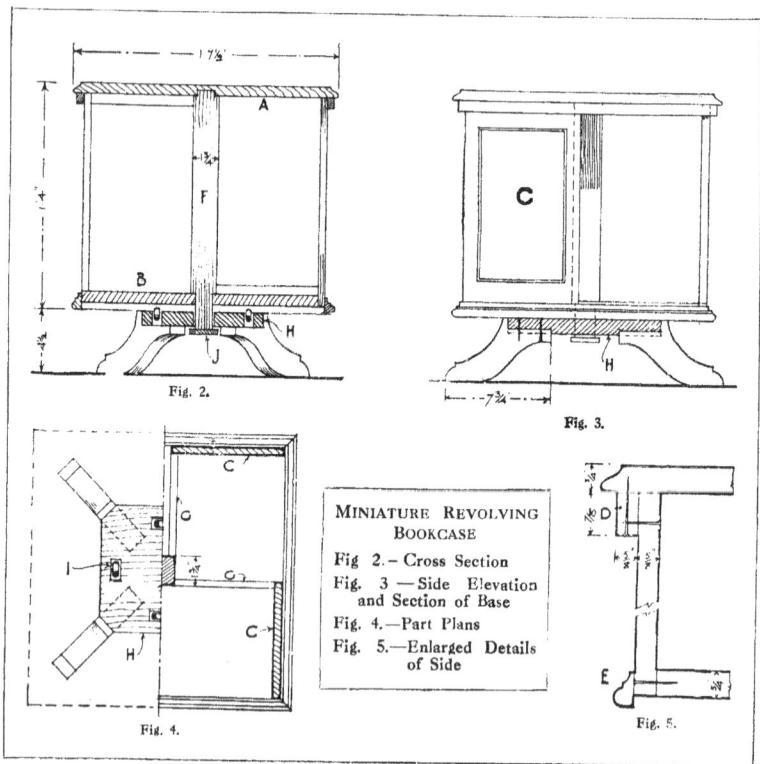

MINIATURE REVOLVING BOOKCASE

Fig 2.— Cross Section
Fig. 3 — Side Elevation and Section of Base
Fig. 4.—Part Plans
Fig. 5.—Enlarged Details of Side

For heavy wear the bottom shelf, if not of hardwood, should have a metal track on its underside to prevent the rollers from wearing a rut into it, as might happen after a time.

A 3-FT. REVOLVING BOOKCASE

A revolving bookcase of neat design is illustrated by Fig. 6, the chief eleva-

tion of the top at B (Fig. 8). Fig. 16 is also a section and gives details of both inner and outer cases; it corresponds with C in Fig. 9. Fig. 17 is a detail of the corner D in Fig. 10, while a section through the plinths, block and underframing, as at E (Fig. 8), is shown in Fig. 18. The remaining illustrations show respectively the steel pivot plates (Fig. 19) and one of the friction-rollers in its mount

REVOLVING BOOKCASES

(Fig. 20). In some revolving bookcases the actual case revolves round an iron standard mounted on cross legs, but in the design here illustrated the actual or inner case is pivoted between the fixed base and the top. Details of the pivot plates are given in Fig. 19, and the way in which these plates are mounted is shown in the section (Fig. 8); these plates are 2 in. in diameter.

As the construction embodies both an outer and inner case, the outer case remaining stationary while the inner one revolves, the design lends itself to more ornamental treatment than is otherwise possible. The corner pilasters (3 in. × ½ in.) may, for example, be sunk, inlaid, incised, carved, or decorated in other ways (see section in Fig. 16), and the upright slats can be moulded or their appearance otherwise improved.

The wiser plan when constructing the bookcase is to make the inner case first. The pivot counterparts are then attached to its top and bottom and the whole revolved on a drawing-board or on the

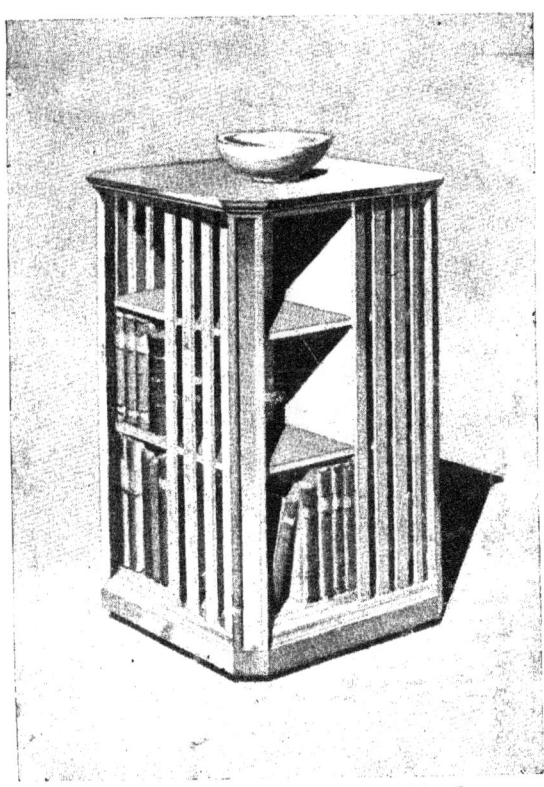

Fig. 6.—3-ft. Bookcase with Inner Revolving Part

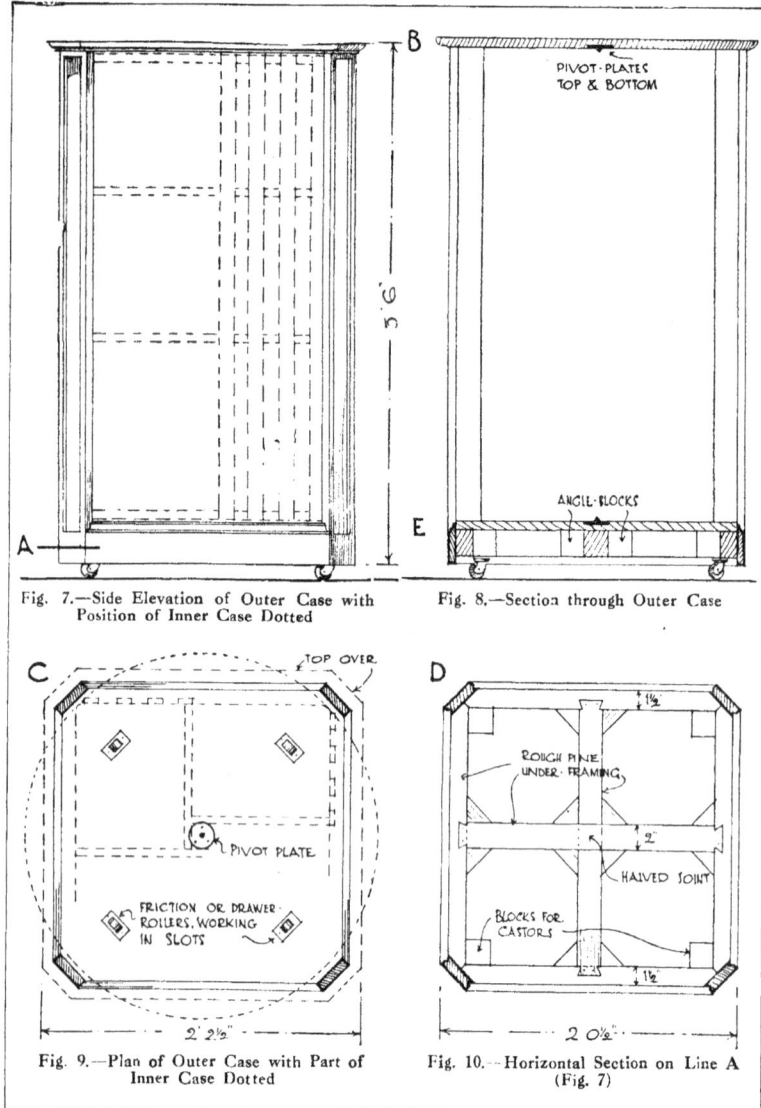

Fig. 7.—Side Elevation of Outer Case with Position of Inner Case Dotted

Fig. 8.—Section through Outer Case

Fig. 9.—Plan of Outer Case with Part of Inner Case Dotted

Fig. 10.—Horizontal Section on Line A (Fig. 7)

REVOLVING BOOKCASES

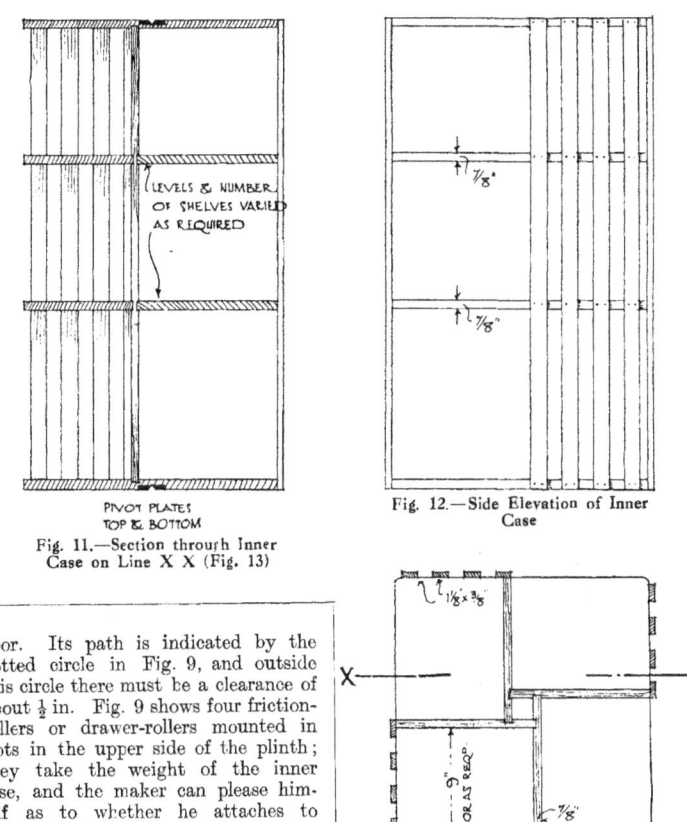

Fig. 11.—Section through Inner Case on Line X X (Fig. 13)

Fig. 12.—Side Elevation of Inner Case

Fig. 13.—Plan of Inner Case

floor. Its path is indicated by the dotted circle in Fig. 9, and outside this circle there must be a clearance of about ½ in. Fig. 9 shows four friction-rollers or drawer-rollers mounted in slots in the upper side of the plinth; they take the weight of the inner case, and the maker can please himself as to whether he attaches to the underside of the inner case an annular iron band to travel over the friction-rollers and save wear. Special care should be taken to see that the friction-rollers are mounted as shown in Fig. 9, the axis of each one being in a line radiating from the centre; otherwise the case will not revolve freely, and there may be an unpleasant squeak when the inner case is moved.

In general, the construction of both the outer and inner cases will be obvious from the illustrations. The divisions of the inner case are housed into its base, as shown in Fig. 14. The dimensions of the various parts are indicated in the illustrations. Fig. 10 shows the strong construction of the plinth or base of the outer case, the cross-pieces being halved

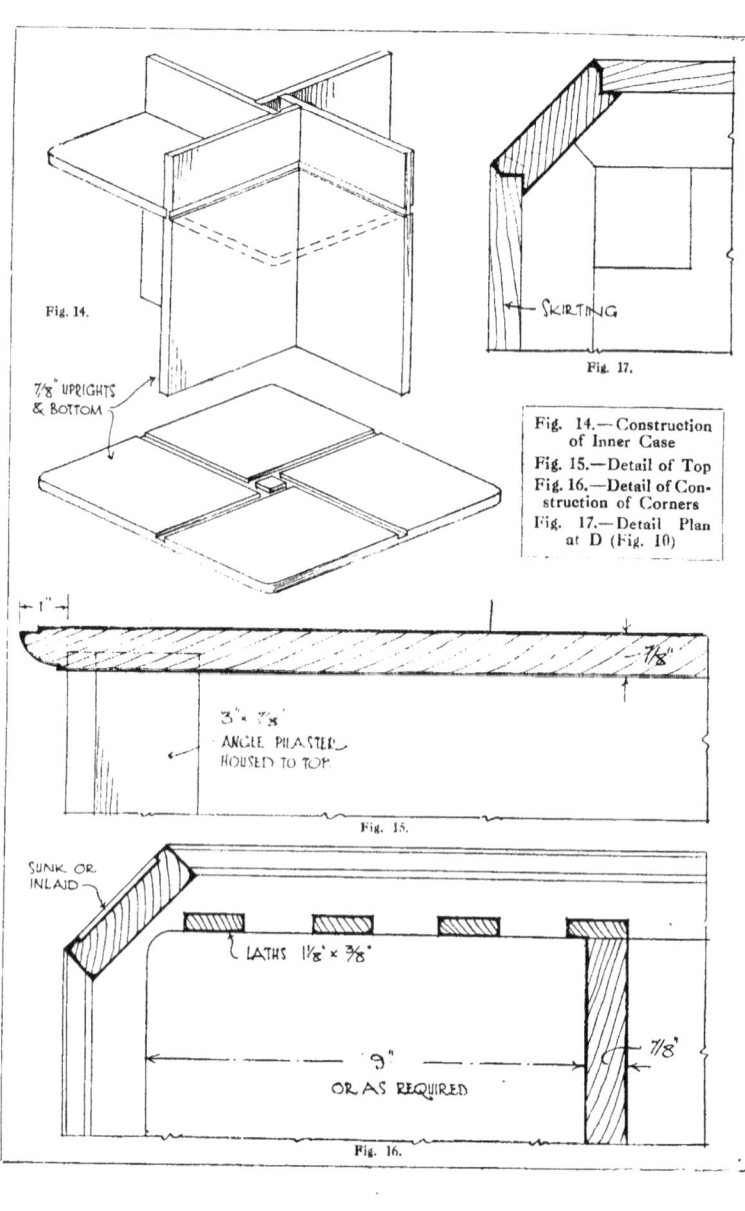

Fig. 14.—Construction of Inner Case
Fig. 15.—Detail of Top
Fig. 16.—Detail of Construction of Corners
Fig. 17.—Detail Plan at D (Fig. 10)

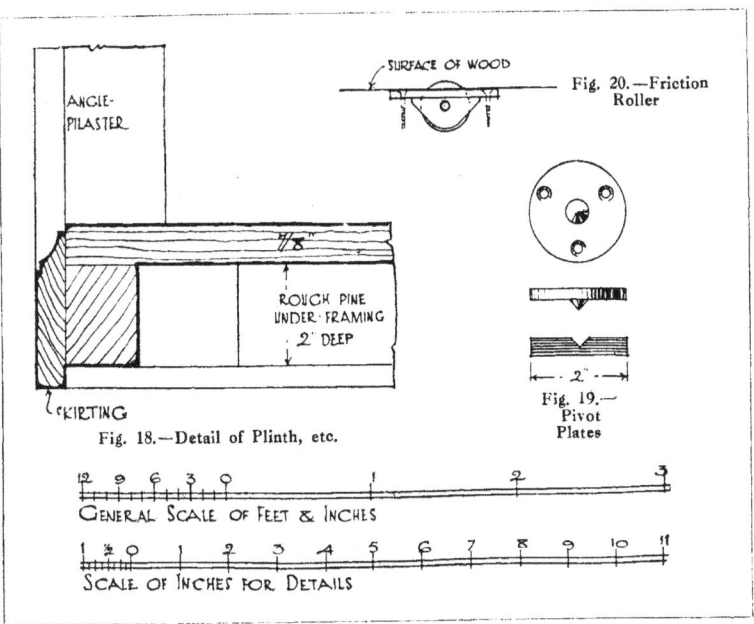

Fig. 20.—Friction Roller

Fig. 19.—Pivot Plates

Fig. 18.—Detail of Plinth, etc.

together at the centre and dovetailed into the side pieces, at which places they are further strengthened with triangular blocks. The four other corners are strengthened with square blocks, and to these are attached the castors which render the whole piece of furniture portable.

Tall Bookcases

OPEN-FRONTED BOOKCASE WITH CUPBOARD

The open bookcase and magazine cupboard shown by Fig. 1 should not present any special difficulties to the worker with average skill, having been designed with a view to simplicity of construction and economy of labour. No elaborate mouldings or curved work have been introduced, and the finished article should be particularly acceptable in the living room. It is of oak throughout, with the door panels of the lower cupboard inlaid with rosewood, ebony and holly. It should be pointed out at the outset, however, that if this inlay is considered beyond the worker, an excellent effect could be obtained by converting the design into a stencilled pattern. The necessary elevations and a vertical section are shown in Figs. 2 to 5. The main dimensions are 5 ft. 6 in. high, 2 ft. 6 in. wide, and 12 in. deep.

Fig. 1.—Open-fronted Bookcase with Cupboard

Work should be commenced with the lower cupboard, this being built up in the usual method of carcase construction. The sides, of ¾-in. material, have a solid bottom lap-dovetailed into them, and are connected by two rails jointed to them in a similar manner at the top (see Fig. 6). The simple ¾-in. plinth consists of strips 3 in. wide mitred round and screwed to the bottom. The top of this lower cupboard may have its edges square with the edges slightly rounded, or a small hollow may be worked on both edges, as shown in Fig. 7. It is secured to the top rails with screws. The carcase back should, if possible, be a framed one, divided by muntins into three vertical panels. The doors are framed up plain, and are rebated to receive the panels, which, after the execution of the inlay, are beaded in from the back. The meeting-stile of the right-hand door is fitted with a plain astragal. The stand on which the cupboard rests is simple in construction, and is screwed to the plinth. Rough thumb-slots are cut in the rails.

The upper carcase is constructed along similar lines to the lower, the two shelves being tenoned right through the sides, and the tenons wedged diagonally. The back in this case is of matched oak boarding, screwed in at the top and bottom. The shaped rails below the cornice and plinth are simply but effectively decorated by means of a chamfered pattern (see Fig. 8), which should be carefully cut with a sharp chisel. The upper and lower carcases are simply screwed together.

A pattern for the inlay on the doors is given by Fig. 9. This should be drawn full-size and traced on to the panels. A separate tracing is made for each piece, which is cut out with a fret-saw, placed in position, marked round, and a recess cut for it. It should be noted that the stems, which are of ebony, should be inlaid and cleaned off first, as the leaves

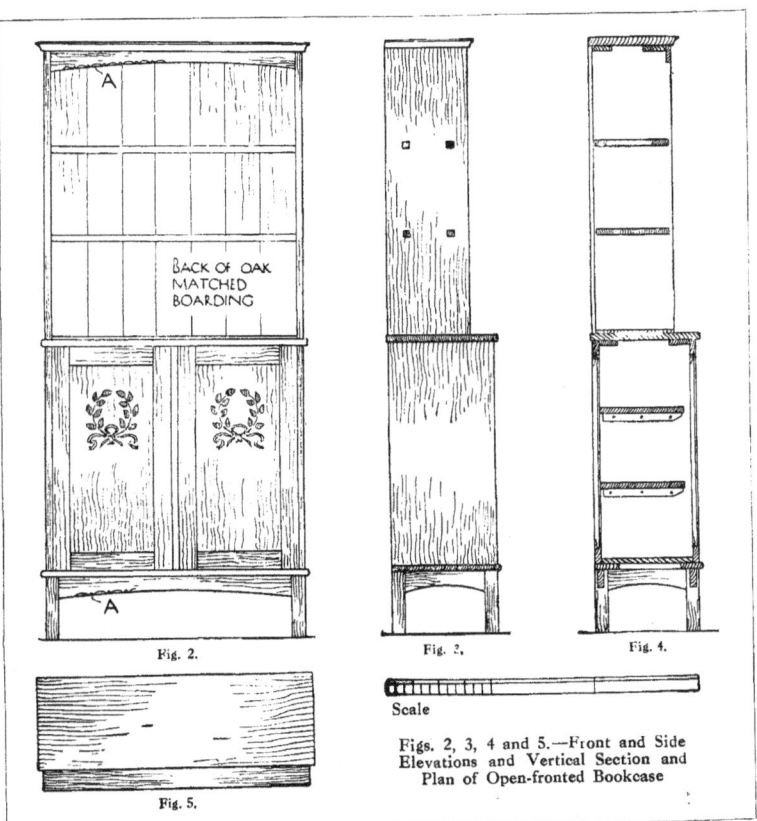

Figs. 2, 3, 4 and 5.—Front and Side Elevations and Vertical Section and Plan of Open-fronted Bookcase

(of rosewood) are partly inlaid into the stems themselves. The ribbons should be cut from holly. The interior of the magazine cupboard is a matter for individual requirements; the shelves rest on fillets screwed to the inside of the ends.

The most suitable finish for the bookcase, after thoroughly cleaning up, would

second a side elevation, and the third a vertical section. From the section it will be seen that the case is made up of two carcases. The lower part is enclosed by two doors with veneered panels, as shown in Fig. 10, and is supported by a base consisting of a pine frame mortised and tenoned together, with a moulding mitred round the edges of the front and

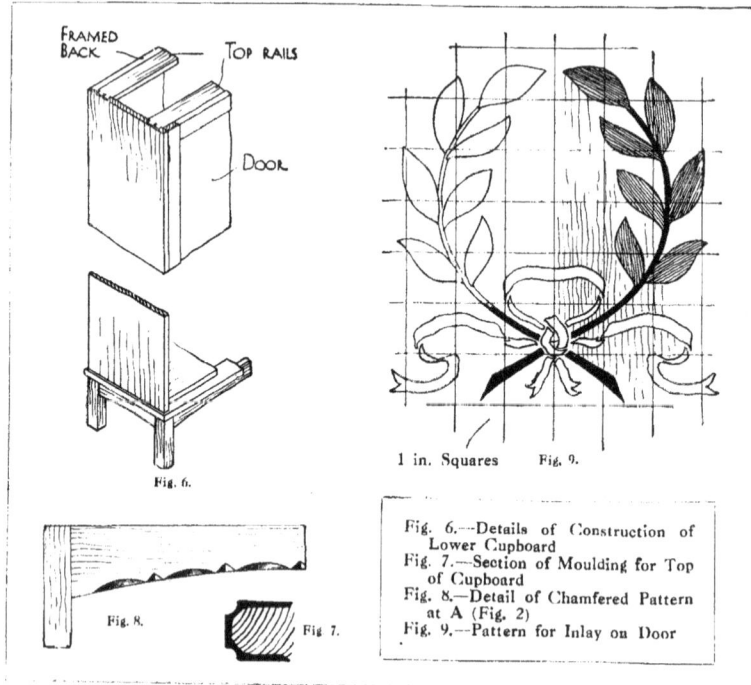

Fig. 6.—Details of Construction of Lower Cupboard
Fig. 7.—Section of Moulding for Top of Cupboard
Fig. 8.—Detail of Chamfered Pattern at A (Fig. 2)
Fig. 9.—Pattern for Inlay on Door

be to fume it a golden brown, and wax-polish it.

BOOKCASE WITH GLAZED DOORS AND CUPBOARDS

Mahogany is the wood suggested for the bookcase shown by Figs. 10 to 12. The first figure is a front elevation, the

the ends. Four tapered feet are fixed to the frame at the corners. The upper part is enclosed by two glass doors, divided by astragals in the positions indicated in Fig. 10. A loose cornice and pediment complete the upper part.

Construction should be commenced with the lower part. Plane up the two gables, and square them to 2 ft. long by

TALL BOOKCASES

1 ft. 2 in. wide by $\frac{7}{8}$ in. thick. Rebate the back edges to receive the back, which is $\frac{3}{8}$ in. thick and tongued and grooved, as shown in Figs. 13 and 14. The top and bottom, of $\frac{5}{8}$-in. pine, are dovetailed to the gables. They should be flush at the front edges, and kept in at the back to allow the back to overlap. The back

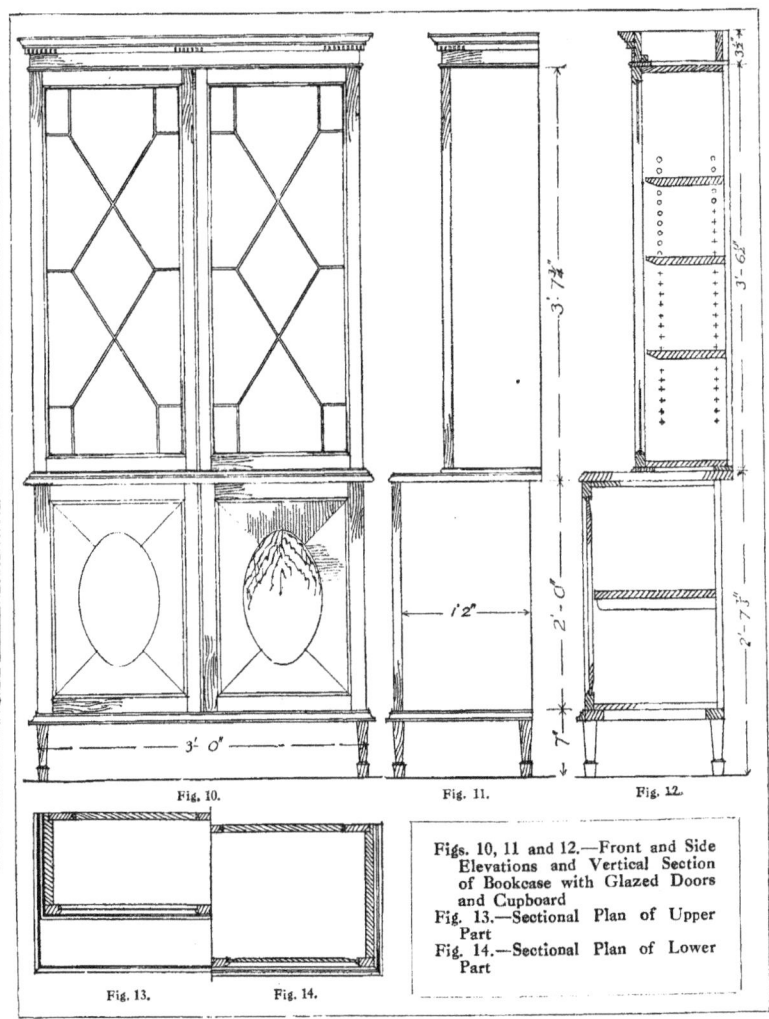

Figs. 10, 11 and 12.—Front and Side Elevations and Vertical Section of Bookcase with Glazed Doors and Cupboard
Fig. 13.—Sectional Plan of Upper Part
Fig. 14.—Sectional Plan of Lower Part

consists of three muntins, 3 in. wide, and two panels which are tongued to the muntins; the joints are broken with a bead. A shelf ⅞ in. thick rests on fillets

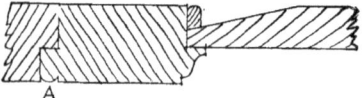

Fig. 15.—Enlarged Part Section of Lower Doors

the corners, with the grain running in the direction shown in Fig. 10. Mortise and tenon a frame together for the base ⅞ in. thick. Then mitre and glue a mould-

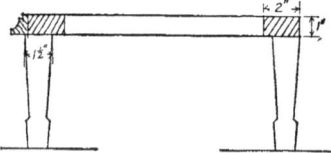

Fig. 16.—Cross Section of Base

screwed to the gables. The shelf may be bevelled away on the underside at the front to give it a thinner appearance. The two doors are mortised and tenoned together, the stiles and rails being 2 in. wide, except the two meeting-stiles, which should be kept ¼ in. wider for the rebates and bead A (Fig. 15). A moulding is run on inside the edges, and a rebate made for the panel, which is fixed with a bead on the inside (see Fig. 15).

The panels are veneered (the subject of veneering is dealt with in a later section), as shown in Fig. 10. Sound African mahogany, ½ in. thick, should be used for a foundation for the veneer, and the surface gone over with a toothing plane before veneering. Begin by laying the piece for the oval, allowing a good margin, which can be afterwards cut off by placing a thin pine mould cut to the size over the veneer, and drawing a sharp chisel round the edge. A showy curl veneer should be used for the oval, the two diameters of which are 1 ft. 2 in.

ing round the edges of the front and ends.

The shaped feet (see Fig. 16) are screwed to the frame. The top of the lower part (Fig. 17) is ⅞ in. thick, and projects over the gables at the front to cover in the doors; it also projects 1¼ in. over the back. The two gables of the upper part should be squared up to 3 ft. 6 in. long by 9½ in. wide by ⅞ in. thick, and rebated on the back edges for the back, similar to the lower gables. The top and bottom are dovetailed to the gables as already described for the lower carcase. The three movable shelves are ⅞ in. thick, are bevelled on the underside, and a moulding is run on the edge (see Fig. 18). Bore holes on the inside of the gables 1 in. apart for the brass studs (Fig. 19), which support the shelves. Sink the studs into the shelves at B (Fig. 18). The stiles and rails of the astragal doors (see Fig. 10) are 1¾ in. wide by 1 in. thick. Frame up the doors before fixing in the astragals, which are made up in two pieces, C and D

Fig. 17.—Section of Moulding

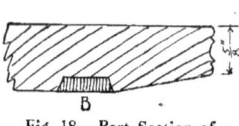

Fig. 18.—Part Section of Shelf

Fig. 19.—Shelf Support

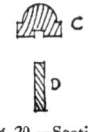

Fig. 20.—Section of Astragal

and 8½ in. It can be rubbed down with a hammer. The veneer round the edges of the oval should be straight grained to show a contrast. It should be mitred at

(Fig. 20). The moulded piece C can be bought ready made from any dealer. Fig. 21 is an enlarged section of the glass doors. Draw the design on a board, and

TALL BOOKCASES

make up the four corners E (Fig. 22) with the pieces D (Fig. 20), dovetailing them together at the corners. The other pieces are next glued in position. All the joints should be strengthened by gluing on pieces of strong tape. Fig. 23 is an enlarged view of an angle piece joined to a square corner. The corners and middle pieces should be mortised to the edges of which the various mouldings are glued. The front and ends of the frame F (Fig. 25) are $3\frac{1}{8}$ in. wide by $\frac{3}{4}$ in. thick, and are dovetailed at the corners. The back of the frame is kept 1 in. in from the back, and is fixed with a dovetailed groove. The frieze G (Fig. 25) is $1\frac{1}{2}$ in. wide by $\frac{1}{4}$ in. thick, glued and mitred at the corners. The piece for the dentils H is next glued

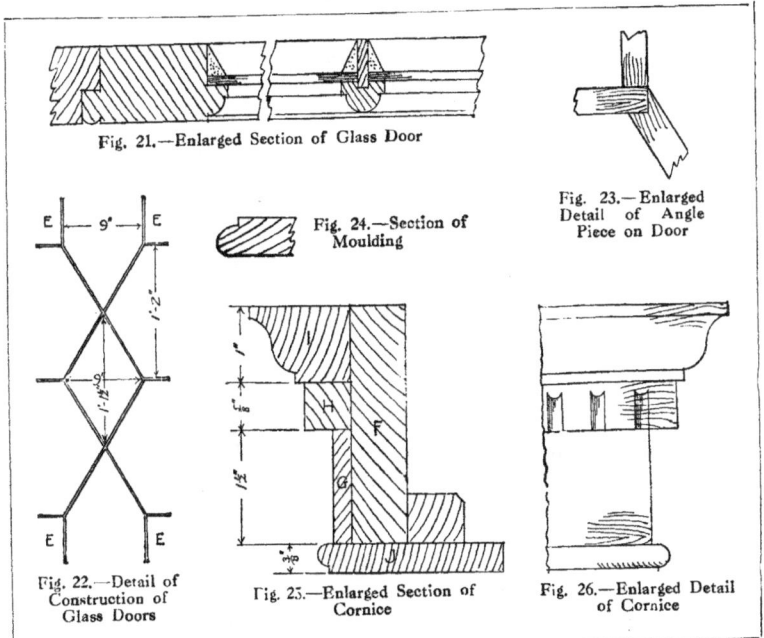

Fig. 21.—Enlarged Section of Glass Door

Fig. 23.—Enlarged Detail of Angle Piece on Door

Fig. 24.—Section of Moulding

Fig. 22.—Detail of Construction of Glass Doors

Fig. 25.—Enlarged Section of Cornice

Fig. 26.—Enlarged Detail of Cornice

the stiles and rails. The moulded pieces are next glued to the pieces D, mitreing them at the corners, and to the sash moulding on the stiles and rails.

The glass is bedded in with putty, the latter being coloured to match the wood. A moulding (Fig. 24), $2\frac{1}{2}$ in. wide by $\frac{1}{2}$ in. thick, is mitred and glued to the top of the lower part of the bookcase to form a base for the upper carcase. The cornice consists of a separate frame of pine to the top edge of the frieze, the dentils being cut with a gouge, as shown in Fig. 26. The top moulding I comes next, and the bottom piece J is glued to the edges of the frieze. Flush bolts should be fitted to the edges of the left-hand doors at the top and bottom. Brass locks and hinges to the doors complete the fittings for the bookcase, care being taken in their selection to see that their size is proportionate to that of the bookcase.

A BOOKCASE BUREAU

The bookcase bureau is a valuable type of furniture in both large and small houses, as it lends itself readily to decorative treatment, and its usefulness is beyond doubt of great value whether it is placed in the study or library of a large house, or in the living room of a small house or modest flat. There are but few homes where it is not desired to accommodate a few books or port-

Fig. 27.—Bookcase Bureau

TALL BOOKCASES

folios and the necessary equipment for writing.

To dip into the history of the bureau one has to traverse the three last centuries, for it was during the seventeenth century that the bureau as a separate piece of furniture was first produced. At the beginning of the eighteenth century the bureau was surmounted by a bookcase with glazed doors instead of the fitted cupboard; and later in the century Chippendale, Sheraton, and the other master craftsmen still further developed the bookcase bureau until they produced models which still stand to-day as the best of their kind.

Figs. 28 and 29.—Front and Side Elevations of Bookcase Bureau

Fig. 27 is a reproduction of a perspective sketch of a modern bookcase bureau based on traditional lines, and embodying legitimate to take the decorative detail of an earlier period, and use it in conjunction with a later arrangement or type of

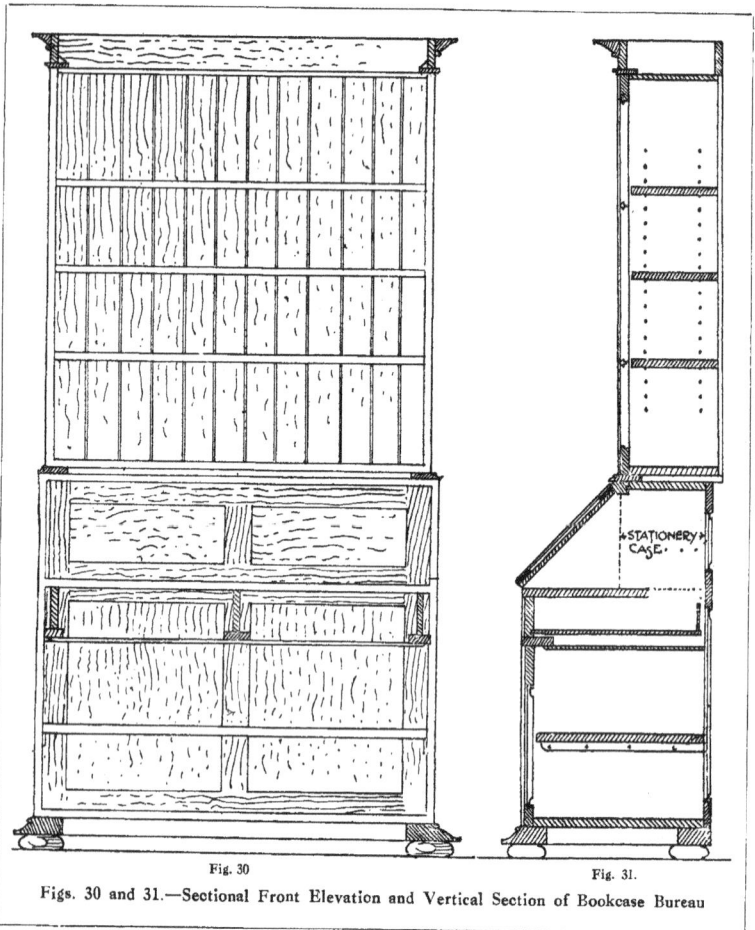

Figs. 30 and 31.—Sectional Front Elevation and Vertical Section of Bookcase Bureau

some of the decorative features of the William and Mary period in the bottom part. It is generally recognised as quite furniture, such as has been done in the present instance. It forms a most useful and decorative piece of furniture, and

TALL BOOKCASES

does not present any very difficult constructive features. Figs. 28 and 29 show the front and side elevations, and two sections are given by Figs. 30 and 31. An enlarged detail is shown (Fig. 32) of the bottom part of the carcase, the main feature of which is a heavy base moulding with turned ball feet.

The carcase should be made with the sides shaped, as shown in the perspective sketch (Fig. 27), with the table part slip-dovetailed in. A rail is tenoned in between the drawers and doors. The carcase bottom should be set back to allow the doors to close over the bottom, and the base mouldings can be mitred and screwed underneath the carcase bottom. The ball feet would, of course, simply be screwed up from underneath.

Reference to the enlarged detail (Fig. 32) will show the actual arrangements of the tenons and mortises, which are reduced on the inside to allow the rebates to be cut. Fig. 33 shows a suggested arrangement for the stationery case; this should be made as a separate fitting, and placed in position from the back. It is usual to make it slightly shorter than is really necessary, and the small resultant spaces can then be filled in with beads to give it a neat appearance. The sliders or "loopers," as they are frequently called, which pull out in order to support the fall or writing flap, are shown in the end view of the bookcase bureau. They should be prepared of straight-grained wood tongued into the front pieces, or clamped as explained on a much earlier page.

Fig. 32.—Detail of Construction of Lower Doors

It is a good plan to keep the straight-grained wood slightly under the front piece, so that the top edge can be covered with baize for the front of the fall to rest on.

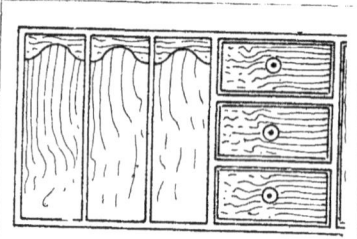

Fig. 33.—Part Front Elevation of Stationery Case

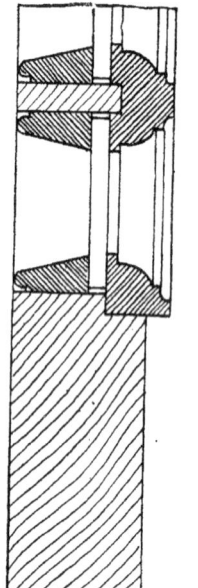

Fig. 34.—Enlarged Sectional Detail of Top Door

The bureau fall is fairly straightforward; it is panelled up, and is hinged to the table part. It is necessary to work rebates on both sides and the top edge, which leaves a projecting part to rest on the carcase edges. The fall is panelled up and made quite flush on the inside, and a lipping must then be made for the lining of the table part. Cross-banded saw-cut veneer about 1 in. wide, glued all round, provides an excellent lipping, and for the lining either billiard-table cloth or leather is suitable. If leather is employed, morocco stained and dressed to the required colour is the best to use; but for purposes of economy "roan" is largely used. Roan leather is similar to morocco in general appearance; but it is, of course, cheaper and inferior in quality. A still cheaper treatment is to use "skiver" material; but its use is not recommended, as there is not much substance in the material, and it soon gets rubbed and presents a dingy appearance. It is usual to have tooled borders to the lining, which must be done by a properly qualified table liner. These borders are made by means of heated dies pressed into the surface of the leather, which impress the leather with a pattern. The pattern is frequently gilded; but a good appearance is effected by leaving the pattern quite plain, which is commonly known as "blind tooling."

The construction of the upper carcase or bookcase part is straightforward. Both the carcase top and bottom should be lap-dovetailed into the carcase ends, and the base moulding attached to the bureau or bottom part. A matched back is illustrated as an alternative to a panelled back. The latter is the most satisfactory, as it keeps the carcase quite square and rigid; but if care is taken with a matched back it is quite satisfactory. In Fig. 34 is shown an enlarged working detail of the door frame. Ordinary oblong frames are made to the required size, with rebates on the inside edges. Bars or slats are then fitted into the design shown, and the mouldings then mitred into the rebates; the cross mouldings also are mitred and glued on to the bars or slats. At the centre an astragal moulding is rebated into the left-hand shutting stile, and fitted over the left-hand door to conceal any opening. In the sectional view is indicated the arrangement for adjusting the shelves to any required spacing; ⅜-in. holes are bored 1½ in. from centre to centre, and wooden struts or pins are made to fit in. The outside of the stud should be made about ½ in. in diameter, and this leaves a shoulder or collar to prevent it passing too far into the prepared holes. Boxing up is employed for the cornice, which is completed by adding the frieze moulding on the oak.

The completed job should be fumed with ammonia, and then slightly french-polished to fix the colour. A good tone may be imparted to the work by finishing off with a mixture of wax and turpentine, rubbed well in with soft cotton rags until a good, even polish is obtained.

Fig. 35.—Simple Bookcase Bureau

SIMPLE BOOKCASE BUREAU

The half-tone reproduction (Fig. 35) together with the dimensioned detail drawings are sufficiently explanatory of this simple bookcase bureau without further description. Two elevations, front and half back, are given by Figs. 36 and 37, and Fig. 38 shows a vertical section.

From a study of the drawings it will be seen that the construction is on particularly simple lines. Figs. 39 and 40 show the methods of fixing the shelves and top, and it will be observed that all joints are avoided. A detail of the hinged writing flap is shown by Fig. 41. The shelf to which the flap is hinged is though this usually takes the form of a wardrobe there is no reason why a bookcase should not come under the arrangement. Fitted furniture is economical because of its simple construction, and it provides good accommodation in recesses and corners where in the usual way a good deal of space is lost. Where

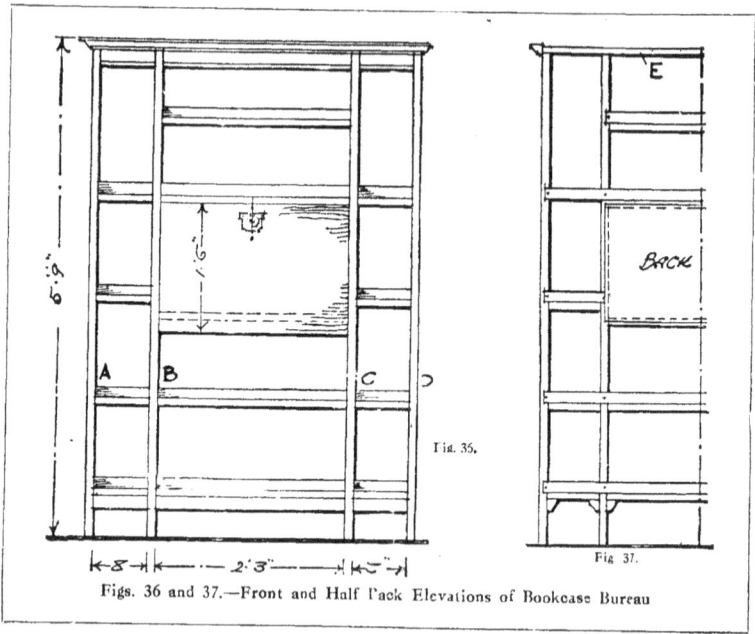

Figs. 36 and 37.—Front and Half Back Elevations of Bookcase Bureau

housed into the two centre uprights, as shown by Fig. 42. Fillets are let into the backs of the four uprights A B C D (Fig. 36), these latter being notched for this purpose, as shown by the detail (Fig. 43). The positions of the fillets are clearly shown in the sectional view (Fig. 38).

FITTED BOOKCASE CABINET

The modern house usually has one or more pieces of fitted furniture, and such work is introduced by the builder or owner as a permanent feature of the house, much less work can be put in than is indicated in the bookcase shown by Fig. 44 and which has panelled backs. Figs. 45 and 46 show front and back respectively.

The fitment should be made in two parts. The bottom part should have a bottom grooved into both the pilasters with the projecting square part supported on fillets attached to the wall, like a low skirting board. A carcase top rail about 8 in. wide should be dovetailed into the

be made to fit the front part and also the wall line. This is attached to the front

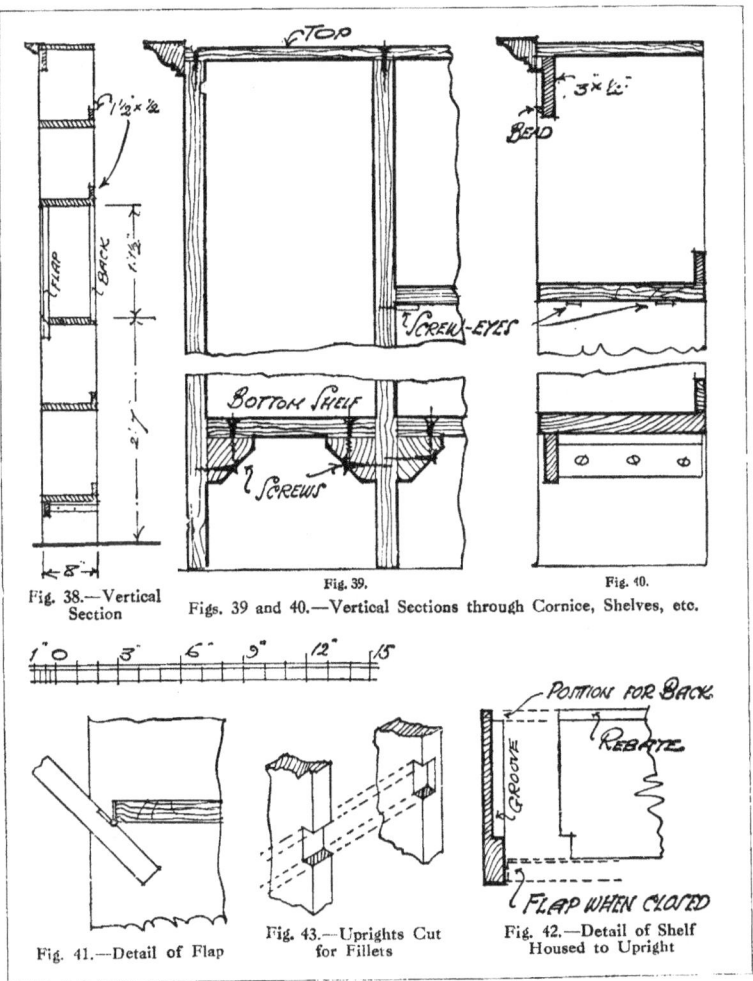

Fig. 38.—Vertical Section

Figs. 39 and 40.—Vertical Sections through Cornice, Shelves, etc.

Fig. 41.—Detail of Flap

Fig. 43.—Uprights Cut for Fillets

Fig. 42.—Detail of Shelf Housed to Upright

pilasters in order to keep them in proper position, and the moulded parts should

rail, and may be supported in the angle by means of wall fillets. It will be seen that after the bottom carcase has been fixed to the wall, a skirting board is mitred round, the top edge of the moulding being made level with the top side of the bottom carcase. The door frame is fairly simple, and for painted work it should be made with through mortise-and-tenoned joints. A bolection moulding is then mitred round in order to form a rebate to receive the panel.

Fig. 44.—Fitted Bookcase Upright

To construct the upper portion a full top should be employed similar to that used for the shelf of the top part. The top should be dovetailed down and the shelf should be grooved into the pilasters on the inside. Both should be supported in the angle by means of narrow bevelled fillets. The arch should be fitted between the pilasters, and to make a neat job it should be laid over the edge of the top, necessitating the latter being set back. A full cornice is hardly necessary. A rail the full width of the frieze and cornice moulding should be mitred together, tongued and blocked, and then the frieze and cornice mouldings can be mitred round and glued. When quite dry it can be screwed in position from the inside. It should here be mentioned that the pilasters are intended to be dowelled down into the moulded bottom, thus obviating the necessity for an additional solid bottom.

The barred doors in the top part should first be dry mortised and tenoned with a wide rail to allow the curves to be cut from the solid. Long and short shouldered mortise-and-tenon joints are necessary in order that the shoulders will fit both the sight line and also the rebate. A straight bar should then be tenoned into the top and bottom rails. When carefully fitted, this should be removed and the two short bars likewise fitted. These also can then be removed and the halving completed preparatory to gluing up the doors with the bars in position. When the doors are dry the front bar mouldings can then be mitred and glued to the bars. Astragal mouldings are usual with such work, but for painted work they look quite well if made flat, the sharp edges being rounded off after the doors have been glasspapered. An astragal moulding should be fitted to the right-hand door in order to overlap the shutting stile of the left-hand one.

The construction of this bookcase cabinet as a separate piece of furniture is shown in the drawings (Figs. 47 to 49). It will be seen that back frames are introduced to give the necessary rigidity. At B (Fig. 47) is shown a part plan of the plinth frame. This is through-dovetailed in the angle, and the two short returns should have lap dovetails. The centre front piece is then mitred and tongued to the two short returns. Afterwards the moulding is mitred round as indicated in the part plan, and if the long rails are made rather wider, they can be notched to receive the moulding and thus yield a level surface on top without the necessity for gluing on separate slips.

The portion of this figure marked A shows a section through the bottom part. Figs. 48 and 49 are enlarged details of

TALL BOOKCASES

this part. The backs are panelled as shown, and a solid top should be dovetailed into the pilasters and screwed down to the backs.

receive the shelf, which should also be sub-tenoned into the edges of the pilasters. This should be finally secured by screwing the shelf through the backs.

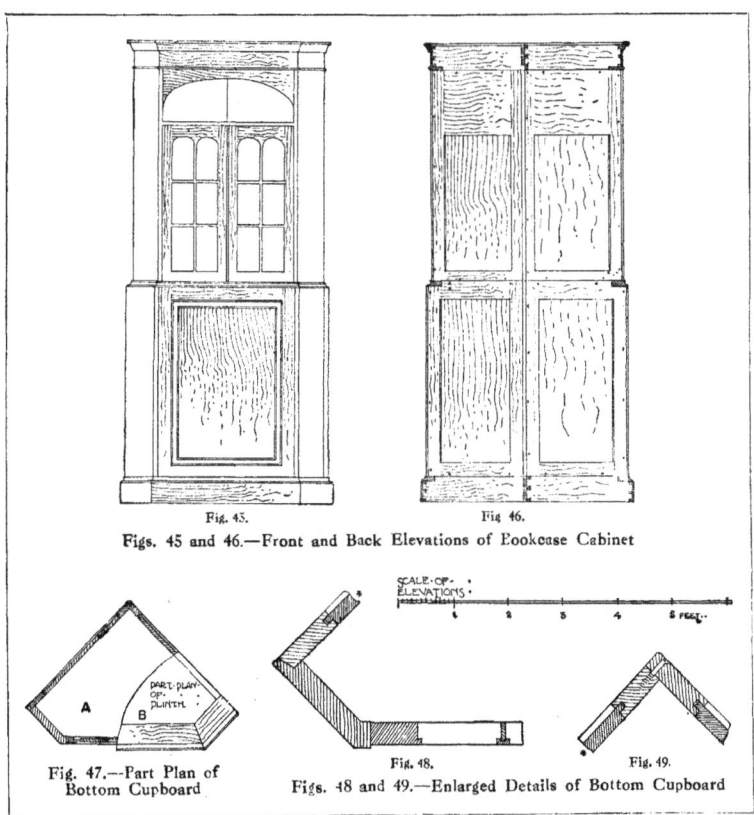

Figs. 45 and 46.—Front and Back Elevations of Bookcase Cabinet

Fig. 47.—Part Plan of Bottom Cupboard

Figs. 48 and 49.—Enlarged Details of Bottom Cupboard

The bottom is dealt with similarly. The base moulding of the top part should be made about 3 in. wide and mitred round to show as indicated. The top carcase should be constructed similarly to the bottom, and the centre part should be cut away to receive the arch. It is also necessary to groove the pilasters to

The cornice is made as a box with the frieze moulding glued round on the underside. The back view shows the cornice moulding glued round to form a rebate at the top which receives a dust-board. Shelves about $\frac{5}{8}$ in. thick should be fitted on fillets, the front edges lining up with the bars.

Hall Furniture

SMALL HALL TABLE

A SMALL table, suitable for the hall, that may be made of bass wood, American whitewood, or any similar softwood, is shown by Fig. 1. Front and side elevations and vertical section and plan are shown by Figs. 2 to 5.

The pieces required should be faced true, and gauged and planed to a thickness of about ¾ in., after which the curves should be marked and sawn out, and the fret ornament cut. Some of the straight parts which join the curves should be finished with the chisel and a small thumb-plane or spokeshave; generally this will be found more satisfactory than trying to finish with a file. The large curve can be finished with a spokeshave, and the smaller ones with a file, or these may be worked by overhand paring with a keen chisel and finishing with No. 1 glass-paper. The thumb moulding shown round the edge of the top may be worked

Fig. 1.—Small Hall Table

by means of a scratch tool. The two standards are connected by means of a 2-in. by ¾-in. rail, as at A (Fig. 2), and have mortises that allow a whole-thickness tenon to pass through, and they are finally secured with small oak wedges. The top on its underside is grooved to a depth of about ¼-in., so as to receive the top ends of the standards. The top and the standards can be fixed rigidly together by gluing a few angle blocks to them. The back piece and the top are secured with glue, and by inserting a few screws from the back. The front rail B (Fig. 2) should be fixed to the standards and top by angle blocks glued in the inner angles, and by driving in a few small sprigs or screws after the glue has set. It has a hole about 3½ in. by 13 in. for the drawer in the centre. The top should overhang at the back a little, as shown at c (Fig. 4).

The drawer (Figs. 5, 6 and 7) has a chamfered front, overlapping the hole in the front rail to the extent of ½ in. all

HALL FURNITURE

round. Its sides and bottom should be housed ¼ in. into the front, as in Fig. 6. The runner D (Fig. 7) is rebated or built up of two pieces as shown, so as to receive a suitable handle should be screwed on, and the table may be finished in any of the usual ways.

The design for the fret ornament in the

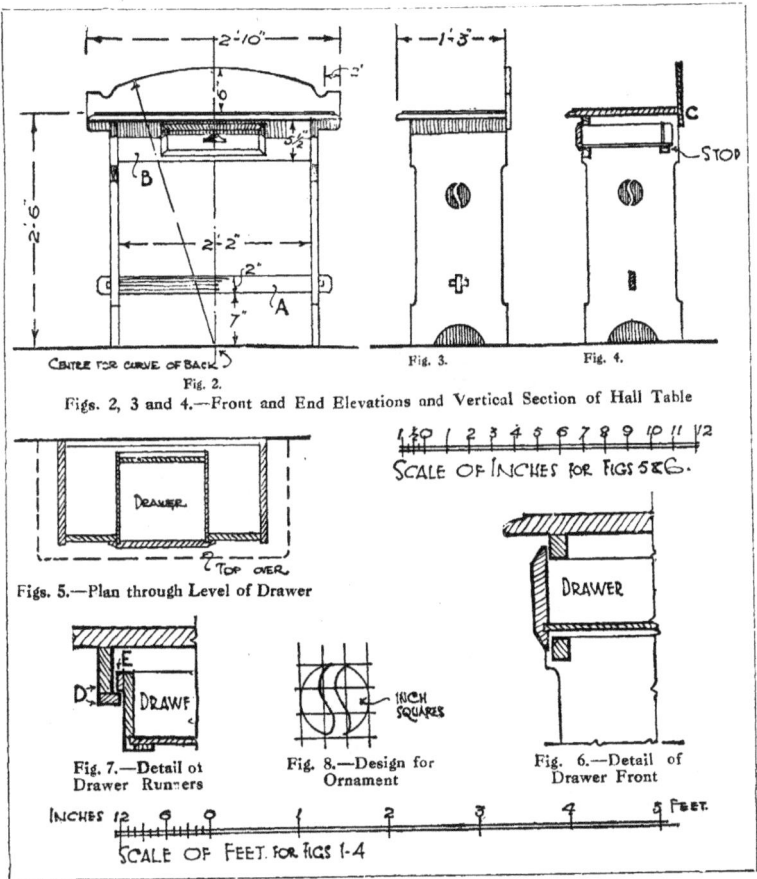

Figs. 2, 3 and 4.—Front and End Elevations and Vertical Section of Hall Table

Figs. 5.—Plan through Level of Drawer

Fig. 7.—Detail of Drawer Runners

Fig. 8.—Design for Ornament

Fig. 6.—Detail of Drawer Front

fillet, which is glued and sprigged on to the sides of the drawer, as shown at E. The drawer should fit quite loosely, and can have a stop, as noted in Fig. 4, to prevent its being pulled too far out. A standards is shown by Fig. 8. The half-tone reproduction (Fig. 1) shows a diamond-shaped piercing in the middle of the back top piece, which might be added if desired.

SHELF BRACKET FOR HALL

A useful shelf bracket for the hall is illustrated by Fig. 9. Figs. 10, 11 and 12 show front elevation, vertical section and plan.

The two side supporting pieces are cut from ¾-in. or 1-in. stuff set out as shown in Figs. 13, 14 and 15. These drawings can easily be enlarged to full-size by means of the inch squares into which they have been divided. The scrollwork is cut with a band-saw, the rough edges being afterwards cleaned with a spokeshave, file, and glasspaper. Two rails, as at A and B (Fig. 11), connect the supports, being let into them and fixed with 1-in. screws. The lower rail should be immediately above the skirting of the hall. The shelf is finished to 10 in. by ⅞ in., moulded on the exposed edges, and fixed to each support with 1¼-in. screws. Under its front edge and ¼ in. behind the front top edge of the uprights is fixed a 1½-in. by ¾-in. front rail as at C. This can be secured either by means of blocks at the back, or by letting it ¼ in. into the uprights at its ends.

The bracket is fixed to the wall by means of screws driven through the rails into wooden plugs fixed in the wall, the supports being cut away to fit over the skirting. Fig. 14 shows how, when the outline of the shaped support has been set out once, it can be traced and reversed as at D, this enabling the pair to be cut very economically from one piece of wood ; this method also ensures symmetry and continuity of curve.

Fig. 9.—Shelf Bracket for Hall

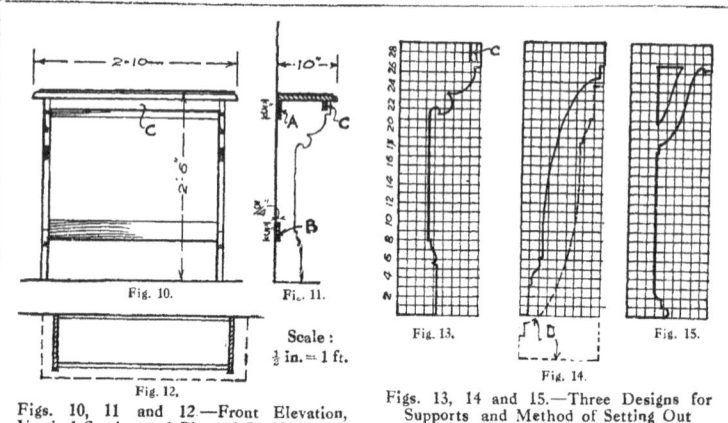

Figs. 10, 11 and 12.—Front Elevation, Vertical Section and Plan of Shelf Bracket

Figs. 13, 14 and 15.—Three Designs for Supports and Method of Setting Out

HALL FURNITURE

HALL TABLE

The dimensions of the hall table shown by Figs. 16, 17 and 18 are 3 ft. 4 in. by 2 ft. by 2 ft. 4 in. high; but these may be altered as desired, if proper care is taken to do so proportionately. The table essentially consists of two framed ends the following parts: head, 3 in. by $2\frac{1}{4}$ in.; foot, $3\frac{1}{2}$ in. by $2\frac{1}{4}$ in. (both with shaped overhanging ends); two stiles with shaped outer edges cut of 4-in. by $1\frac{3}{4}$-in. material; a cross-rail, 3 in. by $1\frac{1}{4}$ in., at a height of $10\frac{1}{2}$ in. from the floor; and a curved spandrel filling to the head out of 5-in. by 1-in. material. The remaining parts to

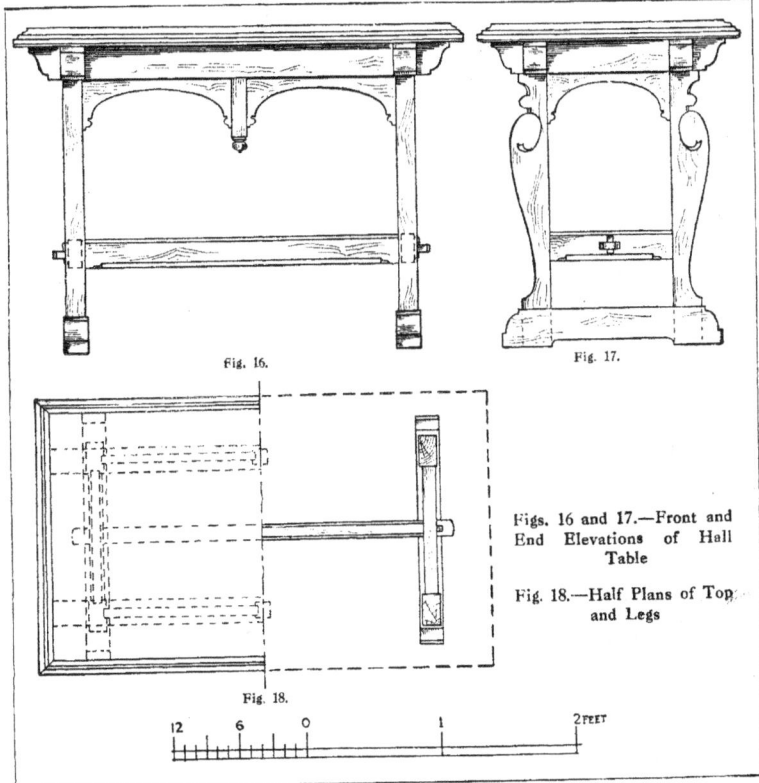

Figs. 16 and 17.—Front and End Elevations of Hall Table

Fig. 18.—Half Plans of Top and Legs

with shaped stiles, connected by longitudinal rails at their heads, and strutted apart by a single stretcher with pinned tenons, allowing the shoulders to be drawn close. Each end frame consists of complete the frame are: head stretchers, 3 in. by $2\frac{1}{4}$ in.; single intermediate stretcher, 3 in. by $1\frac{3}{4}$ in.; pendant pieces, $1\frac{3}{4}$ in. square; and spandrel fillings of the same depth as in the end frames.

The method of construction is as follows: The material for the whole is prepared to dimensions, and the templates for the shaped parts cut in cardboard (or if for repetition work in thin wood). Taking

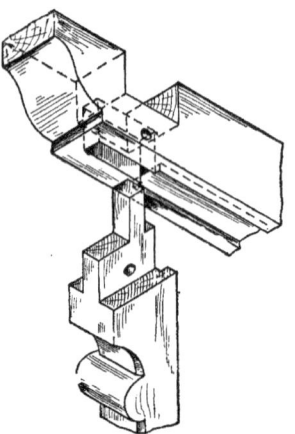

Fig. 19.—Enlarged Detail of Head Rail and Leg

first the end frames, set out the head and foot rails by measuring to dead lengths, marking the position of mortises, housing and halvings (see Fig. 19), and tracing out the moulded ends and sinkings to the centre of feet. Similarly mark out the stiles and cross-rails for tenoning, mortising and housing, with the outline of the outer edges of the stiles. Treat the stretchers in the same way, using throughout a scribing knife for the shoulder lines, and mortise gauge for mortises and tenons. Set out the pendant pieces (providing for a wedged tenon through the top rail), and also the spandrel fillings for the whole.

Begin work by preparing the principal mortises and tenons. Afterwards cut the halvings and the small mortise through the halving of the long rails. Sink the housings for the spandrels, then follow with the moulded ends, etc., to rails, and shaped edges to the stiles. Groove the top rails to receive the fixing buttons for securing the top. Next chamfer the cross-rails (in the end frames) and the single stretcher; "square turn" the drops to the pendant pieces, try the whole frame together, and, if satisfactory, clean up the parts ready for assembling. Glue and wedge up the end frames, cutting back the tenon ends $\frac{1}{8}$ in., so that subsequent shrinkage will not cause them to bear on the floor. Connect the end frames with the stretcher, gluing and draw-pinning as in Figs. 16, 17 and 18. Wedge the pendant pieces to the top rails, again cutting back the tenons and wedges slightly to prevent bearing against the top. Slide the spandrels into position sidewise, then drop the top rail and its connected parts into the halvings and housings prepared for them (gluing the halving and tenon), and finally wedge the latter and cut back slightly as before. If oak or pitch-pine is used for the frame, every tenoned joint should be also neatly pinned with $\frac{3}{8}$-in. diameter pins (preferably draw-bored) within $\frac{5}{8}$ in. from the shoulder.

The top is now prepared from $\frac{7}{8}$-in. material, and, if possible, in one piece. The dimensions given in this case would usually entail jointing, which should be grooved and cross-tongued, with the grooves stopped short of the ends, and 3-in. by $\frac{3}{8}$-in. dowels placed at each end

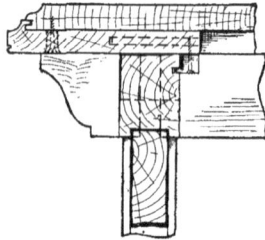

Fig. 20.—Enlarged Detail of Top

(near to the moulded edge), and at 9-in. intervals along the joint. Underneath this $\frac{7}{8}$-in. surface piece is a moulded margin prepared from 1$\frac{1}{4}$-in. stuff, of a width sufficient to extend 1$\frac{1}{2}$ in. beyond the frame inwards. This margin is tongued

HALL FURNITURE

at the edge as shown, being reduced to ⅞ in. thick, and fixed to the top by one row of slotted screws, as in Fig. 20, and the long margins connected by one or more cross stretchers, mortised and tenoned, but not glued, and left ⅛ in. clear at the shoulders. A single screw at the centre of this length keeps the top from lifting, and ensures shrinkage or expansion equally in each direction. The whole of the top thus prepared is fixed to the frame with small hardwood turn-buttons, tongued into the grooves previously prepared in the top rails. The top as completed with the margins is then perfectly free to expand or contract without deterioration to mitres or damage to top surface. Care should be taken to choose material whose grain gives no tendency to lift at the edges (see Fig. 20), or otherwise the tongued-edge joint must be strong enough to prevent it.

The table might be suitably constructed either entirely in oak or mahogany, or with oak or pitch-pine frame and mahogany top. In any case, well-seasoned and dry material is essential.

HALL TABLE WITH FRETTED ENDS

A hall table of entirely different style and construction to the one just described, is shown by the photographic repro-

Fig. 21.—Hall Table with Fretted Ends

duction (Fig. 21). The dimensions and details necessary for making it are clearly shown by the drawings, (Figs. 22 to 27). Suitable woods to use are either black walnut or mahogany. The legs are of 1½-in. square stuff, tapered off equally all round below the drawer rails, the reduction being to 1 in. at the neck of the foot, which is shaped and slightly rounded underneath as shown. At the ends the legs are connected by means of a rail A

1 in. thick and 7 in. deep, stub-tenoned in position, and at the top by a rail B 1½ in. by ¾ in. deep, as in Fig. 23, slightly tenoned to their upper extremities. The deep rail A should be flush on the inside with the legs, as it will form one side of the drawer space. The void between A and B is filled in with a ¼-in. hardwood panel, fretted to a very

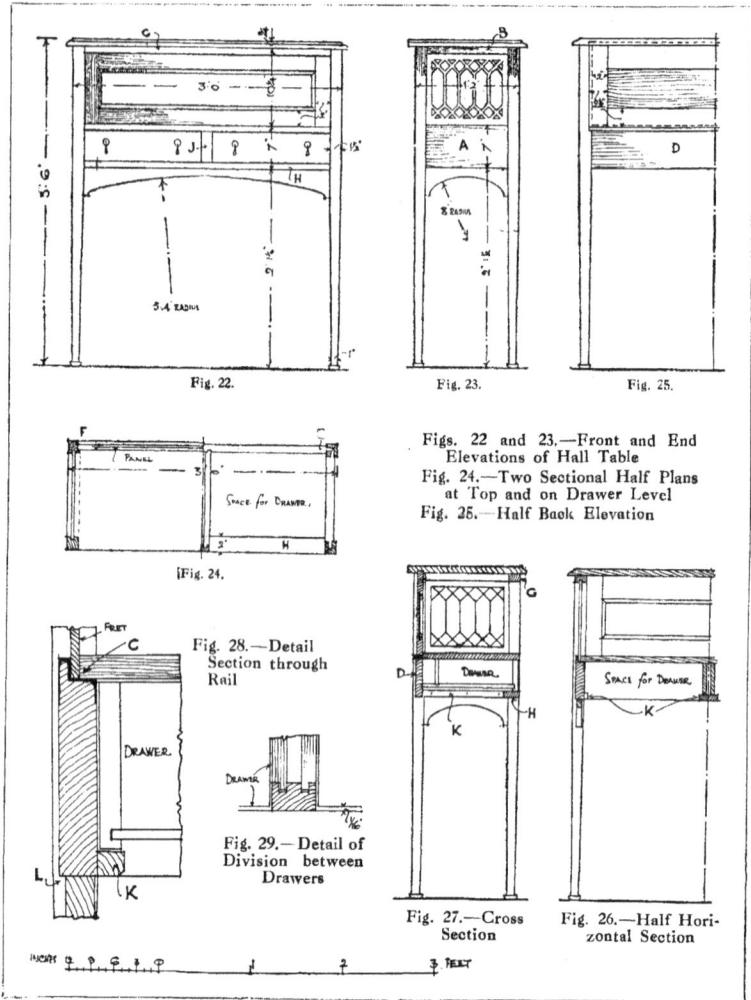

Figs. 22 and 23.—Front and End Elevations of Hall Table
Fig. 24.—Two Sectional Half Plans at Top and on Drawer Level
Fig. 25.—Half Back Elevation
Fig. 28.—Detail Section through Rail
Fig. 29.—Detail of Division between Drawers
Fig. 27.—Cross Section
Fig. 26.—Half Horizontal Section

HALL FURNITURE

simple geometric pattern, and fitted into grooves in the legs and top rail and into part of a rebate, as at C in Fig. 28.

At the back the legs are joined up first of all by means of a 6¼-in. rail, as at D in Figs. 25 and 27, tenoned as at E in Fig. 24. Over this and into the rebates at the ends C (Fig. 28) fits a ¾-in. lower shelf, having all its edges flush with the outer faces of

dovetailed to the tops of the front legs. The top shelf is secured by oblique screwing from behind the various rails. Before this can be done, the 2-in. by ¾-in. drawer rail H (Figs. 22, 24 and 27) must be framed in position, and also a vertical division as at J (Fig. 22). If this is made 1½ in. wide as shown, to match the legs, it can be built up as in Fig. 29, the upright J

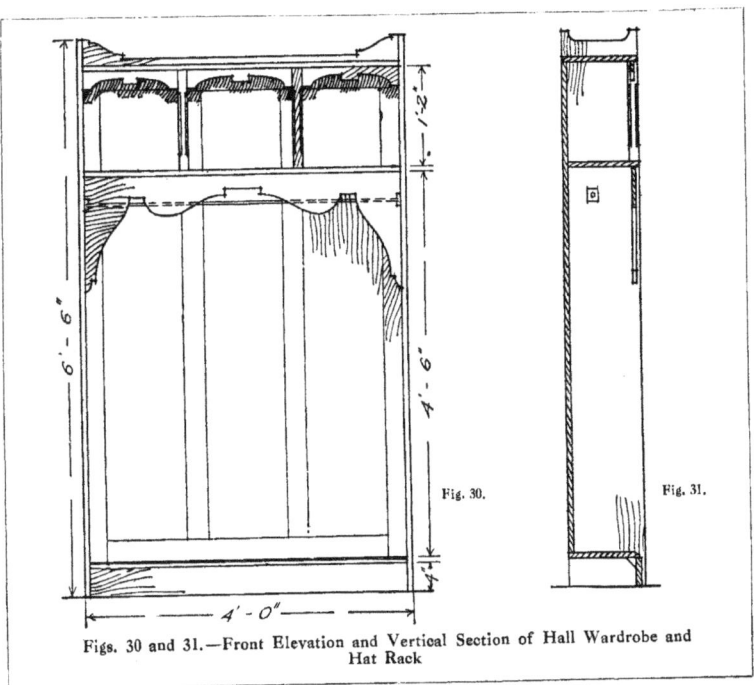

Figs. 30 and 31.—Front Elevation and Vertical Section of Hall Wardrobe and Hat Rack

the legs, round which it is cut and into which it should be notched ¼ in. deep. Its top back edge is rebated as just above D (Fig. 27) to take a long narrow piece of ¾-in. moulded and panelled framing, let into rebates in the back legs F (Fig. 24) and with its top housed slightly into the top shelf, which is ¾ in. thick and moulded. This shelf is finished along the front with a 1½-in. by ¾-in. rail G (Figs. 22 and 27)

being stub-tenoned top and bottom. As a matter of fact, this could be reduced to one thickness of about ¾ in., thereby simplifying the work. It must be let into the back rail, and oak runners for the drawers should be screwed on, as at K in Figs. 26, 27 and 28. There is nothing special about the drawers, which it will be best to arrange ⅟₁₆ in. or so behind the framing when closed. The only portion not already described is the set of three arch or spandrel pieces, which are cut out of stuff 3½ in. by ⅝ in. to curves of the radii given in Figs. 22 and 23. They should be housed ¼ in. into the legs at the ends, and butted against the rails above them, their faces being ⅛ in. behind those of the rails L (Fig. 28). All the parts should be fitted together complete, then taken to pieces, and all except the outside surfaces of the legs bodied in with polish, glued up, cleaned off where necessary, and the polishing finished.

Should a larger table be desired, this

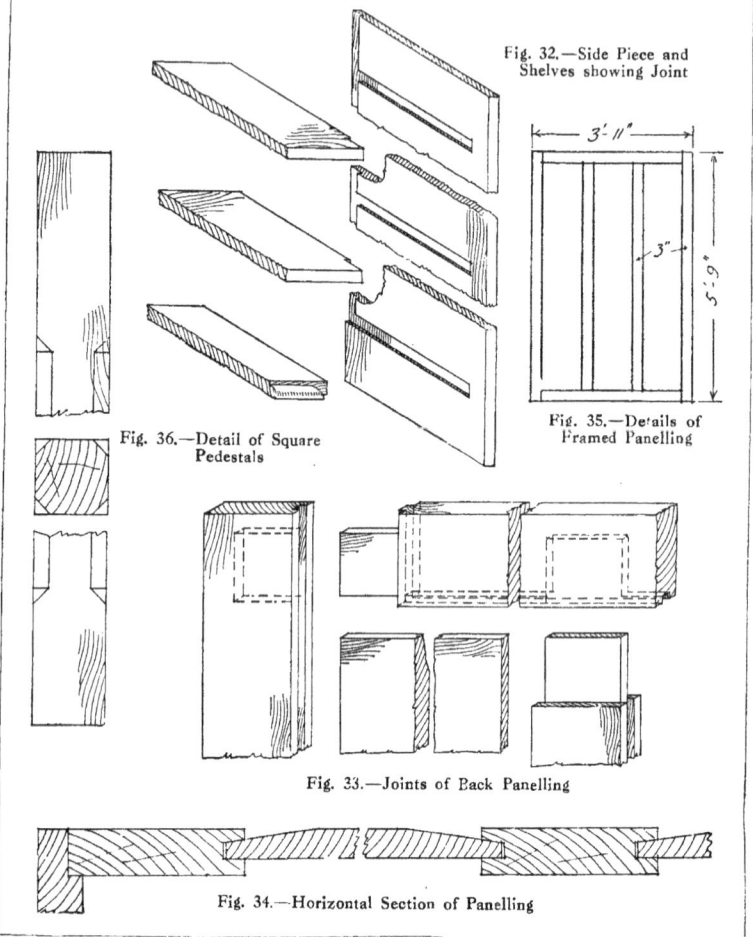

Fig. 32.—Side Piece and Shelves showing Joint

Fig. 35.—Details of Framed Panelling

Fig. 36.—Detail of Square Pedestals

Fig. 33.—Joints of Back Panelling

Fig. 34.—Horizontal Section of Panelling

HALL FURNITURE

design might be increased in height, and ties or rails introduced between the legs about 9 in. above the floor; or another shelf could be introduced at this level. Solid panels to match that of the back might be substituted for the fretwork, or this could be introduced at the back as well.

HALL WARDROBE AND HALL RACK

The useful piece of furniture shown in front elevation and section by Figs. 30 and 31 is especially designed for holding ladies' and gentlemen's hats as well as other clothing. A good appearance will be given if it is finished with white enamel. It is very light in construction, all the boards being

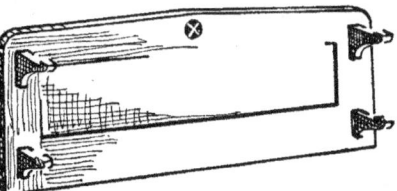

Fig. 37.—Hall Rack

First prepare the two side boards, and mark the three grooves in each piece to receive the shelves. These grooves are ¼ in. deep, and are stopped 1¼ in. from the front edge. The back edge is then rebated ¾ in. wide, to the same depth as the grooves to receive the frame for the back panelling and the wall piece at the top. The shelves are next prepared, and are 3 ft. 11 in. long, the pieces being notched out to fit the stopped grooves. It will be seen that the top shelf is made the full width of the side boards, the middle shelf ⅜ in. narrower to allow for the back panelling, and the lower shelf ¾ in. narrower in the front, the edge being moulded. Fig. 32 shows the grooves in

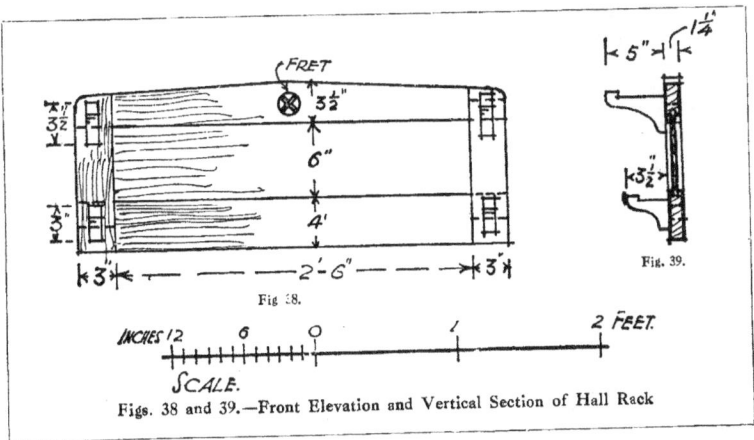

Figs. 38 and 39.—Front Elevation and Vertical Section of Hall Rack

made of material finished at ⅜-in. thickness. Bass wood or good yellow deal is recommended for strong and light construction. If yellow deal is used it can be obtained approximately 11 in. wide, and should be of good quality.

the side pieces and the shape of the shelves. The patterns at the top ends of the side boards are then cut to shape, and all pieces smoothed up and fixed together. For rigid fixing, the joints should be glued and nailed with 1½-in. oval brads.

The back frame, which fits between the top and bottom shelves, is made of material finished at 3 in. wide and ¾ in. thick. The tenons need not be carried right through, and allowance is also made for the ¹⁄₁₆-in. plough grooves, which should be about ⅜ in. deep, as shown in Fig. 33. The panels should be ½ in. thick, and bevelled at the back to fit the plough grooves. They should be fitted so as to

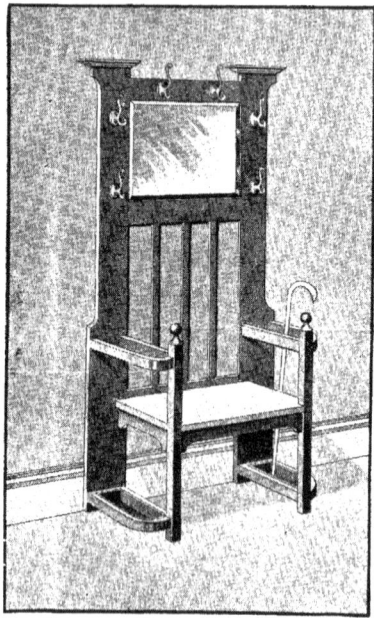

Fig 40.—Hall Stand and Seat

allow for any expansion or shrinkage in their widths, as shown in Fig. 34. Fig. 35 shows the framed panelling ready for fixing. Glue and fasten with brads or fine screws. The 1¼-in. square pedestals (see Fig. 36) for the hat racks are then fitted in and bradded. A brass rod with sliding coat-hooks is then fixed with small blocks as shown. The toe piece is fitted and fastened beneath the edge of the bottom shelf. The top wall piece is then cut to shape and fastened. All the ornamental brackets are ⅝ in. thick, and fixed with glue and brads ⅜ in. from the front edges of the wardrobe.

HALL RACK FOR STICKS

The simple rack shown by Fig. 37 is primarily intended for the accommodation of sticks, golf-clubs, etc., but with slight modification it could be utilised for other purposes. For instance, rails might be put across the brackets and it then could be used for hats. Fig. 38 is a front elevation and Fig. 39 a vertical section. The construction is so apparent that further description is unnecessary. The choice of wood is a matter that can be left to the taste of the maker.

HALL STAND AND SEAT

Oak fumed and wax-polished should be used for the hall stand and seat shown by Fig. 40.

Front, side and back elevations are shown by Figs. 41, 42 and 43 respectively.

The stand is made with a framed and panelled back, to the upper part of which a bevelled-edge mirror is fitted. The seat projects from the framed back, and is supported by front legs, which are connected to the back by framework.

The framed and panelled back is made with two stiles A (Fig. 43), which are 5 ft. 11¼ in. long by 6 in. wide at the bottom, shaped out to 5 in. wide above the seat by 1 in. thick. The stiles are connected by a top rail B, which is 2 ft. 2 in. long by 3 in. deep by 1 in. thick ; lower rail C, 2 ft. 2 in. long by 4 in. deep by 1 in. thick ; and a bottom rail D, 2 ft. 2 in. long by 2 in. deep by 1 in. thick. The rails are mortised and tenoned into the stiles, the joints being arranged as shown. The bottom edges of the tenons on the top rail, both edges of the tenons on the lower rail, and the top edges of the tenons on the bottom rail should be haunched down ¼ in., to allow for the depth of the rebates for the mirror and the grooves for the panels. The space between the stiles and the lower and

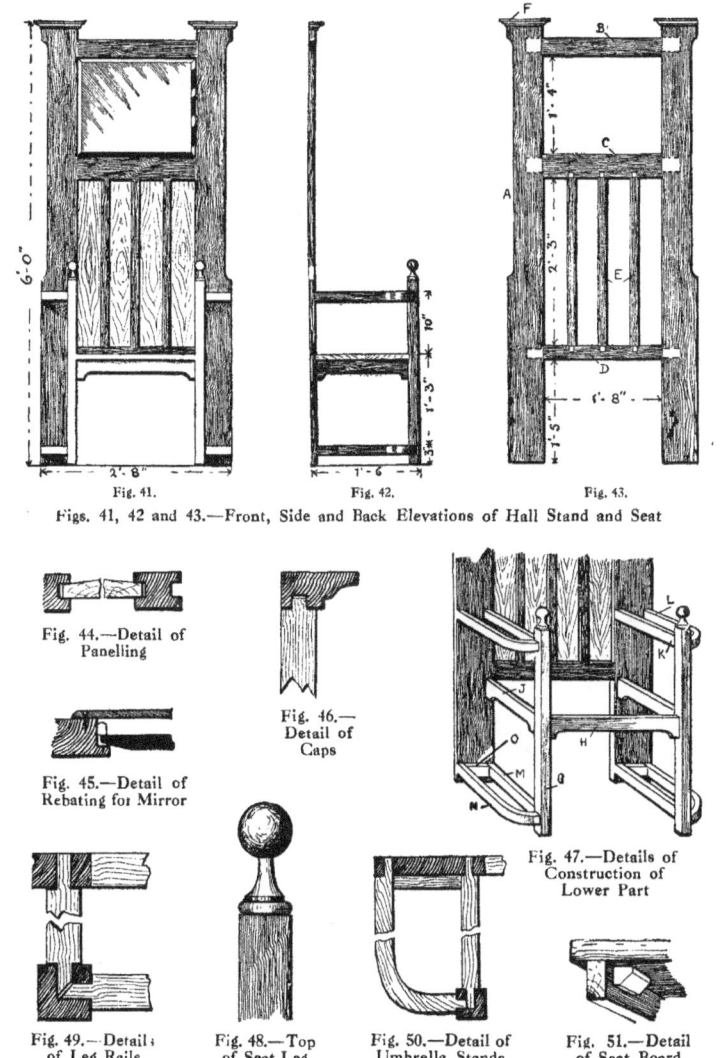

Figs. 41, 42 and 43.—Front, Side and Back Elevations of Hall Stand and Seat

Fig. 44.—Detail of Panelling

Fig. 45.—Detail of Rebating for Mirror

Fig. 46.—Detail of Caps

Fig. 47.—Details of Construction of Lower Part

Fig. 49.—Details of Leg Rails

Fig. 48.—Top of Seat Leg

Fig. 50.—Detail of Umbrella Stands

Fig. 51.—Detail of Seat Board

bottom rails is panelled, the panelling being divided by the small upright rails E, which are 2 ft. 5 in. long by 1½ in. wide by 1 in. thick, and are tenoned into the lower and bottom rails, as shown in Fig. 43. The panels should be ⅜ in. thick, being grooved ¼ in. into the edges of the framework, as shown in Fig. 44.

The edges of the framework round the opening for the mirror are rebated ¾ in. by

Fig. 52.—Hat and Umbrella Stand

¼ in. to receive the mirror, as shown in Fig. 45. The top ends of the stiles are finished with moulded caps F, which are 8½ in. long by 2¼ in. wide by 1 in. thick. The front and end edges of the caps are moulded, and the caps are mortised and tenoned to the top ends of stiles, as in Fig. 48. The legs G (Fig. 47) of the seat are 2 ft. 9 in. long by 1½ in. square, and the top ends are turned to the shape shown in Fig. 48. They are framed together by the front leg rail H, and are connected to the back framework by the side leg rails J. The front leg rail is 1 ft. 10 in. long, and the side leg rails are 1 ft. 5½ in. long by 3 in. deep, shaped out to 2 in. deep in the middle by 1 in. thick. The leg rails are mortised and tenoned into the legs, as shown in Fig. 49, the ends of the tenons being mitred together, and the side leg rails are tenoned into the back framework as shown.

The stick and umbrella stands at the sides are formed by connecting the top ends of the legs to the back with a straight rail K and a shaped rail L, the sticks and umbrellas being placed in the space between the rails. The rails are each 1½ in. deep by 1 in. wide in section, and they are framed into the back and into the legs, as shown in Fig. 50. Metal drip pans are fitted at the bottom of the stands, and the framework into which they fit consists of a straight rail M, an outer shaped rail N, and a filling piece O. The rails are similar to those at the top of the legs, and are fixed in a similar manner. The filling piece O is of a similar section to the rails, and it simply fits between the rails, being secured to the back of the stand.

The seat board is 1 ft. 11 in. long by 1 ft. 5 in. wide by 1 in. thick; it fits over the legs and rests on the leg rails, to which it is secured with wood glue blocks, as shown in Fig. 51, while screws are driven through the back of the stand into the back edge of the seat. The mirror, which is fitted to the back of the stand, fits into the rebates prepared for its reception, and is fixed with small fillet pieces, as shown in Fig. 45, while a thin protective wood back is screwed on behind the mirror.

HAT AND UMBRELLA STAND

The hat and umbrella stand shown by Fig. 52 has two parts, the upright frame at the back, and a cupboard and drawer in front. These two parts are connected by curved rods for holding umbrellas, and also by means of boards at the bottom, as shown at A (Figs. 53, 54 and 55). Other details of construction are shown in Figs. 56, 57 and 58.

To construct the stand, begin with the back framework, as in Fig. 58. This consists of 1-in. framing forming seven panels

HALL FURNITURE

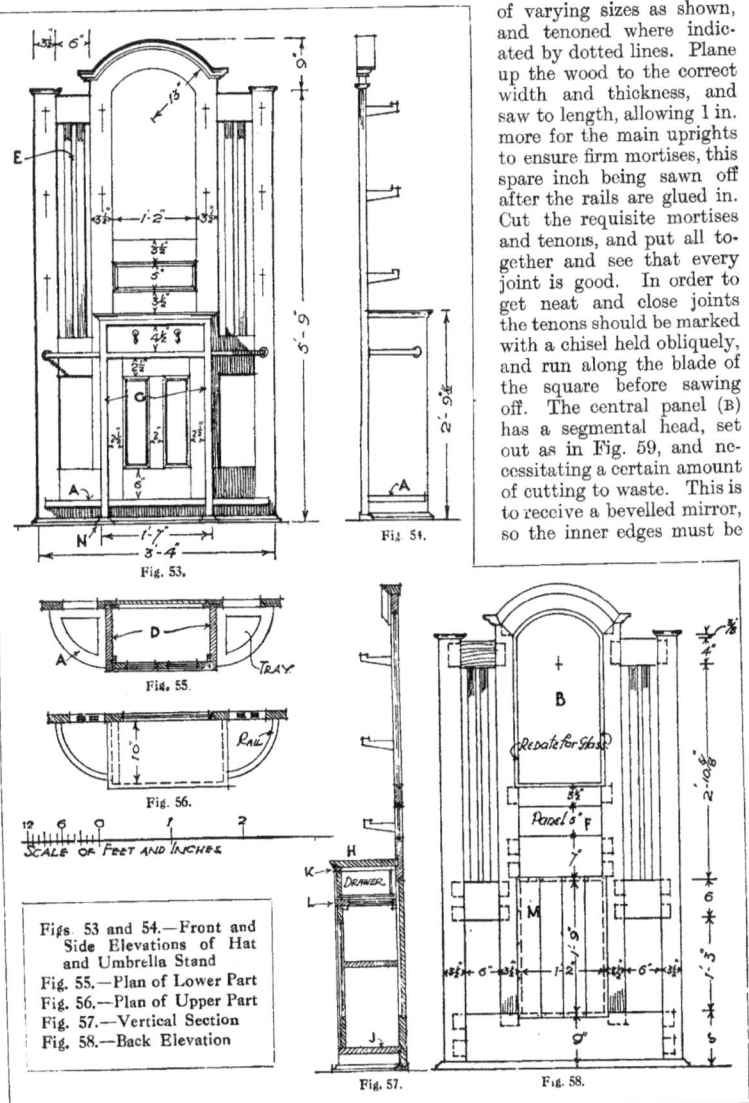

Figs. 53 and 54.—Front and Side Elevations of Hat and Umbrella Stand
Fig. 55.—Plan of Lower Part
Fig. 56.—Plan of Upper Part
Fig. 57.—Vertical Section
Fig. 58.—Back Elevation

of varying sizes as shown, and tenoned where indicated by dotted lines. Plane up the wood to the correct width and thickness, and saw to length, allowing 1 in. more for the main uprights to ensure firm mortises, this spare inch being sawn off after the rails are glued in. Cut the requisite mortises and tenons, and put all together and see that every joint is good. In order to get neat and close joints the tenons should be marked with a chisel held obliquely, and run along the blade of the square before sawing off. The central panel (B) has a segmental head, set out as in Fig. 59, and necessitating a certain amount of cutting to waste. This is to receive a bevelled mirror, so the inner edges must be rebated, as shown at C in the same figure. The framework must be grooved to receive the bottom boards A (Fig. 53, etc.) and the sides of the cupboard D (Fig. 55). When all are cut and fitted glue up the whole, adding four 1½-in. by ⅝-in. laths as at E in Figs. 53 and 59, and a panel under the mirror space F (Fig. 58), and cramp up.

Now prepare the box, etc., in 1-in. stuff. It consists of solid sides G (Fig. 53), bottom and moulded top H and J (Fig. 57), a rail 1¼ in. wide and one 2 in. wide K and L, a panelled door, and an ordinary drawer with runners, as well as a shelf across the cupboard if required. The whole is housed together and into the back framing, and the small shelves are housed into the upright sides. The cupboard back is filled with tongued boarding let into rebates, as at M in Fig. 58. The whole is finished by the addition of moulded cappings (Fig. 60), and a rebated and chamfered base to the back (Fig. 61), mitreing with a grooved and chamfered base to the cupboard sides, as at N in Fig. 53. The boards A for the bottom should be rounded as shown, and hollows sunk ¾ in. to receive pans for drips. The curved brass or oxidised tube may be obtained from an ironmonger, together with rings or plates to cover its junctions with the woodwork. A pattern drawn full-size should be supplied. Let the centre of the curved tube be drawn from a 9-in. radius, and allow ¾ in. at each end beyond the quadrant for insertion. Drive the brass rail into the front legs, and cramp up the cupboard, etc., with the back frame and bottom boards. Secure the bottom board to the back and the box to the rails, with screws from the back.

The mirror should be fixed by means of wedges, as at C in Fig. 59, the back board being kept quite clear of it.

Brass or oxidised hooks may be screwed on ; or these can very suitably be formed in wood as shown, tenoned right through the framing, and wedged from the back. Cut a paper pattern of the sunk hollows in the bottom board, and get an ironmonger to make two zinc trays 1 in. high, with a beading on the tops, and the stand is complete.

HALL SEAT IN OAK

The introduction of lobby halls in even comparatively small houses has provided greater scope for hall furniture than has hitherto prevailed in the long passages of the older houses. In the latter, opportunities were exhausted after a hall stand and chairs, with perhaps a small narrow table, were introduced. Perhaps the most decorative piece of furniture in an old-fashioned hall is a good grandfather clock, and next to this must be placed the hall settle. Its value as a decorative piece of furniture will be generally admitted, and if it is provided with a hinged lift-up seat, its usefulness is increased, and one has both seat and chest. In some cases the peculiar plan of a hall is such as to favour the introduction of a fitted hall seat, and in this connection it may be noted that with but little variation the design shown by Fig. 62 could be modified to suit the changed conditions. In the case of a recess, it is a good plan to have a panelled back, and also panelled instead of shaped sides, such as are illustrated. Figs. 63 and 64 are front and end elevations, and a vertical section is given by Fig. 65. Two views of the back are shown by Fig. 66.

When constructing the settle the ends should first be jointed up with dowelled joints, so that two ends can be cut from one piece. The best plan is to first cut a piece of stiff brown paper exactly the shape of one end to form a template. It is then an easy matter to obtain the necessary size for jointing the wood sufficient to cut one in the other as indicated by Fig. 67. After jointing, the wood should be levelled on both sides, and the shapes marked out by means of the brown-paper template. To shape the ends they should be hand-screwed together and both planed, spokeshaved, filed, and glass-papered in turn, the bottoms being sawn and planed true and square. By practising this method both ends are obtained exactly alike and with the edges square and sharp. Should they be made separ-

HALL FURNITURE

ately there is always the risk of variation, which may cause the settle to "wind" when glued up. It is, of course, also an additional advantage to have the edges perfectly square and sharp in the first instance.

The chief part of the settle is the back, and, as will be seen from Fig. 68, the top or cap moulding D is made separately, and dowelled on to the back frame. The back is made with six panels, and should preferably be mortised and tenoned together. It will be necessary to make the outside stiles wider than the muntins, as the back screws into rebates made in the ends. This detail is indicated in Fig. 69. It is advantageous to bevel the rebate as shown, as by this means the remaining part of the end is strengthened, and is less liable to break away than is the case when the rebate is made square with a resultant narrow slip remaining on the end.

The moulded edge to the stiles and rails, shown in Fig. 68, should properly be worked with a scratch-stock, the ends "running out," which necessitates carving with gouges to finish the mouldings. A pleasing character is given to the work by this particular detail; but alternately an ovolo could well be used, which would be run through the muntin and scratched at intervals on the stiles and rails. The correct finish to a moulding of this type is, of course, the mason's mitre, which again gives more character to an oak job than ordinary mitreing. It will be seen that the panels are placed in position before the frame is glued up, and when the latter has been effected the back frame can be levelled on both sides and squared up. The front frame is made on similar lines to the back, and then the seat and frame can be proceeded with.

The plan (Fig. 70) shows a three-sided

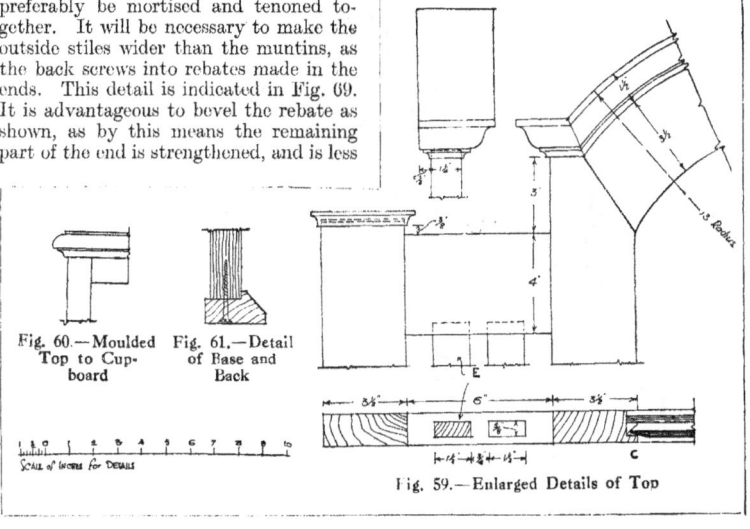

Fig. 60.—Moulded Top to Cupboard

Fig. 61.—Detail of Base and Back

Fig. 59.—Enlarged Details of Top

seat frame which is mortised and tenoned together to receive a hinged lid or seat. The latter is cut from solid stuff, and then the ends are clamped to ensure flatness. A curve is introduced at the front, and, as will be seen, it projects at the front and facilitates opening the lid. An enlarged detail (see Fig. 71) indicates the correct position of the hinges. When fitting these, a marked gauge should be set from the edge of the hinge to the centre of the knuckle. This is used on the edges, and the thickness of one wing is then gauged on the seat and rail. The bottom is made either of solid oak or American whitewood faced up with American oak.

After the back seat, front, and bottom have been properly marked, they can be squared up to their finished sizes and prepared for attachment to the ends. The seat frame should first be dowelled into the ends (Fig. 72), then the front frame should be dealt with likewise, and finally the bottoms; ⅜-in. dowels should be used, and care should be taken to bore and fit carefully in order to make a strong, rigid seat. When the parts have been glued together the seat frame is screwed from the back, and the bottom is screwed up to the front frame. To further strengthen the job, neat angle-blocks should be glued in the angles underneath the seat and also underneath the bottom.

A most important part of cabinet-work is the finish imparted to the work. Should English or European oak be used, fuming and waxing can be employed to advantage.

OLD-STYLE SETTLE

Hooded seats or settles such as that illustrated by Fig. 73 are still to be found in old farmhouses and inns. They are essentially picturesque, and well adapted for use in a hall. To be appropriate in appearance, modern replicas should be quite simple in design, but of fairly heavy construction. The ideal material of which to construct it would be oak; but selected pine treated with a water-stain and slightly waxed would be quite suitable. The

Fig. 62.—Hall Seat in Oak

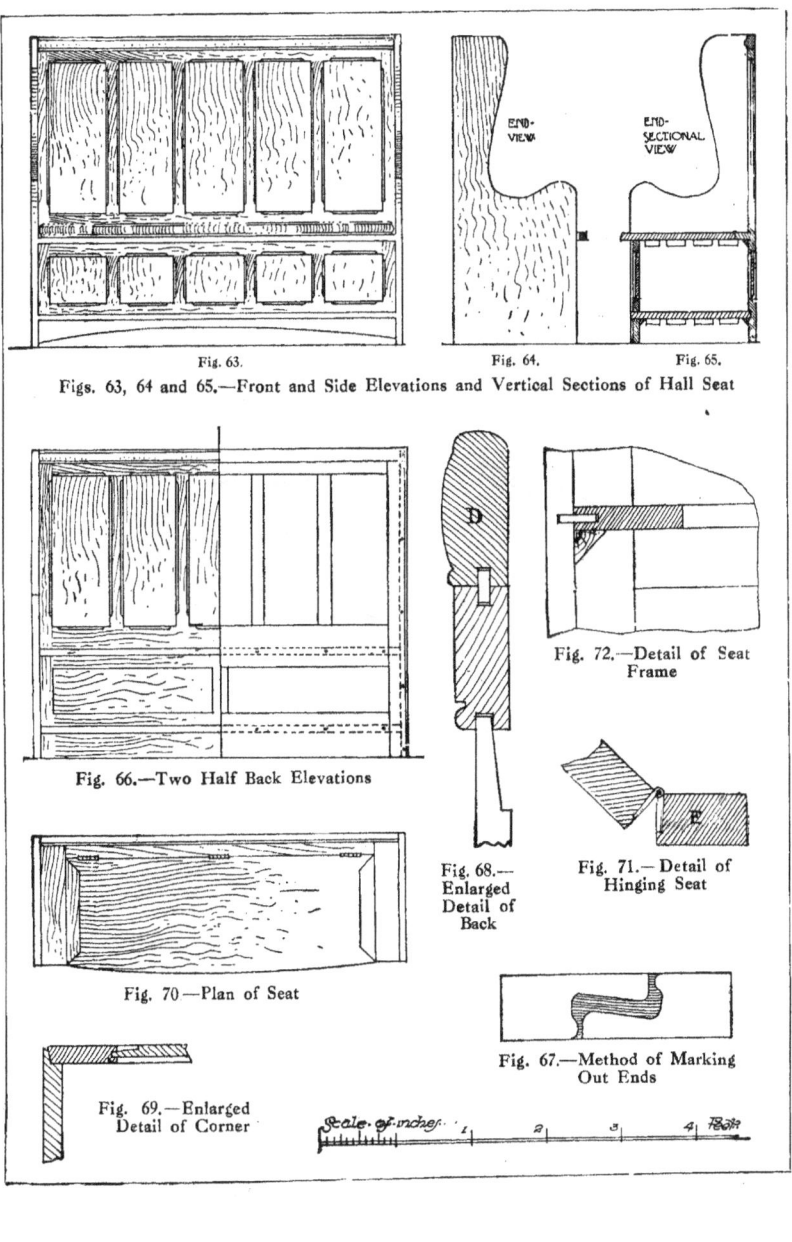

Fig. 63.

Fig. 64.

Fig. 65.

Figs. 63, 64 and 65.—Front and Side Elevations and Vertical Sections of Hall Seat

Fig. 66.—Two Half Back Elevations

Fig. 68.—Enlarged Detail of Back

Fig. 71.—Detail of Hinging Seat

Fig. 72.—Detail of Seat Frame

Fig. 70.—Plan of Seat

Fig. 67.—Method of Marking Out Ends

Fig. 69.—Enlarged Detail of Corner

THE PRACTICAL WOODWORKER

drawers under the seat are useful, although not essential parts of the design.

Front and end elevations and sectional plan are shown by Figs. 74, 75 and 76 respectively.

To begin the work, the ends should be prepared from stuff not less than 1¼ in. thick, built up of three widths of about 8¼ in. each, tongued together and shaped, as shown in Fig. 75. From this the outline of the back edges can be readily obtained, while the large curve of the front and above this will ultimately be fixed a raking top at least 1 in. thick, moulded all round, as shown in Fig. 80. Into this the ends and rail should be housed or tongued. If this is not done, ledges should be fixed as at D (Fig. 77), to prevent the ends from warping through lack of stiffening.

The seat E (Fig. 77) should also be of substantial thickness, rounded on the front (Fig. 79), and finishing flush with the ends at the back (Fig. 81). It slopes ¾ in. towards the back, and should be housed

Fig. 73.—Old-style Settle

can be enlarged from Fig. 78, by first of all setting out the series of inch squares there given. In the same way the slighter curve below seat level can be obtained from Fig. 79, the series of squares working downwards from the top of the seat, which is 1 ft. 6 in. above the floor at the front. If preferred, the three pieces constituting each end can be dovetail-keyed together with hardwood, as shown in Fig. 75. At the top the ends are connected by means of a 4-in. by 1-in. rail as at A in Fig. 77, dovetailed as at B in Fig. 80, ¼ in. into the ends. Under it in the centre is a shaped standard or support F (Figs. 74 and 77), fitted close up to its underside and notched to suit two longitudinal drawer rails shown in Fig. 79, one G 1¼ in. by ¾ in., and the other H 2 in. by 1 in., both being housed into the ends. The lower part of the work is stiffened by means of a 2½-in. by 1½-in. tie J (Figs. 74, 76 and 77) taken completely through the ends and central standard, and rounded, mortised, and wedged, as in Fig. 82. Drawer divisions or guides should be fitted

HALL FURNITURE

from front to back, as at K in Figs. 74 and 76, and drawer-runners as in Fig. 79 screwed on.

Below the seat, the back is filled in with ¾-in. panelled framing in three long divisions, its top fixed against a fillet, as at L in Fig. 81, while above is a piece of stout 1-in. panelling, having square edges to the framing, but with the panels moulded on the front, as in Figs. 74 and 82, a moulded and bottom. It will be found advisable to cut the central standard slightly shorter than the ends, in order to obviate any possibility of the settle rocking on it.

SIMPLE LOBBY GLASS WITH COAT HOOKS

In many modern houses of the smaller type, the entrance passages or lobbies are

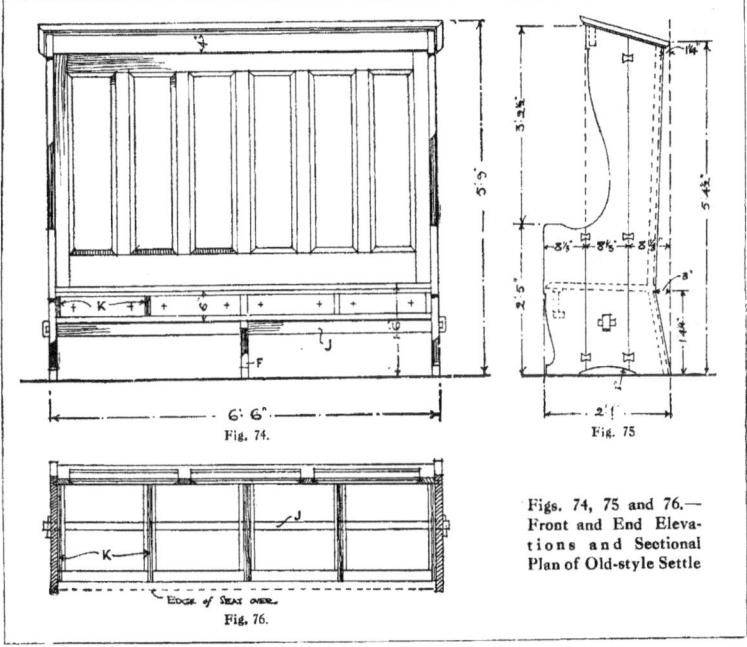

Figs. 74, 75 and 76.—Front and End Elevations and Sectional Plan of Old-style Settle

fillet as noted in the latter figure being planted on the horizontal edges only of all the back panels. This framing should be housed to the ends, seat, and top, or tongued as in Figs. 80, 81 and 82.

Alternatively the back might be filled in with boarding having ploughed edges joined up with very wide tongues (leaving, say, 1 in. between the boards), this necessitating a ledge or rail across the top

so narrow that to place a hall stand in such a contracted space is almost impossible. Yet it is desirable to have something on which to hang hats, coats, etc. A mirror is also almost indispensable.

The hat and coat rack shown by Fig. 83 is designed to take up as little room as possible, and if a small umbrella stand is placed underneath, it will be found much more convenient than the orthodox

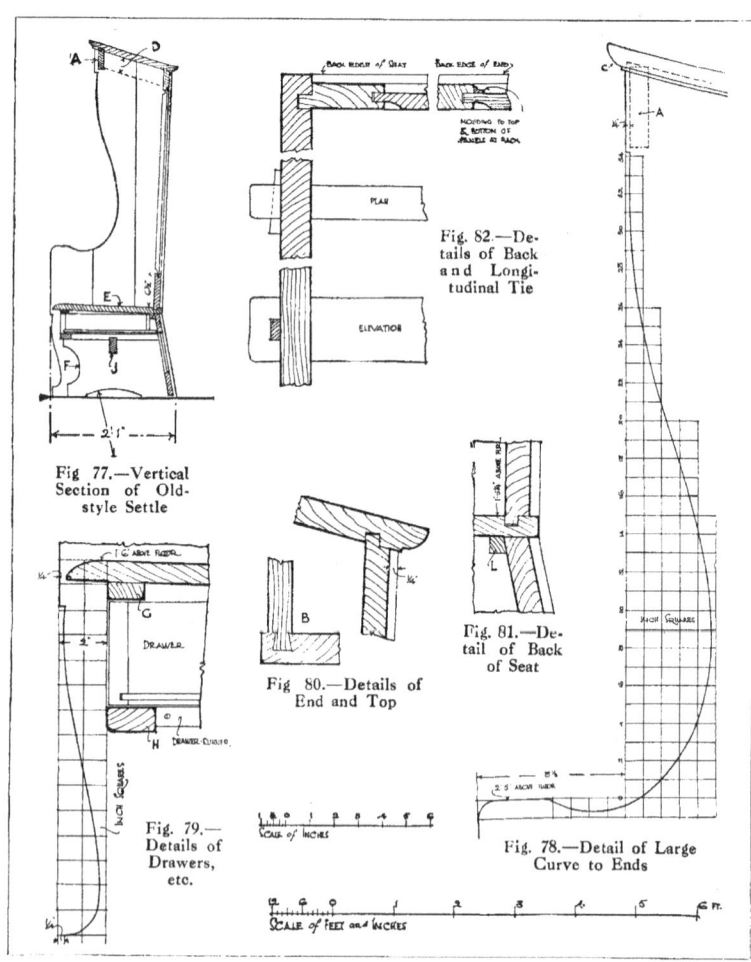

Fig. 77.—Vertical Section of Old-style Settle

Fig. 82.—Details of Back and Longitudinal Tie

Fig. 80.—Details of End and Top

Fig. 81.—Detail of Back of Seat

Fig. 79.—Details of Drawers, etc.

Fig. 78.—Detail of Large Curve to Ends

hall stand. An end elevation and cross sectional plan are shown by Figs. 84 and 85.

In selecting the wood, oak is undoubtedly the most appropriate; but canary, or even any of the softwoods, painted white would look very well. If oak is used, it should be stained dark and french-polished or carefully varnished. The construction has been kept as simple as possible, so that anyone with the least elementary knowledge of woodwork can start on the work with the fullest confidence of success. All dimensions and details of construction are given by Figs. 86, 87 and 88.

HALL FURNITURE

The frame is made out of wood of the same section, all the joints being simple half-laps, as shown by the dotted lines. The cut pieces and laths fit into notches cut for them in the rails. The centre-piece in the panels can be cut out of a piece of wood of the same section as that for the frame, by sawing a piece of the required length down the centre, thus forming two pieces ready for cutting into

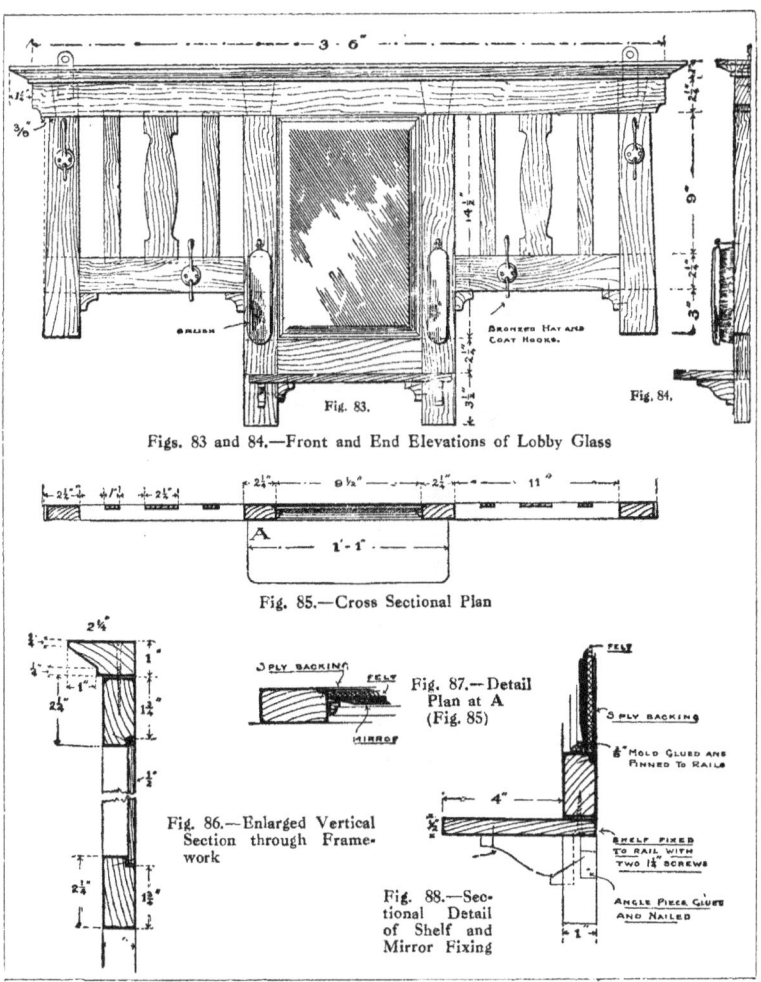

Figs. 83 and 84.—Front and End Elevations of Lobby Glass

Fig. 85.—Cross Sectional Plan

Fig. 86.—Enlarged Vertical Section through Framework

Fig. 87.—Detail Plan at A (Fig. 85)

Fig. 88.—Sectional Detail of Shelf and Mirror Fixing

shape with the fret-saw or spokeshave. A small moulding is planted on round the opening in the centre to receive the mirror. This moulding could be run on the frame by those who are a little more experienced in the work. In forming the cornice, having cut the wood to the required length and squared it on all faces, set the stop of the rebate plane to make a rebate 1 in. wide, and the depth stop set to make the rebate ¼ in. deep. When the rebate is formed take off the width stop, but retain the depth gauge ; and after adjusting the plane iron so that no more wood can be removed from the shoulder of the rebate, proceed to form the slope of the cornice by planing away the wood until ¼ in. remains on the face of the outside edge. The returns of the cornice can be easily worked with the aid of a tenon saw and a large chisel.

Two pieces of wood 10 ft. long by 2¼ in. wide and 1 in. deep will be sufficient to make all the frame ; but a special piece will be required for the shelf and brackets supporting the shelf. About 4 ft. of moulding will be required for planting on round the mirror.

SIMPLE UMBRELLA STAND IN OAK

The general dimensions of the simple umbrella stand shown by Fig. 89 are 2 ft. 6 in. long over the posts by 10 in. deep and 2 ft. 4 in. high from floor to top rail. Front and end elevations and plan are given by Figs. 90, 91 and 92.

To proceed with its construction first prepare the four posts ; square them up to 1¼ in. by 1¼ in. and mortise for the top and bottom rails, which are 1¾ in. by ⅞ in. and 2 in. by ⅞ in. respectively. Tenon the rails to the posts (see Fig. 93), keeping the latter ⅛ in. in advance of the rails. Fig. 94 gives a section of the bottom rails which

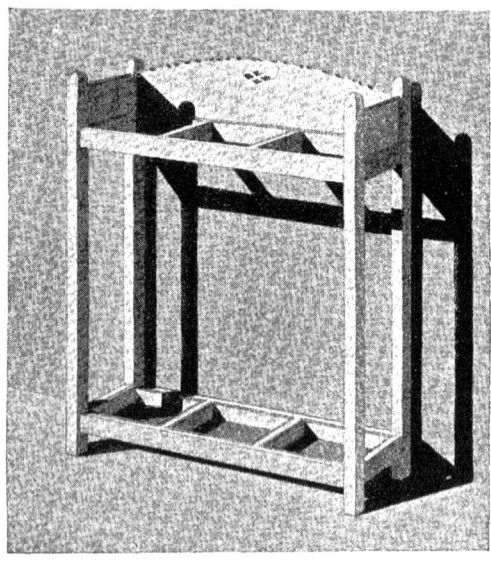

Fig. 89.—Simple Umbrella Stand

HALL FURNITURE

are 2 in. deep by 1 in. thick, and are rebated to receive the ½-in. pine bottom D, which is fitted and fixed with screws to the bottom rails. The cross-rails 1¾ in. deep The tops of the latter are shaped and chamfered, as shown in Fig. 95, while the shaped back is decorated by means of a chamfered pattern along its upper edge

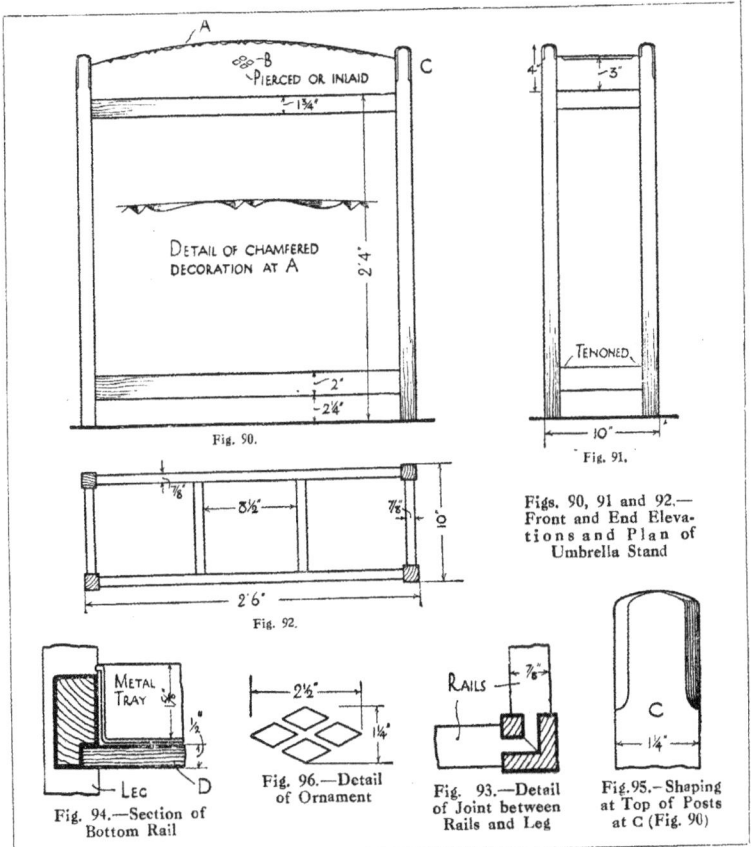

Figs. 90, 91 and 92.—Front and End Elevations and Plan of Umbrella Stand

Fig. 94.—Section of Bottom Rail

Fig. 96.—Detail of Ornament

Fig. 93.—Detail of Joint between Rails and Leg

Fig. 95.—Shaping at Top of Posts at C (Fig. 90)

by ⅞ in. thick are stub-tenoned to the long rails at top and bottom. Between the posts above the top rails are fitted a shaped back and two side pieces (see Figs. 90 and 91). These are of ½-in. material and are housed into the posts. (see Fig. 90). The diamond shaped decoration at B may either be pierced or may be inlaid with ebony. A detail of this is given by Fig. 96.

The zinc pans fit between the bottom rails, as shown in Fig. 94.

Dressers and Sideboards

MODERN KITCHEN CABINET OR DRESSER

A CABINET useful for kitchen or living room, and designed to hold all necessary utensils and materials for preparing food, is shown by Fig. 1. It occupies very little space while affording the maximum amount of accommodation. It could be placed with ease in the recess formed at the side of a fireplace.

The lower portion is divided up into

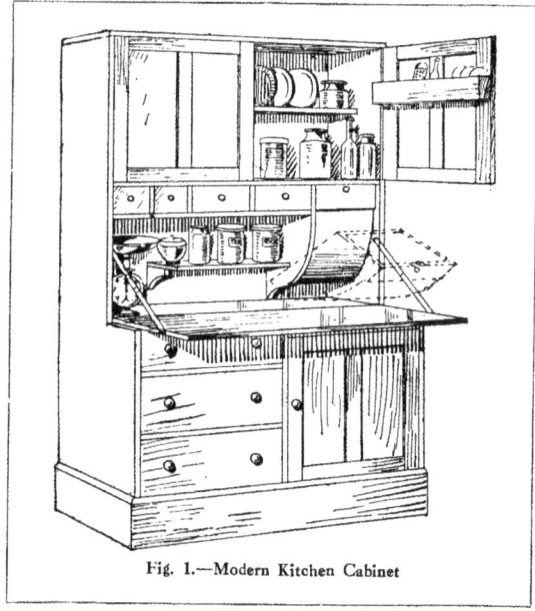

Fig. 1.—Modern Kitchen Cabinet

three drawers on the left side, the top one being for cutlery, and divided into three divisions and lined with green baize. On the right-hand side is a cupboard with shelf for storing pots and pans; the pastry-board slides in a recess above the door. The upper part, enclosed by a hinged flap, contains two small and two large drawers for spices and such commodities as are used in cooking. On the right-hand side is a flour bin pivoted at the bottom, and kept in position when closed by a strong snap-catch. This bin when in use is lowered until it rests on the open flap and permits of easy access for removing the flour. Below the drawers is a small shelf for tins, etc., and on the left is space for a weighing machine. Above is another cupboard with shelf enclosed by two doors. On the doors are fixed two wooden trays for small articles. The shelf has a raised fillet to keep plates from slipping when standing on edge. The constructional work is of the simplest order, and only a few details need be outlined.

The sides should be $1\frac{1}{8}$ in. thick, tongued and grooved to the $\frac{7}{8}$-in. thick top. The drawer and door rails and bearers are $2\frac{1}{4}$ in. by $\frac{7}{8}$ in., and housed

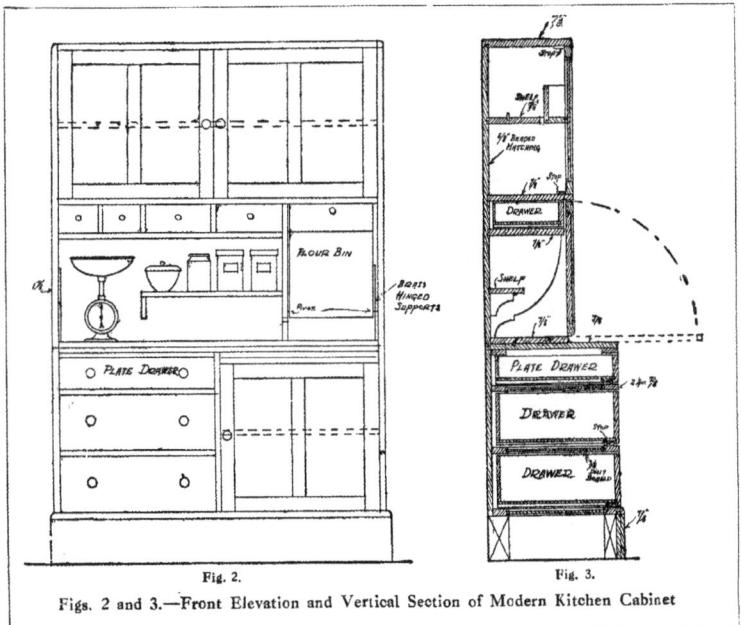

Figs. 2 and 3.—Front Elevation and Vertical Section of Modern Kitchen Cabinet

into the sides. The doors are framed up with $2\frac{1}{4}$-in. by $\frac{7}{8}$-in. stiles and rails, and the panel-fillings of $\frac{5}{8}$ in. are tongued and grooved into framing. The drawers have $\frac{7}{8}$-in. fronts, lap-dovetailed to the $\frac{3}{8}$-in. sides. A plinth, $\frac{7}{8}$ in. thick, is tongued under the bottom bearer. A study of the scale drawings (Figs. 2 and 3) will render these instructions clear.

The general woodwork is deal, painted

THE PRACTICAL WOODWORKER

white, the flap of teak and unpainted inside.

KITCHEN DRESSER WITH ENCLOSED MANGLE

In many small cottage homes a mangle is a necessity, but, as a rule, not an ornament, and the dresser shown by Fig. 4 has been designed to cover it whilst not in use. It will be understood that the mangle is

Fig. 4.—Kitchen Dresser with Enclosed Mangle

by nature of an accessory, and that with a little modification the dresser could be utilised for other purposes. Mangles are usually obtainable locally, and the general dimensions of them when folded are: Height from floor to top, 2 ft. 3½ in.; length of top, 3 ft. ½ in.; and 1 ft. 8¼ in. wide. Should there be any variation from these sizes due allowance would have to be made. Part front elevation and end elevation are shown by Figs. 5 and 6.

The upper part of the dresser, with shelves, is separate from the lower part, and is fixed with holdfasts and screws to the wall, the latter being drilled and plugged to receive the iron holdfasts. The lower part of the dresser (Figs. 7 and 8) is made with the ends to fold inwards against the front, which is made to imitate doors and drawers. Thus, when not in use it can be placed flat against a wall. The front and ends are kept in position by iron stays. The loose top simply rests on the front and ends. The height of the dresser top is about 8 in. higher than the mangle top, so that, if desired, any articles may be placed out of sight by simply raising the front edge of the top. The hollowing out of the lower ends of the upper part A in the end elevation (Figs. 4 and 6) allows for the handle of the mangle to turn.

The complete dresser may be made of pine or deal, painted or stained to match walnut or mahogany. The main dimensions are: Total height, 6 ft. 9 in.; height of lower part, 3 ft.; and extreme width across the front, 4 ft. The back of the upper part B in the part front elevation (Fig. 5) and the sham door panels are made of ½-in. matchboarding, and the remaining parts of 1-in. stuff, finishing when planed about ¾ in. full. The trouble of planing the wood may be avoided by purchasing good sound flooring boards and jointing them to the requisite widths. Most local timber merchants keep these in stock.

In making the dresser the top part with shelves may be first taken in hand. The ends have a rebate worked in the back edges to receive the matchboarded back. The shelves, of course, will be the thickness of the back, less in width than the ends. The latter must be dovetailed grooved across to receive the ends of shelves (Fig. 9). The groove in the ends must be stopped ¼ in. from the front edge, so that the dovetail will not show at the front. The top C (Fig. 5) may be grooved likewise to receive the top parts of the ends.

DRESSERS AND SIDEBOARDS

When the top, shelves, and ends are fixed with glue and nails, next fit in the matchboarding back B. This may pass down behind the top of the lower part. When fixing to the wall due regard must be paid to the weight of crockery it will be likely to contain. The front of the lower part, from the floor to the top. The double centre stile is tenoned into the top and bottom rails F and G. A plinth H, $\frac{3}{4}$ in. thick, with bevelled top edge, is planted on the bottom rail G. The imitation bearers J are strips about $\frac{1}{8}$ in. thick and $\frac{7}{8}$ in. wide, and are planted on the face of

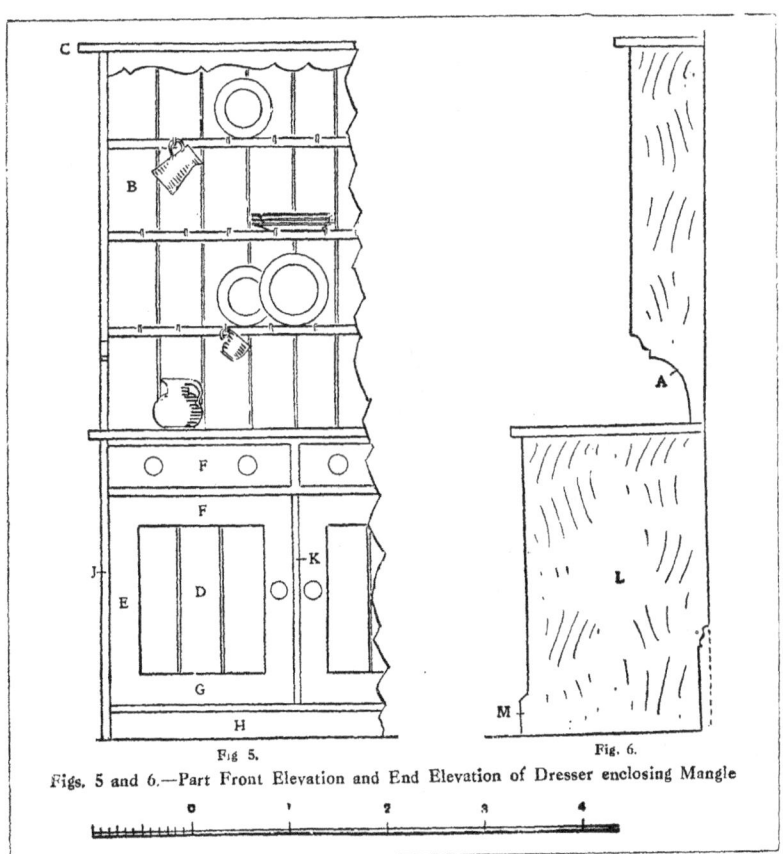

Figs. 5 and 6.—Part Front Elevation and End Elevation of Dresser enclosing Mangle

in imitation of doors and drawers, should be framed together with mortises and tenons, grooves being ploughed in the stiles and rails to receive the panels D (Fig. 5). The two outer stiles E extend the framing and secured with glue and brads; likewise K, about $\frac{3}{8}$ in. wide, $\frac{1}{2}$ in. round in section. The ends L have a piece M glued on the front edge, so that the plinth H can butt against them. The ends L (Fig. 6) are fixed to the front framing with hinges, as shown by Fig. 10. The iron angle stay (Fig. 11) may be made of stout wire, or, better still, by a smith, of ¼-in. iron rod, and connected to the front and ends with iron screw eyelets, which can be had from most ironmongers.

Four blocks O, or two battens about 2 in. wide, should be fixed to the underside of the top, as shown in Fig. 12. These will keep the top in the proper position. The dresser may be made 3 in. or 6 in. narrower or wider if desired. Knobs as shown (Fig. 13) may be used, or brass handles. Hooks

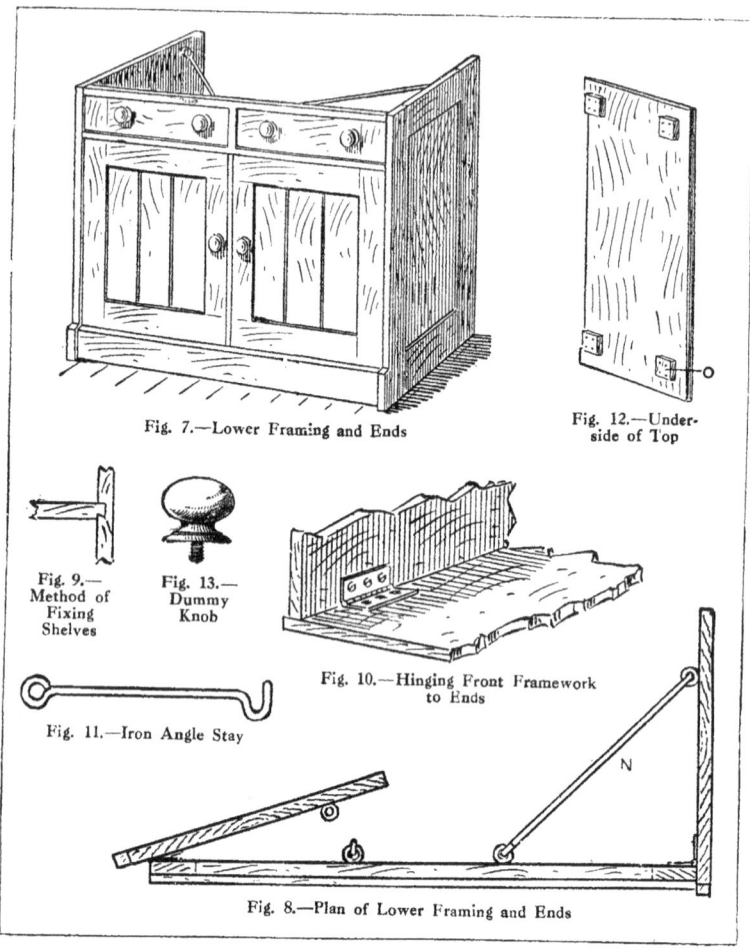

Fig. 7.—Lower Framing and Ends

Fig. 12.—Underside of Top

Fig. 9.—Method of Fixing Shelves

Fig. 13.—Dummy Knob

Fig. 10.—Hinging Front Framework to Ends

Fig. 11.—Iron Angle Stay

Fig. 8.—Plan of Lower Framing and Ends

DRESSERS AND SIDEBOARDS 793

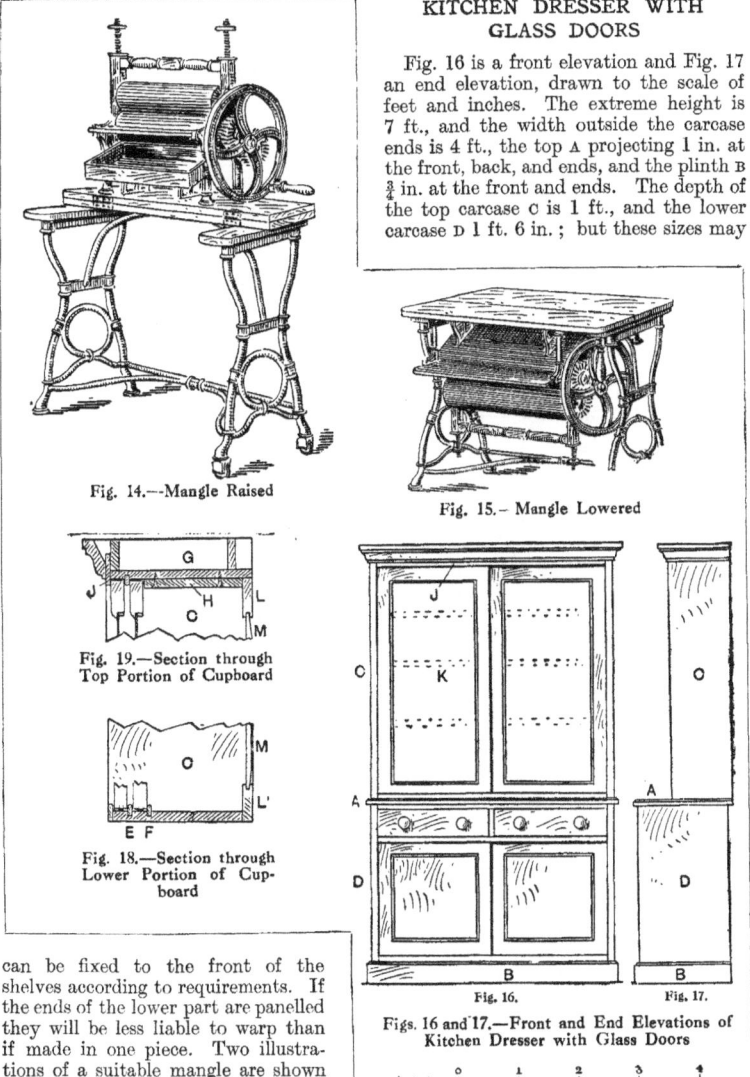

KITCHEN DRESSER WITH GLASS DOORS

Fig. 16 is a front elevation and Fig. 17 an end elevation, drawn to the scale of feet and inches. The extreme height is 7 ft., and the width outside the carcase ends is 4 ft., the top A projecting 1 in. at the front, back, and ends, and the plinth B ¾ in. at the front and ends. The depth of the top carcase C is 1 ft., and the lower carcase D 1 ft. 6 in.; but these sizes may

Fig. 14.—Mangle Raised

Fig. 15.—Mangle Lowered

Fig. 19.—Section through Top Portion of Cupboard

Fig. 18.—Section through Lower Portion of Cupboard

can be fixed to the front of the shelves according to requirements. If the ends of the lower part are panelled they will be less liable to warp than if made in one piece. Two illustrations of a suitable mangle are shown by Figs. 14 and 15.

Figs. 16 and 17.—Front and End Elevations of Kitchen Dresser with Glass Doors

be increased or diminished according to requirements, remembering that one door has to pass behind the other. To keep the doors in their right track, grooves E and F (Fig. 18) are ploughed in the bottom of the top carcase, and hardwood strips are inserted as shown. For the top of the doors a similar groove and strip are provided in the detachable cornice G (Fig. 19). The back of the inner door slides against the edge of the carcase top H, and the shelves are fixtures, then matchboarding running from the top to the bottom will serve. In constructing the lower carcase (Figs. 16 and 17) the plinth B is detachable like the cornice, and the doors are pushed up from below and then dropped on the plinth. The fillet E (Fig. 18) coming between the two doors causes a gap extending from the top to the bottom; this must be closed by a strip fixed to the inner side of the front door.

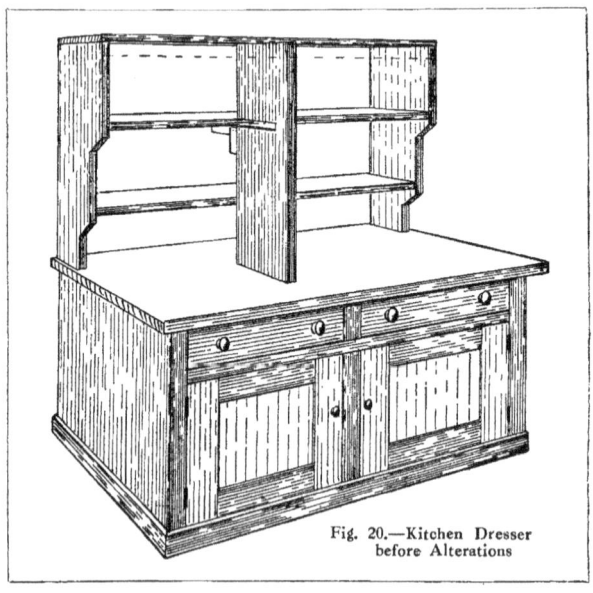

Fig. 20.—Kitchen Dresser before Alterations

front of the outer door against a fillet J (Figs. 16 and 19) fixed behind the cornice moulding. The doors are put in place, and the cornice is dropped over them and then secured with screws from the underside of the top H. If the shelves K are movable like a bookcase, it will be necessary to make the carcase back L (Fig. 19) in one large frame with a centre stile and a cross-rail, with $\frac{1}{2}$-in. thick panels M inserted in ploughed grooves, so as to make the top carcase rigid. But if the

To allow the doors to slide freely, rollers should be fixed to the bottom edges, and to make a substantial job the carcase ends and doors should be about $1\frac{1}{8}$ in. thick.

IMPROVED KITCHEN DRESSER

Utility should be the keynote of modern kitchen furniture, and with this object in mind a design is shown for the conversion of the ordinary kitchen dresser into a real labour-saving piece of furniture. Fig. 20 shows an ordinary type of kitchen dresser in process of transformation and which, actually (for the purpose it is supposed to fulfil) is more or less useless. The same dresser converted into a really useful article is shown by Fig. 21. It will be noticed that the front of the shelves has been filled with doors, and the shelves widened so that they are deep enough to hold plates flat. The drawers and cupflat chisel or a screwdriver to avoid breaking them, for the wood will come in useful in other places. Carefully note where the beading is bradded, and exert most pressure quite close up. Next fit two division boards cut from $\frac{3}{4}$-in. by 11-in. stuff as shown. Slots should be cut in these boards to allow of them being pushed right back to the wall. These slots will require careful marking out, and the best way is to commence with the top

Fig. 21.—Kitchen Dresser with Alterations Complete

boards underneath are arranged to enable their contents to be reached without trouble, and, above all, the surface for dust collecting is reduced to a minimum. Front and end elevations are given by Figs. 22 and 23.

Commencing then with an ordinary dresser, as shown by Fig. 20, first remove all the beading placed on the front of the shelves to keep the plates in place. These pieces should be carefully raised with a slot, as shown at a (Fig. 24). The distance to the line should be measured from the shelf, and the position of the groove determined by placing the board quite upright with the edge against the shelf; the thickness may then be marked off. To make sure that the shelf is quite at right angles, place the try-square on as shown in Fig. 20. If there is any inclination, this must be allowed for. The groove should be sawn out close up to the line and the waste carefully removed. When this groove is done, place the board in position and push the groove on the shelf, so that the second groove may be marked off. Cut this out in the same way, and finally the bottom one, if there is a third shelf, may be marked out and cut. The second division board may be marked off from the first if it fits, and any adjustment may be made. These boards should have a space of 2 ft. if the dresser is a 5-ft. length, used at any rate for the two division pieces. The latter pieces should be 2 ft. apart in the centre, leaving about 1 ft. 2 in. or so for the side openings, as shown by Fig. 25. This frame when placed against the division boards will leave a space at each end, as shown in the side view (Fig. 26); this space has now to be filled up. First of all screw or nail a length of the same material on to the top board of the dresser, as shown at B (Fig 27), and

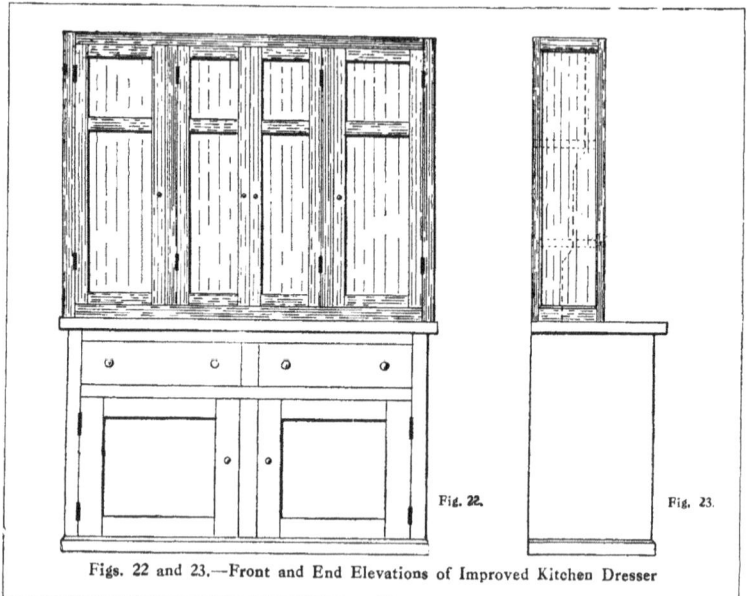

Figs. 22 and 23.—Front and End Elevations of Improved Kitchen Dresser

as is usually the case. If longer, a space of 2 ft. 6 in. would do.

The next stage is to make a framework to hold the doors. This should be made from 2¼-in. by 1¼-in. batten planed down to 2 in. by 1 in. Two lengths will be required for the top and the bottom, these being 2 in. longer than the distance between the uprights holding the shelves. Mortise-and-tenon joints are preferable for the corners, but halving joints may be also another length at the top, as at C. Next cut some lengths to fit between the two uprights, and shape them at the inside ends, with a corresponding sloping notch cut out of the sides. If it is not desired to cut the dresser—and in a rented house this may not be advisable—the pieces should be supported as shown in Fig. 28; but in each case the level of the top of the cross-rails must be on a line with the underside of the existing shelves. The front frame should be lightly bradded or screwed into position, with the division boards placed exactly in the centre of the division uprights, and then a thin board prepared to fit in the space at each end, as shown in Fig. 29. The boards should be about ¼ in. thick, and should fit tightly to allow for inevitable shrinkage.

The whole of the work may now be secured with nails and screws, but it

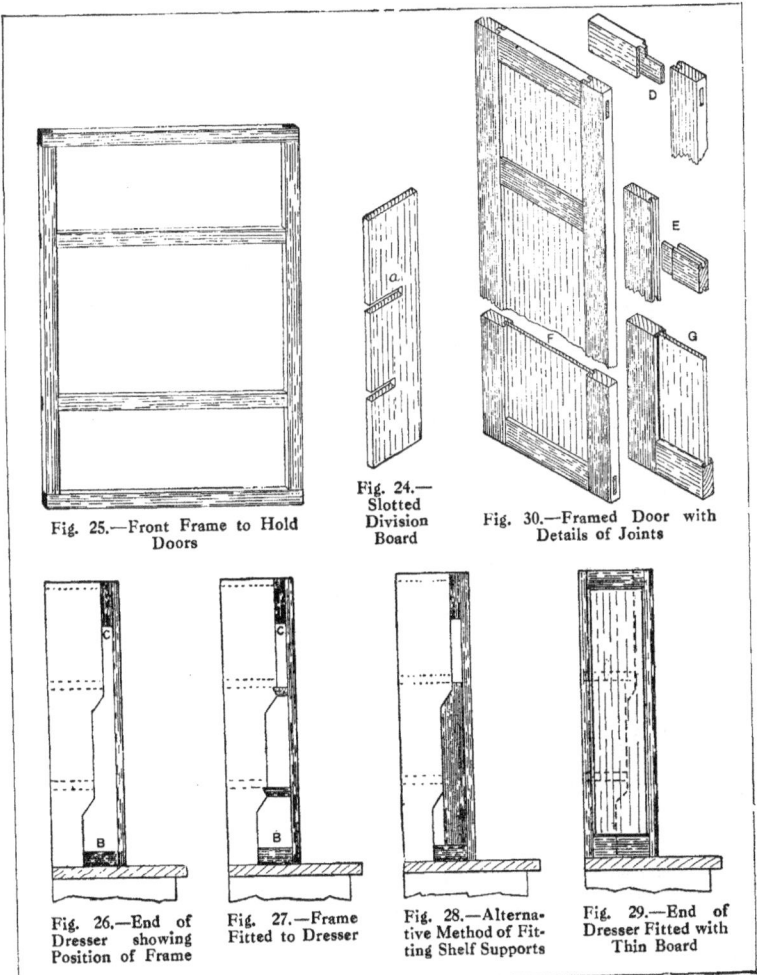

Fig. 24.—Slotted Division Board

Fig. 25.—Front Frame to Hold Doors

Fig. 30.—Framed Door with Details of Joints

Fig. 26.—End of Dresser showing Position of Frame

Fig. 27.—Frame Fitted to Dresser

Fig. 28.—Alternative Method of Fitting Shelf Supports

Fig. 29.—End of Dresser Fitted with Thin Board

would be easier to leave this until the doors are made and hinged, so that the hinge slots may be cut in the front frame.

The best form of door, and the one which will well repay for labour in appearance and wear, is the framed and panelled door, as shown in detail by Fig. 30. The joint for the corners is shown at D. It is

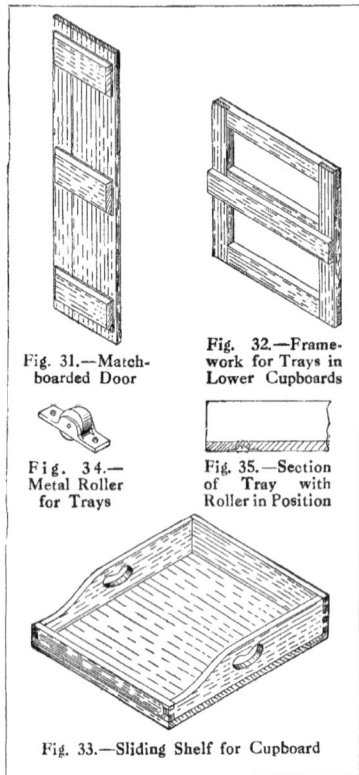

Fig. 31.—Matchboarded Door

Fig. 32.—Framework for Trays in Lower Cupboards

Fig. 34.—Metal Roller for Trays

Fig. 35.—Section of Tray with Roller in Position

Fig. 33.—Sliding Shelf for Cupboard

called a haunched mortise-and-tenon joint, and is no more difficult to make than the ordinary form; it only requires a little more care in setting out. The joint at E is an ordinary mortise-and-tenon.

There are two methods of fitting the panel, the best being shown in section at F, where the panel of $\frac{1}{4}$-in. wood fits in a groove cut inside the framing. The alternative method, which is much simpler, is shown in section at G, the panel in this case being made to fit the inside of the frame and kept in position by beading. There are four doors to make, the centre opening being fitted with a double door, as shown in Fig. 22. Ordinary butt hinges and any kind of suitable fastening should be used. As an alternative to the framed door, the matchboarding door made as shown by Fig. 31 may be used. This is not so strong and does not look so workmanlike, but it will answer the purpose.

The shelves should now be made up to the full width of the space, and should rest on the lengths at each end already fixed in position, and on fillets of $\frac{7}{8}$-in. wood nailed on to the division boards. These shelves will be of varying widths, and probably of $\frac{7}{8}$-in. thick board to match the thickness of the original shelves. This will now complete the upper structure, and the lower portion may be tackled.

It is suggested that the drawers should be fitted with sliding compartments. The internal fittings should be arranged to fit in with the particular requirements of the house. The cupboards of these dressers are not usually convenient; they go back a fair depth, and it is not easy to get at the contents; therefore, the shelves are dispensed with and sliding shelves substituted. A framework flush with the door frames must be made and provided with runners, as shown in Fig. 32. The sliding shelves are made as in Fig. 33. These will run much more easily if fitted with rollers (Fig. 34), a section of the fitting in position being given by Fig. 35. No difficulty should be experienced here, as the work of making the trays will be quite easy. The advantage of these trays will be found when they are stocked with articles, such as tea-things, etc., for they may be washed up, placed on the tray, and put in the cupboard ready for use again. The lower portion of the cupboard doors may, if desired, be filled with a frame to hold various articles as suggested for the kitchen table; but, of course, the use to

DRESSERS AND SIDEBOARDS

which the movable shelves will be put must be considered first to see if there will be room. Figs. 36 to 41. The dresser should be made chiefly of good northern pine, the top of the lower portion being of birch.

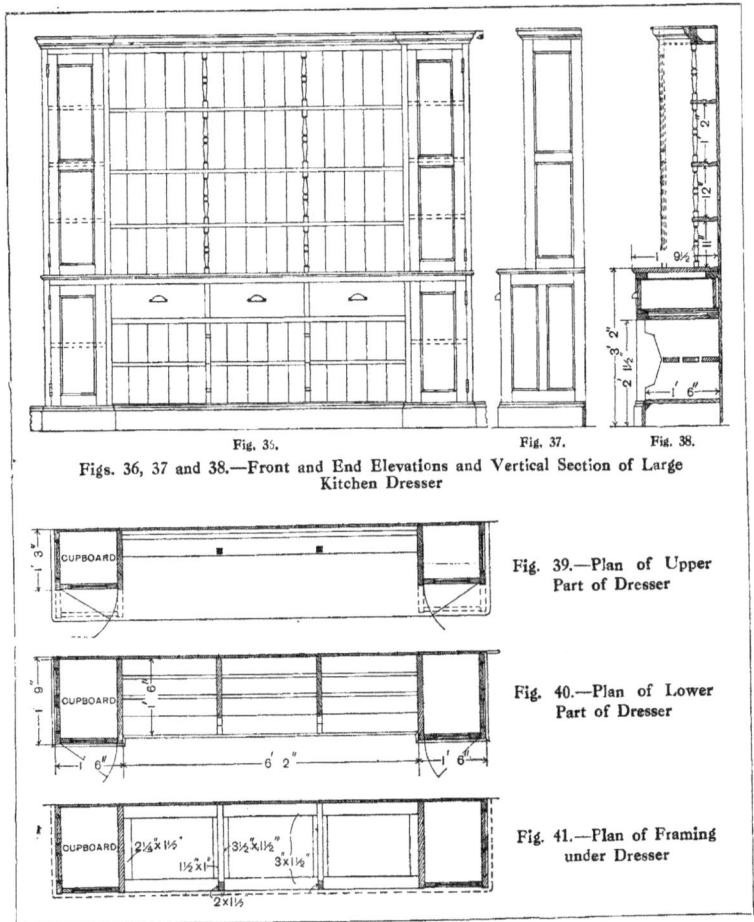

Figs. 36, 37 and 38.—Front and End Elevations and Vertical Section of Large Kitchen Dresser

Fig. 39.—Plan of Upper Part of Dresser

Fig. 40.—Plan of Lower Part of Dresser

Fig. 41.—Plan of Framing under Dresser

LARGE KITCHEN DRESSER

A kitchen dresser suitable for a town house or a country mansion is shown by The material required for the following members is $1\frac{3}{8}$ in. thick, finished: The two plain ends to the top of the cupboard, shown in Fig. 30, and the ends of the lower part shown in Fig. 40, two standards, with shaped front, shown on section (*see* Fig. 38), and in the enlarged section (Fig. 42). The material required for pot-boards is as follows: One piece 6 ft. 4 in. by 18 in. by ⅞ in. thick; and two pieces

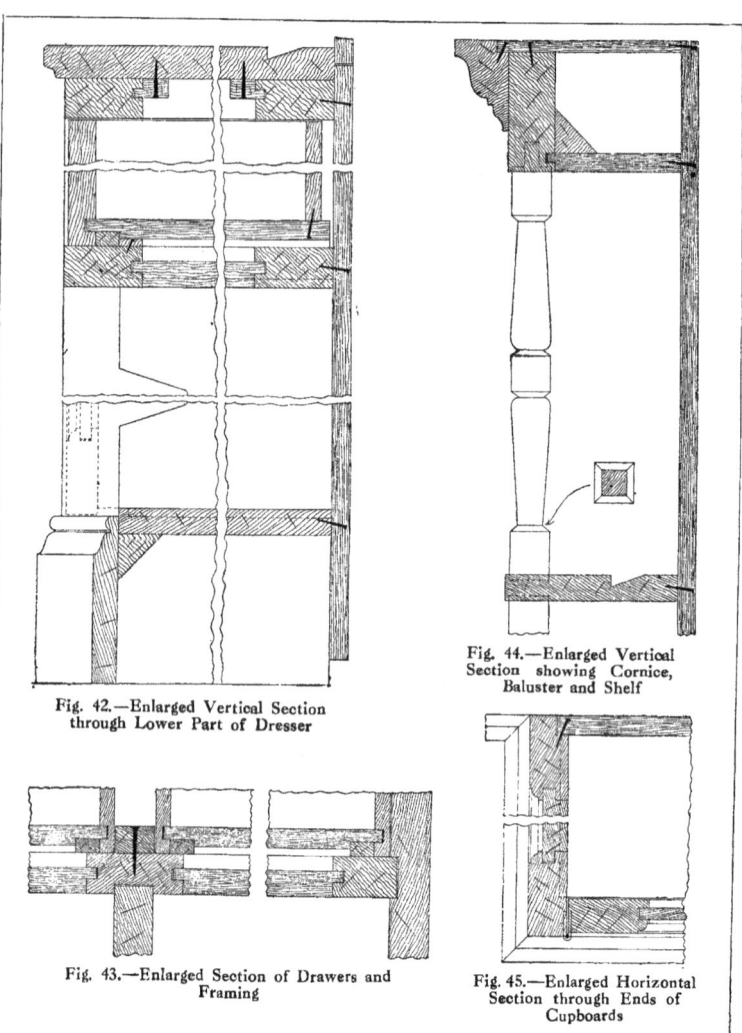

Fig. 42.—Enlarged Vertical Section through Lower Part of Dresser

Fig. 43.—Enlarged Section of Drawers and Framing

Fig. 44.—Enlarged Vertical Section showing Cornice, Baluster and Shelf

Fig. 45.—Enlarged Horizontal Section through Ends of Cupboards

DRESSERS AND SIDEBOARDS

1 ft. 5 in. by 20 in. by $\frac{7}{8}$ in. thick. The two shelves of the lower cupboard are each 1 ft. 5 in. by 20 in. by $\frac{7}{8}$ in.; the six shelves for the top cupboard each 1 ft. 5 in. by 13 in. by $\frac{7}{8}$ in. The three panels in the framing, forming dust-proof divisions between the drawers and the lower cupboard, as shown on section (Fig. 38), and on the plan of the framing (Fig. 41) and enlarged section (Fig. 43), are each 1 ft. 11 in. by 16 in. by $\frac{3}{8}$ in. thick, finished: three drawer bottoms, each 2 ft. 1 in. by 20 in. by $\frac{1}{2}$ in. thick, finished (see the enlarged vertical section illustrated by Fig. 42). The birch top should be cut on 2 in. longer than the required length, which is 9 ft. 4 in. by 22 in. by $1\frac{1}{8}$ in., finished thickness, as shown in Fig. 42. The whole is grooved for cross-tongueing, the groove in the birch top to be stopped 3 in. from each end. The eight balusters are turned, as shown in Fig. 44. The panels in the framing at the ends are flush on the inside, as shown in Fig. 45.

The trellis pieces at the open portion of the lower part of the dresser are cut in lengths fitting between the standards and ends of the cupboards, and are housed in $\frac{1}{2}$ in. at each end, as shown by Fig. 38. The bottom rails of the lower portion of the dresser are dovetailed at the ends. Fig. 46 shows the construction of the front and back rails of the dresser under the birch top, as well as the construction of the two inner ends of the cupboard. The top rail at front and back is dovetailed to the two outside ends. The lower rail at front and back under the drawers is tenoned and mortised; the shoulder inside the rail being housed in the end to the same depth as the rail forming the runner. The two muntins between the three drawers are tenoned, mortised, and housed, as before described. The shaped standards are housed in the pot-board (stop-housing) at the front, as shown by dotted lines in Fig. 42. The pot-board of the two end cupboards is tongued as shown in Fig. 47. The shelves in the cupboards are housed in the ends as shown by dotted lines in Fig. 45.

The rail forming the runner for the drawers is grooved on the underside to

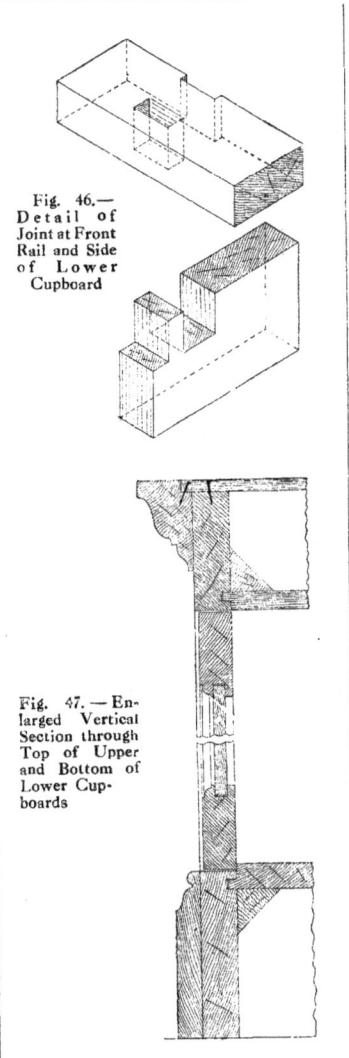

Fig. 46.—Detail of Joint at Front Rail and Side of Lower Cupboard

Fig. 47.—Enlarged Vertical Section through Top of Upper and Bottom of Lower Cupboards

receive the top end of the standard as shown in Figs. 42 and 43. The top rails under the cornice are dovetailed. The three shelves at the top portion of the dresser are sunk, as shown in Fig. 44. The three shelves are housed ½ in. deep into the ends of the cupboards, the housing being cut to fit the sinking in the shelf. The two top balusters are tenoned into the top rail, and are housed in as shown in Fig. 44. The four ends of the lower cupboard run down to the floor, and three bearers, each 5 in. by 1½ in., are fixed under the potboard, and glue-blocked as shown in the various sections. The four ends of the top cupboard are housed ½ in. into the top of the lower portion of the dresser, and stopped. The sinking for plates at the top (Fig. 42) is stopped between the two ends of the cupboard. The birch top is buttoned down, as shown in Fig. 42. The doors are hung with two 3-in. steel-butts, each door being fitted with a small mortise lock and drop handle, while each drawer is fitted with an ordinary grip handle or with turned wood-knobs. Stop-drawers at the front are shown in Fig. 42.

The front and ends of the dresser should be painted in three oils of an approved tint, or grained; the whole being twice varnished.

KITCHEN DRESSER WITH ENCLOSED CUPBOARDS

A kitchen dresser of a similar type to the one last described but of more simple construction is shown in front elevation by Fig. 48.

Figs. 49 and 50 show two vertical sections, and plans of the upper and lower parts are given by Figs. 51 and 52. This dresser could be adapted for a position against a blank wall or could be placed in a recess. Selected red deal or pitchpine would be suitable woods.

The lower portion consists of cupboards and drawers. The doors of the cupboards should be 1 in. thick framed up with panels moulded on the face, as shown in Fig. 53. The drawers should be fitted with 1 in. fronts, and the top above the drawers (see Fig. 54) should be 1 in. thick with plain moulding on the edges secured to the framing below. The upper portion of shelving should preferably be made separate from the lower portion, as the dresser will then be more portable than if constructed in one piece. The sides of the shelving should be 1 in. thick, shaped as shown, and fitted with two tiers of shelving supported with turned balusters ¾ in. square. The top cornice (Fig. 55) should be cut out of 1½-in. stuff, blocked at intervals for strengthening purposes. Below this are fixed cut and shaped heads ½ in. thick housed into brackets and side checks. The back is covered with ½-in. V-jointed boarding in narrow widths. The lower cupboards should be fitted with brass latches and the drawers with plain drop handles; brass hooks for cups and jugs should be fixed on the edges of the shelving. The dresser, when finished, should be either painted to match the existing woodwork or stained and twice varnished.

SMALL SIDEBOARD

A pleasing design for a single sideboard is shown by the half-tone reproduction (Fig. 56). Figs. 57, 58 and 59 show front elevation, vertical section and plan respectively. Of the four uprights the two at the back can be quite plain and finished about 2 in. by 1½ in. The front uprights are 2 in. square (finished), and have chamfers, as at A in Fig. 60, stopped 12 in. above the floor B (Fig. 57) and running into the small turned finials at the tops. One of the latter is shown to a large scale in Figs. 61 and 62, the octagonal section formed by the chamfers being finished with a slight hollow, as at C in both figures. Above this the uprights are round-turned to the design given. At a height of 7 in. above the floor the front legs are sunk $\frac{1}{16}$ in. all round, and thence tapered downwards to 1¼ in. square. Three ⅞-in. or ¾-in. shelves will be required, and they should be moulded, as in Fig. 63, on three sides. Along the front and ends they are supported by means of ⅞-in. by 2-in. rails, as at D in Figs. 58 and 63. These rails are tenoned into the uprights, the front two

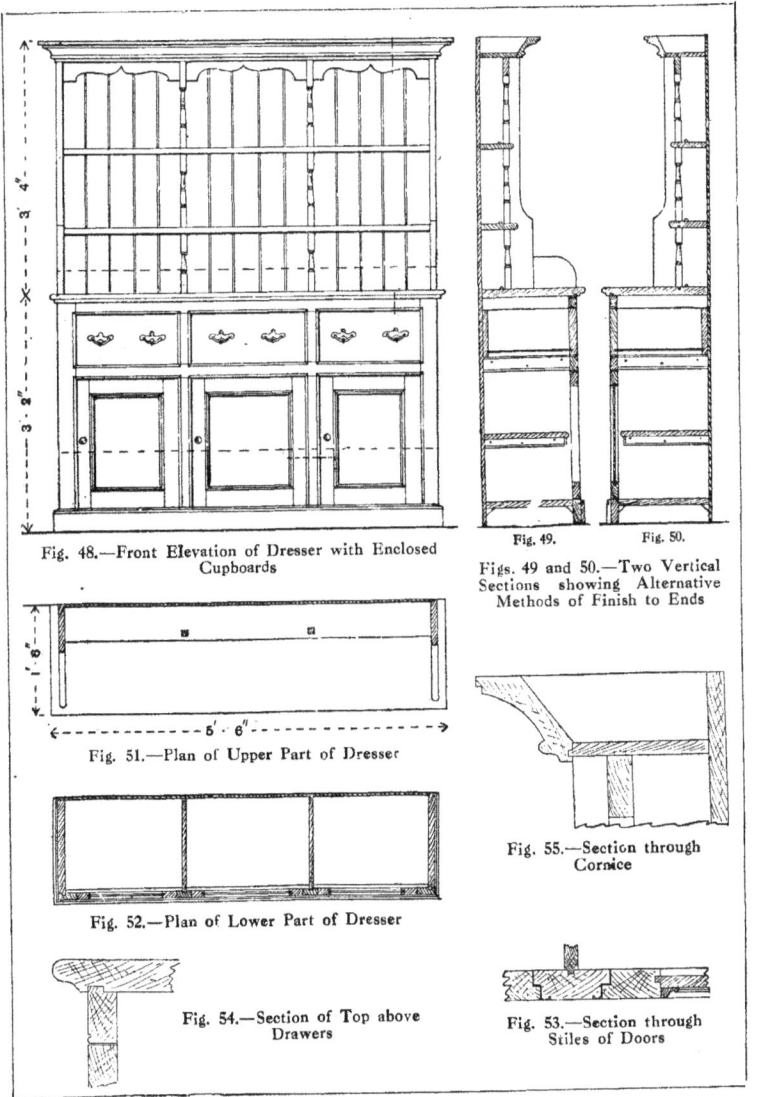

Fig. 48.—Front Elevation of Dresser with Enclosed Cupboards

Figs. 49 and 50.—Two Vertical Sections showing Alternative Methods of Finish to Ends

Fig. 51.—Plan of Upper Part of Dresser

Fig. 52.—Plan of Lower Part of Dresser

Fig. 54.—Section of Top above Drawers

Fig. 55.—Section through Cornice

Fig. 53.—Section through Stiles of Doors

THE PRACTICAL WOODWORKER

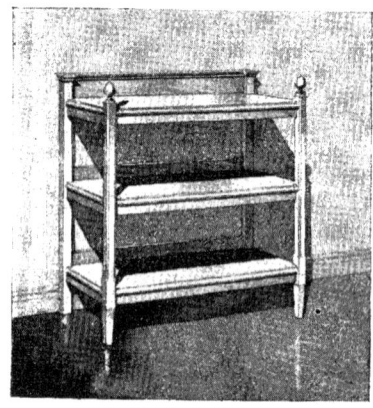

Fig. 56.—Small Sideboard

close intervals from behind, their ends being first halved or notched into the back uprights as in Fig. 59, and the whole finished flush at the back. The top shelf is treated in exactly the same manner, except that its rail F (Fig. 58) is 5 in. deep, and is finished with a small capping mould either rebated or planted in position and continued over the back uprights by means of flat, solid caps $3\frac{1}{2}$ in. by 3 in., moulded and mitred as required, and sunk underneath to fit $\frac{1}{4}$ in. over the posts.

SIDEBOARD DRESSER

A sideboard dresser which harmonises admirably with old-world interiors is shown by Fig. 64. From the point of view of utility it must be confessed that a sideboard dresser of this type is not so of which take two rails at each level, the tenons being arranged as in Fig. 60, in order that the longest rails may be jointed the farthest into the uprights. When the rails and uprights have been framed up, the shelves can be cut away at the corners as necessary, carefully fitted into position, and screwed from the underside obliquely through the rails.

A skirting being desirable along the back edge of each shelf, this is made to take the place of the rail which would otherwise be necessary below the shelf to ensure the required amount of rigidity. For the two lower shelves this skirting takes the form of pieces $\frac{7}{8}$ in. by 3 in., having their lower edges flush with the undersides of the shelves E (Fig. 58), to which latter the rails are screwed at

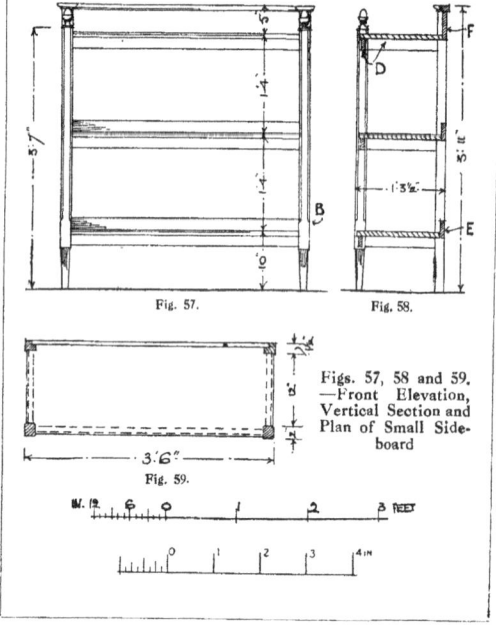

Figs. 57, 58 and 59.—Front Elevation, Vertical Section and Plan of Small Sideboard

DRESSERS AND SIDEBOARDS

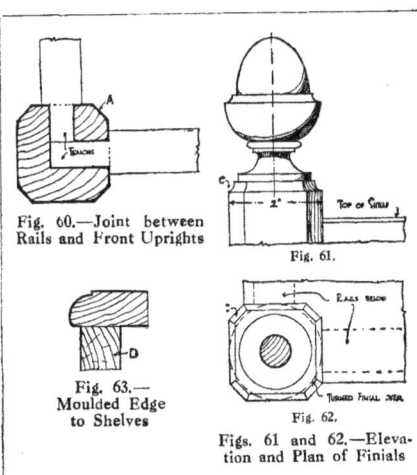

Fig. 60.—Joint between Rails and Front Uprights

Fig. 61.

Fig. 63.—Moulded Edge to Shelves

Fig. 62.

Figs. 61 and 62.—Elevation and Plan of Finials

satisfactory as one designed along Sheraton or Chippendale lines ; but it should be pointed out that many people prefer a good display of china to provision of cellaret drawers and other fittings. A sideboard dresser of this type provides a fair amount of drawer accommodation for linen and cutlery, and the cupboards in the top part serve admirably as receptacles of small articles of plate, cruets, etc.

The constructive features of the sideboard dresser shown in front elevation by Fig. 65 do not present any special difficulties. A half-sectional plan through the drawers is shown in Fig. 66, illustrating the construction of the divisions. It will be noticed that a clamp is fixed to the front of the division at each end of this and the corresponding one ; on the other half, tenons are cut which fit into the top rails and bottom of the dresser. The divisions should be grooved into the back and finally secured by screwing through. Fig. 67 shows the connection of the shelf to the legs. Both ends of the bottom part should be tenoned into the legs, and the span rail of the front should be tenoned to the bottom previous to tenoning this part into both the front and back legs. The insides of the carcase ends should be grooved to receive the ends of the bottom. An enlarged detail of one corner of the drawer part, with broken corner mouldings fixed, is shown in Fig. 68. This detail also serves for the cupboard doors in the upper part.

To construct the top part, the best plan is to carry each end right through from top to bottom ; all shelves are then slip-dovetailed between the ends (see Fig. 69), and the cupboard bottoms dovetailed up. To bind the top part together the span rails are also slip-dovetailed between the carcase ends and made flush at the front. An enlarged detail is shown by Fig. 70 illustrating the method of fixing the cornice moulding round. The latter is allowed to project above the ends in order to receive the dust-board, which is screwed down and levelled off. The matched back with V joints is quite suitable for a sideboard of this type, and an enlarged detail of the matching is shown by Fig. 71. Fig. 72 shows the construction of the cupboard doors, made in one piece with

Fig. 64.—Sideboard Dresser

clamps at each end. Round the bottom of the top part a small half-round moulding should be rebated and mitred, which forms a neat finish between the upper and lower part.

The metal-work suggested for the sideboard is armour-bright iron. The handles could be of a ring shape as shown, or handles with pear-shape drops could be introduced with advantage.

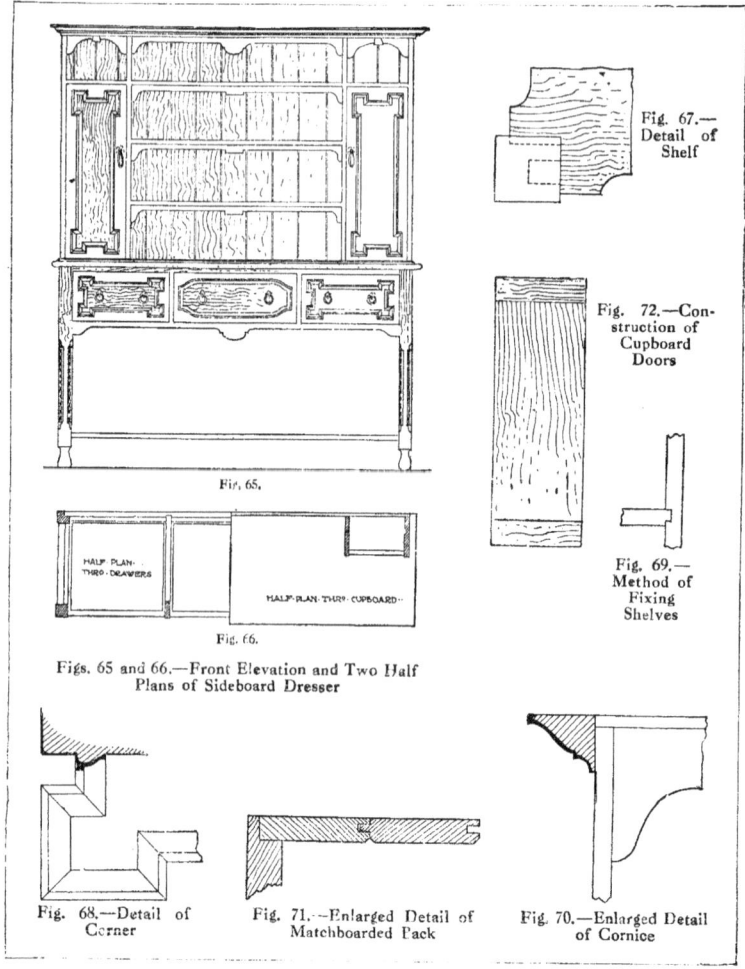

Fig. 67.—Detail of Shelf

Fig. 72.—Construction of Cupboard Doors

Fig. 69.—Method of Fixing Shelves

Figs. 65 and 66.—Front Elevation and Two Half Plans of Sideboard Dresser

Fig. 68.—Detail of Corner

Fig. 71.—Enlarged Detail of Matchboarded Back

Fig. 70.—Enlarged Detail of Cornice

DRESSERS AND SIDEBOARDS

ANOTHER SIDEBOARD DRESSER

The constructional work of the further example of sideboard dresser shown by Fig. 73 is on identically the same lines as the preceding one, and therefore no useful purpose would be served by giving details. This sideboard is simply included here as presenting an alternative design, and the tone reproduction (Fig. 74). Two elevations and an enlarged vertical section are shown by Figs. 75, 76 and 77.

The dresser is made in two distinct portions, the lower one having four front legs 2 in. or $2\frac{1}{4}$ in. square, but circular-turned at a point just above the floor, as in Fig. 78. There are also four 2-in. or $2\frac{1}{4}$-in. by $1\frac{1}{2}$-in. back legs, not turned at

Fig. 73.—Alternative Design of Sideboard Dresser

craftsman who desires to make it should study the construction in conjunction with that just described.

DRESSER SIDEBOARD WITH SLIDING DOORS

An oak dresser, fitted at the top with sliding glazed doors, is shown in the half-

all. These eight legs are connected up by means of top and drawer rails at the front, back and ends, as at A and B in Fig. 78, and as shown in section by Fig. 77. The drawer spaces should be fitted with the necessary guides, runners, and drawers, the fronts of the latter being recessed when shut, and having a small moulding mitred round them. Panels should be

Fig. 74.—Dresser Sideboard with Sliding Doors

formed at the ends, as at C in Figs. 76 and 79, and mouldings applied to match the drawers, and ultimately ten small cut brackets should be fitted where shown. Near the floor the legs should be connected by means of 1½-in. by 2-in. diagonal braces, as in Fig. 80, halved in the middle where they cross. Similar rails should be framed in as at D in the same figure, to take a central shelf about 1 ft. 3 in. wide. A ¾-in. moulded top will complete the lower half of the dresser.

The upper portion should be built up of sides, top and lowest shelf, finished about ¾ in. thick, the top moulded and made into a cornice by means of a small hollowed fillet, as at E in Fig. 77, which also shows at F the shaped outline for the sides. The latter should be housed ⅜ in. deep into 2-in. by 1-in. moulded feet G (Figs. 77 and 78), the line of which is continued against the back by means of a moulded fillet as at H. If possible, the whole back should be panelled; but in any case the lower open portion should

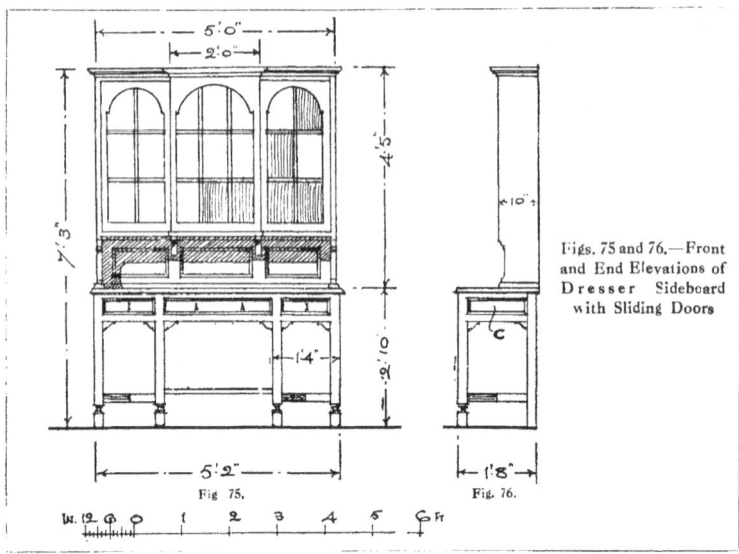

Figs. 75 and 76.—Front and End Elevations of Dresser Sideboard with Sliding Doors

DRESSERS AND SIDEBOARDS

be in three moulded panels, set out to correspond with the glazed divisions above. Two cut brackets and a small top moulding J (Figs. 77 and 78) will complete this portion.

Dealing next with the glazed front, metal tracks will be best for these, although they can be grooved top and bottom to run on rounded oak tongues, as at K in Fig. 77, if desired. Fig. 81 is a detail part plan of this. The small top-rail at L (Fig. 77) as shown should run

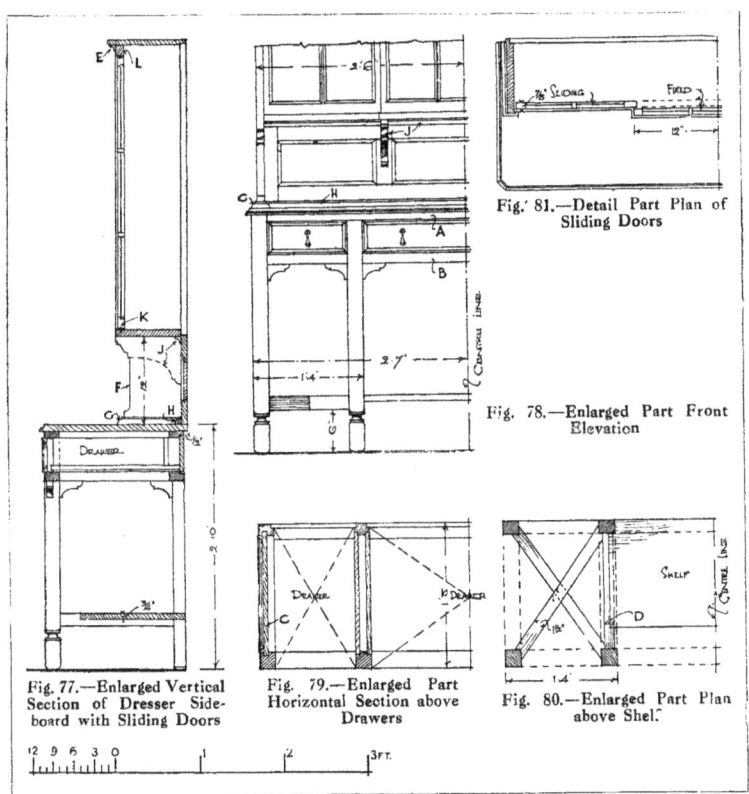

Fig. 81.—Detail Part Plan of Sliding Doors

Fig. 78.—Enlarged Part Front Elevation

Fig. 77.—Enlarged Vertical Section of Dresser Sideboard with Sliding Doors

Fig. 79.—Enlarged Part Horizontal Section above Drawers

Fig. 80.—Enlarged Part Plan above Shelf.

this should be about $\frac{7}{8}$ in. thick, and all well framed in the ordinary manner. The side lights slide towards the centre behind the middle one, which is fixed and projects as shown, the top and bottom shelves being broken out to suit it. It should overlap the side lights $\frac{1}{2}$ in., and right across behind the middle light, and it will be essential to make it exactly parallel to the lower shelf, in order to let the lights slide properly. By opening the side lights it will be quite simple to reach the spaces behind the fixed central portion. If possible, the shelves should coincide with the horizontal glazing-bars in level.

MAHOGANY SIDEBOARD

The eminently useful example of dining-room furniture illustrated in Fig. 82 (finished perspective view) has been designed to show the possibilities of a sideboard which does not involve very shaped edges to the doors and frames. As will be seen from the various views, the shaping is based upon a "repeating" unit, and this detail, as well as the remainder of the design, shows much better in the actual material than in plain black-and-white.

The elevations of the sideboard show the projection of the top part of the back. This is necessary in order to allow for the

Fig. 82.—Mahogany Sideboard

difficult practice or expensive detail, and readers will no doubt admit that the simple lines of the example introduced are much to be preferred to the "many-mirrored" type of sideboard. Front and end elevations are shown by Figs. 83 and 84 on the opposite page.

The decoration of this sideboard is chiefly obtained by the judicious arrangement of well-figured veneers, and an additional decorative feature consists of thickness of the skirting which would otherwise prevent the top part fitting close against the wall. In some instances similar considerations necessitate making the whole of the bottom part flush at the back, in which case the curve shown on the leg would be omitted. This would not seriously affect the appearance of the sideboard, and has the effect of reducing the overhang or back projection of the top part. Two sectional views of the

DRESSERS AND SIDEBOARDS

sideboard are shown by Figs. 86 and 87, which illustrate the construction.

A detail of the decorative shaping used on the doors and frames is also shown in Fig. 86, and this would be executed by

The first step in making the sideboard would be to prepare the four carcase ends, and to dowel the two outside ones into the legs. Before they are glued together, the insides of the ends should

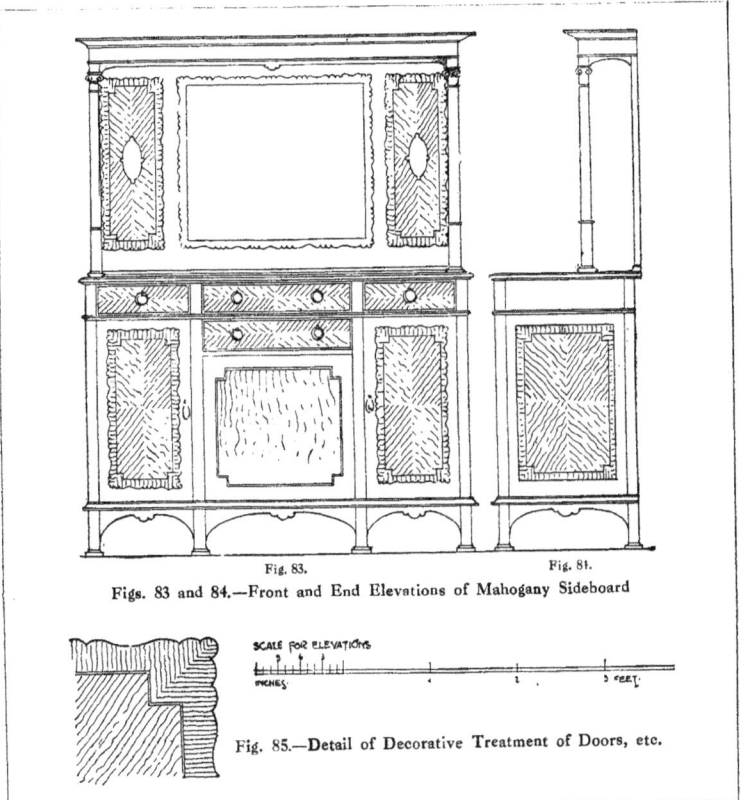

Fig. 83.   Fig. 84.

Figs. 83 and 84.—Front and End Elevations of Mahogany Sideboard

Fig. 85.—Detail of Decorative Treatment of Doors, etc.

simply fret-sawing to the shape shown and finishing with fine files and glass-paper. The shaped part is, of course, only about 1 in. thick, and represents the projecting parts of the framing forming the rebate.

be trenched to receive the drawer runners, as shown in the first sectional view. The inside ends are then dowelled only into the front legs, as they are secured at the back to the main panelled back, there being only six legs. Both sides of the

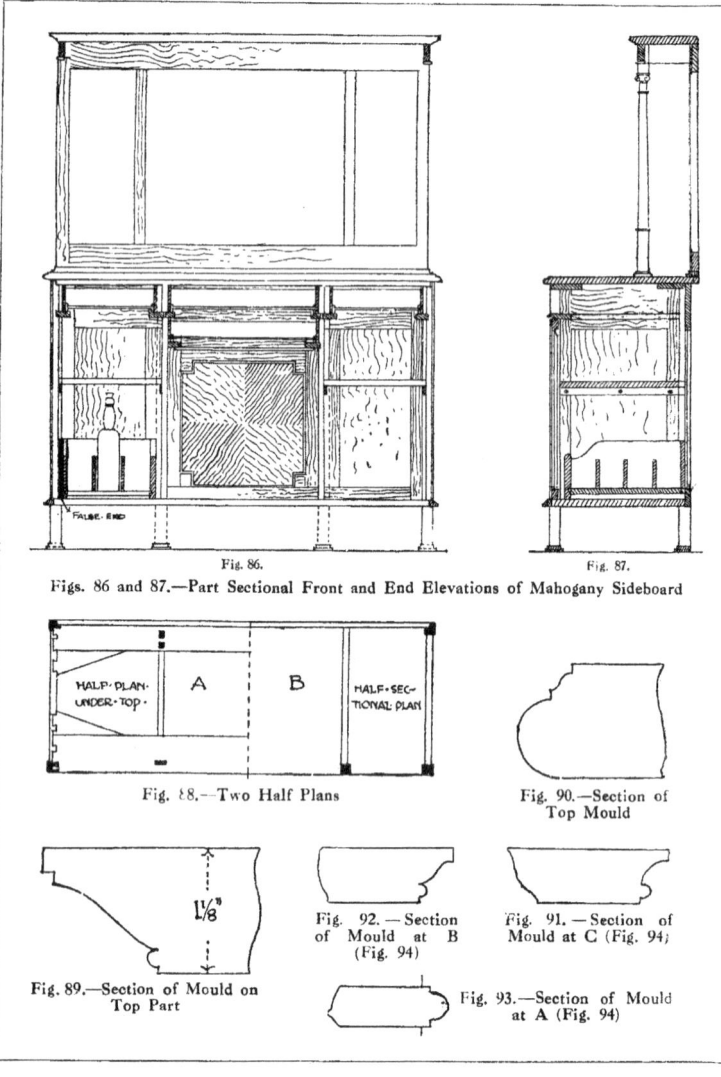

Figs. 86 and 87.—Part Sectional Front and End Elevations of Mahogany Sideboard

Fig. 88.—Two Half Plans

Fig. 89.—Section of Mould on Top Part

Fig. 90.—Section of Top Mould

Fig. 91.—Section of Mould at C (Fig. 94)

Fig. 92.—Section of Mould at B (Fig. 94)

Fig. 93.—Section of Mould at A (Fig. 94)

DRESSERS AND SIDEBOARDS

inside ends must be trenched to receive drawer runners, and the short drawer rails may then be tenoned in between the glued-up ends. The method of attaching the top rail is indicated at A in Fig. 88, from which it will be seen that the ends are pinned through the rails and the latter are dovetailed down into the carcase ends and legs. Triangular brackets are attached to the rails, these serving for additional strength and economise the material. Reference to Fig. 87 shows the bottom running right through underneath the carcase ends. The legs should, of course, be housed to receive it, and the inside legs may be screwed to the carcase bottom underneath the moulding, the latter being fixed after the carcase has been glued together. At the bottom of the left-hand cupboard a cellaret drawer should be introduced; this necessitates the use of a false end (see Fig. 87). The sectional view (Fig. 86) shows the shaped ends for this part, and also the divisions which need not be made the same width of the ends. A necessary feature of a cellaret drawer is the lead lining which is usually soldered in after the woodwork has been completed. The shelf above the cellaret provides for cruets and small articles of plate, and the right-hand cupboard proves useful for reserve bottles, knife-cases and like articles indispensable to a well-equipped dining-room.

The drawers are made in the usual way and veneered with quartered patterns. An added decorative touch is imparted to this part of the work by adding cocked beads which project beyond the face of the work. With cocked beads the face of the drawer front should be in exactly

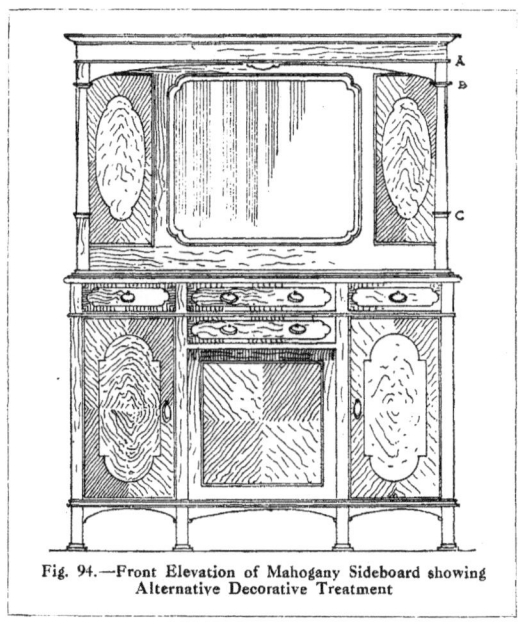

Fig. 94.—Front Elevation of Mahogany Sideboard showing Alternative Decorative Treatment

the same plane as the front legs, and the bead then breaks the joints between them, and also protects the edges of the veneer which would otherwise chip away through coming in contact with the drawer rails. The curved span rails at the bottoms should preferably be made in three pieces, and each one mitred up in order to obviate the short grain which would inevitably break away if the rails were cut from the solid. At the bottoms of the legs small moulded blocks are either screwed or dowelled on to act as feet.

The sectional view (Fig. 87) shows the groundwork of the back frame. This should be made of Honduras mahogany with square edges, and then the front part is faced up with Cuba mahogany. The cornice is made with three rails secret-mitred at the corners with frieze mouldings underneath. A moulded top is prepared to fit right over the frame, and this is secured by pocket-screwing through the insides of the cornice rails. The base moulding is worked in one piece moulded on three sides, and is screwed up to the back frame. To fix effectively the columns, the squares should run to the underside of the moulded top, and to effect this it is necessary to cut this away for the cornice which leaves a projecting horn which may be screwed to the rails. In cases where the top part must be made as a separate feature, a good plan is to mortise and tenon three base mouldings, which act as a sufficient tie or brace for the top part. The shaped rails underneath the frieze moulding are simply fitted in between and then glued up to the moulding.

The centre elliptical shapes in the panels are intended to be executed in curl veneer (described in a later section), and may be cut to the desired shape by placing the two pieces in between two pieces of quarter stuff with pins to secure the whole. The shape may then be fret-sawn and finished with fine files previous to separating them. The quartering should not present any special difficulties, and in this particular instance it would probably economise time to cut in the elliptical centre parts after the quartered veneers had been glued down. The back of the bottom part has necessarily to be made in one piece; this is indicated in the sectional view, from which it will be seen that the top rail has to be made wider in the centre part in order to make the proper margin. The square or broken corners can be added to the rails for purposes of economy. A panelled back of this kind is very strong, and when rebated into the legs, as shown at A in Fig. 88, and screwed to these and the carcase ends great rigidity is obtained.

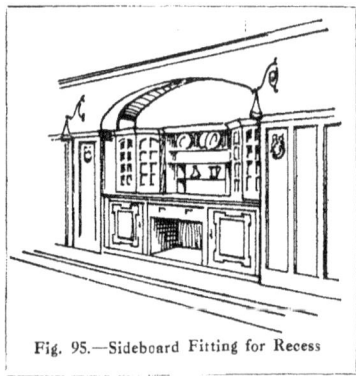

Fig. 95.—Sideboard Fitting for Recess

Details of the moulds are shown by Figs. 89 to 93.

An alternative decorative treatment is indicated in the second elevation shown in Fig. 94. The constructional features are almost identical to those in the first elevation. The veneered designs are different, and flush veneered-doors are substituted for the framed ones. These flush doors are made with clamps mortised and tenoned on, with cocked beads fixed as with the drawers after the veneering has been completed.

SIDEBOARD FITTING FOR A RECESS

Well-planned houses are now frequently arranged with a recess in the dining- or

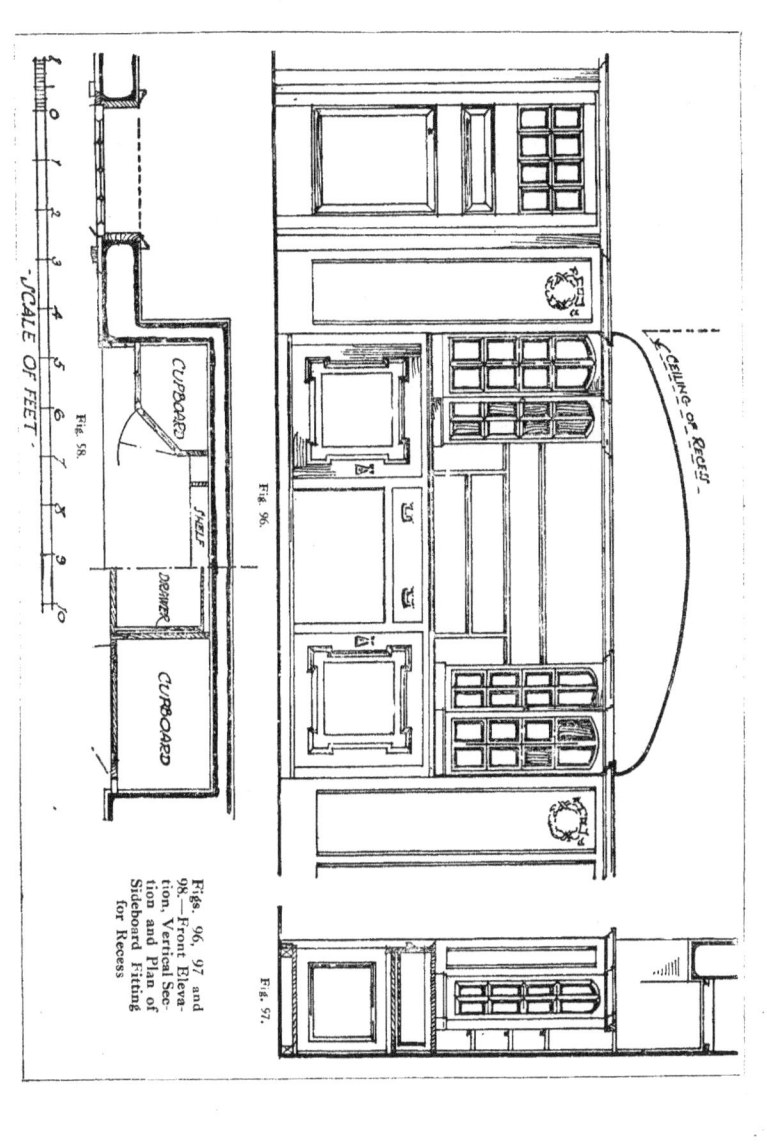

Figs. 96, 97 and 98.—Front Elevation, Vertical Section, and Plan of Sideboard Fitting for Recess

living-room, intended to accommodate a sideboard or similar piece of furniture, and this constitutes not only an economy in space, leaving the whole room free from obstruction, but can be made a picturesque feature of the apartment, second only to the fireplace in importance.

An unpretentious scheme for decorating a room, with special reference to such a recess, having a sideboard fixed permanently in position, is shown in perspective and front elevation by Figs. 95 and 96. A section and plan are shown by Figs. 97 and 98. The walls are covered to a height of 7 ft. with light framing, having canvas of some suitable colour stretched behind it to form panels of this material, some of which are ornamented with a stencilled wreath or festoon as indicated. This framing should be screwed from the front with brass cups and screws to wood plugs or grounds, in order to allow of removal for the purpose of renewing the canvas. At the 7-ft. level a moulded capping is continued round, and the frieze above is plastered in the ordinary way, or rendered and floated only, as is sometimes preferred, to obtain a more interesting texture. The door and linings suggested to be used are shown on the left-hand side of the drawing.

The recess measures 9 ft. across, and is 2 ft. 3 in. deep ; it has a table-top 3 ft. 3 in. above the floor, fitted underneath with a central drawer for tablecloths, and a cupboard on either hand. The doors to each of the latter have raised panels, and the frames are cut to suit the mitres shown for the panel mouldings. A reference to the plan (Fig. 98) will explain the arrangement of the upper part above the table-top, which comprises two angle cupboards with glazed fronts and doors in small panes with wood bars, and shelving fitted in the middle between the cupboards. The moulded capping runs round the top as a finish, and above it is an elliptical or segmental arch, probably only in lath and plaster, to which the small ceiling behind is shown running parallel. The wall behind the cupboards and shelves would be plastered, and the glazing to the door of the room and cupboards might have a few bull's-eyes introduced at random if a quaint effect is desired.

Any description of finish can be employed for the joinery, although it is usual in a room of this description to keep the tones dark or subdued, in order to set off the glass, silver, and linen of the table to the best advantage. A small sketch given by Fig. 95 on page 814 gives some idea of the general appearance when the design is carried out.

Coal-boxes

OAK COAL-BOXES

WOODEN coal-boxes as articles of furniture are a considerable improvement on the metal types. From a decorative point of view, of course, a good brass or copper scuttle is excellent, but so many are made simply of sheet-iron "brassed" over, and they soon look dingy because of the colour wearing off. Wooden coal-boxes can be designed and made to match the other furniture in the room, which is an advantage.

The general shape or design is usually on the lines shown by Fig. 1, but a pleasant variation is to make a pair of folding doors instead of a flap. The example shown in front elevation and section by Figs. 1 and 2 is intended to be made in oak

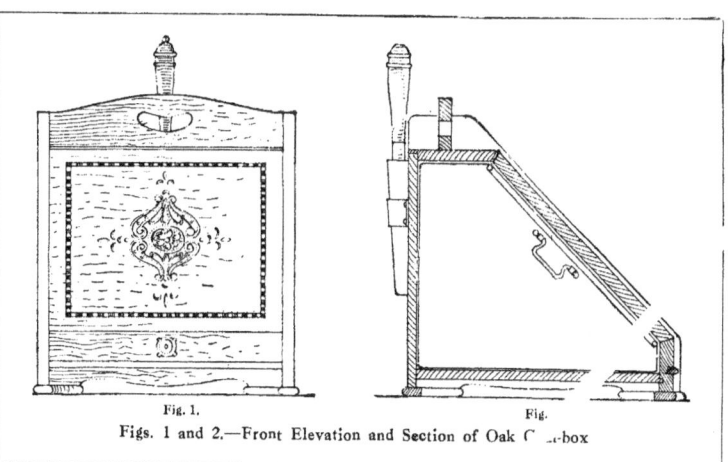

Figs. 1 and 2.—Front Elevation and Section of Oak C_..t-box

inlaid with ebony and rosewood, or dark brown oak and rosewood.

To make the case part, both ends should be planed perfectly flat, and then shaped exactly to the outline shown in the sectional view. Shaping both at the same time ensures exact similarity and much facilitates the work. Both the top and the bottom should be slip-dovetailed

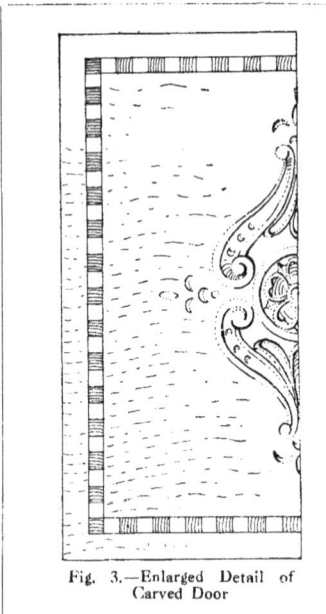

Fig. 3.—Enlarged Detail of Carved Door

in. The bottom front piece should be dowelled in between the sides, and grooved both back and front for the bottom and moulding. Both sides should be rebated on the back edges, and the back piece can then be made to fit exactly, and is then screwed in. The handle piece should be made ½ in. longer than the space between the sides, and is then stop-grooved ¼ in. deep at each side, and inserted before the case is glued up. It will be seen on referring to the sectional view that the fall or flap has the grain running from side to side, with a narrow bottom piece glued on, to which is attached the knob. An ordinary rubbed joint is quite suitable for this part if carefully made. Running the grain from side to side has an additional advantage, as the hinges can be better secured to long-grain wood instead of end-grain wood. The curves underneath the box should be cut with a bow-saw, and filed and glass-papered before the box is glued up. The feet can be made by working a length of wood to the required thickness, afterwards rounding one edge as shown. This is then cut into short lengths as desired, rounding off the ends as required. For instance, the left-hand foot shown in the front elevation (Fig. 1) may be taken as an example. A short length is cut off, and then rounded at each end and screwed up to the box. The return piece in the front is then cut, and one end rounded. The left-hand end of this piece is made dead square, and then a mitre is made, so that it can be fitted into the fixed piece by cutting another small mitre on the side, thus forming a butt-and-mitre joint.

Interlaying is dealt with in a later section, and also carving. The carved centre in this case is adapted from the simple carved designs found on old oak chests, and a study of these will afford much assistance when designing work of this type. To execute this part, half the design (Fig. 3) should be carefully drawn, and then transferred to a smooth chalked surface by means of carbon paper. The outline can then be cut with gouges, and the various reliefs and modelling proceeded with.

The hinge used for the flap is usually

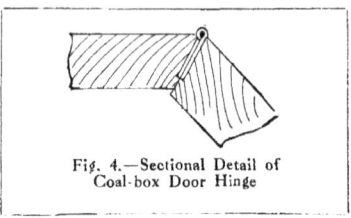

Fig. 4.—Sectional Detail of Coal-box Door Hinge

termed a piano hinge, because of its use in hinging piano falls and tops. The wings or flanges are much thinner than

COAL-BOXES

those used in ordinary hinges, and they may be purchased cut to any required length. As the hinge runs right through the hinging piece on top and the top edge of the flap, the necessary sinking for each flange can be obtained by simply rebating the edges, as is indicated in the section shown (Fig. 4). To obtain the proper gauging for this part, a marking gauge should be set from the edge of the flanges when the hinge is closed to the centre of the pin or knuckle. The gauge is then employed to gauge the rebate lines.

It will be found in actual practice that an iron lining (see Fig. 2) is desirable.

sides, and the bottom lap-dovetailed into the sides. A plinth is formed by working the moulding shown in two lengths, which are rebated in and mitred round after the case has been glued up. The ball feet indicated are then attached by screwing to the bottoms of small blocks glued in the corners. At the top, mouldings are glued round as indicated. The door is made as a frame with a veneered and inlaid panel grooved in before the frame is glued together, and is finished level with the framing at the back.

If desired a pair of folding doors could be fitted. There is not any real need of

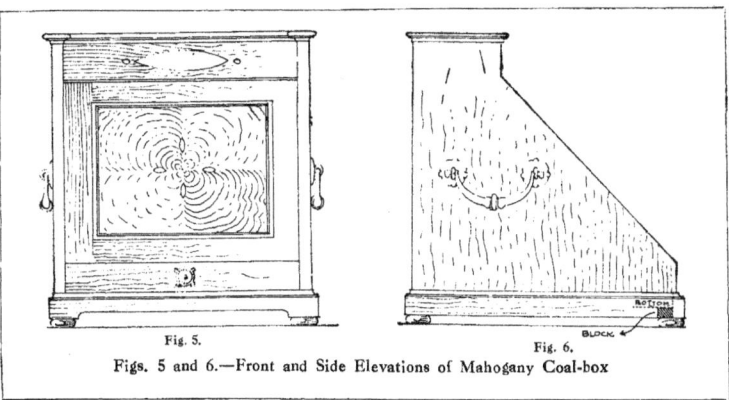

Figs. 5 and 6.—Front and Side Elevations of Mahogany Coal-box

These are usually made with inside handles, which fold down close to the sides when not required for carrying the lining, and have the advantage of enabling one to carry and fill the lining without actually handling the wooden box. Though usually introduced they are not absolutely necessary.

MAHOGANY COAL-BOXES

The construction of the coal-box shown by Figs. 5 and 6, which is intended to be executed in mahogany inlaid with satinwood, is simpler than the preceding one, the top being slip-dovetailed between the separate frames with panels with such small doors; instead, each door should be made from a piece of $\frac{3}{4}$-in. stuff stiffened at the back by means of a pair of clamps each about $1\frac{1}{2}$ in. wide by $\frac{3}{8}$ in. thick, dovetail keyed in flat. Another method of ensuring flat surfaces is to prepare two hardwood clamps each about $1\frac{1}{4}$ in. wide by $\frac{3}{8}$ in. thick. These are rebated and glued at the ends of the doors on the back sides, and then planed off perfectly level all round. These clamps serve to keep the surfaces quite flat and free from casting, and being quite level with the back surfaces, they are not unsightly. In the event of a small pair of doors being introduced, a different method of hinging is adopted, similar to ordinary door hinging. A pair of 1¼-in. or 1½-in. brass butts are necessary for each door. The handles should be secured by sinking the nuts level with the insides of the box, turning them hard up with a forked-end screwdriver. If square nuts are fitted to the pins, ¾-in. holes ₃⁄₁₆ in. deep should be sunk with a centre-bit, and the nuts tightened up finally with a hammer and punch.

COAL CABINET WITH FALLING FRONT

Fig. 7 shows a coal cabinet quite distinct in design from the orthodox coal-box. Front and back elevations and a sectional plan are shown by Figs. 9, 10 and 11 respectively.

The construction will be seen in the

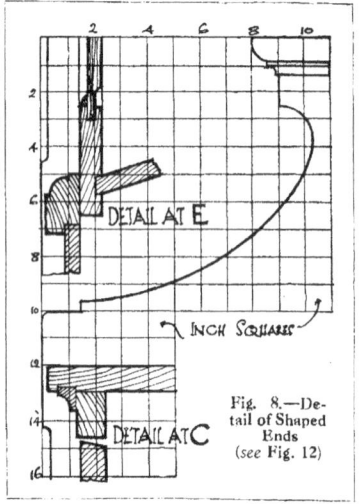

Fig. 8.—Detail of Shaped Ends (see Fig. 12)

Fig. 7.—Coal Cabinet with Falling Front

various details. Each side is made up of two or more widths tongued together, shaped as in Figs 8 and 12, and housed into a small top shelf as at A (Fig. 12), consisting of a moulded shelf proper, made out on its exposed edges by means of a moulded fillet 2 in. by ½ in., as at B. Lower down, the sides are connected by (1) a rail C, 1¼ in. by 1¾ in.; (2) two back rails D, 1½ in. by 2½ in.; (3) a moulded front rail E, 1¼ in. by 2¼ in., with a skirting rebated to it on the underside, as at F in Figs. 9 and 12, and a main top G (Fig. 12), with a small moulding under its front edge. All these connecting portions are housed at least ½ in. into the sides, and the carcase so formed is strengthened on the inside by means of angle-blocks, as shown in Figs. 12 and 13. Further strength is afforded by the filling in of the back, which at the top takes the form of a frame and panel or mirror, and at the bottom consists of light horizontal boarding (Fig. 10). Both frame and boarding should be well screwed into rebates in the back inner edges of the sides.

The outer box, into which the sheet-iron

coal-container fits loosely, should be grooved or tongued together in a simple substantial manner. It has a moulded panelled front, which can be emphasised by screwed in the corresponding positions on the outer sides of the box, the groove at M being continued as at N in Fig. 13, thus enabling the box to be inserted from the

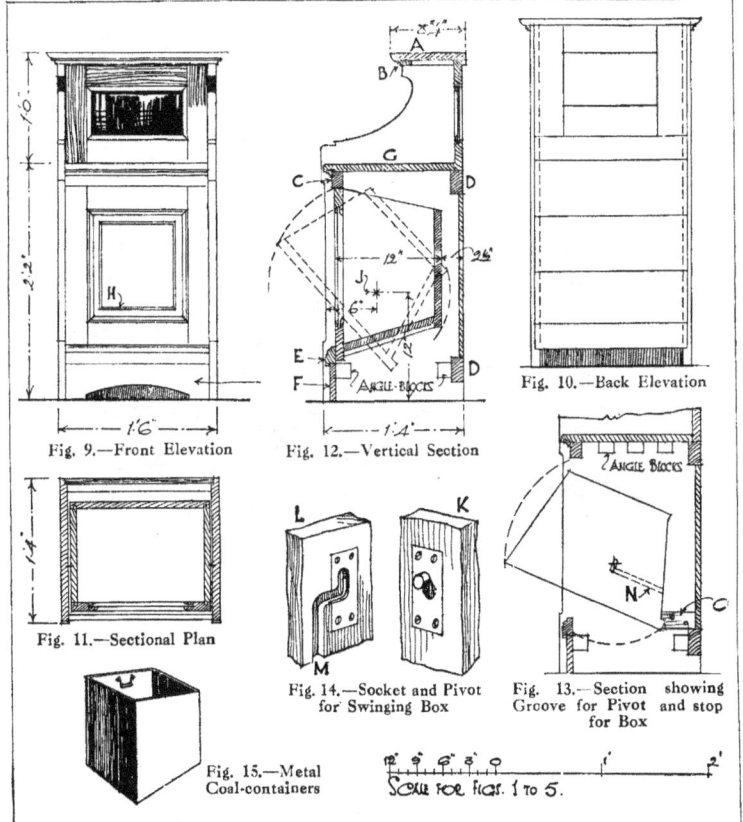

Fig. 9.—Front Elevation
Fig. 10.—Back Elevation
Fig. 11.—Sectional Plan
Fig. 12.—Vertical Section
Fig. 13.—Section showing Groove for Pivot and stop for Box
Fig. 14.—Socket and Pivot for Swinging Box
Fig. 15.—Metal Coal-containers

means of either a raised panel, or a small bead mitred round, as at H in Fig. 9. The point at J in Fig. 12 gives the exact position on the inner faces of the sides of the pivots or centres K (Fig. 14). The plate at L in the same figure is, of course, front of the cabinet, pushed home with the pivots sliding along the groove N, finally dropping into position as shown, when, on being released, it will by its own weight automatically close. A handle will be required near the top for opening, and in order to prevent its swinging too far and depositing its contents on the floor, a couple of rebated stops, as at o (Fig. 13), should be fixed on the sides of the cabinet before the boarded back is finally fixed.

The metal coal-container (Fig. 15) should be galvanised if possible, and it will require a couple of drop-handles at the top for lifting away from the cabinet for refilling. A shovel-holder at the back of the container will also be useful.

from the front edge and ½ in. from the back edge, these back edges being rebated ⅛ in. on the inner side, even with the bottom. The oak rail is also dovetailed into the sides, flush with the front edges, and screwed to the front edge of the bottom (see Fig. 21, where A is the rail, B the bottom, and C the oak side). The two deal rails are dovetailed into the top edges of the oak sides flush with the front edges and the rebates of the back

Fig. 16.

Fig. 17.

Figs. 16 and 17.—Pedestal Coal Cabinet, shown Closed and Open

PEDESTAL COAL CABINET

The photographs reproduced by Figs. 16 and 17 show a coal cabinet of pedestal form. The construction and dimensions are shown in the two elevations, Figs. 18 and 19, and the part underneath plan (Fig. 20).

The two sides of the cabinet are of oak, 1 ft. 6¼ in. long by 1 ft. 1 in. wide by ¾ in. thick finished. The bottom is of deal, 1 ft. 3 in. long by 11½ in. wide by ¾ in. thick finished. The front lower rail A (Fig. 18) is of oak exactly the same length as the bottom by 3 in. wide and ¾ in. thick; and two more rails the same size, but of deal, are required. The bottom is dovetailed into the lower end of the oak sides, ¾ in.

edges; and pieces about 1 in. wide are fitted between screwed to the sides. Screw-holes are made in these and the rails for fixing the oak top of the cabinet (see Fig. 22, where D is the front deal rail, and E the piece screwed to the side). The oak top is 1 ft. 5 in. by 1 ft. 2 in. by ¾ in., and is fixed flush at the back, and to overhang ¾ in. at the front and sides. A moulding to the section shown by Fig. 23 is fixed under the overhanging top, and that shown by Fig. 24 is fixed round the bottom.

The feet are cut from a moulding to the section shown by Fig. 25. Fig. 26 shows the method of marking out, on a piece of moulding 2 ft. 6 in. long, the six pieces which form the front and sides of

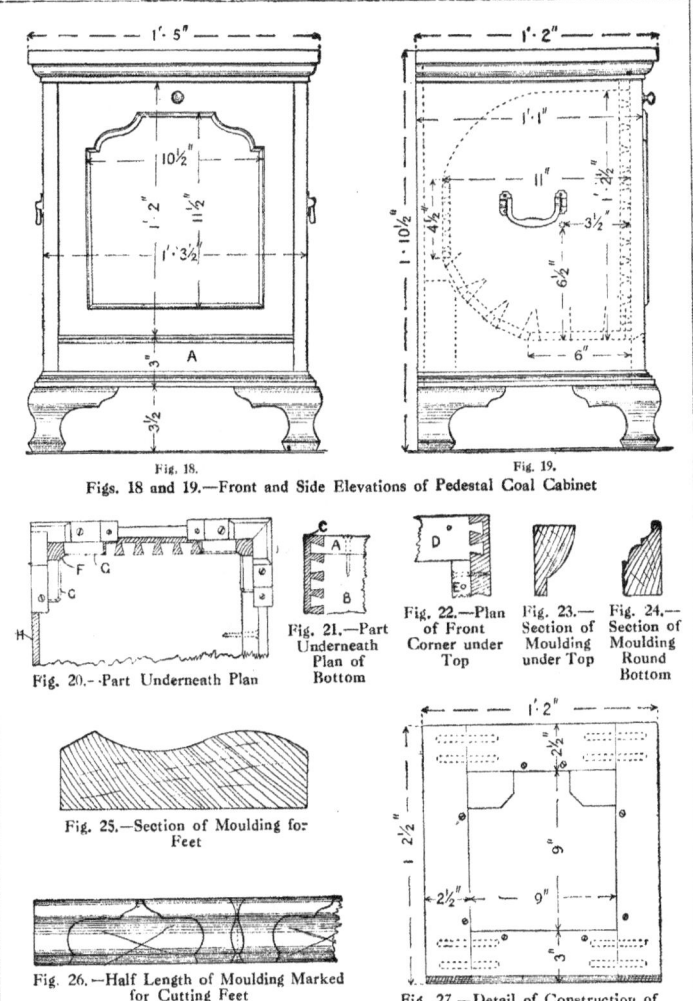

Figs. 18 and 19.—Front and Side Elevations of Pedestal Coal Cabinet

Fig. 20.—Part Underneath Plan

Fig. 21.—Part Underneath Plan of Bottom

Fig. 22.—Plan of Front Corner under Top

Fig. 23.—Section of Moulding under Top

Fig. 24.—Section of Moulding Round Bottom

Fig. 25.—Section of Moulding for Feet

Fig. 26.—Half Length of Moulding Marked for Cutting Feet

Fig. 27.—Detail of Construction of Front Frame

the feet. The dotted line shows the point at which they are mitred, which forms the curves at each side; the other lines which remove the waste are cut with a fret- or bow-saw. The back part of

Fig. 28.—Pair of Movements for Swinging Inner Case

the back feet are of flat deal simply cut slant. Fig. 20 shows the construction of the feet. They are well fitted, and fixed in place with glue and screws. A corner block is glued in each foot, also two other blocks are glued behind the upper part of the feet pieces; F is the corner block of the back foot, and G the other blocks. A back of $\frac{1}{2}$-in. deal H (Fig. 20) is fitted and fixed in the rebate of the sides and to the back edge of the top rail and bottom, which completes the outer case of the cabinet, except the door frame and panel. Fig. 27 shows the dimensions and construction of the frame, which is of $\frac{3}{4}$-in. oak, the joints being dowelled and pieces glued in the top corners; the bottom edge is bevelled to fit against the lower front rail. The panel is of oak $\frac{5}{16}$ in. thick, the dimensions being given in Fig. 18.

The inside case is of whitewood, the dimensions and construction being shown in Fig. 19. The grain of the wood is horizontal all through in this case. The front measures 1 ft. $1\frac{1}{4}$ in. long by 1 ft. 2 in. wide by $\frac{5}{8}$ in. thick; the two sides 11 in. long by 1 ft. 2 in. wide by $\frac{1}{2}$ in. thick; the bottom 6 in. wide, back $4\frac{1}{2}$ in. wide, and three other pieces $2\frac{1}{8}$ in. wide, all the same length as the front piece by $\frac{1}{2}$ in. thick. The sides are dovetailed to the front and back pieces; the bottom is nailed on, and the three other pieces fitted round the lower curve of the sides are

also nailed on. The front frame is fixed to the case with eight screws, as shown in Fig. 27, and the panel is secured with fine panel pins. In Fig. 19 is shown the dotted point for the swivel movement on which the inner case swings. Fig. 28 shows a pair of the movements, two pairs of which are required. They consist of two iron plates $2\frac{1}{4}$ in. by 1 in. by $\frac{1}{8}$ in., with a pin riveted in one, and countersunk screw-holes for fixing. The plate with the hole is fixed inside the outer case, and the one with the pin inside the inner case. It is important that these are accurate, or the cabinet will not keep closed or open as required. Therefore the

Fig. 29.—Pedestal Coal Cabinet—Back View

case should first be swung on nails with the iron lining in, and tried.

A small brass knob is put on the front top rail, and two wood blocks are fixed inside the lower back corners of the outer case to keep the inner one from opening too far, as shown in Fig. 19. A pair of handles are put on the sides, and a set of dome casters on the feet.

Fig. 29 is a photographic reproduction of the back view of the cabinet.

PRINTED BY CASSELL & COMPANY, LIMITED, LA BELLE SAUVAGE LONDON, E.C.4.

www.ingramcontent.com/pod-product-compliance
Lightning Source LLC
Chambersburg PA
CBHW031418150426
43191CB00006B/318